James William Davis

History of the Yorkshire Geological and Polytechnic Society,

1837-1887.

With Biographical Notices of Some of its Members

James William Davis

History of the Yorkshire Geological and Polytechnic Society, 1837-1887.
With Biographical Notices of Some of its Members

ISBN/EAN: 9783744643597

Printed in Europe, USA, Canada, Australia, Japan

Cover: Foto ©ninafisch / pixelio.de

More available books at **www.hansebooks.com**

HISTORY

OF THE

YORKSHIRE

Geological and Polytechnic Society,

1837-1887.

WITH BIOGRAPHICAL NOTICES OF SOME

OF ITS MEMBERS.

BY

JAMES W. DAVIS, F.S.A., F.G.S., F.L.S., &c.,

HONORARY SECRETARY.

Halifax:
WHITLEY AND BOOTH, PRINTERS, CROWN STREET.

1889.

PREFACE.

With the close of the first fifty years of the existence of this Society and the celebration of its Jubilee, came a desire that its history, so far as it could be gleaned, together with some notice of its principal members, should be written; the Council of the Society did me the honour to place this important trust in my hands. The work has presented some difficulties, and reliable information referring to its early years has proved scarce, notwithstanding this it is hoped that a work of some interest, even beyond the circle of the members of the Society, has been produced.

The history of the Yorkshire Geological and Polytechnic Society comprises a period during which the development of Geological science has been very rapid. Little more than twenty years previously William Smith was laboriously laying the foundations of stratigraphical geology, and deducing the sequence of the rocks by comparing those of East Yorkshire with the strata he knew so well in the neighbourhood of Bath. Professor Adam Sedgwick ten years before the foundation of the Society had communicated to the Geological Society of London the result of his researches on the Magnesian Limestone of Yorkshire; and during the early years of the Society's existence Professor John Phillips wrote his classical description of the Sea Coast and the Mountain Limestone of the county. Dean Buckland in 1823 published the Reliquæ Diluviana, in which he recorded the investigation of the Kirkdale Cave, the first systematic exploration of the kind carried out in this country. Since that time a marvellous expansion of the science has taken place, and its ramifications extend over nearly the whole surface of the globe. Together with the advance of scientific knowledge there have been well-marked social changes. The views now held of natural phenomena and the place occupied by man in relation to those phenomena exhibit a greatly extended field, and it cannot be denied that the science to which this Society is especially devoted, has exercised no small influence in the tendency of human thought and speculation during the past half century.

In the preparation of the chapters of this work, the plan adopted has been to adhere to a chronological sequence of events, as far as possible, when treating of its general autonomy or its minor papers and works. But having regard to the great branches of its work it has been found advisable, and it is hoped that the result will prove also, more instructive, to arrange the material so as to form as far as possible a definite history of the growth of the scientific opinion as based from time to time on the discoveries relating to this special subject. Examples of this may be seen in the chapters relating to the investigation of the series of rocks composing the Yorkshire Coalfield. The horizontal and vertical sections made by members of the Society, and the correlation of the several beds of workable coal, preceded the labours of the Geological Survey, and were of the greatest importance ; they afforded no small aid to the Survey and served as a basis on which the more elaborate and finished superstructure was raised, resulting in the great memoir on the Yorkshire Coal-field issued in 1878.

A second example may be cited in the chapter relating the results of the investigations in the domain of man's existence in the country before the historic period. The question of the antiquity of man has been largely discussed on data obtained from Yorkshire Caves ; the probability that man existed coeval with the elephant, the rhinoceros, the Irish elk and the reindeer, and the relation of all of them to the glacial period are matters of deep interest. The accounts of diggings in the Barrows scattered over the county are amongst the earliest and most interesting in the country. The exploration of the Kirkdale Cave by Dean Buckland and the deductions resulting from a study of its contents have served as a model for more recent investigation. Latterly the discovery of Kitchen-middens near

Spurn and Lake-dwellings in Holderness have added much to the interest in prehistoric times in this country.

It is my pleasant duty to express indebtedness to the many friends who have assisted in the preparation of the following pages Without the assistance of my friend Mr. T. W. Embleton, of Methley, the book would certainly never have reached its present extent. Mr. Embleton took an active part in the formation of the Society; he was engaged in the management of the Middleton Collieries, and had a practical knowledge of this most important industry; his experience combined with an active and energetic disposition, was freely placed at the service of the new Society. Many of the newspaper reports of the earliest meetings of the Society were prepared and written by the combined efforts of Mr. Embleton and Mr. Thomas Wilson, the honorary secretary, from notes taken by the former at the meetings; and it was fortunately his habit to preserve particulars of meetings of the Council and of the business of the Society, as well as the correspondence of its members. All this material has been unreservedly placed at my disposal, and elucidated by personal communications, has formed the basis of a tolerably complete conception of the work of the early years of the Society's existence.

It is with no small sense of appreciation that I acknowledge indebtedness to Professor A. H. Green, F.R.S., who, during his residence in Leeds, and whilst the early pages were issuing from the press, kindly offered to read the proofs; and did so until his removal to Oxford, when the accession of new duties, rendered his continuance of this kindness inconvenient, if not impossible.

I have received valuable information and assistance from Mr. Richard Carter of Harrogate, Mr. Richard Reynolds of Leeds, Mr. H. J. Morton of Scarborough, Mr. W. Cheetham, Mr. S. A. Adamson, and Mr. J. E. Bedford of Leeds, and Mr. J. Ray Eddy of Skipton; from Lord Houghton of Fryston Hall, Mr. J. B. Charlesworth of Haddon Hall, Mr. M. Nicholson of Middleton Hall; Mr. G. H. Parke and Mr. William Cash of Halifax; Dr. H. C. Sorby of Sheffield, and from Mr. James B. Jordan of the Mining Record Office, together with many others. I also draw attention, with much pleasure and thankfulness, to the several authors of biographical notices of members of the Society: in each instance they are acknowledged in the context.

The compilation of the list of officers and members has been undertaken by my son Percy; the Index to the volume is due also to him; at my suggestion he cheerfully gave up a holiday in order to prepare it.

CONTENTS.

	Page.
Preface	v.

CHAPTER I.
Formation of the Society; unpublished Records . . . 1

CHAPTER II.
Some of the Founders of the Society . . . 40
  Earl Fitzwilliam, first president.—Thomas Wilson.—Henry Holt.—Thomas Pridgin Teale, M.D.—James Garth Marshall.—Henry Briggs.—Charles Morton.—Joseph Charlesworth: senior and junior.

CHAPTER III.
Proceedings 1839—1840—Rules 65

CHAPTER IV.
Sections to connect the Lancashire with the Yorkshire Coalfield 89

CHAPTER V.
John Phillips, F.R.S. 119

CHAPTER VI.
Adam Sedgwick and William Buckland . 136

CHAPTER VII.
The Museum of the Society 150

CHAPTER VIII.
Proceedings 1841—1848 168

CHAPTER IX.
William Scoresby, the younger, Whalefisher and Clergyman, 1789—1857 200

Chapter X.
Rev. W. Thorp, B.A.—Agricultural Geology, etc.   . 213

Chapter XI.
Biographical Notices   238
    William West, F.R.S.—Henry Hartop.—William Sykes Ward.—Robert Hunt, F.R.S.—Henry Denny.—John Waterhouse, F.R.S.—John Lister, M.D.—William Alexander, M.D.—Blenkinsop and the Leeds Locomotive and Charles J. Brandling.

Chapter XII.
Proceedings 1849—1858   .   .   . 256

Chapter XIII.
Glacial Theories: Cave Exploration and Antiquity of Man . 283

Chapter XIV.
Proceedings 1859—1870   .   .   . 327

Chapter XV.
Proceedings 1871—1877   .   .   . 348

Chapter XVI.
Biographical Notices   369
    Marquis of Ripon, president, K.G., F.R.S.—Lord Houghton, D.C.L.—Viscount Halifax.—Rev. William Thorp, M.A.—Thomas Lister.

Chapter XVII.
The Last Decade 1878—1887   388

Chapter XVIII.
List of Officers and Members of the Society   .   . 437

CHAPTER I.

FORMATION OF THE SOCIETY : UNPUBLISHED RECORDS.

THE Yorkshire Geological and Polytechnic Society originated at a meeting of the coal proprietors of the West Riding, held at Wakefield in the latter part of the year 1837. For a period of nearly forty years the work of the Society was confined to the West Riding, and not until the annual meeting held at Huddersfield in 1876 was its sphere of operations extended so as to embrace the whole county. At a preliminary meeting Thomas Wilson, Esq., of Banks Hall, near Barnsley, occupied the chair; after discussing the question of the formation of the Society, it was stated "that considering the extent and importance of the Yorkshire Coal field; the imperfect information respecting its numerous beds of coal and ironstone; also, that in winning and working these beds a large amount of capital was embarked; extensive machinery and a large population employed; the step was justified." It was expected that great advantages would result from the institution of a Society for collecting and recording Geological and Mechanical information, with the accuracy and minuteness necessary for the successful prosecution of mining operations. It was hoped to attain the objects thus indicated by the formation of a collection of maps, plans, sections, models, mining records, and every kind of information respecting the geological structure of the country; the construction ultimately of a complete geological map; the formation of a museum in which the various fossils and mineral products of the district, as well as drawings and models of machinery, and the tools employed in mining, might be stored. It was decided to hold public meetings in the principal towns of the West Riding at which communications should be received and discussed, and to publish proceedings containing the papers, reports, and transactions of the Society. While these subjects would occupy the principal attention of the Society, it was considered desirable to extend its operation to whatever was connected with the staple manufactures of the Riding, together with the bearings of geology and chemistry upon agriculture, and the application of mechanical inventions to the common arts of life.

A preliminary meeting of coal owners was held at Wakefield, and after considerable discussion, on the proposition of Mr. T. W. Embleton, a committee was formed, and it was decided to issue the following circular calling a meeting of this committee :—

At a meeting of the under-mentioned coal and iron-masters, held at the Strafford Arms Inn, Wakefield, on Friday, the 1st December, 1837 :—

Present: Messrs. Briggs, Embleton, Smithson, John Wilson, Field, Porter, Thorp, Twibell, Stansfield, S. Cooper, W. Cooper, Hopwood, Jos. Charlesworth, Clarke, Biram, Joseph Charlesworth, Jun., and Thomas Wilson.

It having been suggested, that a Society for collecting and recording Geological and Mechanical information, in connection with the Coal Measures and Coal Trade generally of the West Riding of Yorkshire, would be highly desirable. Resolved—That the following gentlemen constitute a Committee, to make the requisite arrangements, and to prepare a scheme for a Society :—

Messrs. Briggs, Embleton, Smithson, John Wilson, Field, Porter, Thorp, Twibell, Jno. Charlesworth, Hartop, Leah, Jno. Chambers, and Matt. Chambers, of Thorncliffe ; Sayle, Jno. Walker, C. Morton, Morley, of Garforth ; Brakenridge, Chambers, Jun., Holmes, S. Clark, of Holmes ; G. Wilson, Stansfield, Samuel Cooper, W. Cooper, Hopwood, James Andrew, Jos. Charlesworth, Jos. Charlesworth, Jun., Clarke, Biram, Thomas Wilson, Henry Holt, William Graham, Christ. Dawson, L. Hird, Casson, Booth, Jeffcock, and Ingham. That the first Meeting of the Committee be held at the Royal Hotel, Wakefield, on Thursday, the 14th December, at 11 o'clock.

(Signed), THOMAS WILSON, CHAIRMAN.

BANKS, NEAR BARNSLEY,
2nd December, 1837.

SIR,

Allow me to solicit your co-operation in forming and supporting the proposed Society. In the present stage of the proceedings, I can only call your attention to the general objects of the Society, and to their great utility in a scientific point of view. In proof of which, if such be necessary, I may appeal to the valuable papers on the Geology of the Northern Coal Field that have appeared in the Natural History Society of Northumberland and Durham, and to the interesting communications on Mechanical subjects that have been made at the meetings of the Polytechnic Society of Cornwall. Without hoping to rival either of these Institutions, it cannot be doubted that a great mass of detached information must exist in the possession of individuals, which, if collected and compared, would throw great light on those points in the coal formation of Yorkshire, about which so much uncertainty at present exists, and, on the other hand, many useful mechanical contrivances, which deserve to be generally known, are confined to the place of their first invention or adoption.

I am, Sir, yours respectfully,

THOMAS WILSON.

Forty gentlemen were present at the meeting on the 14th December, who signified their approval of the objects already foreshadowed and constituted themselves members of the Society, and immediate steps were taken to organize it. The meeting derived much valuable assistance from the advice of Prof. John Phillips, then residing at York, who came over to attend the meeting and help in the formation of the proposed Society. The Rt. Hon. Earl Fitzwilliam, F.R.S., was elected to, and accepted, the office of President, and Thos. Wilson, Esq., of Banks Hall, near Barnsley, that of Secretary.

Prof. Johnston, of Durham, who had been invited to be present at the meeting, but was unable to accept the invitation, was at Leeds the following day reading one of a series of lectures on the geological structure of rocks. Mr. Embleton and others were present, and after the lecture adjourned with the lecturer to Mr. Nunneley's to supper. Prof. Johnston expressed his pleasure that the Society was to be formed, and in a note written to Mr. Embleton the same evening he offered to the new Society a lecture "On the most important objects of such an institution in this district, and the best means of attaining them."

Prof. Johnston at this time exhibited much interest in the geology of the West Riding Coal-field. Along with Mr. Embleton, Mr. West, Mr. J. Garth Marshall, and Dr. Teale he descended several coal-pits and examined the coals *in situ.* It was during a visit to the Deep Coal at Middleton that the earliest record is made of the discovery of fossil fish remains. An examination of the shale forming the roof of the pit and immediately above the coal disclosed the presence of teeth and spines of fish, and further researches resulted in the discovery of numerous other examples. Amongst them the head of a large fish, now in the Museum of the Literary and Philosophical Society at Leeds, which a few years afterwards served as the type of the genus Megalichthys when Prof. Louis Agassiz visited the museum in search of material for his great work on Fossil fishes. Fish-remains were also found above the Better Bed Coal at Low Moor and the Middleton Little Coal and the 40 yards Coal at the same place.

Meanwhile active steps were taken to formulate a code of Rules, and those of the Natural History Society of Northumberland, Durham, and Newcastle-upon-Tyne, supplied by Mr. Hutton served as a good model. Incorporated with the Rules a scheme for the conduct and government of the Society was devised. For these results the new Society was principally indebted to the Honorary Secretary, Mr. Thomas Wilson, Messrs. Embleton, Field and Charlesworth. On the 11th December a meeting of the Committee was held at the Museum of the Philosophical Society at Leeds, and the Rules were presented, passed and adopted in the following form :—

1.—That a Society be formed for collecting and methodising Geological and Mechanical Information in connection with the Coal-Field of Yorkshire; and that it be called "The Geological Society of the West-Riding of Yorkshire."

II.—That the Members of the original Committee, and the

gentlemen now present, together with all who may apply to the Secretary before the next Meeting, be Members of the Society on their conforming to the Rules.

III.—That any person who is desirous of becoming a Member after the next Meeting, must be proposed by a Member, in writing, to the Secretary, and ballotted for at the ensuing General Meeting.

IV.—That the Annual Subscription be Half-a-Guinea, and that it be due on admission, and at the Annual Meeting.

V.—That the Officers of the Society be a President, Vice-Presidents, a Committee of nine, (of whom three shall be a Quorum,) and a Treasurer and Secretary, who shall be ex-officio a Member of the Committee; and that three of the Committee retire annually.

VI.—That the Officers be elected at the Annual Meeting, and be capable of being re-elected.

VII.—That the following Noblemen and Gentlemen be requested to accept their respective Offices :—

PRESIDENT:
Earl Fitzwilliam.

VICE-PRESIDENTS:

Earl of Scarborough,   T. W. Beaumont, Esq.,
Earl of Mexborough,   J. Spencer Stanhope, Esq.,
Earl of Effingham,   R. O. Gascoigne, Esq.,
Lord Wharncliffe,   C. J. Brandling, Esq.,
Lord Stourton,   W. B. Martin, Esq.,
Sir J. L. L. Kaye,   G. L. Fox, Esq.

COMMITTEE:

Rev. S. Sharp,   Mr. Embleton,
Mr. Jno. Charlesworth,   Mr. Field,
Mr. Jos. Charlesworth,   Mr. Biram,
Mr. Hartop,   Mr. Holt.
Mr. Briggs.

TREASURER & SECRETARY:
Mr. Thomas Wilson.

VIII.—That the Meetings be held at Wakefield, on the first Thursdays in March, June, September, and December, at Eleven o'clock.

IX.—That at the Meetings, each Member be allowed to introduce one or more strangers.

X.—That the following Gentlemen be elected Honorary Members :—

Professor Phillips,   Dr. Smith.

That the above Rules be advertised in the Leeds Mercury and Intelligencer, the Sheffield Mercury and Independent, and that they be printed and circulated, and that the parties addressed be requested to signify their wishes, as to becoming Members, to the Secretary, Banks, near Barnsley.

These rules were printed and issued with the following circular to the gentry, colliery proprietors and others who were considered desirable as members of the Society.

BANKS, NEAR BARNSLEY,
16th December, 1837.

I beg to inclose you a Copy of the Rules of "THE GEOLOGICAL SOCIETY OF THE WEST-RIDING OF YORKSHIRE," which were agreed to at a Meeting of Gentlemen interested in the subject, on the 14th instant. Allow me to add, that the objects proposed are highly desirable, and such as can hardly be effected in any other way. The want of accurate information respecting the Yorkshire Coal-Field, has long been felt by the scientific and the practical man : before this can be satisfactorily supplied, a mass of minute detail must be collected, which no individual could obtain, but which may be easily collected by a society that embraces among its members, a number of persons engaged in the working of the minerals in every part of the district. It will only be necessary for the hand of Science to point out the most useful field of inquiry, and a number of pioneers will be immediately at work to make straight her paths. The society may also congratulate itself on having amongst its members a distinguished geologist, whose exertions in the field of Yorkshire Geology are so untiring, and than whom none could be more competent to methodise the information that may be accumulated.

I shall feel obliged by your informing me if I may add your name to the list of Members of the Society, and am

Yours respectfully,

THOMAS WILSON.

On the 25th December, Mr. Embleton sent a copy of the rules of the Society, in which the name is recorded as the "Geological Society," to Prof. Johnston, together with a description of a fossil fish spine from the roof of the 40 yards coal at the Middleton Colliery. Accompanying this letter was a request, that Prof. Johnston would allow his name to be enrolled as a Honorary Member of the Society.

Prof. Johnston to Mr. Embleton.

DURHAM, *31st Dec., 1837.*

MY DEAR SIR,

I am obliged to you for the circular containing the rules of your Society, (Geological I find it is called), for the West Riding. It will give me great pleasure to be enrolled amongst its honorary members, by the side of my friends Phillips and Smith. My impression derived from my conversation with Mr. Hartop, was, that the objects of the Society were to be more extensive, as I think they might with advantage have been, that it was to be a Polytechnic Society, embracing besides the strictly Geological, the practical working, engineering, and economy of the mines and mining products, a wide field which embraces many important considerations, and which will be continually presenting new objects of interest to the community in general, while the researches of pure Geology in reference to a particular district have an obvious boundary and limit, towards which every year will be bringing the Society nearer. It was a general exposition of the important objects which such a Society might embrace that I contemplated in the lecture I requested you to offer to the committee in my name, of course, as the Society is to be purely Geological it would be presumption in me to pretend to direct the mode of their operation, when Phillips and Smith, who are far more able and better qualified than myself, and always on the spot, are members and co-founders with Mr. Wilson and others. You will not, therefore, I hope, think I am less deserving of doing everything I can to forward the views of the Society, if I request Mr. Wilson, through you, not to submit my offer to the committee in its present shape. I shall be happy when I come into that part of the country to give an address or paper on some other subject, but I shall write to Phillips explaining to him that he must do what I offered under a wrong impression. I am at present casting about for the best means of getting up a Polytechnic Society in this district.

I am unwilling to trouble Mr. Wilson with any separate reply to his circular, if you can communicate this present letter to him, I hope he will not consider my not doing so to rise from any want of respect. I am obliged to you for your drawing of the supposed tooth, and am happy to find you are so much on the look out. It is not a tooth, but a dorsal spine, (ichthyodorulite as they used to be called), I think, but is the harbinger of much more you are yet destined to exhume. I find the stuff you scraped of the coal for me of no use, it is so mixed with coal, would you have the goodness to collect me some specimens of the substance on the coal, the thickest layers you can find, and if you have any opportunity, forward them either to Durham or to Newcastle, care of Hutton, or to Mr. Gascoigne's coal office, at the Selby Railway, to the care of Mr. Wharton of Durham, any time during the month of January. I hope however to hear of other discoveries before that time.

With regards to Mrs. Embleton.

Very truly yours,

JAMES F. W. JOHNSTON.

Mr. Embleton forwarded this letter to the Honorary Secretary, Mr. Thomas Wilson, suggesting that the Professor had mistaken the objects of the Society, because at the half-yearly meeting it was intended to unite Geology with Mechanics, as the objects of the Society, and suggesting that should Prof. Phillips be unable to lecture, that Mr. Wilson should endeavour to explain the matter to Prof. Johnston, so that he might still give his proposed lecture.

The substance referred to in Prof. Johnston's letter was a resinous one which Mr. Embleton found in the Deep Coal at Middleton, and other Collieries, and which the Professor, after making analysis of it, named Middletonite, and described as new.

Mr. Wilson to Mr. Embleton.

BANKS, NEAR BARNSLEY,
22nd January, 1838.

DEAR SIR,

I have written to Professor Johnston assuring him that the objects contemplated by our Society are still the same as we at first proposed, as indeed he might have seen from our first Rule—although we have perhaps unfortunately, adopted rather a limited title. You know that we had great difficulty in settling the name, and that a meeting such as ours was, was not the very best for giving the most appropriate designation, inasmuch as many who attended came quite unprepared and were, perhaps naturally enough, from the presence of a geologist led to think more of the Geological department than of any other. I have urged strongly on Professor Johnston the desirableness of his still giving the Lecture as the best means of keeping the Society from the first in the right path, and if you have any communication with him I hope you will urge the point strongly. I think it of great consequence to secure such an exposition of the objects and means of such a Society as he seems to contemplate. I shall be in Leeds on Thursday and Friday, the 1st and 2nd February, at Scarborough's Hotel, if you should happen to be in town on either of those days, I shall be engaged, probably till four or five in the afternoon of Thursday, and from twelve to one or two on Friday, but I should be at liberty in the evening of Thursday or the early part of Friday morning. I propose having a Committee Meeting about the middle of the month, to make our final arrangements for the March meeting. I expect a fair number of subscribers, and I have two papers already promised. There will be a good deal for the Committee to do ; and the most important object for it will be to give the tone to the Society, if we fail in laying before them a well-digested plan of action, the whole thing will break down.

I am, dear Sir, yours truly,

THOMAS WILSON.

After a short delay the following letter was addressed to Prof. Johnston. Though somewhat lengthy it appears advisable to give it in full, because the correspondence expresses the hopes and aspirations of the founders of the Society better than any other material at command.

Mr. Embleton to Prof. Johnston.

NEWCASTLE, *6th February, 1838.*

MY DEAR SIR,

I am obliged by your letter of 31st December, and have communicated with Mr. Wilson on your intended paper, who I hope has by this time written to you. I have to apologise for not having sooner attended to this matter. From the feeling evinced at the meeting it was thought advisable to restrict the designation of the Society to our particular branch of science, although it was seen by the rules that geology alone will not occupy the attention of the members. It was principally from the observation of Prof. Phillip's that the Society would appear to be restricted in its objects—if this really were the case, except for a short period during the infancy of the Society, I do not entertain any hopes that it will go on prosperously or even exist beyond a few years. As you justly observe, its objects, year after year, are becoming fewer and of less interest to the community generally, whereas by having a more extended field of research the converse will take place. I would, therefore, strongly urge upon you the necessity there is that you should give us the paper you originally intended, for it will be the means of imparting a character and tone to the Society that it would not otherwise possess. In fact the very existence and well-being of the Society depends so much upon the manner in which the first meeting is conducted, for from it a sufficient impetus or excitement must be derived to carry us forward to our future proceedings with spirit, that the assistance of persons occupying the higher walks of science is much to be desired to direct the energies of those whose avocations have not permitted them, however willing they may have been, to acquire information beyond what is necessary to enable them to obtain a knowledge of the duties of their profession, and with very few exceptions would, I am sorry to say, seldom attend to anything but the pounds, shillings, and pence side of the question; thus many important facts with which we are familiar, and which to a scientific man would prove of great service, are passed over merely on account of their frequent occurrence—others again which require close and minute investigation are suffered to remain unheeded because no stimulus is at hand to develope them—all this I am sure the Society will be able to effect if once the proper direction be given to its pursuits, and I am equally confident that this direction you will be able to point out to us, and likewise show how we shall best keep in the right path. Your friend Prof. Phillips will be glad to hear that his duties are to be partially lightened by your kindness, for I understand it would be extremely inconvenient, and not accord with his present engagements, to leave London so early as March. If these arguments, poor as they may be, induce you to execute your first promise, I shall feel gratified by hearing that you will be amongst us next month. In the meantime I should be glad to have a few hints for the arrangement of our affairs previously to the meeting, and that for this purpose you would communicate either with Mr. Wilson or myself. I have forwarded to you some more specimens of the resinous substances on our coal, the layers are the thickest we could procure. I hear that at Hebburn Colliery they occasionally find the same substance in their layers, if I can get any specimens while I am here I will send some. We have no fresh discoveries in our "*fish bed*" of any consequence, beyond a fragment of a jaw with four or five teeth of the same kind, but considerably smaller than those you have, a small cusped tooth as on the margin, and a fragment which I take for a small vertebræ. Would you tell me which work you consider the best to enable one to study these remains, that by M. Agassiz I believe is unfinished. I am sorry I have not had an opportunity of calling upon you while I have been at Newcastle.

I am, &c.,

THOS. W. EMBLETON.

This letter seems to have had the desired effect, and Prof. Johnston decided to prepare his lecture.

The first general meeting of the members was held at Wakefield on March 1st, 1838, to which the geological section of the Leeds Philosophical and Literary Society was invited through Mr. W. West. About one hundred persons were present. The President, Earl Fitzwilliam, was unable to be present, and the chair was occupied by Mr. C. J. Brandling, of Middleton. Mr. Embleton has furnished from his note book the following account of the meeting. " Several general resolutions were passed. Mr. Hartop read a paper on the Geology of the Don in reference to a 'heave,' as he termed it, in the coal measures, but the nature of which did not appear. The Rev. Wm. Thorp read a notice of the Yorkshire Coal-field generally ; it contained many details which must have cost him much time to collect and arrange ; on the whole it was very valuable. I briefly explained the model (Mr. Embleton had prepared a model of the workings of a coal-pit). Mr. C. Morton noticed an extraordinary variation of the compass by a large mass of iron amounting to 10 tons." There was very little discussion on the papers, which the writer attributed to a want of arrangement on the part of the committee. It was decided to issue the following prospectus of the Geological and Polytechnic Society of the West Riding of Yorkshire :—

The extent and importance of the Yorkshire coal field are well known. Its numerous beds of coal and iron-stone extend under a great portion of the West Riding, and are at once the origin and support of its great and increasing manufactures ; while in the winning and working of them, a large capital, extensive machinery, and a numerous population is employed. It is believed that great advantages would result from the formation of a Society, which would bring together those who are engaged in the practical working of the minerals, and the votaries of general science, and would invite the intelligent and inquiring portion of the public to be present at their discussions.

A short and imperfect sketch of the principal objects which might thus be attained, will show that such a Society would find an ample field for its exertions, without interfering with any existing institution.

First in importance, as in general interest, would be the contributions it would make to the mineral history of the district, for which it would possess peculiar facilities from the mass of minute and local information which its practical members possess, and are hourly acquiring, the collection and methodising of which can alone fully illustrate the Geology of this important formation, and furnish an accurate map of its mineral riches, tracing the various seams of coal and iron-stone through the whole district, and the direction and extent of the faults by which they are disturbed. The opportunities it would possess for forming, almost without expense, a most valuable and complete collection of the Fossil Botany of the county, would be a sufficient inducement to form a museum, even if it were not absolutely necessary for the identification of the strata. While the labours of the practical man were directed to this object, the more speculative of its members might bring the principles and discoveries of chemistry, to investigate the origin and nature of coal and ironstone.

It may be safely asserted that there is no art more indebted to machinery than that of mining. In this department the steam engine would engage much of the Society's attention; and the great results obtained in other districts, would be discussed with reference to their value in a neighbourhood where fuel is so much less costly. Under this head every process in the art of mining would be subjected to the test of science and experience.

The valuable beds of iron-stone with which the county abounds would attract attention to all the arts of making and preparing that most useful of metals.

Urged alike by interest and humanity, the great problem of ventilation would occupy the Society's most anxious hours. It is not perhaps generally known, that to an Association like the present we are indebted for the invention of the safety lamp. In the year 1815, Sir Humphrey Davy was invited by the coal-owners of the North, to experiment on the fire-damp; and in course of a few weeks he produced his safety lamp, in nearly as perfect a state as we now have it. Valuable as that discovery undoubtedly was, it has, unfortunately left much to be desired; it has succeeded in imprisoning the dark spirit of the mine, but it has left his nature unchanged; and too often he bursts his bonds to give devastation to property and destruction to life. It would be a proud triumph to this Society if it should stimulate another Davy to complete the conquest of that dreadful element, by the discovery of a neutralizing principle, for it is this alone that can give perfect security, and relieve the minds of all who are engaged in mining, from the most painful of their anxieties and responsibilities.

It is to be hoped that a Society, whose members employ so numerous a body of the labouring classes, would consider it as one of its most important duties, to give effect to every suggestion for informing the minds, increasing the comforts, and (as the only sure foundation of these), improving the moral and religious habits of that important class of society.

Aware of the importance to a commercial country, of a full and accurate knowledge of all its commercial interests, and painfully remembering how much it has suffered from the ignorance of the legislature on such subjects, the Society would not neglect the great advantages it would enjoy for collecting the fullest statistical details of the great trading interests of the districts.

In conclusion, the Society—having for its objects the advancement and diffusion of knowledge—would make its collections and its discussions as public as possible; would be ready to assist men of science in any investigation connected with the district; would be glad to forward any experiments for which it might have local advantages, and which might be necessary to test particular theories; and would thus form a link in that bright chain of science, which we may soon hope to see run from one end of the empire to the other.

A Meeting of the Council was held at Wakefield, in the Music Hall, on the 7th of June, 1838, and after some discussion the council adjourned for the purpose of seeing some lands on which it was proposed to erect a building suitable for a Museum, one place selected being a field, which was for sale, adjoining Cliff Hill Tree. Afterwards Prof. Johnston delivered his lecture in the Music Hall; the Rev. Wm. Thorp presided, and introduced the lecturer, who gave a very clear and good address. A reporter from the office of the Leeds Intelligencer was engaged to report the lecture, which was afterwards printed in the form of a pamphlet, and circulated amongst the members. The letter following has reference to this as well as other matters.

The Honorary Secretary to Mr. Embleton.

BANKS, *31st June, 1838.*

DEAR SIR,

I shall be obliged by your requesting Mr. Beckwith to make a full transcript of his notes, I have arranged with Prof. Johnston to forward it to him, and he proposes introducing one or two points that he omitted, and perhaps developing some of those he did allude to more fully. We are then to publish it and send the Professor 50 copies. I feel very anxious to secure a paper on the identification of the various coal seams against our next meeting. Would it not be useful if yourself and Messrs. Briggs, Morton, and Holt were to compare notes together. If you think so, I should name it to them, and arrange for the meeting immediately after we have transacted our ordinary business the next time the council meets. I could arrange the meeting so as to suit the convenience of all parties.

I am, dear Sir, yours truly,
Thomas Wilson.

A day or two afterwards, Mr. Embleton received a letter from Prof. Johnston which is printed below, asking for various items of information respecting the Yorkshire coal-field. He was desirous to make his lecture as widely interesting as possible before it was printed.

Prof. Johnston to Mr. Embleton.
Durham, 18th June, 1838.

My Dear Sir,

If I could have met you yesterday afternoon in Leeds I should have saved you the trouble of reading this letter; though the greater of writing to me, I should still have been anxious to impose upon you. I should like to notice in my lecture, when it is printed, the subject of the structure of coal, which I have marked in my notes to be alluded to, but with some other things find I have passed over. Would you favour me with the result of your observation in regard to the Cleet of the coal.

1st.—If it is always parallel to the water level, and at right angles to the dip.

2nd.—If it is uniform in direction in the same seams, the dip being constant, and if it vary with the dip.

3rd.—If it be parallel to the same line or run in the same direction. *(a)* In the different coal seams worked in the same pit. *(b)* In the different layers of the same seam.

4th.—In respect to the dip the coal may be expected to undulate now and then, so that the dip shall slightly vary in different parts of the same seam, but in different seams lying over each other does the general dip always correspond, or does the dip of (a) differ from that of (b) either in intensity, (number of degrees), or in direction. If the whole of the coal measures of a district were deposited during a period of comparative repose, during which there were only gradual risings and fallings of the land, the general dip of all the beds should be pretty nearly uniform, if during the deposition there were occasional convulsions the successive beds should have occasionally different dips.

These points I mean to notice as worthy of investigation since the lecture is to be published, and I should feel obliged to you if you could suggest to me any other topics which may have escaped me that appear to you from your local knowledge to be such as are worthy to occupy the attention of a Society, having for its object the investigation of all the natural phenomena and the development of the mineral resources of the district.

The offer of a drive to Wharncliffe tempted me as you saw to stay longer than I intended in Yorkshire, I got to Durham about five o'clock this morning.

With kind regards to Mrs. Embleton.

Believe me, my dear Sir,
Yours very truly,
JAMES F. W. JOHNSTON.

T. W. Embleton to Prof. Johnston.

MIDDLETON, *22nd June, 1838.*

MY DEAR SIR,

I was favoured with your letter yesterday, I regret I did not meet with you in Leeds on Saturday. I understood you had left your hotel, and I had not an opportunity to call again; I hasten to answer your enquiries. 1st, The "*Cleet*" seldom or ever runs parallel with the water level, and consequently not at right angles to the dip, the general dip being to the S.E. 2nd, It is tolerably uniform in direction in the same seam, but is not affected by the regular dip of the strata. 3rd, It is somewhat different in each seam, worked in the same pit, that is, an upper seam will have the *Cleet* dissimilar to that succeeding it, but the next will have it the same as the first and so on, the different layers in each seam present the same phenomena. 4th, No two water level drifts, commenced from the same points in different seams, will coincide with each other, inasmuch as the thickness between the seams varies. The dip of the coal too is irregular, without any dislocation in the strata being present.

The direction of the Cleet varies at this Colliery from N 20 W to N 32 W., and is not in the least affected by the dip, this is the fraction which is the guide to the workmen in driving their endings (headways) and boards, the former being driven parallel to it, and the latter at right angles. There is, however, another fraction which is not attended to in working the coal, and has not, I think, been much observed. It forms with the Cleet and horizontal parting a rhomboid or cube, as the case may be; with us its course is from N 29 E to N 42 E. This is the result of a few trials, but I do not offer it as anything more than an approximation to the truth. The fraction of the remaining layers I have not ascertained. I find much difficulty in obtaining the angle, owing, I suppose, to the imperfect instruments used. There are 8 layers beginning at the top, the layer No. 1 is very bright and shining, and contains little earthy matter. No. 2 is rather more earthy, and contains bright undulating layers as shown above. No. 3 has a very dull aspect, and is more earthy than either No. 1 or 2. No. 4 is nearly similar to No. 2, but the bright streaks are less continuous and distinct. No. 5 and 7 are similar to No. 3, and so is No. 6 to No. 4. No. 8 is very bright and shining, and unlike what lies above, produces brownish ashes when burnt. What effect may the quantity of earthy matter have on the fraction? With respect to the water levels in two seams at the same place not being coincident with each other, I would observe that Mr. Baddle's opinions never coincide, and this was an argument made use of on a late occasion to show that a water level driven from a certain point in a lower seam, and which was to form the bedding of the coal worked in that seam could not also be the boundary in the upper seams, as the water levels in them would not lie perpendicularly above that in the lower one. Supposing the clays and sandstones which compose the coal measures to have been deposited at the bottom of a lake or sea from running water, it is natural to infer that the matter from which they were formed would accumulate to a greater extent in some situations than in others, and thus cause the difference in depth between any two given seams at places distant, say a few hundred yards, thus we may perhaps account for a sandstone gradually passing into a shale, or *vice versa*.

There are several disputed points in the Yorkshire Coal-field, the most material question for decision is as to the identity between the Middleton Strata and those containing the Lofthouse or Haigh Moor Coal, and particularly whether the Middleton Main Coal is the same as the Lofthouse Coal, and the Lofthouse the same as the Haigh Moor. Till a short time ago the universal opinion was that they are the same but altered in appearance only by Dykes. However, from some circumstances observed lately some think, and indeed with sufficient reason, that they are quite dissimilar, and the Lofthouse or Haigh Moor strata will eventually be found to be superior to the Middleton strata—this point I have hopes will be investigated at our September meeting. Respecting the Dykes it would be material to observe whether they are, as is generally supposed, chiefly downcasts to the South or S.W ; how the inclination of the strata is affected on each side, and whether a large Dyke is always accompanied by a smaller one running parallel with it, but its heave being opposite to the large one, several instances of this I have noticed. I would here too remark that the "Cleet" is very indistinct in the vicinity of Dykes, and in some cases totally obliterated. As to a test for the quality of the air in a colliery which at present is judged of by the colour of the exterior of the flame of the candle, when the blue is so intense as that of burning sulphur we consider it very dangerous, and comparative safety depends on the shadow between that blue tint and the brown or yellowish tint observed when a candle is burning in the open air. So much, however, depends upon the quality and nature of the material of which the candle is composed that different results may be obtained in the same air by using wax candles or tallow candles, and again, separate results may be observed with tallow candles which have cotton and tow wicks, but besides all this the particular shade at which danger commences with each description of candles has to be carried in the eye, at best a *bad memory* to trust to. It has often occurred to me that an instrument might be contrived, which by showing the specific gravity of the air would at once at a given point determine its state of purity. Instruments for ascertaining the quantity of air passing into the workings would be desirable. Another point for investigation would be as to whether the water found in coal when newly opened out, actually exists in it in the state of water or *in any* other form, which, when exposed to the atmospheric air forms water. I have so little to say on this subject, which I am afraid you are already thinking is very fanciful, that I regret having mentioned it, but one or two circumstances struck me as very singular. 1st, the water issuing from coal when first explored by driving the water levels is quite pure and soft like rain water. 2nd, that as the drifts advance, the water still "*follows to the face,*" and the coal gradually becomes dry at a short distance from the face. 3rd, that when the discharge of water is greatest, there we find the least quantity of fire damp. 4th, that when coal is thus dried, no cavities are found in working it subsequently which contain water. This subject is so interesting, I am sure it will repay the Society for bestowing their best attention to it. I have really prolonged my letter so much that I begin to wish I had met with you in Leeds, for I am sure you will lay it aside before you reach the end.

Believe me, dear Sir,
Yours faithfully,
Thos. W. Embleton.

A large amount of information was furnished to Prof. Johnston for his lecture, prior to its publication, by his Yorkshire friends, which was duly incorporated. He appears to have attached considerable importance to it as representing the state of knowledge at that time in coal mining, and all the numerous collateral industries which influenced or depended upon it. The order to print the lecture was placed at the office of the Leeds Intelligencer, and on the 28th July, Mr. Embleton was able to forward proofs to Prof. Johnston for revision by the Coach "Hero," which ran between Leeds and Durham, when railways were not, in this part of the country. In acknowledging the receipt of the proofs, Prof. Johnston incidentally stated that he had lately obtained at Whitehaven a bottle of Petroleum, which exudes in considerable quantities from the roof of one of the seams. The examination of the Petroleum proved very interesting. Prof.

Johnston was at this time acting as Honorary Secretary to the British Association at its meeting in 1838, at Newcastle-on-Tyne. He contributed several papers on fire-damp, the Davy lamp, and on the ventilation of mines to the chemical section of the Association. Mr. Embleton forwarded to Newcastle, specimens of the new metal Middletonite, to be exhibited at the British Association.

At the General Meeting held at Wakefield on September 6th, 1838, the chair was occupied by the Hon. W. S. Lascelles, M.P. After a number of fossils from the Chevet Rock had been presented to the Society by Lady Pilkington, the chairman called upon Henry Briggs, Esq., of Overton, to read a paper on the Strata between Flockton and Middleton Coals. Other important business was transacted. G. B. Greenough, after his election as an honorary member, gave an address on the proposed museum. A report of this meeting was prepared by Mr. Thos. W. Embleton, assisted by Mr. Chas. Morton, and sent to some of the principal newspapers. The following is abstracted from the "Sheffield Independent" of September 22nd :—

The third meeting of the Geological and Polytechnic Society of the West Riding of Yorkshire, was held in the Music Saloon, Wakefield, on Thursday, the 6th of September. The Hon. W. S. Lascelles, M.P., presided, and in an appropriate address, apologised for taking the chair on such an occasion, as he had no pretensions to the name of a practical geologist. He remarked generally on the great utility of the science, and alluded to its importance in connexion with the extensive mining and manufacturing district. He expressed his conviction that the pursuit of geology is in no way hostile to but entirely in unison with the interests of religion.

After the election of new members, and other preliminary business had been concluded, the Secretary read a communication from Dr. Walker, of Huddersfield, describing two fossils recently found by him, which were further illustrated by drawings.

The Rev. S. Sharp directed attention to some fossils from the Chevet Rock, presented by Lady Pilkington ; and, in moving the thanks of the meeting to her Ladyship, he expressed a hope that ladies and gentlemen connected with the society would furnish the museum with specimens from the strata in the vicinity of their respective residences.

The object of Mr. Henry Briggs's paper was to prove the non-identity of the seams of coal now working under the names of the Haigh Moor and Rothwell Haigh, or Middleton, which have hitherto been thought by many practical men to be the same. For this purpose, Mr. Briggs had prepared a map, on a large scale, of the country in the neighbourhood of Leeds and Wakefield, on which were shown the outbreaks of the various rock formations, between which the different beds of coal are found, and, in the course of his observations, exhibited sections of the country in several directions to exemplify his line of argument. He first adduced the Flockton bed as an intermediate coal, easily recognised in different localities, and attempted to prove that the Haigh Moor lies *above*, and the Rothwell Haigh *below* that particular seam. With this view, he traced the Flockton coal through a large district, and rendered certain its identity by several facts, and by the production of fossil shells which are found immediately above this seam ; then by a section of nine miles of the country easterly from the village of Middleton to Mr. Fenton's colliery near Newmarket, and afterwards by another section from Dewsbury to Lee Fair, he showed that the Haigh Moor coal is situated about 100 yards above the Flockton. After tracing the Flockton coal as far as Drighlington and Gildersome, Mr. Briggs gave a section of about six miles of the country from those places to Middleton and Rothwell Haigh, by which he showed that the seam known by both these latter names, is situated about 80 yards *below* the Flockton bed ; and that, therefore, the two seams under consideration must be totally distinct, and about 180 yards apart. In the course of his observations, Mr. Briggs also exhibited a diagram of a distraction or throw, existing in the Haigh Moor coal, and combatted the formerly received opinion of its being a throw *down* of this coal, as the inclination of this distraction affords good evidence that it is *upwards* ; and that the deep coal working on the opposite side, is an entirely different bed. He also submitted for inspection an interesting section of the strata in Earl Fitzwilliam's property, near Rotherham, with an addition of a deeper series in the vicinity of Halifax, to a total depth of 930 yards, containing 21 workable seams of coal, and an aggregate thickness of 73 feet ; and concluded by suggesting as an interesting object of inquiry, the correspondence of the coal seams in this neighbourhood, with those in the southern part of Yorkshire ; and, at the same time, hazarded a few conjectures on this head, in order that the curiosity of the members of the Society might be excited to further investigation, the result of which might be brought forward at some future meeting. Mr. Briggs also mentioned having met with a spring of mineral water at about 100 yards from the surface, in boring at Newton, near Castleford; a small quantity of which had been analyzed by Mr. Dawson, the chemist of Wakefield, who, from 2 ounces of the water, had obtained $18\frac{1}{2}$ grains of chloride of sodium, or common salt, with a small admixture of magnesia and lime.

Mr. Morton, of Newmarket, then made some observations on Mr. Briggs' paper. He alluded to the commonly received notion that the Middleton coal is the same bed as the Haigh Moor coal, and considered it of importance that the truth or falsity of this opinion should be investigated. For this purpose he exhibited three surface sections. The first taken in a N.W. direction from the lawns near Ardsley to the West Pit at Middleton, showing the rapid rise to the north of the Haigh Moor coal, and its outbreak on Ardsley Common ; and he contended that the measures further to the north were the Middleton measures, dipping southward under the Haigh Moor, or Ardsley measures. The second section, in a N.E. direction from Ardsley to the Victoria Pit, on Rothwell Haigh, exhibited the basset of the Haigh Moor coal, near Thorp, and that of the great quarrystone beneath, which forms the upper stratum of the Robin Hood and Rothwell Haigh collieries. This section crosses the great fault that separates the Lofthouse from the Robin Hood colliery. It has hitherto been considered a downcast fault to the east, throwing the Haigh Moor coal down to the level of the Middleton coal. Mr. Morton stated that there is no evidence to support this assumption ; but, on the contrary, the head or leader of the fault is that of an upcast to the east, and Mr. Morton opinion is that instead of the fault in question having depressed the Haigh Moor measures about 120 yards, as previously supposed, it has elevated the Middleton measures in an easterly direction. The third section commenced near the River

Calder at Newmarket, and taking a N.W. course to Rhodes Green, Rothwell, terminated at the Victoria pit on Rothwell Haigh. This section represented the rise of the Newmarket or Haigh Moor coal to the northward, until it appears at the surface in the escarpment of the hill south of Rothwell. The latter village stands upon the Middleton and Rothwell Haigh great quarry-stone, which, rising northward, also forms the upper stratum of the Victoria pit, where the Middleton coal is nearly 170 yards deep. The section clearly showed that the Rothwell Haigh measures dip under, and lie beneath the Newmarket measures. It follows, therefore, that wheresoever the Haigh Moor or Lofthouse coal exists, the Rothwell Haigh or Middleton coal also exists at a depth probably of 180 yards lower down. He further contended, that without going into minute detail, but merely by referring to the geological map of Yorkshire, the non-identity of these two coal beds would be apparent. Ardsley, Lofthouse-gate, and Newmarket stand upon what Dr. Smith calls the Woolley Edge Rock formation. Middleton, Thorp, and Rothwell Haigh stand upon a deeper formation, viz. the Bradgate. The Haigh Moor coal forms the base of the Woolley Edge Rock, while the Middleton coal lies nearly at the bottom of the Bradgate Rock; so that to identify the two beds of coal would be to identify also these two rock formations; an assimilation altogether at variance with the geographical and geological structure of the district. Finally, Mr. Morton stated that the fossils of the Haigh Moor measures are different from those of the Middleton measures. The former abound in ferns and stigmaria; the latter are characterised by a profusion of calamites, mussel shells, and fishes. The stigmaria, which are so plentiful in the former, are rarely if ever found in the latter; while the mussel binds, and the fish shales of the Middleton and Rothwell Haigh Collieries are never found in sinking to the Haigh Moor coal.

Mr. Embleton remarked, that after the clear manner in which the non-identity of the Lofthouse coal and the Middleton Main coal had been established, he would only make one observation on the section No. I., exhibited by Mr. Morton. Mr. Morton alluded to the probability of the existence of a throw or dyke between Middleton and Ardsley, this he (Mr. E.) could assure the meeting was actually the case, and that the throw had been met with in the Middleton colliery, and also in a colliery to the west of Middleton, where the coal had been worked up to it for a considerable distance. At Middleton, the throw was evidently a downcast to the south, as the fissure of it was first met with on the roof of the coal; if the fissure had been first found in the floor, then it would have been an upcast, and would have destroyed the theory of Mr. Briggs and Mr. Morton. This was the only gap in Mr. Morton's section which required filling up, and a knowledge of the existence of this throw was enough of itself to prove the non-identity of the two seams, and of course, when this was done it was evident that the seams lying above the Haigh Moor coal were not the same as those found above the Middleton Main coal. Mr. Embleton begged to call the attention of the meeting to the patent safety fuse of Mr. Davy, of Camborne, in the county of Cornwall, which he assured the meeting would tend to diminish the many serious accidents from the premature ignition of gunpowder in blasting rocks and coal. In appearance, it was similar to turned cord, and enclosed a cylinder of gunpowder of 3-16ths of an inch in diameter. No "Spindle" being required, all accidents arising from the friction of the "stemming" against it was prevented. It was well adapted to conveying fire to charge under water. It had been introduced into Cornwall, and wherever it had been used, accidents had visibly diminished. Mr. Embleton then produced specimens of Middletonite, a new mineral which he discovered at Middleton colliery about five years ago, and which had lately been analysed by Professor Johnston, and found to be a peculiar compound of oxygen, hydrogen, and carbon, and closely allied to oil of turpentine. The professor considered it to be an altered resin belonging to one of those trees, from which it seems probable coal may have been formed. In confirmation of this, Mr. Embleton stated that it was found in thin layers in the coal, that the thin layers were not continuous, and that the resin appeared to lie on the bark of the tree from which it had exuded, for when the separation between this substance and the coal was minutely examined, it was not a plain surface, but exhibited some indentations, as are found in making a section of the bark of some trees.

The Chairman requested Mr. Fourness, of Leeds, to explain to the meeting the nature of his invention for ventilating mines.

Mr. Fourness stated that as the model of his ventilating machine was still at Newcastle, he was unable to enter so fully into its merits as he could wish. He, however, drew a diagram to show the nature of the invention, which consisted of a fan of a certain description to be turned by a steam-engine, which would cause it to make 600 revolutions a minute. He said he felt fully confident that he could ventilate any mine, however fiery, with his machine, in a manner that would be perfectly satisfactory to the proprietors. Mr. Fourness also entered into calculations, showing the superiority of his plan over any other method now employed in the ventilation of mines.

Mr. Morton adverted to the ebbing and flowing of the fire-damp in coal mines according to the barometric state of the atmosphere, and seemed impressed with the importance of keeping up an unintermittent current of pure air through the workings, in order to clear them of this dangerous gas. He thought the construction and application of the ventilating machine prevented it from sustaining a constant atmospheric current. Every stoppage of the engine would necessarily stop the ventilator, and thereby produce a check in the air underground, which would soon be dangerously felt in a fiery mine. To these objections, the furnaces at present in use are not liable; for, if the furnace only be kept burning, the current of air continually moves onward through the workings. In cases of emergency, where a mine is full of fire-damp, and when it would be dangerous to kindle a furnace, the ventilating machine is highly useful for drawing out the inflammable gas without explosion; but as a permanent substitute for a well-constructed furnace, the ventilator does not seem to be well adapted. He thought the ventilator was an old invention, and exhibited a plate and description of the the machine in an early edition of Emerson's Mechanics.

A memorial to the Board of Ordnance, to expedite the publication of their Map of the West Riding, was laid on the table, and signed by the members.

G. B. Greenough, Esq., in returning thanks for having been

elected an honorary member of the society, expressed the high pleasure it gave him to meet any body of men associated together for the discovery and dissemination of truth; and his gratification was increased, when they had in view the cultivation and diffusion of geological knowledge. The study of geology had been to him, through life, the source of much happiness; and he earnestly recommended the pursuit of this science, as tending to enlighten and enrich the people. He cordially approved of the objects of the society, and advised the members to occupy themselves as much as possible in the examination of the geological structure of this particular district. He expressed his surprise that geology should ever have been considered inimical to religion, and concurred with the chairman in his sentiments on this subject. He then alluded to the deficiencies and inaccuracies of many of our geographical maps, and, considering it highly essential that the observations of geologists should be faithfully laid down and recorded; he rejoiced at the cooperation of local societies with the British Association in urging upon government the desirableness of speedily completing and publishing the ordnance surveys.

A vote of thanks to the chairman having been proposed, Mr. Lascelles returned thanks, and again adverted to the necessity of observing the geological phenomena in the district with the greatest attention; after which the meeting broke up, and a party of the members retired to the Strafford Arms, where a dinner had been provided for them, and was of the most sumptuous description. Venison, game, and dessert had been liberally sent by Earl Fitzwilliam, the president, and Mr. Beaumont. Several speeches were made during the evening, amongst others, one by G. B. Greenough, Esq., on the utility of museums, an abstract of which will be found in a succeeding chapter.

The fourth quarterly meeting of this Society was held at Wakefield, in the Music Saloon, at 12 o'clock on Thursday, December 6th, 1838. The Rt. Hon. Lord Wharncliffe occupied the chair, and was accompanied on the platform by the Hon. J. S. Wortley, Mr. J. C. Brandling, Mr. Godfrey Wentworth, the Rev. S. Sharp, Mr. Thomas Wilson, Rev. W. Thorp, and others. At this meeting Mr.

Fletcher, of Broomsgrove, near Worcester, gave an account of a new safety lamp which he had invented, the principal of which was that when the presence of fire-damp was indicated by increased flame inside the lamp, a thread was burnt which let down a door both at the top and bottom of the lamp, and thus excluded the air and extinguished the flame. Mr. Fletcher also proposed to light mines by conveying fire-damp in pipes, in a similar manner to the one employed in conveying coal-gas for the illumination of streets. The following report of the meeting is from the *Leeds Intelligencer* of December 15th.

Mr. Morton, of Newmarket, in commenting upon Mr. Fletcher's statements, described the casualties and injuries to which the Davy Lamp is subject in the hands of a collier. He said the " Davy" is unsafe when either the lamp or the inflammable gas is in motion, and that a current of gas moving against a lamp at the rate of five feet per second, is liable to be exploded by the passage of the flame from the inside to the outside of the wire gauze cage. He explained the additions and improvements made by Dr. Clanney and by Upton on the Davy Lamp, and he considered that the lamp constructed by Mr. Fletcher is an ingenious combination of Davy's, Clanney's, and Upton's principles. Mr. Morton recommended Mr. Fletcher to devote his talents and attention to the simplification and perfection of his invention, rather than to the lighting of mines by means of the fire-damp. " Similar schemes," he said, " have previously been attempted and have completely failed, owing to the uncertain supply of the gas, its very weak illuminating power, and the complexity and expense of the apparatus requisite for its collection and distribution."

Mr. Embleton, of Middleton, considered all the proposals hitherto made for applying the fire-damp of coal-mines as a lighting agent, to be quite impracticable.

Mr. Hartop thought the Davy-lamp might be made perfectly safe by surrounding one-half of the circumference of the wire gauze with a shield, but Mr. Morton said that it was proved to be unsafe in an inflammable current even with the addition of the shield originally suggested by Davy, and just mentioned by Mr. Hartop.

Mr. Henry Holt exhibited and explained plans and drawings of Hague's Patent Pumping Apparatus, which he recommended as a substitute for the common pumping engine; after which a conversation ensued between Mr. Holt and Mr. Hartop, relative to the application and economy of this machine; which ended in a request from the meeting that Mr. Holt would institute a further examination into the merits of the invention, more especially with reference to its effective power, first cost, wear and tear, and its general adaptation to coal mines. Mr. Holt promised to comply with the request, and lay the result of his inquiries before a future meeting.

Mr. Briggs, of Overton, produced a model of an improvement which he had made in the pulley frame placed at the top of a pit for drawing coals, the principle of which he described. He also exhibited some round and flat rope, constructed of wire, which he had himself made, after reading a description of those used in the Hungarian mines. He stated that a wire rope of one inch circumference is equal in strength to a hemp rope of four inches; that the wire rope is lighter than, and as pliable as the hemp, and will perform nearly double the work.

The Rev. W. Thorp, of Womersley, read a paper on the Yorkshire and Lancashire coal fields. Mr. Thorp's lines of argument tended to prove that there were many data in favour of the identity of the two coal fields; in fact, that at one time they were a continuous tract. It is impossible to give more than a meagre outline of the large mass of information that he had collected on the subject, especially as much of that information requires to be elucidated by the numerous sections he exhibited. He first described and traced on his map the various axes of elevation in the two coal fields, and showed the effects produced by those elevations. Again, he followed the line of Millstone Grit which underlies both the Yorkshire and Lancashire coal fields, and next, the range of two seams of millstone grit coal, better known in this neighbourhood by the name of the Halifax beds—beds similar to those he pointed out as occuring in Lancashire, under the same peculiar circumstances in which they are found in Yorkshire. He noticed also the singular fact of the deposit of marine shells (Pecten papyraceus) in this part of the millstone grit formation. He also pointed out the appearance of the flagstone in each field, as another proof of their identity in structure.

A number of new members were proposed and elected, and several valuable donations of Geological specimens, &c., were announced; a vote of thanks to the noble chairman terminated the proceedings, and the members adjourned to dine together at the Strafford Arms.

The early months of 1839 were occupied by the enthusiastic founders of the Society in making arrangements for succeeding meetings; and the preliminary discussion relative to the formation of the museum. The most devoted attention was shown to the interests of the Society at its frequent council meetings, more especially by the Rev. W. Thorp, Messrs. Embleton, Briggs, Hartop, Morton, and above all by the honorary secretary, Mr. Thos. Wilson. Besides the constant care these gentlemen gave to the details of the organization and management of the affairs of the Society, they were the most frequent contributors of papers at its quarterly meetings, and from their practical knowledge of the stratification of the district, and their experience in the economic and commercial value of the mining industries, they were able to contribute most valuable information to the discussions which generally arose when papers were read. The influence of the Society was widely felt, and communications were made with neighbouring counties, as well as those situated at a greater distance. The Geologists in Lancashire, with Mr. Edward W. Binney and Mr. Bowman at their head, formed a society on the lines so successfully laid down by their Yorkshire friends. The Society had its centre at Manchester, but adopting the peripatetic method of our Society it wisely decided to hold a certain proportion of its meetings in neighbouring towns.

A Report on the state and prospects of the Society was prepared by the council, and presented at the meeting held at Wakefield, on the 7th March, 1839. From this it is gathered that "the Council have great pleasure in being able to congratulate the members on its condition and prospects; and they entertain a confident hope, that if it continue to be animated by the same spirit that has hitherto characterized all its proceedings, it will not fail to accomplish the important ends for which it was established.

To acquire a perfect knowledge of the mineral riches that lie beneath our feet, and to improve the arts which are employed in raising them to the surface and fitting them for the use of man, were the two main objects for which the Geological and Polytechnic Society was instituted, objects which though local and limited in their extent, are yet of great national importance ; but which as they require exact local knowledge, and the collection of an infinite number of minute details, can only be attained by a local Society.

The interest which has for many years attached to the study of the structure of the earth, and the spirit in which it has latterly been conducted, leave little room to doubt, that ere long the general principles of Geology will be established on the sure basis of induction ; but while the attention of Geologists, whether as individuals or as societies, is engrossed with the pursuit of these objects, there is some risk that this more minute examination of local phenomena would be neglected, which is necessary to call forth for the use of man, in their fullest extent and at the least cost, those hidden treasures which the great Architect of the Universe has placed beneath our feet. It is in this that we behold the proper sphere of action of all local Societies, and for this they possess peculiar advantages.

It is our lot to inhabit one of the most important mineral districts in the kingdom, with which, whether we be landowners, merchants, manufacturers or tradesmen, our interests are intimately connected. We may not suffer its resources to remain neglected or wasted, as they must be if pursued with imperfect knowledge, when a little exertion and expense are all that are required to prevent this evil. Much no doubt may be expected from the gratuitous exertions and offerings of individuals, but much will remain that can only be accomplished by a liberal expenditure. Though an abundant collection of the fossils of the district may safely be calculated upon, and models of various improved machines be presented ; though plans and sections and minute details may be accumulated, yet it will be necessary to provide the means of preserving and arranging the one, and of combining and uniting the other on one general map, while the purchasing of a library is an object that should not be overlooked.

To meet these expenses, the Society must rely on its annual

subscriptions ; and as the subscription has been fixed at the low rate of half-a-guinea, with the view of placing the advantages of the Institution within the reach of as large a class as possible, it is only by a corresponding increase in number, that the Society can obtain the requisite funds. Although the present number of subscribers, which is 163, may be deemed satisfactory, considering the short period of the Society's existence, yet when the great wealth and extent of the district are taken into account, there can be no doubt that a large accession of members may be obtained. The Council, therefore, earnestly recommend to every member, to institute an active canvass in his respective neighbourhood.

The experience of the past year has suggested some alterations in the rules of the Society, which the Council, after mature deliberation, venture to recommend. It has been found that much uncertainty prevails as to the time at which the annual subscription falls due ; and it is therefore recommended that the practice of the Society should be assimilated to that of other Institutions, and that the subscriptions should be due on the 1st of January.

The Council has also bestowed considerable reflection on the propriety of holding some of its meetings at other places ; and the result of their deliberations is to recommend that the June and December meetings be held in turn in the great towns of the Riding. By this means it is hoped that a wider interest in the Society will be awakened and sustained, at the same time that information respecting the more remote localities will be more easily obtained in the neighbourhood to which it refers. It is also very desirable that the Annual Meeting should be held at a period of the year when the attendance of the President and Vice-presidents may reasonably be calculated upon ; and when an opportunity would be offered for sending invitations to the scientific strangers who attend the meetings of the British Association ; which would be accomplished by allowing the Council to fix such day in the month of August or September, as would suit the engagements of those who might promise to attend.

There is no point which has been more earnestly urged on the attention of the Council, and none to which they have more devoted their thoughts, than the collection of a complete series of the organic remains with which the Coal formation abounds. Anxious to lose no time in this most desirable measure, the Council have hired a building for a temporary museum, where they may arrange the fossils that may be presented to them, until such time as the subscriptions for a museum shall enable them to erect a suitable building. Mr. H. Holt has kindly undertaken the office of curator ; and it is requested that all donations may be directed to him. As the value of these fossils depends upon their systematic arrangement, it becomes an object of immediate importance to provide cases for their reception, and to construct these so as not to be unworthy of a permanent museum, will require about £500. The Council have pleasure in announcing that a subscription for this purpose has been commenced, headed by Earl Fitzwilliam with a donation of £50.

The Council may appeal with confidence to the proceedings of the past year, in proof of the utility of the Society. They regret that the funds have not permitted them to print all the papers that have hitherto been read ; but they have felt it due to the kindness and liberality with which Prof. Johnston entered into the views of the Society at its establishment, and still more to its own intrinsic merits, to publish his masterly and luminous address at the Society's second meeting; and they have great pleasure in placing in the hands of the members and the public, so comprehensive an exposition of the objects of the society.

From its own members the most valuable communications have been received, both in the Geological and Polytechnic department. Two papers by Rev. W. Thorp, the fruits of long and minute examination of the geology of the Riding, exhibit a complete view of present aspect and condition of the coal field ; and endeavour to show the circumstances that attended on, or preceded its origin.

By the paper of Mr. Briggs on the non-identity of the "Haigh Moor" and "Rothwell-Haigh" seams, a commencement has been made in that minute examination and connection of local phenomena, by which alone the coal measures in one part of the district can be identified with those of another. It is hoped that this plan, so important for mining pursuits, and so easy to those who are engaged in them, will be followed up by other members.

Mr. Hartop's paper on the great heave in the valley of the Don, describes a dislocation of the strata of enormous extent and of very great interest.

In the Polytechnic department, Mr. Embleton and Mr. Briggs have exhibited and explained the Safety fuse and Iron ropes: the former of which has been for some time in use in Cornwall, and the latter have recently been introduced abroad.

In this branch also, two communications have been made on the important subjects of ventilation and the safety lamp. Both of these came from strangers, one from a gentleman who, from philanthropic motives alone, had turned his attention to the prevention of accident from fire-damp. It is one of the advantages of this Institution, that it offers an opportunity for speculative and ingenious men to make known their various plans for the improvement of the art of mining. It will ever be the wish of the Society to receive such suggestions with attention, and to discuss them with candour.

Since the establishment of this Society, one having precisely the same objects, has been formed in the neighbouring county of Lancaster. It will be the interest of both Societies to maintain a constant and friendly intercourse, and the proceedings and investigations of each Society may be expected to throw light on the inquiries of the other."

At the same meeting Mr. T. W. Embleton read a paper on the strata between the Bradford Rock and the Forty Yards Coal at Middleton, and Mr. Henry Hartop communicated one on a new mode of judging High Pressure Boilers. The paper by Mr. Embleton was illustrated by a number of specimens of the rocks passed through in sinking a shaft from the surface to the first workable coal in the Middleton Colliery, and confirmed the observations made by Mr. Henry Briggs, which were the subject of a paper communicated to the society at a previous meeting. The author insists on a careful comparison, not only of the several beds of shale sandstone or coal composing sections in various localities, but also of the fossils usually found in the roof of the coal. Notwithstanding the most careful examinations mistakes were liable to arise, and many perplexing circumstances have to be taken into account, for instance a thick bed of sandstone exists in one district, but at a very short distance it has become comparatively thin, or has split up into several thin beds with intercalating shales. The author further suggests that all the sections should be made on the same scale, viz., 1 inch to 1 yard, and that a uniform scheme of colours should be used to indicate the several groups of strata; the fossils found in each successive stratum should be recorded on the sheet opposite the stratum from which they have been got; so that a correct record of the horizon and the locality should be secured and confusion prevented when the specimens were placed in the museum. The several strata passed through in sinking the shaft are given in detail, and the fossils found in them are stated. In a bed of bituminous shale above coal No. 25, "there were found four or five kinds of teeth belonging to as many species of fish, and an endless profusion of fragments of bones. I have succeeded in obtaining four small jaws (spines) in almost a perfect state of preservation with the teeth attached. In passing I would remark that this shale is highly bituminous, affording, when distilled, an intensely luminous gas and a large proportion of tar. In both respects it is not inferior to the best stone coal. This stratum is of so peculiar a nature and so decidedly distinct from any other stratum in the section that I am led to believe that the same features will be found wherever it occurs, and if so will form a good point from which to compare other sections." Mr. Embleton concludes his paper by a number of philosophical deductions respecting the formation and deposition of the several beds forming the West Riding Coal-field. He expresses a strong opinion that the coal seams are the result of the growth and decay of vegetation on the area over which the coal is now found to extend, whilst of the sandstones and shales he is of opinion that they exhibit abundant evidence of having being rolled in water, and transported from more or less remote districts before being deposited where they are now found.

On the 3rd of May, 1839, an important meeting of the council was held, at which, Messrs. Embleton and Morton were requested to confer with the Lancashire Society as to the scales to be adopted for sections and plans. An active canvass was decided upon to obtain money to purchase cases for the museum. It was also considered that it was very desirable that some of the proceedings and papers should be printed if the funds of the Society would afford the means to do so.

The next quarterly meeting was held at the Cutlers' Hall, Sheffield, on the 6th June. The chair was occupied by Lord Howard. The society met as usual at 12.0 noon. At four the members adjourned to the Tontine Hotel, where they dined, the tickets, as the circular quaintly puts it, 6s. 6d. each, including a pint of wine, were to be had at the Inn. The following report of the meeting is abstracted from the *Sheffield and Rotherham Independent* of the 8th of June, 1839.—The attendance at the forenoon meeting was highly respectable. Lord Howard having addressed the meeting, twenty-eight gentlemen were elected members of the society.

Mr. T. W. Embleton, of Middleton, briefly remarked that at present there was no survey of the county on a large scale, such as was necessary to an accurate delineation of the geological features of the country. He hoped that, by the assistance of similar societies to this, in urging the matter on the attention of government, this important work might be promoted. He moved the adoption of a petition to the House of Commons, for a new ordnance survey of the Northern Counties on the scale of six inches to a mile.

The Rev. W. Thorp, of Womersley, seconded the motion.

The petition was read by the Secretary, and adopted. It set forth that the coal fields of this district extend over 462 miles, and contain many beds of coal and iron-stone of great importance to the manufactures of the country. That the risk and loss of capital in mining are greatly increased by the want of accurate knowledge of the condition of the minerals, and of records of former workings. That the objects of this Society are chiefly to obtain correct information on these subjects, and to record it for the public use ; and that most of the gentlemen interested in the mining operations of the district have joined the Society. That a map on a large scale is necessary, because it is only on such a map that it is possible to lay down intelligibly and accurately the extent of seam, and the magnitude and bearing of faults and workings. That this object is so important in a national point of view, that it ought to be done at the national expense; and as the ordnance surveys of Ireland are on a scale of six inches to a mile, the petitioners prayed that the legislature would authorise a similar survey of the northern counties of England.

Mr. H. Hartop, then moved, and Mr. C. Morton. seconded a resolution to invite the British Association to hold their next meeting in one of the towns of the West Riding, which was unanimously agreed to.

The Rev. W. Thorp read a paper on the Geology of the neighbourhood of Sheffield. It was largely illustrated by diagrams and sections, and resulted in a discussion of some of the points raised, more especially with reference to the much disputed faults in the valley of the Don. The paper was not printed, Mr. Thorp retaining it for a proposed work on the West Riding Coal-field. Messrs. Hartop, Morton, and Prof. Johnston spoke.

Mr. Charles Morton then proceeded to read a paper on the Utility of Geology, as applied to Mining, Agriculture, and the Arts. He remarked, that geologists had too long been considered to be mere antiquarian theorists; but his object was to show the high utility of geology. He adverted to the internal condition of the earth, as capable of being known from its exterior surface, and to the immense losses which had been caused by the ignorant search for minerals, in situations where a geologist would at once know they could not be found. He adverted, also, to other cases, where the science of geology had enabled man to reach valuable minerals, in situations where ignorant persons had long been convinced they did not exist, or were inaccessible. Such was the discovery of the Warwickshire coal-field, under the red sandstone, and the Hetton and other Durham coals, which had been reached through the limestone. In reference to railway operations, he remarked on the importance of going in the longitudinal direction of the strata. The case of the North Midland was a remarkable illustration of this. The line followed the rule he had described, and went chiefly through soft cuttings. But the opposition had attempted to bring it by a route which would have intersected the rocks almost at right angles. He adverted, also, to the advantages which geology would confer on architecture ; and on agriculture, in reference to manuring and draining ; and the great value of geological knowledge to colonists. He referred to Dr. Smith, "who may be regarded as the father of English geology, and who has collected an immense amount of knowledge on the subject, which it is feared that his embarrassed circumstances will render him unable to bring before the world." Mr. Morton recommended this as an exceedingly fit case for the liberal interposition of government. In various respects, the government was then encouraging the increase of geological knowledge, which he hailed as a favourable sign of the times.

On the motion of Mr. Embleton, seconded by Mr. Wilson, the thanks of the society were voted to the Rev. Mr. Thorp and Mr. Morton, for their valuable and interesting papers.

Mr. Hall then exhibited a patent hydraulic belt for raising water. The machinery consists of a cylinder working in the water, and another corresponding to it, a little above the point to which the water is to be raised. A woollen belt passing under the lower and over the upper cylinder is moved by their revolutions, and brings up great quantities of water, which is thrown off by the working of the belt over the upper cylinder. By this cheap and simple machinery, it was explained that water had been raised to the height of 130 feet by a seven inch band, at the rate of 80 gallons per minute.

The Chairman then announced the adjournment of the meeting to seven o'clock in the evening. At four o'clock, about 60 gentlemen sat down to an ordinary at the Tontine, when Lord Howard presided, and his Lordship took occasion to remark upon the importance of the Society, so capable of rendering great services to the neighbourhood, being adequately supported by all persons resident within the sphere of its operations. The interesting proceedings of this morning convinced him of the great utility of this Society, and made him regret that he had been absent from the former meetings.

In the evening, Lord Howard, on taking the chair, expressed his gratification to see so large an audience. He remarked, that we so constantly use coal, that we seldom think of its original formation, or of the hand that formed it; and yet we could scarcely find in nature a greater proof of the wisdom and goodness of the Creator than in the ample provision he had made in the bowels of the earth for our advantage. He had no doubt that the lecture of the learned Professor would have the effect of causing them to think of coal, its origin, and its uses, with much juster views than they had been accustomed to.

Professor Johnston then proceeded to deliver an elaborate and most interesting lecture on the origin of coal. He first proved, by a variety of botanical and chemical arguments, that it is of vegetable origin; he then showed that it was formed by the decay of vegetable substances. In this branch of the enquiry, the Professor explained minutely the composition of different kinds of coal, and showed that the varieties are caused by the different stages of vegetable decay, to the continued progress of which operation, he attributed the generation of the fatal gases that occur in coal mines. The last branch of enquiry was, whether the masses of vegetable matter which form coal had grown on the spot where they are deposited, or had been carried into hollows by inundations, and then settled in the masses in which they are found. The lecturer stated minutely the arguments alleged for and against each of these theories, and concluded that the balance of evidence was in favour of the theory that they had grown upon the spot. The lecturer concluded with a few observations on the vast masses of vegetable matter which had been laid up in store for the use of man, and the proof which the subject afforded of infinite wisdom and beneficent design.

The Lecturer concluded a little before ten o'clock, when a vote of thanks was moved by Mr. Embleton, and seconded by Mr. Morton, who described the lecture as one of the most interesting and instructive discourses that he had ever heard or read on the subject. The table of chemical gradations from vegetable matter, through the different varieties of lignite and brown coal, down to cannel, and true-caking coal, was both original and beautiful, and as clearly established the vegetable origin of coal, by chemical reasoning, as it had previously been proved by geological arguments.

FORMATION OF THE SOCIETY : UNPUBLISHED RECORDS. 39

After a vote of thanks to the noble chairman had been passed, the meeting separated.

On the 5th September, 1839, the president, Earl Fitzwilliam, presided at a meeting held at Wakefield. The Rev. W. Thorp read a paper on the Coal measures South and North of the River Calder, and Dr. Wright explained a model of a gin, which had been constructed by his father.

The foundation and early history of the society comprised in the two first years of its existence have now been traced. During this time the proceedings of the society were unpublished, and the sources of information have been restricted ; without the help, so generously afforded by Mr. T. W. Embleton, any connected history would have been impossible, except of the most meagre description, and it has been a fortunate circumstance in connection with this part of the Society's history, that Mr. Embleton, during the first five years of Society's existence, carefully preserved the published reports and printed rules, together with an almost daily record in his diary of the meetings, and doings of the council and its several members, all which have been unreservedly placed at the disposal of the writer.

CHAPTER II.

SOME OF THE FOUNDERS OF THE SOCIETY.

The biographical notices of members of the Society which follow have been kindly prepared by those whose names are attached. It has not been considered desirable to include a detailed description of the special work done by each member, in connection with the institution and rise of the Society; that will be found in its proper place in other pages. Neither does it appear desirable that the notice should be restricted to the scientific side of the individual's character, but rather that it should present as varied and full a picture of him as may be consistent with the space at our disposal, and the information and knowledge possessed by the biographer.

The Society, during its existence of more than half a century has had two presidents; first, Earl Fitzwilliam, K.G., who was elected at its first meeting in 1837, and continued to hold and adorn the office until his death in 1857; and second, the Marquis of Ripon, K.G., who, as Viscount Goderich, M.P., was elected in 1858, and continues still, without intermission, after a period of more than 30 years, to occupy the position. The Society has been fortunate in being presided over by two gentlemen, who, whilst an ornament to their high position and estate, have placed their wide knowledge and accumulated experience at the disposal of the council and the members. Both imbued with a thorough sympathy with everything calculated to be of use to their fellows, they have always encouraged the spread of education, and sought by all the means in their power to infuse a love of learning in those with whom they have associated. This Society is, at any rate, a living witness of the success of those efforts.

The memoir, relating to the first president of the Society, which immediately follows is from the pen of the Rev. Alfred Gatty, M.A., vicar of Ecclesfield, whose works on archæological and topographical subjects are well known and appreciated.

EARL FITZWILLIAM, K.G., FIRST PRESIDENT.

Charles William Wentworth, fifth Earl Fitzwilliam, was born in Grosvenor Square, on 4th May, 1786, and was the only child of William, the fourth Earl, his mother being Lady Charlotte Ponsonby, second daughter of the Earl of Bessborough.

It is somewhat remarkable, that amongst all the fine portraits, old and modern, which grace the walls of the grand mansion at Wentworth, there is no likeness in mature life of the distinguished nobleman, who is the subject of this brief memoir. There is the lovely picture of a child, standing with a lamb by his side, which was painted by Sir Joshua Reynolds. This is hung over the fireplace in the state drawing-room, and represents the late Earl, when about six years old. When he was sixteen he was painted by Hopner, and the likeness is at Wentworth. Of course he was subjected to the ordinary education becoming his station, and at Eton his likeness was added to the head-master's collection of portraits of distinguished sixth form boys. He did not graduate at either university; for into both domestic and public life he entered, at a very early age. He had married, and become a member of the House of Commons, as Lord Milton (his father being still alive), before he had attained his majority. He married an honourable lady, Mary Dundas, fourth daughter of Thomas, first Lord Dundas, on 8th July, 1806; and it was in the following year that he offered himself as a candidate to represent in Parliament the undivided county of York, in the Whig interest, in opposition to the Honourable H. Lascelles, who was a Tory; and a more memorable contest was never fought by political rivals to secure the coveted prize.

The county returned two members, and the three competitors were Mr. Wilberforce, the Hon. H. Lascelles, and Lord Milton; and Wilberforce being the people's favourite, and a native of Hull, polled 11,808 votes, his expenses being chiefly defrayed by public subscription, Viscount Milton gained 11,177 votes, including about 9,000 plumpers, and Mr. Lascelles found only 10,990 supporters. The polling lasted for a fortnight, and the cost of bringing the constituents to the poll, and then maintaining them, for they were in no hurry to return home, was so extravagant, that the election is said to have cost each of the noble families of Fitzwilliam and Lascelles no less a sum than £100,000.

Lord Milton's first speech in the House of Commons was in favour of religious freedom, a principle which he always advocated, although he was himself a consistent churchman, a great promoter of the building and supporting of new churches, and he held that the church rate was as reasonable a tax as the rate for maintaining the poor; and he would have had this rate continued for the maintenance of the national churches, which, being open to all, he thought were entitled to national support.

In 1812, 1818, 1820 and 1826, Lord Milton was returned to Parliament as a member for Yorkshire without opposition.

In 1830 he did not again offer himself to the Yorkshire constituency, in consequence of his father's failing health, but joined Lord Althorp in seeking election for Northamptonshire, where there was a keen political struggle ; for a Tory squirearchy was abundant in that county. The large possessions of Earl Fitzwilliam, connected with the Milton estate, near Peterborough, made it important that a member of his family should represent this neighbourhood; but it so happened, that prior to the election, Lady Milton became fatally ill, and their son, the Hon. W. Wentworth, who was only eighteen years old, took the place of his father, who was disabled by this domestic affliction ; and he addressed the various constituencies of the county with such energy and eloquence that he secured Lord Milton's return. Lady Milton died on 1st November, 1830, and his lordship continued to represent Northamptonshire until he succeeded to the earldom on 8th February, 1833, when his father died at the advanced age of 85.

Although the late Earl was never attached to any ministry, during the fifty years that he occupied a conspicuous position in political life, twenty-three years of which he was the undisturbed member for Yorkshire, he nevertheless commanded public attention, and exercised considerable influence by the very decided opinions that he held on the national interests of the day, and the boldness with which he expressed them.

This was made especially apparent in 1832, when Lord Grey resigned the premiership, on the King refusing to create some fifty peers to secure the passing of his great Reform Bill in the House of Lords. There was so much indignation in the country against both King and Lords, that the Duke of Wellington came to the rescue, and offered to serve either as the head, or a subordinate in a government, which would provide a majority of peers that would pass a Reform Bill, which would be Lord Grey's own measure, with some amendments.

This loyal effort on the Duke's part, to stand by the King in an emergency, was interpreted by Lord Fitzwilliam as a concession made to obtain place and power for himself and party, and he denounced the proceedings, as a change of policy suggested by a desire for personal advantage. But of such conduct the Duke was quite incapable; and the occurrence is only mentioned as an instance of the independence and purity of Lord Fitzwilliam's own political life. In fact, being a Whig trained in the political school of Burke, he shared in that statesman's horror of the excesses of the great French Revolution, and was not at first eager for any sweeping reform of parliamentary representation; but there was ample room for improvement, and for this his lordship strove.

As early as in the year 1820, he was both a Free Trader and a Reformer, but he knew where to stop; and when, in 1831, he published "An Address to the landowners of Great Britain on the Corn Laws," it was against a sliding scale that he principally combated; and after Peel's measure for a total repeal of the duty on the importation of foreign corn had been passed, he maintained that a moderate fixed duty would have been preferable. The Dissenters having their disabilities removed in 1828, and the Roman Catholics being relieved in 1829, had his hearty approval; and a fairer and more honourable representative of the old Whig school of politicians than the late Earl Fitzwilliam, it would be difficult to select.

Reverting to the early life of the noble Earl, it may be said, that when he came of age, as Lord Milton, the festivities celebrated on the properties, to which he was heir, corresponded in their *largesse* with the amount of their inheritance. Being the sole offspring of his parents, his prospective property, with its responsibilities, was a very serious charge to contemplate. In the earlier history of the Fitzwilliam family, we find them owning the Sprotborough estate, near Doncaster; but in the Tudor days, their principal seat, purchased in 1500, was at Milton, near Peterborough, where the mansion is a most interesting house, of much architectural beauty, and still showing no signs of dilapidation or decay in the fine oolitic stone of which it is built.

The grandfather of the nobleman of whom we write married in 1744 Lady Anne Watson Wentworth, eldest daughter of the Marquis of Rockingham; and her son William, fourth Earl Fitzwilliam, inherited from his uncle, Charles, second Marquis of Rockingham and Lady Anne Wentworth's brother, the vast Wentworth property and the Irish estates, both of which had belonged to the great Lord Strafford and his son. The manors of Ecclesall, Bingley, and Badsworth, were included in the dowry of Miss Bright, who married the second Marquis, and left no family, and so they passed to his nephew, the fourth Earl. The Malton estate must also be included in this great inheritance; but it was not merely the wide acreage of land that constituted the value of these possessions, for underneath much of the soil were beds of coal and iron which had only been superficially worked, and therefore still contained a mine of wealth. The whole properties were a magnificent succession for an only son, and his majority had to be duly celebrated.

The writer has a friend, now in his ninety-third year, who well remembers being taken by his father into Wentworth Park, to witness the unlimited hospitality that was dispensed on the occasion of Lord Milton coming of age. It was a literal fulfilment of the invitation given to all comers by a Fitzwilliam, Lord of Elmsley and Sprotborough, which was formerly engraved on a cross that stood in the High street of the village:—

"Whoso is hungry and lists to eate,
Let him come to Sprotburgh to his meate;
And for a night, and for a day,
His horse shall have both corn and hay,
And no man shall ask him when he goeth away."

The festivities that took place in the Park, as well remembered by our venerable witness, must be regarded as arranged by the servants, who were not restricted in the hospitalities they offered to all comers, without respect for social distinction. Oxen were roasted whole on spits, formed of young fir trees; and the best ales from the extensive cellars under the great house flowed in dangerous plenty for the crowds, who came to the general festival. There may have been cases of excess; but this outdoor hospitality fully expressed that spirit of generosity which has ever characterized this noble family, without regard to class or station.

When Earl Fitzwilliam entered into possession of his estates in 1833, he was a widower, with a numerous family of children. His eldest son, Lord Milton, had married, in this same year, Lady Selina Jenkinson, second daughter of Charles, third Earl of Liverpool; and, to the great grief of his family, he died on 8th November, 1835, of typhus fever; a posthumous daughter ultimately married the son and heir of Lord Portman; and his widow married secondly, in 1845, George Savile Foljambe, Esq., of Osberton, Notts. The present peer, who became Lord Milton, married in 1838 Lady Francis Douglas, eldest daughter of the Earl of Morton; and there were two other sons, the Honourable George, and the Honourable Charles William, as well as six daughters. The eldest of these, Lady Charlotte, will be recalled by all who knew her with the highest respect and admiration. No lady could have filled a mother's vacant place with more graceful fitness; and her father must have felt the great comfort and support of her rule over his stately home.

Lord Fitzwilliam thoroughly maintained all the traditions of the noble ancestry whom he succeeded. A good horse, and he was a great rider, pleased him, as it did the Earl of Strafford beforetime; who, when Lord Deputy in Ireland, had sixty valuable horses in his stable; and yet the subject of this notice had the appearance and manner of a thorough statesman, and man of science, rather than a representative of sport. It may be said, that when his lordship became possessed of his Yorkshire property, the coal and iron trades were in their comparative infancy. The wealthy capitalist and the limited company had not arisen, and the mining engineer did not exist. But iron was beginning to supersede wood in various departments of construction; and coal was being consumed in larger quantities, owing to the increase and extension of population and trade. The great landowners, in the middle ages, being the only persons who could employ labour extensively, were accustomed to work the mineral beds superficially; and Lord Fitzwilliam took great interest, and incurred great responsibilities, without always reaping a beneficial return, both in mining operations and iron works, which were carried on by his agents. Geology was a favourite study with him, as well as the science of agriculture; and his knowledge was practically applied to the management of his Coollattin estate in Ireland, as well as his property in England.

Earl Fitzwilliam was the first president of the British Association for the advancement of science, founded at York in 1831. In conjunction with the Rev. W. Vernon Harcourt, third son of the Archbishop of York, and Professor John Phillips, who acted as secretary, his Lordship assisted in preparing the scheme for its formation and the rules for its guidance.

Six years later, in 1837, his lordship took an equally active part in the institution of the West Riding Geological and Polytechnic Society, and accepted an invitation to preside over it. He held the position of president up to the time of his decease in 1857. He presided at nearly all its annual meetings, and took a deep interest in the general proceedings of the Society. He subscribed freely to a museum at Wakefield, and contributed many geological specimens from the neighbourhood of his own residence. He showed at the meetings of its members how well he was acquainted with geology, as a science, and especially in its application to mining purposes in his own district, and also its important bearing on agriculture. He strongly supported the proposal, that this Society should be amalgamated with the Yorkshire Agricultural Society, and that they should form an united museum at York; but this was ultimately declined in 1841. The study and attention thus bestowed upon science have resulted in the fact, that the miner and ironworker on the Wentworth estate have had their safety and comfort regarded and secured with as much care as the labourer can enjoy, who works in the garden or on the farm.

SOME OF THE FOUNDERS OF THE SOCIETY. 47

We can remember a menagerie in the grounds of Wentworth, which no longer exists, but, in the late Earl's life, it afforded him much interest ; and amongst the specimens was said to have been a chimpanzee, one of the finest specimens that had been brought to England. The animal became ill and died, but not before it had received the best medical attention of the neighbourhood.

This noble family may justly be proud of their connection with the name and property of the ill-used minister of Charles I. ; and so, in 1807, William, the fourth Earl Fitzwilliam, preferred the name of Wentworth to that of his own family, and it has ever since been borne by all his descendants. When the present Earl's elder brother was living, he was called "Mr. Wentworth," as Viscount Milton's eldest son. Hence, it was a subject of considerable annoyance, when in 1847 Sir John Byng, who had been created Baron Strafford in 1835, was elevated to the title of Earl of Strafford. The late Earl Fitzwilliam naturally felt that this trenched on a grand name inseparably connected with his Wentworth estate, and he remonstrated with the Prime Minister, and even addressed the Throne, but the patent had been already granted, and Lord John Russell reminded the Earl that he had the substance and the other the shadow *(nominis umbra)*. This incident was the cause of his lordship restoring the old name of "Wentworth Woodhouse" to the mansion ; but several milestones in the neighbourhood still record on the roadside the distance from "Wentworth House." Being a judicious patron of art the Earl made valuable additions to both the pictures and sculptures at Wentworth, and he paved the grand saloon with marble, in completion of the architect Flitcroft's design, after removing a fine oak floor.

As Lord Fitzwilliam was an accomplished horseman, he rode great distances ; for instance, from Wentworth to Milton in one day, which covers a distance of not less than eighty miles ; and he would ride from London to Eton and back on a visit to his three sons when at school. And it is remarkable that a feat of horsemanship was immediately connected with his decease; for, notwithstanding the affliction during several years of a very painful disease, which required severe surgical treatment, and that he had attained the allotted term of human life, he still preserved his bodily activity, and was at his ease on horseback.

In the summer of 1857, a visit to Wentworth Woodhouse from the Queen and the Prince Consort was arranged ; and, prior to this event, his lordship went to stay with his kinsman, Lord Dundas, at Marsh Hall, near Guisborough, on the Yorkshire coast. Being fond of sea bathing he very much enjoyed this opportunity, and after taking a bath he actually came out of the water, remounted his horse, and swam it out to sea.

It was a violent, and as it proved, a fatal action for a septuagenarian. A shivering attack was followed by serious illness, which made it difficult to transport him to his home ; but this was effected under medical superintendence, and the royal visit was of course indefinitely postponed. A paralytic seizure rendered the case hopeless ; and on Sunday, 4th October, 1857, surrounded by his children, and his sons and daughters-in-law, the good Earl passed peacefully and without pain, into the other world, universally respected, and by those near to him beloved.

The property, both in England and Ireland, which belonged to Lord Strafford, remained with the earldom ; the Milton estate was appropriated to the Honourable George W. Fitzwilliam ; and the Badsworth estate to the Honourable Charles W. Fitzwilliam, brothers of the present Earl.

We rather linger over Lord Fitzwilliam's character. He was a man singularly thoughtful and just, as well as generous. Being thoroughly domestic, the smallest affair that touched his home received his attention. He exercised great bounty, but it was not bestowed indiscriminately, or without enquiry. As a landlord he had vast experience, owing to the great variety of his possessions, which included lands, mines, factories, houses, &c. ; and all who were under him felt the benefit of being in the hands of a proprietor, who could and would investigate all cases that were brought before him. In a word, he was a man invested with great responsibilities, and his whole life showed that he felt their importance and their claim upon his time and thoughts.

At a meeting of the society, held in the Philosophical Hall,

SOME OF THE FOUNDERS OF THE SOCIETY. 49

Leeds, on January 28th, 1858, Thomas Wilson, Esq. was in the chair, and in opening the proceedings, referred to the death of Earl Fitzwilliam. "He was sure that those present that day would all join with him in deeply regretting the loss the society had sustained by the death of their first and only president, Earl Fitzwilliam. That nobleman took an active part in the business of the society throughout its existence. Not only was he most liberal whenever the society applied to him, offering as he did, the sum of £500, towards the establishment of a museum, if it could be carried out; but he attended the meetings and did everything to further the interests of the Society." At a succeeding meeting on December 8th, 1858, in proposing that Viscount Goderich be his Lordship's successor, an affectionate tribute was paid to the deceased nobleman by the members attending the meeting.

The three following biographical notices have been contributed in each instance by the son of the member. That of the late Thomas Wilson, one of the founders, and the first honorary secretary of the society, is by Mr. Henry Wilson, M.A., Head Master of Malvern Link School. The notice of Henry Holt, also one of the founders of the society, by Mr. H. P. Holt, C.E., F.G.S., &c., of Didsbury, Manchester; and for that of Thomas Pridgin Teale, F.R.S., &c., the society is indebted to his son, Mr. T. Pridgin Teale, M.D., F.R.S., of Leeds.

THOMAS WILSON, M.A.

Thomas Wilson, youngest but only surviving son of Daniel Wilson, a member of a family settled for some generations at Featherstone, near Pontefract, was born at Leatherhead, Surrey, where his father was in practice as a surgeon, on 26th Sep., 1800. Before long his father retired from practice, returned to Yorkshire, and joined his brother Thomas in the lease of the Silkstone collieries. The son went to a school kept by Mr. Snowden, at Doncaster, and then to Richmond School, at that time under the Rev. James Tate, the most brilliant teacher of his day. From thence he went to Catherine Hall, Cambridge, where he graduated B.A. 1823, M.A. 1826. After keeping his terms at the Middle Temple, on the death of his father and uncle, he succeeded to their business, and settled at Banks

Hall. Here he soon distinguished himself by the enlarged and comprehensive views he took of trade and manufactures, and of legislation in relation to them, and was elected chairman of the Association of Coal-owners of the Barnsley district. He promoted in every way the welfare and advancement of his workpeople, over whom he exercised the greatest influence. He was an ardent Liberal and Free Trader, and acted as chairman of Lord Morpeth's local committee. Especially he was one of the earliest to recognize the importance of education, and was the friend and fellow-labourer of James Simpson, of Edinburgh, Samuel Wilderspin, Sir Thomas Wyse, and the still living and venerable Sir Edward Baines, in their efforts to spread a desire to receive, and an improved method of communicating knowledge. He was an original member of the British Association for the advancement of Science. He was one of the earliest promoters of the Barnsley Mechanics' Institution. He joined a few other gentlemen in founding the Yorkshire Union of Mechanics' Institutions, on the committee of which he served for 38 years, and appeared at every annual meeting as long as he lived. He was one of the founders of the West Riding Geological and Polytechnic Society, and acted as its honorary secretary and treasurer from its inception in 1837, until September, 1842, when his resignation was reluctantly accepted, and Mr. J. Travis Clay was elected to the offices. During Mr. Wilson's secretaryship, the society assumed and maintained a most important position. He was indefatigable in his attention to its interests; and the correspondence printed in a previous and succeeding chapters proves how judicious and painstaking was his management of its affairs. After his resignation of the offices of honorary secretary and treasurer, Mr. Wilson was elected a vice-president, a position he held to the time of his death. On several occasions he presided at its meetings, and when, as happened at one or two periods of the society's history, its vigour seemed to be waning, or there was a lack of interest in its proceedings, he was always ready to give every assistance in his power, and with wise council, the result of a long and ripe experience to urge the younger members of the society to renewed efforts. After the death of Mr. Denny in 1871, who had been for many years the assistant secretary of the society, Mr. Wilson presided at a meeting held in July, 1871, to consider the steps necessary to place the society on a sounder basis, and took an active part in carrying out the resolutions of the meeting.

On the expiration of his lease of the Silkstone Collieries, Mr. Wilson opened a fresh pit in the neighbourhood, but the venture proved unsuccessful, and in 1842 he was elected, out of many candidates, auditor of the Aire and Calder Navigation Company, a post he held for 34 years. Here he displayed the same energy and breadth of view which he had shown in his own affairs. He was ever on the watch to prevent undue interference by railways or other competing systems, and convinced that canals filled a very important part in the communications of the country, but that owing to their isolated action they were falling into the power of railways, which thus acquired a monopoly, he was instrumental in forming an Association of Canals, to which he acted as secretary. For his services in this capacity he received a service of plate. He was also a director of the Goole Steam Shipping Company.

Mr. Wilson was welcomed to Leeds by all friends of reform and education. He was immediately elected on the council of the Leeds Mechanics' Institution, which he attended most assiduously for many years, and he was president for two years. He was also for many years on the council of the Leeds Philosophical and Literary Society, of which he was joint secretary at the time of his death. He also took part in establishing the Yorkshire College of Science, the scheme for University extension, the local examinations by the Universities of Oxford and Cambridge, the examinations by the Society of Arts and the Department of Science and Art, and the Leeds Educational Council. It was while attending a meeting of the last body, four days before his death, that the first symptoms of his approaching end appeared. He also assisted in forming the Charitable Enquiry and Local Improvement Societies, and was many years an assiduous member of the council of the Leeds Chamber of Commerce.

Mr. Wilson was a sound classical scholar, and a man of wide reading and information. He held very independent views, in many respects in advance of his time, and was totally unmoved by popular applause or dissent. His mind was eminently impartial and judicial, but from constitutional shyness and reserve he never could be prevailed on to speak in public. Though not generally popular, he was the object of warm attachment in his circle of intimate friends. He died on the 17th January, 1876, in his 76th year. Mr. Wilson married in 1830 Elizabeth, second daughter of Elias Inchbald, of Old Malton Abbey, and great niece of the celebrated Mrs. Inchbald, by whom he had six children. Henry, M.A. St. Cath. Coll. Cambridge, many years head master of Malvern Link School. Herbert, M.A. Fellow of Mag. Coll. Cambridge, and of the Bengal Civil Service, died of sunstroke in 1866. Arthur died young from an accident. Edward is a member of the firm of Newstead and Wilson, solicitors, Leeds, and colonel of the Leeds Rifle Volunteers. Kenneth, M.A. St. John's Coll. Cambridge, classical master at the College, Wellington, New Zealand. Miss Lucy Wilson is well known as a speaker and writer on behalf of education, women's suffrage, and kindred topics.

Henry Holt.

Henry Holt, the third and youngest son of Elias Holt, of Notton, in the Parish of Royston, Yorkshire, was born on May 16th, 1812. His father was agent for the late Godfrey Wentworth, Esq., of Woolley Park, near Wakefield, and also farmed the Notton Estate on his own account. The son was educated by the late Rev. T. Westmorland, then Vicar of Sandal Magna, near Wakefield; afterwards, owing to his father's failing health, he became his assistant.

He studied geology and mineralogy, especially that of Yorkshire, with the late Mr. William Smith and Professor Phillips, and then adopted the profession of a Mining Engineer and Surveyor, as well as a Land and Mineral Agent, at Wakefield. He was actively engaged on surveying and levelling for projected lines of railways in the district, and largely employed professionally in giving evidence before committees of both Houses of Parliament, more especially regarding the minerals opened out by the railways.

He married Helen, the second daughter of Henry Hartop, of Barnburgh Hall, near Doncaster, in October, 1817, and afterwards lived in South Parade, Wakefield.

He had the management of the minerals of several estates, among them being those of Sir George Armytage, Bart., Sir John L. L. Kaye, Bart., the University College, Oxford, &c. He was consulting engineer for several collieries amongst others Stanley, Ingham's, Flockton, &c. He was also much engaged in arbitrations, respecting land and minerals, and valuations of property.

In 1862, he moved his residence to Headingley, near Leeds, still retaining his offices in Wakefield. Soon after this, owing to over-work his health failed and he took his chief assistant, Mr. Rowland Childe, of Wakefield, into partnership, and partially retired from business. He then travelled for a time, with a view to restore his health. He left Headingley early in 1869, and went to reside at Southport, where he rallied for a time, but died very suddenly on October 2nd, 1869. He was buried at Thornes Church, near Wakefield. He left a widow and two sons living.

Mr. Holt took a great interest in geology, and became a member of the West Riding Geological and Polytechnic Society in the year 1837.

In 1844, he was elected a member of the council of the society, and retained that position until 1869, the year of his death. Mr. Holt exhibited great interest in the society during its earlier years, and gave much assistance in the preparation of the section across the coal-field, in conjunction with the observations made by the Lancashire Geologists. He, together with Mr. Charles Morton, prepared reports on the sections, which were duly presented to the society. His name will be found frequently mentioned in the pages of this work.

Dr. Teale, whilst forwarding the following notice, wrote as follows :—

38, COOKRIDGE STREET, LEEDS,
December 27th, 1877.

DEAR SIR,

I cannot do better than send you a short biography of my father, published in 1865, two years before his death, and in the preparation of which I believe he assisted. I do not know that I can add to it anything of importance, I believe that he was the first person seriously to maintain the post glacial existence in these islands of the great pachyderms, and to suggest that they might even have been coeval with man.

Yours faithfully,
T. PRIDGIN TEALE.

Mr. James W. Davis.

THOMAS PRIDGIN TEALE, F.R.S.

Thomas Pridgin Teale, the eldest son of Thomas Teale, Esq., a surgeon in extensive practice at Leeds, was born in that town on the first day of the present century. He received his early education at the Grammar School at Heath, near Halifax, and continued his studies at the Leeds Grammar School until his eighteenth year, when he began his medical studies at the Leeds General Infirmary, and spent the session of 1819-20 in the University of Edinburgh. During the three following winters Mr. Teale attended the practice of Guy's and St. Thomas's Hospitals, where he was a pupil of Sir Astley Cooper, Mr. Green, and other distinguished teachers. These studies were followed by a residence in Paris, where he had the advantage of the practical instructions of Dupuytren and Lisfranc. At a comparatively early age Mr. Teale had given proofs of that keen interest in operative surgery which is the first condition of success. He was elected a member of the Royal College of Surgeons in 1823, and about the same time, when only about twenty-two years old, was noticed as the first provincial surgeon in England who had performed the operation of tying the sub-clavian artery for axillary aneurism. The promise of such a beginning was well sustained throughout Mr. Teale's subsequent practice.

Having settled as a practitioner in his native town, he married in 1827, the eldest daughter of the Rev. Charles Isherwood, M.A., of Brotherton, in Yorkshire. In 1831 he took, in conjunction with several other friends, an active part in the foundation of the Leeds School of Medicine, and at its opening, in the autumn of the same year, delivered the introductory lecture. This school has now, during thirty-four years, steadily maintained its high character for efficiency, and among the several causes that have combined to produce such a result, must be reckoned the services of Mr. Teale, whilst he was a lecturer on anatomy and physiology. The business of the session (October, 1865), was inaugurated by Mr. Paget, of St. Bartholomew's Hospital, in a newly-erected building of chastely-ornamental architecture, and furnished with appliances for medical teaching. In 1837 Mr. Teale joined the newly-formed West Riding Geological and Polytechnic Society, and took an active interest in its proceedings. He occasionally presided at its meetings. On Dec. 6th, 1839, he contributed a valuable paper to the proceedings of the Society on the Fossil Ichthyology of the Yorkshire Coal-field.

Mr. Teale belonged to the numerous class of medical men who, while faithfully devoted to their professions, have found relief from study in the variety afforded by other scientific pursuits. He was long well known, in and far beyond his native town, as one of the chief contributors to the more than ordinary success of the Leeds Philosophical Society, in which he held, for upwards of thirty years, the office of honorary curator of the Zoological Department. He was elected president in the years 1860 and 1861. Among his numerous papers read before this Society may be found some of an original character and special interest. In the transactions for 1837, we may notice an account of a beautiful Zoophyte—the Alcyonella—which was discovered in 1835 in ponds near Leeds, and had not been previously recognized as a British animal. The same volume contains also Mr. Teale's anatomical description, with illustrated plates, of Actinia. These have been largely made use of in systematic works on comparative anatomy, since published, both at home and abroad. On the 9th May, 1838, Mr. Teale read a paper on Stigmaria at a meeting of the Geological Section of the Society.

In 1856 Mr. Teale read before the West Riding Geological and Polytechnic Society a paper on a geological deposit in the valley of the Aire, near Leeds, in which bones of the hippopotamus major and the mammoth had recently been found The object of the paper was to show that this deposit was newer than the northern drift which it overlaid, and, consequently, that these great northern pachyderms had not become extinct until post glacial times. This view, now generally regarded as confirmed by numerous later and independent observations, was, at the date of the reading of the paper, regarded as a geological heresy. In the same paper the opinion was advanced that, hereafter, these extinct pachyderms might be proved to have been coeval with man. A description of the superficial deposits in the valley of the Aire was read before the British Association at Leeds in 1858, and published in the report for that year.

In 1843 Mr. Teale was elected a Fellow of the Royal College of Surgeons. He had the honour of being appointed, by the Queen, a member of the General Medical Council, at its institution in 1858. In 1862 he was elected a Fellow of the Royal Society. Having held, during a period of thirty-one years, the office of surgeon to the Leeds General Infirmary, he resigned it in 1864, when he was appointed consulting surgeon.

Mr. Teale is the author of several works of great practical value. His earliest production is a small volume on Neuralgic Diseases dependent upon Irritation of the Spinal Marrow, and Ganglia of the Sympathetic Nerve. In the course of his practice the writer had been convinced that the difficulty and embarrassment attendant on the diagnosis and treatment of the several neuralgic affections, arose from mistaken views of their pathology. They had too often been regarded as actual diseases of those nervous filaments which are the immediate seat of the neuralgia, instead of being considered as sympathetic of disease in the larger nervous masses from which those filaments are derived. Hence the treatment was, too frequently, local and superficial. By this publication Mr. Teale contributed to more scientific views of neuralgic diseases and to a successful mode of treatment, based upon a large induction from well-recorded cases.

In 1846 Mr. Teale published a Practical Treatise on Abdominal Hernia, with numerous illustrations. This is a complete and valuable text book on the subject, and gives the results of extensive experience. With regard to the taxis, Mr. Teale states that, in several cases, he has succeeded in reducing the herniæ by placing the aponeurosis in a state of tension, after he had failed in his attempts whilst the muscles were relaxed. He gives a full account of M. Gerdy's operation for obliterating the hernial aperture by the cutaneous plug, a radical method of cure which, with some modifications, has since been practised by Wutzer and others. Mr. Teale was favourable to the plan of reducing strangulated hernia, when practicable, without opening the sac.

In 1855, Mr. Teale contributed to the Medical and Chirurgical Society a paper, on a plastic operation for the restoration of the lower lip, which was followed in 1857, by the contribution to the Medical Times and Gazette of a series of papers and illustrative cases on plastic operations for the restoration of lower lip, and for the relief of several deformities of the face and neck. By one of the operations described in these papers, the terrible disfigurement from eversion and drawing down of the lower lip towards the sternum, in consequence of severe burns is removed. The features are brought nearly to their natural appearance, and the power of retaining the saliva is restored.

Mr. Teale's latest work, entitled 'Amputation by a long and a short Rectangular Flap,' added greatly to his already high reputation as a surgeon. Dissatisfied with the results of the high double flap operation by transfixion, the author returned to the old circular method, which he considered preferable. But the imperfect condition of stumps resulting from both these methods and the high rate of mortality, induced him to devise the plan of operating by a long and short rectangular flap, which has already been very favourably received by the profession. Its advantages are, that a long flap, formed of parts generally devoid of large blood vessels and nerves, is made to fold over the ends of the bones, whilst the larger blood vessels and nerves are contained in the shorter flap; a long flap does not undergo retraction during the healing process, a stump is obtained which will bear pressure on the end, and the mortality of the operation is diminished.

Besides the works already mentioned, Mr. Teale has written several papers, which would amply repay notice, if our limits permitted any further analyses.

He contributed to the Medical Times and Gazette 'On the Lines of Incision for Partial Amputation of the Foot'; 'A Case of Ovariotomy'; 'Aneursion treated by Pressure'; 'On the operation

F

for Stone in the Bladder'; and 'On the statistics of Amputation.' We have also to mention the article 'Fistula Intestinal,' contributed to the Cyclopædia of Practical Surgery; and the 'Retrospective Address in Surgery,' delivered before the Provincial Medical Association, and published in their Transactions. Mr. Teale died December 31st, 1867.

JAMES GARTH MARSHALL.

The following letter needs no comment. The paragraphs which follow have been for the most part extracted from the *Leeds Mercury*, dated October 24th, 1873.

LOUGHRIGG BROW, AMBLESIDE,
8th April, 1888.
DEAR MR. DAVIS,

I have only just heard from my cousin, to whom I forwarded your enquiry about my uncle, James Garth Marshall, and I am sorry he says he cannot give you any information about his scientific investigations or work. There was a notice of him in the *Leeds Mercury*, and I write to Mr. Talbot Baines, asking him to send you a copy, if still to be got, or give you the date, but I fear it will say little, if anything, about the scientific side of his life.

I know he was a companion to Adam Sedgwick in his exploration of this hilly country, and did some investigation on his own account. He also made some elaborate experiments on the result of long heating of powdered rocks from this country under pressure, but whether the results were worth anything or not I do not know.

His specimens were all given to the Yorkshire College, and Professor Green may be able to tell you something.

Yours,
STEPHEN A. MARSHALL.

Mr. J. Garth Marshall was born February 20th, 1802. He was third son of John Marshall, founder of the family. By nature extremely shy, remarkable rather for weight of ideas than fluency of speech, and yet, notwithstanding the obvious effort which public speaking always cost him, he never hesitated to take his stand among the advocates of whatever was progressive, whether in politics or in social affairs. Among the earliest advocates of popular and ultimately of state education, he showed the value which he put upon the instruction of the young by erecting, along with other members of his firm, schools in Holbeck, intended for the multitudes of children who have passed through their extensive factories ; and he personally attended to them. He built and endowed the church of St. John the Evangelist, Holbeck, 1850, of which, Sir G. Scott was the architect, and the Rev. W. Banks was afterwards incumbent. From 1847 he represented Leeds in Parliament as representative of state education in the House of Commons until 1852, and then retired, his place being taken by Rt. Hon. M. Talbot Baines. Afterwards he supported Mr. Edward Baines. He was in favour of the ballot, and supported Mr. Hall's scheme when the Reform Bill was passed in 1867. He founded the Leeds Social Improvement Society. He was a county magistrate and deputy lieutenant. His scientific and mechanical knowledge was considerable. The latter found ample scope in connection with his professional business, and the former in literary contributions on geology and other branches of science, read before the Yorkshire Geological and Polytechnic Society, the Leeds Philosophical Society, and other institutions. For many years he acted as one of the honorary curators of the Philosophical Society.

Mr. Marshall was one of the founders of the West Riding Geological and Polytechnic Society, and a vice-president to the time of his death. When, in 1843, it was proposed to remove the contents of the museum from Wakefield to some Philosophical Society in the West Riding, Mr. Marshall was active in assisting in the negotiations to transfer the collections to Leeds, and after their removal became joint curator along with Mr. Embleton, and for the thirty succeeding years held the office. Occasionally he presided at the meetings of the society. He married the daughter of Lord Monteagle ; his brother, Mr. H. C. Marshall married her sister.

Disraeli in 'Sybil' gives a description of the Marshall works. Although singularly retiring in manner, and not fluent as an orator, Mr. Marshall, when he spoke in public was always listened to with marked respect; his opinions being invariably based upon solid information and independent thought. Like his father he had no

60   SOME OF THE FOUNDERS OF THE SOCIETY.

passion for honour or popularity, yet earned a gratifying measure of both by virtue of the inflexible honesty of his character, his judicious generosity of disposition, and sterling abilities. He died October 22nd, 1873, at Monk Coniston, Ambleside, after a short illness.

HENRY BRIGGS.

It is a pleasure to express indebtedness to Mr. A. C. Briggs, for the following brief memoir of his grandfather's life. Mr. Henry Briggs was one of the originators of the society, and took part along with Mr. Thomas Wilson, Mr. T. W. Embleton, and others, in calling the first meeting to consider the desirability of such a society. From that time to that of his death he always took a lively interest in the proceedings of the society. He was a member of its council and the local secretary for Wakefield and district. The proceedings of the society received several contributions from his pen, and on more than one occasion he presided over its meetings.

REDBANK, NEWTON PARK, LEEDS,
29th January, 1888.
DEAR SIR,

I duly received your letter of the 21st, but have not until to-day been able to answer it at all fully.

My grandfather's life appears to have been a very uneventful one, and I can hardly think that a mere statement of dates of birth, marriage, and death, &c., can be of much interest to the public. However, what information I can get, I gladly place at your disposal.

My grandfather, Henry Briggs, was third son of Rawdon Briggs, Esq., Deputy Lieutenant for the West Riding of York, and was born at Ward's End, Halifax, August 10th, 1797, married on June 3rd, 1824, at Thornhill, Marianne, daughter of James Milnes, Esq., of Flockton Manor. He died 4th October, 1868, whilst on a visit to my father's house at Dundee. Shortly after his marriage he went to live at Overton House, near Flockton, and became interested in the Flockton Collieries, the firm being then Briggs & Stansfeld, in 1844 or 1845 he withdrew from that business, which was after that time carried on by the firm of Milnes Stansfeld & Co., and he commenced under the style of Henry Briggs, Son, & Có., the Whitwood Collieries, near Normanton, now among the largest in Yorkshire. His partners were his elder brother, Mr. William Briggs, banker, of Halifax, and Mr. Samuel Fletcher Tonge, also of Halifax, and later, my father, the late Mr. Henry Currer Briggs. In 1865, a scheme proposed by my father was carried out, and this business was transferred to a limited company, (in which however the old partners reserved the greater portion of the shares), the peculiar feature of which was that the workpeople were given an interest in the profits, if any, beyond 10 per cent. per annum, which was first payable on the shares. This co-operative system was warmly approved by my grandfather, and it was worked successfully till 1874, that is long after his death. He took a warm interest in the welfare of his workpeople, and was very generous and kind to the poor, but as he never took part in public life, and was a modest man, his name was never brought before the public. He took a great interest in scientific matters and in agriculture, and always farmed a great deal of land, in conjunction with his collieries. He was a unitarian all his life.

I am, dear Sir, yours faithfully,

A. C. BRIGGS.

CHARLES MORTON.

2, WESTBOURNE VILLAS, SCARBOROUGH,
May 30th, 1888.

MY DEAR SIR,

I must apologise for my long neglect of my promise to send you such particulars of my late brother Charles' life as I am able to give. My sister-in-law and nephew have both been away in the south of France, and I hoped they might be able to help me, but they cannot add much to my little store of knowledge.

My brother, Charles Morton, was born October 1st, 1811, in Sheffield. He was a pupil of the Rev. Peter Wright, of Sheffield, who educated nearly all the men of note in that town. At the age of thirteen he was apprenticed to Mr. Leather, engineer and surveyor, of Sheffield (brother, I believe, of George Leather, C.E., of the Aire and Calder Co., Leeds), but was afterwards 'turned over' to Mr. Stobart, of Bunker's Hill, Chester-le-Street, Durham (the colliery agent of the Earl of Durham), to whom he was articled, and with whom he lived. At the end of his apprenticeship he went to Edinburgh University for several sessions, and there, I believe, he took honours in chemistry and geology, and in mathematics. He returned to Sheffield, and I know had much to do, for a time, with the Chapeltown Ironworks, near that town now the property of Newton, Chambers and Co., of Thorncliff. He also, for a time, was acting for Messrs. Chambers of the Holmes Colliery, near Rotherham. He took an active part as scientific witness in the parliamentary contest for, what was then, the new Gas Light Co., of Sheffield (the present Sheffield United Gas Co.) ; also as a witness for the Leeds Gas Co., then seeking additional powers from parliament.

My brother was the first to bring the science of geology before a popular audience in Sheffield. He gave a course of lectures to the Mechanics' Institute (which society he took chief part in founding), and these lectures were highly appreciated, although with many they were most objectionable, as a denial of the Mosaic record. I believe it is a fact that Dr. Holland, a medical man much respected in Sheffield, and my brother were pelted with rotten eggs during their delivery.

In 1836, my brother came to New Market House, near Wakefield, as manager of Messrs. Charlesworths' Collieries. He held this appointment 3 years, until his health gave way. It was whilst residing at New Market House that Mr. Morton became associated with the gentlemen, some of whom have been already mentioned, in the formation of the society. He was from the first a member of the council, and his active and energetic sympathy conduced in no small degree to place the society in the high position it almost immediately assumed. Mr. Morton contributed a number of important papers to its meetings, which are recorded in the proceedings of the society, (and in other parts of this work); he took great interest in the preparation of the geological sections to connect the Yorkshire with the Lancashire coal-fields, and in December, 1839, presented a report on the subject, which led to much discussion, and eventually to the active preparation of the sections. The museum formed at Wakefield always secured his hearty co-operation.

He was afterwards manager for Mr. Thos. Wilson, of Darton Colliery, at the close of Mr. Wilson's colliery work. This was only for a brief period. On leaving Mr. Wilson, he and the late Mr. Henry Briggs sank the Whitwood Colliery, and for some years they were in partnership there. In 1852 he was appointed, on the recommendation of the late Earl Fitzwilliam, one of the first four government inspectors under the Mines' Regulation Act. His colleagues were Mr. Blackwell, Mr. Mathias Dunn and Mr. Dickinson. Mr. Herbert Mackworth soon afterwards was appointed in Mr. Blackwell's post. My brother's district to look after comprised Yorkshire, Nottinghamshire, Warwickshire, Somersetshire, South Wales, Derbyshire, Leicestershire, South Staffordshire, Wiltshire, and Cornwall. It was subsequently reduced to Yorkshire only. On the occasion of the last great accident at the Oaks Colliery, Barnsley, his health broke down, and he resigned his office. He died in Southport, 3rd Nov., 1882. Age, 71. I have some lines written by the late Paul Rogers, of Sheffield (then a working man of that town), the inspiration being from hearing my brother's geological lectures.

Yours very truly,

James W. Davis, Esq. H. J. MORTON.

JOSEPH CHARLESWORTH: SENIOR AND JUNIOR.

The following brief notice of Messrs. Joseph Charlesworth, father and son, who took part in the formation of the Society, has been contributed by Mr. J. B. Charlesworth, J.P., of Hatfield Hall, near Wakefield. It will perhaps be most fitting to give the letter affording the information as it was received.

BLAIRADAM HOUSE, KINROSSSHIRE, N.B.
August 22nd, 1888.

DEAR SIR,

Your letter has been forwarded to me here, and I have the pleasure of forwarding to you what I know of the two Joseph Charlesworth's you mention, and if you think it worth using, you can put it in any form you like.

In 1700 John Charlesworth was a master mason, that is, an architect and contractor combined, at Halifax, and was succeeded in his business by a son John, who was father of Joseph Charlesworth, born in 1749, and who came to Wakefield in 1780, and commenced working collieries, indeed commenced the business, which has been in the family ever since. He died at Kettlethorpe Hall in 1820. In 1814 this Joseph Charlesworth purchased the Lofthouse Estate, and gave it to his son Joseph, who was born in 1778, and died in 1845, and is the Joseph Charlesworth, senior, you mention. His eldest son, Joseph, is the one called junior by you. He was born in 1817 and died in 1858. I am the second son of Joseph, senior, and brother of Joseph, junior. They both lived quiet, retired lives, took no active part in politics, and did not indeed place themselves before the public, but enjoyed the repose and pursuits of a country life, and promoting a kind feeling and good understanding between themselves and their workmen and others in the neighbourhood. At the death of my brother in 1858, it was considered by all in the district that the workmen had lost their best friend. They worked four collieries between Leeds and Wakefield, and two in the neighbourhood of Rotherham.

Yours very truly,
J. B. CHARLESWORTH.

CHAPTER III.

PROCEEDINGS 1839—1840.

Meanwhile active preparations were in progress to secure a good meeting at Leeds. The Philosophical and Literary Society, as on previous occasions, gave the free use of their rooms, and a joint committee of the Geological and Polytechnic Society and the Leeds Society was appointed; the latter represented by Dr. Teale and. Mr. Marshall. On the 1st November a meeting of the council of the Geological Society was held at its rooms at Wakefield. The museum occupied a considerable amount of attention, and Messrs. Briggs and Embleton were appointed a sub-committee to make alterations. It was decided to request Lord Wharncliffe to preside, and Professor Phillips to read a paper. These gentlemen were communicated with by the honorary secretary, and a few days later Mr. Wilson wrote to Mr. Embleton as follows :—

Mr. Wilson to Mr. Embleton.

LEEDS, *11th November, 1839.*

DEAR SIR,

I have received an answer from Lord Wharncliffe stating his inability to be present at our meeting. Professor Phillips too regrets that he will be unable to attend, as well from engagements as from his being unequal at present to appear in public so soon after his uncle's death. This leads me to hope that you will exert yourself to give us a paper. If you can do so we shall have enough with ourselves for two meetings, Mr. Teale, Mr. Thorp, Mr. Hartop, yourself, and Mr. Morton. Mr. Sopwith, I fear, will not be able to attend. Have you arranged for a reporter? we must have his assistance without payment, on condition of giving him the printing. Be kind enough to let me know what you will do for us in the way of a paper.

I am, dear Sir, yours truly,

THOMAS WILSON.

Mr. Embleton represented the Society at a meeting of the joint local committee, when arrangements were made which will be best understood by a perusal of the following correspondence between Mr. Embleton and Mr. Wilson, the secretary. A few days after this correspondence Mr. Embleton was requested by the local committee to invite the Rev. Dr. Hook, vicar of Leeds, to preside at the meeting, an invitation which the vicar readily accepted.

Mr. Embleton to Mr. Wilson.

LEEDS, *23rd November, 1839.*

DEAR SIR,

We have had another meeting of the local committee to-day. The reporter chosen is Mr. Beckwith. The ordinary to be at Scarborough's Hotel for forty, at the usual charge. We have also arranged that an invitation be sent to each member and subscriber of the Literary and Philosophical Society, requesting their attendance. Also tickets of admission, (after some description), to the council and office-bearers of the Literary Institution and of the Mechanics' Institute. It was deemed advisable to meet again before the 5th December, the date to be determined upon according to circumstances. How would it suit for the meeting to be on the evening of the 4th inst., we could then collect the opinions of the members of council about the sections if they were also summoned, and we could discuss this matter with our affectionate brotherhood of Manchester. Can you get any names of parties to dine, could a request to that effect be inserted in the circular calling the meeting. This would much ease the labours of the dinner committee, whose duties up to this date have been truly onerous. In the circular too we might detail the programme of proceedings.

Mr. Teale is anxious to know where he is to be placed, for it will be necessary that his preparations be commenced on the day before the meeting, there are so many drawings, etc., to exhibit, of the Megalichthys and other hard named fishes, his paper will occupy it is said one-and-a-half hours, discussion say a half-hour, the business of the meeting a half-hour, with a paper by Mr. Hartop, will be sufficient for the morning feast, then Mr. Morton and Mr. Thorp will be left for the evening. How would this arrangement suit, pray let me know before Wednesday, that I may set Mr. Teale at rest as to his fate on the eventful day. Since the aristocracy are to be absent how eloquent we shall be.

Mr. Walker proposes to publish a geological map, and thereby supersede our labours, I wished him to attend on the 29th if the council sits on that day.

I am, dear Sir, yours very truly,

THOMAS W. EMBLETON.

Mr. Wilson to Mr. Embleton.

BANKS, *23rd November, 1839.*

MY DEAR SIR,

I did not receive your letter until my return home late last night, too late to reply in time for to-day's meeting. You would see by the Mercury and Intelligencer that I had advertised the papers; but I did not distribute them into morning and evening work, thinking that next week would be soon enough. I have no answer from Lord Stourton, so I have written to Mr. Lascelles, and hope for his reply in a day or two. I will print the circulars at Barnsley, and forward you 200 or more if you want them. I should like to have a few minutes conversation about the reporters, &c., with you. I shall be in Leeds on Monday, from 10 to 2, at Scarborough Hotel, if you could spare a short time. I have this difficulty about them; if one gives a report the first Saturday, the other will want to do so; but how to get the matter ready I don't know. Tell those who find fault with you that Mr. Lascelles is a vice-president. You have a slight taste of the delights of being secretary to a voluntary association. I wish those who find fault, and do nothing else, would just try the office for a short time. They would probably find it very easy to do many things wrong and leave more undone. I will call a council meeting for Tuesday next, you will consider this as your notice, for three o'clock.

I am, dear Sir, yours truly,

T. W. Embleton, Esq.   THOMAS WILSON.

LEEDS, *Monday.*

P.S.—Finding I could not post this in time for you to receive it this morning, I have kept it to post at Leeds. I will write as soon as I know who is to be the chairman. Will the circulars be wanted or will the Literary and Philosophical Society furnish their own? Be good enough to let me know this as soon as possible. Let it be considered that Mr. Teale takes the first paper in the morning, on account of his diagrams, &c.

At the meeting, held at Leeds on December 6th, 1839, the vicar, the Rev. W. F. Hook, D.D., occupied the chair, and opened the proceedings by making the observations following :—Gentlemen, having been requested by your committee to preside at the West Riding Geological Society, I have done myself the honour of acceding to the request, though I must, without any affectation, repeat to you what I said to them, that I am conscious of my inability to discharge the duties of the office with credit to myself or with satisfaction to you, since my acquaintance with geology is merely such as might be expected from any person acquainted with the literature of his country, and I speak in the presence of gentlemen who have sounded the depths and shoals of the science. But thus much I may be permitted to say, that it is a science sublime as well as interesting and important; interesting it is to have the mind carried back to the revolutions of those distant eras when the seeds were sown, if I may so say, of those fields of coal, of which we are reaping the harvest, which ministers a supply to so many human wants, and to which we especially owe the prosperity of the district of which we are the inhabitants. Of its importance I need not speak to practical men, it is at once admitted by the miner, the chemist, the agriculturist, the builder, and the engineer. Sublime it is, for what can be more sublime to the dwellers upon earth than the archæology of the globe. Gentlemen, you are aware that scarcely half-a-century has elapsed since geology began to be studied scientifically; and owing to the crude and conflicting theories of these geologists, who ventured to theorize before they had collected facts or collated the observations of practical men, some prejudice for a time was excited against it, but that prejudice is passing away, and the object with geologists seems to be merely to collect phenomena, to classify and compare them. I believe that I have now the pleasure of addressing gentlemen who aspire to no higher honour than that of being collectors and collators of facts. Gentlemen with whom persons who fear lest the study of geology shall be detrimental to the cause of religion, however excellent they may be, I profess to have no sympathy. My faith in the inspiration of Holy Scripture is such that I am certain the discoveries of science will only tend to the confirmation of its unassailable veracity. To the theories of many geologists I may be opposed, and I may be so on scientific principles, because I find that in the year 1806, the French Institute counted not fewer than eighty theories, supposed to be hostile to scripture history, of all which theories scarcely a vestige is now to be traced, scarcely a record has been preserved. To show, however, that there is nothing in the cosmogony of the bible repugnant to the real discoveries of geology, I would refer you to the commencement of Dr. Buckland's Bridgewater Treatise, and especially to Dr. Pusey's valuable note appended to it. The very learned Professor of Hebrew there states it as his opinion that the first two verses of Genesis contains merely a summary statement of what is related in detail in the rest of the chapter, and that the time of the creation is not defined. We are told only of what we are concerned to know, that all things were created by God. The rest may have been left indefinite, as so many other things have been, that there may be free scope for the exercise of those high endowments with which our Maker has blessed our species, namely, our reason and our imagination. But were the interpretations to which I have alluded merely the conjecture of Dr. Pusey or Dr. Buckland to meet an apparent difficulty, after the discoveries of geology, I for my part, should attach to it no importance whatever : nay, I should be the foremost to contend against it. But I find it to have been a very general opinion among the fathers or early writers of the christian church. The learned Professor of Hebrew refers to some of these writers. I may add that I find Justin Martyr in the second century, and Gregory Nazianzen in the fourth, expressing their belief that an indefinite period elapsed between the original creation, and that disposition of things of which we have the narrative in the book of Genesis. Their judgment was, of course, on that point unprejudiced and independent, and therefore all must admit that in such a case their authority is great. We may indeed conclude, that if the discoveries of geology are opposed to some modern interpretations of scripture, they are not opposed to scripture rightly interpreted. Opposed, I ought rather to say that the investigations of geology are in perfect accordance with scripture, for when scripture tells us of the deluge, the geologist is able to comment upon the fact by pointing to the valleys of denudation, and by calling attention to those pinnacles of granite which are found standing insulated and detached from the neighbouring mountains, to the boulder stones and other diluvial deposits, to the fossils of later date, to the surface of the earth moulded at a comparatively late period, all tending, as the celebrated French geologist remarks, to show that the last revolution that disturbed the surface of the globe is not of very ancient date. Nay, Gentlemen, when we reflect on what has been, when we hear geology speaking of the primeval revolutions in this globe, of the series of past disruptions, elevations, dislocations, when we hear it discoursing of central heat, we are better prepared to listen to the inspired penman when he tells us that as the world which once was, being overflowed with water, perished, so the heavens and the earth which are now, are kept in store, reserved against fire; when he thus tells us that another revolution is approaching, not of water but fire. After these observations gentlemen, I shall conclude my address with saying that I, for one, will bid you God-speed, geology can give no results hostile to revelation. A discrepancy will never be found between the words and the works of Almighty God.

Mr. Charles Morton intimated that a deputation from the Manchester Geological Society attended the meeting in the hope of promoting that union which it was at all times desirable should exist between the two societies. This was the first step towards it; they had been at the trouble of coming over, and he trusted that in future the members of the two societies would interchange visits, and that gentlemen would be deputed from this meeting to visit the Manchester Society at its next meeting. A great ridge of hills divided the places of their meeting, but it was their interest and it would be the duty of each society to investigate, not only the ridge itself, but the hills in its vicinity and the strata on each side of it. He begged leave to move 'That the gentlemen who compose the deputation from the Manchester Geological Society, Mr. E. W. Binney, the secretary, and Mr. J. E. Bowman be elected honorary members of this Society.' The resolution was seconded by Mr. H. Briggs, and unanimously agreed to.

A highly philosophical paper was read at this meeting by Mr. T. P. Teale, F.L.S., on the Fossil Ichthyology of the Yorkshire Coal-field, in which the interdependence of the science of Geology and Practical Mining were stated and insisted upon. It is necessary to recollect, the only knowledge of the extent and relationship of the several beds of coal was derived from the comparison of sections obtained in sinking pits, or, in rare instances, in following the outcrop of the coal along the hillsides. It is therefore not surprising to find the learned author observing that, within the sphere of the Society's operations, there are few objects of greater practical importance than the identification of strata. It was formerly imagined that the valuable beds of coal worked at Middleton, Haigh Moor and Lofthouse, in this neighbourhood, were identical; but it has now been demonstrated, by means of this Society, that the Main Coal of Middleton is not identical with that of Haigh Moor and Lofthouse. But he understood that all are not yet agreed whether the Middleton beds occupy a position higher or lower in the series than those of Haigh Moor and Lofthouse. 'It is however, evident, that if the Middleton beds are lower than the others, there must be at Haigh Moor and Lofthouse, beneath the beds now worked, beds continuous with those at Middleton; and on the other hand, if the Middleton beds are higher in the scale, there must be at Middleton, beneath the present works, beds continuous with those of Haigh Moor and Lofthouse.' It is clear the existence of the Society was in rapid progress of justification, for it was a fact of no trifling importance to the mining fraternity, and equally so to the owners of the land, that it should be proved that such important beds of coal as those named, were independent beds on different horizons, and not a continuous seam. The study of the organic remains in the several beds was a useful adjunct in the determination of the identity of beds in widely separated areas. Mr. Teale instances a remarkable illustration of this fact in our own district. At Moortown, three miles north of Leeds, is a bed of black earthy-looking substance, about four inches in thickness; and this is identical with the beds of coal, several feet in thickness, which are worked at Halifax, and supply the extensive manufacturing districts of Bradford and Halifax with the greater part of their fuel. But how do we know the thin bed of black earth at Moortown to be the same bed as the coal at Halifax? Their appearance, or in other words, their physical characters do not enable us thus to decide. It is from their being accompanied by a particular fossil, the Pecten papyraceus, which is now known to be characteristic of this bed. The author goes on to explain that this characteristic fossil has been traced in the roof of the coal seam from Moortown, Kirkstall, Idle, Bradford, and Halifax. A point of considerable interest, as a matter of history, is embodied in the foregoing observation, that fifty years ago the manufacturing towns of Bradford and Halifax obtained their principal supply of coal from the Halifax beds; it indicates very forcibly the immense increase that has taken place during that period in the industries of those towns. Mr. Teale enumerated four genera of ganoid, and seven genera of placoid fishes. The following account of the identification of the genus Megalichthys is interesting. "The earliest known specimens of this fossil are some in the Leeds Museum, of which a description was sent upwards of fifteen years ago, by the late Edward S. George, to the Geological Society of London, at which time they were regarded as the remains of a Saurian reptile. In 1833, at the Limestone quarries at Burdichouse, near Edinburgh, were discovered, in great abundance, teeth, scales and bones of large size. These formed the subject of several papers to the Royal Society of Edinburgh, in the earlier of which they were described as the remains of reptiles. In 1834, at the Meeting of the British Association at Edinburgh, these fossils, which by this time had excited great interest amongst naturalists, were shown to M. Agassiz. This gentleman immediately doubted their reptilian character, and advanced the opinion that they belonged to fishes, to that family of the ganoid order, which he had denominated Sauroid, from their numerous affinities to Saurian reptiles, and which have as their living type or representative, the Lepidosteus. But of the truth or fallacy of this opinion, no positive evidence could be adduced, for the scales and the teeth had never yet been found at Burdiehouse in connection. A few days afterwards, M. Agassiz, in company with Prof. Buckland, visited the Leeds Museum, and I well remember the delight, the ecstatic delight, evinced by the distinguished naturalist of Neufchatel, when he first beheld the splendid head of this animal in the Leeds Museum. Here, said he, we have the same scales and the same teeth as those of Burdiehouse, conjoined in the same individual. It is therefore no longer a conjecture that they might belong to the same animal. And in these selfsame specimens we have the hyoid and branchiostic apparatus of bones; it is therefore no longer a conjecture that the Burdiehouse fossils were the remains of fishes and not of reptiles. To them M. Agassiz assigned the name Megalichthys." Besides the remains of Megalichthys, Mr. Teale exhibited and described fossil remains, which he attributed to the genera Acanthodes, Platysomus and Holoptychius amongst the Ganoids and of the Placoid order, Gyracanthus, Hybodus (Ctenacanthus) Pleuracanthus, Helodus, Ctenoptychius, Ctenodus and Diplodus. He then remarked, 'I have now endeavoured to bring into view the scattered fragments of our knowledge of the fossil Ichthyology of this district, and have attempted to assign to each element of this knowledge its proper position in the large Zoological group of fishes : it must however be evident, that we have as yet but entered upon the very threshold of the investigation. Much remains to be accomplished before we have completed even the first stage of the enquiry, namely, the determination of all the genera and species of fishes which exist in the neighbouring strata, and the distinguishing characteristics of each. When this shall have been accomplished, it will be necessary to proceed to the second important consideration, as to the precise range and circumstances peculiar to each individual species. The result of these investigations will afford many and valuable applications, and throw light on that most interesting of all the geological epochs, the carboniferous era.'

A discussion was introduced by Mr. Henry Hartop on the boilers of steam engines and the construction of engine chimneys. The question mainly turned on the relative merits of the waggon boiler invented by Mr. Watt's, and a new boiler recently come into general use in Cornwall, and consequently styled the Cornish boiler. The author considered the latter more economical, but also expressed an opinion that there was more danger in its use, because the internal flue was found to collapse ; this he attributed in a great measure to carelessness, the supply of water was interrupted and the flue became red hot and collapsed, or water was admitted and caused an explosion.

Mr. J. Garth Marshall stated that he was convinced of the superiority of the Cornish boiler, and had erected boilers of that shape. He suggested that greater strength might be obtained by " staying" them.

The Rev. Theo. Barnes said that the improvement found in the Cornish boiler was due to Mr. Hornblower. It was at first doubted that his invention would affect the saving that he predicted, and many were reluctant to try it, upon which he made proposals to put up the boilers at his own cost, and to take 10 per cent. annually upon the increased profits, the quantity of work done being registered by a counter. When he returned at the end of a year, it was found that the profits had really been very great, for they had been enabled to work mines that had been previously abandoned ; and as the mining proprietors did not like to pay him such large sums as the original agreement would entitle him to, a fresh arrangement was made by which they were at liberty to use his invention on payment of a definite sum.

Mr. Charles Morton rose to suggest that as in Yorkshire no man knew what his neighbours were doing with respect to the fixing of their steam boilers, the form of their boilers, or the work their boilers can do, that it would be an advantage if some system like that pursued in Cornwall were adopted. The statistics of the Cornish engines were generally very complete, and he would therefore suggest that returns should be made by the coal-owners and others, of the form and construction of their boilers, their mode of firing, the number of horses' power of the engine, the quality and quantity of the coal consumed, the cost of working, the quantity of work done, and the amount per annum that it cost to keep the boiler or engine in repair, and the circumstances under which accidents occur. This might be done very economically, by this Society sending out sheets to the proprietors of engines, to be filled up with the particulars required. They might or might not fill them up as they pleased, but great good would arise if they did so.

Mr. William West had a strong impression that societies like this might obtain information where individuals failed. He was desirous to ascertain the proportion of fuel consumed to the quantity of water evaporated from the boiler, and this information he had sought in vain. If the Society should take up the enquiries suggested by Mr. Morton, he hoped this question would be included.

Mr. T. W. Embleton spoke of the importance of Mr. West's suggestion. At present nothing was known in Yorkshire as to the quantity of coal consumed by engines. After some remarks from Mr. Marsh and Mr. Hartop, the meeting separated for dinner at three o'clock at Scarborough's Hotel. At seven o'clock the members re-assembled, and the Rev. Dr. Hook resumed the chair. Papers were read by Mr. Charles Morton on Safety Lamps, and by Mr. T. W. Embleton on the succession of the strata in the Northern Yorkshire Coal-field. In connection with the former Mr. W. Sykes Ward, of Leeds, introduced and explained an oxy-hydrogen lamp, which he stated would burn without communication with atmospheric air.

Mr. Embleton confined his paper to a consideration of the order of the various seams of coal found in the townships of Whitwood, Methley, Stanley, Wrenthorpe, Lofthouse, Rothwell, Ardsley, Middleton, and Beeston. It would be of great importance to the Society if the order of the seams of coal were determined in each district, and it was the only sure foundation for comparison with distant parts of the coal-field. It was only by a careful collection of shaft sections that many important questions in local geology could be satisfactorily cleared up. As for instance the thinning or thickening of certain seams in particular directions ; the existence of seams at one colliery which were not found in an adjoining one ; the origin of coal itself. Comparisons of such sections would set at rest the long agitated discussion as to the origin of cannel coal, which, as asserted by many, is only to be found in the vicinity of throws or dykes. Professor Johnston was of opinion that it was the result of a higher state of decomposition of the vegetable matter composing it, than was the common coal. The subject required further investigation. The workable seams in the townships before-mentioned on the Stanley Shale Coal, Stanley Main Coal, Warrenhouse Coal, Lofthouse or Haigh Moor Coal, the Fish Coal, the Forty Yards Coal, the Yard Coal or Little Coal, and the Main or Deep Coal of the Rothwell Haigh and Middleton Collieries, the Eleven Yards Coal, and the Beeston Coal. Of these seams the Forty Yards Coal, the Yard Coal, the Main Coal and the Beeston Coal supply Leeds with fuel, both for domestic and for manufacturing purposes. The necessity which manufacturers had for rendering assistance to this Society was very obvious. The Stanley seams occupying the highest position in the district were first minutely described, these seams are worked at Hatfield Colliery, Auchthorpe Colliery, and the Victoria Colliery, the seams are usually 17 yards apart; the upper seams 2ft. 6in. thick, the under one very variable, and composed of three or more beds separated by argillaceous bands. The next section was at Whitwood, East of Stanley. The strata were compared with those at Stanley and the similarity fully established; but there was here another deeper bed. At Wrenthorpe the sinking of the shaft was commenced just at the outbreak of the Stanley Main Coal, and continued to a depth of 186 yards. This shaft passed through the Whitwood Lower Coal, and also the Haigh Moor Coal. By the Newmarket section, the Lofthouse Coal was proved to be the same as the Haigh Moor; the lower seam at Whitwood, the middle seam at Wrenthorpe, and the Warrenhouse Coal at Newmarket were also shown to be identical. The northern outbreak of the Lofthouse Coal was traced from Rothwell to Ardsley, and the fact insisted upon of the occurrence a few hundred yards beyond that outbreak of a peculiar yellowish sandstone rock, commonly called the *quarrystone*. This is called by Dr. Smith the Bradgate Rock, but Mr. Thorp has proved that the Bradgate Rock is much deeper. The Thornhill Lees or Middleton Rock was given as more distinctive. In two sections of strata below the Haigh Moor Coal the author pointed out the situation of this rock, and thus fixed its position with regard to the old and inferior seams. He likewise compared this section with the Middleton section, and assigned the position of the Fish Coal and the Forty Yards Coal; the former seam being 80 yards below the Haigh Moor Coal. The roof of the Fish Coal consists of bituminous shale 6 inches in thickness, from which nearly the whole of the specimens described by Mr. Teale were obtained. A remarkable fact of the thinning away of sandstone was mentioned; two of the Middleton pits are 300 yards apart; in one, the quarrystone or rock is 16 yards thick, in the other only two yards; although the depth from the surface to the first seam is the same at both pits. Then followed a description of the Yard Coal at Middleton the Main Coal, the Eleven Yards Coal, and lastly the Beeston Coal. The section at Beeston was similar to that at Middleton. Other seams were known to exist below the Beeston seam, but Mr. Embleton deferred a consideration of them to a future opportunity.

No sooner was the Leeds meeting over before preparation was being made for the next quarterly meeting to be held in March, at Bradford. Mr. Embleton was requested to visit that town, and to assist in the arrangements for the meeting. Mr. S. Sharp, the president of the Literary and Philosophical Society, took an energetic interest in the meeting, and secured the attendance of the Vicar of Bradford, the Rev. Dr. Scoresby, to preside. On the 13th January Mr. Wilson wrote to Mr. Embleton the letter following :—

Mr. Wilson to Mr. Embleton.

BANKS, *13th January, 1840.*

MY DEAR SIR,

I quite forgot, on Friday, to tell you why you had not received the Calamite on Wednesday last as I promised. The morning was so frosty and the roads so rough that I rode to Barnsley to meet the coach instead of driving, and could not therefore very well convey the box. I now have it at Mr. Cross's, where you will find it when it is convenient to send for it.

I should be glad to borrow your Lindley and Hutton for a week, at any time when you can, without inconvenience, spare it, and shall be happy to lend you Mammatt's work on the Ashby Coal-field in return. As I am coming to Leeds, almost every week, I could convey them without any risk.

I should be glad to know the exact cost of the Leeds Cases.

Mr. Denny seemed to speak in doubt when he stated it at £150.

I shall be happy to hear the result of your visit to Bradford particularly in the matter of papers. With Mr. Thorp, and Mr. Hartop on iron (if he will undertake it) we might do for the morning, but we have nothing for an evening meeting.

It is a matter too, that requires some consideration, whether we should in any case agree to an evening meeting of our own at Bradford. If we do, we seem to establish a fixed custom, which it may be difficult to abandon, and yet not easy to maintain. I should prefer the evening to be devoted to a meeting of the Philosophical Society, when we might attend as audience, and they play the fiddle ; and I think this would suit the president of the Literary and Philosophical Society of Bradford. You can sound him on the subject.

I am, my dear Sir, yours sincerely,

THOMAS WILSON.

The Bradford meeting was held on March 11th, 1840, and the Vicar of Bradford, the Rev. Dr. Scoresby, presided, and gave an address, which he concluded in the following terms :—" In a mental point of view, geology, in common with other sciences, tends to improve the powers of the mind, to elevate our tastes, and to withdraw us from pursuits of less dignified or less useful character, as well as to promote the good of society generally, and in its ultimate practical results, the national prosperity, I cannot, therefore, do otherwise than wish this Society all the success which its most sanguine friends can desire." A paper by the Rev. Mr. Thorp on the section across the coal-field led to some discussion, and papers were read on the effect of aqueous vapour in the atmosphere as applied to Blast Furnaces in the manufacture of Pig Iron, by Henry Leah, of Byerley Hall, and on the proportion of Sulphur in Coal by W. West, F.R.S.

Mr. Leah's paper was read to confute arguments advanced by Mr. Dawson, the president of the Society of Iron Masters of the counties of York and Derby, who had laid down the hypothesis that "the atmosphere in its different circumstances, acquires a different affinity for the oxygen or hydrogen part of the water, and converts it into air as circumstances require." Mr. Dawson considered his observations confirmed by some eudiometrical experiments of Dr. Priestley ; by the notion of Dr. Girtanner that atmospheric air was composed of oxygen and hydrogen gases in very near the same proportion as water ; and by additional experiments with the eudiometer by Mr. Humboldt. " By the aid of these high authorities he satisfactorily concluded that the atmosphere is a chemical composition or solution of gases ; that it may be, and frequently is, composed of oxygen and hydrogen, the proportional parts of which are subject to considerable variation in different seasons and temperatures ; and hence together with the spontaneous evaporation of water, he deduces the principal cause of its greater or less fitness for the purposes of combustion, particularly as applied to the production of iron from the blast furnaces." The author went on to prove that this hypothesis from every point of view, is wholly inadmissible. He contended that the atmosphere is not a chemical, but a mechanical mixture of gases, and supported Mr. Dalton's theory of the properties of that mixture, "that mixed gases neither attract nor repel each other," and further quotes Mr. Henry's paper read to the Royal Society, that Dalton's theory is far better adapted than any former one for explaining the relation of mixed gases to each other, and especially the relation between gases and water, and consequently that the amount of gas absorbed by water depends altogether on the pressure applied. After stating the result of numerous experiments he advises the use of the hot air blast in furnaces for smelting iron as more economical than cold air. Mr. Hartop and others contended that iron made with the hot blast was inferior in strength, and that objects manufactured from it were much inferior in this respect to others made from cold blast iron.

The tenth general meeting was held at Sheffield on the 4th June, 1840, and Mr. W. Bennett Martin, of Worsborough Hall, presided. · Papers were read by Rev. W. Thorp ' On the disturbances in the district of the valley of the Don,' and an animated discussion arose as to whether they were due to a folding of the strata forming a synclinal trough, a lateral pressure, or a vertical pressure which had produced a fault, each theory having its exponent. Messrs. Morton and Holt produced a report on the proposed line of sections which will be found elsewhere, and Mr. Sopwith exhibited a model of the Forest of Dean and an isothermal projection of the mining district of Alston Moor.

Messrs. Embleton, Morton, Briggs, Holt, Hartop and Wilson were appointed a committee to draw up rules for the government of the Society to be considered at the next annual meeting; and the Rev. W. Thorp, Mr. Hartop and Mr. Lucas were appointed a deputation to represent the Society at the meeting of the British Association at Glasgow.

Mr. Wilson to Mr. Embleton.

BANKS, NEAR BARNSLEY,
20th July, 1840.

DEAR SIR,

I am anxious to hear from Professor Sedgwick, in answer to a letter I wrote him a few days since, before I call a council, as his reply will probably influence our decision as to the time of holding the annual meeting. It is not easy to know what to do, and I shall be glad if you will weigh the question well in all its bearings, that we may not hastily decide.

Professor Phillips has abandoned the Geological Report for the Agricultural Society, and Mr. Thorp asks if it is probable that his undertaking the district between the Aire and the Don would attract to us the patronage of the country gentlemen. This is a most valuable and seasonable suggestion, and I have of course requested him to set to work directly. I have written to the secretary of the Agricultural Society for a few copies of their committee's report, in the hope that he will, when he sends them, ask our co-operation. I had previously hinted to Mr. Wentworth that we might be of use to them. Through this means, the presence of the savants, of our president, and a little judicious puffing, we might I think collect a good many of the recusant at our meeting, and it has struck me that if we were to have a grand dinner in the Exchange Rooms, for one hundred persons, and work hard to get tickets taken, we should muster a good party, and hook in a large addition of subscribers.

There is no doubt of Lord Fitzwilliam's attendance, and his family. Lord Wharncliffe is to be the new president of the Agricultural Society, and might therefore be induced to come, perhaps Earl Spencer might be persuaded, then we are sure of Mr. Brandling, Mr. Wentworth, Mr. Blayds, and Sir F. L. Wood. Of course the price of our tickets must be 15s. or 20s. If in addition, Lord Fitzwilliam invite Dr. Buckland and Murchison, we should be bunglers if we did not muster a large audience to hear such lions roar.

Lord Fitzwilliam is expected at Wentworth in a fortnight, and I dare say would attend a council meeting if we thought it necessary, it might be useful to ask him to do do so, and then to advertise the plan of operations in all the county newspapers.

I am much puzzled about fixing the day, Professor Sedgwick cannot leave Norwich till 1st October, I have asked on what day he can be here, the 2nd is Friday, Wakefield market-day ; Saturday would not be a good day, on account of the parties returning home to a distance ; and Monday is late, as the British Association break up on the 24th September. I expect to hear from Mr. Sopwith about Dr. Buckland's attendance shortly. For matter we should be well off, the Report on the Railway, Mr. Thorp's Geologico-Agricultural Paper, and Mr. Holt's on the Ingleton Coal-field, this last would rouse Sedgwick if the others did not.

Mr. Swanwick promises the sections on Wednesday next, so that when the council meet they might arrange the committee meeting ; should not Mr. Atkinson be associated with the committee, for the sake of the Derbyshire geology.

I will meet you as early as possible on the day of the council meeting, and bring a person to help us with labelling, &c., that we may get all our specimens ready as you suggested. We can lock them up in the room over the council room. I will also endeavour to get the Elsecar Coal and Iron Fossils sent previously. Do you know anybody that would collect for us the Limestone Fossils ? Mr. Thorp has often promised, but it is too much to expect him to look after this part of the work.

I am, my dear Sir, yours sincerely,
Thos. W. Embleton, Esq. THOMAS WILSON.

The annual meeting in 1840 was held at Wakefield, the birth-place of the Society, on the 5th October. The president, Earl Fitzwilliam occupied the chair, and gave an address, in which the following passages occur :—' When last we had the pleasure of meeting here, our Society had not assumed a very solid form ; but from what I have observed and heard of the proceedings at other places since that time, I have derived much gratification, and feel now an assurance that we shall assume that position which will enable us to confer great and lasting benefit on the country with which we are connected. I well remember that at that time a notion was entertained that this was a society the sole object of which was to advance the knowledge and interests of those who were more particularly connected with collieries. Upon the present occasion I believe we shall have a practical refutation of the idea that our views are confined to such limited objects, for I understand that in the course of our discussion this morning you will have one paper, at least, read, which has a very different object in view, and which will tend rather to show the connection which geology has with the cultivation of the earth itself. And I trust too, if we are not led to do so on the present occasion, yet that in the course of time we may pursue our operations in other parts of the Riding which are unconnected with the coal-field. I mean that part in which what is called the Mountain Limestone particularly prevails. I am not sure whether our excellent friend Professor Sedgwick is just now in the room, but every one will feel great gratification in learning that he is in the town, and I trust that, in addition to the general information which he will be able to give you, he will particularly advert to that part which forms much the largest portion of the Riding of which he is a most distinguished native and ornament.'

The annual report showed that the number of members had increased from 200 to 280 during the year, and that there was a balance in the hands of the treasurer of about £150. The annual subscription had hitherto been 10s. 6d. ; it was now decided to make an extra charge of 2s. 6d. to cover the cost of the proceedings of the Society, and to issue them periodically so that the members might have a permanent record of the papers that were read, and the discussions that took place.

In the Geological department valuable contributions had been made by the Rev. W. Thorp on the Disturbance of the Strata in the valley of the Don, and subjects relating to the Lancashire and Yorkshire Coal-fields, and Mr. T. P. Teale on the Fossil Fishes of the Coal-field. The Committee appointed to recommend a line of section had produced two reports, and the extensive section of the minerals on the Wentworth House estate, and a part of the same section in the neighbourhood of Darton, had been described by Mr. Biram and Mr. Morton. In the Polytechnic department the value of the application of Chemistry to Geology was illustrated by Mr. West on the proportion of Sulphur in Coals, and Mr. Teale's paper on the influence of atmospheric moisture on the manufacture of Iron. Mr. Hartop has contributed observations on the form of Boilers, and Mr. Morton's remarks on Mr. Fletcher's Safety Lamp, and Mr. Sykes Ward's application of the Drummond light forcibly exhibited the two great defects of the most valuable invention of Davy. The methods of recording and delineating geological and mining operations and information were fully explained by Mr. Sopwith in his description of the principle of Isometric projection, and by the exhibition of his admirable model of the Forest of Dean.

The Council 'regretted that the number of those who contribute papers is so small. There must be in the ranks of the Society many who in the course of their daily experience are constantly meeting with important information, but who, it is believed, are deterred from coming forward by the supposition that only a long and elaborate paper is worthy of the Society's attention ; such an opinion cannot be too soon abandoned, nor can they be too often reminded that the communication of any *fact* connected with the objects of the Society, however simple and briefly related, is of great importance.' This paragraph so thoroughly expresses the feelings of the Council at the present day, that it appears desirable to give the extract *in extenso*, as that the members may take note of one of the difficulties which has remained with those more particularly interested in its proceedings, from its institution, through half a century to the present time.

The report concludes with a reference to the museum which it was decided to form. " In the commencement of the Society's career, the council, indulging the hope of being able to erect a suitable museum, had been enabled by the liberality of their noble president to purchase a site; but finding themselves at present disappointed in their expectations, they have considered it advisable to accept an advantageous offer for its disposal. In the meantime they have not neglected an object so important, but have fitted up the temporary museum with cases, and can now invite the members to inspect it. The collection, notwithstanding the short time since the cases were completed, amounts to nearly 1000 specimens, and contains many very valuable fossils, and the members are earnestly invited to renewed exertions to add to its stores.

A revised Code of Rules was presented and adopted by the meeting, one of which provided that the property of the Society should be vested in twelve trustees. By the power afforded under Rule VII. Mr. James Heywood, vice-president of the Manchester Geological Society, was elected an honorary member. It will be noticed that the name of the Society now indicates not only the Geological but also the Polytechnic side of its work, the latter term having been omitted when the first brief rules were drawn.

The following are the rules presented by the committee appointed at the last meeting :—

RULES.

1. The title of the Society shall be the Geological and Polytechnic Society of the West Riding of Yorkshire.

2. The objects of the Society shall be, 1st, the investigation of the Geology of the West Riding, with the accuracy and minuteness necessary for the successful prosecution of mining and agriculture; 2nd, the improvement of the arts of mining and metallurgy, and their dependent manufactures, and of the machinery and tools employed therein; and 3rd, the amelioration of the condition of the population connected therewith.

3. The means by which it shall pursue these objects shall be the collection of maps, plans, sections, models, mining records, and every kind of information respecting the geological structure and mineral resources of the country; the construction of a complete geological map or model, with a book of reference; the formation of a museum, as well of the various fossil and mineral products of the

country, as of drawings and models of the machinery and tools employed in mining and manufacturing; the holding of public meetings for discussing topics connected with these various subjects, the publication of papers, reports, and transactions, and the corresponding and co-operating with the Metropolitan and other similar Societies for the advancement of their common object.

4. Every candidate for admission into the Society must be proposed by two members at a General Meeting, and elected by a majority of the votes of the members present. Note.—Each member will have the privilege of admitting ladies and children at the Quarterly Meetings.

5. Notice of his having been elected shall be sent by the Secretary to each member, with a copy of the laws and of the following declaration, which he shall be requested to sign and return to the Secretary.

To the Council of the Geological and Polytechnic Society
of the West Riding of Yorkshire.

'I do hereby declare that as a member of the above Society, I will conform to its laws, and endeavour to promote its objects.'

Dated. Signed.

6. Any member may withdraw from the Society by giving notice in writing of his intention to the Secretary, and paying up his subscription to the end of the current year.

7. Any individual who resides out of the West Riding of Yorkshire, and is distinguished for the pursuit of the objects contemplated by the Society, or who may render any services to the Society, may be elected an Honorary Member, in the same form as an Ordinary Member.

8. The Annual Subscription shall be Half-a-guinea, and 2s. 6d. for the Reports, which shall be payable in advance on the 1st January in each year. Note.—Members who are elected at the December meetings shall not be liable to subscriptions until the 1st January following.

9. If any member allow his subscription to be in arrear for more than one year, and, after receiving notice from the Secretary, do not pay it within one month, the Council may erase his name from the List of Subscribers.

10. No new rule shall be passed, nor any rule altered, except at a General Meeting, nor unless a notice in writing, signed by six members, have been given at the preceding Quarterly Meeting, and afterwards inserted in the circulars calling the meeting.

11. The Officers of the Society shall be a president, vice-president, and twelve trustees, a secretary, a treasurer, and two honorary curators, and a council of twelve members in addition to the officers.

12. The Officers shall be elected by vote at the Annual Meeting, they shall be re-eligible, and shall continue in office until their successors are appointed.

13. ELECTION OF OFFICERS.—At the June meeting lists shall be prepared on which any member may enter the name of any member of the Society for any office, and at the annual meeting the lists so prepared shall be marked by the members present, and those whose names have the greatest number of marks shall be declared elected to their respective offices.

14. The museum and property of the Society shall be vested in the Trustees, and as soon as the number by death or resignation, is reduced to three, a new trust deed shall be executed.

15. The Council, of whom three shall be a quorum, shall meet once a month. They shall have the entire control of the property and the management of the business and funds of the Society. They may exchange or present duplicate specimens ; offer premiums for Essays or Inventions ; present copies of the Transactions to individuals and Societies ; supply vacancies in the officers until the annual meeting be held ; and they shall present a report to the annual meeting on the condition of the museum and property, and on the position and prospects of the Society.

16. The President, Secretary, or any three of the Council, may at any time call a Council Meeting, by notice through the post-office seven days previous, stating the objects of the meeting.

17. The Treasurer shall keep an account of all moneys paid and received for the Society ; produce his vouchers and accounts whenever required by the Council, and present the accounts for the year ending June 30th, together with an abstract, before the Meeting of the

Council in August, that they may be examined before being submitted to the auditors.

18. All moneys received for the Society shall be paid into such bank as the Council shall appoint, and no sum exceeding two pounds shall be paid without an order of the Council.

19. The Annual Abstract of the Accounts shall be prepared so as to show the expenditure of the Society under the most important heads; viz., rent, salaries, purchase of collections, printing transactions, &c., &c., and it shall be presented at the Annual Meeting, and printed with the report of the Council.

20. The Secretary shall take minutes of the proceedings of the General, Special, and Annual Meetings, and of the Meetings of the Council, and enter them regularly in the minute book; he shall conduct the correspondence of the Society under the superintendence of the Council, and shall prepare and bring before the Council everything that relates to the business of the Society, and carry their directions into effect.

21. General Meetings of the Society shall be held on the first Wednesday in March, June, and December, in the principal towns of the county, for transacting the business of the Society and for discussion. The Members present at each Meeting shall fix the place where the next Meeting shall be held.

22. The Annual Meeting shall be held in Wakefield in the autumn at such time as the Council may appoint, when the officers and two auditors shall be elected, the accounts and reports received, and the general business of the Society transacted.

23. A Special General Meeting may at any time be called by the President, the Council, or any twelve Members, in the same form as presented in Rule 16.

24. At all General Meetings the President, if present, shall take the chair, or in his absence a chairman shall be elected. All questions shall be decided by a majority of the votes of the Members present, the Chairman, if necessary, having the casting vote.

25. Those Members who intend reading papers must give two month's notice of their intention to the Secretary, and send in their

papers for the inspection of the Council, one month previous to the Meeting at which they are to be read.

26. The Society shall not be dissolved except at a Special General Meeting called for the purpose (of which three months' notice shall be given to each Member by the post), and by a majority of three-fourths of the Members present ; and in case of the dissolution of the Society, its collections shall not be sold, but presented to some local, or permanent Institution.

It was proposed by Mr. Wilson, seconded by Mr. Hartop, "That the above Rules be adopted," and carried unanimously.

CHAPTER IV.

SECTIONS TO CONNECT THE LANCASHIRE WITH THE YORKSHIRE
COAL-FIELD.

The appointment of Messrs. Morton and Embleton, on the 3rd May, 1839, to confer with the members of the Lancashire Society as to the formation of a section across the Penine Chain, so as to connect the Yorkshire and Lancashire Coal-fields, was duly acted upon by those gentlemen. The scheme was mutually satisfactory, and the general principle agreed to. Active steps were taken to form a section on the Yorkshire area, and amongst the most energetic in carrying it out was the Rev. William Thorp. The following letter from this gentleman, addressed to Mr. Embleton, expresses very well the eager spirit in which the work was prosecuted, and the care which was taken to verify every item of information by a practical study of the rocks and other strata exposed in the district.

Rev. W. Thorp to Mr. Embleton.
WOMERSLEY VICARAGE,
Wednesday, 19th July, 1839.
DEAR SIR,

How is your geological section coming on at Leeds? Have you begun the map yet, and what state of progress is it in? I have been hard at work this last six weeks, having been staying in the neighbourhood of Barnsley, and therefore have had a fine opportunity of visiting the western portion of our Coal-field. I am daily expecting the section from Mr. Williamson, which is 10 yards long, of the Lancashire Coal-field, as he has promised to lend it me, and to let me have a copy, and I mean to be over in Lancashire the first week in next month. I have been engaged with the strata between the Bradgate

I

rock and the flagstone; commencing at Sheffield, and going north up to the Calder. It appears that at Sheffield there are in that thickness four beds worked; further north, at Silkstone, there are three beds; but if a line be drawn down Clayton valley to near Chevet Hall, there are on the south side of this line as at Whitley Hall no less than nine beds worked, some of which are entirely different deposits, and others are continuous from one part of the Coal-field to the other. I mean to run over the country on the south side of the Calder after returning from Manchester; and there are two or three difficulties which, perhaps, you could assist me in solving. 1. George's paper must be wrong at page 163, where he says that the Mirfield Moor Coal is only 52 yards above Royds Coal; that the Mirfield Moor Coal is, I believe, identical with your Middleton Main Coal, and is the Lepton Edge or Blocking Coal of Flockton; and it is impossible, from a view of the country, that it can be only that distance above the Royds Coal. 2nd. Can you trace, as he says, page 165, the Stone Coal, or Upper Flockton, by Adwalton, through Birstall, Morley, Batley and Dewsbury, and can you obtain for me any section through it at any of the first four mentioned places; at Dewsbury, or rather Thornhill, I have a section through it? 3. There is another difficulty about the Thornhill Lees Rock, which, if you could determine for me, would save much trouble. This rock is not known in any of the Silkstone sections, or further south as in Lord Fitzwilliam's section. It is not the Bradgate Rock, for this latter lays immediately above the Parkgate Coal of Silkstone, and is certainly the Crow Coal of Flockton,—there is no doubt of this—and George says, page 165, 'that 50 yards above (the Cromwell Coal) is a coal of very variable thickness and quality, in some situations it is 9 feet, &c., it occurs at Daw Green, and is the Two Yards Coal of Birkenshaw and Gomersall.' Now, query, is the Gomersall Coal the Crow Coal (or Floating bed, or Lousey bed, for they are all one) of Flockton, and is the Gomersal Coal the first coal of your section, 'got formerly for the ironstone above it?' If it is not, the rock in your section is not the Bradgate Rock. 4. Can you get a section above your coal near you, so as to see what has become of the Old Flockton beds? I doubt that Coal in the boring, page 186-7, at Simpson's Spring, being the Upper Flockton.

I had another round with Hartop, at Mr. Wilson's, of Banks; Morton was there, and it was after dinner, and we kept him in good humour. He says that there has been a lateral movement, as well as a vertical one, and that the bord and end of the coal has been moved round. I wish that you would be kind enough when in Leeds to ask Mr. Denny to let me have a boring below the Low Moor Coal, which he promised me. Perhaps you could write which is the Low Moor Coal in the boring, for I am ignorant of its range through Leeds town. What authority have you for your rock (at the top of the Middleton West Pit) being the Bradgate; if Smith's map is the only one it is not to be relied upon, for he makes the Horbury Rock, which has the Haigh Moor Coal under it, the Bradgate? I can point out twenty errors in his map. I am about to exchange borings with Mr. Briggs for the Glass Houghton and Fairburn ones, so as to complete a section to the Millstone grit North over Bramham Moor. I believe in this line there is a great thinning away, but not further west. Please direct to me, under cover, to Rt. Hon. Lord Hawke, Womersley Park, Pontefract. P.S.—Can you get borings from Beeston to Royds.

        Excusing this trouble, Believe me,

                Very truly yours,

                      WM. THORP.

Further correspondence of a similar character took place, and Mr. Thorp was indefatigable in his investigations; he paid a visit to the Lancashire side of the hills, but does not appear to have gained so much information as he wished, the time at his disposal being too short to allow a detailed survey of the district to be made.

On the 11th October following, a meeting of the council was held at the Museum, Wakefield, at which, along with other business, resolutions were adopted with regard to the proposed sections. The Rev. Samuel Sharp was in the chair.

The secretary having read a letter from Mr. Binney, Secretary to the Manchester Geological and Polytechnic Society, expressing their readiness to co-operate with this society in fixing scales for maps, plans, and sections, and in procuring a section across the Penine Chain. It was resolved—

1. That Messrs. Morton and Embleton be requested to prepare a report on the scales most suitable for plans, sections, and maps, both for record and publication, that they communicate it to the Manchester Geological Society, and report to the general meeting at Leeds.

2. That the same gentlemen, together with the Rev. W. Thorp, Mr. Hartop, and Mr. Holt, be a committee to report on the best line of section on the eastern side of the hills, and to prepare a plan of operations, in conjunction with the Manchester Society, which may be laid before the next meeting.

Mr. Charles Morton to Mr. Embleton.

DARTON COLLIERIES, NEAR BARNSLEY,
28th October, 1839.

MY DEAR SIR,

I have written to all our colleagues on the section committee, but have not yet received an answer, therefore I cannot name a day for our meeting. I have also written to Mr. Binney, of Manchester, on this subject, and respecting the scales. A copy of our line of section has also been sent to Professor Phillips and Mr. De La Beche, with a request that they will give us the benefit of their opinion and advice thereon. Mr. Wilson will most likely call a council meeting for Friday next, if so, I shall probably have the pleasure of seeing you at Wakefield along with the other councillors. With respect to the Leeds meeting, I presume you may consider yourself the "Plenipotentiary" of the Society; and, in the exercise of your high powers, let me beg of you not to forget the dinner for the ladies as well as for the gentlemen, you know that I have pledged myself to bring this matter before the notice of our august councillors, and I shall most assuredly redeem my pledge, notwithstanding that such an innovation may be sneered at and resisted as a dangerous organic change. I should think it will be proper for you to make arrangements for a reporter to attend our meeting, it would indeed be a loss to the public to allow such flowers of eloquence to 'blush unseen, and waste their sweetness on the desert air.' Give my kind respects to Mrs. Embleton and Miss Easton, and to Miss Emily Easton, if she has not departed for cannie Newcastle.

Subjoined you have the borings which I promised to send you.
Believe me, dear Sir, yours sincerely,
CHAS. MORTON.

The Committee appointed on the 11th October to report on the best line of section across the Penine Chain, in conjunction with the Geological Society of Manchester, prepared a report to be submitted to the meeting at Leeds, and an invitation was sent to the Manchester Society to send representatives to the meeting. This invitation was accepted, and Messrs. J. E. Bowman and Edward W. Binney were appointed. A meeting of the Council was held on the 4th December at which those gentlemen were present, introduced by the following letter from Captain Brown:—

Mr. Brown to Mr. Embleton.

MANCHESTER NATURAL HISTORY SOCIETY, PETER STREET,
4th December, 1839.
DEAR SIR,

I beg leave to introduce you to the bearers, my friends Mr. Bowman and Mr. Binney, who are sent as members of the deputation to attend the meeting at Leeds to-morrow, they are both very intelligent geologists, and I am sure you will find them so.

I am sorry to say, that my time here has been so absorbed by my duties, that I have not had time to give that attention to the fossils which you sent me that they deserve, however, I shall in a week or two turn my attention to the subject, and write you concerning them.

I have been only able to get out two numbers of my 'Fossil Conchology,' and one of my 'Recent Shells,' since I came here. They are just now sent by Mr. Bowman to Mr. John Calvert, 10, Commercial Street, who will send your copies to you.

Do you never come to Manchester, when you do, I shall be most happy to see you.

Excuse haste, while I am, yours faithfully,
THOS. BROWN.

The proposed sections and scales were thoroughly discussed, and Mr. Morton was entrusted with the task of introducing the subject at the public meeting on the following day.

At the commencement of the meeting, Messrs. Binney and Bowman were elected honorary members of the society, and during the course of the subsequent proceedings Mr. Charles Morton made a report of the result of the previous day's discussion. The Manchester Geological Society at its last meeting had decided to assist in forming the section, and to continue the Yorkshire section on the Lancashire side of the Penine Chain. There were no accurate sections on a large scale across the island at this latitude, and it was considered that the completion of even one section across Yorkshire and Lancashire would throw so much light on the structure and stratification of the two coal fields, and of the ridge of hills which divides them, that great benefit would be conferred on geological science generally, and to the members of these two societies in particular. Three different lines of sections had been proposed, but it was desirable to concentrate all the energies of the society upon one of them. Such a section should be carried on in a north-easterly direction, this being the line of the greatest dip of the strata; and its latitude should not be further north than Leeds, nor further south than Sheffield, otherwise it would be beyond the limit of the Yorkshire coal-field altogether. Perhaps the best line would be an intermediate one, that is, in the latitude of Barnsley, for the stratification of this coal-field is probably more fully developed between Penistone and Goole than in any other direction. The information which this section should contain ought to be local and in detail, not as geological sections too often are, composed of vague generalities, and a mixture of half fact and half fiction. The surface of the country should be carefully levelled and laid down, towns, villages, roads, rivers, collieries, &c., should be noticed, vertical sections of pits, boreholes, quarries and cliffs should be delineated, the insertion of the bassets or outcrops of coal, ironstone, and other remarkable strata should be marked down, with their names and thickness, the crossing of faults or throws, should be registered, and the extent of the dislocation up or down should be stated, the continuous position and dip of the different beds (where these can be correctly ascertained,) should be drawn. The sources from whence the requisite information may be obtained are various and numerous, and the means of executing both this and other lines of section are in the societies own hands. The distance from the Penine Chain at the Sheffield and Manchester Railway Tunnel to the Holderness coast is about 70 miles, and if ten members of the society would each undertake 7 miles, the whole length might be completed within a reasonable time. Each individual would have to level his own portion either with a spirit-level or theodolite, and to measure it with the chain or take its lengths from accurate township maps. Each would lay down on paper his observations and results, and their respective sheets, when joined together, would form the section required. Respecting the scales of these sections much may be said, Mr. De la Beche recommends that the scales of lengths and depths should be equal, but this suggestion cannot always be beneficially acted upon, and it certainly cannot in the present instance. The summit of the ridge near Penistone is probably about 1800 feet or one-third of a mile above the sea, consequently if an uniform scale of three inches to a mile were adopted, the length of our section when laid down on paper, would be 17½ feet, and its height only 1 inch. The most likely scale for length is 3 inches to a mile, and for depth 1 inch to 50 feet, which would make the length of the sheet 17½ feet, and its depth 3 feet. As before stated these different lines of section have been proposed, which may be named the Leeds line, the Barnsley line, and the Sheffield line. The first to commence at the Leeds and Manchester Tunnel at Todmorden, and proceed by Halifax, Leeds, Aberford, and Pocklington, to Barmston, on the Holderness Coast. The second to commence at the Sheffield and Manchester Railway Tunnel, near Penistone, and proceed near Darton, north of Barnsley, Brierley, Swinefleet near Goole, Cave sands and Cottingham to Aldborough, on the same coast. The third to commence at the central axis of the Penine Chain, near Castleton, and proceed by Sheffield, Maltby, Tickhill, Bawtry, north of Gainsboro', Caistor, to the mouth of the Humber, below Grimsby. The second or Barnsley line is preferable because it crosses the coal-field in the direction in which its peculiar stratification and richness is most fully exhibited, and because the means of obtaining accurate geographical and geological information are more abundant, and more accessible to the members of this society than on either of the other lines. The Barnsley line would possess the advantage of having the millstone grit and flagstone strata beautifully illustrated by the great tunnel sinkings and cuttings on the railway near Penistone. The Wortley and Bradgate rocks, containing the valuable and important beds of coal known by the names of the Flockton, Parkgate, and Silkstone beds, with their associated strata of iron-stone, would be clearly exhibited by the sinkings in Mr. Wilson's Pits, near Darton, which are the deepest in the county. The Woolley Edge rocks, containing the thick Barnsley coal and other seams, would be not less distinctly illustrated by the borings and sinkings of the same gentleman near Staincross. Further eastward the Chevet and Ackworth rocks would be delineated by borings already in possession of members of the society, and the magnesian limestone by borings made near Womersley, under the immediate inspection of the Rev. W. Thorp, at Swinefleet, the section would pass the very deep borehole recently made by Messrs. Egremont and Company through the new red sandstone and its associated beds of gypsum, and across the the Cave and Holderness districts; considerable geological information may be gained by examining the county with the writings of Prof. Phillips and Mr. Harcourt for guide books. Mr. Morton further stated that the Barnsley line, if continued westwards, would cross Lancashire in a more advantageous locality for investigating and illustrating that coal-field than either of the other lines, and he concluded his report by reading an extract from a letter written by Mr. Greenough, on the subject of these sections, wherein he recommends the adoption of the Barnsley line, but advises the society to confine its attention solely to the coal measures, and deprecates the extension of this, or any other section across the New Red Sandstone, Oolite and Chalk districts of the East Riding.

Mr. E. W. Binney expressed his opinion that the scale of the sections proposed in the report would not answer the purpose, especially on the Lancashire side of the ridge. To attempt to display the Lancashire Coal-field in a section of three inches to the mile, would be futile indeed. In the rich part of the Coal-field, about Ashton and Dukinfield, they would have forty-five seams of coal within about a mile and a half. With regard to the particular line to be adopted, he thought it should be along the line of the Sheffield and Manchester Railway, as then they would have the plans drawn and the sections correctly taken. If the northern (or Leeds) line mentioned in the report were chosen, it would go through the unprofitable part of the Lancashire Coal-field, and it would be 150 yards below the Sheffield Coal about Ormskirk. It would not suit either the line or dip of Lancashire. In that county the dip was generally to the South West, so that to follow the proposed north line would take the range of the coal instead of the dip. The southern (or Sheffield) line suggested would cut out the Lancashire Coal-field nearly altogether, and would extend into Flintshire, and into the Silurian or Slate system of rocks. The middle (or Barnsley) line which had been pointed out was not, perhaps, the best that could be chosen, but for the reasons he had stated it was preferable to either of the others. Perhaps the best plan would be to take a line from the central axis near Salter's Brook to Mottram, and then diverge into two lines, so as to embrace the whole of the great Lancashire Coal-field. On the Lancashire side there would not be more than fifty miles of coal-field to traverse, which would give only five miles to each of ten persons, instead of seven as on the Yorkshire side. With respect to the sections, he thought they ought to represent the "cleet" of the coal amongst the other particulars. In the Lancashire Coal-field some of the different beds were not to be identified by either fossils or anything else, so that the *cleets*, which were in Lancashire very useful, might not avail in Yorkshire. The Pecten which Mr. Teale had stated was to be found only over one description of coal in Yorkshire, was distinctly found over three kinds in Lancashire. Therefore neither salt water nor fresh water shells would serve them in Lancashire to the same extent as in Yorkshire, but still they might be useful.

Mr. Embleton spoke in favour of the Barnsley line, and hoped that some understanding would be arrived at with the Manchester gentlemen as to the line of section to be adopted. Mr. Bull said he would be glad to assist in the cost of the undertaking, and recommended that at the end of every quarter of a mile marked on the section, a permanent bench-mark should be put down in the ground, which could be referred to at any time hereafter. Mr. S. D. Martin offered to undertake a portion of the section. Mr. Hartop did not think it desirable to prescribe any definite line of section for the Lancashire Society to adopt. The Lancashire gentlemen should be at liberty to select their own line, and that without reference to what should be done on the Yorkshire side. If they selected a line which passed at right angles with their minerals, it was not essential that it should meet the Yorkshire one in the centre of the Penine Chain. There might be opportunities of uniting the two lines by particular observations, and if each could be so drawn as to give the gentlemen on each side of the ridge an opportunity of taking that direction which was best for their particular Coal-fields, it would be better than adopting one continuous line.

A resolution was eventually agreed to on the proposition of Mr. Morton, seconded by Mr. Embleton, " That the Council be empowered to proceed with the section from the eastern end of the tunnel of the Sheffield and Manchester Railway at Dunford Bridge, across the Yorkshire Coal-field, in conjunction with the Manchester Geological Society, in such manner as they shall consider most likely to attain the desired objects."

In order to appreciate the value of the sections which the Society had thus resolved to undertake and which its members proceeded to map and determine, it is necessary to consider the position of geological science, more especially as applied to mining industries, half a century ago. Exactly forty years before the date of the meeting at Leeds, the venerable William Smith published the first parts of his map of the Strata of England, which was not completed until the year 1815. During these years geologists were divided between the hostile theories of Hutton and Werner. The latter was Professor of Mineralogy at Freiburg in Germany, and the study of the rocks in his vicinity led him to propound a theory that all rocks were of aqueous origin ; that originally they were all dissolved in the ocean, and were precipitated and deposited in the order in which they now exist, so that formations exist universally over the surface of the globe. Dr. Hutton, of Edinburgh, on the other hand, arrived at independent and very different conclusions, he taught that the forces now in existence and operating on the surface of the earth were sufficient to account for all the past geological changes on the globe. The action of rain and frost in loosening the particles of soil and rock, their removal and carriage to more or less distant areas by streams and rivers, the abrading action of the waves, were agencies constantly at work and capable of producing great geological changes. These operations during untold ages removed mountains, and reduced the land surfaces beneath the level of the sea, whilst the material so removed went to form new areas of land. The successive alternations of sea and land could be traced in the sequence of the rocks; and the power of volcanic action was recognized as frequently assisting in the elevation of an old sea bottom to form dry land. The frequent occurrence of granite and other crystalline rocks was accepted as proof of this action. The Huttonian theory, though fixed on so solid a basis that it may be regarded as the groundwork of every succeeding speculation and as the foundation on which the superstructure of modern geological science has been erected, took no cognizance of the fossil remains of animals and plants contained in the rocks, and it remained for William Smith to discover that each stratum of rock has its characteristic and peculiar fossils. He was a native of Oxfordshire, and was trained to the profession of a land surveyor and civil engineer. During his early years he collected fossils from the Oolitic rocks, near Bath, and his practical and thoughtful method of studying them, led him to the conclusion that each stratum was characterized more or less by fossils peculiar to it, and that these did not extend to the beds above or below. Whilst maturing this discovery his professional duties called him to Yorkshire, and his attachment to geological science, soon led to the investigation of the secondary strata of this great county, and he was surprised and delighted to find that his observations in the Midlands were confirmed and substantiated in Yorkshire; he found the same groups of fossils in their respective beds of rock, shale, or limestone, and came to the conclusion that those beds extended across the country from Dorsetshire to Yorkshire, and that they could everywhere be distinguished by the fossils they contained. Visits to all parts of the country soon convinced Smith that his discovery applied to all the stratified rocks;

and the older rocks of north-west Yorkshire and the Lake district were recognized as the equivalents of those of Wales. The old red sandstone and the great carboniferous series were defined, and together with the intermediate beds were carefully indicated on his several maps.

In 1832 Sir Henry de la Beche proposed to the Board of the Ordnance Survey that he should colour the ordnance map of Somerset, Devon and Cornwall geologically, and a sum of £300 was placed at his disposal for the purpose. With this amount De la Beche went to work, contributing, however, a much larger sum from his own private resources; and in a few years gained so much ground that he and his staff of surveyors were recognised as the Ordnance Geological Survey. Their efforts were in the first years confined to representing by colour, the relative areas of the several series of formations. At the meeting of the British Association at Edinburgh in 1834 resolutions were adopted, and a deputation appointed, to impress on the Government the necessity of a Geological Survey of the northern half of this island, and in 1835 the deputation waited on Mr. Spring Rice, the Chancellor of the Exchequer, but with slight advantage. In 1835 also De la Beche made a representation to the same eminent financier that the work of the survey should be extended so as to embrace a museum, which should contain all British materials which were useful from an economic point of view. Sandstones, cements, and materials useful for building purposes; metals, ores, and minerals having a commercial value; and every other substance used in industrial operations were to be collected and placed in the proposed museum. Such collections it was contended would be of the greatest value to the people engaged in these industries, and would afford a great amount of practical information not otherwise accessible. This recommendation was adopted, and a house in Craig's Court, Charing Cross, was placed at the disposal of the survey. Large numbers of specimens were speedily forthcoming, and the house adjoining was added to the one already occupied. This additional accommodation was soon inadequate for the requirements of the survey, and in 1845 the building, now occupied in Jermyn Street, was authorized to be used for the exhibition of specimens which had been collected, and also as a school of applied science. The Geological Survey was transferred in 1844 from the Ordnance Department to that of Woods and Forests. The Chief Commissioner of the latter was the late Earl of Carlisle, who was a member of this Society. Another prominent member of the Government, then occupying the office of Chancellor of the Exchequer, was the late Lord Halifax (then Sir Charles Wood), whom this Society numbered amongst its vice-presidents. During the alterations which were necessary to adapt the building in Jermyn Street for museum purposes, the following letter was addressed by Lord Carlisle to Sir Charles Wood. 'It has been settled that my department is to build a museum of Economic Geology. The rent of the building in Piccadilly, which the public will have to pay to the crown, is calculated at about £2000 a year. There has been a plan for having shops in the lower story, which might bring in £750 a year ; but the conductor of the museum, Sir H. de la Beche, and the Economic Radicals, are vehement against said shops ; and Hume says if I do not assure him that they are given up, he will this session move an address to the crown. Will you let me throw over the shops ?' To which Sir Charles Wood replied, 'If you wish me to denationalize to such an extent this *shopkeeping* nation, I cannot resist you.'

The staff of the survey in 1839 consisted of six assistant Geologists, with Sir H. de la Beche at their head. There was also a laboratory under the charge of Mr. Richard Phillips ; and a room, set apart for the collection and preservation of mining plans and other documents relating thereto, was denominated the Mining Record Office.

It is evident from the foregoing brief epitome of the state of Geological Science before the foundation of this Society in the West Riding of Yorkshire, that the accurate information respecting the Yorkshire Coal-field was a comparatively small item ; and this observation applies with equal force to that of Lancashire. The want of authentic information resulted in the expenditure of thousands of pounds sterling in fruitless searches and borings for coal, where the most rudimentary geological knowledge would have made it abundantly evident that the longed-for coal seams could by no means be present. It is not an uncommon incident to find heaps of shale still existing on Millstone Grit areas which are miles from the outcrop of the nearest coal-seam, and which are the result of borings and drivings in search of that article, prosecuted many years ago. The presence of a dark coloured shale was looked upon by the practical man of those days as evidence of the existence of coal in its vicinity, and on the surface of formations, lower in the scale than the millstone grits, there may be repeatedly found the shale-heap, indicative of the vain search for coal. A story is told of Prof. Sedgwick, who, during a visit to Leicestershire, saw an engine and gearing at the top of an adjacent hill which he was informed was a coal pit. On visiting the place and making the ascent of the hill he found Lias shale with numerous fossils, 'Why,' says he, 'this is Lias'! 'Lias' says the enraged proprietor, 'you're a liar, and you're all liars together'! But all the same the man ruined himself. Prof. Jukes cites a story which Dean Buckland used to tell, of Lord Oxford sinking on some property in Oxfordshire, on the Kimmeridge or Oxford Clay, by the advice of a 'Great practical man' and in opposition to all Buckland could say, who offered to be broiled on the first ton of coals raised there, and Conybeare made a caricature of that distinguished divine and geologist frizzling in his own fat. These are instances outside our county, but equally egregious blunders can be found in plenty in it. Even in the coal district there was a blissful amount of ignorance as to the sequence of the coal-seams; the occurrence of faults was well known, but their effect in the strata was a matter of surmise to the practical miner, and instances may be given in which much time and money have been expended in the vain search for a coal-seam, which has been thrown out by faults though it may exist, at a considerable depth, a field-length away.

During the first thirty years of the present century " was a time of marvellous vigour in the history of geology. It was during that time that the science took shape and dignity. Amid the conflict of opposing schools progress had been steady and rapid. Every year broadened the base on which the infant science was being built up. The rocks of England and Wales were arranged in their order of age, the outlines traced by Smith having been more and more filled in. Excellent service had been done by the handbook of Conybeare and

Phillips, while Boué, Jamieson, Macculloch, and others had made known the rocks of large tracts of Scotland;"* Greenough, Buckland, Fitton, Horner, De la Beche, Johnston, Sedgwick, and others had been steadily working in England and Wales; and Scrope had given to the world his researches on the extinct Volcanoes of Central France. But a vast deal remained to be accomplished. The field was still in a sense newly discovered, it stretched over a wide area, and lay open to anyone, who with active feet, good eyes, and shrewd head, chose to enter it, and the enthusiasm of those who were already at work within its borders sufficed not only to inspirit their own labours, but to attract and stimulate other fellow-workers from the outer world.

The members of the society who undertook to prepare sections and map their respective districts, did so knowing the difficult and frequently perplexing nature of the ground. In the eastern part of the district they had the advantage of such detailed sections as had been preserved of borings and sinkings, and of some valuable but more or less indiscriminate information gathered from the practical working of the several coal seams. Westwards the courses of the streams, the larger valleys, and the gritstone escarpments forming the brow of the hills succeeding each other in a regularly constituted series were all to be carefully measured, localized and mapped. Observations on dips, strikes and faults had to be made and recorded. Taken in the aggregate and remembering that the members of the Society who devoted themselves to this work were working from a pure desire to extend the boundaries of knowledge, animated by a noble enthusiasm for the new branch of science which they banded themselves together to prosecute, and that their only reward arose from the satisfaction of having prosecuted their investigations to a successful issue, and added some facts to the gradually accumulating mass of information respecting the structure of the earth's surface. When all these circumstances are considered, it must be granted that their work was calculated to be of great benefit to the community at large, and reflects the greatest credit on the energy of the young Society, and of those members especially who mainly prosecuted the the work.

---

*Mem. of Sir R. Murchison, by Dr. A. Giekie, 1875. p 111.

Meanwhile the Geologists of Lancashire had organized a Society for the prosecution of the science in that county, and had their headquarters in Manchester. The first quarterly meeting of the members of the Manchester Geological Society was held on the 30th January, 1840, and in compliance with an invitation that some of the members of the West Riding Society would attend, Messrs. Embleton, Morton and Wilson were present. On the proposition of Dr. Black, the three were elected honorary members of the Society. After papers had been read by Mr. J. Hawkshaw and Mr. J. E. Bowman a long discussion took place on the proposed line of sections across the Lancashire and Yorkshire Coal-field, and on the scale to which the sections should be drawn. Eventually Mr. Hawkshaw proposed that the horizontal scale be four inches to the mile, and the vertical be one hundred feet to the inch. This was agreed to by the meeting, the representatives of this Society gracefully acquiescing in the arrangement.

Notwithstanding the apparent unanimity of opinion respecting the direction the proposed sections should follow, which was expressed at the Leeds meeting, there were individual opinions respecting the matter which were sufficiently important to merit attention. Members of the Society had paid special attention or gained greater knowledge of some one district than another, and could see advantages in that area which were not apparent to others who had not the same thorough knowledge of it; and the result was that the members combated their several views with much pertinacity, and there was a keen struggle before the final decision was arrived at.

The next general meeting of the members was held at Bradford, on the 11th of March, 1840, at 12 o'clock. The Rev. Dr. Scoresby, Vicar of Bradford, occupied the chair, and gave an admirable address. A special effort was made by the secretary and council to have a thorough expression of opinion respecting the proposed sections, and it was decided that the evening meeting should be devoted to a discussion of the question. The Rev. William Thorp, of Womersley, read a paper on the subject in which he considered the general principles which should govern the minds of the members in deciding so important a question. The section should be made in some district where it would be at right angles to the 'line of strike' of the different beds. After considering the general formation of the coal-field, its basin-shaped form, and the varying dip of its rocks and coals, Mr. Thorp proceeded to recommend a line through Rotherham, commencing with the red-rock near that town, over the coal district on the south side of the Don, over the roadstone near Tidswell, and the mountain limestone near Buxton; this line would embrace fourteen workable seams of coal. He ridiculed the line suggested by Mr. Morton through Barnsley and Penistone, in which there were only six beds of coal worked, the total thickness of which was about 24 feet. He remarks "Surely the Lancashire gentleman would exclaim upon an inspection of the completed section, that we must have made a mistake! That while they had fifty worked beds, amounting to 150 feet of solid coal, we had only six diminutive, forsooth riding coals, amounting to 24 feet; they would say that their great coal-field can certainly have no relationship with that of Yorkshire, at least if it has, that of Yorkshire is only the fag end of it." The direction suggested by the Manchester Geological Society to take a line from the central axis near Saltersbrooke to Mottram, and then to diverge into two lines so as to embrace the whole coal-field of Lancashire, Mr. Thorp pointed out several reasons why this suggested line on the Lancashire side should not be adopted, amongst others, that it omitted the higher strata of the seams in the Oldham district; there was also a section of the Dukinfield district which had been already published by Mr. Elias Hall, which was very correct and and of great merit; and Mr. Heywood was preparing for publication in the Literary and Philosophical transactions of Manchester some sections in the same district. The section towards Derbyshire would have the advantage of obtaining details of the mountain limestone series of that county, which would make it valuable not only to the two societies but to all who study the science. "Again there is a system of transverse and longitudinal valleys in the Yorkshire coal-field, to which none other in the British Islands are exactly analogous; a study of these valleys, with their relation to the Derbyshire axis, the passage of large bodies of water from the west, and the diluvium which they severally contain, would well repay the labour bestowed, for if a true theory of the formation of these valleys could be made,

K

it would afford a clue to the interpretation of the mode of action which elevated our continents. Those within the area of the Coal Field scarcely contain any diluvium, but those of Derbyshire abound with pebbles left above the highest flood-mark."

Mr. H. Hartop pointed out some difficulties attending the line of section proposed by the Rev. Mr. Thorp, but with some deviation to avoid the dislocation in the valley of the Don he should be prepared to support it.

Mr. T. W. Embleton pointed out that the object of the section was not to get the best series illustrating the Yorkshire Coal-field, but to afford the means of comparison between that and the Lancashire Coal-field. To effect this the section across Yorkshire should commence near the same point as the one across Lancashire. He agreed with Mr. Thorp that it should embrace the full dip of the strata, as this would allow more strata to be intersected than any other direction. The line proposed by Mr. Morton and himself has this recommendation, and it had the advantage of starting eastwards from the same point as the Lancashire section did westwards. Mr. Thorp's objection that on the Barnsley line, some of the seams of coal and some of the rock formations were only slightly developed, stood for nothing, for no one line could be selected where every stratum was developed to its greatest extent. Of course other sections would be commenced, and which would with advantage be carried through those parts of the Coal-field where some coals attained their greatest thickness ; but as before observed, this section was merely to assist in instituting a comparison between the two Coal-fields, and as such could not be made with advantage to the Society unless the line proposed at the Leeds meeting be adopted.

After dining the meeting was resumed at 6.0 p.m., and the gentlemen interested in the proposed sections, promised to further discuss them. A good deal of practical information on the subject was elicited ; but the meeting was unable to come to a decision on a subject that involved so many points of detail, and the matter was referred to the committee on the sections, for further consideration and report.

On April 25th the genial and hospitable secretary, Mr. Wilson, invited the Council of the Society to meet at his residence, Banks Hall, to further discuss the line the sections should take.

The following extract from a letter from Mr. Wilson to Mr. Embleton, dated April 6th, 1840, is interesting.—" Mr. Holt proposes Monday, the 27th instant, for the meeting at Banks, which will also suit Mr. Briggs and Mr. Morton. If I hear from you that it is inconvenient to you, I will immediately inform Messrs. Thorp and Hartop. I propose that we should breakfast at half-past nine, as you are so far off, I hope you will come the night before. I have suggested that we should meet alternately at three or four places in this neighbourhood, instead of Wakefield, once a month. Do you not think we should work better in this way, having more time for our deliberations." All the gentlemen named accepted the invitation, and after partaking of the good cheer provided, proceeded with all due decorum and wisdom to the solution of the much debated problem. Mr. Hartop advocated his scheme for the South of Barnsley, which would enable the council to incorporate the Wentworth House section, which had been made several years previously, had since been improved upon and corrected, and was then probably as accurate as any section existing. Mr. Thorp hesitated to advocate his line towards Derbyshire, and did not appear to have made up his mind about any of them. Whilst Mr. Holt, with much skill and pertinacity proposed that the section should extend from the border of the county through Northowram, thence to Flockton, and across to Woolley, and eastwards to the escarpment of the Permian Limestone. After much consultation and reference to maps, the latter line was finally decided upon. Messrs. Morton and Holt were requested to report fully on the subject at the next quarterly meeting of the members in June.

The report was presented in due course, and is printed in the proceedings of the society issued to the members, pp. 18-24. After recapitulating the lines of sections which had been suggested for the consideration of the council, they report that after very careful examination they have determined to recommend to the society the adoption of the one commencing near Halifax, and proceeding in a south-easterly direction towards Doncaster, which, whilst it developes our own coal measures to the fullest extent, does not altogether lose sight of the original object, for, if continued westwards to the summit of the Penine Chain it would connect a similar line of section on the eastern side, and thus connect the Yorkshire with the Lancashire Coal-field ; they further considered it advisable to confine the attention of the society exclusively to that part of the section which traverses the coal measures, without regard to the Magnesian Limestone and Red Marl deposits that lie further to the east, in the hope that by concentration of the society's energies to one portion only, they would more speedily and more accurately carry out the fundamental object of the society, namely, the thorough examination and elucidation of the Yorkshire Coal-field.

The following is an outline of the direction which it was now proposed that the sections should take :—

" The line of section proposed by me commences in Northowram on the flagstone, wherein lie the Halifax hard and soft bed of coal. It then crosses a district of table land, composed of flagstone, to the most westerly escarpment of the Wortley Rock, in which are deposited a bed of first rate Furnace Coal, the Low Moor Better Bed, and a Coal accompanied by an excellent black ironstone, the Low Moor Black Bed. Passing south of Norwood Green, where coals are worked by Sir George Armytage's lessee and others, the line reaches Bailiff Bridge, where a great dislocation down to the west occurs, running parallel with the valley that extends from Brighouse to Low Moor. The bold cliff of Clifton is next mounted, and the line proceeds by Woolrow, and crosses the Leeds and Elland turnpike road, about half way between the village of Clifton and the Pack Horse. The Low Moor Black Bed and Better Bed underlie this township, and an accurate knowledge of them may be obtained from the colliery workings of Mr. Walker, and from borings which have recently been made near the line of section. The levels in this part range a few degrees East of North. Entering the township of Hartshead the line traverses three quarters of a mile of unexplored ground, in which the marked lines of springs, and other circumstances, indicate considerable dislocations at right angles with each other. The site of Hartshead Colliery is next crossed. Here the Blocking Coal is worked, and a large dislocation runs almost due North and South.

The levels first range nearly East, and afterwards nearly North. A short distance further the escarpment of the Lime Coal is met with, and next, the escarpment of the Cromwell Bed, which, I believe, is identical with the Park Gate Coal. Proceeding to the division of the townships of Hartshead and Mirfield, and near the old Huddersfield and Leeds road, a considerable 'throw' up to the South is found. The extent of this elevation is supposed to be not less than one hundred yards, which opinion is corroborated by the levels. The line of section then intersects another outcrop of the Blocking Coal, which may be traced through the village of Mirfield to the south side of the river Calder, where it has been worked by the Wheatley's and the Walker's. In the township of Thornhill the ground rises southward from the river, and sufficient cover is obtained for the Lime Coal or Wheatley's Three-quarters Coal and the Cromwell Bed, which have been worked for many years by Messrs. Wheatley. I have taken many lines of water levels here, but I have not been able to ascertain the average dip of the strata, owing to their distracted state. From this high ground the line of section descends the dell in Mr. Ingham's estate, where the Cromwell Bed is worked; and further on it crosses the outcrop of the Flockton Coal; then climbs the bold escarpment of Bradgate Rock, on which stands the village of Thornhill, and proceeds along a plain about a quarter of a mile in length to another escarpment, on the brink of which are Mr. Ingham's Collieries working the Flockton Thin Coal. A deeply denuded valley separates this cliff from the rising ground of Emroyd, under which Messrs. Briggs and Stansfield are working a seam of coal that lies about eighty-one yards below the Flockton Thin Coal. The levels in Emroyd Colliery generally range nearly East and West. Having attained the summit of the Emroyd ridge at a point about half way between Overton and Middlestown the line of section descends into the Coxley valley, passes through the steep wood on the opposite side, and goes over another hill between Midgley and Netherton, into the Bullcliffe Wood valley. It then traverses an elevated ground in the township of Bretton, crossing the Denby Dale road at Sunwood, and proceeds towards Woolley. The district between Middleton and Bretton is almost unexplored; the geological information respecting it is very scanty; and the outcrops of the coals, if any occur, are distant from the present line of section. Near the division of the townships of Bretton and Woolley is a bed of coal worked by Mr. Twedale. The coal is near the surface, and I think it is probably a part of the Barnsley Thick Bed. The latter, however, has not yet been found in its full thickness farther north than Darton. Passing along the extensive and bold escarpment of Woolley Edge, the line of section goes near the outcrops of Beamshaw, Winter, and Woodmoor coals, which have been worked in this locality by Messrs. Charlesworth, for a distance of three-quarters of a mile on the line of section. From the elevated summit of Woolley Edge, the line proceeds through the village of Woolley, along a gentle slope of unexplored ground; but there is little doubt that the strata here dip conformably with the fall of the ground. The Sheffield and Wakefield turnpike road is crossed near Riding's Quarry, (which, I think is a western outlier of the Chevet Rock formation). Notton Park is next passed through, and at the intersection of the line with the Staincross and Royston Road, the two beds of coal, supposed to be the Thick Coal of the Chevet Rock, and the Woodmoor bed, have been bored to. Parts of the townships of Royston and Carlton are then traversed, where there is no positive information concerning the coals; though I have little doubt that the Thick Coal just mentioned and the Woodmoor Coal are here, and at no great depth. After crossing the Barnsley canal, the line of section is carried through the township of Shafton, and here I am unable to lay before the society further plans, except those derived from published maps, on a small scale; for I am informed that there is no township plan of Shafton. I recommended that the line should proceed in the same direction, through the townships of Cudworth, Darfield, Billingley, and Bolton-upon-Dearne, to the Magnesian Limestone ridge; but Mr. Thorp is of opinion that a better development of the strata may be had by curving the line in Woolley to the north-east, and passing through Notton, Royston, Shafton, Brierley, Great Houghton, and Clayton-in-the-Clay, to the Magnesian Limestone. There is however little geological interest between Notton and the limestone ridge, so far as regards coal beds, there being only two workable seams."

The committee recommended that the section should embrace the various details mentioned in the committee's report at Leeds, namely, that the surface of the country should be carefully levelled and laid down, that towns, villages, roads, rivers, canals, collieries, boreholes, and township boundaries should be noticed, the vertical sections of pits and boreholes should be delineated, that the intersection of basset or outcrop of coal, ironstone and other strata should be marked down, that the crossing of faults or throws should be registered, and the extent of the dislocation stated, and that the continuous position and dip of the different beds should be drawn as far as they can be correctly ascertained. It was also recommended that a map or plan of the ground on each side the line of section to the extent of five or ten chains should be made, and that the scale of lengths should be 264 feet (or 4 chains) to 1 inch, and that of depths be 40 feet to 1 inch. It is further requested that members who may furnish details of sinkings or borings should draw them on an uniform scale of 8 feet to 1 inch. The section as proposed was 25 miles in length, and comprised between 3,000 and 4,000 feet of strata. "In a work so extensive it is obvious that the combined talent and exertion of all the geologists in the society will be required to accomplish it. The committee had the satisfaction to announce that the following gentlemen had volunteered to assist in the preparation of the several portions of the section:—In the townships of Northowram and Hipperholme, Mr. Martin; in Clifton and Hartshead, Mr. Holt; in Mirfield, Mr. Bull; in Thornhill and Shitlington, Mr. Briggs; in Bretton, Crigglestone and Woolley, Mr. Morton and Mr. Embleton; in Notton, Roystone and Shafton, Mr. Hall; in Brierley and Great Houghton, Mr. Hartop; and in Clayton and South Elmsall, Mr. Thorp.

At this time the Midland Railway was in progress, designated the North Midland at that time, and the council of the society made a request to Mr. Swanwick, the engineer to the line, that he would allow a number of the members to inspect the cuttings along the route. This permission was readily granted, and the 25th June, 1840, fixed for the visit. The members met at the Scarborough Hotel, at Leeds, and breakfasted between 6 and 7 in the morning.

At 7-30 the party was conveyed in a special train from the station of the company, and stopped first at at the Altofts Cutting, the section exposed therein was minutely examined, and the party again steamed along. Derby was reached in time to dine and leave at 5 p.m. to return to Leeds, which place was reached at 9 p.m. Mr. Swanwick furnished the members with copies of the sections which had been seen during the day. The Rev. W. Thorp, Messrs. Morton, Holt, Embleton ,and Wilson were requested to prepare a report of the excursion, and on September 7th, they met at the house of Mr. Embleton, and drew up a report covering the ground between Leeds and Rotherham. Some of the sections were revisited on foot to make sure of the sections, and the report as full and correct as possible.

On the 2nd December, at a meeting held at Doncaster, the report was presented. It is stated that unfortunately some portions of the line had become grown over or covered with soil before the excursion was made, and a second cause of incompleteness was that the railway passes through certain districts of which geologically, scarcely anything at that time was known. The terminus was then adjoining Hunslet Lane in Leeds; the surface being forty or fifty yards above the Black Bed Coal of Low Moor. The strata dip moderately towards the south east. The cutting in Hunslet Moor exhibits the Beeston Coal five or six feet in thickness. It is seventy or eighty yards above the Black Bed. The Beeston Coal had been previously worked, and in cutting this part of the railway several old pits were discovered; nearer the village of Hunslet a fault throws the Beeston Coal to a depth of forty-five yards beneath its normal position. In the Woodhouse Hill cutting the Middleton Main Coal is seen near Jeffery Bridge, a couple of faults depress this coal respectively thirty-five and forty yards, and a thick bed of sandstone occupies the principal part of the cutting. A third fault near the south end of the cutting re-elevates the strata about thirty yards. Two of these faults were observed at the Middleton Collieries, and the Middleton Rock was shown to be identical with the rock exposed in the cutting. Similar beds occur in the Woodlesford Cutting until they are cut off by a fault near the bridge; from this point the sides of the excavation are entirely sandstone. In the Methley Cutting a coal seam is considered to correspond with a coal seam in the Whitwood borings. The railway after crossing the River Calder enters the excavation near Normanton, "which is one of considerable interest, because of the dislocations cut through and the alternation of bind and sandstone beds here exhibited. Sudden and unaccountable changes from sandstone to shale, and *vice versa*, are often observed in sinkings near to each other ; but in this cutting the passage from one to the other is distinctly seen. In the first part of the excavation the strata *rise* rapidly to the south until we reach the road leading from Normanton to Newland, where a fault occurs which reverses their position, causing them to *dip* to the south. In the northern portion of the cutting beds of bind predominate ; but these gradually disappear and are replaced by sandstone in the southern portion. Further on two dislocations are seen near to each other ; the first is a throw *down* to the south, the second a throw up." At the entrance of the Oakenshaw Cutting are three beds of coal rising rapidly to the southwards, supposed to be the Sharlston Beds. These are succeeded by a bed of hard white sandstone of great value to the contractors in building bridges and stations. Within half a mile from the point where the line crosses the Wakefield and Pontefract turnpike, a fault re-introduces the Sharlston Coals. The railway enters the Chevet Rock near Walton, the Chevet Tunnel being cut through the same rock, as are also the three cuttings at Cudworth. The Notton High Bridge Cutting exposes several faults and a Bed of Coal, three feet thick, supposed to be the Shafton Coal ; teeth and scales of fish were found in the roof of it. Darfield Tunnel is in the Chevet Rock, which is also worked in quarries near Darfield Station. The report on the further extension of the line was deferred.

The Lancashire and Yorkshire Railway was also in progress, and Mr. Embleton and Mr. Holt, with the permission of the engineer, Mr. Gooch, visited and made drawings of the principal sections along the line. A month or two afterwards arrangements were made for the members of the Society to visit the line, and ten members availed themselves of the opportunity. A railway carriage and horse was placed at their disposal.

The following letters are interesting, and illustrate the activity of some of the members in scientific work :—

Mr. Embleton to Mr. Wilson.

DEAR SIR,
22nd September, 1840.

I duly received your enclosures, and I have to-day heard from Mr. Gooch, he forwards a letter to the resident engineers, (Messrs. Burke, Scott, Young, and Dickinson), to allow the society to inspect the cuttings and take tracings of the plans. I have written to Messrs. Morton, Holt, Thorp, Hartop, H. Teal, J. G. Marshall, Briggs and Brackenridge, fixing 29th, Tuesday next, for the excursion, to meet at the Strafford Arms, Wakefield, to breakfast at 7 a.m., business at 8. I have mentioned to Messrs. Holt and Morton that it would be advisable to lay our plans the evening before.

Yesterday Mr. Holt and I had a very long day on the North Midland, we talk of finishing the inspection to Barnsley or beyond next Monday, so that we could easily reach Wakefield in the evening, and consider our arrangements for the next day. This we can settle definitely on Friday, Mr. H. Morton cannot give us any help with the sections, Mr Holt promised to find some one in Wakefield, which he has not done, so I must endeavour to engage a person here, I have also written to Mr. Burke, to request him to furnish tracings of the line. Could we invite him to our meeting on Friday?

Yours faithfully,

THOS. W. EMBLETON.

The letter following bears same date as the above, and must have crossed, it is dated from the meeting of the British Association, at Glasgow, 22nd September, 1840.

Mr. Wilson to Mr. Embleton.

MY DEAR SIR,

I have invited Mr. James G. Marshall and Mr. West to join the Railway excursion, and should be obliged if you would send them notice of the arrangements. The latter I had named it to long ago, and before I knew that the number would be so limited, and I thought it would not be safe therefore to omit him. I have neglected to see Mr. Perring about a reporter, and should be greatly obliged if you would do so when you happen to be in Leeds.

The meeting here appears to be very fully attended, and few of the great lights with the exception of Hershell and Sedgwick are absent, and there is no want of most interesting matter for the consideration of the section. Professor Johnston read his paper on Organic Chemisty, Part. I, which we had enjoyed at Sheffield, and was highly complimented on it, and a very interesting discussion followed. There was also on Saturday an exhibition of maps and models that was full of interest, unfortunately I was obliged to leave the section before it was finished, and before the question of uniformity of scales came on, and none of our society were present besides myself, they having all joined the geological trip to Arran.

I have not yet seen Dr. Buckland, as I waited for Mr. Sopwith's instructions, and he has not arrived. Mr. Greenough cannot yet say whether he can come to our meeting or not. The next meeting of the Association is to be at Plymouth.

I am, my dear Sir, yours sincerely,

THOMAS WILSON.

Those taking part in the excursion met at the time appointed, and after partaking of breakfast at the Strafford Arms, Wakefield, at 7 a.m., the party set off in their "one-horse chaise," and had a good day's geologizing along the line, the cuttings were examined and notes taken. The excursion led to the desire that the works should be measured and reduced to scale, and in October Mr. Embleton was requested to obtain the services of some competent surveyor, and ten guineas were placed at his disposal for the purpose. A request preferred to Mr. H. J. Morton was declined.

Subsequently the services of Mr. Bull were secured, and sections of the cuttings on the railway exposed between Hebden Bridge and Normanton were obtained.

At the meeting of the British Association at Glasgow in 1840, which was attended by representatives of this Society, a committee was appointed for the purpose of collecting and preserving a regular series of sections of railway cuttings, which, by their intersection of mineral districts or of rocks presenting any remarkable geological features, may afford useful information, and be worthy of being kept as geological and mining records, and a sum of £200 was placed at the disposal of the committee. This committee in due course prepared sheets on which the sections could be copied and uniform results obtained. The scale was 40 feet to one inch both horizontal and vertical. Already the members of this Society had made some progress in the direction indicated to the committee of the association, and it would appear that an object so easy of attainment, and of such importance and utility, would scarcely require the assistance or pressure of the British Association to secure its being effectually carried out. Such, however, was not the case. Great energy was expended in the formation of new railways, and on many lines no measures had been taken to preserve a regular and systematic record of the geological sections exposed during their formation, and in other cases where the sections had been carefully measured and preserved, they were on such a varied series of scales that their utility was greatly reduced. It was difficult to convince those not intimately acquainted with the facts and truths of geological science of the value of such sections and records; and of the loss and inconvenience resulting from the want of the particular information they afforded. In the West Riding where so much of the prosperity of its inhabitants depends on the products of mining, the sections exposed by railway cuttings, together with the sections exposed in sinking shafts and pits or borings, were recognised of the utmost value in determining the sequence and lie of the beds; but even where the advantages were so apparent many sections were allowed to become obscured and lost before any attempt was made to record them; how much greater then must have been the neglect in more remote districts where there was no mining operations carried on. The importance of the knowledge from an agricultural point of view is equally great; the nature and depth of the soil, the substratum of rock or clay, and the general structure of the district is valuable in proportion as it is known and appreciated, and the relation which was then discovered existing between chemistry and agriculture rendered a knowledge of the geological structure of a country of still greater importance. Railway sections in a flat country afford evidence, which can with difficulty be otherwise obtained of the relation and spread of derivative strata, such as glacial clays or drift, to the older rocks which they overlie, and the consequent change in the character of the superimposed soils.

Meanwhile the work in connection with the great line of sections joining the Lancashire and Yorkshire Coal-fields was in active progress and the annual report of the council presented 27th September, 1843, states "That two of the sections are now completed, namely, that surveyed by Mr. Bull, which includes the township of Mirfield ; and the one by Mr. T. W. Hall, comprising the townships of Bretton-West, Crigglestone, Wortley, Notton, Roystone, Shafton, Brierley, and Great Houghton ; extending over a distance of 9 miles and exhibiting a noble instance of individual exertion to the advancement of scientific knowledge." The remaining contributors to the section are urged to proceed as rapidly as may be consistent with correct work.

At the next meeting of the society at Huddersfield, in December, 1843, Mr. Henry Briggs exhibited and explained the portion of the line of section he had undertaken, comprehending the township of Thornhill and the hamlet of Netherton. The portion of the section extending through the townships of Clifton and Hartshead had also been completed by Mr. Henry Holt, and was exhibited at the same meeting. The portion of the section undertaken by the Rev. W. Thorp, viz., Clayton and South Elmsall, and that of Messrs. Morton and Embleton were already completed, and the whole series, together with numerous sections of pits and borings, were available for reference by members of the Society.

The Rev. W. Thorp had prepared an independent series of sections for the illustration of his work on the West Riding Coal-field, a notice of which will be found on another page. The sections were printed and sold, and until the more elaborate and complete ones, issued by the Geological Survey, were available, Mr. Thorp's sections were greatly prized.

In 1852 the quarter sheets of the Geological Survey 81 N.E. and 82 N.W., bordering on the county of Derbyshire, were coloured geologically, the first by Professor John Phillips, and the latter by Professor Phillips and Warrington W. Smyth. Other quarter sheets bordering on the Lancashire districts were coloured by Mr. W. T. Aveline and Professor Edward Hull in 1863 ; but it was not until 1866-7 that the Geological Survey of the Yorkshire Coal-field was systematically commenced. The survey of the West Riding Coal-field was made under the superintendence of Professor A. H. Green, assisted by Messrs. R. Russell, J. R. Dakyns, J. C. Ward, C. Fox-Strangways, W. H Dalton, and T. S. Holmes. Several small memoirs were issued explanatory of quarter sheets from time to time as the work progressed, the whole culminating in the great memoir published in 1878, under the editorship, and in great part written by, Professor Green. In the dedicatory notice preceding the work, Mr. Bristow states that "it is a pleasant duty to acknowledge the valuable assistance which the officers of the Geological Survey have received from colliery proprietors and others who have given information, without which the memoir could not have been made as complete as it now is." The members of the survey collected and recorded all the information that could be obtained from workings in the pits, information which will be of great value, when the beds of coal now worked are finished and others at a greater depth have to be sought for; but at the same time information having heretofore a precarious existence, and liable to be lost when the colliery to which they belong is exhausted. From what has already been stated it may easily be conceived that the work done by the members of this Society in the collection and comparison of sections obtained in sinking pits and trial borings; in the correlation and identification of the several coal seams; in the formation of horizontal sections; and observations made during the progress of railway undertakings would be of no small value to the Geological Surveyors, and a reference to the memoir will show how readily these observations have been placed at their disposal.

It must not be supposed, however, that this branch of the Society's work is completed. In the introduction to the Survey memoir will be found this paragraph,—"The Yorkshire Coal-field is comparatively speaking virgin ground, along its western and northern outcrops mining operations have been indeed vigorously carried on, but these are, so to speak, bassett workings, exceeding in very few instances a depth of 200 yards; the great spread of exposed Coal Measures in the centre of the basin is untouched, and the portion beneath the Magnesian Limestone is pierced by only a few shafts."

CHAPTER V.

JOHN PHILLIPS, F.R.S.

No geologist has been more intimately associated with Yorkshire Geology than the late Professor Phillips. He came to this county in company with his uncle, William Smith, in the year 1819, and from that time for the succeeding twenty years had his residence at York. It was principally through his efforts that the geological structure of the secondary rocks on the Yorkshire coast, and the mountain limestone and associated strata of the Yorkshire dales were worked out, and in addition to his well-known larger works on Yorkshire Geology and Scenery, he contributed a large number of papers to the societies and magazines of the day. Professor Phillips took a great interest in the formation of this Society, and assisted by his presence and counsel in all its initial stages. He frequently afterwards attended its meetings, and several of his contributions will be found printed in the "Proceedings."

Fortunately, a short time before his death, Professor Phillips contributed an account of his early life to the Athenæum newspaper, which was published on May 2nd, 1874, this presents so graphic a picture of the formation of his scientific tastes during the early years of his life, that it is ventured to reprint it in full :—

"I was born on the happy Christmas Day, 1800, at Marden, in Wiltshire, the moment being noted by my father with the exactitude suited to a horoscope. He was the youngest son of a Welsh family settled for very many generations on their own property at Blaen-y-Ddol, in Carmarthenshire, and some other farms near it. On their possessions, much reduced from their ancient extent, my grandfather died in the beginning of this century. My father, born in 1769, was trained for the church, in which some of his relations had place, but this plan was not carried out. He came to England, was appointed an officer of excise, and married the sister of dear old Wm. Smith, of Churchill, in Oxfordshire. My first teachings were under his eye, and I may say hand, for he now and then employed the *argumentum baculinum*, though very gently. But he died when I was seven years old ; my mother soon after ; and my subsequent life was under the friendly charge of my great relative, a civil engineer in full practice, known as 'Strata Smith.' When I was nine years of age my uncle Smith took me by the hand while walking over some cornbrash fields, near Bath, and showed me the pentacrinite joints. He afterwards immersed them in vinegar to show the extrication of carbonic acid, and the flotation or swimming of the fossils. Before my tenth year, I had passed through four schools, after which I entered the long-forgotten but much-to-be-commended old school at Holt Spa, in Wiltshire. Lately I rode through the village, and was sorry to find the place deprived of all that could be interesting to me. At Holt School, a small microscope was given to me, and from that day I never ceased to scrutinize with magnifiers plants, insects and shells. In after-life this set me on making lenses, microscopes, telescopes, thermometers, barometers, electrophori, anemometers, and every kind of instrument wanted in my researches. When you see me now, $\chi\alpha\lambda\epsilon\pi\hat{\omega}\varsigma\ \beta\alpha\delta\iota\zeta\omega\nu$ tired with the ascent of Gea Fell, and the rough path to Zmūtt Glacier, you will hardly credit me as the winner of many a race and the first in many a desperate leap. My work at this school was incessant for five years, I took the greatest delight in Latin, French, and Mathematics, and had the usual lessons in Drawing, we were required to write a good deal of Latin, especially our Sunday theme, of such I wrote many for my idle associates. I worked through Mole's Algebra and Simpson's Euclid, the first two books completely, and selections of the others. The French master was a charming old Abbé, a refugee, whose patience and good nature, and perseverance were quite above praise ; we spoke and wrote French in abundance ; of Greek I learned merely the rudiments to be expanded in after-life ; I did not work at German till some years later ; Italian I merely looked at.

"From the tragedies and comedies of school, I passed to a most pleasant interlude by accepting a twelve months' invitation to the home of my ever-honoured friend, the Rev. Benjamin Richardson, of Fairleigh Castle, near Bath, one of the best naturalists in the West of England, a man of excellent education, and a certain generosity of mind very rare and very precious. Educated in Christ's Church, he retained much of the indefinable air of a gentleman of old Oxford, but mixed with this there was a singular attachment to rural life and farming operations. Looking back through the vista of half-a-century, among the ranks of my many kind and accomplished friends I find no such man, and to my daily and hourly intercourse with him, to his talk on plants, shells, or fossils, to his curiously rich old library, and sympathy with all good knowledge I may justly attribute whatever may be thought to have been my own success in following pursuits which he opened to my mind.

"From the rectory at Farleigh, where science and literature were seen under colours most attractive to youth, I was transferred by the good old Bath coach to my uncle Smith's large house, which looked out on the Thames from the eastern end of Buckingham Street. Here a kind of life awaited me which, remembered at this long distance of time, excites sometimes my wonder, at other times my amusement, not seldom regret, but always my thankfulness. Here was a man in the exercise of a lucrative and honourable profession, who had for many years given every spare moment and every spare shilling to the execution of that vast work, 'The Map of the Strata of England and Wales.' After that was published in 1815 he continued his labours in more detail, and issued twenty-one English county maps, coloured geologically after personal examination in each district. His home was full of maps, sections, models, and collections of fossils ; and his hourly talk was of the laws of stratification, the succession of organic life, the practical value of geology, its importance in agriculture, engineering, and commerce, its connection with physical geography, the occupations of different people and the distribution of different races. In this happy dream of the future expansion of geology his actual professional work was often forgotten, until at length he had thrown into the gulf of the strata all his

M

little patrimony and all his little gains, and he gave up his London residence and wandered at his own sweet will among those rocks which had been so fatal to his prosperity though so favourable to his renown. In all this contest for knowledge, under difficulties of no ordinary kind, I had my share ; from the hour I entered his house in London, and for many years after he quitted it, we were never separated in act or thought ; in every drawing or calculation which his profession required, in every survey for canal or drainage, or railway or mine, I had my share of work ; for every book, map, and tour my pencil was at his command ; and thus my mind was moulded on his, and it seemed to be my destiny to mix as he had done the activity of professional life with the interminable studies of geology. Thus passed the time till the spring of 1824, when, by the invitation of the Yorkshire Philosophical Society, then lately established, my uncle went to York to deliver a course of lectures on geology, and I was his companion. This was the crisis of my life. From that hour the acquisitions I had made in natural history and 'fossilogy', as we then termed the magnificent branch of study now known as palæontology, brought me perpetual engagements in Yorkshire to arrange museums, and give lectures on their contents to members of Literary and Philosophical Societies. In this manner most of the Yorkshire towns which were active in promoting museums of natural history and geology were repeatedly visited. York, Scarbro', Hull, Leeds, Halifax, and Sheffield became scenes of most valuable friendships, and the great county in which thirty thoughtful years were afterwards passed, became known to me as probably to no others. The generous Yorkshire people gave no stinted remuneration for my efforts to be useful, and I employed freely all the funds which came to my hands in acquiring new and strengthening old knowledge, so as to be able to offer instruction in almost any department of nature, but especially in Zoology and Geology. By degrees Birmingham, Manchester, Liverpool, Chester, Newcastle, and other places offered me advantages of the same kind as those which always welcomed me at home, and when in 1831 the British Association was formed my circle of operations had reached the University College, London, then under the wardenship of Mr. Leonard Horner. At this time I had been resident in York for five years, having the care of the Yorkshire Museum and the office of secretary of the Yorkshire Philosophical Society. In this capacity it was my good fortune to be associated with Mr. W. V. Harcourt, the first president of that Society, and to assist in the establishment of the great association which he had so large a share in organising, with Brewster, Forbes, Johnstone, Murchison, and Daubeny. After this the whole book of my life has been open for the public to read. Educated in no college I have professed geology in three universities, and in each have found this branch of science firmly supported by scholars, philosophers, and divines."

In the preface to the first edition of that delightful book, "The Rivers, Mountains, and Sea Coasts of Yorkshire," published in 1852, Professor Phillips says:—"From childhood my attention has been fixed on the great county in which most of the labours and enjoyments of my life have been experienced. Long before my eyes rested on the mountains of the North of England, the mighty form of Ingleborough was engraved in my imagination by many a vivid description, and when I crossed the old Gothic bridge and beheld the glorious church which is the pride and veneration of Yorkshire it was but the realisation of a long-indulged dream of boyhood. There is indeed a large harvest to reap and much inducement to gather it. The physical geography and scenery of the county had been too little considered; the various elements of climate which reign on its long line of romantic coast, its broad fertile valleys and ranges of barren mountains (but little inferior to their neighbours in Cumberland) had not been recorded; the vast spaces of new land which art and nature had conquered from the sea, had yielded more rents than reflections; the roads and camps of the Romans, and the earlier sites of Brigantian tribes are travelled over, with little thought of the ages to which they belong." It appears to have been in this spirit that Professor Phillips on his entry into Yorkshire in 1819 pursued his geological and other scientific investigations, and he has recorded in the introduction to the second volume of his "Geology of Yorkshire," his journeyings to and fro in pursuit of geological knowledge. He says:—"In 1819, I made, under the guidance of my uncle, William Smith, my first examination of the limestone of Yorkshire, and learned from Mr. Francis Gill, of the Auld Gang Lead Mines, the succession of the strata in Swaledale, for comparison with the very different series I had before seen at Bristol, in the Forest of Dean, and near Pontypool."

In 1821 Phillips passed through the limestone tract of Derbyshire, and over the summit ridge of millstone grit at Penistone into Yorkshire, and then spent four months in exploring the district round Halifax, Todmorden, Burnley, Skipton, and Settle. From Settle he went to Kirby Lonsdale, and attentively surveyed the line of the great Craven fault, and from Kirby Lonsdale into Westmoreland. Thence northwards he followed the basaltic line of the Roman wall, and skirting the Cheviot Hills, returned by Newcastle and Durham to Barnard Castle. Thence he travelled by Brignell Arkendale, Reeth, Leyburn, Masham, Ripon, Ripley, Harrogate and Harewood to Leeds, where he found Mr. E. S. George engaged in the details of local geology, and employing himself in making a manuscript geological map of the vicinity. It was during this tour in Northumberland that the observations were made, which were the groundwork of William Smith's geological map of the county. After again visiting Swaledale, his wanderings for this year closed at Nottingham.

Early in 1822, Professor Phillips repeated his visit to many places already named, and after spending many months at Hesket Newmarket, he joined Mr. Smith at Kirby Lonsdale, from which delightful station a large region of slate, limestone, and millstone grit was minutely explored, and abundant fossils collected.

In 1824 he walked from Kirby Lonsdale to York, chiefly following the valley of the Aire, "and it was in arranging the small collection then belonging to the Yorkshire Philosophical Society, and in drawing for Mr. Smith's lectures that I first resolved to follow out the recommendation of the Council of that Society, and to devote a considerable portion of my time to the illustrations of the geology of Yorkshire. My lamented friend, Mr. E. S. George, walked with me to Greenhow Hill and through a part of Wharfedale, one of the most instructive short journeys I ever made, and the first in which I used the mountain barometer, an instrument of inestimable value where exactness is desired in investigating a complicated series of rocks in a district like that of the Yorkshire dales."

In the following year he again visited the mountain limestone districts of Derbyshire and North Yorkshire, making sections of strata and accumulating materials for his "Geology of the Mountain Limestone." In 1826 Professor Phillips became permanently attached to the Yorkshire Philosophical Society, and made a long pedestrian tour in Scotland.

The following account of a visit to the York Museum, given by Sir Roderick Murchison in the year 1826, is interesting :—" Phillips, then a youth, was engaged in arranging a small museum at York. He recommended me strongly to his uncle, Wm. Smith, who was then living at Scarbro', and had little intercourse with the Geological Society, for he thought that Greenough and others in taking from him the main materials of his original geological map of England had done him an injustice. The unpretending country land surveyor, who had really the highest merit of them all, had been somewhat snubbed by such men as Dr. M'Culloch and others, who, having a superior acquaintance with the chemical composition of rocks and minerals, did not appreciate the broad views of Smith. From the moment I had my first walk with Wm. Smith, then about sixty years old, I felt that he was just the man after my own heart; and he, on his part, seeing that I had, as he said, an eye for a country, took to me and gave me most valuable lessons. Thus he made me thoroughly acquainted with all the strata north and south of Scarbro'. He afterwards accompanied me in a boat all along the coast, stopping and sleeping at Robin Hood's Bay. Not only did I then learn the exact position of the beds of poor coal which crop out in that tract of the eastern moorlands, but collecting with him the characteristic fossils from the calcareous grit down to the lias, I saw how clearly strata must alone be identified by their fossils, inasmuch as here, instead of oolitic limestones like those of the south, we had sandstones, grits, and shales, which though closely resembling the beds of the old coal, were the precise equivalents of the Oolitic series of the south. Smith walked stoutly with me all under the cliffs from Robin Hood's Bay to Whitby, making me well note the characteristic fossils of each formation."

Prof. Phillips records the visit of Sir Roderick Murchison to the York Museum in the following terms :—"In a bright afternoon of early summer, while engaged in museum arrangements, a man of cheerful and distinguished aspect was presented to me by the president of the Yorkshire Philosophical Society (Mr. W. Vernon Harcourt) as Mr. Murchison, a friend of Buckland, desirous of consulting our collection. The museum was tolerably well supplied with Oolitic fossils, especially those of the Coralline Oolite and Calcareous Grit of Yorkshire. Some of these were amusing enough. A diligent collector at Malton, who supplied the museum with specimens, sometimes brought what were called beetles, made by painting and varnishing parts of shells and crustaceans. After examining the fossils with care, Murchison would see these curiosities. As it happened they were laid contemptuously at the base of vertical cases and were rather difficult to get out. 'Never mind,' said the old soldier, ' we will lie down and reconnoitre on the floor.' I knew then that geology had gained a resolute disciple, possibly a master workman."

In 1827 he examined Dr. Henry's collection at Manchester, and made some geological excursions with him; ascended Pendle Hill, and partially explored the limestone tract of Bolland. He also, in company with his friend Mr. George, completed a survey of the Cumbrian slates, and a leisurely review of the Craven fault and its attendant phenomena enabled him to draw up for the Geological Society a memoir of that district which is printed in the Transactions, N.S., Vol. III. The years 1828 and part of 1829, were devoted to the preparation of the first volume of the " Illustrations of the Geology of Yorkshire." The latter part of the year was devoted to an examination of the Eifel and various parts of Germany, and to visits to some museums and friends at Bristol and Bath. In 1830 another Continental tour, and in 1831 he says :—"My leisure was almost wholly occupied by the preliminary arrangements of the first meeting of the British Association for the advancement of science.

In 1831 Phillips accompanied Murchison to explore the district of Collie Weston and Ketton. It was in the cool spring time, and they had a pleasant walk along the high grounds overlooking the Willand, cigars contending with endless discussions on the rocks and their relationship to Alpine limestones, which had then begun to be recognized. They made careful measures of the slatey and sandy beds full of shells which there overlie the ironstone and the lias, contemplating a joint memoir as to their position and numerous fossil contents.

Dr. Giekie, in his "Life of Sir Roderick Murchison," has recorded the latter's recollections of the first meeting of the British Association at York :—"This first gathering of men of science to give a more systematic direction to their researches, to gather funds for carrying out analyses and enquiries, to gain strength and influence by union, and to make their voice tell in all those public affairs in which science ought to tell, came about in this wise. Assemblies of 'naturforscher' had been for two years or more in existence in Germany, having begun in Hamburg. Thereon, Sir David Brewster wrote an article in the *Edinburgh Philosophical Journal* suggesting that such a meeting should be tried in Britain. On this the Rev. Wm. Vernon (afterwards Vernon Harcourt), the third son of the Archbishop of York, and a Prebendary of York, not only made the real beginning by proposing that we should meet at York, but by engaging his father to act as a patron, and by inducing Earl Fitzwilliam to be the president, he gave at once a *locus standi* and respectability to the project. But he did more, for he elaborated a constitution of that which he considered must become a parliament of science such as Bacon had imagined, and was thus our law-giver. The project thus elaborated having been transmitted to me in London in the spring of 1831, when I was president of the Geological Society, I at once eagerly supported it ; nay, more, I wrote and lithographed an appeal to all my scientific friends, particularly the geologists, urging them to join this new association. But notwithstanding my energy, the scheme was for the most part pooh-poohed, and among my own associates I only induced Mr. Greenough, Dr. Daubeny, Sir Philip Egerton, and Mr. Yates to follow suit. John Phillips, of York, the nephew of Wm. Smith, and the curator of the York Museum, had very much to do in the origin of this concern, for he co-operated warmly with Wm. Vernon, and when we got together at York was the secretary and factotum. He had already corresponded with me in London, and stimulated me with a ready-made prospectus. I may say that it was the cheerful and engaging manners of young Phillips that went far in cementing us, and even then he gave signs of the eminence to which he afterwards arose in the numerous years in which he was the most efficient assistant general secretary of the body, until when, as the distinguished Reader of Geology in the University of Oxford, he presided over the British Association at Birmingham. When, however, we were congregated from all parts, the feebleness of the body scientific was too apparent. From London we had no strong men of other branches of science, and I was but a young president of the geologists; from Cambridge no one, but apologies from Whewell, Sedgwick, and others; from Oxford we had Daubeny only, with apologies from Buckland and others. On the other hand, we had the Provost of Trinty College, Dublin, Dr. Lloyd, Dr. Dalton (from Manchester), and Sir David Brewster from Edinburgh. Thus there was just a nucleus, which, if well managed, might roll on to be a large ball, and admirably was it conducted by Wm. Vernon, for after opening the meeting in an earnest, solemn manner, the good Lord Fitzwilliam handed over the whole control to Harcourt, and left us. For my own part, I had plenty of matter wherewith to keep my geological section alive, as, besides those I have mentioned, we had a tower of strength in old Wm. Smith, the father of English geology, and then resident at Scarbro'; James Forbes, Tom Allen the minerologist, and Johnstone the chemist, from Edinburgh; to say nothing of Harry Witham of Lartington (now an author on "Fossil Flora") and others, including Wm. Hutton, of Newcastle-on-Tyne, then strong upon his 'whin sill.' After all we were but a meagre squad to represent British science, and I never felt humbler in my life than when Harcourt, in an opening address, referred to me as representing London. Indeed, Wm. Conybeare, afterwards Dean of Llandaff, had quizzed us unmercifully, as well as W. Broderip and Stokes and other men of science. The first of these had said that if a central part of England were chosen for the meeting, and the science of London and the south were to be weighed against the science of the north, the meeting ought to be held in the Zoological Gardens of the Regent's Park. It required, therefore, no little pluck to fight up against all this opposition, and all I can claim credit for is that I was a hearty supporter of the scheme—*Coûte que coûte*. This first gathering was in short much like what takes place at small continental meetings. We had no regular sections, but worked on harmoniously with our small affairs *in cumulo*. The excellent archbishop was of great social use, and gave a dignity to the proceedings; whilst Lord Morpeth, then the young member for Yorkshire, incited us by speeches as to our future. It was then and there resolved that we were ever to be Provincials. Old Dalton insisted on this, saying that we should lose all the object of diffusing knowledge if we ever met in the metropolis. With all our efforts, however, we might not have succeeded had not my dear friend, Dr. Daubeny, boldly suggested (and he had no authority whatever) that we should hold our second meeting in the University of Oxford. It was that second meeting which consolidated us, and enabled us to take up a proper position. Then it was that seeing the thing was going to succeed, the men of science of the metropolis and those of the Universities joined us."

At the close of the meeting Murchison again accompanied Mr. Smith to Scarbro', and renewed his acquaintance with the rocks on the Yorkshire coast. It does not require a stretch of the imagination to picture Murchison among these Yorkshire cliffs with the kindly old man as his guide, who, though he had done more for geology than any man then living, was spending the remainder of his days in humble quiet at Scarbro', and it was during these wanderings that Murchison conceived the idea of obtaining for Mr. Smith the appointment of geological colourer of the ordnance maps, with a salary of £100 per annum.

In 1831, Professor Phillips was also investigating the neighbourhood of Halifax, and was enabled through Mr. C. Rawson to add materially to his knowledge of the lower coal system, and "to demonstrate the occurrence of a marine calcareous bed with fossils of the Mountain Limestone amongst the Coal Series." In 1832, he surveyed the vicinity of Harrogate, and made abundant observations in the dales and amongst the hills to the northwards. His leisure in 1833 was similarly employed, and every visible bed of rock or shale in the great Yorkshire mountains was measured and recorded.

The latter part of this year was spent to a large extent in Teesdale, and on the Fells near its source. In 1834-5 much attention was given to the districts between Wharfedale and Nidderdale, and Nidderdale and Uredale, for the purpose of completing his views of the Millstone Grit Series and the limestone of Upper Nidderdale. He also made satisfactory examinations of the Craven country between Skipton, Settle, and Slaidburn on the one hand, and Cracoe, Burnsall, and Bolton Bridge on the other. In his capacity of secretary, he attended the meeting of the British Association in Dublin, and had opportunities of greatly improving his knowledge of the Mountain Limestone, and inspecting the collections, and profiting by the intercourse with Mr. Griffith, Captain Portlock, and other Irish scientists. After the meeting a party of geologists assembled at Florence Court, the hospitable mansion of the Earl of Enniskillen, "where Lord Coles' rich collection was open to me, and I could discuss the subject of his work on the Mountain Limestone with Professor Sedgwick, Mr. Murchison, Mr. Griffith, Sir Phillip Egerton, and M. Agassiz. Explorations of three of the fine mountains which are visible from Florence Court gave us a complete section of the limestone series in Ireland, and while the forms of Ben Jochlin, Kulkeagh, and Belmore, seemed copied from Penyghent, Wildboar Fell, Water Crag, their constituent rocks were found closely analogous." Enriched with specimens, drawings, and new knowledge from this interesting region, he returned to Yorkshire, and prepared for publication his work on the "Mountain Limestone District," which was published in the following year. In addition to the stratigraphical descriptions, the work contains descriptions and figures of hundreds of species of fossils ranging over the whole series of the animal kingdom comprised in the strata between the Silurian rocks of Howgill Fells, to the base of the coal measures. During his repeated peregrinations, Phillips made many friends, and he especially records his obligation to Mr. Gibson, of Hebden Bridge; Mr. Looney, of Manchester; and to Mr. Gilbertson, of Preston, for the examination and use of their collections of fossils; the magnificent collection of the latter gentleman serving to a large extent for the illustration of Professor Phillips' work. In 1882 Professor Phillips contributed to the Philosophical

Magazine, observations made in the neighbourhood of Ferrybridge in the years 1826-8, and in 1832 on the Lower or Ganister Coal Series of Yorkshire. In 1831 he contributed to the British Association an account of the geology of Yorkshire, and in 1841 he acceded to the request of Mr. De La Beche that he would describe the palæozoic fossils of Cornwall, Devon, and West Somerset, for the newly-organized Geological Survey. Some years later he was associated with Mr. Warrington Smyth in the Geological Survey of quarter sheets 81 north-east and 82 north-west, which overlap to a small extent the boundaries of Yorkshire, and were published in 1852. In the following year he issued his map of the Geology of Yorkshire, on the scale of five inches to a mile. In 1852 "The Rivers, Mountains, and Sea Coasts of Yorkshire" was published, and had a wide circulation.

Dr. John Evans, in his anniversary address as President of the Geological Society of London in 1875, remarking upon the life of Professor Phillips, says :—"It was in the year 1828, that he had become a Fellow of this Society, and in 1834 he was elected a Fellow of the Royal Society, and accepted the Professorship of Geology in Kings' College, London, an appointment which he held for six years. In 1844 he was appointed Professor of Geology in Trinity College, Dublin. Nine years later Professor Phillips virtually attained the position which he ever since occupied with so much advantage to the progress of science. In the autumn of 1853 Mr. Henry Strickland came to a melancholy end, in a manner which gave to the scientific men of that day almost as severe a shock as that produced on our minds by the sad death of Professor Phillips ; Mr. Strickland was examining the geological structure of a railway cutting, when he was knocked down and killed by a passing train. The deceased gentleman had been engaged for some time lecturing on geology at Oxford, in place of Dr. Buckland, who was then unable from ill-health to perform the duties of his readership. Professor Phillips accepted the position thus vacated, and afterwards, on the death of Dr. Buckland in 1856, succeeded to the post of Reader in Geology in the University of Oxford. Of the mode in which he performed the duties of that important office there can be but one opinion. As a lecturer his qualifications were always of the highest order ; his knowledge, most

various and profound, was communicated in a lucid and genial style, which not only rivetted the attention of his hearers, but imparted to them some of his own enthusiasm. But perhaps the greatest service that he rendered to geology during his residence at Oxford was the aid afforded by him in the foundation and arrangement of the new museum belonging to the University, which now contains one of the finest and best collection to be found in this country. From each University, of Dublin, Cambridge, or Oxford, he received the honorary degree either of LL.D., or D.C.L. In 1845 the Wollaston Medal was awarded to Professor Phillips, then at the University of Dublin, for the services he had rendered to geology by his various published works. In the years 1859-60 he was President of the Geological Society, to which during the course of his membership he communicated several papers; of these perhaps the most important are on a group of slate rocks in Yorkshire, and on some sections of the strata near Oxford. He made some communications to the Royal Society in connection with the planet Mars, the appearances of which he long and carefully studied. Meteorology was also one of his studies at a time when it was little thought of, and during his residence at York a consecutive series of meteorological observations were made for several years. Professor Phillips was also associated with General Sabine in the Magnetic Survey of the British Isles, and with Mr. Blackwell in the enquiry into the nature of Fire-Damp in Coal Mines, which led to the appointment of the existing staff of inspectors. As Secretary to the British Association he arranged and edited no fewer than 27 volumes of the reports of that body of which he was President for the year 1864. The year after the publication of Darwin's "Origin of Species," Professor Phillips wrote a work entitled "Life on the Earth : its Origin and Succession," in which he attempted to show the fallacy of Darwin's investigations. After reviewing in detail the difficulties attendant on the development of a higher form from a lower, Professor Phillips continues (p. 211) :—
"If it is not possible in the existing ocean, among the innumerable and variable radiated, amorphozoan and foraminiferous animals, to construct one chain of easily graduated life, from the fertile cell to the prolific ovarium and digestive stomach, it must be quite vain to

look for such evidence in the fossil state. In the face of the assumption requisite to imagine such a chain, we cannot venture to adopt it as a probable hypothesis, and thus the idea of one general oceanic germ of life, whether we like it or not, must be abandoned. Reasoning of the same kind will convince us that to derive by any probable steps any one great division of the animal kingdom from another, involves too much hazardous assumption to be adopted by a prudent inquirer."

From this extract it is clear that to the mind of Professor Phillips, in 1860, the difficulties in connection with the acceptance of Darwin's theory of evolution quite outweighed the simplicity and beauty of the conception, and he felt bound to reject it. But in the short space of a dozen years, the labours of many naturalists, in most cases equally unbelieving, had produced such a mass of confirmatory evidence, that the theory was generally accepted by the scientific workers of every country. In 1873, at the meeting of the British Association at Bradford, the ever-increasing mass of evidence in favour of natural selection and development had produced their natural result, and we find the Professor in his presidential address to the geological section discoursing as follows[*] :—" But concurrently with the apparent perpetuity of similar forms and ways of life another general idea comes into notice. No two plants are more than alike ; no two men have more than a family resemblance ; the offspring is not in all respects an exact copy of the parent. A general reference to some earlier type accompanied by special diversity in every case ('descent with modification') is recognised in the case of every living being.

"Similitude, not identity, is the effect of natural agencies in the continuation of life forms, the small differences from identity being due to limited physical conditions, in harmony with the general law that organic structures are adapted to the exigencies of being. Moreover, the structures are adapted to new conditions ; if the conditions change, the structures change also, but not suddenly ; the plant or animal may survive in presence of slowly altered circumstances, but must perish under critical inversions. These adapta-

---

[*] Brit. Assoc. Report, 1873. Trans. of the Sections, pp. 73, 74.

tions, so necessary to the preservation of a race, are they restricted within narrow limits? or is it possible that in the course of long-enduring time, step by step and grain by grain, one form of life can be changed, and has been changed to another, and adapted to fulfil quite different functions? Is it thus that innumerable forms of plants and animals have been 'developed' in the course of ages upon ages from a few original types?

"This question of development might be safely left to the prudent researches of physiology and anatomy, were it not the case that palæontology furnishes a vast range of evidence on the real succession in time of organic structures, which on the whole indicate more and more variety and adaptation, and in certain aspects a growing advance in the energies of life. Thus at first only invertebrate animals appear in the catalogue of the inhabitants of the sea; then fishes are added, and reptiles and the higher vertebrata succeed; man comes at last to contemplate and in some degree to govern the whole.

"The various hypothetical threads by which many good naturalists hoped to unite the countless facts of biological change into a harmonious system have culminated in Darwinism, which takes for its basis the facts already stated, and proposes to explain the analogies of organic structures by reference to a common origin, and their differences to small, mostly congenital modifications which are integrated in particular directions by external physical conditions, involving a 'struggle for existence.' Geology is interested in the question of development, and in the particular exposition of it by the great naturalist whose name it bears, because it alone possesses the history of the development *in time*, and it is to inconceivably long periods of time, and to the accumulated effect of small but almost infinitely numerous changes in certain directions, that the full effect of the transformations is attributed.

"For us therefore, at present it is to collect with fidelity the evidence which our researches must certainly yield, to trace the relation of forms to time generally, and physical conditions locally, to determine the life periods of species, genera and families in different regions, to consider the cases of temporary interruption and occasional recurrence of races, and how far by uniting the results obtained in different regions the alleged 'imperfection of the geological record' can be remedied."

In addition to works and papers already mentioned by Professor Phillips, he wrote in 1837 a "Treatise on Geology" (which was re-issued in a larger form in 1852), and a "Guide to Geology" reached its fifth edition in 1864. In 1869 he published a "Description of Vesuvius," and in 1871 "The Geology of Oxford and the Valley of the Thames," besides several minor papers. While still in the full activity of mind and health of body, although already in his 74th year, an accidental fall downstairs, when engaged in conversation with a friend, produced injuries from which he never rallied, and which on the following day resulted in his death.

Dr. Evans concludes his address with the following observations:—" Of the personal qualities of one who was so well-known to the Society I need hardly speak. Eminently judicious, ever courteous, genial, and conciliatory, he gained the affections of all with whom he was brought in contact; whilst in cases where conflicting views required to be reduced into harmony and strong feelings to be smoothed, his tact and judgment were often able to prevail where the more strenuous efforts of others would have been powerless."

Professor Phillips was an indefatigable worker, he never tired in his efforts to spread abroad that love of nature which so thoroughly imbued his own existence. By example and teaching, whether orally or with the pen, his single aim was the advancement of those branches of knowledge which had proved so ennobling to his own existence. Never married, he was wedded to his science, and in all his labours, whether as an original investigator, an organiser of the means for encouragement and assistance of his fellow-workers, or (more important than either), as an inculcator of a true knowledge and love of scientific method in the youthful minds of those entrusted to his care, at the College or elsewhere he was always earnest and sincere.

CHAPTER VI.

ADAM SEDGWICK AND WILLIAM BUCKLAND.

Adam Sedgwick was born on the 22nd of March, 1785, at Dent. His father was the vicar of the parish; a man of great local influence and of considerable learning. The Sedgwicks belonged to that fine old race of small landed proprietors named "Statesmen," which is now fast disappearing even from the northern dales. Among them the Sedgwicks held a prominent place, their names occurring in the register of Dent as far back as 1672. In 1756 Sedgwick's father entered as an undergraduate at St. Catherine's College in Cambridge. He took holy orders and returned to his native place, and became Vicar of Dent. The childhood of his son Adam was spent among the hearty, straightforward dalesmen, and he was a general favourite with them all. He delighted in every kind of sport and outdoor exercise, and he had always a quick eye for anything curious and unusual which he might come across in his scrambles amongst the crags and fells which surrounded the valley. His education was begun under his father's eye in the Old Grammar School at Dent. He afterwards went to the Sedbergh School, which had a high reputation and was attended at that time by the sons of most of the leading statesmen, as well as by many others who have made their mark in the world. He boarded along with three other boys at a farmhouse kept by a Quaker. "We were treated by the family," he says, "with infinite kindness, and our happy freedom made us the the envy of our schoolfellows." It was here he gained the habit of early rising, which he kept all through his after life to the very last. From Sedbergh he went to Cambridge, where he entered Trinity College in 1804. He read chiefly mathematics, and during the vacations continued his studies with the self-taught mathematician,

Matthew Dawson. In 1808 he took his degree, when he was classed as fifth wrangler, and in the following year he was elected a Fellow in Trinity College, of which he became subsequently assistant tutor. He threw himself energetically into the ordinary work of the University until in 1818 he was appointed Woodwardian Professor of Geology in the room of Professor Hailstone. In the same year he was elected a Fellow of the Royal Society and of the Geological Society of London. In 1819, he, in conjunction with others, was mainly instrumental in founding the Cambridge Philosophical Society, of which he was one of the first secretaries, his colleague in that office being Professor Lee. When appointed to the Woodwardian Chair, he modestly said that he knew nothing about geology; he had not paid special attention to the subject; his studies had been classics and mathematics, in both of which he was among the first men of his year, but there is evidence from many sources that he had long been an intelligent observer of geological phenomena, and whilst wandering amongst the streams and crags of his native Yorkshire, he had made observations on the stratification of the rocks and the occurrence of fossils. But whatever may have been his defects in this respect, he set himself most energetically to supply them. Almost immediately after his appointment he started with Professor Henslow to investigate the geology of the Isle of Wight, and upon the materials collected in this excursion his first course of lectures were founded. From this time he allowed no opportunity of acquiring knowledge to escape him, and as early as May, 1820, he communicated to Cambridge Philosophical Society his first paper, in which he treats of the physical structure of Devon and Cornwall. Early in his scientific career he visited Paris in successive winters, where he benefited by the instructions, and enjoyed the friendship, of Cuvier, De Blainville, and of other eminent men who were then at the head of science in France. In a syllabus published in 1821, for the use of his geological class, he gave the classification of the sedimentary rocks, which still holds good on all the chief points. The older Palæozoic Rocks had not then been worked out; he was himself the first to put them in order some ten years later. He did some good practical and original work on the phenomena connected with trap dykes in Yorkshire and Durham; and in a paper published on this subject he refers them to an igneous origin, and points out that they are of all ages. In describing the columnar structure, it did not escape his notice that the prisms were arranged at right angles to the cooling surfaces. He also mentions that the common mode of weathering into great balls was by the exfoliation of successive layers from the faces of the joints. He fully recognised the value of palæontological evidence. As early as 1822 he wrote to the Editor of the "Annals of Philosophy," stating his view of the "importance of an intimate acquaintance with certain branches of natural history. Without such knowledge it must be impossible to ascertain the physical circumstances under which our newer strata had been deposited. To complete the zoological history of any one of these forms many details are yet wanting." He afterwards carefully collected fossils, and referred them to the best authorities he could find on each special group, but whilst he appealed to palæontological evidence he fully recognised that the first thing was to get the rocks into the right order in the field. As a geological investigator and writer the chief object which he appears to have set before him was, as he himself used to say, "the unravelling of the story of the older Palæozoic Rocks." The structure of the Cumbrian Mountains and their surrounding carboniferous margin formed the subject of more than one able paper. At this time he inclined to the opinion that Mountain Chains were the result of somewhat rapid upheaval, an opinion which in after years he considerably modified. From Cumberland he soon extended his examinations of the carboniferous rocks over a considerable area of the Yorkshire moorlands. He also investigated the Isle of Arran, and in conjunction with Sir R. Murchison published many sketches of the Geology of the Eastern Alps. It was about this time that he devoted considerable attention to the Magnesian Limestone of the north of England, and described the results of his investigations in the transactions of the Geological Society of London. He traced the character and extent of this formation, which had previously been indicated by Wm. Smith under the name of the Pontefract Rock, throughout the whole of Yorkshire and Durham. He was the first to notice the peculiar concretionary structure which characterises some portions of the formation, and his classification of the series is the one that is still held, with slight modification. His description of the Magnesian Limestone must be regarded as the most complete production of Professor Sedgwick's pen, and there was probably nothing published at that period of geological history which can be compared to Sedgwick's Monographs for thorough completeness and mastery of his subject. The great unconformity between the Coal Measures and the Magnesian Limestone is pointed out by Professor Sedgwick. He says:—" After the production of the rocks of the carboniferous order, the earth's surface appears to have been acted upon by powerfully disturbing forces, which, not only in the British Islands but throughout the greater part of the European basis, produced a series of formations of very great extent and complexity of structure. These deposits, known in our country by the name of New Red Sandstone and Red Marl, and when considered on an extensive scale comprising all the formations between the Coal Measures and the Lias, notwithstanding their violent mechanical origin have several characters in common which enables us to connect them together, and for general purposes of comparison to register them as one group;" and he continues:—" We have no right to assume, nor is there any reason to believe that such disturbing forces either acted uniformly or simultaneously throughout the world. Formations which in one country are unconformable may in another be parallel to each other, and so intimately connected as to appear the production of one epoch." It was probably the observation of the remarkable formations presented by the concretionary character of the Magnesian Limestone that induced Sedgwick to turn his attention to the causes of these peculiarities, and led to the production of his paper on the "Structure of large Mineral Masses, and especially on the chemical changes produced in the aggregation of stratified rocks during different periods after their deposition," which was read at the Geological Society in 1835. It contains an excellent discussion on the phenomena of metamorphism, concretionary structure, cleavage, and joints. The terms "cleavage" and "strike" were first introduced into geological literature in this paper. Meanwhile he had been engaged, sometimes alone, sometimes in company with Sir

Roderick Murchison, in the investigation of the geological structure of Wales, Sedgwick commencing his work from the base of those disturbed and obscure rocks, and working upwards, whilst Murchison principally concentrated his efforts on the upper members of the group, and gradually worked downwards. In 1832, Prof. Sedgwick communicated to the British Association the first results of his labours, and in the following year read papers to the Cambridge Philosophical Society. In 1835 he communicated a joint paper with Murchison at the British Association in Dublin, giving a general account of the combined results of their labours, by which it was supposed that the Cambrian and Silurian systems were definitely established as distinct and successive series of formations. It was soon found, however, that the actual boundary between the two systems had not been accurately ascertained, and gradually a controversy arose on this subject, which remained unsettled so long as the authors lived.

After the publication of Young & Bird's "Geology of the Yorkshire Coast," Sedgwick published a paper in which he endeavoured to make up for the deficiency of the book by a correlation of the beds observed by him on the Yorkshire coast, and those occurring in other parts of England. In all his writings he exhibits an indefatigable energy in the observation of facts, a penetrating sagacity in grasping their significance, and the broadest possible power of generalization; and a list of his works exhibits an extraordinary variety in the range of his researches. Whilst in the exercise of his functions as Professor of Geology at Cambridge, he took an intense interest in the Woodwardian Museum connected with his Professorship. On his receiving the appointment, the collection of which he was put in charge consisted solely of the original collections of British and Foreign fossils and minerals, brought together in the 17th century by Dr. Woodward. From the first he set himself vigorously to the task of forming a museum worthy of the University. With this view wherever he went he collected rock specimens and fossils, and used all his influence with the University authorities to induce them to make purchases of fine specimens or collections too costly to be secured at his own expense. Among the most important

of these acquisitions may be mentioned the collection of Count
Munster's Duplicate Fossils, the Image Collection of Chalk Fossils,
Fletcher's "Silurian Collection" and the Leckenby Collection of Oolite
Fossils chiefly from Yorkshire. The last-mentioned magnificent
series was purchased with funds subscribed in response to an appeal
made by Professor Sedgwick, in which he speaks in a most touching
manner of his being prevented by the infirmities of age from enriching
the collections by his personal efforts. For many years the great
accumulation of specimens had no fitting place for their reception,
the only apartment assigned to him for this purpose being a room in
which the specimens were stored, generally in packages in which
they had come to Cambridge. Such a state of things was most
unsatisfactory, and Professor Sedgwick exerted all his influence to
put an end to it. In 1842 he obtained possession of the fine suite
of rooms under the new building of the University Library, in which the
collections are at present displayed, and he devoted himself with his
accustomed enthusiasm to the task of arranging the specimens in a
manner best adapted to advance the study of geology in the University.
He secured the assistance of a succession of able coadjutors in the
persons of Ansted, Jukes, Salter, M'Coy, Barrett, and Seeley, under
whose hands the treasures of the museum were gradually brought
into order, and in many cases described. The Palæozoic Fossils gave
origin to the descriptive catalogue of Professor M'Coy, published in
1851-5, and to the contributions to British Palæontology of the same
author; whilst at a later period Professor Seeley published catalogues
of the reptilia of the secondary strata, and Ornithosauria from the
Cambridge Greensand founded on the specimens contained in the
museum. In an index supplement prepared by Mr. Salter, Professor
Sedgwick wrote an elaborate preface, in which he explained his
views as to the nomenclature and classification of the palæozoic
rocks, and which may serve as a summing up of his side of the
question at issue between Cambria and Siluria. In this preface
Professor Sedgwick expressed himself as follows :—" There were three
important hopes which possessed my heart in the earliest years of my
Professorship, 1st, that I might be enabled to bring together a
collection worthy of the University, and illustrative of all the depart-

ments of the science it was my duty to study and to teach; 2nd, that a geological museum might be built by the University amply capable of containing its future collections; and lastly, that I might bring together a class of students who would listen to my teachings, support me by their sympathy, and help me by the labour of their hands. It now makes me happy to say that all these hopes have for many years been amply realised."

The following letter, written to Professor Louis Agassiz, exhibits Sedgwick's views as to the new theory of evolution which a few years later found so able an advocate in Charles Darwin.

Sedgwick to Agassiz.*

TRINITY COLLEGE, CAMBRIDGE,
April 10th, 1845.

MY DEAR PROFESSOR,

The British Association is to meet here about the middle of June, and I trust that the occurrence will again bring you to England, and give me the great happiness of entertaining you in Trinity College. Indeed, I wish very much to see you, for many years have now elapsed since I last had that pleasure. May God preserve your life, which has been spent in promoting the great ends of truth and knowledge.

Your great work on fossil fishes is now before me, and I also possess the first number of your monograph upon the Fossils of the Old Red Sandstone. I trust the new numbers will follow the first in rapid succession. I love now and then to find a resting-place, and your works always give me one. The opinions of Geoffroy St. Hilaire and his dark school seem to be gaining some ground in England. I detest them, because I think them untrue. They shut out all argument from design and all notion of a creative Providence, and in so doing they appear to me to deprive all physiology of its life and strength, and language of its beauty and meaning. I am as much offended in taste by the turgid mystical bombast of Geoffroy as I am disgusted by his cold and irrational materialism. When men of his school talk of the elective affinity of organic types, I hear a jargon I cannot comprehend, and I turn from it in disgust; and when they

---

* Louis Agassiz, his life and correspondence by E. C. Agassiz, London, 1885, p. 383.

talk of spontaneous generation and transmutation of species they seem to me to try nature by a hypothesis, and not to try their hypothesis by nature. Where are their facts on which to form an inductive truth? I deny their startling condition. "Oh, but," they reply, "we have progressive development in geology." Now, I allow, as all geologists must do, a kind of progressive development. For example, the first fish are below the reptiles, and the first reptiles older than man. I say we have successive forms of animal life adapted to successive conditions, so far proving design, and not derived in natural succession in the ordinary way by generation. But if no single fact in actual nature allows us to suppose that the new species and orders were produced successively in the natural way, how did they begin? I reply, by a way out of and above common known material nature, and this way I call creation. Generation and creation are two distinct ideas and must be described by two distinct words, unless we wish to introduce utter confusion of thought and language. In this view I think you agree with me, for I spoke to you on the subject when we met, alas! ten years since, at Dublin.

He then proposes a number of questions to Professor Agassiz relating to the types of fishes found in several formations, and requests his opinion as to the probability of their being successively derived one from another, and as to whether the Saurians found in more recent formations could have been developed from the Sauroid or any other type of fish.

He concludes by reiterating the hope that Professor Agassiz may revisit this country, and signs himself his most faithful and most grateful friend.

In February, 1851, the Council of the Geological Society of London awarded to Professor Sedgwick the Wollaston Medal, the highest however in their power to bestow, in recognition of the value of his original researches in developing the geological structure of the British Isles, the Alps, and the Rheinish provinces. Twelve years later, in 1863, he received from the Royal Society the Copley Gold Medal for his observations and discoveries in the Geology of the Palæozoic Series of Rocks, and more especially for his determination of the characters of the Devonian System, by observations on the order and superposition of the Killas Rocks and their Fossils in Devonshire. Subsequently to this date his geological writings were few. His health had never been very robust, and for several years before his death he may be said to have been a habitual invalid, compelled to pay the strictest attention to his diet in order to avoid serious illness.

A year and a half before his death he wrote a letter to Professor Agassiz, from which the following is extracted. It exhibits his sense of declining health, and the keen hope of happiness in a future state. It is dated from The Close, Norwich, August 9th, 1871* :—

. . . . . As for myself, at present I can do nothing except hobble daily on my stick from my house to the Cathedral, for I am afflicted by a painful lameness in my left knee. The load of years begins to press upon me, (I am now toiling through my 87th year), and my sight is both dim and irritable, so that as a matter of necessity I am generally compelled to employ an amanuensis. That part is now filled by a niece, who is to me in the place of a dear daughter.

I need not tell you that the meetings of the British Association are still continued, and the last session (this year at Edinburgh) only ended yesterday. . . . It is a great pleasure to me, my dear friend, to see again by the vision of memory that fine youthful person, that benevolent face, and to hear again, as it were, the cheerful ring of the sweet and powerful voice by which you made the old Scotchman start and stare while you were bringing to life again the fishes of their old red sandstone. I must be content with the visions of memory and the feelings they again kindle in my heart, for it will never be my happiness to see your face again in this world; but let me as a Christian man hope that we may meet hereafter in heaven, and see such visions of God's glory in the moral and material universe as shall reduce to a mere germ everything that has been elaborated by the skill of man or revealed to God's creatures.

I send you an old man's blessing, and remain,

Your affectionate friend,

ADAM SEDGWICK.

---

* *Op. cit.*, p. 687.

For many years he constantly referred to his sense of increasing infirmities of age, and declared that they would compel him to resign his professorship. Nevertheless, being convinced by his friends that his resignation would be injurious to the cause of science in the University of Cambridge, he continued to occupy the chair until his death, which took place on the 27th of January, 1873, in his rooms in Trinity College, and when he was within six weeks of completing his 88th year.

"Professor Sedgwick's was a nature charged to the full with human sympathy. Bring joy near him and he rejoiced; bring sorrow before him and his pity overflowed in consolation. Out of the fulness of his heart his mouth spoke unmeasured, unpremeditated words of gladness or of sympathy, and though the friends of his youth passed away as shadows, he ever gathered round him the young and happy and caught some of their life. Full of interest in all that was going on around him, the brave old man died in harness, and in 1873 was buried with the great men among whose memories he had so long lived. A simple ' A. S.' marks the spot where his body was laid in the chapel of Trinity College, Cambridge." (Professor Hughes.)

At Dent, his native place, his memory is held dear. A huge unhewn mass of granite has been erected in the centre of the village to his memory, marked with the single words "Adam Sedgwick."

WILLIAM BUCKLAND.

William Buckland was born at Axminster, March 12th, 1784. After spending some time at the ancient Grammar School at Tiverton, in 1798 he entered St. Mary's College, Winchester, and in 1801 Corpus Christi College, Oxford, as a scholar on the Exeter foundation. He attended the lectures of Dr. Kidd, Professor of Mineralogy, and manifested a strong bias towards the study of natural history and geology. He was associated in his researches with Mr. Broderip, and acquired much knowledge from the Rev. J. Townend, the friend of William Smith. He afterwards made long excursions on horseback throughout the greater part of the South-west of England, and collected large quantities of fossils. In 1813, on the resignation of Dr. Kidd, he was appointed Professor of Mineralogy at Oxford.

Buckland quickly awakened great admiration for, and interest in Geology in the University, which led to the appointment of a reader for Geology in 1819. At that period the science of Geology was looked upon with great suspicion, and most people held that its teachings were contrary to the Mosaic Record. The eloquence and straightforwardness of Buckland in confuting these ideas served to render the science much more popular. In his *Vindiciæ Geologiæ*, Dr. Buckland observes :—" If by utility is meant subserviency to the common purposes of life (though it may be easily shewn that geology had shrunk from a comparison with few other sciences even in this respect), yet such views should be altogether objected to *in limine* as unworthy and unphilosophical. The claims of geology may be made to rest on a much higher basis. The utility of science is founded upon other and nobler views than those of mere pecuniary profit and tangible advantage. The human mind has an appetite for truth of every kind, physical as well as moral, and the real utility of science is to afford gratification to this appetite. The real question, then, more especially in this place, ought surely to be, how far the objects of geology are of sufficient interest and importance to be worthy of this large and rational species of curiosity, and how far the investigations are calculated to call into action the higher powers of the mind." He then proceeded to dwell on those wonderful phenomena, organic and physical, which are the objects of the geologists' study, and adds :—" Surely these will be admitted to be objects of sufficient magnitude and grandeur to create an adequate interest to engage us in their investigation."

In 1818, Dr. Buckland was elected a Fellow of the Royal Society, and in 1824 was President of the Geological Society of London. In April, 1825, a Charter of Incorporation of the Geological Society was obtained from George III, and in it Dr. Buckland was appointed first President. Soon after he married Miss Moreland, of Abingdon, an estimable lady, who shared and appreciated his scientific toil, whilst she lightened the anxieties of life and spread a charm over home occupations by her devoted affection. In 1832 he was President of the British Association at the second meeting, which was held in Oxford, and in 1847 was appointed a Trustee of the British

Museum, in which, as well as the Museum of Practical Geology, in Jermyn Street, he had for several years taken a keen interest. In 1845 he was appointed, on the recommendation of Sir Robert Peel, to the Deanery of Westminster, a position he held to the time of his death.

Dr. Buckland influenced the progress of Geological Science, not only by his writings, but still more, probably, by the inimitable lectures which he gave at Oxford. He combined a most playful fancy with the most profound wisdom, and roused an amount of enthusiasm in his students, which made them speedy converts to his science, and enthusiastic workers in after years. Murchison thus describes a visit to Dr. Buckland at Oxford.* "On repairing from the Star Inn to Buckland's domicile, I never can forget the scene which awaited me. Having by direction of the Janitor climbed up a narrow staircase, I entered a long corridor-like room (now all destroyed), which was filled with rocks, shells, and bones in dire confusion, and in a sort of sanctum at the end was my friend in his black gown, looking like a necromancer, sitting on the one only rickety chair not covered with fossils, and cleaning out a fossil bone from the matrix."

In 1814, in company with Mr. Greenough, Dr. Buckland visited an insulated group of rocks of Slate and Greenstone, in Cumberland and Westmoreland, on the east side of Appleby. These rocks encircle two beds of granite, which differ from that of Shap Fell; on the east side Old Red Sandstone is interposed between the Slates and the Mountain Limestone of Cross Fell; but on the west there are evidences of considerable disturbance. The thick beds of Limestone and Red Sandstone of the east are absent, and the Red Sandstone of the plain of Carlisle is in juxtaposition, except in a few places, with the Greenstones and Slates, or against the truncated extremities of the Lower Limestone. The result of his investigations was, that the Carlisle Red Sandstone was proved to be the same with that of the plains of Cheshire, Lancashire, and Yorkshire, and is geologically a deposit more recent than the Magnesian Limestone which is incumbent on the upper strata of the principal coal-fields.

In 1816 he described the curious bodies which are so common in the chalk of the East Riding of Yorkshire, known under the name

* Life of Murchison, by Geikie, vol. i., p. 125.

of Paramoudra. The animal nature of these bodies, and their spongiferous character, was pointed out and insisted upon. In 1823 Dr. Buckland published the results of his work in the Kirkdale Cave, which will be found referred to on another page. The *Reliquiæ Diluvianæ* will always associate Dr. Buckland with Yorkshire Geology, and though the accident of his birth chanced to take place in another county, it cannot be inappropriate that this short notice of him should be given amongst other Yorkshire Geologists.

During the next two or three years Dr. Buckland examined and identified a considerable number of the remains of extinct animals found in the Wealden of this country by Mr. Mantell and others; amongst them the remains of Megalosaurus. Mr. Crawford had been investigating the River Gravels along the course of the Irrawaddy, and found a large collection of Fossil Bones which he had brought to this country, and submitted for examination to Dr. Buckland. In these he found evidence of similar animals to those which he had already discovered in the Yorkshire Cave. Two species of mastodon, one of hippopotamus, one of rhinoceros, exhibited a similar character to those from Kirkdale, and appeared to indicate that the warmer climate which existed in this country at the period those animals lived extended also to India.

In 1829 he described and named the Pterodactylus macronyx, discovered by Miss Mary Anning in the blue lias of Lyme Regis. At the same time he described a bed of Coprolites or fossil fœces, which he had discovered in the same district; it extended for many miles, and was several inches in thickness. This discovery was the result of Dr. Buckland's previous identification of the Album Græcum as excrementious matter of hyænas in the Cave of Kirkdale, and glancing as it were over the long series of organic life and death, he concludes that "in formations of all ages, from the first creation of vertebral animals to the comparatively recent period at which hyænas accumulated Album Græcum in their antediluvian dens, the fœces of aquatic and terrestrial animals have been preserved, the coprolites being records of warfare waged by successive generations of inhabitants of our planets on one another, the imperishable phospate of lime derived from their digested skeletons having become embalmed in the substance and foundations of the everlasting hills, the carnivora in each period of the world's history fulfilling their destined office to check excess in the progress of life and maintain the balance of creation," a truly wonderful generalisation to be derived from so humble an origin! Thirteen years after the publication of the memoir on Kirkdale Cave, Dr. Buckland was requested to undertake, and contributed, one of the Bridgewater Treatises, viz., that on Mineralogy and Geology.

Dr. Buckland died in 1856. He was one of those great intellectual organisers of the early history of geological science who are long since dead. He took no small part in laying a just and true foundation of the science, and whilst always earnestly in search of the truth, perhaps no man more strongly expressed the opinions that he from time to time held, or was more ready when he discovered errors to accept a new and more truthful theory. He frankly acknowledged any original misconception, and assiduously endeavoured to advocate more correct opinions derived from greater knowledge, however opposed they may have been to those he had previously held. His views of diluvial action, insisted upon with all the natural fervour of his energetic character, were quickly modified when Agassiz made his appearance in this country, and propounded his glacial theories. No one welcomed him more zealously, or aided him more energetically in working out those theories than Dr. Buckland.

He was of a very cheerful disposition, and cultivated the humorous side in all things. He possessed great bodily strength, which made him equal to any amount of exertion, and many stories are told of his geological escapades.

CHAPTER VII.

THE MUSEUM OF THE SOCIETY.

The Committee of the Society was very actively engaged during the early part of the year 1838, in soliciting subscriptions for the erection of a Museum. Several meetings were held, and inquiries were instituted, as to the best method of gaining this object. At a meeting of the Committee, held at the Strafford Arms, Wakefield, on the 15th of March, Mr. C. J. Brandling presiding, and Messrs. Thorpe, Wilson, Field, Briggs, and Embleton present, it was determined in the first place to apply to the Earl of Harewood and Earl Fitzwilliam, to ascertain from them the amount of support that might be expected for the projected Museum of the Society, and then to send the list to Mr. Beaumont, and afterwards to the Vice-presidents, and lastly, after the amount had been ascertained, to print a prospectus with the subscribers' names attached for general circulation in the district. The result of the appeal was, that Earl Fitzwilliam promised £500 in three items, viz. : £300 for himself, and £100 each for Lord Milton and Mr. Fitzwilliam. The Earl of Harewood deferred promising anything. The Vice-presidents were communicated with twice but without result. It was then decided to issue a circular letter to all who were interested in the work proposed to be achieved, of which the following is a copy :—

Wakefield, 15th March, 1838.

SIR,

At a meeting of the Council, held this day, it was unanimously resolved "That to enable the Society fully to accomplish its objects, it is desirable that it should immediately possess a museum, in which it might collect and arrange the Fossil Flora of the district, and that the proposals for a subscription to erect a museum, &c., which the secretary has just read, be printed and circulated amongst the gentlemen of the Riding."

In pursuance of the above resolution I have the honour of forwarding to you a copy of the proposals for a subscription, with a list of the noblemen and gentlemen who have already consented to become officers of the Society ; and I also enclose a "Statement of the objects of the Society," from which you will perceive that they are such as to entitle it to the support of the great landed and commercial interests of the Riding. I have further to request you will be pleased, at your earliest convenience, to signify your intentions to the Secretary, Banks, near Barnsley.

I have the honour to be, your obedient humble servant,

C. J. BRANDLING, Chairman.

PROPOSALS FOR A SUBSCRIPTION TO ERECT A MUSEUM FOR THE GEOLOGICAL AND POLYTECHNIC SOCIETY OF THE WEST RIDING OF YORKSHIRE.

To investigate the geology of the Yorkshire Coal Fields is one of the first objects which the Society proposed to accomplish ; but before it can ascertain the number of seams of Coal and Ironstone which the district contains, and trace and identify at least each workable seam throughout the whole of its ranges, it will be necessary to collect an immense number of plans, sections, and minute details. At the same time a complete and classified collection of the Fossils of the Coal-field, arranged according to the strata in which they are found, will be required ; and this part of its duties has been already urged on the council by its noble President, and by Professors Buckland and Phillips. That the Society would soon be presented with a very extensive and valuable collection of these Fossils, and of numerous materials for a Geological Map of the district, if it were only in possession of suitable apartments, there cannot be a doubt, when we consider how many of its members are engaged in the practical operations of mining.

It is highly desirable that the Society should possess a spacious Museum, a Library, and Lecture Room for its public meetings, with apartments for the person who may have the immediate care of its collections. From the promises of support which the Society has already received, and from the interest it has excited in the short interval since its establishment, there would be no difficulty in raising such a sum as would provide these accommodations on a moderate scale, and so far as they are essential ; but the Council cannot help thinking that for such an object subscriptions on a liberal scale would be obtained, which would enable them at the same time to erect a building that would be an ornament to the town. It is obvious that the funds of the Society must be wholly inadequate to such a purpose, as the subscription has been fixed at the lowest possible rate, with the hope of extending its advantages as widely as possible. The Council therefore appeal with confidence to the liberality and public spirit of the gentlemen of the county, whose interests are so intimately connected with the objects of the Society, to enable them to provide a suite of rooms that shall be convenient for their purposes, and an ornament to the metropolis of the riding.

President, Right Hon. the Earl Fitzwilliam ; Vice-Presidents, Right Hon. the Earl of Effingham, Right Hon. the Lord Stourton, Right Hon. the Lord Wharncliffe, Sir John Lister Lister Kaye, Bart., Sir Francis Lindley Wood, Bart., T. W. Beaumont, Esq., C. J. Brandling, Esq., G. L. Fox, Esq., M.P., W. B. Martin, Esq., J. S. Stanhope, Esq. ; Treasurer and Secretary, T. Wilson.

Subscriptions will be received by the Yorkshire District Bank at all its branches.

Following the promulgation of this circular, enquiries were addressed as to the best style and arrangement for a Museum to the Officers of Philosophical or Naturalist Societies, at Leeds, York, Newcastle, and more distant places. On March 28th, 1838, Mr. Thos. P. Teale furnished particulars as to the original cost of the Leeds Museum.—"The first cost of the Hall was £7,100, and eighteen months afterwards, in 1826, alterations were made at an additional expense of £1438." On the ground floor there is a lecture room, 43 feet square, vestibule, library and laboratory, besides apartments in the yard for the assistant curator. Above were three rooms used as a Museum, in which were the Geological, Zoological and Antiquarian collections. After animadverting on the evil of building by "contract," he continues :—" Allow me to suggest that your

Museum should be lighted from above, in order to have as much room as possible on the walls for cases. I think the plan of cases for the exhibition of geological specimens as adopted at York a very good one. Care should be taken that the cases are not too lofty, for it is desirable that the upper row of shelves should be of such a height that the specimens placed therein may be readily seen and reached. I think 8 feet a convenient height for the cases, immediately resting upon these cases a light gallery can be placed, containing cases 8 feet high, and again another gallery with cases if necessary. This plan secures the greatest economy of wall room, and the area of the museum can be left open for large specimens, which may be either grouped on the floor or on tables. This plan is adopted in the museum at Guy's Hospital, which is the best arranged of any museum I know."

Active preparations were made for the third quarterly meeting of the members, held at Wakefield, in the Music Saloon, on September 6th, 1838. Several committee meetings were held and invitations were forwarded by the President, Earl Fitzwilliam, to Professors Buckland, Sedgwick, and G. B. Greenough, Esq., the latter of whom attended. The question of the museum occupied much attention, and the officers of the Society having made unavailing efforts to obtain funds necessary to erect a new building adapted for the purpose, at length decided on the 31st August to instruct two of their number, Messrs. Sharp and Holt, to seek out a room which could be used temporarily for a museum. During succeeding weeks several properties were visited, all more or less unsuitable, and those which might have served the purpose were too expensive. Eventually a warehouse in Westgate, Wakefield, was fixed upon and an engagement entered into to rent it. The property has since been adapted for a dwelling, and it is at present occupied by Dr. Wright.

Mr. G. B. Greenough was elected an honorary member of the Society. He was one of the founders and the first President of the Geological Society of London. His amiable disposition and genial hospitality did much towards rendering the newly organised Society so successful and popular as it has since been.

At the meeting referred to above, in reply to a question from one of the members, Mr. Greenough said, "since Mr. Morton has thought

o

it of sufficient importance to ask my advice respecting the proposed museum, I rise willingly and respond immediately to his desire, though I may perhaps repeat what I have already stated to some in conversation. I have had a great deal to do with museums, and possess one which is very copious; and I will state to you what has occurred to me as being the most important in the formation of such a museum as will be best adapted to a society constituted like the present. Let your museum be strictly local. Do not mark out for yourselves more than you can conveniently compass. It is a common fault with local societies that they set out by pretending to do too much, and they often end in doing little or nothing. By limiting your sphere your labours will become of much greater utility. The field of your exertions is the most interesting that can be found for a geologist; it has hitherto been scarcely known, and is of the highest importance in a commercial point of view. If you attempt to get together a general collection, you will find it attended with great expense and labour, and you will get into an endless labyrinth; whilst, if you confine and localise your object, your efforts will be of incalculable service both to geological science and to the district which is the scene of your operations. I cannot therefore too much press on your attention that you should form quite a local museum. I should recommend you to keep within the county at any rate, but in preference to the West Riding; and if you can well illustrate that portion, I mean the Coal Field and Lead Measures, you will accomplish a very important work. There can be no difficulty in forming a museum. I am sure you will have specimens pouring in upon you in greater numbers than you want; but let those you retain be good ones. Do not encumber yourselves with useless trash. Reject all imperfect specimens, and those whose locality is not accurately marked, or you will get into great confusion. Let every member send sections and illustrating series of specimens from his own immediate neighbourhood, and make interest with his friends that they may assist him and send him descriptions and illustrations of other parts, and you will in a short time have an excellent collection If, after you have explored and investigated this district, and got it as it were represented in your museum, you think of extending your researches to other parts, by all means do so. Every specimen should be ticketed, and its position in the strata, and its geographical situation, for instance, the parish or part of the parish where it was found, clearly marked down. As to the arrangement of the specimens, it is not so important that they should be classed according to this or that system, as that they should be so distributed that you can find each one so soon as you shall want it for inspection. This is the really useful and essential point in the arrangement of a museum. What, for instance, would a tradesman do in his shop if he did not know the exact situation of each article therein, and produce it to a customer within a minute after he was asked for it? He could not go on. So with a museum, every specimen should be so placed that it can be immediately produced when required; if it cannot be made available, the collection loses its utility. If an ordinary tradesman knows where all his wares are to be had at a moment's notice, a curator ought surely to know the situation of, and be able to produce any required specimens in the same short space of time. It is a mere matter of business. Having long had a considerable museum of my own, and having spent 40 years of my life in the study of geology, I have endeavoured to render mine as useful as possible. I have arranged it at different times, according to different systems, and I have found that the only way to render a museum practically useful is to have it arranged as I have just stated. Mr. Greenough concluded by observing, that no other district afforded such means for collecting a valuable museum as the West Riding of Yorkshire.

On the 18th December a meeting of the council was held, at which the institution of the museum occupied the attention of those present. It was decided that Messrs. Briggs, Embleton, Holt, Morton, and the Rev. S. Sharp be a commmittee to superintend the alteration of the present cases and to order additional ones; and that the sum of £50 in addition to the special subscription be placed at their disposal. It was further resolved that Messrs. Briggs, Embleton and Morton be requested to draw up instructions for the architect in preparing a plan and estimate for a museum, specifying the nature and extent of the accommodation required, and the best method of arranging the cases.

A letter dated December 21st from the Honorary Secretary to Mr. Embleton contains the following paragraphs which explain the above resolutions, he says :—" I calculate we shall have a balance of £100, when the amounts are balanced at the end of the year. We have therefore added £50 to the subscriptions for cases, which amounted to £97, making a total of £147. We have spent £63, and the alterations will cost £10, leaving a balance of £74, so that we may order four more sets which we propose to do shortly. We thought your alterations most admirable and satisfactory. Mr. Chantrell has offered to be our architect gratis. Why then should we not have a plan for a museum? If we had one, at least the ground plan, fixed, we could adapt our cases to it. We have accordingly appointed a committee to prepare instructions for the architect, and I should wish to lay before him the ground-plans and sections of the museums at Newcastle, York and Leeds, with working drawings of the cases and tables. The two latter I think I can get. Can you procure the former?"

The work at the museum in the early part of 1840 appears to have progressed rapidly, and the numerous specimens which had already been presented to the society were labelled, classified, and placed in the new cases. The work entailed a considerable amount of time and attention, both of which were ungrudgingly given by some of the more active members of the society, amongst whom the Honorary Secretary, Mr. Thomas Wilson, and the gentlemen named in the above resolutions were prominent. On the 28th January, a man and his wife were engaged to reside on the premises as caretakers.

The cases gradually got into order, and the number of specimens presented to the Society having been labelled and placed in their proper sequence in the cases, it became necessary to make a further purchase of new ones. To these the following letter refers :—

Mr. Embleton to Mr. Wilson.

MIDDLETON, *4th July, 1840.*

DEAR SIR,

I have been unable to see Mr. Batty till to-day ; I have ordered of him 20 feet of Cases according to the plans of those at Leeds, with the exception of the omission of one of the beads at the door.

He refused to execute the work for less than the sum mentioned to you, viz. : £11 10s. for two lights; he charges also for the back, £1 5s., making £35 15s. 0d. for the whole, for this sum he agrees to convey them and to fix them in the Museum at Wakefield without further cost. He proposes to finish them in six weeks, so that we shall have sufficient time to fill them with specimens before the meeting. We must also pay for the whitewashing and varnishing, which will amount to 20s. If Mr. Batty does his work well I think his charges are very moderate, I shall have an opportunity of inspecting the work as it proceeds. The Rule you have I believe is mine, for I have found it missing since the trip to Derby.

I fear I cannot fix a day to meet you at Wakefield, for I am under promise to hold myself in readiness to spend a week from home either this week or next, but I will write to you as soon as I am able to say with certainty when I can see you.

T. W. EMBLETON.

At a meeting held at Halifax, on March 3rd, 1841, a paper was read by Mr. T. W. Embleton, who had been curator of the museum from its inception, "On the Museum of the Society and on the various objects which it is desirable that it should contain." After an appeal for better premises than those occupied by the Society at Wakefield, the curator states objections urged by people against sending specimens to the museum, and says that everything is worth sending ; nothing is too common or will be rejected. He urges that the facilities for obtaining specimens are very great in some instances In quarries, railway and canal cuttings opportunities are afforded for making collections of different rocks and the fossils they contain, but it is necessary to remember that when they are completed we are probably for ever debarred making further collections of their organic treasures. In coal or iron mines, when once the shaft is sunk, we are precluded from knowing the organic contents of the strata passed through ; there is still, however, the roof of the coal and its floor and the ironstone and its matrix for research, and these should not be neglected. "The contents of the museum are not numerous nor have the donors been many. About 1000 specimens have been numbered and are entered in the catalogue, and about as many more remain to be arranged ; but these specimens, excellent and unique as many of them are of their kind, illustrate but a small part, and that imperfectly, of the Coal-field. They consist of a few remains of fishes and of shells, of various species of calamites, sphenopteris, neuropteris, pecopteris, lepidodendron, ulodendron, lepidostrobus, sigillaria, &c., some of which are quite new ; specimens illustrative of strata passed through in sinking shafts, and specimens of building stones." Mr. Embleton next proceeds to enumerate those objects essentially necessary to render the museum practically useful. A complete collection of the fossil-fish remains found in the district ; it is on the roof of the coal that the greater portion of these remains have been found ; they do not frequently exist at any great height above the coal, but just where the coal separates from the stone. " The search for them is best made when the coal has been recently removed and the roof is smooth. We should be careful to note under what circumstances they exist in the greatest abundance, and whether, as up to this period has always been held, they are nowhere present in the roof of the coal except it contains a notable proportion of bitumen." The relative abundance of fish remains above cannel and common coal is a subject of interest amongst others. The most perfect specimens of fishes are in the Leeds Museum ; they were obtained from Middleton Main and Low Moor beds, and these beds should supply specimens for the Wakefield Museum. The Flockton Collieries, Rothwell Haigh, the roof of the Stanley Shale Coal, and others are rich in fish remains ; and probably they may be found in greater or less abundance over nearly the whole of the Yorkshire Coal seams. Fossil shells are wanted, they are fairly abundant. Some extend for miles in a continuous layer ; others are found imbedded in shale one by one in a peculiar manner, the hinge always being the lowest, &c., others in ironstone. Do the fish and shells occur in the same beds, and are they associated with Entomostraca ? The fossil remains of plants were much needed. The microscopical investigation of the structure of fossil plants was at that time unknown, and the author laments the entire absence of all those data which guide a botanist in the investigation of recent plants.

Collections of minerals, coal, iron, lead, copper, building stones and road-making materials, together with tables and sections of borings and sinkings drawn to scale ; safety lamps of varied construction, and models of machinery all come within the area proposed to be covered by the museum.

It was early in this year that the proposition was made to amalgamate this Society with the Yorkshire Agricultural Society, one of the stipulations being that the two societies should have a combined museum to be placed at York. This proposition caused considerable discussion, and was eventually declined by the council of our society. The curator, and others of the council most interested in the museum and its contents, met frequently at the museum and arranged and labelled the specimens. During June, Mr. Wilson engaged a young man to collect fossils for the museum at the rate of 21s. per week for himself, and his personal expenses. He visited the the pits at Elsecar and near Sheffield, and collected fossil ferns. His engagement did not last long, being determined by his acceptance of a situation as engine-driver.

Mr. Wilson to Mr. Embleton.

BANKS, *August 26th, 1841.*

MY DEAR SIR,

Dr. Buckland expresses a wish to be at our Annual Meeting, but cannot promise as his engagements are not quite at his disposal. He wishes us therefore to fix the time independently of him, and let him know, and he says the week between the 19th and 26th September will be most likely to find him at liberty. I have written to Lord Fitzwilliam to ask if Thursday the 23rd will suit him, and if it will, I think the council should decide on that day. I shall call a special council meeting as soon as I have his Lordship's answer. In the meantime can you spare a day, say early in the week, to complete the arrangements of the Museum. We might venture, I think, while you were arranging the remaining fossils, to be writing the names and the donors' names for those that are placed. I should be glad if you could order some cards, such as you think likely, and bring them with you. Mr. Briggs would, I dare say, assist us, and Mr. Holt might perhaps lend us one of his assistants for a day, for such a purpose. Or we might name these fossils on paper, and hire a person to copy them neatly at his leisure. We should also select a decent box for Exeter, and then we should immediately get a good selection in return. I hope Mr. Batty has completed the cases. You will perhaps think it desirable to remind Messrs. Leah and Hird of their promise of fossils, &c., and request them to send what they have immediately. Our council meeting might be on Friday, the 3rd September, it would not require to be a long one, and would therefore not be inconvenient to those who attend the Wakefield market. Can you bring the Wortley Fire Clays?

I am, my dear Sir, yours sincerely,

THOMAS WILSON.

P.S.—I shall have very shortly to make up my accounts for the auditor. Can you get in the Leeds subscriptions?

P.P.S.—Had we not better have a great many of the cards ready printed? It would be clearer, more ready, and no great expense, and the "Presented by" may stimulate others through their 'love of approbation' as the Phrenologists say, to go and do likewise.

On September 3rd a meeting of the Council was held, and the remainder of the day Messrs. Thorp, Briggs, Wilson and Embleton spent in the museum.

Mr. Wilson to Mr. Embleton.

BANKS, *8th September, 1841.*

MY DEAR SIR,

If you are disengaged on Saturday next, I could meet you at the museum at 10 o'clock, and we could set some one to work lettering the specimens. I feel almost sure of Dr. Buckland; Lord Fitzwilliam would write to invite him yesterday. Mr. Sopwith has also promised to come, and offered four papers. I have chosen one "On preserving Railway Sections, Sinkings and Borings."

Mr. Hartop tells me that there is great probability that Mr. W. V. Harcourt will be at Wentworth at the time, as the Hearths at Elsecar will be ready to be opened, under which they deposited a number of substances to test the action of great and continued heat.

I have written to all our architects to announce Mr. Waller's paper, and to beg for specimens of building stones, viz., Messrs. Chantrell, Moffatt, Hindle and Sharp; to Messrs. Chambers, and to

Mr. Booth for specimens of minerals and manufacture at their two works ; to Mr. Briar for fossils generally. Mr. Hartop I saw, and he has promised both fossils and a collection of minerals and iron.

I am, my dear Sir, yours sincerely,

THOMAS WILSON.

The principal contributors of specimens to the museum at this time were Earl Fitzwilliam, Rev. T. Barnes, and Messrs. Morton, Farrer and Embleton. At the annual meeting held at Wakefield on the 23rd September, 1841, Earl Fitzwilliam in the chair, it was stated in the report that " the Council cannot but express regret that the museum has not received those contributions from the Society at large which might be made with so much ease by each member, and which collectively would be so much value to the Society. In the meantime the Council would earnestly invite the members to an inspection of their collection, which has been carefully arranged by Mr. Embleton, and will be found, even in its present imperfect state, well worth a visit." In the early part of the following year, the Council decided to appoint a Resident Curator, whose duty it should be to systematically arrange the numerous specimens in the museum, secure further contributions, and generally to take charge of the collections. It was thought desirable that the appointment should, in the first instance, be a temporary one ; but with a view to its permanent continuance if experience rendered that course desirable. Mr. Martin Simpson of Whitby received the first appointment. Shortly after entering the service of the Society the following correspondence took place :—

Mr. Wilson to Mr. Embleton.

LEEDS, *7th May, 1842.*

MY DEAR SIR,

Mr. Simpson, our new curator, has applied to me for the catalogue of the museum, that he may commence arranging and naming the fossils, how far he is equal to the latter task we shall soon judge. I think the catalogue is in your hands, and should be glad if you could send it down to the office, when I will call for it, as well as the section, which I did not get yesterday, as I was suddenly called in another direction.

I hope you will be able to attend our council meeting on the 17th, that we may make some satisfactory arrangement with our sub-curator, and prepare a plan for his operations. You are aware that our next meeting is to be either immediately before or after the Manchester gathering, we must therefore fill our cases, and get into a creditable appearance. If you should be engaged on the 17th, perhaps you would name some other day when we might meet.

I should be glad if you would also send me the sections of the railways that they may be forwarded to the Museum of Economic Geology.

I am, my dear Sir, yours truly,

THOMAS WILSON.

Mr. Simpson to Mr. Embleton.

MUSEUM, WAKEFIELD, *May 18th, 1842.*

SIR,

The Council of the Geological and Polytechnic Society have requested me to see you respecting the Catalogue of Fossils and other matters connected with the museum. During the last week I have been examining and arranging some of the fossils, but am unable to apply their proper labels until I know something respecting their localities, and the beds from which they have been procured.

It is the wish of the Council that the duplicate specimens should be made up into collections, to be exchanged for those of other formations, or localities. In order to do this, as well as to preserve various other specimens which may be sent to the museum, cabinets will be almost indispensable. I suppose plain well-made cabinets, about four feet long, and two feet broad, would be the most appropriate. These when placed back to back, in the middle of a room of similar dimensions to the one we at present occupy, would leave a suitable passage on either side; and ultimately they might be surmounted with glass-cases. The room, I believe, would admit of eighteen such cabinets, which might be procured in pairs as they become necessary. This, however, can be a matter for future consideration. But as we are about to make an inventory of the property of the Society, and as I wish to hasten the business of labelling the fossils, it seems necessary that I should see you without delay.

It would have been a great advantage if I could have seen you at the museum, which I hoped to have done yesterday, but if you are not likely to be at the museum soon, I shall be glad to wait upon you at any time you may appoint.

I have the honour to be Sir, your obedient servant,

MARTIN SIMPSON, Curator.

Mr. Simpson to Mr. Embleton.

WHITBY, *August 16th, 1842.*

SIR,

I found it necessary to come over here without waiting for the council meeting. I have been negotiating with the Whitby Philosophical Society for an exchange of specimens, by which I hope both museums will be greatly benefited. They have a large collection of duplicates but they are unarranged, and I shall have them to select. I shall get what I can, but to examine the whole would be almost equal to arranging their museum, a work much heavier than I can of course undertake. They will be glad to receive our remains of fishes and plants. Since coming here I have had an expedition 12 or 14 miles into the country, to a bed of the Inferior Oolite (*Dogger*), and obtained nearly 1000 specimens, some of them rare and valuable, but the greater part, as may be expected, are duplicates, many of these and the inferior specimens I shall endeavour to leave here, and get for them what I can. It is a pity our funds are not better, that we might have purchased the rarer species, but we must be content for the present. The plants of the sandstone beds I fear are beyond my reach. The Lias fossils are scarce along the coast, all being sold to the dealers.

Yours truly,

MARTIN SIMPSON.

New cases were added to the museum in the latter part of 1842, at a cost of £38 5s., for the accommodation of the ever increasing collection of fossils. In September the Hon. Secretary, Mr. Wilson, resigned his office, and Mr. J. Travis Clay, of Rastrick, was appointed his successor. When Mr. Simpson had held his post for one year, a meeting of the Council was called to consider the propriety of continuing the expense of a paid curator. The meeting was held on the

3rd April, and it was the opinion of the Council that the year's experience of a resident curator had not proved satisfactory. The appointment involved a considerable expenditure, and the Council were of opinion that the increased outlay did not secure advantages of corresponding value ; and whilst they were very anxious to expand the usefulness of the museum, which now contained many valuable collections, they did not feel warranted in sanctioning such an encroachment on the funds of the Society as this system of management required. It was therefore decided to give the resident curator three months' notice that his engagement would then terminate ; and in July of the same year he returned to Whitby. Meanwhile a meeting was called by Mr. Clay to consider the best mode of conducting the future operations of the Society. The following letter on the subject was addressed by the honorary secretary to Mr. Embleton :—

Mr. Clay to Mr. Embleton.

RASTRICK, NEAR HUDDERSFIELD,

2nd May, 1843.

MY DEAR SIR,

I was sorry that you could not give us your company at Wakefield yesterday. We mustered better than usual, Mr. Hartop, Mr. Briggs, Mr. Wilson, Mr. Morton and myself. You are aware of Mr. Simpson's notice to leave which expires in about two months, and this leads to a consideration as to the future management of the society.

The museum at Wakefield appears to me to be nearly a useless expense, no one can visit it, and it creates no interest in favour of the society. My own opinion is that a removal of head-quarters would be a good thing, and the suggestion was favourably received. What do you think of Leeds? There are many more persons there likely to take an interest in the society; and as I cannot give the time required by the secretaryship, it is a much likelier place to find a successor, or an active assistant.

The next quarterly meeting will fall at Leeds, the first Wednesday in June, and the whole of this month is full of engagements with me, Mr. Wilson has kindly offered to do what he can to assist me, and I have to request you to do me the same kind office. A local committee was appointed to co-operate with the Philosophical and Literary Society, including yourself, Mr. Wilson, Mr. J. G. Marshall, Mr. Geo. Shaw, Mr. Teale, Mr. West, and Mr. Maclean. Mr. West informs me he is very unwell, confined to the house and cannot assist us, which I regret, as I had hoped he would have filled the chair, and perhaps have read a paper.

I sent Mr. Todd the number of the Transactions which you mentioned.

I am, very truly yours,

J. TRAVIS CLAY.

Shortly afterwards it was decided that enquiries should be instituted as to the possibility of placing the collections under the care of some Philosophical Society in the West Riding; and that of Leeds was chosen as the fittest and most satisfactory. The appended letter from the honorary secretary explains the reasons which influenced the council in arriving at this important conclusion.

Mr. Clay to Mr. Embleton.

RASTRICK, NEAR HUDDERSFIELD,

11th September, 1843.

SIR,

I beg to hand you a copy of a resolution of the Council passed this day, and to request your co-operation and assistance in carrying the same into effect :—" The best mode of maintaining the Museum of the Society in a state of efficiency having been taken into consideration, it is the opinion of the Council that the expenses attendant upon the present system of management are not compensated by adequate advantages, and that it is desirable that some plan be adopted by which the sphere of its usefulness may be increased without encroaching so much upon the funds of the Society as is involved by the appointment of a permanent Curator."

The following gentlemen were appointed a committee to consider whether any satisfactory arrangement could be made for placing the collection under the care of some Philosophical Society in the West Riding, which could afford the requisite accommodation, viz. :—

Mr. J. G. Marshall, Mr. Embleton, Mr. Briggs, Dr. Chadwick, Mr. West, Mr. Holt, Mr. Thos. Wilson, Mr. W. T. Hall, and the Secretary.

I am, yours faithfully,

J. TRAVIS CLAY.

Accordingly the Leeds Philosophical and Literary Society being communicated with, a joint committee of the two societies was appointed, and met on the 23rd September, 1843. The Rev. R. W. Hamilton was in the chair, and Messrs. J. G. Marshall, T. P. Teale, W. Sykes Ward, W. West, Thos. Wilson, and J. Travis Clay were present. The following minutes were unanimously agreed upon as the basis for the proposed arrangement:—

"That such an arrangement as is proposed is regarded by us as very desirable.

That the curators of the two societies agree in the appointment of the sub-curator of the Leeds Philosophical and Literary Society, the latter society receiving any amount of compensation which may be due in respect of the increased labours of the sub-curator.

That the geological curator of the Leeds Philosophical and Literary Society be, *ex-officio*, one of the two curators of the West Riding Geological and Polytechnic Society during the proposed arangement.

That the notice to terminate the proposed arrangement be one full year's notice by either party.

That the sum of £30 per annum appears a reasonable amount to be paid by the West Riding Society to the Leeds Society for rent, and for compensation for extra labour, &c.

That the whole expense of removing the museum from Wakefield and its setting up in the Philosophical Hall, be borne by the West Riding Geological and Polytechnic Society, as well as the expense of its further alterations.

That the right of entrance and admission to the united museum be the same to the members of both societies."

This proposed scheme of transfer having been submitted at a general meeting of the members held on the 6th December following, it was proposed by Mr. Pitt, and seconded by Mr. Morton, and carried unanimously—

"That the specimens composing the museum of this Society be removed to the apartments of the Leeds Philosophical and Literary Society, and that they be kept there as a separate collection, and remain the property of the West Riding Geological and Polytechnic Society, and be reclaimable at pleasure, on due notice, and that the following gentlemen be requested to carry the foregoing resolution into effect, and that they be appointed a committee to make the needful arrangements, viz., Mr. Briggs, Mr. Holt, Mr. Morton, Mr. J. G. Marshall, Mr. Embleton, Mr. J. W. Leather, Mr. Teale, and Mr. Thos. Wilson."

At a meeting of the joint sub-committees of the two societies, held on the 4th March, 1844, Mr. J. G. Marshall in the chair, it was resolved after the confirmation of the previous minutes,

"That the room now occupied as the Antiquities Room be appropriated for the museum of the Geological and Polytechnic Society, except that the mummy shall remain in its present position.

That in order to meet the outlay attendant upon the removal of the specimens from the Antiquities Room, and providing suitable accommodation for them elsewhere, the Geological and Polytechnic Society shall contribute the sum of fifteen pounds towards the expense.

That, in order to diminish such expenses, a temporary interchange of such cases as may be suitable is advised."

At the annual meeting of the Society, held on the 18th December following, it was reported that the museum had been transferred to the apartments set apart at the Philosophical and Literary Society at Leeds. Messrs. T. W. Embleton and J. Garth Marshall were appointed honorary curators, and the hope expressed that the geological collection of the two societies would be more interesting and beneficial now they were in a sense combined, than either would have been separately.

CHAPTER VIII.

PROCEEDINGS 1841—1848.

During the year 1841, the number of members was increased to 326, a gain of 46. The statement of accounts showed a balance in favour of the society of more than £15. The amount of subscriptions owing for the current and previous year was large, and the difficulty of collecting subscriptions from members who reside at varying distances extending over the whole West Riding is stated, and an appeal made to members to regularly transmit their subscriptions to the treasurer. Three hundred and fifty-nine pounds had been expended in land, on which to build a museum, and an expense of nearly one hundred and fifty pounds had been incurred during the preceding year for cases erected in the museum. The former item was met by a loan from the president. The papers read at the society's meetings formed a valuable series relating to the geology and kindred subjects in the West Riding. Rev. Wm. Thorp read papers, comprising three Reports on the Agriculture of Yorkshire, geologically considered, and one on Illustrations of Yorkshire Geology. The latter was not published in the proceedings, Mr. Thorp's intention being to issue a memoir on the Yorkshire Coal-field, similar to the work on the Mountain Limestone, by Professor John Phillips. Mr. Embleton read a paper on the Museum of the Society, and a Report on the Geology of the North Midland Railway, which are spoken of more fully in another page. Dr. Wm. Alexander at a meeting at Halifax, held in March, 1841, read a paper on the Mineral Springs in the Parish of Halifax, geologically considered. He gave a description of the stratification of the Parish, and the relation the several springs afterwards described bear to the strata. The geology of the Parish had not hitherto been described, and the paper exhibits evidence of much research and outdoor investigation. Situated westward of the Coalfield proper, the Parish of Halifax presents a bold and mountainous aspect; the deeply excavated and sloping valleys contrasting well with the outlines of the hilly ridges. Whilst the coals are thin and comparatively unimportant, the sandstone and flag quarries gave employment to 1,200 persons, and furnished large supplies of freestone, and flagstone or slate. The several measures of the Millstone Grits and Lower Coal Measures were traced through the parish; together with a description of the localities near Todmorden and Hebden Bridge, where the formation of the railway line had exhibited highly fossiliferous Yoredale Shales and thin Limestones. From these, Mr. J. Gibson of Hebden Bridge, collected more than one hundred species of mollusca. In a letter addressed to Dr. Alexander, Mr. Gibson gives the following details of the discovery of the fossils. " In the railway excavation at Millwood near Todmorden, the shale is of a bluish-grey colour, and very smooth to the touch ; it contains several fossils not found in any other locality, particularly Goniatites proteus, which is in shapeless masses of dark-coloured limestone. This stone is full of shells laid in every direction, and strongly cemented together, so that it is almost impossible to procure perfect specimens. In Hoolebottom Clough a few fossils of rare occurrence are met with, but our favourite localities are Crimsworth Dean and Higher Wood, where most of the fossils, recorded in a list appended to the paper, were obtained. The shales here constitute three principal varieties ; first, blue-grey, coarse-grained and micaeous, containing no organic remains, but iron-pyrites in a nodular form ; second, black sandy and coarse-grained, containing a few crinoidal columns ; third, very dark-coloured and fine-grained, containing vegetable remains, such as lepidodendron, calamites, &c. In the same shale are shapeless masses of hard limestone, containing besides dicotyledonous wood, a heterogenous mass of shells, such as orthoceras, nautilus, goniatites, melania, buccinum, pecten, inoceramus, &c., some of them in a beautiful state of preservation."

Having given a description of the strata of the parish, Dr. Alexander stated that "the loose soils, beds of gravel, and porous
P

ragstone of this neighbourhood readily absorb water, which descends until its downward progress is arrested by a stratum of clay, compact sandstone, or some other impermeable material, where it accumulates, forming a subterranean sheet of water, beneath which *bearing level*, practical well-sinkers know there is no occasion to go for a permanent supply of water. On Norland Moor there are two or three natural springs, shooting up their flowing streams into the air. In common with other hilly districts the parish abounds with springs, some of which from the medicinal nature of the substances held in solution, obtain the name of mineral or spa waters; besides others, which being free from mineral substances, are practically pure and used for domestic purposes." Amongst the Spa Wells described in the paper are those a quarter of a mile S. of Elland, one at Erringden, St. Helen's, Holywell at Stainland, the Swift Cross Spa in Soyland, the Upper Ellistones Farm Well in Greetland, Booth Dean Spa in Rishworth, and the Widdop Ochre Spring in Heptonstall. "The town of Halifax is abundantly supplied by the rains from two springs in Ovenden, from whence the water is conducted by drains and collected into two large reservoirs, which were commenced by voluntary subscriptions in 1826 at the suggestion of Mr. M. Garlick, for the charitable purpose of giving employment to the poor, who were then suffering from a general depression in trade." They will contain nearly 5,000,000 gallons of water. Besides there is the Well Head Spring with an average discharge of 80,000 gallons per day, which after supplying several private residences at the south and west end, is distributed from a large cistern to the lower parts of the town.

The Horley Green Spring was considered the most important in the Parish, it contained considerable quantities of iron, whose presence was attributed to the large quantities of iron pyrites, distributed in the strata from which the water springs; a gallon of this water, analysed by Mr. W. West, was found to contain 40.77 grains of iron. Other sources are referred to, and the author concludes by a reference to the "never failing" springs of hard and soft water at Elland.

Preparations were made for the succeeding meeting at Leeds, and the following letter was addressed by :—

Mr. Wilson to Mr. Embleton.

BANKS, *3rd May, 1841.*

MY DEAR SIR,

I sent to you on Saturday the Reports of our Wakefield meeting, those of the Doncaster and Halifax meetings will be out in a fortnight. Mr. Morton thinks his paper should not be printed, what is your opinion?

Dr. Buckland promises to come to Leeds if he is not called away to South Wales at the time. I should have been glad to have kept him for the annual meeting, but Mr. Sopwith having urged him to come to Leeds I had no choice but following his lead.

How many extra copies of your paper on the museum should be printed. We ought to have them for distribution to other societies, as well as to our members.

The Council inclined to ask Mr. Barnes to preside, if you think you can get the local committee together soon, it would be well to take their advice. Would Mr. J. G. Marshall take the chair? Can you get us any papers from Mr. West, Mr. W. S. Ward, or from any other person.

I hope the local committee will canvass hard; Mr. Teale suggests the addition to it of Mr. George Shaw, Mr. Edward Waud, now in Leeds, G. W. Birchoff, N. P. Simes, and Rev. J. Holroyd, the last is not a member. Mr. Teale himself is so busy preparing a Report for a Medical work that he cannot give us any time. He will however canvass for us.

I am, my dear Sir, yours sincerely,

THOMAS WILSON, Secretary.

Mr. Embleton to Mr. Wilson.

5th May, 1841.

MY DEAR SIR,

I have been so much from home lately that I have not had an opportunity of attending to your letters. It would be quite convenient to me to meet the Agricultural Society's Committee on the 17th inst. The resolution relative to the museum is rather out of place, as we do not know how many or what duplicates we have, but something should be done towards an arrangement of what we have before June, if Dr. Buckland is to visit the museum. I could perhaps devote a couple of days to the object, and much might be done even in that short time if Mr. Holt will join me, but Mr. Morton must not rely on me for any assistance in the next section of your Railway Report. I have read the reports and will forward them to-day. Probably the printing of Mr. Morton's paper might be left to his own discretion; it does not comprise any new matter, but shows clearly the facts in favour of the theory he adopts. As to my own paper I shall be glad before it is printed if you will take the trouble to enlarge it or amend it in any way you think proper. It was hastily written and cannot be printed as read. I have written to Mr. Marshall to know when it will be convenient for him to attend the first meeting of the Local Committee, and when I hear from him I will write to the rest. Mr. Brandling is not at home. I have some further evidence about the non-identity of the Haigh Moor Coal and the Middleton Main Coal, but not far enough advanced for a paper.

T. W. EMBLETON.

Mr. Wilson to Mr. Embleton.

BANKS, *6th May, 1841.*

MY DEAR SIR,

I shall be glad to meet you at Lockwood's Hotel, (White Swan), Pavement, York, at 12 o'clock on Monday week, the 17th Inst. We are to meet the Agricultural Committee at 2. I hope Mr. Thorp will come, he seems now rather to incline. I infer from his letters that they will make the Museum at York a *sine qua non*, if there is to be an united Museum. I do not think this necessary, but we can hear their arguments. If you should arrive before 12, I shall be heard of at Messrs. Tweedy & Wilson's Bank, in High Ousegate, and should be glad to consult with you as to the whole of the questions that are likely to arise, before Mr. Thorp arrives.

Mr. Sopwith I fear cannot come to Leeds, and he says Dr. Buckland's lectures do not end till the middle of June, I have nothing yet promised but the Report on the North Midland Railway, unless Mr. Sopwith comes. I have written to ask Mr. Teale, who cannot help; Mr. West, who does not answer; Mr. Holt, who says he has not data; and Mr. Billington, who promises one for the next meeting.

Could Mr. Chantrell be spurred up; Mr. Thorp says flatly he has not time, as he has the Agricultural Society's Report to prepare, and he wont be at the trouble to correct his former papers for the press. An evening meeting seems out of the question.

I called on Mr. Holmes, Draper, School Close, to-day, to see his lamp, in hopes it might do to exhibit, but I fear it is only Upton and Roberts over again, without any security. He has promised to see you with it, if you think it will do to exhibit, be good enough to let me know. It might be laid on the table to look at, and he might explain it briefly, without our advertising it. Our brethren at Manchester are I think ahead of us now, they seem to have no difficulty in getting papers. We will settle about the museum when we meet at York.

I am, my dear Sir, yours sincerely,

THOMAS WILSON.

A meeting of the Local Committee was held at Leeds on May 19th, and it was decided amongst other things to invite the Rev. Theophilus Barnes to take the chair, which in due course he accepted; the meeting was held early in the following month at the Philosophical Hall, Leeds. The Rev. Chairman gave an interesting address on the objects and prospects of the Society. Papers were read by Mr. Charles Todd, of the firm of Shepherd and Todd, makers of locomotive engines at Leeds, on experiments illustrating the relative strength of Pig Iron, of various qualities, which gave rise to an important discussion of the question. Mr. Henry Hartop "On the presence of Titanium in Blast Furnaces," exhibited a large specimen of cubes of Titanium, with crystals of iron in contact with it, obtained from a Welsh Blast Furnace. Mr. Hartop also drew attention to a Slab of Ironstone, embedded in which were numbers of mussels (anthracosia), which had apparently been suddenly fixed in the matrix whilst in a feeding position, that is with the open margins of the shell upwards, whilst in another iron seam about one hundred yards deeper, an immense number of mussels were found extended on their sides with every appearance of having been floated into position when dead. Mr. Hartop had living specimens of the pond mussel for comparison which seemed to confirm the truth of his observation.

At the evening meeting Mr. John Holmes produced the Safety Lamp referred to in Mr. Wilson's letter, in which he had introduced a modification of the principle of Messrs. Upton and Roberts Lamp. The improvement consisted in an apparatus for regulating the admission of air. Mr. Holmes was recommended to continue his experiments.

An interesting paper was afterwards read by Mr. J. Travis Clay of Rastrick, describing the occurrence of Boulders of Granite and other Crystalline Rocks in the valley of the Calder. The stream at Cromwell Bottom near Elland has cut through a deep alluvial soil six feet in thickness, beneath which is a bed of large pebbles and boulders the majority of which are coarse-grained sandstone from the Millstone Grit Series, but mingled with these are many rounded fragments of Granite and other Crystalline Rocks, whose original site is far distant; beneath the gravel is a considerable thickness of soft peaty clay. The total absence of similar Granitoid Boulders on or near the surface of the surrounding country was stated by the author, and the opinion expressed that those now in the bottom of the valley were brought there by icebergs when the land was at a much lower elevation than at present, and the valley of the Calder formed an inlet from the sea.

At the annual meeting, held on the 23rd September, 1841, at which the President, Earl Fitzwilliam presided, the Rev. William Thorp, of Womersley, read a continuation of his Illustrations of Yorkshire Geology, which were not printed in the proceedings of the society. Mr. Lawrence, of Leicester, exhibited some fossil fruits from the coal formations of Lancashire, and wished for information as to their occurrence in Yorkshire. Mr. Embleton stated in reply to Mr. Sopwith that plants were frequently found fossil in the actual coal, as for example in the Haigh Moor Coal, at Ardsley, and the Stanley Main Coal, near Wakefield, and that their presence was always an indication of the inferiority of the coal containing them. Dr. Buckland, who was expected to attend the meeting, was examining the evidence of the action of glaciers on the mountains of Cumberland and Westmoreland in company with Mr. Hopkins, and sent an apology.

Mr. W. Wallen, F.S.A., of Huddersfield, read a paper, entitled

"An elucidation of the geometical principles of Gothic architecture."
A series of models illustrating some of the more intricate forms of geological stratification were exhibited by Mr. Thomas Sopwith, of Newcastle, and the same gentleman also exhibited several electrotype copies of fossils in the Museum of Economic Geology, then in Craig's Court, London. The thin deposit of copper which is formed on the wax or plaster cast from the original fossils conveys an exact idea of the minutest details of structure, and Mr. Sopwith pointed out that by these means correct copies of the best specimens of fossils could be multiplied to an indefinite extent, at a small expense, and every village museum might thus obtain electrotyped fossils, corresponding to those which adorn the cabinets of the Geological Society, or of the most careful amateurs. The electrotypes were made by Mr. T. B. Jordan. Examples of medals and some ornamental objects were also exhibited, and the application of this new and interesting art was shown to be capable of embracing a wide and useful range of objects. The most elaborate work of art could be copied as easily as a plain sheet. "Engraved copper plates can be copied for eight shillings for each pound of copper, that is to say, four shillings for the matrix, and four shillings for the copy, as the first of these containing the lines in relief, is nearly as heavy as the second, or copy for engraving from. Thus a copper plate which has cost £100 to engrave, may be faithfully copied for as many shillings. The process is applicable to many elaborate forms of metallic vessels, and hence, we may conclude that it will, ere long, find its way into the workshops of our manufacturers." It is interesting to consider the enormous use made of this process since the few examples, regarded as curiosities, were exhibited at the meeting in 1841, and how well conceived were the expectations of the author.

Thomas Sopwith, M.A., F.R.S., was born at Newcastle-on-Tyne in January, 1803, and was a member of a firm of large cabinet and upholstery manufacturers. He gave considerable attention to mining and railway engineering, and attained some skill in these branches of knowledge. His reputation as a geologist was also great. He invented and constructed a number of large Geological Models of mining districts, now placed in the Museum of Practical Geology in

London and elsewhere. In 1838 he was appointed Commissioner for the Crown under the Dean Forest Mining Act, and the models prepared in connection with this office were exhibited at meetings of this Society. At the meeting of the British Association at Newcastle he was instrumental in causing the formation of the present Mining Records Office. In 1845 he was appointed to the management of Mr. W. B. Beaumont's large mining property in Allandale, and from that time to the time of his death in January, 1879, he resided at Allan Heads.

Mr. Sopwith contributed to the same meeting a paper on the Preservation of Railway Sections, and of Accounts of Borings, Sinkings, &c., in elucidation of the measures recently taken by the British Association, in which he urged that a systematic record should be kept of all the sections exposed in the formation of new railway lines. Whether regarded from an economic or scientific point of view, exposures of this kind are of great use and interest, " they form instructive pages in the book of nature, opened by the Engineer, and presented in an attractive form to the perusal of the Geologist." The opportunity is often of but short duration, and the silent operations of nature clothe the rocks and soils in grasses, mosses and lichens, and close the volume to the geologist, exemplifying the common but too often forgotten adage, that opportunity neglected can seldom be regained.

It was proposed to hold the meeting of the British Association at York in the year 1843, and an invitation was given to its Council by the city authorities and the Philosophical Society. The latter sought to enlist the sympathy and co-operation of kindred societies in Yorkshire, and appealed to the Yorkshire Geological Society to help them. Mr. Wilson, on receipt of this communication addressed the following letter to Mr. Embleton :—

BANKS, *27th, 1843*.

MY DEAR SIR,

I received a few days since a circular from the Yorkshire Philosophical Society, asking us and the other Scientific Institutions of the country, to join them in inviting the British Association to York in 1843, and to assist in raising the guarantee fund of £500,

I have written to Mr. Lucas, Mr. Sharp, and Mr. West, to ascertain the views of the Philosophical Societies of Sheffield, Bradford, and Leeds. The latter Society's Council meet to-morrow evening, (Friday), I fear you will not be able to attend. I have suggested that if the object is merely, by a loan of a share of the honour, to draw from us a portion of the money to be spent in York, it is not worth while to stir in the matter, but that if there be a disposition to form a permanent union of the Philosophical Societies, for mutual advice, assistance and improvement, it would be well to enter into the consideration of the question, and I have proposed a Meeting of Deputies at Normanton, to deliberate on the matter. I have further hinted that the proposition should comprise the Leeds Society.

I must of course call a Council Meeting shortly, but I should like to know what day will suit you. If Tuesday, the 8th February will not, pray name any earlier day, and I will send out the circulars forthwith.

I have asked Mr. West to bring the Smoke Consuming question before us at Sheffield. If you have an opportunity, pray second my solicitation.

I am, my dear Sir, yours sincerely,

THOMAS WILSON.

At the meeting in March, 1842, held at Sheffield, Mr. William Lee, of Sheffield, read a paper on the Fossil Footprints of the Carboniferous System. The author premised that during the last fourteen years footprints of animals, upon the New Red Sandstone, had been found in Saxony, the United States, and various parts of England. Being at Brighouse in 1836, and visiting the quarries in that district, he found large slabs of stone covered with footprints between Brighouse and Rastrick. Many of the tracks were in straight lines up and down the surface, whilst some of them diverged across in an oblique direction, proving, as he considered, that the animals had walked up and down a sloping beach of fine sand to and from water. In 1839, during the excavation of a new coal pit near Sheffield, at a depth of 270 feet, he discovered footprints on fine grey quartose sandstone. They were of a small animal, the length of the stride being about one inch and a half. The impression of the toe nails was sharp and distinct. From some of the marks indented lines extend backwards, as though the feet had been drawn along the surface. In 1840 similar impressions were found on slabs of stone at Hill Bridge, near Owlerton; and the following year at Fullwood Head, west from Sheffield, footprints occurred on some beds of brown sandstone, along with worm-tracks. Upon one he deciphered forty continuous impressions of the same track, the distance between the footsteps being about one inch; and at Walkley, a stratum containing similar footprints was found in 1841. From an examination of these footprints and a comparison with the feet of many recent reptiles, of some of which Mr. Lee had made casts, he was convinced that the tracks were those of a small reptile, probably lacertian. The author refers to the description by Prof. Hitchcock of Ornithicnites found in the valley of Connecticut, and considers that these footprints may be referred to a species very similar. The specimens are from sandstones, the equivalent of the Elland Flag Rock, and he considers that they are almost peculiar to the Lower, or Ganister Coal Series.

At the annual meeting held at Wakefield in September, 1842, it was stated in the Report of the Council that the number of members had been increased to 329; 33 new members having been elected, 24 resigned, and 5 removed by death. During the year the quarterly meetings had been regularly held, at Huddersfield, Sheffield, and two meetings at Wakefield, at all of which communications of interest and importance were read; many of them are of considerable practical value, and justified the existence of the Society as an exponent, in addition to geological subjects, of the various subjects connected with the trade of the West Riding, more especially that of coal mining. The Council report, with much regret, Mr. Wilson's resignation of the offices of secretary and treasurer, which he had most efficiently filled since the formation of the Society. To his zealous and indefatigable exertions, the success which had attended the operations of the Society were in a great degree to be attributed, and great regret was expressed at the loss of so able and willing a gentleman. The establishment of a Museum of geological specimens, and more particularly of those peculiar to the district, had always been considered of primary importance, and in order that the numerous specimens which had already been contributed to the Museum at Wakefield might be systematically arranged, the Council decided to engage a resident curator for a temporary period, with the view of permanently continuing the appointment, if experience should render that course advisable. Liberal contributions of fossils were acknowledged, and a hope expressed that members who were able to afford assistance of this kind would do so. Professor Liebig, of Giessen; Professor Daubeny, of Oxford; and Dr. Lyon Playfair, were elected honorary members of the Society. The office vacated by Mr. Wilson was filled by the election of Mr. Joseph Travis Clay, of Rastrick, as honorary secretary and treasurer; and Messrs. T. W. Embleton and Mr. Henry Holt were re-elected honorary curators. The financial statement showed an expenditure cf £175 9s. 9d., (with a balance of £11 in the hands of the treasurer), £45 of which had been expended in the purchase of cases, maps, etc., for the Museum. During the following year, 18 new members were elected, and 11 resigned, but the list was carefully corrected, and a number of names erased, who, from removal or other causes, had ceased to qualify, and the number now on the books was 299. Four meetings were held during the year, at Bradford, Halifax, Leeds, and Doncaster, the one at Doncaster in August being a combined meeting of this Society with that of the Yorkshire Agricultural Society, to hear a paper by the Rev. William Thorp, on the best modes of judging of the fertility of soils. A general feeling of gratification was expressed at the co-operation of the two Societies (which have many subjects of common interest), and the Council looked forward with pleasure to the prospect of future opportunites of interchanging information of a mutually interesting character. Twelve papers were read during the year, and the Council considered that they indicated that the enquiring spirit which so peculiarly marked that age was fully developed in the West Riding, and must be highly satisfactory to every supporter of the Geological and Polytechnic Society. It was reported that progress had been made with the line of section connecting the West Riding Coal-field with that of Lancashire. Two of the divisions were completed, viz., that surveyed by Mr. Bull, which includes the township of Mirfield ; and one by Mr. T. W. Hall, comprising the townships of Bretton West, Crigglestone, Wortley, Nutton, Royston, Shafton, Brierley, and Great Houghton, extending over a distance of upwards of nine miles, and exhibiting a noble instance of the devotion of individual exertion to the advancement of scientific knowledge. The other gentlemen who had so liberally undertaken to perform the remaining portions were earnestly desired to complete them before the lapse of another summer. A resident curator had been appointed, at a salary of £50 a year, to take charge of the museum at Wakefield ; but the Council found after a year's experience that the additional expense provided no corresponding benefit, they had, therefore, instituted an enquiry as to the possibility of placing the collection under the charge of some West Riding Philosophical Society, with the expectation that if a satisfactory arrangement of this nature could be made, the occasional services of scientists would afford the aid required for classification, and also allow an increased expenditure in collecting specimens. The British Association for the Advancement of Science had determined to hold its next meeting in Yorkshire, in the autumn of 1844, and it was hoped that the members of this Society would do all in their power to render that meeting a success. The subscriptions collected during this year amounted to £109 0s. 6d., and after paying the expenses there was a balance due to the treasurer of £2 14s. 1d. Mr. Clay was re-elected honorary secretary and treasurer ; Messrs. Embleton and Holt curators.

At the following meeting on the 6th of December, Mr. Briggs exhibited and explained that portion of the line of section which had been placed in his charge, comprehending the township of Thornhill and the hamlet of Netherton ; and Mr. Henry Holt also placed his portion of the section, including the townships of Clifton and Hartshead, on the table. The thanks of the Society were given to Mr. Ingham, for a collection of coal measure Fossil Plants ; to Mr. W. Bean, of Scarborough, for a collection of Oolitic Fossils; and to Mr. Simpson, for the remains of an Ichthyosaurus and other Liassic Fossils. At the annual meeting held in 1844 at Wakefield, Mr. Clay presented a report for the past year. The Society had had three meetings during the year, the fourth having been given up to afford the members greater opportunity to be present at the meeting of the British Association at York. The Council reported that arrangements had been made, in accordance with the resolution passed at the last annual meeting, for the removal of the Museum to the Hall of the Philosophical and Literary Society at Leeds, and that the specimens had been placed there in a separate apartment, and arrangements made for their safe custody, details of which will be found on another page. The members were congratulated on the amount of observation which had been made in several new lines of railway in process of formation in the district. "Such a favourable opportunity for examining the structure of this interesting portion of the county may probably never occur again, and the facilities which are afforded, if properly cultivated, will afford opportunities for the collection of a mass of information of the greatest practical importance." The balance sheet showed a deficit of rather more than £16, and the subscriptions amounted to only £104. Mr. Clay resigned his position as honorary secretary and treasurer, and the Rev. William Thorp, of Womersley Vicarage, was unanimously elected to occupy the vacated offices. In accordance with the arrangements with the Philosophical Society at Leeds, Mr. J. Garth Marshall was elected honorary curator, along with Mr. Embleton.

A brief notice of Mr. James Garth Marshall has already been given. It may be supplemented by the following observations :—He was elected a Fellow of the Geological Society in 1833. He inherited from his father a love of science, especially of geology, for the study of which his residence among the mountains of the north of England afforded him many facilities. These he turned to good account during the many years in which he resided in his paternal home at Halsteads-on-Ulswater, where he made and recorded a valuable series of meteorological observations, including the rainfall on Swarth Fell, and afterwards at Coniston. He traced the Bala or Coniston Limestone across the country near his home, and paid close attention to the metamorphic and granitic rocks of the district, his observations leading him to an opinion which has been adopted by many geologists, viz., that the so-called granitic neuclei are often only the completely changed portions of the neighbouring strata, there being frequently between the wholly re-constituted granite and original stratified mass some incompletely altered rocks of the kind usually termed metamorphic. He brought forward some experimental results in confirmation of his opinion, which he also supported by a considerable experience in the volcanic regions of Europe. Mr. Marshall's papers on this subject will be found in the reports of meetings of the British Association for the years 1839, 1858, and 1861. The explanation offered by Mr. Marshall of these phenomena proceeds on the supposition that the strata of the district had been exposed to the action of the general heat of the globe by reason of the depression to which they had been subject, that this general heat has been productive of effects varying with the nature of the rock, and graduated by the scale of applied heat, granite being the extreme term of metamorphism, viz., complete fusion followed by re-crystallisation, the whole metamorphic tract being subsequently subject to displacement. Professor Phillips, in his presidential address to the Geological Society in the year 1859, whilst referring in eulogistic terms to the researches of Mr. Marshall, says :—" The general conclusion to which Mr. Marshall has been conducted in the course of his long study and intimate knowledge of the Lake Mountains is thus expressed. The phenomena observed may be best explained by the supposition that the whole series of rocks (granites included) are metamorphic sedimentary strata *in situ*, or in their original order of position, and that the slatey rocks alternating with the porphyries are to be accounted for on the supposition that they are by chemical composition less fusible, less easily acted upon by heat than the porphyritic beds, and have therefore been only hardened, retaining the cleavage and stratified structure, whilst the more fusible rocks have been changed into porphyries. This supposed original inequality in the degree of fusibility has been in some degree submitted to the test of experiment. Portions of the Skiddaw slate, green slate, and porphyritic bands in powder have been placed in crucibles and gradually heated ; at a good red heat the porphyry puffed up, fused and ran over the edge of the crucible in the shape of a brown glassy slag ; at a white heat the Skiddaw slate fused into a grey glassy slag ; and lastly, at a strong white heat the green roofing slate also fused into a black glassy slag. Thus the slate rocks appear to be decidedly less fusible, less easily acted upon by heat than the porphyries. The same result was obtained in fusing fragments of Skiddaw slate, Skiddaw granite, and porphyry, in a common reverberatory furnace. A white heat was required to fuse them, but the granite and porphyry melted much more readily than the clay slate when pressure was employed to consolidate the powders of granite, Skiddaw slate, and porphyry in strong tubes, and the compressed mass was secured by screwing down. The melting occurred in each case at a lower heat with pressure than without. A red heat was sufficient to fuse them, when slowly cooled they resumed a stony texture and did not resemble the glassy slags produced by fusion without pressure. A large mass of syenite of Charnwood Forest was melted in the reverberatory furnace and slowly cooled. It showed every gradation of texture from that of glassy slag to stony, granular, and even porphyritic structure. By exposing glassy slag to heat below fusion for two or three weeks, a stony texture is found to be induced. It is much to be wished that experiments of this kind may be repeated under pressure, and, if practical, in presence of moisture, for in every view of the Plutonic rocks moisture must be conceived to have been present. According to the theory of a cooling globe, the influence of the atmosphere and ocean must have been very strongly felt in the formation of compounds by consolidation from fusion, while, according to the theory of volcanic heat being generated from the contact of water and unoxidised bases of alkalies, earths, and metals, some trace of water should appear, as, in fact, it does in the minerals crystalised in lava."

No report was presented in 1845, but at a meeting of the Council held at the Philosophical Hall in Leeds, on Monday, February 3rd, it was resolved that the services of a paid secretary are essential to the prosperity of the society, and that as the present funds are inadequate to the payment of a liberal salary to a competent person, the following gentlemen be appointed a committee to consider the propriety of proposing such a reduction in the amount of subscription as may induce a large increase in the number of members, and that the committee be instructed to communicate with the president on the subject. The committee to consist of Messrs. H. Briggs, T. Wilson, C. Morton, W. West, Rev. W. Thorp, and Messrs. H. Hartop, W. T. Hall and J. T. Clay.

At the annual meeting, held at Sheffield in October, 1846, the President, Earl Fitzwilliam, as was usual, occupied the chair. The condition of the Society during the past two years was considered satisfactory and encouraging. Owing to the change of the office of secretary, the printed transactions of the Society, as well as the moneys due, had got considerably in arrear; the Council were happy to state that these defects had been remedied. The debts of the Society were all paid off, and sufficient money collected to permit its affairs to be conducted with ease and satisfaction. The objects for which the Society was instituted continued to excite great interest, and the meetings held at the several towns had been numerously attended. An increased number of valuable communications had been made, which were published in the reports. The Council desired to express their warmest acknowledgments and gratitude to their enlightened and most noble President for his kind attention to the Society, and especially for so repeatedly presiding at its meetings. The subscriptions collected during the year 1846 amounted to £180; of this nearly £29 had been expended in fitting up geological cases. and towards erecting a new gallery in the Society's Room at the Philosophical Hall. The cash in the hands of the treasurer amounted to a little over £5. During the year it had been decided to appoint an assistant secretary, at a salary of £50 per annum, and Mr. Henry Denny, the curator at the Philosophical Hall, had accepted the office. Dr. Alexander, at Halifax; Mr. Thomas Pitt, at Huddersfield; Mr. Phineas Beaumont, at Sheffield; and Mr. George C. Walker, at Doncaster, were re-appointed local treasurers. At the annual meeting for the year 1847 the balance sheet presented by the treasurer was very satisfactory. £223 had been collected in subscriptions (in great part consisting of subscriptions due for previous years), and when all indebtedness had been removed, a balance remained in the treasurer's hands of nearly £58. This financial prosperity appears to be mostly due to the exertions of Mr. Henry Denny, the assistant secretary, who at that time and for many succeeding years took an active and careful interest in the welfare of the Society.

At a meeting at Wakefield, held in July, 1842, Mr. Henry Hartop read a paper, on the relative properties of Iron made by the use of cold and hot air blasts in the smelting furnace. In 1829 the use of hot air in the smelting furnace for the manufacture of cast iron was introduced at the Clyde Ironworks, near Glasgow, and at the fourth meeting of the British Association, held at Edinburgh in 1834, Dr. Clarke gave an account of its success, and stated that whereas with the cold air blast eight tons of coal were required to make one ton of iron, with a heat of 300 degrees Fahrenheit five tons produced a ton of iron to which must be added 8 cwts. of coal for heating the iron. In 1833, the temperature of the air was increased to 600 degrees, and it was found that raw coal (coke having been previously used), might be used, which reduced the quantity of coal required to 2 tons 5 cwts. per ton of iron made. In the following year, Mr. Hartop, at a meeting of the Association at Dublin, stated that Dr. Clark was in error, and that five tons of coal with a cold blast would reduce one ton of iron, and that the amount with the hot blast was 2 tons 15 cwts., which caused a saving of 12s. 6d. per ton of pig iron. But against this there was a deterioration of value in the iron of 17s. 6d. per ton, and in the succeeding seven years the difference in the value had been increased to 32s. 6d. per ton. The iron made with the hot blast is inferior to that made with the cold blast in the following particulars:—Its greater weakness under impact, greater loss in re-melting, (amounting to 2 cwts. per ton), and the great irregularity in the contraction of castings when cooling. From these and other circumstances he considered it a debt due to the iron trade to call attention to it, and after reading his paper at the British Association at Dublin, its importance was at once recognised, and a sum of money appropriated for making needful experiments which were carried into execution by Mr. Fairbairn, the Engineer, of Manchester. Mr. Fairbairn experienced a difficulty in ascertaining the composition of the irons experimented upon, in consequence of many of the manufacturers being unwilling to give information, but the result of his experiments went to prove the correctness of the views he had stated, and the strength of cold blast iron was in all instances greater than that manufactured with the hot blast, and the results

Q

accruing from the use of railway chairs made with the hot blast iron proved that they were much more liable to break than those manufactured in the old way. Reference was made to the paper prepared by Mr. Todd and read at a meeting held at Leeds in 1841, in which the iron prepared with a cold blast was shown to be relatively much stronger than the other. Considerable discussion occurred on the conclusion of the paper, and considering that the quantity of iron produced in Great Britain had increased from 653,000 tons in 1830 to 1,396,000 tons in 1840, the subject was of sufficient importance to be adjourned to another meeting, when the whole question could be more fully discussed. On the 14th December, Mr. W. Graham communicated a paper on the same subject in which he contended that the iron produced by the hot blast was superior to that produced from the cold blast, his experiments being conducted on irons which had been bent until they had broken. Mr. Hartop contended that the paper was no answer to the one he had read six months before, and that the cold blast irons had been produced at Mr. Graham's works, whilst it was a notorious fact that they were not capable of producing good qualities by that process, those works being essentially hot blast system. He stated that the iron manufacturers in the neighbourhood of Bradford and Low Moor had had the courage to continue to make on the cold blast system during a series of years of depression, the result of which was that the miners in the vicinity of Bradford had been nearly fully employed throughout the three years, while the miners in other parts of the iron districts were only half employed. The matter was adjourned to the evening meeting, and a long discussion followed on the relative merits of the two methods of manufacture, one party contending that there were plenty of purposes to which the hot blast iron might be applied, and it was preferable because it was cheaper; the other contending that there was no use to which it could be put with advantage, the cheapness of production being more than counterbalanced by its decrease afterwards.

At the same meeting the Rev. Dr. Scoresby, who occupied the chair, explained a practical method of determining the qualities of Iron and Steel, and the degrees of hardness of the latter. The principle which he submitted bore on · the determination of the different qualities of the different kinds of cast and malleable iron, as produced from the different ores in the neighbourhood. His test was a magnetic one. A piece of iron was capable, by mere proximity to a magnet and still more by contact, of exhibiting very powerful magnetic phenomena. This was the case in different degrees with all ferruginous substances, whether in ore or in a metallic state, as malleable or cast iron and steel. By this means they called forth a latent principle within it, and those irons of the purest character, or most perfectly ferruginous, were capable of the highest development of magnetic condition. A piece of cast iron brought in contact with the magnet would be found to exhibit the magnetic character in a much inferior degree to that which malleable iron did, and a piece of steel exhibited a slighter degree than cast iron. There was a less tendency to get magnetism by juxtaposition than in iron, but there was a greater tendency to retain it; for whilst the iron lost its power by removal from the magnet the steel did not. The more imperfect the iron the less were its capabilities for showing the magnetic action. Cast iron has susceptibility to the magnetic influence, but in a degree of capability very different from that of malleable iron, which, if pure quality and soft, would be found to possess the highest capacity for the magnetic condition. When he discovered these facts he drew the inference that that which was most perfectly iron would show the highest development to the magnetic condition, and therefore that the iron which should exhibit the highest capabilities would be the best iron. A number of experiments were shown to illustrate these propositions, and he proved that the best iron had decidedly the highest magnetic capacity, and that this capacity was analogous to the respective values of the article in commerce. The commercial value of these observations was duly appreciated, and a year afterwards, at a meeting held at Huddersfield in December, 1843, at which the Rev. W. Scoresby presided, he stated many discoveries of the highest order had arisen from the observations of minute circumstances, and he urged the younger, members in particular not to refrain from communicating any new observations from the idea that they were of trifling importance. The experiments recording the investigation of the qualities of iron and steel by magnetism which he had laid before the Society some months since had been continued, and the course of experiments was now completed. The expectation which he had formed of the utility of this test had been fully realised. In wrought-iron he was able to discriminate the quality very accurately, and he had been equally successful with steel, but a greater difficulty attended his observations on cast-iron, though a considerable degree of accuracy had been attained. A manufacturer of tools at Sheffield had had a quantity of foreign iron put into his hands which appeared to him well fitted for steel, though much lower in price than that which he habitually used. He converted it and manufactured the steel into tools, which were apparently of the best quality, but he was fearful of injuring the character of his articles, and being still doubtful whether it was safe to send them out to his customers, he requested him (Dr. Scoresby), to examine them, and on submitting them to the test, he found that although the steel of which they were made was lower by £10 per ton than what the manufacturer had usually given it was in every respect of equal quality.

In July, 1842, Mr. Richard Solly, of Sheffield, read a short paper on, and exhibited specimens of iron pins, which, originally fibrous, had become granular and brittle by being subjected to great vibration at a temperature of about 100° Fahrenheit. The pins had been used to hold down the brasses over the neck at the end of a shaft turning a mule, and revolving nearly 300 times per minute. The vibration was very great and continuous, and after two months it was found that the pins had lost their fibrous texture and become brittle and granular, with the result that they broke. Mr. Solly stated that this was a not infrequent occurrence in the axle-trees of railway carriages, and he had examined broken axle-trees at Derby, all of which presented a similar crystalline appearance. He had been told by Mr. Newlay, a wire-rope manufacturer, that granular iron, by being constantly bent backwards and forwards, became fibrous. The question had attracted some attention, and he thought was a subject peculiarly fitted to a Polytechnic Society, and he hoped the Society would give it attention.

Mr. Wilson, at the same meeting exhibited a head of a spear which had been found 24 feet below the surface, in the valley of the Calder, near Fairy's Hill. Mr. James Hammerton, of Hellifield Peel, near Skipton, contributed a paper on " Arboriculture." This was a lengthy paper, illustrated by several plates exhibiting various structures of wood. He was of opinion that in the management of plantations too many trees were frequently allowed to grow, which prevented any of them arriving at maturity, and his contention was, that by cutting out the weaker trees so as to leave plenty of space for those which it was intended to become mature, a great advantage accrued both in securing good plantations and in the sale of the timber. He quoted Mr. Major, of Nosthrop, in support of his argument. Mr. Major said, " I find wherever my profession calls me I observe very great and glaring defects in plantations, arising in nine cases out of ten from the want of early and judicious thinnings. Now could we persuade persons who have the management of plantations to commence thinning a few years after planting, and to continue to do so once in two or three years as it is necessary, the defects I complain of would be prevented, and the object I have in view effectually attained. We generally find plantations wholly neglected for the space of fifteen or twenty years, sometimes even longer, and that though the trees were planted at no greater distance than three or four feet from each other ; such management must cause the branches to decay and fall off, and consequently leave the trees little better than naked poles, miserably ill-calculated to form a screen or to ornament the surrounding landscape." If trees are planted, and too many are kept on the ground and allowed to stand without any being taken away, a mortification of the root takes place, and the whole plantation suffers in health and becomes stunted in growth ; and, moreover, there is no mode of thinning it afterwards to keep a proper crop of trees on the ground. He argues that the increased area which is allowed to a tree more than compensates for the removal of the others by the much quicker growth it can make, in consequence of having a larger area from which the roots may obtain nourishment. If trees stand too near to each other they cannot throw out leaves sufficient to obtain support from the air ; the tops only being exposed to the light are drawn up, and the trees, if not thinned out, become too tall to be supported by the strength of their bole. Mr. Hammerton incidentally mentions some of the largest trees in the country, and awards the palm to the Cowthorpe Oak in this county, which, within eight feet of the ground, has a circumference of sixteen yards. This is by far the largest tree in the British Islands, and is said to be 600 years old.

Mr. Thomas Sopwith exhibited a model of the strata near the Coal and Ironworks at Ebbw Vale, in Monmouthshire, in which the workings of the successive beds were accurately laid down, and could be inspected with the greatest ease. Dr. Buckland, who was present, said that whoever saw such a model as this could not fail to understand the nature of a coal-field. Now that we had the means it would be a sin on the part of the nation to neglect the opportunity thus afforded for making an accurate register of the state of our mining districts. If such registers had been kept of ancient workings in the principal coal-fields of England they would have been the means of preserving the lives of hundreds of miners, and have prevented the loss of an immense amount of property.

Mr. B. Byrom, of Wentworth, contributed a paper on the Reciprocal Propelling Powers of Fluids, and certain Rotary Machines upon each other. The object of this communication was to elucidate certain principles of action, and proper construction of machines which derive their motion from the oblique impulse of the atmosphere or water, and the construction of the sails of windmills are entered into with considerable detail. An important feature in this paper is the application of similar rotary machinery in order to propel boats through water, and with the aid of tin models which he had prepared, he showed that a screw propeller might be used in urging small boats through water with considerable celerity. The success attending his experiments in propelling upon water, induced him to turn his attention to the same principle to propel air, and he exhibited models which clearly illustrated the great capability of a wheel of this construction. By obtaining considerable velocity, he found he could readily cause a current of air to pass through a building at the rate of nine hundred to a thousand feet per minute, and he could not doubt of its great applicability for ventilating public buildings, the holds of ships, and also for mines. The construction was simple and economical, the space required small, and the current of air which it propelled exceeded that of any other application with which he was acquainted. Mr. Martin J. Roberts described a process of blasting by means of galvanism, which he had invented and adopted in Cornwall, by which greater safety in firing gunpowder in mines was secured.

Mr. William West, of Leeds, at the next meeting, called attention to a peculiar action of water upon a lead cistern. Mr. West had been requested to provide a remedy for the corrosion of certain cisterns at a gentleman's house. One of them had been five years in its present position, and in certain spots on the bottom the lead was greatly reduced in thickness. There were patches of efflorescent deposits of carbonate of lead, under which the lead was so soft as to be easily scraped with a nail into a hollow. For some time this phenomenon was very puzzling, but eventually Mr. West found that the water before reaching the cistern passed through an iron pipe which had become rusted, and he found that a portion of the rust being carried forward by the water into the cistern settled to the bottom, and caused the peculiar action which he described.

Dr. James Inglis, of Halifax, contributed a paper by Mr. Simpson, the late curator of the Society, in which he gave the result of some observations which he had made in the Stanley Shale and Flockton Stone or Fish Coal, Mr. Simpson's attention having been directed to the Fishes of the Yorkshire Coal Strata by a fine collection presented to the museum by Mr. Embleton. He had examined the dark shale brought out in sinking a shaft at Stanley, in which he found not only detached teeth and scales of fishes but also numerous coprolites in the highest state of preservation. He also collected a number of similar specimens at Newton Lane-end, Grove Colliery, and Westgate Common. The shale containing these remains forms the roof of the Stanley Shale Coal, and is six or eight inches thick. Above the six inches containing fish remains there are numerous examples of the dispersed remains of molluscous animals, and nodular masses of ironstone, rich in a small species of unio ; but they do not occur in the fish shale. The Flockton Stone or Fish Coal is more bituminous than the Stanley Coal. It is frequently used in the manufacture of gas, but when burned leaves a large quantity of fine brown ashes. A resinous substance called Middletonite is found in it, which is supposed to be of vegetable origin, and has been mentioned in a previous chapter. The remains of fishes in this bed, as in the Stanley Shale, are disseminated throughout the entire mass, but certain layers may be observed in which they are more abundant. The parts are, as in the former, all detached. He also found coprolites in the coal, but not so well preserved as the former ones. His examples were collected from Overton and Middleton. At Dewsbury, compressed shells occur in this bed, but the fishes are absent, and he remarks that the fish remains seem to be of very local origin, for, whilst they are abundant at Sir John Kaye's pit at Overton, none could be found at the pit of Messrs. Stansfield and Briggs, a mile distant. Dr. Inglis gave a description of the Halifax Hard and Soft Bed Coals, with the general character of the fauna and flora which characterised them, remarking on the peculiar fact that in the same pit at one time is discovered a conglomeration of marine remains, as of Goniatites, Nautilus, Orthoceras, Pectens, etc., whilst a little lower down in the same series we come upon a whole stratum of fresh water mussels, and these in such a perfect state of preservation as to lead to the inference that they were embedded during a period of considerable tranquility. He remarked upon the necessity of combining the invaluable information which had been secured in mining operations in the West Riding, for, with the exception of two or three short essays in the proceedings of this Society and some observations in the *Encyclopædia Metropolitana*, he knew of no other published accounts of this coalfield. His paper concluded with a description of a new species of Nautilus which he had found in the shales in the upper of the Halifax Coal Beds. The fossil was the property, and was located in the Museum, of the Halifax Literary and Philosophical Society, after whose late president and founder Dr. Inglis had named it, *Nautilus Rawsoni*.

At the first meeting of the Society in March, 1844, a paper was contributed by Mr. E. W. Binney, of Manchester, in which he described some fossil trees found standing upright in the Lancashire Coal-field. He alluded to trees found in cutting the Manchester and Bolton Railway, described by the late Mr. Bowman, who considered they afforded positive proof that the trees forming the beds of coal upon which they stood had grown upon the spot where they were found. The specimens described by Mr. Binney had been principally found in the roofs immediately above seams of coal, and were referred to the genus Sigillaria. He next described a singular genus of supposed coal plants, (Stigmaria) and stated that he had found evidence of that fossil in the floors on which the coal rested, in all the seams examined by him, nearly 100 in number, in the Lancashire Coal-field. Fossil trees found at St. Helens exhibited the stems of Sigillaria absolutely united to the roots of Stigmaria, thus first proving the identity of these two plants. Mr. Binney supposed that remains of Sigillaria were the chief constituents of the beds of coal resting on floors containing Stigmaria; that this vegetable matter had undoubtedly grown on the spot where it is found, and was not drifted from a distance, and that each seam of coal indicated a period of repose of the earth's crust, during which a separate marine forest of vegetation grew, in the successive subsidences of the area on which the coal measures were formed; the sandy and argillaceous strata having been accumulated during subsidences of the earth's crust beneath the sea, whilst the coal seams themselves were the product of plants grown during periods of repose when the surface was elevated.

At the meetings held in 1845 and two succeeding years, Mr. William Sykes Ward, of Leeds, contributed a number of important papers, mostly on physical subjects. He was of an inventive disposition, and took out several patents for improvements in machinery, and for applications of electricity to industrial purposes. Amongst others, he contributed a paper on vibrations producing sound, a subject on which he had expended considerable experimental attention, which led him to adopt the theory of a direct progressive motion rather than the undulatory theory for the transmission of sound. In March, 1846, he read a paper on the comparative economy of various methods of applying power for locomotion on railways, and particu-

R

larly on the atmospheric system, in which he advocated the use of an atmospheric engine as being both less expensive and affording more rapid transit over a line of moderate length, say up to 20 or 30 miles. He compared in an elaborate manner the saving that would be effected by such an engine as compared with the stationary engines and ropes which were used between Euston Square and Camden Town Stations of the London and Birmingham Railway; and also with the engines driven directly by steam. He had taken out a patent in June, 1845, for improvements in exhausting air from tubes or vessels for the purpose of working atmospheric railways, but whether it was ever practically applied does not appear. In March, 1847, he contributed a paper on the strength of materials, and the following year on a process of smelting iron with anthracite coal and the hot blast, and the use made of the gaseous escape from the blast furnaces at Ystalyfera Ironworks, near Swansea; and on a mechanical communication for the working of signals and brakes on railways. The latter was an ingenious application of torsion rods extending beneath the carriages for communicating signals between the guards and engine drivers on railway trains, or for the application of brakes; and he strongly advocates that the three carriages next the engine should be supplied with self-acting brakes, and that the last three should have brakes worked by the guard, so that greater safety might be ensured than could possibly exist with the single brake on the van as then used.

Dr. J. D. Heaton, of Leeds, was elected a member of the Society in 1845, and contributed two papers on the mutual relations of animal and vegetable existence, and on the distinctive characters of animals and vegetables, in which he accepted the theory that in the early geological world a large quantity of carbonic acid existed in the air, and that if the vegetation of the coal period, or some similar phenomenon had not happened, the existence of animals would have been impossible, and he further considers that had animals never been created, vegetation must in time have exhausted the air of carbonic acid, plants would then have ceased to exist; but by the introduction of animals the balance necessary to continue vegetable and animal life combined was secured.

Mr. Henry Briggs contributed a paper on "Lime and its uses in Agriculture," in which he gave a series of analyses of the Limestones obtained from the Chalk, the Magnesian Limestone, and the Carboniferous Limestone, pointing out that the upper beds of the Magnesian Limestone contained only a minute trace of Magnesia, whilst Carbonate of Lime existed to the extent of 94 per cent. ; in the lower thick-bedded Magnesian Limestone the proportion of Carbonate of Lime amounted to 62 per cent., and that of Magnesia to 36. He advised the use of lime for districts in which the water (which he took as a fair guide) contained very little, especially mentioning the districts bordering on the Penine Chain.

In 1845 Professor John Phillips, of York, contributed two papers, one of which was on " The Remains of Microscopic Animals in the Rocks of Yorkshire," and the other on " Observations on the Process of Petrifaction." In the latter he alluded to a subterranean forest which had recently been found in the neighbourhood of Ferrybridge, whilst cutting the Aire and Calder Canal. The soil was alluvial. The forest was composed mostly of hazel bushes, containing fine clusters of nuts, at a depth of about fourteen feet. In some instances the wood remained unchanged, whilst in others the external part was converted to stone, but in all instances the bark retained its vegetable character. On examining the nuts he found the external shells were entirely unaltered, but the kernels were converted into stone. He had examined a portion of the wood so converted into stone under a microscope, and it presented as beautiful and as perfect a specimen of hazel wood as could be seen. With respect to the nuts he believed that the change was owing to their having been permeated by water that had passed over a bed of limestone. The Professor next described an ancient boat which had been found embedded in the banks of the Calder near Stanley Ferry, and also the lower jaw of a red deer found a few years ago embedded in Hatfield Chase. The jaw bones and teeth of the latter were quite flexible : they had lost the whole of their hardening earth and retained the gelatine. The latter had become tanned by the peat, and thus the whole was actually converted into leather, and was as pliable and flexible as a piece of ordinarily prepared leather. In the former paper Professor

Phillips described the manner in which he had obtained the microscopic animals which are the subject of his paper. He did this by examination of thin slices cut for the microscope, by incineration, by pulverising and washing such substances as chalk, or by distilling chemically some parts of a rock and leaving others for examination in a finely divided state, the result being that an immense number of foraminifera had been found in nearly all the formations. It had been ascertained that in the secondary strata below the chalk, particularly in the oolites of Yorkshire and Stonesfield, many foraminifera occur. They were found in the chalk, especially in the south of England, and in Tertiary Strata. The Mountain Limestone of Yorkshire consisted principally of two varieties, the oolitic and the compact. In the former, consisting of grains or ova, minute foraminifera, bits of coral or encrinites were usually found in the centre of the grains. In the compact rocks he found precisely the same things, such as Foraminifera, small Milleporidæ, minute Cyathophylla, and Calamoporæ, and other objects. In the brown clouded marbles of Beetham Fell they are so plentiful as to crowd the field of the microscope. In the Magnesian Limestone he had not been so successful. The compact parts of the rock seem to consist of earthy grains embedded in a cement of crystalline Carbonate of Lime, which is a very general character of the so-called earthy limestones. The nodular lias beds of Yorkshire he had not yet examined. Some of the oolitic beds of Yorkshire are remarkably rich in minute organisms, and numerous foraminifera, principally of the form of Textilaria, occur. These are frequently so numerous that a million may be found in one cubic inch. The oolitic grains in the north of England are separately suspended in a connected mass of clear crystalline Carbonate of Lime, which is not a character found in other parts of the country. The Yorkshire Chalk contains minute foraminifera, especially of the genera Rotalia and Textilaria. He rarely found the spicules of sponges in this rock. The flints did not contain so many organisms as those of the south of England, but specimens with a peculiar cloudy, mottled, textural arrangement contain several kinds of minute structures, the so-called Xanthidia being the most remarkable. Speaking generally, Professor Phillips found that the greater the power and clearness of the microscope and the more organisms he could distinguish. Sixteen years before Professor Phillips published a description of lacustrine deposits, a quarter of a mile north of Bridlington; but until within a few years his microscope was inadequate to the research. He had recently repeated his examinations, and had found a considerable number of loricated infusoria, five species of the genera Navicula, Cocconema, Bacillaria, and Eunotia; he had also discovered a new species of the rare genus Campilodiscus in this marl. Specimens of Gaillonella, Lyxidicula and Sydenera were also found. It appears from the researches of Ehrenberg that the Bridlington species are nearly all living at the present day, and though he considers it somewhat difficult to be assured of this perfect identity, still observation appears to agree in the statement that no clear or certain mark of distinction between the fossil and recent specimens can be distinguished.

Mr. William West, F.R.S., at the same meeting exhibited a number of experiments, illustrating some peculiar states of water at high temperature, and upon the freezing of water in red-hot vessels, and the Rev. Dr. Scoresby gave extemporaneously his observations on the currents and phosphorescence of the Atlantic. The Reverend gentleman was also present at the evening meeting and contributed observations on the falling or shooting stars at Rheims and Paris, and other subjects which had been dealt with at the previous British Association Meeting at Cambridge. Mr. Henry Denny then read a paper on the fossil animal exuvia of the Yorkshire Coal-field. After noticing the abundance and elegance of its fossil plants, he remarked that the remains from the animal kingdom were very rare, but that a many ichthyological specimens had been obtained. The first well-authenticated remains of fish were the heads of Megalichthys, from the Low Moor and Waterloo Collieries. The highest class of vertebrate animals found in the coal measures is that of fishes. On the Continent, between Coblentz and Cologne, there is a brown coal formation, or as it is termed paper coal, of more recent origin than our coal measures, in which are found, besides fishes, batrachian reptiles. In the Yorkshire coal measures we cannot lay claim to any quadrupedal or reptilian remains. The fishes occurring are mostly

Placoidians or Ganoidians, and the former specimens consist of either teeth or dorsal spines. Of these fine specimens of Gyracanthus formosus and Pleuracanthus planus have been found at Middleton and Adwalton; Ctenacanthus brevis and Orthocanthus cylindricus in the stone coal at Adwalton; a species of Helodus and Ctenoptychius pectenatus at Middleton; and a unique specimen of Ctenodus cristatus upon a piece of coal from Tong, preserved in the Museum of the Leeds Philosophical Society. Teeth of Diplodus and Hybodus also occur at Middleton, and Agassiz enumerates Petalodus acuminatus from Leeds, and Carcharopsis prototypus, which Mr. Denny had not been able to trace. Of the ganoids, specimens of the genus Megalichthys appeared to have been extensively distributed through the coal-fields of Great Britain, more especially in the cannel or stone coal; the first examples, as well as the most celebrated, being the nearly perfect head and portion of the body of Megalichthys hibberti, from Low Moor, deposited in the Museum at the Leeds Philosophical Society in 1823. Since that period, numerous scales and teeth have been detected at Middleton and Adwalton, from the latter locality, several large teeth two inches in length have been obtained by Mr. Drabble, of Leeds, who was informed by one of the pitmen that a large mass of scales, in length equal to one of the corves, had been brought up and broken to fragments at the pit's mouth. Several small jaws have also been obtained from the fish coal at Middleton, but the species to which the belong has not been determined. Numbers of small teeth have been obtained in the small coal at Stanley, Newton, and Overton, associated with coprolites; also at Rothwell Haigh, and in the roof of the better bed coal at Low Moor. Scales of Acanthodes and Holoptychius are not uncommon in the Middleton fish coal. Agassiz also mentions the species of Platysomus, and Diplopteris as also occurring, but where he could not ascertain. The last fish he named was Cœlacanthus Phillipsii, of which the tail was found in the centre of a baum pot near Halifax, and is now in the Museum of the Philosophical Society of that town. Mr. Denny then proceeds to enumerate the species of fossil mollusca which have been found in the West Riding, including those commonly known from the marine beds of Halifax, and the fresh-water iron-stone containing unios. He states that Captain Brown, of Manchester, has enumerated 12 species of unios under the genus Pachyodon,* viz., six from Low Moor, five from Middleton, and one from Wakefield. The crustacea are restricted to one small creature, Cypris arcuata, which occurs along with the unios. The total remains found in the Yorkshire coal-field are stated to be, of fish 17 species, cephalopods 5, mollusca 17, crustacea 1, total 40.

Several interesting papers were read on subjects that do not appear to have been contemplated as within the scope of the Society at its formation, but which nevertheless are of considerable interest. Amongst others, Dr. Alexander, of Halifax, read a paper on disinfecting agents, in which, after enumerating the several disinfectants at that time available, he expressed the opinion that chloride of lime stood before all others in efficacy. Mr. James Heywood, of Sheffield, also read a paper on Malaria and disinfectants; and a second one on the clover sickness of certain soils, an investigation into the causes producing the failure of the red clover crop, in which he expresses the opinion that the failure of clover is owing to a deficiency of soluble potash in the soil at the time the plant requires this material, and he advocates the application of stable manure so as to restore the potash (taken from the plants by the animals), to it. Mr. West contributed a paper on the action of certain waters in forming incrustations in boilers, gave some analyses, and recommended the application of chloride of calcium for preventing incrustation. Mr. Henry Briggs contributed a paper recommending the growth of flax in Great Britain and Ireland to take the place of cotton, giving a number of statistics to show that its growth and manufacture would be a great benefit to the country, and would afford more employment to the workpeople, in proportion to the money expended, than the growth of cereals.

---

* See Transactions, Manchester Geological Society.

CHAPTER IX.

WILLIAM SCORESBY, THE YOUNGER, WHALEFISHER AND CLERGYMAN.
1789—1857.

The following interesting memoir has been written by Mr. J. Arthur Binns, of Bradford, whose name has long been known to the literary world as that of a poet of much excellence and refinement.

We are told that the name of Scoresby has been counted amongst those of the dignitaries of the North of England for six centuries past. Those who bore it, however, may be passed over until we come to William Scoresby, of Cropton, near Whitby, in Yorkshire, who was born in 1760, and was father of Dr Scoresby, Whalefisher and Vicar of Bradford. This district, it will be remembered, is noted for another great name associated with navigation, that of Captain Cook, whose early life was spent at Staithes on the same coast, and who after a distinguished career of science and discovery, both in the Polar and Pacific Oceans, found his fate at the hands of savages in the Sandwich Islands, when our Vicar's father was about twenty years of age.

After a short training in agricultural life, William Scoresby apprenticed himself to a shipowner, and sailed on his first voyage when in his twentieth year. He had troubles enough whilst gaining his experience at sea. He was once a prisoner of war in Andalusia, and the character and variety of his experiences on his homeward voyage after his escape appear to have made him somewhat tired of his life afloat. For three or four years he settled down in his native village. Then he married. After a short time his adventurous spirit reasserted itself, and after some hesitation he chose for his vocation the whale fishery, which was then an exceedingly prosperous branch of trade for people of sea-going pursuits. At this time Whitby ships had been employed as whalers for more than thirty years, and when William Scoresby began, about twenty vessels were annually despatched from that port in quest of whales. He, himself, made his first expedition in the ship "Henrietta," which started for Greenland in 1785. It was not till 1791 that he was appointed to the command of a ship, and he is known to have complained of having married before he was well able to support a wife. One can scarcely be astonished at this, if, as his son writes in his autobiography, during the six years which preceded his father's appointment to the command of a vessel in 1791, his receipts for the whole of the voyages were only sixty pounds.

On the 5th October, 1789, our William Scoresby was born. Physically and mentally he appears to have been of a timid and delicate constitution. His mother was a singularly pious woman, and the impression of her kindly life and teaching was very lasting on the mind of her son. This comes out very clearly in his manuscript autobiography, especially in the wonderful veneration with which he regarded Sunday. Once, he tells us, he found on that sacred day a penknife with six blades, perfectly new ; he picked it up and carried it about, conscience-stricken, for a week, at the end of which time he threw it into the river near the place where it was found.

The lessons of his schoolmaster were of a different order, and enforced in a different way. The cane and the ferule, both of which are stated to have been of unusual magnitude, were constantly applied, and Scoresby and his companions were frequently locked in the school through hours of darkness, or strapped to a bench, or with a cord fastened to their thumbs and fixed to a pulley, hoisted up so as to leave their toes alone upon the ground, a class of punishment in which modern schoolmasters would scarcely dare to indulge.

When the boy was ten years old, his father, who had resigned his command of the "Henrietta," undertook the charge of a ship sailing from the Thames, the "Dundee," of London. He called in Whitby Roads in 1800, to take leave of his wife and family, who resided at Whitby. William went at his father's invitation to see the ship, and contrived so to manage circumstances that instead of returning to his mother and his family, his father took him along to

s

Greenland. In the life which he wrote of his father half-a-century afterwards, he gives a picturesque account of an attack upon the ship by an enemy, which attack suddenly came to an end on the opening of the ports of the "Dundee," and the revelation of her cannon. It further appears that the father, even after starting for Greenland with William, had entertained the idea of leaving the boy in Shetland until his return, but again the son out-manœuvred the father, and succeeded in remaining on board the vessel.

In 1806, being then 16 years of age, he was appointed to be chief officer of his ship, the "Resolution," and sailed in that capacity under his father's orders. The ship forced her way through "an icy barrier of extraordinary tenaciousness and compactness," and speedily left the rest of the whaling fleet far behind. Here she reached a region in the 80th parallel, described by Captain Scoresby as a sea of open water, never before or since navigated. They continued their course until, with not even a whaling vessel within three hundred miles of them, the sea began to freeze, and they retraced their course after having reached the highest northern latitude, ($81°\ 12'\ 24''$), ever reached by ordinary sailing. The point attained by Admiral Parry in 1827, ($82°\ 45'$), was reached by travelling across the ice.

In the intervals of his voyages, the younger Scoresby was industriously carrying on studies mainly of a scientific character, his genius and predilections being eminently in that direction. In this way he utilised the time in winter, during which his sea-work was impossible, and, notably at Edinburgh during two winters, he made remarkable progress. His studies included natural history, mathematics, and logic in particular. Anatomy and gymnastics completed his ordinary routine. The time that could be spared beyond what these required was spent in extending his notes on natural history, which he had habitually made from the first.

It was during the voyage of 1806 that his first step in practical science appears to have been taken. While delayed in Balta Sound, Mr. Scoresby made a survey of the harbour, of which there was no chart, and drew out directions for the navigation. In 1807, when the gigantic contest between France and Prussia was in progress, Mr. Scoresby was at Copenhagen. This beautiful city was bombarded on the 2nd September in that year, and the British sailors engaged in the Greenland trade were called upon to assist in bringing the fleet captured from the Danes into British Ports. Scoresby was the first volunteer to offer his services for the purpose. On the way home he was transferred to another ship, which appears to have been the home of nearly all the evils then characteristic of the British naval service. On board this vessel were fifty seamen, eighty pikemen, five hundred soldiers, fifty women and several children, and Scoresby and his companions suffered many hardships. They were insulted, ill-treated and robbed by the crew, and were refused redress by the officers. The vessel narrowly escaped shipwreck on approaching England. Regarding this incident Scoresby says, " for my own part I was calm and collected. Death seemed inevitable. Yet I had a sort of vague and inexplicable confidence that the merciful God would save us for the sake of so large a number of souls." Further, " I felt a degree of thankfulness to Almighty God for the deliverance, but it was far from the sanctified thankfulness experienced by a true disciple of Christ." It is very characteristic that, even at this early time, he should have analysed so keenly the exact nature and extent of his gratitude.

In 1808 Scoresby was introduced to Sir Joseph Banks, one of the leaders of contemporary science. During this and the following year, he began also to give special attention to the natural history of the Polar regions, and the collection of many hitherto unknown specimens of plants. Meteorology also interested him ; he discovered and microscopically examined the different forms of snowflakes, making drawings of many, and noting the atmospheric and other surroundings which might be supposed to influence them.

In 1809 he had a narrow escape from death, the boat in which he was whale fishing having been struck by one of his intended victims. The bottom of the boat was driven in, but assistance was fortunately at hand, and its occupants were saved.

Professor Jameson, the chief under whom he studied natural history at Edinburgh, always interested himself in Scoresby's pursuits. Scoresby lent him his diary, which contained descriptions of the whale, and his journal on meteorology. Jameson introduced him into society, Scoresby's extreme diffidence making this, to use his own words, inconceivably painful. He had, he says, such a degrading sense of his own inferiority, that he could not summon vanity enough to imagine himself the object of any attention. This passed away in time to a certain extent, but never completely. Professor Jameson caused several parts of Scoresby's manuscripts to be laid before the Wernerian, now the Royal Physical Society, of which he was president. The articles mainly dealt with meteorology, the description and figuring of snow crystals, and remarks on the whale, with drawings of the animal; and he was elected a member of this Society. On the whole, Edinburgh seems to have delighted him. He says himself that on entering the northern capital he had not a single literary acquaintance in the place; he quitted it enriched by the friendship of some of the most eminent men of science in the Scottish metropolis. In 1810 he made the acquaintance of Dr. Stuart, of Luss, whose house, on the shore of Loch Lomond, appears to have been a place to which people of scientific or literary culture naturally made their way. Scoresby's taste for science was now thoroughly developed. He was associated with Sir Thomas McDougall Brisbane, while on this Northern excursion, in taking astronomical observations in the Isle of Bute, Sir Thomas having an excellent observatory at Mount Stuart, in that island. Returning to London, he records that he visited Sir Joseph Banks weekly, and particularly notes that he was constantly present at Sir Joseph's conversaziones on the *sabbath* evenings.

On the 5th October, 1810, his 21st birthday, Mr. Scoresby was appointed to the command of the "Resolution," his father retiring in his favour. His first voyage was a success, and he began to look forward to marriage. He married his first love, Mary Eliza Lockwood, in 1811. His autobiography at this time reads somewhat curiously. He tells us that while externally his conduct was moral and exemplary, he was an utter stranger to the spirit of piety. Persons of eminent sanctity assured him that to be in a state of safety for eternity some renovation of heart and "alterative" in unholy desire must be necessary. He tried to discover the way of salvation, but, while wishing to be religious, he was not willing to give up worldly pleasures. His life was a constant struggle between the convictions of conscience and the power of sin. He confesses that he rather looked to his union with his wife, who was not only of pious habits, but had a deep knowledge and experience in religion, and was a member of a dissenting congregation, to help him out of his unconverted state.

In 1812, he was again successful as a whale fisher, and in that year his first child was born. For ten years he remained connected with the "Resolution," eight years under his father's command, and two as commander himself. He records with pride that during the whole of those ten years the ship never met with any accident, or suffered damage. Nor did she ever fail to surpass all the other ships in the port, which were seven or eight in number, in her catch of whales.

In 1813 he took command of another vessel, the "Esk," and sailed on his first voyage in her in March of that year. It was very successful commercially, but the ship had a narrow escape from being crushed in the ice. It was on this voyage that he contrived the instrument named by him the 'marine diver,' by which he investigated the temperature of water at and beneath the surface, and settled the fact that the temperature was warmer below than at the surface, which was the reverse of every former experiment performed in any other part of the globe.

In 1814 he read before the Wernerian Society a paper entitled "A Description of the Polar Ice," which attracted considerable attention amongst the scientific men of the day. Baron Von Buch speaks of the paper and its author in high terms, placing him as a navigator in the same rank with Hudson, Dampier and Cook.

In 1815 he was less successful as a whaler, but he records in his journal that God was beginning to call him by the voice of his Providence to other work. 1815 and 1816 saw considerable progress with his "Account of the Arctic Regions," which was published in 1820, and received with marked approval by competent judges both in England and on the Continent. This must ever remain one of the most interesting and valuable of his books.

In 1817 he had attained a position of great eminence in the scientific world. On the subject of the North Seas his word was law. It is perhaps not too much to say that out of suggestions made by him to Sir Joseph Banks, the new interest in Arctic discovery was awakened, which afterwards took visible form in the expeditions of Ross and his adventurous successors to the regions of the Pole.

In 1819 he was elected a Fellow of the Royal Society of Edinburgh. The greater part of the same year was spent in superintending the building of the "Baffin," a vessel designed by a Liverpool firm for his use in the whale fishery, and esteemed at the time one of the finest in the service. While sailing in her, Mr. Scoresby made observations of "singular appearances presented by the coast line and also by fleets of ships and masses of ice, under circumstances of remarkable atmospheric reflections and refractions." One of these, new to the world, was the ice-blink, a peculiar reflection, or rather various reflections, in the heavens, revealing the existence, and to a large extent the character, of the ice-fields on the surface of the sea.

Scoresby the father, and Scoresby the son, suggested to the Board of Trade, in the year 1821, a thorough search and exploration of the coasts on the south and east of Spitzbergen, for the discovery of some more abundant fishing station, and the greater safety and prosperity of the whale fishery in general, but nothing came of it. The government of the day, with the usual inability of governments to avail themselves of real opportunities for usefulness, allowed the chance to go by, with a final intimation "that the Admiralty had no authority to dispose of his Majesty's property to private ships."

In 1829 the father died, having for six years before his death given up all connection with a seafaring life.

Undiscouraged by official neglect, Mr. Scoresby now prepared for work on his own account. The whales, which had previously left Jan Mayen, now fled from Spitzbergen, and had to be followed to the East Coast of Greenland. Of this coast little was known, except what had been discovered by Hudson 200 years before (1607), and it was very imperfectly and erroneously laid down in the maps. He determined upon an exploration which should not only trace the route of the whales, but also serve his purpose of making scientific, geographic, and hydrographic enquiries. In the course of these investigations he discovered that the charts then existing were wrong in the 75th parallel by about 7°, and that the charts published for the use of whale fishers were erroneous by 820 miles of longitude, or nearly 14°. He was also greatly interested in the fate of the ancient colonists who had settled eight centuries before on the unfrequented east coast, and of whom all trace had long been lost. Although his search for them was fruitless, he never ceased to believe that some descendants of that hardy race still existed in the region which he was unable to reach. His faith was not altogether without warrant, as he did discover several domestic implements which indicated European knowledge ; amongst others a piece of unicorn's horn, bearing marks of a drill, and a wooden coffin, neither of which could properly, in his judgment, be ascribed to an unenlightened people.

After the "Baffin" left Greenland, Mr. Scoresby surveyed the coast line for 400 miles direct, but if the bends of the coast are taken into account, probably twice that distance was actually measured. He mapped and named the whole of the coast, using at least fifty different stations, and his map bears the names which he gave to the various sounds, bays, and headlands. Soon afterwards the government sent out an expedition to examine the same coast, Mr. Scoresby having in the meantime published his own results, but although there was practically no difference in the results of the two investigators, Mr. Scoresby's work was ignored when the official report was printed.

Returning to England he found that his wife was dead.

It was in 1822 that he compiled his Seaman's Prayer Book. In 1824, whilst staying in Edinburgh, he made the acquaintance of Sir Walter Scott, but declined to meet him at dinner on Sunday. Clearly this touch of self-denial was somewhat of a trial to him, as he acknowledges that 'in this instance the privation was greater than on any previous occasion.'

Mr. Scoresby's last voyage was not a commercial success, nor was much added by it to scientific knowledge. In fact his Arctic work was coming to a close. He had settled, after much meditation, that his real work, the one to which he was called, was the Christian ministry, and he determined to qualify himself for its requirements. He entered himself at Cambridge as a ten years' man. The principal difficulty was want of knowledge in Latin and Greek. His friend, Archdeacon Wrangham, advised him to go and study with a country clergyman near York ; this he did, and in 1823 his name was entered at Christ's College, Cambridge. A letter, written to Archdeacon Wrangham about this time, refers to his having relinquished an employment which for eleven years had produced him an average income of £800 per annum. As for many years afterwards his earnings from the clerical profession were less than a tithe of this, we may fairly assume that it was not with the prospect, or in the hope of emolument, that he exchanged the deck for the pulpit. Religion, as he conceived it, had now for a long time grown to be his chief interest and purpose in life, and it always remained so, although the scientific side of him refused to be suppressed. From Whitby he wrote to his sister, Mrs. Clark, in 1824, detailing to her with great carefulness the nature and practice of religious life, and he lays, as usual, the greatest possible stress on the observance of the sabbath.

His first position in the ministry was that of Curate at Bessingby, near Bridlington. Here he devoted himself to religious work, attending carefully to preaching, teaching, and visiting his people. But he also wrote many interesting papers on magnetism for the Edinburgh Philosophical Journal, and one long article on the Polar Regions for the Edinburgh Encyclopædia. 1827 was a notable year for him. The Institute of France elected him one of its corresponding members, and the Chaplaincy of the Mariners' Floating Church in Liverpool, the one thing most of all to his mind, was offered to him and accepted. The Mariners' Church was a ship of war, fitted up for the purpose of accommodating over a thousand persons, the greater number of those who attended of course being sailors. It was in this Church that Rammohun Roy first attended divine worship in England. Very interesting to note is the homely, yet admirable and effective way in which, while minister of the Mariners' Church at Liverpool, Mr. Scoresby used the language of nautical men for the purpose of influencing the minds of the sailors in the direction of religion.

At the first meeting of the British Association for the advancement of science, which was held at York, on the 27th February, 1831, Mr. Scoresby was elected to the sub-committee of the Section of Mathematical and Physical Science, and to the work of that association, especially in enquiries relating to magnetism, he was faithful for the rest of his life.

He married for a second time in June, 1828, his wife being Elizabeth Fitzgerald, an Irish lady. It soon became apparent that she could not live in the climate of the North, and that he must therefore give up the chaplaincy of the Mariners' Church. The result was his removal to Exeter, much to the regret of his friends in Liverpool. He took the degree of B.D. in 1834. For seven years he remained in Exeter, busy with his favourite work, but his life was saddened by domestic suffering. His two sons, the children of his first wife, one sixteen years of age and the other ten, the former a student of medicine at Edinburgh, died in these Exeter days, and while broken by this bereavement he had a severe fall from his horse, which rendered him incapable of discharging his clerical duties. In 1839 he took his degree of D.D., and after once refusing to accept the position of Vicar of Bradford, at last, in an evil hour for himself, he consented to do so. He was installed Vicar on the 17th July, 1839. Here he found church accommodation inadequate, church influence in the parish very small, and especially a want of discipline, arrangement and regard to ecclesiastical order, which was intensely repugnant to him. Besides this, the income was very inadequate. The captain's instinct awoke, and he determined to set things in order. His parish was his ship, and he was responsible for its proper government. As a first, and as he believed, an indispensable step, a church-rate was proposed. The people were as determined as the vicar, and it was refused by a majority exceeding two thousand. Rough protestors against such an impost threatened revenge, the vicar's troubles became greater and more various, and quarrels arose with new local churches on account of fees which he claimed as payable by them to the parish church. Dr. Scoresby believed that he was bound to maintain the rights of the mother church, whatever new ones might be erected within the parochial limits, and he refused to divide with them certain fees which had hitherto been shared equally with what were known as the "ancient chapels." This led to quarrels with the local gentry, and one of the new churches which had been licensed for public worship was closed. The Bishop was appealed to, and he ruled generally in favour of the vicar. But such success neither helped Dr. Scoresby in his real work, nor made his personal position more tolerable. Add to these troubles the fact that the manufacturing districts throughout the North of England were in a very agitated state. Chartism was starting into life. The rains of 1836 recalled to men's memories the old history of the deluge. Wheat reached a prohibitory price, and in 1840, when the agitation for the repeal of the corn laws sprang into being, born out of the suffering of an impoverished kingdom, the discontent of the people was universal and intense. And in few places did it take an angrier form than at Bradford. Still the vicar persevered, and wrestled with unswerving courage against his difficulties. It was without avail. The antagonism between him and the people manifested itself in many ways. The local gentry and clergy opposed him. Between the vicar and the pronounced dissenters there was a great gulf drawn. The working people saw in him an embodiment of authority and power which they believed to be ruinous, and which they heartily and openly detested and fought against. In 1844 the conflict had passed beyond his endurance His health, if not his spirit, gave way, and he resigned his charge. He was induced to withdraw his resignation, and for six months he sought change and rest in America. He returned only to find himself in the old vortex of contention, and he finally gave up the struggle in 1846, thus bringing to an end the seven stormiest and most painful years of his life.

Whilst he was on a visit to America in 1847 his wife died in Ireland. It was on his return journey in 1848 that he accomplished the feat, so graphically described at the time in "Household Words," of measuring, whilst lashed to the mast of the vessel, the height of the stormiest Atlantic waves. He was married for the third time, in September 1849, to Georgiana, the youngest daughter of William Ker, of Roxburgh and Torquay. At Torquay he built himself a house, and spent in scientific and religious work the tranquil evening of his life.

Dr. Scoresby's published works, including his papers contributed to the Philosophical Journals, exceed a hundred in number. Those by which he is most generally known are, of course, the Account of the Arctic Regions, and his Memorials of the Sea. But his scientific observations and enquiries were unusually wide and far reaching. Including his "Journal of a Voyage to Australia and Round the World for magnetical research," which was published in 1859, two years after his death, they cover a period of forty-nine years, his first paper "Meteorological Journals," (Whitby to Greenland and back), having been published in the Memoirs of the Wernerian Society in 1810. Interesting as his narratives are when they deal with the fascinations of the extreme north, so wild and weird and solitary, and greatly as they touch us by their revelations of the daring and resource of the men who sought and found its secluded fastnesses, they yield in importance to the magnetical investigations which formed the chief labour and purpose of his life. These first come to the front when at 29 years of age, he wrote his paper " On the anomaly in the variation of the Magnetic Needle as observed on shipboard." This appeared in 1819 in the "Philosophical Transactions." Thenceforward, throughout his life, whatever else in science awoke his interest, this remained his abiding passion. His papers and works on this subject are very numerous, and many of his writings -professedly on other questions deal also with this. In 1822 he published the results of experiments on "The development of magnetical properties in steel and iron by percussion ;" and in the same year he wrote on "The deviation of the compass and its fatal effects." It is not proposed to deal with his magnetical work in a paper so brief as this must be, but several of his papers were read at meetings of this Society, and will be found noticed on other pages. His conclusions are brought to a focus in the "Journal of a Voyage to Australia and Round the World for the purpose of magnetical research." This voyage was undertaken when he was 65 years of age, for the purpose of testing the correctness of theories which he had been long elaborating, and to settle some points in dispute between the Astronomer Royal, then Mr. G. B. Airy, and himself. These differences of opinion had reference to the development of magnetism by percussion, the influence of iron in ships upon the compass, and the variation of the compass with locality, ending in the reversal of polarity between the northern and southern hemispheres. This was the last of the scientific enterprises to which Dr. Scoresby devoted himself, and he did not live to see the results of his investigations in print. The book was published after his death, with an admirable introduction by Mr. Archibald Smith, of Trinity College, Cambridge, who sums up, clearly and ably, the whole of the questions at issue, and shows that on the main points of the contention between Mr. Airy and himself, Dr. Scoresby had been in the right.

He died at Torquay on the 21st March, 1857, being 66 years of age, and having lived a noble, strenuous, and consistent life.

213

CHAPTER X.

REV. W. THORP, B.A.—AGRICULTURAL GEOLOGY, ETC.

The Rev. William Thorp was one of the founders of this Society, and until his death in 1860 took the liveliest interest in its proceedings. His name occurs so frequently in the pages of this work and in the proceedings of the Society that it is unnecessary to say more as to his scientific and literary labours. He was a member of the Council from the first, and on the retirement of Mr. Clay from the office of honorary secretary and treasurer in the year 1844, Mr. Thorp was unanimously requested to occupy the position, which he did, and discharged the responsible duties attached to them for a period covering ten years. From the year 1845, when Mr. Henry Denny was appointed his Assistant Secretary, he received that gentleman's able assistance; and the Society, especially during the earlier years of the decade, was in a most flourishing condition.

Mr. Thorp, at the time this Society was formed, was Vicar of Womersley. He was afterwards presented to the Vicarage of Misson by the late Earl Fitzwilliam. Notwithstanding the most persistent and long-continued efforts to obtain some worthy account of the life of the reverend and learned gentleman, the result has not been commensurate with the desire naturally entertained to place on record a notice worthy of the important position Mr. Thorp occupied in the Society. The following letters therefore are very valuable, and the Society is indebted to the gentlemen who have furnished them.

HATFIELD HALL, WAKEFIELD, *Sept. 9th, 1888.*
MY DEAR SIR,
I knew the Rev. W. Thorp very well, he was Vicar of Womersley, which was in the gift of Lord Hawke, for a number of years. He

was of the family of Thorp's who worked the Gawber Hall Collieries for a long time. The collieries have been worked out, and I do not know that any of the family are still at Barnsley. Mr. Thorp was married and had daughters, who all married in his lifetime. He derived his taste for geology from his associations with the colliery in the neighbourhood of Barnsley. He was greatly respected.

Yours very truly,

J. B. CHARLESWORTH.

Dr. T. Pridgin Teale wrote on September 3rd, 1888 :—

I am sorry that I cannot help you about Mr. Thorp. My father knew him well, and considered him to be a very able geologist. He was also well-informed in medical matters, which he made a sort of hobby.

Mr. Thomas Scattergood records that between 1846 and 1850, when he was house-surgeon to the late Mr. Teale at the Leeds Infirmary, he used frequently to hear him speak of Mr. Thorp. There was evidently considerable intimacy between the two, probably extending to both scientific and social matters.

The Rev. J. R. Baldwin, the present Vicar of Misson, has contributed this interesting letter :—

MISSON VICARAGE, BAWTRY, YORKSHIRE,

September 8th, 1888.

DEAR SIR,

It is now about 28 years since Mr. Thorp died. He was twelve and a half years vicar of this place. He was chiefly remarkable for his liberality, and knowledge of medicine. He gave away every winter a cart-load of coals to all the poor, and if he went into the village with 20s., he seldom brought any back, he had given it all away. One story is characteristic : One day he met a man who never went to church, Mr. Thorp inquired why, he replied, that he had no hat good enough, so Mr. Thorp took off his own, gave it to the man and went home bareheaded ; so too he was as kind in visiting and prescribing for the sick, and giving them all medicine. He was not much of a preacher or reader, &c.

He obtained the extension of the church yard, and the enlargement, almost a re-building, of the national schools.

His death was very sad, he went to Doncaster, to arrange for coals for the poor, and met there one of the school trustees, whose unmerited abuse he so much took to heart, that he died at Doncaster the same day, it was said of heart disease, and was brought home, the first man to be buried in the new church yard. I am sorry my information is so poor. When the church was restored, his four daughters subscribed and placed a stained glass window representing the four evangelists, to his memory. There is a brass tablet in the church to this effect.

His eldest daughter, Mrs. Alexander, was the largest subscriber to the restoration, which I carried out.

He died in 1860, I think !

Yours faithfully,

J. R. BALDWIN.

Prior to 1840 the Yorkshire Agricultural Society had requested Professor John Phillips to prepare a Report on the Geological Constitution of the Soils of the County ; but he, having undertaken, at the request of the Lords' Commissioners of H.M. Treasury, to describe, for the purpose of publication, the Organic Remains of the Older Strata of Cornwall, Devon, and West Somerset, collected by Sir Henry de la Beche and his assistants on the Ordnance Geological Survey, was obliged to decline the work. It was proposed that the Rev. W. Thorp should prepare Reports on the several districts of the county, and this he agreed to do, and an admirable and most useful series of papers was the result.

At the annual meeting, held at Wakefield on October 5th, 1840, the Rev. W. Thorp read the first of a series of papers " On the Agriculture of the West Riding considered geologically." In this paper he took the New Red Sandstone district. The paper is printed *in extenso* in the proceedings of the Society ; but in order to indicate the growing interest in geological work by those more especially engaged in the cultivation of the soil, it appears desirable to give one or two extracts from the paper. The intimate relation which subsists between Agriculture and Geology was evident to every scientific agriculturist ; indeed of such importance was it that a subcommittee had been appointed by the Yorkshire Agricultural Society to obtain an essay on the Agricultural Geology of some part of Yorkshire. In a printed report they state that the object of their appointment was to show in how great a measure soils, and therefore their vegetable products, are modified by the strata on which they rest; and thus to prove to the agriculturist that to farm to advantage it is necessary to be acquainted with the leading geological features of the district in which he resides; the agriculture is already to a considerable extent carried on upon geological principles, though without the knowledge of the occupier of the farm, and in order to carry their purpose into effect six points requiring notice are enumerated, viz., geographical limits of the formation; its general character, such as height and form of hills, or ridges, depths of beds, &c.; its chemical composition; the plants which seem to thrive best upon it; the manures which have been found most applicable; suggesting others which, from their chemical properties, seem likely to supply deficiencies in the soil; and lastly, the insects and diseases which are found most destructive to the crops, with the remedies where known. Mr. Thorp concluded the report by expressing the conviction "that agriculture will never receive its full development until its connection with geology shall be closely examined, and clearly defined. This subject then, being one of vast importance to the agriculturist, I do think it the duty of this Society to afford to the Agricultural Society every assistance in their power towards carrying into effect their great and beneficial undertaking; and for this purpose these papers are written. I hope, therefore, now to be able; 1. To describe the geographical limits not only of the formation, but of each of the beds subordinate to it; to project these upon a map of the scale of six inches to the mile, and to produce vertical sections of the hills, depths of beds, &c. 2. To examine the chemical composition of soils upon the same strata, and to compare the unfertile with the more productive, and 3. To notice the state of agriculture as at present existing over the country described, and offer suggestions for its improvement where required." The paper exhibited much original investigation, and is replete with information; the alluvial deposits of the district receiving proportionate attention with the older rocks; but as the paper is already published it is unnecessary to state more than a bare outline of its contents.

After some remarks by the chairman, Sir Francis L. Wood, and others, Professor Adam Sedgwick said, that having been called on, he should say a few words, though the immediate subject of their discussion was one to which he was almost a stranger, he meant the examination of soils and their bearing on agricultural produce. His pursuit of geology had been on a large scale, and he had studied its relations to great questions both of natural history and of general physics, but its application to the science of Agriculture he had hardly ever touched upon. They were all greatly indebted to Mr. Thorp, for the skill with which he had drawn up his paper, and for the instructive facts and observations he had laid before them. Professor Sedgwick pointed out that a geological map might be of little use to an agriculturist, because the rocks which underlie the surface may have above them soils which have been derived from them by disintregation, or the soil may have come from a distance, and be of quite a different character. It was only by minute details and local investigations like those just read, that he could learn the nature and value of his subsoil. But this knowledge once gained, he was then prepared to receive the contributions of geology, and to turn them to profit. For geology teaches the true principles of irrigation, and determines the distribution of all mineral treasures, and such knowledge must ever have an important bearing on the economical labours of the agriculturist. He suggested the formation of experimental gardens on a large scale where every variety of seed might have a fair trial in combination with every variety of soil. Every variety of manure might in time also have its proper trial, and out of the combined results some practical conclusions might surely be arrived at. When the first series of results had given them experimentally the quantity of produce under given conditions of cultivation, the experiments might again be followed out by ascertaining the successive rates of exhaustion by the repetition of the same crops, as well as the best succession of crops to secure permanent fertility. These were noble experiments, and they were of a nature not to be expected from the practical farmer. If made at all, at least if made practically, it could only be by the combined efforts and capital of a society of gentlemen deeply interested in agriculture, such as he had the honour of addressing. He also addressed some opinions to the meeting on the advantages of scientific draining, and the advantage of a knowledge of geology in making artesian wells to obtain water. As an illustration he mentioned very extensive sinkings which had been made on the Bedford level in search of water which had all failed. Any practical geologist would have predicted this result because the sub-stratum of all that district is Oxford Clay, and is of such enormous thickness that it has never been pierced through by any sinking. On the other hand, the wells in Essex, which pierced the London Clay and reached the permeable beds below were exactly in accordance with scientific knowledge, and of inestimable value. In the district first referred to, the geological map had taught the farmer, years before the knowledge was turned to any good account, that his light, dry, turf fenlands was underlaid by an inexhaustible supply of clay, which might at a small expense be got to the surface and mixed with the turf. By this treatment, adopted only a few years ago, thousands of acres of dry turf soil gained at once tenacity and fertility, and were loaded year by year with the richest crops of corn. As an example of this kind the Professor quoted an estate near Downham, which, not long since might have been purchased for £1300, and was now let for £1300 a year.

The meeting after adjourning for dinner was resumed in the evening, and the subject was further discussed.

At the following meeting held in December, E. B. Beaumont, Esq. occupied the chair, and referred to the paper read by Mr. Thorp at its last meeting, and enlarged on the advantage of every farmer being made acquainted with the scientific basis of his farming, and knowing the geological character and the chemical constituents of his soil. A second contribution was made by Mr. Thorp at this meeting on the agricultural geology of the West Riding. The subject of his paper was the Magnesian Limestone District; it occupied the whole of the morning sitting, and exhibited in a clear and most practical manner the geological features of the district; all the information which the author had been able to accumulate from the experience of such chemists as Sir. H. Davy, Prof. Liebig, and his own observations is duly chronicled. The analysis of soils, the elements removed from the soils by the crops, the quality and quantity of manure necessary to replace the absorbed elements and restore fertility to the soil, are exhaustively treated. The preservation and use of manures resulting from cattle, horses and men, are dealt with and compared with those derived at great expense from foreign sources. The state of agriculture on the district under observation is described and suggestions offered for its improvement. The rotation of crops and keeping sheep and cattle are strongly insisted upon, and the rev. lecturer concludes " In fact the great secret in agriculture is to follow the indications of Providence. It has, however, ordained a great circle of transmutations. Vegetables collect food from inorganic bodies, while animals derive sustenance from vegetables; the decay of both affords a fresh supply of nutrition to vegetables. The atmosphere is a vehicle for the supply of one substance, the earth of another, and one remaining constituent has been left to be adduced by man. In some countries man does follow the suggestions of the laws of nature. But in England which has risen to a pinnacle unattained by any nation in the world in the arts and in commerce, agriculture languishes! And why do we hear of agricultural distress in the midst of continual demand for agricultural produce ? Why is she obliged to import not only a large proportion of corn, but an enormous quantity of manures to raise her own corn ? The reason is obvious. Those employed in the agricolation of Great Britain undervalue those substances which constitute the chief food of the vegetable kingdom, and therefore the agriculture of England is inferior to that of China, Belgium, and several other countries of the continent of Europe."

This passage, with some modifications, might very well be applied to the state of agriculture at the present time, and it appears that fifty years ago the farmers were in as poor a condition as they are now; it still remains a question for the scientific agriculturist whether all the manures are used in cultivation which might be. At any rate, in a thickly populated district as the West Riding is, where great quantities of refuse are constantly accumulated which are admirably fitted for manures, whether some method cannot be devised by which they may be rendered serviceable to the agriculturist, at a sufficiently small cost to make their use remunerative.

Mr. J. W. Childers, M.P., who was present at the meeting, expressed his gratification in having heard the useful paper of Mr. Thorp. He said "an arrangement had been made last year with a member of the Society, Prof. Phillips, to go over the same district as that described by Mr. Thorp, and to report upon it; but his being employed by the government in the county of Cornwall, had interfered with the plan. It had occurred to him whether it would not be possible, especially considering the intimate connection between this Society and the Yorkshire Agricultural Society, to meet together at the same time, and to devote one part of the day to discussion, and the other to the show of cattle. What the Yorkshire Agricultural Society had at heart exactly corresponded with the subjects on which Mr. Thorp had treated; and therefore he thought they might, with great propriety, co-operate together. He observed that this Society was called a West Riding one, but if the Council would consent to change the title to "Yorkshire" there would be no difficulty in meeting the Society at Hull next year.

This idea of Mr. Childers, that an union of the two societies should be considered, appears to have led to the Agricultural Society making certain proposals to the Geological Society which are embodied in a letter from Mr. Wilson to Mr. Embleton.

LEEDS, *20th January, 1841.*

MY DEAR SIR,

The Council at their last meeting yesterday decided upon adjourning to Tuesday next at 3 o'clock, then to hold a special meeting, to consider the following propositions, which at an interview with Mr. Thorp were made to us by Messrs. Legard, Thompson, and E. B. Beaumont:—

1st.—That the subscription of each member of our Society being raised to £1 per annum, the members of our Society should be members of theirs, and *vice versâ.*

2nd.—Each Society to retain its own officers, funds, &c., and that we should hold our meetings annually, conjointly with theirs; the expense of publishing the Transactions of both Societies and of a Curator to be borne equally.

3rd.—That they will assist us in raising subscriptions towards the museum, they having already £1000 funded which might be appropriated to this purpose.

4th.—They much wish, and would strenuously urge that the museum be at York.

To have had a proposition like this submitted is a great acknowledgment of our utility, I do not however think we can accept it in its present form, but I think we may accomplish the great object we have in common by some other means. The first proposition would expose us to the danger of having no new members, parties would rather prefer the Agricultural as the more honorary and popular Society. The second we may do without the others. The third's tempting bid would not, I think, really answer our purpose. The fourth would be fatal to us.

It appears to me desirable that a committee should be appointed to meet their committee and discuss the points formally, and either come to a conclusion or prepare a scheme for the sanction of both Societies.

I was sorry to hear that illness has kept you away from us. I hope you are recovered, and that you will if possible attend the meeting on Tuesday. Mr. Thorp, yourself, and one or two more should be the committee.

I am, my dear Sir, yours sincerely,

THOMAS WILSON.

A Council Meeting was held on the 26th January, 1841, to consider the proposals of the Yorkshire Agricultural Society, and, after discussing the question, Messrs. Thorp, Wilson and Embleton were appointed a sub-committee to meet a committee of the other Society, and ascertain more definitely their wishes. Nothing further appears to have happened in connection with the matter for two or three months. On the 29th April Mr. Wilson wrote to Mr. Embleton, and amongst other subjects said : " Sir J. Johnston proposes our meeting the Agricultural Society's Committee at York between the 17th and 20th May. Will the 17th suit you ? the 18th is the Council Meeting when we could report proceedings, and, if necessary, receive further instructions. I have written to Mr. Thorp, but he says he won't go, as you and I are opposed to a museum at York, and that others make it a *sine quâ non*. I have replied that we are open to conviction, and that there are many other points beside the museum for us to discuss, and have strongly urged his going. He has undertaken to assist them with their geological report for Hull; and has already met them on that business. Let me hear from you as soon as you can. I am, my dear Sir, yours sincerely,

THOMAS WILSON.

The meeting of the joint committees was duly held at York, and a report of the meeting and proposals was prepared, to be submitted to the meeting of the members of the Geological Society, at Leeds, on June 3rd, 1841. The report was as follows :—It has not been the practice of the Council to lay a report before the Society except at the annual meetings; but a question of great interest and importance has long occupied their attention, on which it is now desirable that the opinion of the Society should be expressed. From its earliest establishment the great object of the Society has been to pursue the study of local geology, and to direct the knowledge thus acquired to the advancement of every art to which it was applicable. No sooner, therefore, was it aware that the Yorkshire Agricultural Society had directed its attention to the important aid which geology might render to agriculture, and had appointed a committee of Agricultural Geology, than the Council offered to lend it every assistance within the sphere of the Society's operations; and at the same time they gladly availed themselves of an offer made by the Rev. William Thorp, to draw up a report on the geology as connected with agriculture, of particular formations in the West Riding. Of the very admirable manner in which these reports were executed it is unnecessary for the Council to speak, since they have already called forth the warmest eulogiums of the leading members of the Yorkshire Agricultural Society, and have mainly led to their making the proposal which the Council now wish to receive the careful consideration of the Society. It is proposed then that a joint meeting of the two societies should be held once a year; that at this meeting papers should be read on the application of Geology to Agriculture; and that the reading should be followed by discussions.

The Council believing that such a meeting would be productive of very beneficial results, recommend that the Society should hold a special meeting at Hull, in August, and it will then be seen whether the result of that experiment will be such as to induce both Societies to wish for its continuance in future years.

Mr. Embleton then moved "that a special meeting of the Society be held at Hull on Tuesday, August 3rd, concurrently with the meeting of the Yorkshire Agricultural Society." He said he thought it was right to state, that the Agricultural Society had expressed its willingness to give the members of the Geological Society every accommodation they might desire. He thought it was for the interests of the two Societies that they should meet together. The connection between them was very intimate, for this Society would not only be able to point out to them the exact local geological position of the various soils, but the particular kind of manures applicable to them, so as to secure a proper treatment of the land; and the Agricultural Society, in return, would no doubt be quite willing to afford them whatever information would tend to promote the prosperity and usefulness of this Society. Seconded by Mr. Hartop, the resolution was carried unanimously.

In due course the combined meeting was held, the Agricultural Society placed 100 tickets at the disposal of the members of this Society for admission to the Show, and invited a similar number to dinner. The meeting was held the evening before the show. The members of the two Societies dined together in the Public Rooms, and then adjourned to the Theatre of the Literary and Philosophical Society of Hull, which with the Museum was kindly placed at their disposal. The President, Earl Fitzwilliam, occupied the chair, and called on the Rev. W. Thorp to read his paper, which formed the third on a similar subject which he had prepared. It was on the Agricultural Geology of part of the Wold District of Yorkshire, and of the Oolite in the neighbourhood of South Cave, &c. He began with a quotation from Professor Rennie, "next indeed to the knowledge of what is best to be done in practice, is the knowledge of the reasons why one mode of agriculture is better than another mode. Now these reasons are in fact the science, and the farmer who does not know a good and satisfactory reason, beyond the use of wont or hap-hazard experience, for adopting certain rotations of crops, for limeing one sort of soil and not limeing another sort, for planting or sowing thinly rather than closely, and in short for all the various processes and operations, must be pronounced to know little more than half his own business. I think therefore no more important subject can occupy the attention of the agriculturist than an enquiry into the reasons why the chief processes of agriculture are more successful in some instances than in others, for if these reasons are once discovered, and the facts connected with them established beyond controversy, like many of the facts in practical chemistry and practical mechanics, then the farmer will have a sure guide in his operations, and will be as superior to the old farmer of hap-hazard experience as the modern mariner with his compass is to the mariner of olden time, who dare not advance out of sight of land for fear of losing himself in the pathless ocean." In order, however, to discover the reasons why one mode of farming is better than another, it will be necessary to ascertain the difference of the circumstances under which these different modes are performed, and the aptly acknowledged principles to local circumstances ; for on a comparison of several modes of farming, it may be found that each has been made under a diversity of soils, sub-soils, climate, manures applied, and crops produced ; so that it becomes requisite to study the agriculture of particular districts in relation to those phenomena ; or in other words to apply to the investigation of the subject the cognate sciences of Geology, Chemistry, and Physiological Botany. The several formations between the Lias and the Diluvium of Holderness are described, and the characters of the soils are explained ; this part of the subject being illustrated by sections of the rocks, and a map enlarged from that of the Rev. W. Harcourt published in the Annals of Philosophy, Vol. XI., p. 435. An exhaustive enquiry into the nature of the growth of plants, and the sources from whence their substance and nutriment is derived follows ; and numerous analysis of soils from various parts of the district made by Mr. J. Spencer, are dealt with. The rarity of crops from different parts of the East Riding are next considered, and compared with crops from similar formations in other parts of England. Then follows some suggestions for improvement, and especial stress is given to the necessity to cultivate additional green crops ; for we may lay it down as an axiom, that as the perfection of stock husbandry is the production of the greatest amount of flesh from the smallest quantity of food, so that of culture is to obtain the greatest amount of produce in the shortest space of time from the smallest quantity of land. The improvements suggested are already performed in various parts of England, and therefore the land in those parts does actually produce the crops mentioned; and not only by the introduction of other green crops than those now produced is there a greater amount of produce, but the land, if they are consumed upon it, is thus manured in the cheapest mode. It is by growing great quantities of green food and roots that the Belgian outstrips the English farmer in the great number of stock kept, the dung collected from them, and as a certain consequence, the corn produced. A beast for every three acres of land being with them a common proportion, and in small farms the proportion is greater; hence on every hundred acres there ought to be thirty-three beasts, or an equivalent number of sheep, say two hundred.

One suggestion made by Mr. Thorp is very strongly insisted on, he says there is scarcely one farm yard in ten which is spouted round to keep off the rain-water which descends upon the roofs of the buildings; there is not one in one hundred which has its floor impervious to water; and fewer still which have the plane of the floor so inclined that the liquid portion will drain off, and be collected in a reservoir, instead of being evaporated into the atmosphere. In addition to this reservoir separate tanks are required for the cowhouses and stables, with partitions, to enable the recently made urine to be preserved until it is neutralised. But where is there a homestead which has all these three conditions fulfilled? The total loss in England has been estimated at one-third of the value of the whole manure made, and this at £21,000,000, or the loss at £7,000,000 annually! If chemistry teaches anything valuable to agriculture, it is the above suggestion; and if it be true "that the chief art of agriculture depends on the collection and preservation of those manures which contain ammonia in the greatest quantity," surely this ought to be done. The paper covers more than 60 pages, and is full of valuable information and statistics, the farming in

Yorkshire is compared with that of other parts of England, and with that of other countries; and much consideration is given to rotation of crops, and the comparative cost and yield of manures.

On the 27th of August, 1842, Mr. Embleton received the letter which follows from Mr. Wilson :—

MY DEAR SIR,

Mr. Sopwith sends me a letter of Dr. Buckland's, saying that Liebig and Playfair are at Oxford, and that he has persuaded them to come to our meeting with him, if it be on the 6th September. I have to save time written to Lord Fitzwilliam, and hope he will agree to the day, and I have also, for the same reason, and because I have some grounds to think Mr. Clay may be from home, taken upon me to call a Council Meeting at 4 o'clock on Tuesday next.

I have asked Mr. Thorp to get ready a Geological Paper, as well as one on Clover; Mr. Hammerton is to treat of Arboriculture; and Mr. Walker has another Architectural Paper; Mr. Sopwith offers his new Model of Dean Forest, and one of the Somersetshire Coal-field, with a paper.

I have proposed to Lord Fitzwilliam an evening meeting also. I hope you will be at Wakefield on Tuesday.

Yours sincerely,

THOMAS WILSON.

Mr. Thorp still continued his researches in Agricultural Geology, and at once accepted the invitation of Mr. Wilson to prepare a paper on the failure of the red and white clover upon certain soils. Dr. Buckland, Professor Liebig, Dr. Daubeny, and Dr. Lyon Playfair were present at the meeting. Professor Liebig expressed the pleasure with which he had heard the Rev. W. Thorp's paper. He spoke in German, and the text of his speech was not preserved. Dr. Daubeny also spoke, and Dr. Buckland said it was indeed a matter of great importance that agriculture had attained the position which it now enjoyed; that chemical investigation was being applied so successfully to those pursuits on which the growth of the food on which mankind depended. Mr. Thorp had given an able analysis of Professor Liebig's work, which had opened a new field for scientific research; but the facts now brought forward proved that something more was requisite than a knowledge of the chemical constituents of the soil; for it appeared that while crops of clover had failed on soil which apparently contained every element of nutrition, they had flourished on land which was inferior in this respect; and it followed that the mechanical condition of the soil, i.e., its compact or loose state was a matter to be attended to in considering the causes of fertility and barrenness. He had lately seen an instance corroborative of Mr. Thorp's views, where a sandy soil had become compact from the constant treading of horses, and now for the first time was covered with a luxuriant crop of White Clover.

In the annual report presented to the members of the society the following month at Wakefield, Earl Fitzwilliam presiding, the valuable papers of Mr. Thorp are referred to as having opened up a new field for the labours of the society, the importance of which it was not easy to overrate, since thereby the Yorkshire Agriculturist would not only be made acquainted with the geological character of the soil he cultivated, but also with those principles of cultivation which the recent discoveries of science had suggested. If the result anticipated were gained, the society would have reason to congratulate itself on having lent its willing aid to forward so desirable a result.

On the 15th July, 1843, Mr. Clay issued a circular to the members of the Society, in which it is intimated that the members of the Yorkshire Agricultural Society and of the Geological Society would again hold a conjoint meeting on August 1st, at Doncaster, at the Mansion House, at half-past two, when the Right Honourable the Earl Fitzwilliam would take the chair. At that meeting Mr. Thorp gave an account of the mode of management pursued at Glasnevin Model Farm, and contributed a valuable paper, the result of much original research, " On the indications which are guides in judging of the fertility or barrenness of the soil." A prize of £50 had been offered by the Royal Agricultural Society of England for an essay to explain the productiveness of soils by obvious signs whether of colour, consistence or vegetation. In this paper Mr. Thorp showed that all these qualities depend on the geological structure of the ground, and illustrated his subject by reference to the districts of Yorkshire, which offer great variations in productiveness as they do in geological constitution. Lord Morpeth, Earl Spencer, and others spoke to the utility of the paper.

At a meeting of the Council of the Society, held at the Philosophical Hall, Leeds, on July 10th, 1844, it was resolved "That the Council have seen with great pleasure the prospectus of a publication by the Rev. W. Thorp, illustrative of the Geology of the Yorkshire Coal-field, in which the papers read by him at various meetings of the Society will be comprehended ; and the Council have much satisfaction in recommending the work to the support, not only of every member of the Society, but also of all persons interested in Science and Manufactures." The work was advertised as in one volume, quarto, " which will form a continuation of, and be printed uniformly with, Professor Phillips work on the Mountain Limestone District of Yorkshire." It is stated to include " a description of the various beds of Coal, Ironstone, Flagstone, Sandstone, and Fire Clays with their organic remains, which would be traced from place to place, and laid down on a map, and drawings given of the different genera of fossil-vegetables, and all the species of fishes and shells hitherto discovered; the tracts of coal next to be brought into operation after the exhaustion of the collieries now at work ; the extension of the coal beds beneath the Permian Limestone is to be examined ; the relationship of the Yorkshire Coal-field to those of Lancashire and Derbyshire is to be discovered, also the Agricultural Geology of the district, the whole to be accompanied by a Geological Map." Subscribers were requested to communicate with Messrs. E. Baines and Sons, the cost to be 30s. if 500 were subscribed for, and £2 if there were fewer ; with the prospectus is a list of 66 subscribers. The sections were published, but repeated enquiries for the book have not led to its discovery ; and it appears very probable that the list of subscribers never reached a sufficiently high number to warrant the author in proceeding with its publication.

The diagrammatic section of the Coal-field of the West Riding, accompanied by a second vertical section extending from east to west, is of peculiar interest, not only because it was the first effort to illustrate a most complex and difficult geological area, but from the unique way in which the several pit sections are laid down. Not only is the diagram an epitomised series of sections in one line in any direction but it also forms a sort of ground plan of the whole of the area of the Coal-field, and shows the relative position of the pits and sections superficially, at the same time that the relative position and thickness of the strata vertically are exhibited.

At the meeting held on December 18th, 1844, the newly elected secretary, the Rev. W. Thorp, read a paper on the causes of the different rates of mortality in some of the most populous towns in the West Riding of Yorkshire. In this paper the author endeavours to show that the character of the strata on which towns are erected exercises a great influence on the health of the inhabitants. "Halifax and Huddersfield, both large manufacturing towns of the same staple article, and with a dense population of above 100,000 persons in each, (i.e., in the Registrar General's districts), have exactly the same rates of mortality. That is, taking the population and the number of deaths in each district, and dividing the one by the other, the rate of mortality in each is 2.1 per cent. per annum, or 1 in 48 dying for the three years past, or as far as we have any authentic information from registration. These towns moreover are extremely healthy, being more so than any of the large towns in England, with the exception of Kidderminster. They are even more healthy than the rural districts of Thorne and Doncaster, and of Selby, Goole and Pontefract. The *cause* why Halifax and Huddersfield possess similar degrees of healthiness is, that they are built upon the same geological strata; and why they are so healthy is, that they rest upon the millstone grit," which secures good natural drainage, forms good building stone, of which houses are erected with walls 15 inches thick, and proportionably large rooms. The water is purer and more plentiful, and there is less of exhalation and miasmata, and therefore a purer air. "Leeds and Sheffield, both manufacturing towns of different staple commodities, the one of flax and woollens, and the other of steel and iron; the one containing twice the amount of population to the other have likewise their rates of mortality or degrees of unhealthiness for the same three years exactly alike, viz., 2.7 per cent. per annum, or 1 in every 38 persons dying. These two towns are, however, exceedingly unhealthy, and supposing their population to be equal to that of Huddersfield and

Halifax, in every ten years 17430 persons more in proportion would be destroyed by disease." Leeds and Sheffield are built upon exactly the same strata which are continuous from one place to the other, and the reason of their unhealthiness is because they are located upon 'clays and binds' of the coal formation, which presents certain conditions prejudicial to health. The strata are more or less impervious to water, and consequently the drainage is less efficient. The houses are built of brick, and the rooms are smaller, and there are large numbers of cellar dwellings. The sewerage being defective, there is more malaria and all its evil consequences. Hull and Newcastle built on clays are more unhealthy than Leeds and Sheffield; whilst the Oolite regions, which are very porous and consequently healthy, of Easingwold, Helmsley, Pickering, Malton, &c., stand as low as 1 in 55, and are more healthy than Huddersfield and Halifax.

On the conclusion of Mr. Thorp's paper, Dr. Crowther stated that in his opinion a deficiency of water caused a great mortality. He had no faith in the notion that high and airy situations were always the best. Ardsley, a supposed healthy situation on a hill, was hardly ever free from typhus fever, whilst at Wakefield, in the valley, there was scarcely ever a case ; thus, in his opinion, proving that it was water, and plenty of it, which was wanted. He did not think the quality was so much an object as the quantity. Mr. Crowther further stated that some thirty years ago an epidemic broke out every year at Daw Green, near Dewsbury. The inhabitants had an ashes heap, and it was customary to remove the ashes every May, and immediately the disease was raging. One year it was removed at Christmas, and the following summer the place was healthy. The ashes were always afterwards removed at Christmas. He maintained that the drainage of towns had much influence upon health. In his opinion no good would be done until the legislature compelled towns to apply proper drainage. None but compulsory measures would effect the desired good. Mr. C. Morton asked the author of the paper if there was any established relation between mortality and the geological position of towns. Mr. Briggs considered that the quality of water had more to do with the health of the inhabitants of a district than was generally thought, and Dr. Inglis, of Halifax, stated that the quality of water either increased or decreased mortality to a considerable extent; the doctor instanced a village near Halifax where the water was bad, and the inhabitants were never free from disease. Mr. Clay considered there was most typhus on the brow of hills looking south, and supported Dr. Inglis and Mr. Briggs with respect to the quality of the water. The Rev. Mr. Thorp said that if the rates of mortality from the fifth report of the Registrar General were examined, there would be found very great variations according to locality, such as neither density of population nor droughts could account for, and this paper sought to establish a connection between the degree of salubrity of any place and its geological site.

These data are interesting for comparison at the present time, they preceded the passing of the Corporation Acts, and indicate the state of the towns in draining and other matters. The application of systems of drainage, extensive water supplies carried long distances from favourable situations, and general attention to cleanliness has to a great extent rendered the death-rate independent of the geological formation on which the town may chance to be built, and to-day there is little difference in the average mortality of the large towns.

At a meeting of the Society held at York in July, 1846, Earl Fitzwilliam in the chair, the honorary secretary, the Rev. W. Thorp, contributed a paper entitled Illustrations of the Geology of the Yorkshire Coal-field. He observed that this coal-field, whilst being one of the largest, has hitherto been less exhausted of its minerals than any other in Great Britain. The towns of Sheffield, Leeds, Barnsley, Bradford, Halifax and Huddersfield owe their existence to this coal-field. About four million tons of coal are annually raised, and owing to the want of cheap and quick communication to the sea, nearly all this coal is consumed in the district, in this respect differing largely from Northumberland and Durham, which annually export about seven million tons. Some of the lower portions of the strata of this coal-field are prolonged into Derbyshire, and others into Lancashire. The vertical thickness of the whole strata he calculated to be about 1200 yards, which may be divided into three parts:— The lowest, about 200 yards in thickness, does not produce coal of any great value; the middle portion, prolonged into Derbyshire, is about 600 yards thick, and contains the most productive and richest number of coal-seams; the upper portion, of about 300 yards, consisting entirely of coarser arenaceous beds, the coals covering only small areas. The several seams of coal, their position, quantity and quality, were described in great detail, and illustrated by reference to various sections. The average vertical thickness of solid coal in Yorkshire is stated to be from 90 to 100 feet; and Humboldt asserts that in the temperate zone the growth for 100 years of the forests upon any given part would not cover it seven lines in thickness with carbon; therefore, in order to account for the enormous quantities and sizes of the plants which compose the coal strata, we must enquire into the forces which are concerned in the organizations of plants. A great quantity of carbonic acid in the atmosphere, together with an increase of temperature, have been assigned as sufficient causes for this luxurious vegetation; and from the researches of Dr. Draper, of New York, light, or rather the tithonic rays, are the active agents in the growth of all vegetation; he asserted that the sun is one of the periodical stars, and that for a series of years or centuries it may increase in brilliancy, and then decrease, which would affect the rate of vegetable growth, and the character and constitution of the atmosphere. It has been objected that such alternations would require long periods of time, but "of one thing we may rest assured that no matter how great the periods that may be required for the phenomena of the universe to transpire, there has been and will be time enough for their endless repetition." The paper was listened to by Professor Phillips, Sir Roderick I. Murchison, and Dr. Buckland. At its conclusion Professor Phillips congratulated the Society on hearing the result of many years' hard work among the coal-fields in Yorkshire, and he hoped that Mr. Thorp would publish the result of his experiences at length in the transactions of the Society. Dr. Buckland, Dean of Westminster, offered some remarks in favour of the theory that coal was a vegetable construction. He affirmed it to be the unanimous opinion of competent persons that the coal-fields were derived from vegetable origin grown upon the spot, and after seeing Mr. Thorp's sections he was confirmed in that opinion. Sir Roderick Murchison dissented from the opinion that the Yorkshire Coal-field was a deposit of jungles, forests, peat bogs, and morasses of vegetables grown upon the spot. He argued that it was a deposit of matter drifted from a distance, and he asserted this after having accompanied Mr. Thorp in his travels. To a large portion of the tract under consideration he could bear ample testimony as to its accuracy. The Coal-fields of the North of England, such as Newcastle and Durham for instance, which he had lately examined, were most certainly the result of matter drifted from a distance. Professor Phillips begged to observe that when the facts or phenomena were self-evident geologists were willing to agree, but where they offered somewhat doubtful characters, then they were compelled to differ, and could be allowed to do so. The fact was he thought to a certain extent both theories were correct ; in some instances coal-fields were derived from vegetables which had grown on the spot, and in others they were the accumulation of vegetable substances transported from other localites by the actions of floods. Earl Fitzwilliam considered the students of geology were too apt to draw hasty conclusions, as they were ignorant of the mighty power which had been at work in the formation of the crust of the earth.

The following year Mr. Thorp presented another paper on " The Ventilation of Coal Mines." About this time several explosions had occurred, with considerable loss of life. Only a few days previously to his reading the paper, the Oaks Pit, near Barnsley, was destroyed, with a loss of 73 lives, and much public attention was directed to these casualties. Mr. Thorp stated that nothing could be more simple than the principle upon which coal mines are ventilated. Atmospheric air descends by one shaft, called the 'down-cast' shaft, is made to circulate through the subterranean workings, and to ascend at another shaft, the 'up-cast' shaft. The ascending current of air is made lighter usually by a fire placed in the up-cast shaft, and the efficiency of the ventilation of the mine will be in proportion to the heat of this ascending current. It becomes, therefore, an object of the first importance to obtain a rapid and warm current of air in the up-cast shaft, and here occurs a difficulty not usually acknowledged by viewers and overlookers of collieries. To obtain good ventilation the dimensions of the fire should have a direct proportion to the area of the shaft through which the ascending current of air has to rise ; otherwise, the fuel in the grate not being sufficient to rarify the whole portion of the air in the flue, the rising current of heated air is met by a descending current of cold air, and the circulation is impeded. This is a common defect in the construction of house chimneys, and the smoke made by the descending current is borne back into the room. Treadgold's rule, applicable to these cases, is to multiply by seventeen the length of the fireplace in inches, and divide by the square root of the height of the chimney in feet, and the quotient is the area in inches for the aperture of the chimney. A fire at the bottom of a pit having a fireplace twelve feet, or one hundred and forty-four inches wide, and a chimney three hundred feet high, requires an aperture of only one hundred and forty-four inches, or one foot square ; and as the shafts are often eight feet in diameter and a hundred yards in length, there should be two or three fires to render the ventilation good. In Yorkshire the long method of getting coal is adopted, and of this there are two modifications, one with single board gates, the air being drawn from one to another across the banks where the men are working, and is used where there is little fire-damp ; another has double board gates, the air being coursed up one and down another, and drawn across the banks where the men are working. The great objections to these systems is that while the whole air sent down ventilates in one body the whole mine ; if a considerable explosion takes place in any part of it nearly the whole of the persons usually perish ; the ventilation is stopped, and those who are not burnt or killed by the force of the explosion are suffocated for the want of pure air. Mr. Buddle, of Newcastle, has devised a new scheme for working coal mines in panel work, and instead of the working surface being in one extensive area, it is divided into quadrangular panels, each containing eight to twelve acres, and round each is a solid wall of coal forty to fifty yards thick. Through these walls roads and air-courses are driven in order to work the coal contained within each, and thus they are connected together with the shaft. The advantage of this method is that there is less pressure on the coal ; in case of casualty the accident is localised, and can be cut off from the remainder of the pit. The ventilation of the other panels can be continued without detriment, and thus practically instead of the air being required to circulate twenty or thirty miles, as is frequently the case under the ordinary system of working, it is cut off into separate lengths of three or four miles each. Mr. Thorp stated that if there had been a separate air-course from the downcast pit to the workings south of the throw, during the explosion at the Oaks Pit, a great many lives would have been saved. Objection was taken to the custom of keeping the air in the goafs or worked out parts of the pit where the roof has fallen in, walled up or "dead," as it is termed. They considered it was much preferable to keep a circulation of air through them, and carry away any slight accumulations of gas rather than confine them, with the great risk at some time of their bursting forth and setting fire to the pit. Another danger reverted to is due to sudden small outbursts of gas called "blowers," which give no notice of their approach, but insidiously accumulate, often during the night, a very considerable quantity of gas. In board gates it is usual for the men to fire the gas, which is accumulated, but in the neighbourhood of goafs, or where the ventilation of the pit is not very perfect, this is an extremely dangerous operation. The paper was concluded by suggestions calculated to diminish the risk of accident. The most important were considered to be the appointment of Government Inspectors, who should make an absolute rule that the ventilation in every mine should be conducted on the best principles known, and all reasonable means of preventing accidents should be enforced; the size of the furnace should be increased so as to secure proper ventilation; and the coal worked in detached portions of moderate size, so that no air-course shall be of greater length than four miles; that the goafs should receive greater attention, and if walled in the present manner should be carefully tested at frequent intervals for the presence of fire-damp, and no naked lights should be used.

A communication by the Rev. William Thorp, on the iron-stones in the Oolitic district of Yorkshire, was made at Pontefract in 1855, in which he compared the iron-stones of North Yorkshire with those of the Yorkshire coal-field. In order to show the comparative value of the oolitic iron-stones, he enumerates the beds of iron-stone which were then worked in the West Riding, the principal of which is the one overlying the Black Bed Coal of Low Moor. The yield from this bed is about 1,000 tons per acre, and its extent is about six or seven miles. The musselband iron-stone above the Upper Flockton Coal can be traced over a tract of country about 15 miles in length, extending from Flockton to Tankersley Park; the yield from this bed is about 1,200 tons per acre. A third iron-stone occurs above the Swallow Wood Coal, worked by Earl Fitzwilliam, which is about seven inches thick, and yields 600 tons per acre ; six other iron-stones above the Ashton common coal, the Abdy. and the Kent's thin coal, all near Rotherham, the black mine above Park Gate Coal, and the bands above the Thorncliffe thin coal, and the Silkstone Coal.

In 1848, Mr. Thorp was asked by a friend of Mr. Osbaldiston, to go to Ebberstone Lodge, in the Vale of Pickering, to ascertain if there was any probability of finding coal. A bore hole had been made to the extent of 140 yards, and at a depth of 43 yards, coal 2 feet thick had been found of very inferior quality, and they were wishful to ascertain whether the coal measures were within workable distance. Mr. Thorp advised the boring to be abandoned, when he was requested to inspect an ironstone 6 feet thick, recently found in another portion of the estate. He accordingly made a tour into the valley of the Esk, and much to his surprise found that 6 feet of solid ironstone, with 10 yards of intervening strata dividing it midway, occurred in the district. The yield from this he estimated at 2½ tons per cubic yard, or 24,000 tons per acre, the value of the ironstone being 11s. per ton, and the cost of getting, 20d. per ton. The ironstone was carried into Durham to be smelted. This bed of ironstone is between 60 and 80 yards below the alum shale, or Upper Lias beds of Phillips. Mr. Thorp proceeded to enquire the extent of the ironstone, and was convinced that it could not extend to any great distance southward, the entire Lias series in the neighbourhood of Pocklington being only 25 yards thick, but northwards, about four miles south of Middlesbro, under the Stapylton Estate, and at Eston Hall, it is 14 feet thick of clear ironstone. Professor Phillips and Mr. Holt had affirmed that the iron on these estates alone would amount to 3,000,000 tons. It is exceedingly rich in iron, containing 45 per cent.; while none of the Yorkshire ironstones in the coal district contain more than 33 per cent. The ironstone in Eskdale is a firm, heavy, dark-coloured rock. The one at Eston is reddish-white, not particularly heavy, and looks in appearance like a ferruginous limestone. Mr. Thorp considered it probable that the ironstone of the Oolites of Northamptonshire is on the same geological horizon, and he concludes by stating that it is his opinion that this ironstone may be continuous from the valley of the Esk, for a distance 12 or 14 miles to Eston, and that wherever the bottom of the oolite can be approached large deposits of iron may be expected, but that southwards it is almost certain that this deposit has disappeared, although it may reappear in Northamptonshire.

Other references to the papers and work of Mr. Thorp will be found in previous and following pages.

CHAPTER XI.

BIOGRAPHICAL NOTICES.

The principal facts of the following biographical notice of William West have been prepared by Mr. William Cheetham, of Horsforth. On the basis so prepared Mr. Richard Reynolds, of Leeds, has added some further information respecting Mr. West's connection with the Chemical Society of London.

WILLIAM WEST, F.R.S.

William West, F.R.S., was born at Wandsworth, in Surrey, in 1792, and in 1816 he settled in Leeds as a wholesale and retail chemist and druggist. From that time he devoted a large share of his time to the pursuit of chemical and other sciences, and became associated with many societies established for the promotion of such objects. He cultivated chemical analyses as a profession, and in connection with this enjoyed great public confidence, being often retained in legal cases as a scientific witness. Mr. West ultimately gave up business, continuing only his professional work, and in recognition of his attainments in chemical science he was elected a Fellow of the Royal Society in the year 1846.

He was one of the earliest and most active of the members of the West Riding Geological and Polytechnic Society, and held the office of Vice-President. In 1819 he was one of the founders of the Leeds Philosophical and Literary Society, to which he contributed a large number of papers, and he was successively Honorary Secretary and a Vice-President. He held the office of President at the time of his death in 1851, which occurred at his residence Highfield House, Hunslet. He was an original member of the Leeds Mechanics' Institute, and one of its governing body. The Institute of Civil Engineers elected him an Associate in 1842, and awarded to him in 1846 the Telford Silver Medal for his paper on "Water for Locomotive

Engines." For many years Mr. West held the post of Lecturer on Chemistry in the Leeds School of Medicine.

Professor Daubeny, F.R.S., President of the Chemical Society, thus mentioned Mr. West in the obituary notice of deceased Fellows of that Society, which he laid before the Annual Meeting in 1852. After naming many circumstances already detailed in the present notice, he remarked, my own acquaintance with Mr. West dates as far back as the period when he formed, with myself, one of that little band of promoters or cultivators of science, who, obedient to the summons of Sir David Brewster, assembled at York in 1831, and whilst there, in spite of the smallness of our numbers (which, however, besides the illustrious philosopher. who first projected the meeting, included the names of Dalton, of Murchison, of Forbes, and of Sowerby) had the boldness to organize the scheme of that great scientific association, which next year obtained its full development at Oxford, and has since been welcomed in almost every large city of the British dominions.

Mr. West's first paper before the Leeds Philosophical and Literary Society was read in 1819, on some Colours for Painting found at Pompei, followed in the ensuing ten years by papers on substances from which a blue precipitate may be produced by means of heat :— On the Atomic Theory. On Iodine and notice of the ignition of Charcoal by the Galvanic Battery. On Mental Originality. The Twentieth Century, in verse. On the Varieties of Water.

1830. On the Decline of the Roman Empire, as related by Gibbon.
1831. On the Boiling point of Water under certain circumstances, with Memorandum of Experiments.
1832. Miscellaneous Chemical Observations, with Experiments.
1833. On the Intellectual Capacity of the Negro. On Hints in Support of Materiality of Caloric.
1834. He gave an account of the Meeting of the British Association at Edinburgh ; also a Paper on the Temperature of the Tunnel of the Leeds and Selby Railway.
1835. On the Detection of Arsenic.
1837. On Chemical Notation, Isomorphism and Isomerism.
1838. He gave a summary of the Proceedings of the British Assoc-

iation at Liverpool, and made arrangements for a Meeting of the Association at Leeds.

1840. A Paper with Practical Hints on Steam Engines, Boilers, Locomotive Engines and Railways.

1842. A Review of Professor Whewell's Philosophy of the Inductive Sciences.

Three Lectures on Chemical Analysis were given in 1845.

1847. A Paper on a Comparison between the Modern Languages of Europe.

His last lecture was delivered in 1851, the subject being " Explosions in Coal Mines : causes and preventions."

Some of the Papers after 1837, were read before the members of the West Riding Geological and Polytechnic Society, as well as at the meeting of the Leeds Philosophical and Literary Society.

He also contributed Papers to our Society on the Proportion of Sulphur in Iron. On a remarkable case of the action of Spring-water on Lead. On some peculiar states of Water at High Temperature, and on the Freezing of Water in Red-hot Vessels. On the Chemical Analysis of Water for Steam Engines. Remedies for Incrustation in Boilers, and notice of a remarkable case of crust composed of Sulphate of Lime.

Mr. West's activity of mind, and earnestness of purpose were not confined to scientific subjects. He was a member of the Town Council for Hunslet Ward from 1844 to 1850, and was for many years local secretary to the Anti-Slavery Society. A sincere member of the Society of Friends, he took much interest in the cause of peace, and was a delegate to the Peace Congress held in Paris in 1849, in which Mr. Cobden took a prominent part. One of Mr. West's sons, Mr. Tuffen West, displayed such conspicuous ability as a draughtsman in relation to natural history, that the leading work of this class came from his hands for many years.

HENRY HARTOP.

SEAMER LODGE, SCARBOROUGH,
DEAR SIR, *September 7th, 1888.*

I am sorry not to have sent the very scanty information I have got sooner. My uncle has only sent me the dates of Henry Hartop's birth and death. He was born at Brightside, near Sheffield, January 25th, 1786. His father had ironworks at Attercliff, where he was during the earlier part of his life. He afterwards had the Milton Ironworks. After that he became mineral agent to Lord Fitzwilliam. I believe he was a member of the Geological Society from its formation, and took a great interest in all branches of science. He died April 18th, 1865.

Yours very truly,

H. J. Morton, Esq.   T. HARTOP HOLT.

W. SYKES WARD.

Mr. Richard Reynolds, of Cliff Lodge, Leeds, has contributed the following brief notice of Mr. W. Sykes Ward, who was for a period of sixteen years Honorary Secretary. During this time the late Mr. Denny was Assistant Secretary, and to the latter the greater part of the energy infused into the Society must be attributed. Mr. Ward was not possessed of great powers of organization, but was peculiarly ingenious in speculation and experiment.

Mr. William Sykes Ward was the son of a solicitor practising in Leeds, and became his father's associate and successor in that profession. This social position permitted him to employ both leisure and pecuniary means in the pursuit of such arts and science as attracted his interest.

Mr. Ward took an active part in the work of the Leeds Philosophical and Literary Society, of which he was an Honorary Secretary from 1840 to 1869, communicating many papers to its meetings. He was an enthusiastic lover and student of music. In such matters as telegraphy, atmospheric railways, photography, and various chemical subjects Mr. Ward was an early explorer. He was one of the earliest elected Fellows of the Chemical Society of London.

Mr. Ward became a member of the West Riding Geological and Polytechnic Society in 1842, and in 1848 he was elected a Member of its Council, whilst in 1855 he accepted the office of Honorary Secretary, an office which he held until the year 1870.

The following is a list of the papers which he read before the Society, some of which will be noticed at length on other pages :—

1845. On Vibrations producing Sound.

1846. On the comparative economy of various methods of applying power for Locomotion on Railways, and particularly on the Atmospheric System.

1847. On the Strength of Materials. On a New Galvanometer, and of some of the phenomena of Voltaic Currents.

1848. On a mechanical communication for the working of Signals and Brakes on Railways.

1849. On Improvements in the Galvanometer, and on the comparative Economy of various Voltaic arrangements.

1850. On a New Gas Stove.

1851. On the use of the Barometer in Coal Mines, and a cheap form of instrument for that purpose.

1853. On a new Thermostat for regulating Ventilation.

1855. On the Collodio-Albumen Photographic Process as applicable for copying mechanical and scientific objects.

In 1845, Mr. Ward obtained a patent "for improvements in exhausting air from tubes or vessels for the purpose of working atmospheric railways, and for other purposes." The paper which he communicated to the Society in the following year showed that he was a sanguine supporter of the atmospheric system of propulsion, which was still a possible rival of the locomotive for the working of railways. Mr. Ward did not refuse to admit that the locomotive had the advantage in duty performed on a level road, but he thought that the slipping of its wheels in ascending an incline would result in a preference for the atmospheric system.

From failing health, Mr. Ward spent the last few years of his life in retirement, continuing, however, his scientific pursuits. He died in 1885.

The succeeding memoir of Robert Hunt, F.R.S., has been derived from the article by Mr. T. W. Newton, in the "Western Antiquary," issued December, 1887; and a contribution to "The Biograph and Review" for August, 1881; both kindly placed at the disposal of the writer by Mr. James B. Jordan, of the School of Mines, London.

ROBERT HUNT, F.R.S.

Robert Hunt was born on the 6th September, 1807, at Devonport. His father, who was an officer of the navy, lost his life through the foundering of H.M.S. "Moncheron," in the Grecian Archipelago, shortly before his birth. He was educated in his native town, and subsequently at Penzance. At the age of 13 he was sent to London and placed with a chemist at the West End. He remained in this situation about a year and a half, and then returned to Penzance. He afterwards returned again to London, and went as a pupil to Dr. Charles Smith, with whom he remained five or six years, and during this time gained a tolerably good knowledge of pharmacy and dispensing chemistry. An attack of illness rendered it necessary that Hunt should again leave London, and he returned to Cornwall, and the death of his grandfather gave him possesion of a small property on the banks of the River Foy. He spent several months in pedestrian travel through the country, and gleaned a large number of stories from the country people, which many years afterwards were published under the title of "Romances and Drolls of Devon and Cornwall." On returning to London he secured a situation with a firm of chemical manufacturers, and from this time seems to have devoted his attention to scientific pursuits. He was impressed by the discovery of Daguerre, and made many experiments in photography, some of his results being published in the *Philosophical Magazine*. In 1840 he received the appointment of secretary to the Royal Cornwall Polytechnic Society, and this brought him into close relationship with the miners of the Western Counties. The work of this office, combined with constant travelling and lecturing on scientific and other subjects, resulted in the acquisition of a great deal of knowledge relating to mines and mining, and in the year 1845 he received the appointment from Sir Henry De La Beche of Keeper of the Mining Records under the Geological Survey. On the establishment of the Government School of Mines in 1851 he was appointed Lecturer on Mechanical Science, and two years later Lecturer on Physics. His main work has been in connection with the Mining Record Office, and he compiled and published a great number of statistics relating to mines. Towards the close of his life he published a large work on "British Mining ; a Treatise on the Metalliferous Mines in the United Kingdom," in which he says :— "Until 1845 no successful effort had been attempted to obtain reliable returns of the quantities of metalliferous ores obtained annually from the mines of the United Kingdom." To obtain these returns he devoted all his tact and energy. There was at that time no law to compel owners of mines to give returns of their production. It was with this object that he repeatedly visited this Society, and papers will be found, referred to on other pages, in which he gives the result of his investigations in the coal district of the West Riding of Yorkshire. So far as this district was concerned he received every help and encouragement from the members of this Society, as well as other large coal owners in the district. In 1854 Mr. Hunt was elected a Fellow of the Royal Society. He was the author of the " Poetry of Science ; or, Studies of the Physical Phenomena of Nature ;" the first edition published in 1846, and afterwards followed by two others. The work is full of poetic imagery, and exhibits high imaginative power. In 1849 he wrote "Panthea, the Spirit of Nature," a work which has been characterised as philosophy and poetry finely blended, the grand truths and noble sentiments expressed in it being full of the language of beauty and eloquence. In addition to many papers on photography he edited three editions of "Ure's Dictionary of Arts, Manufactures, and Mines." His personal characteristics rendered him deservedly popular. He was fluent of speech, courteous in bearing, and exhibited an unvarying readiness to place his knowledge and influence at the services of others, and at the meetings of this Society his presence was always appreciated and cordially welcomed.

Robert Hunt died on the 17th October, at his house, 26, St. Leonard's Terrace, Chelsea, London, in the eighty-first year of his age, and was buried in Brompton Cemetery.

The succeeding biographical notice of Mr. Henry Denny is contributed by his son, Professor Alfred Denny, of Firth College, Sheffield.

HENRY DENNY, A.L.S.

During the first thirty years of its existence, the Yorkshire Geological and Polytechnic Society had few, if any, more devoted members than Henry Denny, who was not only a frequent contributor to its "Proceedings," but also acted as assistant secretary from the year 1845 up to the time of his death in 1871.

Henry Denny was born in Norwich, in 1803, and there the early part of his life was passed. At an early age he showed a taste for natural history pursuits, and coming in contact with Kirby and Curtis, and numerous other well-known entomologists then living in the neighbourhood of his native country, he soon developed into an indefatigable student of entomology. Although in after years his surroundings compelled him to extend his attention to all branches of natural history, yet, insects, the subjects of his first love, continued to hold the foremost place in his affections. The friendship of the veteran entomologist, Kirby, was perhaps one of the most important features of his youth, and the status which he afterwards attained among the entomologists of this country was in no small degree due to the early training and patronage extended to him by this distinguished man of science. In 1821 he was for some month's Mr. Kirby's guest at Barham Rectory, and it was during this period of daily intercourse with the venerable "father of British Entomologists" that he received the foundation of his scientific training. Mr. Denny's reputation as an entomologist was based chiefly on the publication of two original monographs, both of which have been regarded as authorities. The first of these, the "Monographia Pselaphidarum et Scydmænidarum Britanniæ" appeared in 1825, when the author was only 22 years of age, and is dedicated to his patron, the Rev. W. Kirby. This work was the first distinct notice issued from the press of this country bearing upon the groups of insects in question. Shortly after the publication of this work it happened that the Leeds Philosophical Society decided to appoint a Curator to take charge of the Society's Museum which was then in embryo, and on the recommendation of several leading scientists of that day, including Sir J. E. Smith, (Founder of the Linnean Society), Rev. W. Kirby and Mr. Curtis, Mr. Denny was elected to the appointment, and came to Leeds in the summer of 1826. Here he entered upon his duties (which were destined to occupy the remainder of his life), with that zeal and enthusiasm which can only be exhibited by one whose work is a labour of love. The Museum was at that time of very small dimensions, and its imperfections were so numerous as to give Mr. Denny plenty of scope for his ardour for long years to come. Wherever he found missing links in the collections he never rested until he had obtained some object that would help to make the chain complete; and in this way the work continued for a period of 45 years; the indefatigable Curator never was so happy as when acquiring some fresh object to add to the collections which constitute one of the most extensive of our provincial Museums.

Of his publications, the most important and extensive was the "Monographia Anoplurarum Britanniæ," which is an illustrated monograph of the British species of parasitic insects, (Lice), belonging to the group Anoplura of Leach. This almost untrodden path in entomological science Mr. Denny made almost entirely his own in this country, and a large proportion of the British Anoplura were described and figured by him for the first time. In the preface of his Monograph he states that during its progress he had to contend with repeated rebukes of his friends for entering upon the investigation of a tribe whose very name is sufficient to create feelings of disgust. The preparation of this treatise occupied his leisure hours for a period of fifteen years, the idea being first conceived in 1827, and the work published in 1842. During its progress the amount of material to be dealt with increased to such an extent beyond what was calculated upon, that the publication of the work at the prices originally announced in the prospectus could not be carried out without serious loss. While in this dilemma the British Association met at Glasgow, and on the proposal of Sir William Jardine, a grant of £50 was made for the purpose of furthering our knowledge of the British Anoplura. Sir William Jardine, Mr. W. Yarrell, Dr. Edwin Lankester, and Mr. P. S. Salby were appointed trustees in connection with the grant, and the sum was placed at Mr. Denny's disposal. The work is illustrated by highly magnified figures, drawn and engraved from nature by the author, who was a gifted draughtsman, and frequently prepared illustrations for the transactions of the Societies with which he was connected. Among other things he executed plates for Kirby & Spence's well-known Introduction to

Entomology. After the publication of his work on British Anoplura, Mr. Denny continued to enrich his collection with Anoplura from all parts of the world, with the intention of publishing a companion Monograph on Exotic Anoplura. He made drawings and commenced the engraving of these on the same plan as his published work, but these were never finished, and after his death Professor Westwood, of Oxford, purchased both the collection and unfinished plates with a view to completing the work. The estimated expense of finishing the work was found to be so considerable as to deter the Professor from undertaking such a speculation, and the collection and plates are now in the University Museum. In the formation of a collection of such unpopular creatures as the Anoplura, Mr. Denny had very few rivals, and he received great assistance from all parts of the world. Of the numerous sources through which his collection was enriched it may be stated that Charles Darwin added to it specimens collected during the voyage of the "Beagle"; Sir John Richardson and Sir J. Ross from the Arctic Regions; Dr. Livingstone from Central Africa; and at home the Officers in the Gardens of the Zoological Society were specially requested by the late Prince Consort to give Mr. Denny all the assistance in their power.

Among other things Mr. Denny was an enthusiastic Botanist, and in 1832 was elected Lecturer on Botany in the Leeds School of Medicine, which appointment he occupied for a long term of years. He was personally acquainted with many of the most distinguished Botanists of his day.

In 1845 his connection with the Yorkshire Geological and Polytechnic Society commenced, and during the remainder of his life he took the deepest interest in this Society's welfare. About the last work executed before his death was the preparation for the press of the annual volume of Proceedings of this Society. In the year 1845 he presented his first communication to the Society on Fossil Animal Exuviæ of the Yorkshire Coal-field; and from this time down to 1870 the Proceedings contain records of his numerous contributions. In 1843 he was elected an Associate of the Linnean Society. He was also a Corresponding Member of the Academy of Natural Sciences of Philadelphia; Honorary Member of the Philosophical Society of

Dickinson College, Carlisle, Pennsylvania; of the Yorkshire Philosophical Society; of the Blackmore Museum, Salisbury; and of the Norfolk and Norwich Museum.

His life was a singularly busy one and so entirely devoted to the fulfilment of his numerous official duties that of his private life there is very little to record. Upon all occasions his manner was kindly, obliging, and courteous to an extent which endeared him to all who knew him. He was an earnest and laborious student, but ever ready to meet any demand made from any source upon his stores of scientific knowledge, especially in aiding the promotion of science in any of its departments.

JOHN WATERHOUSE, F.R.S.

This notice was written by Mr. F. H. Bowman, D.Sc., F.R.S. Ed., a friend and associate of the late Mr. Waterhouse, for the obituary of the Geological Society, from which it has been mainly derived for the present work.

John Waterhouse, F.R.S., F.G.S., was born at Halifax, Yorkshire, on the 3rd August, 1806. Very early in life he evinced a decided taste for scientific studies, and the training which he received at school only served to increase this preference, and enabled him to obtain a sufficient knowledge of mathematical science, which he turned to good account in after years in various branches of physical research to which he gave attention. A certain weakness of constitution, which prevented him in his youth from great physical exertion, only seemed to stimulate his mental activity; and, when in search of change of climate with a view to invigorate his health, he undertook a voyage round the world, the training which he had received and the bent of his mind enabled him to record his observations in a journal which is a storehouse of scientific facts and notices, and which, had his modesty not shrunk from having it printed, would have proved a record of a scientific expedition, when such journeys were far less numerous than at present and attended by far greater inconveniences. During this voyage his love of nature and wide range of his scientific tastes acquired an increased stimulus, and when he returned home his experience in observation and his knowledge of natural phenomena in different parts of the world enabled him to enter with renewed pleasure into the less active study of the physico-mathematical sciences. He established an astronomical and meteorological observatory, and in connection with the latter published a few years ago a complete work on the Meteorology of Halifax, which will continue to be a model for all such local observations. Practical Botany also engaged his attention, and his gardens were distinguished throughout the neighbourhood for the rich variety of their contents, especially in rare plants and exotics, of which he was justly proud. His favourite studies were astronomy, geology, electricity, and light, and in connection with the latter he was identified with the early progress of photography; also with the discovery by the Rev. J. B. Reade, F.R.S., of the method of taking portraits, first upon leather and afterwards upon paper, instead of silver plates or glass, and also the chemical means of giving permanence to such images. He was specially interested in the progress of microscopy, and was himself a skilful observer and an adept at those manipulations which are necessary in the preparation of objects for examination. He was also extremely fond of music, and was a skilful performer on the violincello. Indeed, he seemed able to turn his hands to any pursuit, and such was the aptitude which he possessed for grasping the general principles upon which any practical operation depended, that he speedily was enabled to do with proficiency work which required under ordinary circumstances years of patient labour and practice. As must be expected, he was also identified with those movements which had for their object the spread of scientific knowledge, and in connection with the local Literary and Philosophical Society, of which he was one of the founders, and for many years President, he lectured on more than occasion on various scientific subjects, as well as enriched the museum with many choice objects of natural history collected during his travels. He was also connected with the Mechanics' Institution during its early years, and was active as a Magistrate, being for many years Chairman of the County Bench at Halifax, and a Deputy-Lieutenant for the West Riding. In later years a stroke of paralysis which compelled his retirement into private life only made him appreciate more his beautiful gardens, until a

W

severer form of his malady prevented all mental pursuits, and finally terminated his life on the 13th February, 1879, in the 72nd year of his age. He was a Fellow of the Royal Society, of the Royal Astronomical Society, of the Royal Microscopical Society, and of the Geological Society, and was for many years a Vice-President of this Society. Although a certain timidity of disposition prevented him from making original discoveries, few men were better acquainted with the whole range of scientific enquiry ; and his kind and generous disposition, as well as the means at his command, enabled him to liberally assist many who were pursuing the difficult path of original investigation.

JOHN LISTER, M.D.

It is a pleasure to express indebtedness to Mr. John Lister, M.A., of Shibden Hall, for the following brief memoir of his father, one of a group of learned and industrious scientists who made a reputation for the town of Halifax when science was not so popular as it is to-day.

John Lister, of Shibden Hall, M.D., J.P., was born in London, 18th June, 1802, being the only son of Mr. John Lister, of Swansea and Stockwell, by Ann, his wife, daughter of Mr. Stephen Morris, of St. Marylebone. After attending the usual surgical and medical courses of practice and instruction at St. George's and the Middlesex Hospital, he was admitted a Member of the Royal College of Surgeons in the year 1826. The next year he made his first voyage as a ship-surgeon, on board of one of the East India Company's vessels, and continued in the service of the Company until the year 1832. In 1833 he attended lectures and walked the hospitals in Paris, and in 1842 was admitted to practice medicine by the London College of Physicians. In 1844 he married Louisa Ann, daughter of the late Major Charles Grant, of the Island of St. Vincent, in the West Indies. After his marriage he practised in London, and then at Sandown, in the Isle of Wight. While residing at the latter place he formed a strong and steadfast attachment to the practical study of the science of geology, for which the island offers such abundant facilities. A long ramble, hammer in hand, round the chalk cliffs of the Culvers, or the greensand rocks of Dunnore, was to Dr. Lister supreme enjoyment, and he succeeded in making a valuable collection of the local fossil fauna. Other sciences, astronomy in particular, were industriously pursued, though, naturally, with an enthusiasm subordinate to the dominant hobby. In 1853, Dr. Lister, having succeeded to the estate of his cousin, the late Miss Anne Lister, removed to Shibden Hall. It was, however, his custom to spend the winter season in London, partly in order to enjoy the advantages of attending the meetings of the various learned Societies with which he was connected. He was a Member of the Royal Institution, and Fellow of the Geological, Zoological, Geographical and Anthropological Societies. Thus he became intimately acquainted with many of the leading *savants* of the time, such as Waterhouse Hawkins, Salter, Tennant, &c. Dr. Lister was placed, in his latter days, on the Commission of the Peace for the West Riding, and, moreover, appointed a Visiting Justice. He died very suddenly, at Aberystwith, on the 6th August, 1867, and was buried in St. Anne's Churchyard, Southowram, leaving a widow and two sons and a daughter surviving him.

WILLIAM ALEXANDER, M.D.

Dr. William Alexander was an original member and one of the founders of this Society, and took a great interest in its subsequent proceedings. For many years he occupied the position of Honorary Local Secretary at Halifax, and was a member of the Council from an early period to the time of his death, which took place after an illness of only a few hours, on the 13th of April, 1888, at his residence in Blackwall, Halifax; the worthy Doctor being then in his 82nd year. A few month's before Mr. Alexander's death occurred, the following letter was received, in reply to a request for information respecting the early history of the Society or its Members resident in Halifax.

Dr. Alexander to Mr. Davis.

HALIFAX, *November 23rd, 1887.*

MY DEAR MR. DAVIS,

I must apologise for not answering, at once, your favour of the 5th November. It seems to me a bright idea that you should edit short biographical notices of the members for the Yorkshire Geological and Polytechnic Society, and incorporate a sketch of its history. My cousin, Mr. Christopher Rawson, and the Rev. William Turner and others were very old members of the Society. During the time I lived at Scarborough I knew Phillips and Smith, who chiefly lived there. I might brush up some interesting events *if I had time*, as well as give you an account of my own travels in India, Holland and the Dominion of Canada. I am otherwise engaged just now, but accept my thanks for your proposal, and believe me, yours truly,

WM. ALEXANDER.

The following interesting particulars have been contributed by Mr. Reginald G. Alexander, M.D., son of the late Dr. W. Alexander:—

William Alexander, M.D., of Halifax, born September 3rd, 1806, was the son of Gervase Alexander, M.D., and grandson of Dr. Robert Alexander, of Hopwood Hall, Halifax, and was descended from a long line of medical predecessors. For nearly two centuries there has been no member of the family out of the learned professions of Law, Physic, Divinity, Army and Navy, and in the case of Dr. Robert Alexander occurred the singular coincidence that all the five professions were represented by his five sons. Dr. Robert Alexander (grandfather to the present Dr. Alexander) married Miss Disney, of Pontefract, and the family of Alexander, through the Disney's, are lineally descended from the celebrated Sir Reginald Brage, who, after the battle of Bosworth Field, found the English Crown, gave it to Lord Stanley, who placed it upon the head of King Henry VII., for which service he was created a Baron, and this Baronacy was a few years ago offered by the House of Lords to the Alexander family and declined.

Dr. William Alexander was educated at the University of Edinburgh, where in the year 1830 he graduated M.D., and in 1869 was elected (F.R.C.P) Fellow of the Royal College of Physicians, London. For nearly sixty years he has practised as physician at Halifax, and was connected with the Infirmary for nearly half a century. He has held the post of president of the Halifax Mechanics' Institute, and taken a lively interest in the welfare of the working classes. The Literary and Philosophical Society was founded by his cousin, Mr. Edward Alexander, F.S.A., late registrar of the County Court, and also the Halifax Agricultural Society, together with a few leading Halifax men, all of whom are now dead. Dr. Alexander's cousin was

Mr. Robert Alexander, Q.C., leader of the Northern Circuit, born 1795. Dr. Alexander has taken a deep interest in the West Riding Geological Society, and contributed a paper to their transactions " On the Springs of Halifax geologically considered." He also wrote on the Adulteration of Food and Drinks, and many other papers on Medical and Sanitary Sciences. Iu 1879 he was appointed a Justice of the Peace for Yorkshire (West Riding), and he has served his generation well, and gained the esteem and respect of all classes of the community.

BLENKINSOP AND THE LEEDS LOCOMOTIVE.

Mr. Blenkinsop was born at Walker, in 1782. His cousin, Thomas Barnes, was viewer of Walker Colliery, and when the proper time came, he was put under the care of this relative to learn the business of colliery management. Before he was of age his cousin died, but he had made good use of his opportunities, and although so young, was qualified to take a position of trust and responsibility in his profession. So, at least, thought Mr. Charles J. Brandling, for soon after the death of his teacher, he was appointed viewer of the collieries at Middleton, near Leeds, which had been opened upon an estate derived from the marriage of Ralph Brandling, in the seventeenth century, with Anne, daughter and heiress of John Leghe. At the time of his removal into Yorkshire, in 1801 or 1802, coal-owners and colliery-engineers were engrossed in the study of mechanical haulage. Various attempts were being made to apply steam to that purpose, both in the form of travelling engines drawing waggons behind, and fixed engines pulling them from point to point with ropes. Soon after his settlement at Middleton, a travelling engine was patented, by which Trevithick hoped to solve the problem that was baffling the best mechanics of the country. It did not answer, and a similar want of success attended the racing steam-horse which the same engineer brought out in 1808. Ten years of experiment had failed to overcome the difficulties which beset the application of steam to locomotion, and it appeared as if the fixed engine would be the only means of mechanical transit available. The produce of the Middleton Collieries was conveyed into Leeds, a distance of between three and four miles, in waggons drawn by horses along a railroad, and Mr. Blenkinsop, seeing the failure of Trevithick's efforts, and having a place so suitable at command, began to make experiments on his own account. On the 10th of April, 1811, he obtained a patent for certain mechanical means, by which the conveyance of coal, minerals, and other articles, is facilitated, and the expense is rendered less than heretofore. An engine was built for him by Messrs. Fenton, Murray, and Wood, of Leeds. Following the presumed necessity for a more effectual adhesion between the wheels and the rails than that presented by their mere smooth contact, Mr. Blenkinsop's patent provided a racked or toothed rail, laid along one side of the road, into which the toothed wheel of his locomotive worked, as pinions worked into a rack. The boiler of his engine was supported by a carriage with four wheels, without teeth, and rested immediately on the axles. These wheels were entirely independent of the working parts of the engine, and therefore merely supported its weight on the rails, the progress being effected by means of the cogged wheel working into the cogged rail. The engine was provided with two double-acting cylinders, instead of one as in Trevithick's engine. By this contrivance the fly-wheel was rendered unnecessary, and uniformity of action was secured. The invention of the double cylinder was due to Matthew Murray, of Leeds, one of the best mechanical engineers of his time, Mr. Blenkinsop (who was not himself a mechanic), having consulted him as to all the practical arrangements of his locomotive. The cylinders were placed vertically, and were immersed for a considerable portion of their length in the steam space of the boiler. The boiler was of cast-iron, of the plain cylindrical kind, with one flue, the fire being at one end and the chimney at the other. The connecting rods gave the motion to two pinions by cranks at right angles to each other. The pinions communicated the motion to the wheel, which worked into the toothed rail. Mr. Blenkinsop's engine began running on the railway extending from the Middleton Collieries to Leeds on the 12th of August, 1812. They continued for many years to be the principal curiosities in the neighbourhood, and were visited by strangers from all parts. The locomotive did the work of sixteen horses, and drew twenty-seven waggons, weighing ninety-four tons, on dead levels, at three and a half miles an hour. The engine weighed five tons, and its cost was about £400, to which must be added the expense of laying down a special tooth-racked rail. After they had been working fifteen months between Middleton and Leeds, the Brandling's took one to their collieries at Kenton and Cock's Lodge, in Northumberland, with sixteen waggons, weighing altogether seventy tons. The engine was set going, and the speed realised was not so great as was anticipated, owing to some partial ascents in the railway. Amongst the spectators of this experimental trip was George Stephenson, then engine-wright at Killingworth Colliery, who remarked that he could make a better engine than that to go upon legs, and how, with William Headley and others, he succeeded is now matter of history. Mr. Blenkinsop died at Leeds in January, 1831, at the early age of 48 years, and was buried at Rothwell Church. The engines continued to be employed in the haulage of coal at Middleton for many years, and furnished the first instance of the regular employment of locomotive power for commercial purposes. Mr. Embleton, who succeeded Mr. Blenkinsop in the management of the Middleton Collieries, made several improvements in the structure and working qualities of the engine, and to him is due the first conception of the idea of turning the steam into the funnel and so causing an increased draught, with greater consumption of fuel, and consequently greater power.

CHAPTER XII.

PROCEEDINGS 1849—1858.

During 1849 two meetings were held at Wakefield and Doncaster, and papers were read which were more numerous on the Polytechnic than on the Geological side ; Mr. W. Sykes Ward gave further results of his work on the Galvanometer, and Mr. Henry Denny contributed a paper on the fossil flora of the carboniferous epoch, with especial reference to the Yorkshire Coal-field. At the next meeting held at Halifax, in June, 1850, two papers on electrical subjects were read.

The annual meeting in 1850 was held at Barnsley, Earl Fitzwilliam in the chair, the statement of receipts and expenditure showed a balance in the treasurer's hands of £9 14s. 7d. Mr. William West read a paper on explosions in coal mines, and Mr. W. L. Simpson, of Doncaster, read a communication on the nature, value, and application of fuel. Mr. H. Clifton Sorby, F.G.S., contributed a paper on the contorted stratification of the drift on the coast of Yorkshire, the contortions in the drifts in the neighbourhood of Bridlington were considered to be due to the stranding of icebergs when the bay extended a greater distance inland than it does at present, and it is further argued, that as the contortions occur at all levels throughout the drifts, the action of icebergs is indicated as extending during the whole of the drift period, and not, as has been supposed by some highly distinguished geologists, merely at its close. At the same meeting Mr. Sorby also read a paper on the existence of four crystalline species of carbon, viz., diamond, graphite, hard coke, and charcoal, in which he described experiments which he had made to show their various crystalline forms and mutual relationship.

Dr. Sorby made a communication on the excavation of valleys in the range of flat-topped, tabular hills, extending from Scarborough westward to near Thirsk. They are composed of Calcareous Grit or Coralline Oolite at the top, with Oxford Clay, or some of the softer rocks of the oolitic series beneath. Their formation is traceable to this structure, and it has been considered that the valleys were produced in all probability by the action of streams now running in them, but Dr. Sorby, after a careful consideration, especially of Yedmandale, considered that the phenomena appeared to indicate that they had been washed out by the sea when the land was at a lower level than at the present time, by a current from the north. The larger expansion of the upper part of the valley appears to be better accounted for by this supposition than any other. The excavation took place previously to the time when the chief part of the erratic drift was deposited. He appears to consider that the drift occupying the lower level was beneath the water, whilst the higher parts of the land were above the sea.

In June, 1851, he communicated the result of investigations on the microscopical structure of the Calcareous Grit of the Yorkshire Coast. Good sections of this grit may be seen at Filey, Gristhorpe, and Scarborough. The greater part of it is a sandstone containing a variable quantity of calcareous matter, but a considerable portion contains a great deal, and is much hardened by the infiltration of agate, which has solidified many of the shells and the wood, and filled the chambers of many of the ammonites. It is to this part of the bed that the author calls attention. If the calcareous grit be dissolved in hydrochloric acid there remains portions of agatised shells and a quantity of sandy matter. When this is examined under the microscope it is found to contain a very large quantity of reniform bodies, which are evidently not sand but some kind of of minute organisms converted into agate. These reniform bodies have a structure similar to that frequently seen in large agates, the deposit having begun from the sides and left a vacancy in the centre, which was afterwards filled up with less pure agate in alternating layers. He counted in a space of 1-280th of a square inch no less than forty of these bodies; therefore, there are on a square inch 11,200, and since they are on an average 1-200th of an inch in diameter, there would be about two and a half million in one cubic inch. These small bodies differ altogether from the minute concretions forming the oolitic rocks, which are composed of alternating concentric layers of more or less impure calcareous matter, round grains of sand or fragments of shell or coral, and Dr. Sorby considered he had every reason for thinking these bodies had been minute shells. They may have been foraminifera, although he had been unable to detect any internal divisions into chambers, or anything to indicate that they are detached foraminifera cells such as are sometimes met with. These small shells have been filled with calcareous or silicious infiltrations, as already described, and in the same manner as the chambers of the larger ammonites which are found in the same rock.

Mr. H. C. Sorby, F.G.S., made a communication on the Oscillation of the Currents drifting the sandstone beds of the south-east of Northumberland, and on their general direction in the coal-field in the neighbourhood of Edinburgh. The author in this paper explained that the peculiarities of structure in sandstones indicate the direction and velocity of the currents which deposited them. Tranquil water deposited "level bedded" sandstones. If, however, the current moves over the surface of the sand at the bottom, with a certain moderate velocity, systems of waves are found on it, trending on an average, perpendicular to the line of the current, in the same manner as when a breeze blows over water. When for a short interval the velocity becomes less, these ripples become permanent, and their layers may be deposited conformably over them, gradually becoming level, having a structure which he called "ripple laminated." The author traced all the forms of bedding in sandstones from these small beginnings to "false bedding," and by observing the direction of these markings and beddings infered the direction in which the current moved, and also its velocity. The strata in the neighbourhood of Newcastle and Edinburgh are described; and it is shown that there was a strong current of considerable velocity northwards from the former place, and that near Edinburgh the coal strata exhibited evidence of currents running north with 4° east.

Mr. Theodore West drew attention to a large number of circular cavities on Appletreewick Moor, running in a line nearly east and west, along or near the edges of the limestone beds. Theories as to their formation are discussed, the one accepted being that they are caused by the rock underneath being removed by running water, and the superincumbent mass of limestone falling in, leaving a circular hollow above.

The annual meeting was held at Leeds in December, the Mayor, Mr. John Hope Shaw, in the chair. The treasurer's accounts were presented, and from them we gather that the principal items of expenditure were the assistant secretary's salary and the rent of Museum Rooms at the Philosophical and Literary Society at Leeds, a small balance remained in the hands of the treasurer. A paper was read by Mr. R. Solly, on Observations on the Manufacture of Iron. The several sources of supply of the raw material were enumerated and considered, and the characters of the iron, principally malleable iron, were enumerated. A second paper was read by Mr. T. J. Pearsall, F.C.S., Consulting Chemist to the North Lincolnshire Agricultural Society, on the chemical preparation of Flax for manufacturing purposes. The paper was an exhaustive one, and described with much detail the growth of flax and its subsequent manufacture.

Only one meeting was held in the year 1853, at Doncaster. Messrs. William Beckett, M.P., John Mc. Londesborough, and Peter Fairbairn were elected members amongst others ; and valuable papers were read by the honorary secretary, Mr. W. Sykes Ward, on a new Thermostat for regulating ventilation ; by Mr. H. C. Sorby, F.G.S., of Sheffield, on the Origin of Slatey Cleavage. After stating that Mr. Fox, of Cornwall, and Professor Hunt found that a laminated structure was produced by passing an electric current through clay, the author explained that a distinct relation had been found to exist between the direction of cleavage and the axis of elevation of a cleaved district ; several observers, chiefly Professors Phillips and Sharpe, had shown that the organic remains found in slate rocks, indicate a considerable change in their dimensions, being compassed in a line perpendicular to the cleavage; and Professor Sharpe strongly advocated the theory of the cleavage being produced by this pressure. Mr. Sorby had been for some time studying the microscopical structure of rocks, and being convinced that cleavage must be due to some peculiarity in the arrangement of the particles, he applied this method of research to slate rocks. Rounded and concretionary grains included in the slate matrix were found to be greatly elongated and distorted, or broken up in such a manner as to indicate that there was a considerable change of dimension; the results are summed up in the following sentence :—" I may state my firm conviction that there is abundance of facts to prove that the slate rocks have undergone a very considerable change of dimensions, to which the cleavage is distinctly related, having been greatly compressed in a line perpendicular to its plane, and elongated in that of its dip." Such a change would necessarily alter the arrangement of their ultimate particles from that which is found in rocks not having cleavage, and hence develope a line of structural weakness in the direction in which it occurs.

The Society at this period does not appear to have been in a very flourishing condition. The honorary secretary resided at a considerable distance from the area of its operations, which naturally rendered it difficult for him to give that careful and ready attention to the details of management which are essential to secure success. Mr. Thorp decided to resign his post, and intimated his intention to Mr. Thomas Wilson. The latter communicated with some of the principal members, and sought their help in placing the Society in a position of greater financial security. The letter following was sent to Mr. T. W. Embleton.

Mr. Wilson to Mr. Embleton.

CRIMBLES HOUSE, LEEDS,

MY DEAR SIR, *26th August, 1854.*

Mr. Thorp wrote to me a few days ago, saying that he had written to Mr. Denny, to resign the office of secretary to the Geological Society. He had previously, some two months since, expressed to me an opinion that the Society could not be carried on. I had therefore previously to, and independently of his resignation, turned my thoughts to the present position of the Society and to the consideration of the question, whether it must be given up or could still be carried on. I own to the greatest disinclination to abandon it without every effort being made to continue it, because I conceive it has already been of great service to the cause of local Geology, and may still contribute to its further investigation, while the Polytechnic branch of its operations has been but partially worked and is capable of indefinite extension. I have naturally consulted Mr. Sykes Ward, as the only one in Leeds who has taken an active share in our proceedings, and we have both come to the conclusion that the Society may be carried on, and that the proper course to be pursued is to call together those who have taken an active part in the working of the Society, to decide what is to be done. Of course we shall be prepared to state our views, and others, we hope will be ready with their suggestions for the future working of the Society. We have fixed the meeting for half-past one on Tuesday, the 5th September, at the Philosophical Hall here, and we hope you will be able to attend.

I am, my dear Sir, yours sincerely,

THOMAS WILSON.

The Council Meeting was held on the 5th September, 1854, and the resignation of Rev. W. Thorp was read. It was decided that Mr. W. Sykes Ward should be requested to accept the Honorary Secretaryship, and that there should be a strong endeavour made to increase the number of members of the Society. The Council again met prior to the annual meeting held on the 11th October, and several suggestions were discussed as to the future management and conduct of the Society. Local Secretaries were to be appointed in the large towns, whose duty it should be to collect subscriptions and take charge of their immediate districts. It was suggested that the subscription should be lowered so as to induce the foremen and others connected with mining operations to join the Society. There was, however, a difference of opinion, and no decision was reached.

There was one meeting in 1854, held at Halifax, Mr. John Waterhouse, F.R.S., presided. A letter was read from the Rev. W. Thorp, the Honorary Secretary, tendering his resignation of the office; much regret was expressed, and as a record of the indebtedness of the Society to his many valuable papers, and in consideration of his past labours the following resolution was passed :—" That the warmest thanks of this Society be presented to Mr. Thorp for his services, and especially for his valuable contributions, from the foundation of the Society, on local geology, which have contributed more than those of any other person to a knowledge of this important coal-field."

Mr. William Sykes Ward was elected Honorary Secretary in the place of the Rev. Wm. Thorp. Mr. Embleton and Mr. Marshall remained the curators of the museum. Five local Secretaries and Treasurers were re-appointed, they were :—For Halifax, Dr. Alexander ; Wakefield, Henry Briggs ; Sheffield, H. C. Sorby ; Doncaster, R. D. Baxter ; and Huddersfield, Thos. Pitt. The balance sheet showed a considerable deficiency, and the question was again discussed as to the propriety of lowering the subscription so as to induce a larger number of persons employed in mining operations, &c., to join the Society. But, as at the meeting of the Council, no decision was arrived at. Papers were read by Mr. E. H. Durden on the application of Peat and its Products ; by H. J. Traice on Williamson's improved system of Colliery Ventilation.

During 1855 the Society exhibited greater vitality and three meetings were held, and several important communications were presented to the Society. Dr. Sorby, of Sheffield, read a paper on the motions of waves as illustrating the structure and formation of Stratified Rocks, in which he adduces evidence in support of the theory of "current structures" in rocks of the several geological formations, which the author formulated at a previous meeting of the Society. The action of the waves on the seashore afforded information as to the direction of the open sea, from which tide waves proceed ; line of coasts and portion of sandbanks ; comparative depth of the water and other matter extremely valuable in ascertaining the circumstances under which any particular formation was accumulated.

Mr. E. W. Brayley, F.R.S., of London, spoke on the essential conditions of the Metamorphoses of Rocks, and Mr. Robert Hunt, F.R.S., read a communication on the structural character of Rock, and of mineral deposits as affected by electricity. In the latter paper some interesting experiments are described which illustrate the formation of metallic veins by means of an electric current continuous for a considerable period. Mr. E. H. Durden, of Leeds, read a paper on new materials for the manufacture of paper, and cites straw, peat, wood, and other substances as being extensively used for the purpose.

The Rev. William Thorp brought before the Society a paper on the Ironstones in the Oolitic district of Yorkshire, in which he compared the extent and yield per acre of the West Riding Ironstones with those of Middlesborough and Eskdale. The Low Moor beds yield 1,000 tons per acre, whilst those of Eskdale yield 24,000, and the percentage of iron in the latter is forty-five per cent., while that of the former is thirty-three per cent. The question of the extent of the ironstone in the Liassic rocks is discussed, and the author is convinced that it is of local extent and dies out southwards, though it may re-appear in Northamptonshire.

Mr. James Nasmyth, C.E., of Patricroft, near Manchester, contributed a paper explaining a new System of Puddling Iron by Steam.

The annual meeting held in December, 1855, at the Museum, Leeds, was thinly attended; Henry Briggs, of Outwood Hall, occupied the chair. The retiring officers were re-elected. The balance sheet exhibited much indebtedness, the principal items being, the assistant secretary's salary for a year and a half, a half-year's rent of museum, and Messrs Baines' account for printing, a total of about £120. Papers were read by Mr. R. Carter, C.E., of Halifax, and by Mr. W. Fisher; the former giving his observations on a new boring machine for artesian wells and other purposes; and the latter on a subject that does not appear to have been greatly in harmony with the original objects of the founders of the Society, the subject was the supply of shells, horns, bones, and woods used in the cutlery trades of Sheffield.

At the next meeting, held at Sheffield in July, 1856, the only one during that year, Mr. H. C. Sorby, F.G.S., read a paper on the Origin of the Cleveland Hill Ironstone. If the Ironstone worked at Eston and other places be examined it will be found to contain more or less entire portions of shells, some of their original composition, consisting of Carbonate of lime, others with the Carbonate of Lime replaced by Carbonate of Iron. The microscopical examination of sections of the stone shows clearly that the minute fragments of the shell have been altered in this way, the replacing Carbonate of Iron extending as yellowish obtuse rhombic crystals from the outside to a variable distance inwards, often leaving the centre in its original condition, as clear, colourless Carbonate of Lime, though in many instances the whole is changed; the oolitic grains also appear to have been changed after deposition. The conclusion drawn by the author is that the Oolitic Ironstone was originally Limestone, "interstratified with ordinary clays containing a large amount of the oxides of iron, and also organic matter, which by their mutual reaction, gave rise to a solution of bi-carbonate of iron, that this solution percolated through the limestone, and removing a large part of the Carbonate of Lime by solution, left in its place Carbonate of Iron; and not that the rock was formed as a simple deposit at the bottom of the sea."

Mr. W. Baker, of Sheffield, read a paper on the Purification of Lead by Crystallization.

The next Annual Meeting was held in the Philosophical Hall, Leeds, on January 22nd, 1857, and Mr. John Hope Shaw presided. Earl Fitzwilliam was re-elected President; and Mr. W. Sykes Ward, Honorary Secretary; Messrs. T. W. Embleton and J. G. Marshall, Honorary Curators; and Messrs. Wm. Alexander, M.D., Halifax, Hy. Briggs, Wakefield, H. C. Sorby, Sheffield, and R. D. Baxter, Doncaster, were re-appointed local Treasurers and Secretaries. The financial statement was of a more satisfactory character than the one presented in December 1885, but still left the Society with an indebtedness of more than £50.

The Rev. John Kendrick made some remarks on a hoard of Roman coins, numbering between 1200 and 1300, which had been discovered in an earthen vessel near Warter, in the East Riding, and presented by Lord Londesborough to the museums at York and Leeds. The Rev. D. H. Haigh, of Erdington, contributed an erudite paper on the crosses discovered at Leeds in 1838, with references for comparison with other crosses in the West Riding, and Mr. R. D. Chantrell, architect of London, gave a short paper on the same subject. Mr. Hy. Denny read a paper on the skull of a dog exhumed from the alluvial gravel of Norwich, in 1851. It was found associated with the bones of deer and other animals.

At a subsequent meeting Mr. Thos. Wright, M.A., F.S.A., described some ancient Barrows or Tumuli which had been recently opened in a field near Bridlington by Mr. E. Tindall, and others in land belonging to Yarborough Lloyd, Esq., which resulted in the discovery of bronze fibulæ which Mr. Wright said were undoubtedly Roman. One of the tumuli was nearly forty yards in circumference; it was penetrated from the surface in the centre, and beneath a quantity of boulder or cobble stones there were found five rows of horizontal stones radiating from a centre; at the extremity of two of these an urn was found. The urns were found in hollows of the chalk made for their reception, and above them was extended a slab of stone; they contained a pasty matter, some pieces of leather, and a quantity of hair. An attempt was made, under the direction of Lord Londesborough, to open the Willey-How, a mile from Wold Newton, but after making a considerable trench it was abandoned.

Mr. H. C. Sorby, F.R.S., read a paper on the so-called crag deposit at Bridlington, and the miscroscopic fossils occurring in it. The beds were near the base of the cliff, a quarter of a mile north of the pier. By washing the sandy clay in a fine sieve many foraminifera and entomostraca were easily picked out of the washed sand with a camel's hair brush. The specimens obtained were submitted to Mr. T. Rupert Jones, and he enumerated the following species:— Dentalium communis, Lagena striata, Polymorphina lactea. Quinqueloculina seminulum, Robulina calcar, Truncatulina tuberculata, and also undetermined species of Biloculina, Guttulina, Nonionina, and Triloculina. The entomostraca belonged to two species, Cytheridea Sorbyana and C. concinna, neither of which had been previously known, either living or fossil. This list of fossils is interesting for comparison with the list prepared by the late Dr. Gwyn Jefferies, from specimens collected by Mr. Lamplugh.

A valuable paper was contributed by Mr. Richard Carter, C.E., of Barnsley, on Colliery Ventilation, in which a broad view is taken of the duties of Coal-pit proprietors, in securing for their operatives not only a sufficient supply of fresh air for respiration, but also for the removal of gases given out by the coal and other strata in the mine, which, if not removed, are by their presence and accumulation ever surrounding the entire operations with danger and death. Methods of ventilation are advocated by means of separate air shafts and other arrangements which have since come very generally into operation.

Mr. Thomas Lister, of Barnsley, gave a sketch of that town, including its mineral and manufacturing products, and natural history.

In the district there were fourteen workable beds of coal. The Barnsley Nine Feet Seam was worked at twenty-four pits, and the Silkstone Coal at twelve pits. The greater part of the paper is taken up with an enumeration of the birds found in the neighbourhood, those resident being 102, and visitant 81, a total of 183 in number.

At a subsequent meeting at Huddersfield, on November 5th, 1857, a paper was read from Mr. W. H. Bartholomew, C.E., on improvement in pressure gauges adapted for indicating the pressure of steam in boilers. Mr. J. Brackenridge again introduced the subject of the best mode of working and ventilating coal mines.

The annual meeting held at Leeds on January 28th, 1858, met at 12 o'clock at noon. The chair was occupied by Mr. Thomas Wilson, a Vice-president. On opening the proceedings the chairman remarked that "he was sure that those present that day would all join with him in deeply regretting the loss the Society had sustained by the death of their first and only President, Earl Fitzwilliam. That nobleman took an active part in the business of the Society throughout its existence. Not only was he most liberal when the Society applied to him, offering as he did the sum of £500 towards establishing a Museum if it could be carried out, but he attended the meetings and did everything to further the interests of the Society."

The meeting was a small one, and it was proposed that the next one should be held at Leeds, during the visit of the British Association, which was to meet at Leeds that year. It was stated that there would probably be a large gathering of members, and by that means would be brought about something like a revival in the activity and resources of the Society. There is no record however of such a meeting having taken place, and, indeed, it was not until December 8th that the next meeting was held, and it was at Bradford; the statement of receipts and expenditure was read by the honorary secretary, from which it appears that the total income was £96 4s. 0d., which had all been paid away, and liabilities remained amounting to £55.

The honorary secretary read a communication from Dr. Pritchard, of Filey, on the Discovery of Roman Remains on the Cairn Head immediately above the Brigg. The author, in conjunction with Professor Phillips, had excavated a large barrow, which had been exposed in section by the falling away of a portion of the cliff. Five large stones were found set at 12 or 15 feet apart, they were tooled, and on one of them was a representation of a stag and dog or wolf carved on it; numerous bones, fragments of pottery, charred wood, coins and other objects were found; and amongst them the two stones of a hand mill or quern, about 2 feet in diameter. The author surmises that this may have been the site of a Roman fort, of which there was probably a series extending along the coast to prevent invasions by the Saxons.

The Council of the Society was called together on the 12th November, 1858, to consider the appointment of a President to succeed the late Earl Fitzwilliam, and after discussion it was unanimously decided to recommend Lord Goderich for the office, and at the meeting of the Society subsequently held at Bradford, on Wednesday, December 8th, 1858, at noon; the Mayor, Henry Brown, Esq., presided, and he, having welcomed the Society to Bradford, Mr. Thomas Wilson, in complimentary terms, moved that Viscount Goderich, M.P., be elected President of the Society in place of the late Earl Fitzwilliam, to whom he paid an affectionate tribute. The motion was seconded by Mr. H. Briggs, and carried unanimously.

The Rev. Ed. Trollope, M.A., F.S.A., of Leasingham, read a paper on the Alluvial Lands and Submarine Forests of Lincolnshire. The author described the great buried forests on the coast of Lincolnshire embedded in a deposit of peat, beneath which are sands and gravels containing boulders, large yellow water-worn flints, teeth and bones of elephants and various animals. He quotes the description of De la Pryme in his paper on Hatfield Chase (Phil. Trans. No. 275, p. 980), in which he describes "infinite millions of the roots and bodies of trees, great and little, of most part of the sorts that this island either formerly did, or at present does produce, as firs, oaks, birch, beech, yew, winthorn, willow, ash, &c., the roots of all or most of which stand in the soil in their natural postures, as thick as ever they could grow, as the bodies of most of them lie by their proper roots" De la Pryme describes an oak which was fourteen yards (?) in diameter and forty yards long. The full length of the tree is calculated at 70 yards. The author cites a tree found in 1858 sixty feet long to the collar, from whence sprang two large limbs each large enough for a separate tree ; its diameter was four feet. The reason for the disappearance of these huge forests is considered and attributed to one of three causes, viz : 1st, the interference of the Romans with the natural drainage ; 2nd, a change in the coastal line through the action of the sea ; 3rd, the agency of earthquakes, causing subsidence of the earth. Of these the author is in favour of the latter, and adduces examples in other countries where earthquakes have affected the level of the land ; he also instanced the recorded earthquakes which have occurred in eastern England. In 1048 there was a serious convulsion in Lincolnshire and again in 1117, the latter extending across to Holland. In 1185 Lincoln was much injured by an earthquake, and in 1448 a violent shock was felt in the southern parts of the county. In 1750 a shock occurred throughout Lincolnshire and Northamptonshire, attended by a rumbling noise, chimneys fell, houses tottered, and plates fell from shelves ; and in 1792 Bourne and the neighbouring towns experienced another shock of earthquake. To these phenomena it is considered possible that the land may not only have been submerged but also re-elevated, and as trees cannot flourish whose roots are constantly submerged, the trunks would decay and be blown down by the wind, the prevailing direction of which was from the S.W., the trunks extending towards the north-east.

Mr. T. Wilson referred to a British Bronze Dagger found in excavating at Altofts, near Wakefield, at a depth of twenty-four feet, and Mr. Stephen Eddy, of Skipton, read a paper on the Lead Mining Districts of Yorkshire ; and a paper was read by Mr. Samuel Baines, of Lightcliffe, on the Yorkshire Flagstones and their Fossils.

In March, 1859, Dr. Sorby read a paper on the Structure and Origin of the Millstone Grit in South Yorkshire. He described the constitution of the millstone grits as consisting of grains or pebbles of quartz, cemented together, in some instances, by decomposed felspar, but occasionally actual crystals of felspar were found. This leads to the inference that the sandstones are the result of the decomposition of an older rock which contained these ingredients in large proportions, and the author is of opinion that that rock had been derived from the disintegration of coarse-grained granites. This opinion receives some proof from the fact that he had found a few pebbles of undoubted granite, which are composed of quartz and felspar similar to the grit rocks. Besides the felspar there also occur pebbles of a fine-grained felspathic rock with a few laminæ of mica, and rarer instances of white or brownish orthoclase felspar. The question then arises as to where the land would be situated from which this waste granite was obtained. Mr. Sorby, in a paper read at a previous meeting, had shown that the current which drifted the materials into the present resting-place came from the north-east, and therefore he was led to expect that the ancient land which furnished them lay in the same direction, and the nearest locality at present known from which they could have been derived is situated in Norway or Sweden, unless some south-westward prolongation of that country existed whose disintegration and removal has now given place to the North Sea.

During the decade now under consideration, a large amount of attention was given to the ventilation of mines, and the circumstances attending colliery explosions. Government Inspectors had been appointed, who regularly subjected the mines to inspection, and it was hoped that their influence and recommendations would diminish the frequency and extent of disasters arising from the explosion of fire-damp in mines. Notwithstanding this, some very alarming explosions had occurred during the past few years, and had been the subject of investigation by men of acknowledged eminence in the scientific world. The Oaks Colliery, at Barnsley, which has been previously mentioned, was reported upon by Sir Henry de la Beche and Mr. Warrington W. Smythe, who had previously reported upon an explosion at Risca, in Monmouthshire; Dr. Faraday and Sir Charles Lyell had presented a report on the explosion at Haswell, in Durham, in 1844; and Dr. Playfair on the one at Jarrow. These reports provided subject matter for much discussion on important facts respecting fire damp, choke damp, atmospheric air, combustion, and other agents related to these frightful accidents. Mr. William West, F.R.S., in 1850, gave a report of the circumstances attending explosions. Perhaps one of the most astonishing pieces of evidence adduced was that of Mr. Green, at Risca, who stated that he had many times seen colliers with the safety lamp hung up by them burning, and they working with the naked candle, also burning, close to each other. There appears to have been considerable evidence that the men objected to the use of the safety lamp, partly from the dim light afforded by it, and partly, as in the case of Upton and Roberts' lamp, on account of its weight. The following year, Mr. W. Sykes Ward contributed a paper on the use of the barometer in coal mines, and explained a cheap form of instrument which he had invented for use in the mine, whereby the miner would be able to appreciate the differences in the weight of the atmosphere as indicated by the barometer, which had so much to do with the escape of gas in mines. Mr. James Nasmyth, of Patricroft, read a paper in which he described a steam fan for the better ventilation of mines, which he stated was used in several pits, and was found to produce a better ventilation than the ordinary method of fire at the base of the up-shaft. At the same meeting, Mr. B. Byram described a fan erected for the ventilation of the Hemmingfield Pit, belonging to Earl Fitzwilliam at Elsecar. Earl Fitzwilliam, who presided, stated that there were difficulties in regulating the velocity of the air, which was made to pass through the mine by the fan, but he considered that in case of accident, and the ventilation becoming suspended, the fan was calculated to be of great advantage, as considerable time might elapse before the furnaces could be got into operation. In April, 1852, Dr. George Boddington, of Sutton Coldfield, contributed a paper on the subject of ventilation, his plan being founded on the arterial and venus circulation in the human body, which suggested to his mind a natural mechanism for moving and circulating the atmosphere or gases in a pit. Mr. W. Sykes Ward read a paper on a new thermostat for regulating ventilation, and Mr. W. H. J. Trace explained the principle of Williamson's improved system of colliery ventilation. The practicability of carrying out the views of either was very much doubted by the meeting.

In February, 1857, the great explosion occurred at Lund Hill, by which nearly two hundred people were destroyed. In the following July, Mr. Richard Carter, of Halifax, read a paper to the Society on Colliery Ventilation. He traced the working of collieries through three phases. Half a century previously colliery workings were carried on at comparatively shallow depths, and most of the large establishments, such as Low Moor, Bowling, and Elsecar, had been planted in localities where valuable mineral seams had come to the surface, or lay at a moderate depth only below it. For a long period their operations of acquiring supplies of coal and iron were, therefore, carried on with far less risk and difficulty than they had now to contend with. Soon, however, the invention of the steam engine, and the great quantities of coal required for the manufacturers, led to a bolder system of penetrating the seams by means of shafts traversing the mineral stratum to a greater or less distance; and the necessities of ventilation had ended in something like the scheme of in-take distribution and up-cast, which we find in general operation at the present day; but the proprietor hesitated at the expense of an additional shaft for the purpose of ventilation, and made in its place a shaft by tubbing or bratticing off a portion of the existing shaft, and thus performing all the operations of drawing the coal, taking in air for ventilating the works, and discharging the air after doing so within the area of one small aperture or shaft which, in all probability, was in its dimensions scarcely adequate for any one of the purposes separately. Latterly, the pits have had a second shaft provided for the return of air after ventilating the mine; but there was still a lamentable ignorance on the part of both proprietors and men of the scientific principles which should be applied in obtaining ventilation, and in working the coal. The object of Mr. Carter's paper was to suggest a scientific method of getting rid of the accumulations of gas which always occur with greater or less frequency in the mine, and the plan he suggested was that the gas which is much lighter than atmospheric air and always ascends to the roof of the pit, should be allowed to make an exit at the highest point in the working which appeared to be in the direction it would naturally take, rather than that it should be drawn by a current of air to the up-cast shaft, which was usually placed at the lowest part of the pit. The currents of air having thus swept through the working parts of the mine would collect all the fire-damp in the lateral cavities or goafs, along with any accumulations that might be near the roof of the mine, and carry them to the discharge shaft on the most elevated side of the workings. He considered the extra outlay necessary to provide this up-cast shaft would be compensated by the fewer passages necessary to trap and split up the air so as to ventilate the whole of the mine. On the conclusion of Mr. Carter's paper, Mr. E. W. Binney, F.R.S., of Manchester, contributed a paper on the mixed use of Davy lamps and naked lights in coal mines. He stated that it was a common practice for lamps to be used on the opening of a seam of coal in driving fast places, and where pillars had been robbed or worked back whilst naked lights are in use over the greater part of the mine. The ignorance of the pitmen of the knowledge of fire damp appeared to be of a most alarming character. As an instance of this, he stated that it was the practice of clever practical men to try a place for gas by a naked candle, and as the flame tapered up, cut it off with their hands. Although some men, doubtless, were very clever in escaping being burnt in doing this, their skill must be considered as that of thoroughly reckless men.

Mr. J. Brackenridge, at the next meeting of the Society, contributed his observations on the best mode of working and ventilating mines. He had intended to read it at the previous meeting, but was unable to be present. His principle was very similar to that of Mr. Carter, but he gave rather better definition to his views. He considered that in opening every new mine a way should be driven from the pits' mouth to the furthest and highest extremity intended to be worked, and that there the up-cast shaft should be placed. From that point the actual working of the coal should commence, and should be worked back until the whole of the seam was got. Mr. Brackenridge was convinced that a mine worked on these principles would lead to a saving of the expenses to the coal proprietors, and he had entire confidence that those heart-rending scenes of destruction of property and of lives which they had recently had so much cause to lament would in a great degree be averted. At the conclusion of the paper Mr. Carter stated that he quite agreed with the principle enunciated by Mr. Brackenridge, and was astonished that their two schemes should be almost identical. Mr. Henry Briggs was afraid that Mr. Brackenridge had not made any provision for throws or fractures of the stratum. He thought the suggestion of carrying off the gas to the rise a very excellent one ; still, there were practical difficulties regarding its escape. In his (Mr. Briggs') colliery they found the straight works a very great expense, but they were necessary for the safety and comfort of the men, and therefore expense was a secondary consideration. No doubt the best ventilation was that of the cupola fire, but there was the danger attending it that the men would allow the fire to go down and thus stop the ventilation. There was also considerable difficulty in the propping of various kinds of roofs. In one, as soon as the props were taken away, the roof fell nearest to the working surface ; but in another instance the roof was so hard a rock that they could work seventy yards square without a prop. The roof was a most dangerous cause ; when it did come it brought with it an immense quantity of gas, which was liable to rush upon the men. That was the kind of goaf which required ventilation ; whereas, when the roof fell close, ventilation was unnecessary. There was danger in the continuous working of a mine, because when, as at Lund Hill, a mine was worked night and day, the trap doors were being continually opened, the current of air was as constantly baffled, and the air of the mine became in an impure state. Let that go on long enough and an explosion was inevitable. Beyond doubt the principle of Mr. Brackenridge was the best, of commencing at the far end, in the first instance, and working towards the drawing shaft, because the men were leaving the old workings behind them ; when they were escaping from an explosion there was a clean road for them to run, devoid of old workings. By the old system of working from the down-cast shaft, where one man was burnt by an explosion, twenty to thirty were smothered by the choke damp. In his Whitwood mine, worked upon the principle advocated by Mr. Brackenridge, they had had no miners smothered, and only two or three killed. Mr. Jebson objected to the plan on account of the difficulty of applying it to such large estates as were sometimes worked in the neighbourhood of Barnsley, which often covered an area of 1,000 to 1,500 acres. If they started at the engine pit and pushed their working to the up-cast before they fairly began to get the coal, they would be very expeditious to complete the preliminary work in two years and a half. That was precisely the most dangerous period of a mine, because of the difficulty of expelling the foul air before they had got their straight work completed. After some further observations from Mr. Brooke, Mr. Sykes Ward, and Mr. Carter, Mr. Brackenridge replied that by the mode he recommended there could be no danger in the lower part of the mine, as there would be no old workings in which gas would be generated, and that the quantities given off in making the shaft would be so small that they could be easily dealt with.

Mr. F. H. Pearce, of Bowling, gave the result of some experiments in the ventilation of a pit one hundred and twenty yards deep, of which he had charge. On account of some defect in the pumps water had accumulated in the mine and ascended some distance up the shaft, thus completely stopping the ventilation, and rendering any effort to repair the damage hopeless from the accumulation of choke-damp. He contrived to pass a small steam pipe to the bottom of the seven-inch pipe used for lifting the water, and on turning on the steam the air was drawn from the shaft and purified in an almost extrordinary manner. At the same meeting Mr. J. Jebson, of Mold Green, near Huddersfield, also read a paper on the ventilation of mines, in which he contended for the old system of working and ventilation possessing greater practical advantage than would be likely to accrue from the adoption of the plan suggested by Messrs. Carter and Brackenridge.

Mr. Robert Hunt, F.R.S., Keeper of the Mining Records, con-contributed a paper on the statistical returns of the mineral produce of Yorkshire for the year 1857. The production of lead ore amounted to 12,045 tons, from which 7,875 tons of lead had been obtained. Of the latter amount, Cononley contributed 388 tons, and the mines in the valley of the Wharfe 1,336 tons. The largest amount, however, was obtained from Swaledale and Wensleydale, which contributed 5,365 tons. The iron ore of Yorkshire is the most metalliferous deposit obtained. In the North Riding, in the Eston and Sutton districts, 1,414,155 tons were brought to the surface, as against 1,197,417 tons in 1856. Of the argillaceous iron ores of the West Riding it has not been possible to obtain an equally reliable return to the above. The total quantity of clay iron ore raised in the West Riding, as far as returns have been obtained, was 247,500 tons. The number of furnaces in the Cleveland district which were in blast in 1857 were 23; in the West Riding there were 25. The cold-blast furnaces of the West Riding appear to have produced 63,000 tons of pig-iron. The total produce of the West Riding is estimated at 117,000, and of the North Riding 179,838 tons; an increase of 21,000 tons on the previous year. The exportation of pig-iron from Middlesborough in 1857 was nearly four times as much as in 1855. In the neighbourhood of Halifax, Todmorden, and Huddersfield, 3,560 tons of iron pyrites were raised, valued at £1,572, for the manufacture of sulphuric acid and copperas. The production of coal from 374 collieries existing in the West Riding was 8,875,440 tons. Of this amount, 41,927 tons were sent to London. In addition to these mineral returns, replies had been obtained from 102 quarries in Yorkshire producing building and paving stones, lime, grindstones, and whetstones. Through these, Professor Hunt had been enabled to estimate the value of the stone raised in Yorkshire during 1857, as being £105,374. The total value of all the minerals raised was £3,462,198.

In October, 1850, a valuable paper was read by Mr. W. L. Simpson, C.E., of Thuruscoe Hall, Doncaster, on the nature, value, and application of fuel. The paper treats on the nature of wood, peat, peat-charcoal and coal, and their value as fuel. The most valuable part of the paper is perhaps that in which he speaks of the products resulting from the destructive distillation of coal, namely: coke, tar, ammonia, the hydro-carbons and carbonic acid. He suggests that the coke is of greater value than the coal itself, and can be used in manufactories without the emission of the dense smoke which was so fatal to the health and comfort of large towns. The volatile combustible substances may at the same time be obtained by an enlarged system of gas manufacture, and extensively employed for the development of domestic heat as well as for illuminating purposes. The application of coal-gas for the production of heat, as well as light, is one which demanded strictest attention. The heating value of gas, he considered, is greater than that of coal, and its application easy and economical. Amongst its advantages are the cheerful brilliancy of its flame, the facility with which the supply can be regulated and the temperature kept uniform, and the absence of smoke and soot. He cites, as an instance, Mr. Appold, the inventor of the centrifugal pump, who, at his residence near London, had erected a small gas manufactory in one of his outbuildings, and used its products for every heating purpose throughout his entire premises. By introducing the gas at a number of small orifices, at the back of grates, he obtained a cheerful and exceedingly warm fire. Among other ingenious experiments he had provided each supply pipe with a throttle valve, so delicately suspended as to be opened or closed by the fall or rise of the thermometer, placed on the stairs leading to his rooms, and so admirably can he regulate the temperature by this means, that it did not vary more than three or four degrees during the whole year. A suggestion might be taken from this for the regulation of the temperature in rooms heated by gas at the present time. The ammonia at that time was discharged into the atmosphere. Mr. Simpson suggested a most simple arrangement by which this important production might be economised, and under the form of sulphate of ammonia form a most valuable commercial article. He referred to an ingenious patent recently taken out by Mr. Crole, of the Tottenham Gasworks, by which he passed the ammonia gas through a weak solution of sulphuric acid; the gas uniting with the acid forms sulphate of ammonia in solution. This is evaporated to dryness, and yields 80 ounces per gallon, the commercial value of which is £13 per ton for the purposes of manure. It is needless to remark on the extent to which this operation is carried out in the gasworks now existing, and it is somewhat remarkable that the value of the sulphate of ammonia was so nearly the same at that day as the price now obtained. His paper concludes with a suggestion that in the manufacture of iron, large quantities of combustible gases are eliminated, as attested by the immense volumes of flames which illuminate the country near large iron manufactories. These gases should be collected and applied to heating and illuminating the various buildings connected with the works. Chevalier Bunsen and Dr. Lyon Playfair clearly demonstrated in a report prepared by them on the gases existing in iron furnaces that one of the largest resources of the country is wasted by the neglect of these important considerations. Mr. Simpson had no hesitation in saying that the expense of fuel to produce steam power for the blast and other mechanical operations might be wholly economised from the application of such combustible gases in the place of it. In manufacturing processes we are too apt to attend solely to the production of one commercial article and to neglect others which necessarily arise during its formation. "But in these days when a vast struggle for superiority in commerce and in agriculture, in manufacture and in science, is shaking all European nations to their foundations, the importance of any, even the smallest bye-product cannot be over-rated, and it should be the object of the manufacturer to discover the whole compounds eliminated, and to apply each to its respective purpose; equalising the expense of the generation of all. I might enlarge on the necessity of every manufacturer possessing such a general education in all sciences and all arts as to enable him to observe what the uneducated and consequently prejudiced man would allow to pass by him every day unnoticed."

Mr. James Nasmyth gave a description of an Improved Safety Valve for Steam Boilers, which would open and allow the steam to escape on a certain pressure being reached without the interference of the engine driver. It consisted of a sphere which fit in a circle in the boiler, to which was attached a direct weight placed inside the boiler, so that the engine man would be unable to tamper with it, there being no machinery exposed outside the boiler. Some time afterwards Mr. W. H. Bartholomew, C.E., engineer to the Aire and Calder Navigation Co., explained an improvement in pressure guages. He stated that the engine drivers frequently tampered with the safety valves, and worked the engines at pressures much higher than they ought, thereby endangering not only the boiler, but the lives of the passengers. To obviate this it was proposed to add to the ordinary working index or pointer of the dial a second index, which could be entirely out of the control of the engineer, and which would remain fixed at the maximum pressure attained by advancing with the movable index but not receding. The second index could only be replaced or regulated by the employer, having a key for that purpose. Mr. Nasmyth also read a communication on a new system of puddling iron by steam. The difference between cast iron and malleable or wrought iron is chiefly due to the presence in the former of a considerable quantity of carbon in combination with the iron. To convert cast iron into malleable iron it is requisite that this carbon should be removed. This object is attained by what is termed puddling, a process which Mr. Nasmyth explained with some detail. The improvement he suggested consisted in employing a combined mechanical and chemical action of steam, which is driven beneath the surface of the molten cast iron, and not only throws the metal into violent agitation, but by the intimate contact of the steam with the molten iron the former is decomposed, and the liberated oxygen combines with the carbon and passes off in the form of carbonic acid and carbonic oxide gases, whilst the hydrogen combines with carbon to form carburetted hydrogen, and also with any sulphur which may be present and forms sulphuretted hydrogen. The time necessary to complete this operation is only four or five minutes, and the resulting malleable iron is of first-rate quality.

Mr. Richard Solly, of Sheffield, also contributed a paper, recording some Observations on the Manufacture of Iron, in which he enumerated the principal sources of iron in Great Britain, their comparative values, and the purposes for which they are best adapted. He described the principal processes in the manufacture of iron, and indicated the several qualities resulting from different methods in manipulation.

Mr. Robert Hunt, F.R.S., of London, communicated the result of some experiments which he had made to illustrate the structural characters of rock and of mineral deposits as effected by electricity. Between a zinc and copper plate, properly connected in a vessel prepared for that purpose, a mass of clay in a condition of thin mud was subjected to an electric current. After some weeks the mass of clay was dried, and was found to be indurated in a remarkable manner on one side of the plate, whilst on the other it was laminated, the clay breaking off in thin shales; the depth to which this lamination extended being determined by the length of time the clay was under Voltaic influence. The hardening on the other side was found to be due to the formation of small concretions arranging themselves along tolerably well defined curved lines. Results of this kind appear to show that electricity exerts some powerful influence on the particles of matter grouping themselves in the crystalline rocks, and that concretionary nodules, such as are not unfrequently found in limestone or laminated stone, may be the result of position in regard to the line along which the force of the current of electricity may be acting. In connection with the mineral deposits, all the productive copper mines of Cornwall are found at the juncture of granite and clay-slate, with a main direction from north-east to the south-west. The lead lodes of Yorkshire and the North of England indicate a set of rock conditions of a similar order. At Alston Moor, which Mr. Hunt had recently examined, he found that the lead occurred in different layers of silicious sandstones, limestones, and clays, and that the amount of lead depended to a large extent on the rock through which the vein passes. In the silicious rock the vein is small, and contains but little lead ore; in the argillaceous there is frequently none; but in the limestones it occurs in great abundance. The electricity developed by mineral veins had been investigated by Mr. Fox, Mr. Henwood, Mr. J. A. Phillips, and Mr. Hunt, and they found by connecting two parts of a lode by copper wires to a galvanometer the needle was powerfully deflected, and in some cases it swung round with extraordinary violence. This the author concluded was due to electrical changes going on within the lode itself. That electricity has considerable influence on the formation of mineral lodes, he demonstrated by an experiment which he described; a quantity of clay, in the condition of thin cream, was mixed with a solution of sulphate of copper, and placed between a properly adjusted voltaic pair, which were kept in a state of excitement for more than a year; the water was then evaporated and the mass hardened, and in addition to the lamination and induration already described, there was found a miniature mineral lode formed of the carbonate of copper, interspersed with red oxide and occasionally beautiful particles of native copper. Mr. Hunt concluded by observing that he thought there existed a force beyond that of electricity, which they did not comprehend; but that in such general terms as molecular and catalytic forces there was expressed a set of phenomena which belong to a physical force differing materially from any of those with which science has hitherto made us acquainted. At the same meeting, Mr. E. W. Brayley, F.R.S., of London, delivered a lecture on the essential conditions of the metamorphosis of rocks. It is only printed in brief abstract.

During the same year, Mr. William Baker, of Sheffield, read a paper explaining the process for the purification of lead by crystallization, in which he showed that copper may be separated from lead by the process introduced by Mr. H. L. Pattinson in 1833, for the purpose of obtaining silver from lead ore. At a meeting in Bradford, in 1858, a paper on the lead mining districts of Yorkshire, was read by Mr. Stephen Eddy, of Carlton Grange, Skipton. In the metalliferous portion of the carboniferous rocks, lead occurs in rake veins, pipe or tube veins, and flat veins. The rake vein consists of a rent or fissure of great length, and often unknown depth. The pipe vein, generally occurring in limestone, is an irregular cylindrical tube, which passes more or less diagonally through the strata, whilst the flat vein is seldom met with except in connection with a rake vein, and has always a position conformable to the stratum in which it occurs. Rake veins are the most common, they vary greatly in width, from a foot or two, to as many yards, and then contracting to a mere point. They are generally most expanded in limestone or gritstone, and often scarcely perceptible in shale. The vertical extent of fault or throw most favourable to mining is from 6 to 18 feet, the faults vary greatly in direction. The Old Gang vein in Swaledale has been worked for many miles in length, and can be traced to a much greater distance in a nearly straight line. The lead veins in Swaledale, Arkendale, and Wensleydale, are generally more irregular in size, and the beds of a more uniform thickness than in the three southern districts, Airedale, Wharfedale, and Nidderdale. In the former the lead occurs principally in the limestone beds, whilst in the latter the principal deposits are in gritstone. In the southern area the veins generally run from north-west to south-east, whilst in the northern districts they are north-east to south-west. The Grassington mines yield about two-thirds of the products from the southern fields. The operation is of a very uncertain and speculative character; the best lodes have often great lengths of unproductive ground.

Two elaborate and philosophical papers were communicated during the early portion of the decade by Mr. W. Sykes Ward, of Leeds, the first on improvements in the galvanometer and on the comparative economy of various voltaic arrangements, and the second on some phenomena of dyo-magnetism, with experiments. Mr. Christopher L. Dresser, of Leeds, explained a new and cheap voltaic battery for the production of the electric light. In retorts used for the distillation of coal in the manufacture of gas for illumination, there is deposited a carbonaceous matter, lining the whole with a coating varying in thickness from that of writing paper to several inches. The deposit consists either of minute scales, like a section of a hollow sphere, or thin layers; the scales are deposited on each other until the whole assumes a mammilar appearance, and consists of nearly pure carbon. It will bear the most violent heat with very little waste, and can be obtained at comparatively trifling cost. If cut into sticks about seven inches long, and an inch and an eighth in diameter, they may be used in batteries in place of platinum of equal size, and the resulting electricity appears to be in every way similar and equal in quantity. Mr. Dresser had illuminated his garden and a large field with a battery of 90 plates. The difference in cost between the carbon and platinum negatives would be as £4 is to £60. In a discussion which followed, Mr. Pierceall alluded to the great advantage it would be if lighthouses were illuminated by electricity. Mr. Ward also commended this application, and speaking of electricity for use for ordinary purposes in the place of gas, he showed the fallacy of supposing that this light, however beautiful, would ever supersede ordinary gas for shops or streets.

At a meeting held at Leeds in 1857, Mr. John Hope Shaw presiding, two papers were read on the discovery of some fragments of

Y

ancient crosses at Leeds in 1838, the first by the Rev. Daniel H. Haigh, of Erdington, who, in a long paper, described the principal crosses which occur in the neighbourhood of Leeds. One of the earliest of these was the fragments of a cross found at Dewsbury, which is said to date back to the time of Paulinus, the Roman Missionary. At Collingham, fragments of three or four crosses have been found, probably of about equal antiquity with that of Dewsbury. Others are mentioned at Wycliffe, at Greta Bridge, and Hackness, near Scarborough. Crosses which have been discovered at Rastrick and on Hartshead Moor, near Halifax, are also described. The immediate subject of the paper was the description of six or seven fragments of crosses which had been obtained during a restoration of the Leeds Parish Church, which are attributed to the middle part of the tenth century, and appear to indicate the existence in those times of a considerable religious establishment on the site of this church, which the author, in a learned disquisition, attempts to prove from some historical manuscripts. The second paper is by the architect who had charge of the restoration of the church, Mr. R. D. Chantrell, who, whilst the works were in progress, gave instructions that any carved stones that were found should be brought to him, and the fragments of crosses already mentioned were removed to his residence in London. A description of the crosses follows.

The decade which closed with the year 1858, and the printed proceedings of which form volume V, is principally remarkable for the large space occupied by the consideration of mining operations, and the methods then in vogue for the protection and safety of the miner. General and profound sympathy had been generated by the frightful accidents which had occurred in various parts of the country, and any project which would afford greater security to those engaged in the pits, received eager and most painstaking consideration. That much benefit accrued from the discussion of the subject is shown by repeated evidence of the practical application in the mines of the scientific truths evolved during discussion. The evidence given before the Government Commissioners appointed to enquire the cause of accidents led to beneficial legislation, and produced in the minds of the miners a less reckless disregard of the elementary rules for their own protection and safety.

283

CHAPTER XIII.

GLACIAL THEORIES : CAVE EXPLORATIONS AND ANTIQUITY OF MAN.

Sixteen years previous to the formation of this Society, a cave had been discovered in Kirkdale, three or four miles east of Helmsley, The entrance to the cave was in a large quarry of Oolitic Limestone, and this had been quarried back thirty feet before the present entrance was reached. The entrance was about three feet high and five feet broad ; the cave expands and contracts irregularly in width from two to seven feet, and two to fourteen feet in height, diminishing as it recedes to the interior of the hill. It is twenty feet below the surface, and its course is intersected by vertical fissures. It was not till the summer of 1821 that the existence of animal remains in this cave was suspected. The workmen accidentally discovered amongst the sand and clay, which almost fill the entrance, some fragments of bone. The bottom of the cave, to the average depth of about a foot, was filled with argillaceous and micaceous loam, occasionally interspersed with lenticular beds of sand. Above the mud was a coating of stalactite. The workmen supposed the bones which they found to have belonged to cattle, which had by some means got into the cave from above. They were afterwards noticed by Mr. Harrison, of Kirby Moorside, who collected a large number of them, which were dispersed amongst individuals and afterwards lost. Some of the specimens came into the possession of the Bishop of Oxford, who pre sented a large series to the Museum at Oxford, and Dr. Buckland thus received his first information of the existence of the cave. In its whole extent only a very few large bones have been discovered in even a tolerably perfect condition. Most of them were broken into small angular fragments and chips, which were laid separately in the mud or were invested in the stalagmite, the latter projecting "like the legs of pigeons through a pie-crust into the void space above, have become thinly covered with stalagmite droppings, whilst their lower extremities have no such encrustation, and have simply the mud adhering to them in which they have been embedded." Dr Buckland enumerates eighteen species of animals found in the cave, namely, hyæna, bear, wolf, fox, tiger, weasel, elephant, hippopotamus, rhinoceras, horse, ox, three species of deer, hare, rabbit, water-rat, and mouse. There were also several species of birds. On removing the mud, the floor of the cave was found strewn with the great quantities of teeth and bones, the latter in all instances broken into small fragments. On some of the bones marks may be traced which, on applying one to the other, fit exactly to the canine teeth of the hyæna ; the hyæna's bones were also broken. The most common of the bones are those of the deer, hyæna, and rat. There is evidence that the probable number of individual hyænas could not be less than two or three hundreds in the area explored. Many of them were young, and appear to have fallen a prey to the voracity of their elders ; others are the teeth of aged animals, worn down almost level with the jaws. Of the tiger, two large canine and a few molar teeth were discovered, they indicate that the animal was of a size exceeding that of the Bengal tiger. The evidence of the bear rests on a single tusk. About ten elephants' teeth were found, and these were mostly of young animals. The teeth of hippopotamus were rare ; those of the rhinoceras considerably more common ; some of them very large, indicating full-grown animals. Teeth of deer occur in considerable numbers, and those of the water-rat are common. The bones of the remaining portion of the body are in so broken a condition that it is almost impossible to recognise any of them. From a consideration of these facts Dr. Buckland arrived at the conclusion that the cave at Kirkdale had been inhabited for a long succession of years as a den by hyænas ; and that they, after killing their prey, dragged the bodies into the cave to be eaten ; and it is probable that the carcases of the weak or aged animals served as food for those younger and stronger. Dr. Buckland, after describing the cave and its contents, adduced evidence from caves, fissures, and diluvial gravels in other parts of England and Europe, that they all afford additional proofs of the theory of a universal deluge. He considers that the conditions of the country before and after this deluge were very similar, but that the great flood suddenly interrupted the life of the district and swept away the quadrupeds which had previously inhabited it, to which they never afterwards returned, and in this way the animals found in the Kirkdale Cave came to an untimely end. This opinion was shared by most people of that day, and Mr. Greenhough, the President of the Geological Society of London, may be quoted as affording an admirable summary of the phenomena considered to be derived from this diluvial action. "The universal diffusion of alluvial sand, gravel, etc., proves that at some time or other, an inundation has taken place in all countries, and the presence of similar alluvial deposits, both organic and inorganic, in neighbouring or distant islands, though consisting often of substances foreign to the rocks of which the islands are respectively composed, makes it highly probable at least that these deposits are products of the same inundation. The universal occurrence of mountains and valleys, and the symmetry which pervades their several branches and inosculations, are further proofs not only that the deluge has swept over every part of the globe, but probably the same deluge." Cuvier, in France, who had exhumed immense quantities of animal remains in the Paris Basin, held the same opinion, and few scientific men in those days ventured to differ from it.

Professor Phillips, who wrote a treatise on geology for the *Encyclopædia Brittanica* in the same year as this Society was founded, held some advanced opinions as compared with Dr. Buckland, and a quotation from that work will exhibit the difference made in the public mind during the fifteen years which had elapsed since the publication of *Reliquiæ Diluvianæ* :—" Since the time when the whole stratified crust of the globe was supposed to have subsided from a universal flood of water, the geological effects ascribed to the historical deluge and other violent agitations of water have continually diminished. It is not many years since we were familiar with the doctrine of the excavation of valleys, and the accumulations of detritus over large surfaces of the globe being due to diluvial action,

There are geologists who would gladly expunge the word "diluvial" from our nomenclature, and instead of appealing to one or several general convulsions for the explanation of some striking fact, are willing to believe that small and local forces, operating through long time, are sufficient for the purpose of geological speculation." Mr. Greenough, who has been quoted in confirmation of the views held by Dr. Buckland, declares himself "incapable of distinguishing between the effects of such a deluge or deluges and subsequent phenomena produced by the ordinary agency of running water." The opinion now held with respect to the dispersion of rocks from their original sites to distant situations was that they had been removed, during the submergence of the whole country beneath the sea, by icebergs, and it was considered that the clays of Holderness, containing enclosed masses of granite and syenite brought from Cumberland and Westmoreland ; of porphyritic granite of Shap Fell ; of limestone from the mountain districts of Yorkshire, and many others, were accumulated by this means, and that they passed over the Penine Escarpment at Stainmoor and proceeded down the valleys to their present position. The fact that there are no fragments of these rocks east of the Penine Chain, south of Boulsworth, was accounted for by the range of hills running north and south, and east and west, being so high as to have prevented the glacier passing over.

It was reserved for a Swiss naturalist, M. Louis Agassiz, to dispel the generally accepted but erroneous ideas respecting these accumulations of detritus. Following in the track first indicated by Charpentier, Agassiz in 1836, spent his summer vacation in the valley of the Rhone, and there learnt how the ice of the glaciers carried the masses of rock from the mountains and scattered them over the valley, how the sides of the valley down which the glacier flowed was scoured and grooved by its action, and morainic matter piled high along its slopes, whilst the masses of stone torn by its action from their parent beds were rounded, smoothened, polished and scratched in their transit. From the consideration of the glacial phenomena existing in the Swiss mountains, Agassiz deduced the ancient extension of the glaciers over a much larger area of that country, and his knowledge of the features existing over Europe led him to the conclusion that at one time in the history of the earth the whole northern hemisphere had been enveloped in a great sheet of ice. "The surface of Europe, adorned before by a tropical vegetation, and inhabited by troops of large elephants, enormous hippopotami, and gigantic carnivora, was suddenly buried under a vast mantle of ice, covering alike plains, lakes, seas and plateaus. Upon the life and movement of a powerful creation fell the silence of death. Springs paused, rivers ceased to flow, the rays of the sun, rising upon this frozen shore (if, indeed, it was reached by them), were met only by the breath of the winter from the north, and the thunders of the crevasses as they opened across the surface of this icy sea."*

The views thus expounded by Louis Agassiz were first ridiculed by the geologists all over Europe, and amongst others by Dr. Buckland in England. He was, however, persuaded by Agassiz to visit Switzerland, and speedily became convinced that there was much truth in the theories of his enthusiastic guide. In 1840, Agassiz visited England, to attend the meeting of the British Association at Glasgow. He was convinced that in the Highlands of Scotland, and the mountainous parts of England and Wales, evidence would be found of the truth of his glacial theories. Dr. Buckland volunteered to be his guide in the search for these proofs, and after attending the meeting of the Association they made a tour of the Highlands. At the meeting, Agassiz read a paper on Glacial Phenomena, and the subject was referred to by Sir Roderick Murchison in a letter to Professor Sedgwick descriptive of the meeting. "Agassiz gave us a great field-day on glaciers, and I think we shall end in having a compromise between himself and us of the floating icebergs! I spoke against the general application of his theory."† Agassiz some years after recounted his experience of the meeting, and said, " Among the older naturalists only one stood by me, Dr. Buckland, Dean of Westminster, who had come to Switzerland at my urgent request, for the express purpose of seeing my evidence, and who had been fully convinced of the extension of ice there, consented to accompany me on my glacier hunt in Great Britain. We went first to the Highlands of Scotland, and it

---

* 'Etudies sur les Glaciers, p. 315.
† Life of Sir R. Murchison, by Dr. A. Geikie, 1875, vol. i., p. 307.

is one of the delightful recollections of my life that as we approached the castle of the Duke of Argyll, standing in a valley not unlike some of the Swiss valleys, I said to Buckland, 'Here we shall find our first traces of glaciers'; and as the stage entered the valley we actually drove over an ancient terminal moraine, which spanned the opening of the valley."* Everywhere as he expected, he found proofs of the truth of his glacial theories; and on a subsequent visit to the seat of the Earl of Enniskillen in Ireland, for the purpose of studying the magnificent collection of fossil fishes in the Museum at Florence Court, the same phenomena of lateral and terminal moraines, *roches moutonnées*, polished surfaces and scratches, were observed in that country. It is needless to particularize the progress the glacial theory made. Lyell speedily accepted it, and all the chief geologists came round to the same view. Yorkshire is replete with evidence of glacial action, and the importance of the subject was speedily recognized by this Society, and papers were presented on the subject.

In 1841, at a meeting of this Society, held at Huddersfield, Mr. J. Travis Clay, of Rastrick, read a paper on the Yorkshire Drifts and Gravels, in which he to a large extent accepted the the theory of Professor Phillips. He divided the clays and gravels existing in Yorkshire and Lancashire into three groups; 1st, the unstratified mass of clay, interspersed with boulders and pebbles derived from distant rocks, which covers the Vale of York, and conceals many parts of the regular strata in the east of Yorkshire and also in Lancashire; 2nd, the stratified deposits of sand and gravel which are frequently superimposed upon the first division; and 3rd, the hillocks and terraces of unstratified matter which occur in many of the northern valleys. The first division includes the diluvium of Holderness, and a deposit which Mr. Clay considered precisely similar, covering the whole area of the Vale of York, extending from the Tees and Durham to the boundary of the county. He considered that the large boulders, frequently weighing more than a ton, could not be brought by the agency of water from distant localities, frequently over hills of considerable height; and that, consequently, there must

---

* Louis Agassiz, his life and correspondence, by Eliz. A. Agassiz, 1885, vol. i., p. 307.

have been other agencies, of which he considered the transportation by icebergs to be the most powerful. He further adduced proof of this theory from the occurrence of erratic boulders in the Valley of the Calder in the neighbourhood of Halifax, and considered that it is inconceivable that these boulders could have been brought over the Penine Chain and deposited where they are now found, but that it would be easy, if the land were at a considerably lower elevation than at present, that they should be brought by floating icebergs from the sea and stranded in the narrow inlet which the bed of the river would then form. The superficial gravels and sands which form his second group, he considered afford very strong evidence of the long-continued and comparatively gentle action of water. The third division forming hillocks and terraces of disturbed material, occur in many of the northern valleys, and though they had, until a recent period, escaped attention, he believed that they would furnish a clue by which the difficulties surrounding the question might be unravelled. Referring to the paper recently contributed to the meeting of the British Association at Glasgow, by M. Agassiz, in which he endeavoured to show that a great part of these terraces and deposits have been produced by the action of glaciers, Mr. Clay expressed dissent, and considered that M. Agassiz carried his theory to a most unwarrantable extent when he inferred that great sheets of ice resembling those now existing in Greenland, once covered all the countries in which these unstratified gravels now occur ; but he considered that the evidence was sufficient to prove that towards the close of the Tertiary era the land was at a lower level than at present, and there was a considerable preponderance of water. The mountainous districts of Scotland and the Northern Counties of England were not submerged, but probably covered with perpetual snow, huge glaciers occupying the valleys between, and bringing the spoils derived from the rocky summits down to the sea, which, breaking off as icebergs, floated away bearing the detritus to some distant localities where, by their gradual dissolution, they gave rise to the unstratified masses of clay and boulders. On the re-elevation of the land, the shallower parts would approach the surface, and currents would affect the upper portion of the deposit, stratifying the *débris* and forming layers of sand and gravel. The third division, comprising the hillocks and terraces of unstratified matter, Mr. Clay considered may be true moraines, left by the glaciers as they retreated before the increased temperature attendant upon the gradual elevation of land, and in this way the appearances enumerated may have resulted from the same general cause.

Early in the following year, Mr. Thomas Sopwith, of Newcastle, read a paper before the Society on the evidences of the former existence of glaciers in Great Britain. He traced, in a most forcible manner, the extension of glaciers from the Highlands of Scotland, the Cumbrian mountains, and those of Wales, into every valley near them, and over a much further extent of country than had hitherto been known. He described the action of existing glaciers in Switzerland, the formation of lateral and terminal moraines, instanced the scratching of the surface over which the glacier passed, and the striation of the boulders torn from the rocks in its passage, and gave instances of similar results existing in the North of England, which he attributed to the same cause, and showed the rapid strides which had been made in a short time in the acceptance of the glacial theory.

At the meeting of the Society held in June, 1851, at Sheffield, a paper was read by Mr. H. C. Sorby, on the contorted Stratification of the Drifts of the Coast of Yorkshire. Sir Charles Lyell had communicated a paper to the Geological Society in 1840, on Contorted Stratifications of the Drifts. Since that time a paper had been read by Mr. Trimmer, in which he attempted to explain these phenomena by supposing that masses of ice had been fixed amongst the beds when they were deposited, and that on these subsequently thawing, the strata sunk down into the space they occupied, Lyell's opinion being that they were due to stranded icebergs. Mr. Sorby considered that the contortions were probably due to both these causes, for, in some instances, the contorted strata occupied a very limited area, and the underlying and superimposed strata were laid horizontally above and below. This could only be due to a large mass of ice becoming embedded in the boulder-clays as they were deposited, which subsequently thawed, and the space became filled up with masses of sand

and clay; then the strata deposited above were laid horizontally and evenly above it. In other instances, the sands and clays appear to have been pushed or folded by a lateral force; and these may be due to icebergs borne by the tide and left stranded. Mr. Sorby considers that at this time the chalk wolds were above the sea, and if so, there must have been a kind of bay at Bridlington somewhat similar to the present. He very carefully investigated the directions of the currents in this bay at the period of the drift, as shown by the ripple marks and other evidences, and was led to conclude that a tolerably strong current swept round its shores, and that in the centre it was more tranquil, and had a returning eddy. Comparing the directions of the currents with these contortions, he found that the side on which the pushing force acted in the different parts of the ancient bay agrees with that which would result from the drifting of an iceberg in the line of the current which prevailed. As the contortions are underlaid and surmounted by undisturbed beds, the time when they were formed is fixed within narrow limits. They occur throughout the whole series, and whatever produced them acted during the deposition of every part. If, therefore, it is requisite to consider them to be due to the action of icebergs, it leads to the important theoretical conclusion that they were present during the whole drift period, and not, as has been supposed by some distinguished geologists, merely at its close.

In the following year the Rev. W. Thorp contributed a paper to the proceedings of this Society on the Diluvial and Gravel Beds of Yorkshire and Nottinghamshire, in which he took much the same line of argument as Mr. Clay had done some years previously. The diluvium he stated to consist of an upper and lower deposit, the lower, consisting of clay with boulders scratched underneath, on their long axes, and the upper, of fragments rarely scratched and having much false bedding, indicating rapid currents in water having no great depth. Marine shells, when found, are in a broken state, and lie above the beds containing the bones of mammalia, and the limestone pebbles are in no case perforated by boring lithodomi. In Norfolk the drift reposes upon the forest bed; it also covers up the remains of mammalia at Kirkdale Cave; hence it was deposited over pre-existing dry land, upon which plants were growing and animals dwelling. There are accumulations of this drift in valleys, proving the latter were excavated previously to its deposition. The scratches on the included boulders are ascribed to the action of icebergs or of glaciers; whilst the absence of these scratches in the higher beds indicates the deposit was accumulated under violent aqueous action in shallow water. He agrees with Cumming, Trimmer, and others that at the commencement of the period of the boulder clay formation, the sea and land had the same relative level as at present; that the climate was of an Arctic character, due to a great current originating probably in the North Polar area, together with a modification of the present Gulf Stream; that this was followed by a gradual submergence of the area of the British Isles to an extent in some places of 1,600 feet; that subsequently a gradual emergence of the land took place to the same extent, of which he considers sufficient evidence is afforded by the elevated terraces or extended platform of rolled boulders and gravel, sometimes consisting of re-distributed stones from the boulder clay, in others, of adjacent rocks regularly stratified. During the uprising of the land the severe cold was modified; erratics from distant localities were dropped by the melting of icebergs, while the scratching and grooving action of glaciers in a great measure ceased, and a period ensued which marked the close of the glacial epoch in this country. The gravels extending along the sides of the rivers Aire and Calder were derived from sandstones of the coal district localities in which they occur, intermixed with occasional fragments from the mountain limestone of Craven. This gravel does not extend much north or south of the valleys of the Aire and Calder. Leeds stands upon it, and it occurs on the higher grounds near Rothwell Haigh, at Oulton, and Ferrybridge. He considered that these masses of material were derived from the strata of the district by the waters which were driven eastward during the time of emergence, and down the lines of valleys which then formed the easiest retreat for the retiring waters. The gravels noticed by Mr. Thorp are at a much higher level, and must not be confounded with those previously described by Mr. Clay. which occupy only the bottom of the valley, and contain many boulders which have not been derived from the adjacent strata.

About this time the attention of Mr. Denny was called to the occurrence of some very large bones in a brickfield at Wortley, near Leeds. These occur in the second series of drifts mentioned by Mr. Thorp. The discovery forms the subject of a paper read a year afterwards, in 1853, at a meeting of the Society at Doncaster. The bones were those of hippopotamus, and on careful examination of the clays from which they were obtained it was found that several other bones of the same animal still remained inserted. Evidently the animal had remained where it had died, and the whole of the skeleton was preserved. Ultimately, the remains of two other animals were found, as well as some bones of a fossil elephant (Elephas primigenius), and a jaw with molar teeth of Bos primigenius. These animals were considered by Mr. Denny to represent pre-glacial types, but appear to indicate that they existed after the close of the glacial period; because, agreeing with Mr. Thorp and others that the deposits near Leeds were accumulated at or immediately after the close of the intensely cold period during which the boulder clays were accumulated, it follows that the remains embedded in them must also have existed after the close of the glacial period. This was the third occurrence of hippopotamus in Yorkshire :—first, in the cave at Kirkdale; second, at Overton, near York, where a single molar tooth was found; and the present instance. The remains of the hippopotamus and other animals were deposited in the Society's Museum, located in rooms rented from the Philosophical Society of Leeds, and formed, perhaps, at that time the most important collection of bones of this animal in the kingdom.

Mr. Denny further contributed a paper in 1855 on the claims of the Gigantic Irish Deer, to be considered as contemporary with man. He describes a large number of instances in which remains of *Megaceros Hibernicus*, or the Irish Elk, have been discovered. The first one of which any record has been kept was at Cowthorpe, near Wetherby, in 1744, when a fine head and horns, weighing 68lbs., were found at a depth of six feet in a peat moss. These horns were supposed not to have arrived at their full growth, from the circumstances of their being still covered with a velvet coating. The fossil bones of this animal were considered to be of comparatively modern date from the fact that two-fifths of their substance consists of cartilage and gelatine. Archdeacon Maunsell found this in such large quantity that he made some soup from it, and sent a sample to the Royal Dublin Society. Examples occur of the legs of the elk being found covered with skin and hair, the latter of a tan colour and short. In some instances, as in a bog at Callan, in Tipperary, the horns have been found associated with implements and ornaments used by a man. He cited instances in this country, also, where similar discoveries have been made. Dr. Leigh described a fossil elk, found in the bogs of Lancashire and Cheshire, associated with hippopotamus, and in the same beds a millstone or quern, beads of amber, and human bones were discovered; other instances are cited in support of the relationship; amongst others it is stated that in the same bed of clay at Wortley, near Leeds, in which the bones of four specimens of hippopotamus, and also the mammoth and the urus occurred, an earthern vessel of unbaked clay, without any external markings whatever, also a fragment of pottery with a distinct pattern on its surface, and glazed were found; near to these was a large circular block of gritstone in the centre of which was a hole still containing a piece of iron. The upper surface of the stone was marked with circles, no doubt caused by the friction of some other body revolving upon it. This had probably belonged to a quern, and with the other remains of human construction, apparently attests their contemporaneity. It having been previously shown that these animals were co-existent with the great Irish elk, it follows that man was also.

Archdeacon Maunsell presented to the Royal Dublin Society a rib, in which Dr. Harte, of Dublin, discovered an oval aperture near its lower edge, around which had grown an irregular effusion of callus. This opening was supposed to have been produced by the head of an arrow, and caused at that time a great amount of discussion. Professor Owen and others considered that the incision had probably been made from the point of the antler of another elk, or perhaps by the teeth of some carnivorous animal. Messrs. Richardson, Newman, and others pointed out that the antler of the elk was of too blunt a character to produce such an incision, and would rather have broken the rib than have pierced it. It was further shewn that this incision was in a position where the teeth of an animal could not possibly have made the hole. Mr. Denny was inclined to agree that the incision had been made by the head of an arrow. Mr. Denny chronicled a great number of instances of the discovery of the Irish elk in the peat bogs of Ireland as well as this country, and in association with them, there were frequently found evidences of the apparent co-existence of man. He quotes the opinion, however, of Dr. Ball, of Dublin, who thinks the mere association of human implements with the bones of the deer is no proof of their having been contemporary, but accounts for the circumstances in this way:—With the ancient Irish it was a well-known mode of stratification to build island forts in valleys where a stream ran, surrounded by a stockade of wood, and he supposes they would commence operations by first driving down the wooden posts or palings. Into this was then thrown the earth derived from the formation of a ditch around the whole, which may have been accompanied by heads and bones of the giant deer previously embedded. No doubt, whilst this may have been done, various implements of domestic or warlike use belonging to the people who erected the fortifications, would be accidentally accumulated, along with the matter thrown into the centre. In course of time the whole structure decayed, the mound crumbled and fell, the elk bones being mixed along with the implements of human construction. Thus they would be eventually found associated, apparently furnishing conclusive evidence of their co-existence. The Rev. J. G. Cumming considered that in the Isle of Man the elk existed at the same time as man, but was almost immediately exterminated. Mr. Denny concluded his endeavour to trace the megaceros down to the human era, by stating that he did not consider that man and the megaceros lived on the earth long together, but, on the contrary, he supposed that the last stragglers only, which escaped extermination by physical changes and causes, may have continued to exist down to man's first appearance on the British Isles; and as precisely similar views regarding the extinction of the dinornis in New Zealand had been advocated by Dr. Mantel in one of his last communications to the Geological Society, there needs no apology in concluding with his remarks when speaking of the Moa beds:—"Both these ossiferous deposits, though but of yesterday in geological history, are of immense antiquity in relation to the human inhabitants of the country. I believe that ages ere the advent of the Maories, New Zealand was densely peopled by the stupendous bipeds whose fossil remains are the sole indications of their former existence. That the last of the species was exterminated by human agency, like the dodo and solitaire of the Mauritius, and the gigantic elk of Ireland, there can be no doubt, but ere man began the work of destruction, it is not unphilosophical to assume that physical revolutions, inducing great changes in the relative distribution of land and water in the South Pacific Ocean, may have so circumscribed the geographical limits of the dinornis and palapteryx, as to produce conditions that tended to diminish their numbers preparatory to their final annihilation."

Mr. Thomas Wright, F.S.A., on the remains of a primitive people in the south-east corner of Yorkshire: with some remarks on the Early Ethnology of Britain. The first part of this paper is descriptive of an interesting collection of flint implements found by Mr. Edward Tindall, of Bridlington, and Mr. Thomas Cape, of the same place; they consist principally of arrow-heads, heads which might be attached to spears, fish-hooks, slingstones and chips or flakes. The author was informed by Mr. Tindall "that the arrow-heads and the heads of spears and javelins are found most abundantly in old moor-land, on the sides of rather steep hills; and that when such land is first broken up and tilled they are sometimes found scattered about in considerable numbers. It is evident that they belonged to a tribe confined within this district, because they appear not to be found beyond it. Mr. Tindall further informs me, from his own experience, that the slingstones are found chiefly in and around Flamborough; that in the neighbourhood of Sewerby, about three miles from Flamborough, the rudest of the arrow-heads are found; and that as far as his own observation goes those of most perfect make are found further inland. It appears that in particular fields in the immediate neighbourhood of Bridlington, they are met with in much greater quantities than in other places; in such quantities indeed, that I am assured that a person who looks for them, can hardly, at any time, walk across one of those particular fields without picking up one or two implements of chipped flint." The occurrence of numerous chippings in special localities led the author to the conclusion that they were sites of manufacturies of these implements, and that the people who lived in the district made their own weapons. These observations are interesting at the present time when flint implements are scarce and rarely met with, in comparison to the numbers found in Tindall's time.

A communication was made by Mr. Thomas Pridgin Teale, F.L.S., in which he referred to the discovery of bones of hippopotamus and other animals discovered in a brickfield at Wortley, and previously delineated by Mr. Denny. He described a hewn stone of millstone grit, egg-shaped, truncated at one end, and hollowed out on the flat side, which was apparently an ancient quern or hand mill; with this were also found two pieces of pottery, one of them rudely worked by hand, without decoration; the other, a fragment of glazed pottery, ornamented on the outside with a number of star-like marks, impressed on the soft clay by a hard material. Mr. Teale states that these objects were found at a depth of five or six feet, and were near, though not actually in juxtaposition with the mammalian remains, and he was of opinion that they are of great antiquity, though he states that Mr. James Wardle and others thought that they were of Roman or Anglo-Saxon date.

Mr. Denny, at the Leeds meeting, in 1857, described the skull of a dog exhumed from the alluvial gravel of Norwich in 1851, which is at present located in the museum of the Philosophical Society at Leeds. It had been found, along with the bones of deer and other animals, by some workmen whilst sinking a shaft in the city of Norwich. Citing Professor Owen, he states that there is considerable difficulty in distinguishing the skull of the dog from that of the wolf. Mr. Denny considers that the great size of the canine, the greater size and height of the occipital sagittal crests, and the triangular space between the orbits being narrower and flatter, distinguish the skull of the wolf from that of the dog. In the skull under discussion, these characters were not developed, and Mr. Denny had little doubt that it was a dog resembling the Irish hound, whose remains occur in the bogs of Ireland along with those of the gigantic deer. Mr. Denny,

z

wishing as far as possible to certify his opinion, had written to Dr. Ball, of Trinity College, Dublin, and sent him a sketch of the skull in question, to which Dr. Ball replied :—

Dr. Ball to Mr. Denny.

3, GRANBY ROW, DUBLIN,

July 30th, 1856.

MY DEAR SIR,

The sketch you sent is of the contour of a wolf's head of perhaps two years of age, but if the drawing be correct in the proportions of the teeth, the largest molars and canines are not large enough for a wolf. I would therefore say your specimen is the skull of a dog of a wolfish aspect. I have studied the subject a good deal, and made instructive collections, and have wolves' skulls of many ages, as well as dogs of various breeds, and several of both species from the bogs. I have not yet got any skull of a dog so large as I should suppose our great Irish dogs possessed. I rather imagine these animals were at all times rare and probably the property of great men. If they at all exist at present they are probably in the mountains of the North of Africa, where is to be found a dog possessed of the proportions ascribed to our ancient animal, and knowing from other circumstances that some intercourse existed in remote ages between the North of Africa and Ireland, hence I am led to believe came the great dog in question. Truly yours,

R. BALL.

Mr. Denny, in conclusion, remarks on the scarcity of the remains of dog associated with those of other animals which were undoubtedly domesticated in early ages by man.

At the succeeding meeting, held at Barnsley, Mr. Thos. Wright, M.A,, F.S.A., contributed a paper on some ancient barrows, or tumuli, recently opened in East Yorkshire. On the higher ground to the north of Bridlington is a village called Hunton, near which is a continuous embankment, extending across several fields and enclosing an oblong space. Within this are many pit-formed hollows in the ground, and a number of large barrows scattered about appear to indicate a primeval cemetery. Its position is exactly such a one as the early inhabitants of our island were accustomed to choose for that purpose.

Five of these barrows have been recently opened by Mr. Edward Tindal, of Bridlington. In the first at a depth of 2 feet from the top, the remains of two skeletons were found among burnt earth and a little charcoal. Several chips of flint were picked up, but no other objects of interest. At a short distance are two other mounds in a field belonging to Mr. Y. Lloyd. In these the chalk rock had been first uncovered and hollowed into the form of a bowl, 18 inches deep and 9 feet in diameter. The bodies were placed in this receptacle, and the bowl was filled in with fine mould, and above this was raised the tumulus formed of large chalkstones covered over, when finished, with a coating of rubble and fine soil. This tumulus was about five feet high above the surface. No human remains were found, but a considerable quantity of bones of carnivorous and ruminating animals, and three articles in bronze, one of them a fibulæ, of rather unusual form. In the third barrow, which closely resembled the last, nothing was found except a few fragments of bones, some charcoal, and a quantity of dark-coloured, fatty earth, and four flint implements. The fourth barrow opened by Mr. Tindal was nearly 40 yards in circumference. In this was found two urns of slightly-baked earth, containing some pieces of leather and a quantity of hair. These were placed in hollows made in the chalk for their reception, and were covered by a flat piece of flagstone on one, and a piece of chalk on the other. From the cut and jagged edges of the leather, it was probable that it had belonged to some ornamental part of the dress. The fifth tumulus was similar to those already described. Several urns are described which have been discovered by Mr. Tindal and Mr. Cape, also of Bridlington, in the exploration of other mounds; and the paper concludes with a description of an attempt, with the assistance of Lord Londesborough, to open a large mound known as Willey Houe, about a mile from the village of Wold Newton. A number of men cut a large trench on one side of the tumulus, but after three or four days labour, finding that the work was likely to be of a much more extensive character than was anticipated, the investigation was relinquished.

A tumulus was opened at Thorpe Arch in 1859, a description of which was given by Mr. F. B. Carroll, of Boston Spa. It is on the summit of a small hill adjoining the Walton and Wetherby Road, about eight feet in height, and rather more than two hundred feet in circumference. The centre of the hill was found to be a large heap of boulder stones, some of considerable dimensions, all in a rough and unhewn state. The cairn itself was five feet in height, and twenty-four feet in diameter. The top of the cairn was in the form of a basin, in the bottom of which were found a number of charred bones and small fragments of bronze, somewhat decayed, no doubt the remains of an ornament or coin. Several pieces of flint were found of a rude form. Above the cairn about two feet of earth was deposited, and upon this was piled a heap of stones, leaving a second basin-like cavity, one foot in depth and three feet in diameter. In this occurred a second burial, with bones and flint implements. This was again covered up with earth and a mound of stones. The mounds were considered to be of early British construction.

At a meeting held at Ripon, in April, 1864, the Rev. J. C. Atkinson, of Danby-in-Cleveland, recorded the results of some barrow diggings in that district. The portion of Cleveland investigated consisted of the parishes of Danby, Guisborough, Skelton, and Westerdale, an area comprising about 35,000 to 40,000 acres. The district included in this area constitutes a deep valley, of no great width, running east and west, from which two smaller valleys branch out; the barriers which separate these smaller valleys are narrow, promontory-like ridges with moorland surfaces, and a height of 1,200 or 1,300 feet above sea level. Ancient ramparts and entrenchments are found on these ridges without exception. The most westerly ridge is a regularly-formed camp, with very extensive earthworks upon its extremity, that is, at Crown End, in Westerdale. The other ridges have similar entrenchments; the one between Danby and Fryup Dales has had four separate entrenchments drawn across it. They were considered to be the defences of Celtic settlements. Together with these entrenchments are a large number of tumuli, or barrows; seventy or eighty large ones had been observed, and some hundreds of small ones. These are locally termed houes. The larger ones vary from two or three feet to twelve or fourteen feet in height, and from thirty to ninety feet in diameter. One large pile is probably 150 to

180 feet across. The smaller houes are twelve to eighteen or twenty feet by one and a half to two feet in height. The latter appear to be entirely barren of any remains betokening interment, and are composed of rough stones piled together, often by the side of or above a large slab that has been a fixture in the soil, probably dropped in the place where it is now found by some glacial action. In the larger mounds evidences of burial are found, usually consisting of a stone cist, in which were placed urns. In addition to the primary burial, the mounds appear to have been used for others of a later date, and in one in which the original deposit had been made in the centre of the mound, nine secondary interments were discovered along its side. One of the latter contained a large urn twenty-four inches high by seventeen and a half inches across the mouth, the contained bones being a mere handful. In a comparatively small cairn, with a slight covering of earth, at a point some six or seven feet south of the centre, were found many fragments of urns, accompanied by portions of calcined bones. These had not been broken by recent disturbance, and on continuing the excavation it was clear that repeated burials had been made in this cairn, and every inch seemed to afford some evidence of its repeated disturbance. At the base a small stone covered an urn which appeared to indicate the primary burial, but around it were the ashes of more recent burials. The urn contained besides calcined bones a small barrow-shaped vase, placed bottom upwards, with one of its sides closing the mouth of an incense cup laid sideways. Mr. Atkinson considered that the urn last-mentioned must have been that of a conquering intruder who had been buried in the tumulus erected to some previous chieftain, which would probably account for the fragmentary character of the broken urns. In another houe two urns were found, in one of which was a beautifully wrought war-hammer of fine-grained polished granite, and a rudely-formed incense cup inverted and empty, portions of four bone pins, and some other bone ornaments. No traces of metal implements or ornaments of any kind were found, but stone or flint implements usually accompanied the interment, and the burnt condition of the bones appeared to indicate that in each instance the body had been cremated before burial. In some instances the

urns exhibited a clumsiness of manufacture, together with considerable thickness, and a more obviously rude appearance than any of the others; and these were in every instance found in the centre of the houe, and indicated the first interment. Mr. Atkinson concluded that the most recent interment met with in this portion of Cleveland dates back more than twenty-five centuries, whilst with respect to the earliest they appear to indicate an era so remote that a century or two more or less makes no practical difference.

At a succeeding meeting the same year, the description of some barrows near Bridlington was given by Mr. Edward Tindall. Five of them had been opened in the neighbourhood, and previously described by Mr. Wright. In October, 1857, in conjunction with Captain Collision, Mr. Tindall commenced his investigations. The tumulus opened occupied an elevated position between Bridlington and Buckton. It is about 100 yards in circumference and 9 feet in height. On approaching the centre of the tumulus by means of a trench, a quantity of flint chippings were discovered, amongst which occurred one or two examples of arrow heads. In the centre of the tumulus was a human skeleton. Between the jaws of the skull was found a leaf-shaped arrow head, which appeared to have entered the back of the head and passed forward to the mouth. The skeleton was laid on its back in a trench dug in the chalk, 2 feet wide, 18 inches deep, and $5\frac{1}{2}$ feet in length. On the surface of the chalk surrounding this trench were twelve circular holes, about 9 inches in diameter and 12 inches deep, in which were deposited calcined bones and particles of charcoal. The purpose of this peculiar feature could not be conjectured, they may have either served to have received the ashes of sacrifices at the death of the occupant of the central cist, or may have been food offerings. An urn was found near the skeleton, it was broken, but had contained ashes and a small quantity of burned earth. Mr. Tindal states that the flint implements found in tumuli invariably seemed to indicate more modern and elaborate workmanship than those discovered in the soil overlying chalk, apart from interments. On the conclusion of the paper, the Rev. W. C. Lucas stated that though he had had considerable experience in the investigation of tumuli, he did not remember any instance in which circular holes around the trench had been found.

Mr. Henry Denny, at a meeting at Leeds in August, 1866, read an important paper on early British tumuli on the Hambleton Hills, near Thirsk. In this paper, the area embraced the region occupied by the moors of Boltby, Eskwith, Hawnby and Kepwick Moors, and Southwoods ; the numerous tumuli on which had been examined by the Rev. W. Greenwell, of Durham ; Mr. Craster, of Middlesbro' ; Mr. Verity, of Southwood ; and Mr. Murray, of Daleside. Accompanied by Mr. Fox and Mr. Abraham Horsfall, of Leeds, Mr. Denny had spent some days prosecuting with great zeal the laborious task of grave-digging, with the result that they opened some tumuli, which the author then proceeded to describe. One skeleton which was discovered, that of a female, had round the neck a necklace consisting of about 120 variously-shaped beads of jet and Kimmeridge coal, similar to a necklace found by Mr. Greenwell in Northumberland, the beads of which were also of jet and shale. Several fragments of pottery were found which had apparently been drinking vessels, and urns mixed with bones and chippings of flints. A second tumulus opened near the preceding one, contained, besides the skeleton, a portion of the brow antler of a red deer. No pottery or personal ornaments were found. The body was laid on the surface of the ground, the stones being heaped above it covered with soil. In the village of Hawnby there are numerous indications of tumuli. The locality forms a spur running out from the western side of the Hambleton Hills overhanging the village. It is crossed by an ancient dyke, and on the west side there is a group of tumuli, one large one in the centre, and eight or nine small ones surrounding it. These have been examined by Mr. Murray and Mr. Verity. The larger tumulus was 120 feet in circumference, and 4 feet in height. It contained the skeleton of a young female, evidently of high rank, from the various decorative articles and personal ornaments which accompanied it. At the head was a bowl of thin bronze, with three handles about 11 inches in diameter. It had a wooden cover, with bronze straps arranged in a diamond pattern across it. The young lady's waist had been encircled by a leathern girdle, of which the buckle or clasp was made of two pleats of gold, one of which, set with four garnet-coloured glass ornaments, still remained ; they had been rivetted to the leather with gold rivets.

Near the head were two pins, one of gold, 2 inches in length, with a flat, pear-shaped head; the other silver, of larger size, with two holes perforated through the upper part, probably by a bodkin. There were several rings of silver wire, the ends twisted together; blue glass beads; a portion of a knife; and several much-corroded fragments of iron, a small circular hole perforated in the centre, probably a whorl of a spindle; and an oblong bronze ornament of unknown use. The bones of the body were much decayed. A singular custom was indicated by the cutting edge of the front teeth being filed into three points, a peculiarity which may have denoted the rank or tribe to which the deceased belonged. Mr. Denny remarks that Dr. Barnard Davis records in *Crania Britannica*, the possession of an Ashantee skull, the upper front teeth of which had been chipped to points. This remarkable circumstance shows that a similarity of custom has prevailed between two tribes so widely separated by time and locality as this native of Western Africa of the present day and the young lady of Anglo-Saxon birth, probably interred in the fourth or fifth century of our era, the only difference being that in one the upper front teeth are filed, and in the other the lower.

Of the eight smaller tumuli only two or three contained the remains of interments. In one of them, near the thorax of the body, was found a small circular bronze box, attached to which was a bronze chain, a ring-shaped fibulæ, and a small iron knife. These objects are now in the Leeds Museum. Another tumulus contained a spear head of bronze ten inches long. On the Hambleton training ground are two flat tumuli, one of which is Cleave Dyke. They had been opened by Mr. Greenwell and others, and some particulars were given with respect to their contents. Cleave Dyke entrenchment exhibits a peculiarity of construction. It consists of parallel entrenchments, between which is extended a raised portion at about every three yards. It is somewhat difficult to conceive what can have been the purpose of these divisions; it is surmised that they may either have been used as sunk pits or earthworks in warfare so as to command a better position, or they may have been covered with wattle boughs and formed the rudimentary huts of this ancient British people. The whole district appears to have been very thickly populated.

In December, 1859, a meeting was held at Sheffield, at which Mr. Denny contributed a paper on the geological and archæological contents of the Victoria and Dowkabottom Caves in Craven. To the eastward of Settle, and also near Arncliffe, caves have long been known in the mountain limestone. Hitherto they had been regarded as subterraneous wonders, and had received little or no consideration as the abodes of man and other animals. In August of this year Mr. Denny, accompanied by Mr. O'Callaghan, visited Mr. Jackson, of Settle, who had recently discovered a cave at King's Scar, a mile and a half from Settle, at an elevation of 1,460 feet above sea level. Mr. Jackson had already obtained from the cave ornaments, coins, pottery, and mammalian remains, which were inspected at his house. The cave had probably three entrances, two of which were then partialty closed by the *debris* of the superincumbent precipitous rock. The descent into the cave was rather difficult. Entering by a steep fissure it was necessary to crawl through a low and narrow passage into a cave, in which the visitor could scarcely stand upright; then through a second contracted aperture into a lofty cavern. The floor was covered with stalagmite and clay, and strewn over with blocks of limestone which had fallen from the roof. From this cavern a third and nearly closed passage afforded an entrance to another large compartment. Besides these caves were lateral fissures, whose terminations were unknown. The floor of the cave consisted first of loose stones and loamy soil, beneath which were charcoal ashes mixed with bones, antiquarian relics, and earth; below was clay, stalagmite and rock. In some parts the stalagmite rose to the surface, and immediately beneath was clay, with bones and relics. In other parts the loamy clay with charcoal ashes, containing bones, pottery, and other ancient remains, rested upon a solid limestone floor.

The Dowkabottom Caves, near Arncliffe, are situated on a lofty plateau of the rocky crags of the Kilnsey Range, 1,250 feet above the sea, from which a descent is made into a lofty chamber from whose roof hang large masses of stalactite. Turning by a narrow passage to the left, a large, lofty cave is entered, a considerable portion of the floor of which is covered with stalagmite, owing to the constant flow of a rapid stream of water through it from the extreme end of a narrow gallery of considerable extent. Whitaker, in his "History of Craven," thus describes the scenery in which Dowkabottom Cave is located :—" Dowkabottom Hole is about two miles north from Kilnsey Crag, high up in the hills, and surrounded by cliffs of limestone. The entrance is an oblong chasm in the surface, overhung with ivy and fern ; at the south end is a narrow but lofty opening into a cavern of no great extent. The view downward from the north is tremendous. On this side it is very lofty, and extends to a considerable distance. The rocks at the top, and particularly near the entrance, hang down in the most picturesque shapes, and both these and the sides are covered with petrified moss, richly tinted." In the first chamber of the Dowkabottom Cave some very large stones occupied the surface ; on the removal of these was found a layer of charcoal ashes nearly 2 feet in thickness, amongst which was a fragment of a bronze fibulæ. Mr. Hodgson, who excavated this spot along with Mr. Farrer, of Ingleborough House, discovered the remains of three human skeletons laid in the bed of clay about a foot deep. Underneath the clay was a layer of soft stalagmite, and at the base of this several skulls and bones of the wolf and goat, and the horns of a deer were found. On the first examination of these different caves by Mr. Jackson, the bones and teeth of animals were found, with relics of human art scattered indiscriminately over the floor, or just below the surface in the charcoal ashes previously alluded to, and the first specimens obtained, consisting of various articles of British and Roman art, coins, bones and teeth of the tiger, hyæna, bear, and wild boar, (the latter identified by Dr. Buckland), were deposited in the British Museum, and a description was read before the Society of Antiquaries of London, by Mr. C. R. Smith. The number of personal ornaments and implements of various kinds indicated that the several caves were for a considerable period the abode of human beings. The investigations of Mr. Jackson had resulted in the accumulation of a considerable number of these objects. He found about 24 fibulæ of bronze, and five of iron, of various sizes and appearances, many in fine preservation and highly ornamented, some apparently plated with silver. Two bronze armlets and four fragments of others, two rings, and bronze articles like studs, one long comb, (probably used for the back of the head), and fragments of another. Portions of what appear to have been small-tooth combs made of bone had been found. Six bronze pins, (one of them with a flat head the size of a shilling, and plated), bone needles, bone spoons, with the handles rudely carved, and the bowls with a hole in the centre ; remains of knives, a key, bone arrow heads and other implements, and the head of an adze made of trap ; the canine teeth probably of the wolf, perforated for ornament; fragments of glass, mostly for ornament ; and pottery of the ordinary Roman red or Samian ware ; and some flint and stone implements, together with Roman coins of the date of Trajan and Constantine, were embraced in Mr. Jackson's collection. In the exploration of the Dowkabottom Cave already alluded to, in addition to the bones mentioned, were jaws and skulls of the short-horned ox, the sheep, and the goat, bones of the horse, skulls and jaws of the wild boar, the horns of the red deer, and pottery of Roman character, and other remains of man. It was well known that Yorkshire was inhabited at remote periods by the hyæna, bear, tiger, and wolf; that such animals reside in caves, and their bones were frequently found in a fossil state in the caves in other parts of the country ; and it was probable that the carnivorous species inhabited the caves and carried the remains of other animals into them for food. This conjecture was rendered probable from the fact that when the caves were first discovered the skulls and bones of various animals were strewn over the floors in considerable numbers, but as they were not considered of value in comparison with the relics of human art they were neglected, broken, and destroyed. The animals identified by Mr. Denny, occurring in the Victoria Cave, were the cave tiger, the bear, (Ursus arctos), the badger, hyæna, fox, wild boar, hare, water-rat, short-horned ox, and the horse ; whilst from the Dowkabottom Cave were obtained the wolf, the wild dog, ox, wild boar, water-rat, red deer, sheep, goat, short-horned ox, and the horse. The facies of the two sets of animal remains appears to indicate that whilst the Victoria Cave was occupied by hyænas, and that they dragged into it the remains of other animals brought there for food, the Dowkabottom Cave was not a den of hyænas, but appears to have been the abode of bears and wolves.

In March, 1865, Mr. Farrer, of Ingleborough House, along with Mr. Denny, contributed the results of further explorations in the Dowkabottom Cave. The surface of the western chamber was composed of 14 inches of broken stone, earth, and charcoal, in which were found fragments of pottery, part composed of coarse black earth, and the other of red Samian pottery. Below was a bed of clay 18 inches thick, resting on a stratum of soft stalagmite, about 3 feet thick, in which the bones of several animals were obtained. The soft stalagmite rested on a bed of hard stalagmite, 8 inches in thickness, upon which lay a nearly perfect skeleton of a very fine specimen of the gigantic red deer, with antlers of great beauty. An excavation was made to the depth of 6 feet, passing through clay mixed with stones and gravel; and a boring rod was inserted for a further distance of 6 feet through soft clay, without reaching any bottom. The chamber eastwards from the opening was also examined, and beneath 18 inches of clay the hard stalagmite was dug through down to the rock, 4 yards and a half in thickness. A flint implement was found, along with horns of the red deer, and a portion of the left antler of the gigantic Irish elk (Megaceros Hibernicus), which forms the second instance of the remains occurring in Yorkshire. Shortly before the reading of the paper, whilst exploring the west chamber, about 4 yards from the spot where the skeleton of the red deer was discovered, a slight hollow or grave was disclosed, which had been dug in the hard stalagmite, measuring 1 foot long, 8 inches wide, and 1½ inches in depth, in which were the remains of a skeleton of a child probably 2½ years of age. The bones were in a very imperfect and fragile condition, and were embedded in the superimposed soft stalagmite. The whole of the bones and other objects obtained during these excavations are stated to have been presented to the Museum of the Leeds Philosophical Society by Mr. Farrer. The two chambers extend conjointly 390 feet in length, and as the entrance to another fresh cave had been discovered, additional and important results might be expected, it being Mr. Farrer's intention to make a further examination of the new cave.

At a meeting held at Leeds in May, 1861, the Rev. John Kenrick, F.S.A., of York, contributed a paper on the Rev. Mr. M'Enery's researches in the bone cave of Kent's Hole, near Torquay, and their relation to the archæology and palæontology of Britain. The scene of these researches is somewhat remote from Yorkshire, but the value of the discoveries had a considerable influence on the cave work throughout the whole country, and for this reason it may not be inappropriate to give a short account of the cave. The mountain limestone of South Devon, like that of Yorkshire, is full of ancient water-courses and caves. Kent's Cavern, one of these, is about a mile and a half eastward from Torquay. Like similar caves its floor was more or less covered with stalagmite, and it had been of general interest for centuries before the scientific interest of its contents was discovered. Mr. Northmore, in 1824, was the first to make an investigation of the cave. He had embraced what was called the helioarkite origin of mythology, a religion consisting of the worship of the sun, combined with the deification of Noah as the symbol of the deluge. Mr. Northmore had a belief that this worship had been widely different over the ancient world, and had its share in producing Druidism; its rites were celebrated in caverns, and Mr. Northmore was convinced that he should find in Kent's Hole evidence of the performance of helioarkite and mithraic worship. In the course of his exploration he found a tusk of a hyæna, bones of bears, and others. Mr. Northmore's researches were followed by those of Mr. Trevelyan, who obtained a large number of specimens of the teeth of rhinoceros and other animals, which he took up to London, and submitted to the inspection of Dr. Buckland. At this point Mr. M'Enery took up the investigation and carried it on for several years, and as the result made a large and valuable collection of fossil remains and works of art. He intended to publish a description of his labours, but after two appeals to subscribers was obliged to give it up. His manuscript was sold, along with bundles of sermons, but eventually came to light, and in 1859 was published by Mr. Vivian. Some of the finest and rarest of Mr. M'Enery's specimens found their way to the British Museum. More recently, Mr. Pengelly, F.R.S., of Torquay, had taken great interest in the cave. He was convinced that much remained to be explored and valuable information could be obtained providing a sufficient sum to cover the expenses could be obtained. Beneath the stalagmite is a thick bed of clay, and it is on the surface of this clay that flint implements and other objects attest the presence of man's occupation. The tools are frequently found sticking in the mud, the upper part being embedded in the crust of stalagmite which overlies it at the bottom. At the surface the human remains probably belong to the British or Roman-British period, and embrace pottery, beads, bone pins, and other objects; lower down stone axes, arrow and spear heads, along with the teeth and bones of animals, but no pottery or other art-work indicate an earlier people; whilst lowest of all is a bed containing only animal remains, with the exception, at rare intervals, of an occasional flint. Such was the statement of Mr. M'Enery, and he had no doubt whatever as to the occurrence of flint implements in the lower accumulations, along with those of extinct animals, such as the elephant, rhinoceros, tiger, bear, hyæna, and Machairodus latidens; and he described the flints in this lower deposit as rude compared with those of the upper. Mr. Kenrick entered into an elaborate argument as to the antiquity of man, to which we need not do more than refer at the present time.

At Leeds, in May, 1861, Mr. Henry Denny read a paper on the former existence of the Roebuck in the West Riding of Yorkshire. In the collection of bones, pottery, and other articles which had previously been obtained from the Dowkabottom Cave, and sent by Mr. Farrar to the Leeds Museum, the most valuable specimen was the portion of the skull of a roebuck, with antlers, probably about six years old. Mr. Denny, in 1859, whilst exploring the cave, had found some smaller fragments of jaws and skull of a species of ruminant which he was now able to identify as belonging to the roebuck. The occurrence of the roebuck in the cave was important, and indicated the antiquity of the cave and its contents, as it was known that this animal was contemporary with the rhinoceros, the mammoth, and the megaceros. The number of species of the Cervidæ family now known to have inhabited Yorkshire was five, Megaceros, Strongiloceros, the red deer, the fallow deer, and the roebuck. Some time afterwards Mr. Denny made some observations on the distribution of the extinct bears of Britain, and described a new species. He remarked on the peculiarity that whilst in the north of Europe bears were much more numerous than hyænas, in Britain the latter animal was much more frequently found. The northern limit at present known for the occurrence of the bear was Yorkshire; southwards they were much more abundant. Very few remains of the bear had been found in Ireland, and for some time it was thought not to occur there at all, but in 1846-7 two remarkably fine crania of a gigantic species of bear were discovered seven feet from the surface in a deposit of marl beneath a bog on the borders of Westmeath. These specimens passed into the hands of Dr. Ball, of the Royal Irish Academy, and afterwards Mr. Glennan obtained possession of them, who in the autumn of 1863 lent them to Mr. Denny. The present paper contains a description of the skulls. One of them, the larger, somewhat resembled Ursus maritimus, but had belonged to an animal of much larger size, and this one Mr. Denny proposed to call Ursus planafrons from the peculiarly flat receding form of the anterior portion of the head. The other one was considered by Professor Owen, to whom the specimens were exhibited, to be closely allied to Ursus arctos. Mr. Denny concluded his paper by summarising the extinct forms of animals which had hitherto been found, and the relation that man probably bore to them.

In the Museum at Leeds there was an ordinary socketed celt, with a loop, which had been obtained from Hanwick, in Lincolnshire. It was peculiar from being made of lead, and formed the subject of a communication by Mr. Denny to this Society, in November, 1865. It had been found by Mr. John Green associated with elephants' teeth in gravel at the place named. Mr. Denny found that there were a number of barrows in the district, and he thought it was very probable that this lead celt had been obtained from one of them. Remarking on the occurrence of celts in burial mounds, Mr. Denny mentioned a case in which Mr. Fyffe, after digging for the foundation of a house near Wellington, New Zealand, suddenly came upon a human skeleton, doubtless that of a Maori, which had been buried in a sitting posture, with the arms extended towards the mouth; near was an entire egg of the moa, and between the legs numerous tools of jade. It was probable that the moa's egg was buried with the man to serve as food, and the weapons for use in a future state, and under this supposition indubitable evidence was afforded that the moa and man were contemporary inhabitants of New Zealand. With respect to the lead celt he was of opinion that it had been formed in a mould for casting bronze celts as a *trial celt*. The Rev. W. C. Lucas was cited as having found similar celts in the Channel Islands, which had suggested the same solution for the reason of their occurrence. Before concluding the paper, Mr. Denny stated that in January, 1863, a magnificent skull of Bos primogenius was found beneath 4 feet of peat near the village of Reche, in Cambridgeshire, with the frontal bone on the upper margin of the orbits broken in, and the remains of a flint celt in the orifice, proving that man was co-eval with this great ruminant. At the conclusion of the paper, Mr. John Evans, F.R.S., expressed an opinion that the custom of burying arms with the dead may in some instances have led the representatives of the deceased to have put imitation weapons such as miniature swords or other arms in the grave along with the dead, and it was a matter for consideration whether this unique celt to which their attention had been drawn might not be an imitation after all, though genuine as to its antiquity.

Mr. P. O'Callaghan, of Leeds, contributed a paper on Cromlechs and Rocking Stones, ethnologically and geologically considered. He referred to the researches of the Rev. W. C. Lucas and Sir R. C. Hoare, who, along with others, had clearly proved that the cromlechs were placed over graves. Thirty years previously, when Mr. O'Callaghan resided in Trinidad, he had opportunities of observing the aboriginal, and then nearly extinct tribes of the Caribs. He took great interest in observing the habits and character of these curious beings, and no custom of theirs impressed him more than their mode of disposing of their dead. Soon after life was extinct, and while the body was still warm, it was tied up in the smallest possible compass. The legs were bound up to the thighs, and the elbows fixed between the knees; the face, which had been previously smeared with some reddish paint, was fastened down upon the open palms of the hands, and the hair thickly greased; the body was next tightly swathed in a long piece of coarse cloth; it was then left to cool and stiffen, when it was removed and deposited in a narrow and short grave. If a natural crevice in the rock, or a convenient receptacle under large stones could be found near at hand, they always availed themselves of such a secure protection for the remains of their deceased relatives against the depredations of the ferocious carnivorous animals which infested the surrounding forests. This description applies to the human remains found in the rudest cromlechs in this country, and is probably the most primitive, as it was the most natural way of disposing of the human dead body in man's savage state all over the world. The stones of an artificial cromlech are often comparatively light and easily removed, the natural or indistinctive resource under such insecure conditions would be to conceal it under a mound of earth or heap of stones, and this is probably the origin of the earthen tumulus of which so many occur in this country, and perhaps may be the prototype of those stupendous pyramidal structures of the civilised Egyptians. The occurrence of rocking stones he attributed to glacial action, and considered that they would be carried down by an ice-sheet, and occasionally left balanced on the rocks where they are found.

At the same meeting, Sir John Lubbock, F.R.S., contributed a paper on the "Geological and Archæological Discoveries in Denmark, Switzerland, and France." He first described the lake dwellings discovered in Switzerland in 1853-4. In those years the water in the lakes fell to an extraordinarily low level. Some of the inhabitants on the borders of the lake took advantage of the lowness of the water to increase their gardens by building a wall along the new water-line, and raising the level of the land thus reclaimed by mud dredged from the lake. In the course of this dredging great numbers of wooden piles, horns of deer, and stone implements were found. This speedily became known to the scientific men in Switzerland, and Dr. F. Keller, amongst others, gave the matter much attention. The ancient settlements or lake dwellings were found to be very extensive and must have been constructed by many thousands of persons. Sir John Lubbock gave a detailed account of the discoveries that had been made up to that time which have since been published by Dr. Keller and others. The pile dwellings in Switzerland were probably

AA

erected during the latter part of the stone age and the bronze period. During the stone age the pile dwellings were spread over the whole country, but during the latter period, when bronze was used, they were confined to the lakes of Western Switzerland, and still more recently, when iron was used for the manufacture of their implements, they were found only on the lakes of Bienne and Neuchatel. Far earlier than these remains are those discovered by M. Boucher de Perthes in the year 1846. He found human implements in beds of the drift age, a description of which he published in Antiquitæ Celtiques et Antediluviennes, 1847. For several years M. Perthes received little attention, and by many was looked upon as a madman. It was not until Dr. Faulkner visited his collection at Abbeville, and made known the result of his visit to Dr. Prestwich and Dr. Evans, who immediately proceeded to Abbeville to verify for themselves the discovery of these flint implements, that the tide set in favour of M. Perthes' theories. After the results of these visits had been made known in the Society of Antiquaries and the Royal Society of this country, many other geologists, amongst whom were Sir Charles Lyell, visited the drifts of Amiens and Abbeville, and speedily came to the conclusion that the specimens were genuine. An examination of the collections in the Society of Antiquaries showed that many years previously specimens of similar implements had been found along with bones of extinct animals, at a gravel pit at Oxon, in Suffolk, and had been described in the Archæologia in 1800. Numerous other localities speedily occurred in which the palæolithic or oldest flint implements were found, but it is doubtful whether any specimens of these implements have been found in this county, though the bones of the animals which are found associated in other localities with these old flints, the elephant, rhinoceros, hippopotamus, and others, have been found in Yorkshire in abundance. Sir John Lubbock cites M. Lartet's opinion that the men, whose implements are found in the river gravels are not the oldest men of whom we have evidence, because man is found associated in caves with the great cave bear, (Ursus spelæus), which has not hitherto been authentically discovered in the river gravels and was probably extinct before the man of the river gravels existed.

The Rev. Edward Trollope, at the same meeting, contributed an interesting paper on the historic incidents connected with Lincoln Heath; and at the one next succeeding, the Rev. John Kenrick, of York, described the rise and suppression of the Templars in Yorkshire, a paper in which there is much interesting information with respect to this ancient order, and their settlements at Temple Newsome and other places.

In a paper on the primeval condition of the inhabitants of the British Islands, by Mr. P. O'Callaghan, he considered that it may be possible that gold and copper had been known and partially used long before foreign art had taught the people to convert them to manufactured articles. Gold, though usually found in small quantities, is more generally diffused than perhaps any of the native metals. It is also the most beautiful, and would probably be the most abundant in the first instance. It is not unreasonable to suppose that in these metalliferous islands gold may have been readily converted into personal ornaments, even before the importation of the foreign art of smelting it. We must therefore look upon rudely-formed personal ornaments of gold as amongst the most ancient metallic relics in these islands. According to Irish annals, gold was worked and made into pins to fasten garments seven or eight centuries B.C.; and he considers it at least a curious coincidence that pins, brooches, collars, and torques, are amongst the most ancient articles fabricated from metals in this country. He did not intend to enter into a detailed notice of all the gold ornaments found in this country, but he would cite one peculiar instance, in which a barrow, called the Hill of the Fairies, in Flintshire, had been looked upon for ages with much superstition, and had been avoided by passengers at night. In 1833, an old woman was obliged to pass this way, and she was startled by seeing a spectral figure, clothed in a coat of gold, cross the barrow. This strange story made a considerable stir in the neighbourhood, and the owner of the land determined on removing the mound altogether. In doing so, he found rude urns of unbaked pottery, and burnt bones; but on excavating to the base of the mound he came to a human skeleton, wrapped round the chest with a corselet of the purest gold, embossed with an ornamentation of superior design and workmanship. This precious relic, valued only for its intrinsic worth, was broken up and sold. It has, however, been since recovered in great part and put together so that it can now be seen nearly complete in the British Museum.

At a meeting at Doncaster, in November, 1865, at which Lord Houghton presided, Mr. John Evans, F.R.S., read a paper on the Coins of the Ancient Britons, and more particularly those found in Yorkshire. In the year 600 B.C. a Greek colony was founded at Massilia (Marseilles). It was here the original of all our coinage was introduced about 330 years B.C., the ancient and beautiful Phillipus, on the obverse of which is a bold figure of the head of Apollo encircled with a laurel wreath. These coins were imitated by the native inhabitants of Gaul, and in course of time the imitations came over to Britain and were again imitated in this country. The author opposed the supposition that the art of coining was unknown in Britain until the time of Cæsar, on the ground that if this had been the case we should have had a coinage of the three metals then in use, gold, silver, and bronze; and not one of gold only, if the earlier introduction of money had taken place as already indicated. From the numerous occurrences of coins of Phillip in this country, Mr. Evans was inclined to consider the earlier date of the introduction of the coins the correct one. Mr. Evans referred amongst other discoveries to that in 1827 of a fictile vase in the vicinity of the old Roman road at Lightcliffe, near Halifax, in which were found Roman coins, together with three of the well-known Yorkshire type, with the inscription VOLISIOS, in two lines, across a wreath on the obverse; and a rudely-formed horse and DUMNO-CO-VEROS on the reverse. A fourth coin was a new variety, and evidently a direct descendant of the Macedonian Phillipus, though only the wreath and the horse survive to prove its relationship.

In August, 1866, Mr. John Ffooks read a paper on the Flint Implements and Weapons found at Bridlington. In this paper Mr. Ffooks considered he had discovered characteristics in the flints which indicated different races of people. At some places white flint was used; at others grey. Sometimes both were used by the same people, but there was a marked difference in their form as well as their colour. Then a distinct people had used only red and black-coloured flint. Those who used white flint had a settlement on the cliff at Sewerby and another at Bempton. An ancient British village, of which only a few traces remain, was situated in a field in front of the Rev. Mr. Lloyd's house, the principal part of which has been destroyed by the falling of the cliff that once extended into the bay to an unknown distance. This village was enclosed by an earthwork which commenced at the cliff, and passing round the eastern side of the village was continued in a nearly straight line to Old Bridlington. It was perfect up to the time of the enclosure of the parish about 60 years since, when the present road was formed partly on the line of the embankment. There were also two lines of embankment from the angle at Sewerby leading in a straight line to the Danes Dyke, with a road between them, intended to connect the two lines of entrenchments, and to form a secure passage between them. One of these banks was taken away when the new road was formed, but part of the other bank still remained. The sunk fence in front of Mr. Lloyd's house is a part of the enclosed road, and shows its original level with its exact line of position. Mr. Ffooks made several investigations of these embankments and amongst the tumuli, and gave a detailed description of the result, along with a somewhat sensationally interesting account of the strife which took place between the inhabitants of the several settlements. He concluded by stating that the weapons and implements mentioned in this account of his researches are to be handed over to the trustees to be appointed by the Sailors' Club in Bridlington, in order to preserve them for general inspection, and he trusted they might remain preserved for as many future generations as they have existed during past ones.

At the same meeting a paper was read by Professor Wm. Boyd Dawkins, F.R.S., on the Pleistocene Mammals of Yorkshire. The term pleistocene is regarded as synonymous with those of post-pleistocene, pre-glacial, and glacial, and the animals existing in Yorkshire at this period amount in all to 22 species, nearly half the entire number of the pleistocene mammals whose remains have been found in Britain. They fall into five distinct groups, the first of which are all extinct ; the second at the present day confined to northern climates; the third to southern; the fourth those common to northern and southern; and fifth, those still inhabiting the temperate zones of Europe. Of the first group seven have been found in Yorkshire; of the second two; of the third two; and of the fifth eleven.

At a meeting at Bradford, in March, 1867, the Rev. William Greenwell, Canon of Durham, read a paper on the inhabitants of Yorkshire in pre-Roman times. Of the men who lived when the mammoth, the tichorine rhinoceros, and several extinct mammals existed in Yorkshire, there appeared to be no evidence, and Mr. Greenwell regretted that the celebrated Kirkdale Cave was examined in days when it was never dreamt that man and the mammoth had lived together, and when flints had not become important as evidences of man. It is possible that amongst the large number of animal remains found in the cave some evidence of man might have been obtained. In many parts of England, including Yorkshire, there is abundant evidence of the existence of a people who used only stone implements before the advent of those acquainted with bronze. The former appeared to have possessed distinct physical features as compared with the latter. The sepulchral mounds in which their remains have been found are long in proportion to their breadth, and the interments were always at the east end. "The skulls of the buried people, like the mounds, are long in proportion to their breadth, and also different in many other particulars from the heads of the bronze-using people who lie buried in round barrows. With these earlier interments no object of metal has ever been found, the only implements or weapons being made of flint or bone. The discovery of secondary burials of the people of the age of bronze, evidently introduced into these mounds at a time subsequent to their first erection, proves that they belong to an earlier time than those of the round-headed bronze-using people, and as in no case, and a very large number have been examined, has any article of metal been found in them, it is not an unfair inference to assume that at the time they were raised metal was unknown to the people who erected them." Other features of a very peculiar kind have been observed in the burials of the long barrows, both in

Wiltshire and elsewhere. In one I opened in the North Riding, near Ebberston, there were the remains of about 14 bodies of all ages and of both sexes, and in several of these the state of the bones, broken and widely scattered in fragments, showed that a violent death had overtaken them, and that the flesh had been removed before the bones were interred. Is the conjecture a forced one which suggests that these fractured bones were the relics of persons slain at the funeral of the chief, and eaten by the guests? " Cannibalism has not been so infrequent that we need wonder at such a feast." A mound at Willoughby-on-Wold contained similar broken bones. Over them had been heaped flints and chalk, and upon these wood had been placed, which was set fire to, and the bones were consumed by ignited lime; after this, the material forming the barrow had been heaped. In other barrows the primary burial appears to have been that of a long-headed chieftain, whilst others have been buried in the same mounds with round heads. The latter appear to have been an invading and conquering people. The ancient Briton who occupied this country when Cæsar landed was a man of good stature, with an average height of 5 feet 8 inches, of powerful and symmetrical frame. The lines of the face must have been on the whole harsh and severe, for all the prominent features are strongly developed, and wanting in that softness of outline which adds so much to beauty of form; the mouth was slightly protruberant; eyebrows rugged and projecting; cheekbones high, and the nose prominent and well marked; forehead broad, but low; and the hinder part of the head remarkably broad. The breadth of the skull distinguishes it from that of the modern English head, which in the main is oval; nor does it closely approximate to that of the Irish, Scotch, or Welsh Celt, which is also oval, but somewhat different from the Teutonic. The teeth are usually well preserved, rarely showing any signs of decay, but in old skulls are much worn down. In one instance, near Pickering, hair was found in a barrow, of a light auburn colour and braided in plaits. A portion of woollen fabric made into garments occasionally occurs. In Craven, under a barrow, a coffin made out of a split and hollowed oak tree was exhumed, in which the body had been enveloped from head to foot in a textile woollen fabric. It was in so fragmentary a condition that nothing could be made out as to its shape. Ornaments for personal decoration have frequently been found, large gold torques for the neck are not uncommon, and frequently of beautiful design and workmanship. Similar ornaments, but smaller, adorn the arms and sometimes the ankles. Plating of one metal upon another was done very skilfully, gold has been found plated upon bronze. Necklaces are abundant, and of very various materials, gold, glass, amber, clay, and most frequently jet. In the latter material they have occurred in most varied shapes and ingenious arrangements. It is probable that many of the rings used for bracelets may have served the purpose of money, as well as for decoration. In Nubia, and other parts of Africa, ring money similar to this is used at the present day. Their skill in manufacturing weapons for warfare was very great, and some of their leaf-shaped swords and spear heads exhibit exquisite form and skilful workmanship. They used shields, circular in form, and made of hammered bronze. Specimens of these have been found in Northumberland and Durham. The offensive arms were the sword, spear, javelin, dagger, sling and bow, the first four made in bronze. The sword varies from 20 to 30 inches in length, and was meant for thrusting. The spear and javelin heads are of various sizes, and sometimes have loops at the sides for attachment to the shaft. The usual mode of fixing, however, is by a single rivet through the socket. The dagger is short, broad, and strong, and is frequently found buried with its owner. The arrows were always tipped with flint, no example of a bronze arrow-head having been found. There appears to be little doubt that for purposes where flint was either more useful or more accessible than bronze it continued to be used until the termination of the bronze period. Five examples of a chariot have been found, in each case buried with their owner. The wheels were about 3 feet in diameter, and the rim was of iron. The chariots were small, as were also the horses that pulled them. Associated with them were quantities of rings, bits, and other articles of bronze, sometimes beautifully enamelled, which had formed the trappings of the horses, and ornamental parts of the chariot, and which show to what perfection in metal work these people had arrived. Of the flint implements, one of the commonest is what is termed a thumb-flint, which was probably used for cleaning skins, and for scraping bones. The Esquimaux at the present day use a similar stone for scraping with. Pins were made of both bronze and bone, and grain was bruised by stone pounders, generally water-worn pebbles. Millstones, in the shape of small querns made of sandstone, are also common. The corn was probably grown on terraces made on the sides of the hills which formed their settlements, in a somewhat similar manner to that in which the vine is grown on the banks of the Rhine. The reason for this may have been two-fold. The valleys at that time were subject to constant overflowing of the rivers, and would be too swampy for growing corn, and in the disturbed and unsettled state in which these people existed, it was necessary that their corn-growing land should be in a position where it could be protected. At that time the country presented a very different appearance to its present one, and all the bare millstone grit hills which now grow only heather were clothed with thick forests. In these forests the ancient Briton hunted herds of deer and wild boar, and a small species of ox. It is probable that the Irish elk still existed though rare; the wolf was common, and the beaver occurred in suitable situations; the horse and dog were domesticated; and it is probable that the people possessed large herds of domesticated cattle. There is no evidence that the round-headed Britons indulged in cannibalism, and Mr. Greenwell is of opinion that this custom was unknown to them. He considers that the large megalithic structures at Stonehenge, Avebury, Callernish and Stennis were erected by these people; but nothing of the kind exists in Yorkshire. Their dwellings appeared, from what is left of them, to have consisted of a wall never more than three feet in height, enclosing a circular space 15 feet to 30 feet in diameter, over which was raised a conical roofing of timber covered with turf or thatch. There is generally a hearthstone in the centre. They were great fortifiers, and the whole of the north of England is full of forts and fortlets, the defensive places of the British tribes. It is probable that they raised stockades of timber upon the entrenchments which were formed. It does not appear probable that these entrenchments were erected for combined protection, but rather by each separate small tribe for defence against others in the immediate district. Mr. Greenwell further described the various methods of burial both with and without cremation. At the conclusion of the paper Mr. Fairless Barber drew attention to a number of entrenchments and barrows on Baildon Moor, and suggested that valuable information would be obtained by investigating them.

In October, in the same year, Mr. H. Ecroyd Smith, author of Reliquiæ Isurianæ, gave a description of a Romano-British mosaic pavement discovered at Aldboro'. The site was known in pre-historic Britain as Yseur, the chief city of the warlike Brigantes, the leading people of the island at the Roman advent, whose territory stretched from the Mersey and Humber on the south, up to the Tweed and the Solway, and who far surpassed in their ability and energy all the more southern tribes, a character ably sustained by their successors, and to some extent descendants. The inhabitants of Yorkshire and Lancashire excel all the rest of England, whether we select arts or literature, agriculture or manufactures. On the advent of the Romans the place became known as Isurium Brigantum (Yseur of the Brigantes), and became the capital of the victorious invaders until, after the pacification of the country, the growing necessities of the capital of so important a province of Britain induced removal to a site more accessible to navigation, which was found lower down the river at York; and here uprose the future metropolis, firstly, of the Romans in North Britain; secondly, of the Saxon King of Northumberland or Deira; and lastly, of the great ecclesiastical district than which not even London itself is more famous throughout the national annals. The mosaic pavement is apparently of Romano-British manufacture, probably referable to the end of the third or beginning of the fourth century, and is one of a number which have been found at Aldboro'. It is four feet square, and represents Romulus and Remus suckled by a wolf, and was probably the central portion of a much larger pavement. In 1863 it was purchased and deposited in the museum of the Literary and Philosophical Society of Leeds. The mosaic is made from pieces of blue lias and magnesian limestone. The tesseræ, of a red colour, are artificial, being of baked clay.

At a meeting held at Rotherham in April, 1868, the Rev. R. J. Mapleton, M.A., contributed a lengthy and elaborate paper on the origin and rise of Menhirs or Pillar Stones. In the absence of the author, the paper was read by Mr. Fairless Barber. It was followed by a paper by the Rev. Scott F. Surtees, who described a Roman camp of considerable extent on Sutton Common, near Askern. After describing the station, the author states that this was the seat of the the colony Camulodunum, which had hitherto been located by English authors in the south of France. He gave extracts from various authors to prove that Claudius's campaign was in Brigantia, and that it was here that he met and fought the ancient Britons.

In April, 1869, Mr. Edward Tindall read a paper on the extinct fauna of the East Riding of Yorkshire. Amongst the most interesting of these were enumerated the beaver, the elk or moose dear, and the reindeer. Of the former animal a very fine skull was exhumed during some extensive drainage operations on the banks of a river near Wawne, in the neighbourhood of Beverley, in 1861, by Dr. Brereton. The skull belonged to a mature individual, and it was 6 inches in length and 4 inches in breadth, and was in a tolerable state of preservation. The paper is illustrated by a figure of it. The elk or moose deer was found in the spring of 1822, in drift gravel, whilst constructing a lake at Thorpe Hall, near Bridlington, at a depth of about 4½ feet from the surface ; and in 1868, a horn in the occipital portion of the skull of a female specimen was found near Carnaby. The horn of the reindeer was found in 1860, at the base of the cliff in a lacustrine deposit near the top of the lake at Skipsey. These animals all afford evidence of the severity of the climate which existed during the pleistocene period in this district.

At the same meeting Mr. Denny described the occurrence of flint implements at Adel, near Leeds. In the latter part of the previous year, whilst excavating a small plot of ground at the back of the Reformatory, numerous fragments of flint were found, and various implements of the same material, forming arrow heads, javelin heads, knives, sling stones, and other objects. They were picked up by the boys at the Reformatory, while employed in digging the ground, and would probably have been lost but for the accidental circumstance that one of them was seen by Mr. Twigg, the superintendent, who recognised the similarity they bore to similar objects in the Art

Treasures Exhibition, then opened in Leeds. He stimulated the boys by a trifling reward, and the specimens found were brought to him, and have since been placed in the Museum of the Leeds Philosophical Society. From the limited space in which they all occurred, it would appear to have been the site of a manufactory. The material was brought from a distance, probably the chalk districts about Flamborough. It was probable that other specimens may have been turned up during the enclosure of the moorland at different periods, for in 1815 Thoresby figured in his *Musæum Thoresbyanum* two flint arrow-heads, which were found near Adel Mill. Mr. Denny considered at some length the historical circumstances under which these implements may have been accumulated. He incidentally mentioned that in 1867 a massive gold armilla, whose value as old gold was £18, was found within a few miles of Leeds, and in 1868 an example of gold ring money, or rude ear-ring, weighing 336 grains, was found in a ploughed field at Cawood, which also passed into the hands of a goldsmith at Leeds.

Mr. Thomas W. Tew, of Carleton, near Pontefract, described some bones of Bos longifrons, which were found in April, 1869, whilst some men were excavating sand at Monk Hill, at about a depth of 12 feet from the surface. They got out some of the teeth, horncores, and other bones, when the soil above them fell and the teeth were again buried. The bones were submitted to Professor Owen, who identified them as belonging to the animal named. The bones of reindeer, Bos priscus, and Bos primogenius, have also been found with the specimens described.

The Rev. W. C. Lukis, F.S.A., contributed a description of the stone avenues of Carnac, and other pre-historic monuments of Brittany, which he had recently visited and mapped. He, however, did not attempt to decipher their meaning, but left that for future investigations.

Mr. John Ffooks, who at a previous meeting of the Society had read a paper on the flint implements found at Flamborough Head, laid before the Society the result of his further investigations. He considered that before the use of flint, men would probably use wood, bone, or soft stone for their weapons. These, however, from various causes, would more readily disappear than the harder flint. The first weapons of those early people would naturally be a stone, which they threw, and a stick which they fashioned into the form of a club to strike with, and it is from these primeval implements that Mr. Ffooks traces the advent and use of the several flint implements found in the district. The stick would become a far more deadly weapon if attached to the end of it there was a flint implement, and hence the ingenuity of the people was exercised in attaching flints of various kinds, by thongs or otherwise, to the end of the stick, and so forming, in the first place hatchets, and then spears, darts or javelins, and arrows. The stone thrown from the hand gained greater force when whirled from a sling, hence sling stones. He had found many stones which had evidently been formed for holding in the hand to strike with. These were sharp at one point, whilst the other end was naturally or artificially formed for holding in the hand. Of household implements, he describes knives of various kinds, scrapers, the most important use of which he considered was for splitting willows and stripping off the bark and cleaning them for basket work. They were also probably used for giving an even and plain surface to flat boards, and for this purpose appeared to have been formed straight on one side and oblique on the other. Sharp-pointed flints were used for making small holes in skins through which some kind of thread was passed to fasten the different parts together. He described several kinds of flint fish-hooks, which he considered were adapted for catching the various fish which occur in great abundance in the bay ; and a number of objects of flint, of more or less artistic construction, which were probably used for ornamental dress fastenings. The people were not destitute of refinement, and of the comforts of life ; they joined in communities and built their huts in regular order ; they were acquainted with the uses of fire, and having made bread, it is not likely that their cooking would reach to this extent alone. That they had considerable skill in the manufacture of wicker work is proved by the Romans when they came as conquerors to the island, sending examples of this work to their Imperial city. Altogether they appear to have been a vigorous and intelligent people, who possessed determination to promote their own happiness.

The Rev. J. T. Fowler recorded the discovery of an Anglo-Saxon ring near Driffield, by a ploughman feeling a slight obstruction to his ploughshare, it was a fine specimen of the goldsmiths' work, probably of the seventh or eighth century. A notice was given by Mr. Henry Denny of the discovery of a pair of ancient shoes and a human skeleton, in a pit on Austwick Common, near Clapham. The skeleton occurred at a depth of about ten feet from the original surface, and near it was the pair of shoes, though not connected with it. This is stated to have been the only record of a human body being found in peat in Yorkshire, the description of which is followed by a learned disquisition on the pair of shoes found with it, and old shoes in general. This was followed by an interesting paper on the Runic monuments of Northumbria, by the Rev. Daniel Henry Haigh, of Erdington. The runes are a system of writing which the Jutes, Angles, and Saxons brought with them to England in the fifth century, a system which they had preserved from times of remote antiquity, quite distinct from the old Semitic alphabet, the parent of the alphabets of Greece and Italy. The origin of the system is unknown, and only exists engraved on tombs or stone monuments of other kinds. There are probably a larger number of runic inscriptions in Northumbria than in all England besides, and of several of them the author gave a description.

CHAPTER XIV.

PROCEEDINGS, 1859—1870.

Between 1859-61, a series of papers were communicated by Capt. Drayson, the Astronomer, etc., at the Royal Military Academy, Woolwich, in which he endeavoured to show that the land was raised from the sea by the expansion of the crust of the earth, and that the glacial period, as generally recognised by geologists, was due to the extreme inclination of the orbit of the poles of the earth towards the plane of the sun. He quotes Kepler's third law, that the masses of the planet vary as the square roots of the distance, and endeavours to prove that the density of the earth was at one time considerably greater than it is now; and if that be so, it follows that the earth's orbit must have been less, and that it would have had a correspondingly closer proximity to the sun. The density of the rocky crust of the earth is equal to about $2\frac{1}{2}$ times that of water, the mean density of the whole earth five times the density of water. To the pressure upon the central masses and their condensation is due the increased weight, and before the expansion of the crust of the earth it must have been much greater than at the present time. He adduces the opinion of eminent geologists that during the formation of the gneiss and micacious beds there is no proof of any land having emerged from the water, and it was not until the close of the primary period that any of the continents began to emerge from this universal sea. If therefore at this early period of the earth's history, there had been no elevation of land, the pressure upon the internal and central parts of the globe must have been at its maximum consequently, according to the law of Kepler, the earth must have been much nearer to the sun during the evolution of the rocks above the old red sandstone which Captain Drayson calls secondaries. There was a constant expansion of the earth, and its body became separated by a proportionably greater distance from the sun. During the carboniferous period the growth of plants exceeded in luxuriance the productions of the hottest parts of the globe at the present time; and this, according to the author, is exactly the result that might be expected. In addition to the closer proximity of the earth to the sun, and the inclination of its polar axis, the sun would be for one-fourth of the year constantly above the horizon, and a much greater temperature would be maintained than would be possible at present, so that vegetation would spring up in enormous quantities, and whilst the extent of winter would be equally great and proportionably severe the plants would be frozen, and at the same time preserved by the great covering of snow. During the succeeding epoch, whilst the Permian beds were in process of formation, the earth's crust was greatly disturbed by faults and dislocations. These are all shown to be due to a further expansion of the earth's crust, which appears at this time to have been more abrupt and violent than any either preceding or succeeding it. The greater expansion of the earth removed it still further from the sun, and the decreased temperature rendered possible the existence of the succeeding forms of animal life, which have successively peopled its surface. In more recent times, old coast lines and raised beaches are brought forward as proofs of the further expansion of the earth. Fissures, joints, mineral veins, are all considered in support of this theory. Astronomical arguments are adduced in favour of it, and a comparison is made between the position of the north pole of the planets as compared with that of the earth with regard to the sun. The planet Venus may be taken as an example of his argument. Venus is spherical like the earth, rotates on its axis, has an atmosphere, and in fact appears very like our globe, except that a singular annual variation of climate prevails upon her surface. "If Great Britain were tranferred to the same latitude on Venus that it occupies on our earth, we should have an Arctic climate in winter, during which the sun would be absent nearly 40 days, and thus Scotland, Wales and England would have their glaciers and icebergs formed in winter." In the summer, however, there would prevail a heat of which we have no conception. The sun would then return, and would remain 40 or 50 days entirely above the horizon, day and night, not low down, as is now the case in the Arctic regions, but nearly vertical. Those only who have felt the fierce heat of a tropical sun, which remains scarcely more than 12 hours above the horizon, can imagine what would be the intense furnace-like heat, were the sun to remain nearly vertical during 40 days and nights. The rocks on the surface, and even deep down in the earth, would become heated beyond anything which we have ever seen, whilst the sulphurous strata would be forced into a volcanic condition. These and many other changes are probably occurring in Venus, for on that planet the sun does so remain above the horizon.

In December, 1859, Dr. H. C. Sorby, F.R.S., read a paper on the temperature of the springs in the neighbourhood of Sheffield, in which he showed as the result of a number of experiments that the springs nearest the surface exhibited the greatest difference in temperature in summer and winter, and at the same time had the highest mean temperature. The springs which rise in the district, reaching an elevation of not more than 500 feet, had a mean temperature of $48\frac{1}{4}$ degrees, whilst springs on higher elevations, reaching to 1,275 feet, had an average of about $45\frac{1}{2}$ degrees. Many springs in the neighbourhood of Sheffield are strong chalybeates. As a general rule there is small variation between the summer and winter temperature of these springs, which clearly points to their deep-seated origin, a conclusion which is further established by their temperature being some degrees higher than that of the ordinary springs under similar circumstances. Dr. Sorby concludes that this increased temperature proceeds either from the greater depth from which the waters come, so that they experience the warming effects of the interior of the globe, or else that their temperature is somewhat raised by the oxidation of the pyrites of the subjacent strata, to which, no doubt, their chalybeate character is due.

Dr. C. W. Bingley, of Whitley Hall, recorded the result of some experiments he had made on the properties of the different clays for making firebricks. A considerable difference is well-known to exist in the fire-clays as regards their power to resist heat and withstand any sudden change of temperature when intensely heated, as in the case of the withdrawal of crucibles and the cooling of furnaces. In order to ascertain the degree of fusibility of each kind of clay it was baked or burnt to the state of an ordinary firebrick, from which portions were chipped so as to present several sharp, angular edges. These were placed in crucibles lined with powdered charcoal, and afterwards heated in a wind furnace to the fullest possible extent. After cooling, the comparative value of each was estimated by the degree to which it had resisted fusion, as shown by the thin edges of the broken piece being rounded or rendered translucent. To denote the power of resisting sudden changes of temperature without cracking, a crucible was made of each kind of clay, and after carefully drawing, they were subjected, without previous annealing, to the heat of an intensely heated furnace, and when thoroughly heated to the temperature of the furnace suddenly withdrawn and exposed to a current of cold air. On comparing the results of these experiments, it appeared that those clays which contained the minimum amount of oxides of iron and the alkaline earths are the best adapted to resist fusion, and least liable to crack upon being exposed to any sudden change of temperature, and the clays most serviceable for these purposes are those which approach nearest to the typical composition of one equivalent of allumina combined with two of silicic acid and two of water.

Mr. Samuel Baines read a paper on some differences in the deposition of coal. In a previous paper he had advanced the opinion that the Yorkshire Freestone is an estuarine deposit, and being continuous with the coal series further research has confirmed the opinion that the Coal-field generally is one large estuarine deposit. The formation of the coal he surmised to be due more to the annual fall of foliage than to the stems themselves. The reed-like Calamite has evidently been a water plant from its being found in such abundance in the black shale rather than in the coal itself. The presence of remains of bivalve shells and fish in cannal coal clearly proved that it was formed under water, and ordinary coal was probably accumulated in low, marshy islands or deltas in the mouths or estuaries of large rivers. That it was a very quiet deposit is shown by the absence of water-worn pebbles.

In April, 1860, Mr. John Watson, of Whitby, contributed a paper on the Geology of the Esk Valley, in which he described the several series of rocks composing the Oolitic and Lias formations exhibited there. He described the method of obtaining alum from the Alum Shales of the Lias at the Kettleness Alum Works, now disused. At these Alum Works pieces of lignite had been obtained, weighing two or three hundredweight, completely encrusted with jet about half an inch in thickness. The manufacture of jet ornaments appears to have been known in Whitby since about 1589 ; the use of it subsequently declined, and in 1810 there was no consumption of jet in the town. Now the manufacture of jet was the staple trade of Whitby, and during the previous year (1859) the amount of money turned over at Whitby in jet was £20,000, and it found employment for 800 or 1,000 of the inhabitants. At the conclusion of the paper, Prof. Robert Hunt said he did not think that jet was due directly to the conversion of lignite. He was disposed to believe that the vegetable matter from which jet may have been derived was first converted into a sort of fluid bitumen, which was eventually consolidated into jet ; and he referred to specimens in the museum at Whitby in proof of his argument. Prof. Hunt read a paper on the iron ores of Lincolnshire. He had examined the district about half a mile from the railway station at Kirton-in-Lindsay. The iron ore was found about a foot below the cultivated surface ; in some places it was only necessary to remove a few inches of soil and the iron ore deposit was exposed. It was in a loose state of aggregation, and had the appearance of a ferruginous earth. It varied in depth from two to five feet. Similar superficial deposits occur at Schimthorpe, where the bed was ten or fourteen feet in thickness. The upper part was composed of a black sand, nearly pure peroxide of iron. Lower down it became more indurated. Analyses of several examples of the iron ore were made by Mr. Pattinson, of Newcastle, and Mr. Sollitt, of Hull, the results of which were given. These analyses show that the beds must at one time have been Carbonate of Iron, and it is probable that the long-continued action of percolating water and of atmospheric air has produced the change to oxide. Similar iron workings occur at Stamford and near Peterboro'. They are similar to the deposits so well known in Northamptonshire,

At the succeeding meeting, Mr. Richard Carter, C.E., made some observations on colliery ventilation, in which he enunciated the principles which form the subject of a paper previously referred to. The principle of direct ascending ventilation was then being pursued by several colliery proprietors, and had justified the representations as to its perfect and economical application which he had ventured to make. Mr. W. R. Milner of Wakefield, gave the results of investigations he had made as to the relation of explosions in coal pits, and the state of the barometer at or preceding the time of the explosion, the result of which showed that of 79 explosions, 59 took place when the barometer was lower than it had been 24 hours previously, and 20 when it was higher; 60 when the barometer was lower than it had been 48 hours previously, and 19 when it was higher; 44 of the explosions occurred when the barometer stood lower on the day of the explosion than the mean of the month in which the explosion occurred. The result clearly indicated that a slight difference in barometric pressure produced the escape of the gas, either from the coal or old workings, which had so frequently been attended with fatal results.

Mr. Jepson read a paper on Water Springs and their relation to Manufactures, in which he indicated the most probable situations from which water could be obtained by wells. Incidentally, he remarked on the foolishness of contaminating the rivers with refuse water, and thus depriving everyone on the stream below of the use of it. One cannot help speculating as to the advantage which would be derived by manufacturing towns and commercial districts, if some of the money which has been expended on erecting reservoirs and preserving drainage areas for the supply of pure water, had been expended in conducting the refuse water from those places to the sea, and using the pure water from the streams for manufacturing and domestic purposes.

In May, 1861, a communication was made by the assistant Secretary of the Society, Mr. Denny, suggesting the introduction of the silk-worm into the West Riding. Attempts had been made to introduce the common silk-worm (*Bombyx mori*) into England which had failed. Now there was a second species from Assam (*Bombyx cynthia*) which had been introduced successfully into Germany, Sweden, and Russia, and the experiments which had been made seemed to show that this silk-worm might be cultivated in England. The value of the silk industry in this country was shown by the fact that the exports in 1856 reached the large sum of £3,000,000, and that over 200,000,000 spindles were at work in spinning silk, and it is probable that not less than half-a-million of persons were engaged in the silk industry. The difficulty connected with the growth of the mulberry trees was spoken of, and the result of some experiments made by Mrs. Whitby in the growth of silk appeared to prove that a good strong, sound silk could be produced at a cost that would be very remunerative.

The next meeting was held at Halifax, and was presided over by Mr. John Waterhouse, F.R.S., Mr. Francis A. Leyland read a paper giving some account of the Roman roads in the parish of Halifax, with especial reference to the claims of Almondbury, Slack, and Greetland as the site of Cambodunum. Prior to the Roman invasion the most powerful tribes in England, recorded by Julius Cæsar, were those of Brigantia. The parish of Halifax occupied a large extent of the hilly country on the western confines of Brigantia proper, and was so situated that several ancient roads which were necessary to connect the towns on each side of the Penine Chain must have passed through it. These, during their possession by the ferocious and woad-stained Brigantes, consisted of wretched hovels and palisaded encampments. On the advent of the Romans they quickly gave place to cities and towns of considerable architectural beauty, with public buildings and villas, reminding one of the architecture of Italy. Recent examinations had brought to light several remains of extensive buildings and baths, tesselated pavements and mural decorations, and altars which record the faithfully-performed vow of some favoured individual, or which had been dedicated to Jupiter. The most important city was undoubtedly Eboracum; next in importance was Isurium, or Aldborough, whose former greatness is attested by the extent of its remains and the interesting discoveries which have recently been made there. Its walls were estimated at a mile and a half in circuit. Before the subjugation of the Brigantes it was the capital of the province. The great military road between York and Manchester, traced out by Mr. Leyland, was shown to go by Slack and Castleshaw, with a branch to Greetland and Littleboro'. Mr. Leyland gave a description of the discovery of a Roman altar at Thick Hollins, lying upon the height near Clay House. This altar had been erected at the beginning of the third century, about the time of the expedition of the Emperor Severus and his sons against the Caledonians, and bears an inscription to the effect that it was dedicated by Titus Aurelius Aurelanus to the God of the states of the Brigantes, and to the deities of the Emperor, on behalf of himself and his, in grateful remembrance of their undertakings. The altar was removed by Sir John Savile to Bradley Hall, and has since been deposited in the British Museum. At Slack, which Mr. Leyland considered to be the site of the ancient Cambodunum, large numbers of the foundations of Roman houses have been found, and it has been a common practice for long past to dig for fence-stones from the foundations of these buildings. Subsequently to the reading of this paper investigations have been prosecuted at Slack, and the walls of a Roman bath, and houses with tiled floors have been unearthed. The objects discovered have since been placed in the Museum of the Halifax Literary and Philosophical Society. Discussing the direction of the ancient Roman roads, Mr. Leyland expressed the opinion that whilst they would avail themselves of the ways previously formed by the Brigantes, it is extremely unlikely that their successors would desert the roads made by the greatest road-makers of antiquity for the purpose of forming new ones, and he considered that most of those roads are still used at the present day.

At a meeting of the Society held in March, 1867, Mr. Richard Reynolds described a Fire and Choke Damp Indicator invented by Mr. Ansell, of the Royal Mint. The action of this instrument depends on the permeability of gases through more or less solid substances. The diffusion of fire-damp through a thin pellicle of india-rubber placed across the top of an iron funnel, provided with a U tube, to the end of which a piece of glass tube is fixed in brass, and to these the pole of a battery is attached. In the iron tube is placed mercury, and when diffusion takes place the mercury is pressed up against a platinum point which establishes communication of the electric current. By placing this instrument near the roof of a colliery the presence of fire-damp may be detected with the greatest nicety, and communication made with an electric bell, which at once gives warning of its presence.

The Rev. John S. Tute, in a paper on the Geology of the country near Ripon, described several rocks occurring in the neighbourhood of Ripon, comprising the new Red Sandstone and the Magnesian Limestone. He drew attention to the sparry cavities so characteristic of the latter, and inferred that they had probably arisen from the decay of organic remains. At Aldfield a considerable number of fossil mollusca had been obtained. Below these beds was the Red Grit of the Cayton Gill Beds, the latter at Hampsthwaite and other places being highly fossiliferous. Below these are the Coal measures. Ripon is built upon a thick bed of glacial drift, which lies in a trough between the Magnesian Limestone and the New Red Sandstone. The glacial beds are deposited in the bottoms and on the sides of valleys which were excavated before the glacial period. Eastward the drift passes imperceptibly into the general superficial deposits of the Vale of York. On the sides of the valley of the Ure extensive beds of gravel are located, which were probably derived by the action of water from the glacial beds.

At the same meeting a paper was contributed on the Geology of parts of Yorkshire and Westmoreland, by Prof. T. McKenny Hughes, M.A., of Her Majesty's Geological Survey, in which he called attention to points of special interest, some of which required still further working out. The mountainous districts of Yorkshire, comprising Ingleborough, Whernside, and Penyghent consist chiefly of Yoredale Rocks, capped by Millstone Grit, resting on a great plateau of Mountain Limestone. The great Craven faults bring down the Mountain Limestone against the Silurian Rocks, and the higher formations against the Mountain Limestone. Mr. Hughes considers that the Green Slates and Coniston Limestone at Chapel-le-dale, Kingsdale, and Horton must be referred to the Lower Silurians, and are the equivalents of the Carradoc Sandstone and Bala Limestone of Wales. These rocks were hardened and upheaved, and their edges denuded before the Upper Silurians were deposited. This may be seen near Austwick, where on the south side of Southwaite Farm there is, at the base of the Coniston Flag Series, a red conglomerate resting on shales of Lower Silurians. The division may be equally well seen in other places, and substantiates the classification of Prof. Sedgwick, who separated the Coniston Flags from the Coniston Limestone, placing the former at the base of the Upper Silurian Series of the Lake district. The red conglomerates about Kirby Lonsdale and Sedburgh, regarded as Old Red Sandstone, are evidently the waste of neighbouring land, re-sorted on the sea bottom, formed during the time preceding the growth of the Mountain Limestone. The view of Prof. Ramsay, who regarded these conglomerates as having a glacial origin, was regarded as somewhat doubtful. Prior to the deposition of the Mountain Limestone, the Silurian Rocks were planed down and reduced to a more or less even surface, and indicate an enormous lapse of time between the two formations. The phenomena indicated by the clays and drifts of the glacial period received considerable attention. The drifts appear to be divided into three parts; the lowest is a stiff blue or brown clay of great density and hardness: the next is a common drift of a more arenacious character; and the third consists of morainic matter left by the receding glaciers as the climate grew warmer, something allied to kames and eskers. The direction of the great glaciers descending the deep gorges between the Howgill and Wild Boar Fells, across Grassdale and Dentdale, over the hilly ranges called the Riggs, along Holme Fell to the Lune Valley, is traced by the scratches left on the hill sides where the hard rocks have been bared. The interesting collection of Silurian grits resting on the Mountain Limestone plateau of Norber was described. They were considered to be due to the action of the glacier which filled the valley between Ingleboro' and Pennyghent.

Prof. Louis C. Miall, at the same meeting, read a paper on the great system of Anticlinals in South Craven. They occupy a considerable area south of Settle, extending towards Colne, and are well exposed at Rainhill and Thornton, where the low hills occupying the valley have been extensively quarried. The rocks consist of argillaceous shales passing into black laminated limestone, which rests immediately upon the lower scar limestone, all much contorted. At Slaidburn similar rocks may be seen, and in Lothersdale there is an exposure at Ray Gill, a vast quarry of contorted limestone. The beds are much faulted, and veins of barytes traverse the limestone in the lines of fault. At Park Head Quarry, an anticlinal is manifest, and in the Skipton Rock, limestone has been quarried, so that a considerable surface is exposed, the beds standing at a very high angle towards Bolton Abbey; a good section may be seen at Draughton. Near Bolton Bridge the anticlinal crosses the Wharfe and extends towards Blubber-houses, and thence to Harrogate and Knaresborough. The anticlinals are due to lateral pressure, such as would be caused by unequal resistance to the thrust of a mountain mass. The crust of the earth being in a state of tension, denudation or other agents destroyed its equilibrium and caused lateral motion, and in many cases elevation at the weaker points; and to some such action extending over an indefinite period, the Craven anticlinals are attributed.

Mr. J. W. Salter contributed a paper on Sacocaris, a new genus of Phyllopoda, from the lingula flags. This species had been discovered by Mr. Humfrey, and was the first of its kind that had been discovered on so low a horizon.

Mr. Denny read a paper which had been forwarded to him by Dr. G. Seyffarth, professor in the Concord College, St. Louis, U.S., on the remarkable mummy in the collection of the Literary and Philosophical Society at Leeds, from which it appears that it is the remains of an Egyptian minister born in 1722, B.C., 144 years subsequent to the exodus of the Israelites. The mummy was procured from Gournou, the burial place at Thebes, and transmitted to London for sale. It was purchased by the late Mr. Blaydes, and presented to the museum in 1824. The mummy's name was Enkasiv-Amun, and he was minister during the combined reigns of Osimanphtha and Rameses. An interesting description is given of the hieroglyphics on the clothing of the mummy, illustrated by figures.

On the 3rd September, 1862, the Society appears to have had its first geological excursion; in this respect, following the example of the Manchester Geological Society, which had held occasional field days. The members met at the museum of the Philosophical Society at Halifax at ten o'clock in the morning, and were joined by a number of members of the Manchester Geological Society, including Messrs. Binney, Horsfall, Parker, Hodgson, Knowles, and Atkinson. Chevalier W. P. Barbel de Morny, captain of the Imperial Corps of Miners in Russia; Mr. H. Green; John Waterhouse, F.R.S., Dr. Alexander, Leyland, and Ward, of Halifax; Henry Briggs, P. O'Callaghan, Thomas Wilson, S. Baines, Edward Brook, R. Carter, J. Richardson, E. Woodhead and others were present. The collection of coal plants at the Halifax Museum was examined, and the party proceeded to Swan Bank Colliery, and the outcrops of the Hard and Soft Bed Coals were examined. Numerous examples of goniatites, nautilus, orthoceras, avicula-pecten, etc., were obtained. The Manchester geologists recognised these beds as identical with the lower or Rochdale series of Lancashire. The party proceeded to Mr. Richardson's at Southowram, and inspected his interesting collection of specimens. They then proceeded to some of the flagstone quarries of Southowram and Hipperholme, and afterwards partook of lunch at Holroyd House, the residence of Mr. Baines. The party thence proceeded to Low Moor by rail, and inspected the Low Moor Ironworks, and went down one of the Better Bed Coal pits, under the guidance of Mr. Woodhead. In due course they adjourned to the Railway Hotel and there dined, bringing the day's proceedings to a satisfactory conclusion.

On May 28th, 1863, a meeting was held at Leeds, at which Mr. H. C. Sorby, F.R.S., read a paper on the microscopical structure of Mount Sorrel Syenite, artificially fused and cooled slowly. He was indebted to Mr. James G. Marshall for the material used in his microscopical enquiries. Mr. Marshall had, in some instances, melted as much as a ton of rock, and allowed it to cool very slowly. From this thin sections were prepared for the microscope. The rock is a mixture of reddish felspar, clear green hornblende, and quartz, along with some opaque mineral in a greatly altered state, perhaps originally pyrites, or magnetic oxide of iron. The quartz contains many fluid cavities nearly filled with water, a feature which had been previously described by the author at the Geological Society in London. The cavities indicate that the rock was consolidated under a very great pressure. They show the spontaneous movement of the bubbles which they contain extremely well. The description is given of specimens taken from different parts of the cooled mass, which show no kind of similarity with the natural rock. Where it does resemble a natural rock it is more like basalt than granite, and its structure is identical with some of the stony masses obtained by fusing basalt or basaltic lavas. He was led to the conclusion that the natural rock, before being crystallised, was in a very different condition to the artificial state after melting, which is especially shown by the fluid cavities in the quartz. This water, and the intense pressure under which the rock was formed, are features which the author had been unable to imitate in the artificial product, but he contended that such experiments, and the microscopical examination of the resulting masses, were likely to lead to a far better knowledge of the igneous rocks than we at present possess.

Mr. Denny described a fossil plant which had not hitherto been noticed, from the Carboniferous Sandstone near Leeds. It was apparently the terminal portion of the root of a plant resembling Stigmaria, but differing from it in the scars being elevated above the surface, and of a lozenge-shaped pattern.

Mr. Phillip Cooper read a paper at Huddersfield on the effects of certain geological arrangements on the working of Coal. Contrary to a generally received opinion he considered that faults were beneficial in draining the water from the strata, and thus preventing a large expenditure of money in pumping. He cited a number of instances where a bed of coal became divided by intervening strata, sometimes to a very large extent; due, according to Sir Charles Lyell, to a slow settling of a part of the area of the coal bed after a lower portion had been deposited, together with a subsequent deposition of shale, etc., of which they are formed. He concluded by stating the difficulty there will be in working very deep beds of coal, from the great increase of temperature. At a depth of 4,000 feet the temperature would be 100 to 120 degrees, and hitherto the experience in ventilating mines had been that very little difference in temperature was produced by the influx of fresh air.

In March, 1865, Mr. T. W. Embleton, of Middleton Colliery,

near Leeds, introduced a new Hydraulic Coal-cutting Machine to the members. It was manufactured by Messrs. Garrett, Marshall & Co., of Leeds, and was then at work at Kippax. The machine was worked by water pressure, produced by an engine placed at the bottom of the shaft. The pressure employed varied from 150 to 300 pounds per square inch. It had an 18 inch stroke, and made 25 strokes per minute, using in that time 40 gallons of water. The cutting bar is furnished with three cutters, which effected at one stroke a depth of 3 feet 3 inches. As much as 39 feet in length on the face of the coal had been cut in the above depth in an hour. The cost was less than half that of getting coal by hand labour. The produce of slack was very much less, and the net result was a saving of 10½d. per ton upon the produce.

Mr. Sorby contributed a paper on Impressed Limestone Pebbles, as illustrating a new principle in chemical geology. Much attention had been drawn on the continent to the curious phenomenon of one pebble penetrating another, sometimes to such an extent that it nearly passed through it without there being any apparent fracture. Mr. Sorby considered that this must be explained by the convertibility of mechanical pressure into chemical action, the pebbles being pressed one against the other with great force at a considerable depth below the surface of the earth, and surrounded with water saturated with Carbonate of Lime the limestone would dissolve, so that in time one pebble would penetrate into the other, and Carbonate of Lime would be deposited in a crystalline form elsewhere, where the pressure was less.

In October, 1867, at a meeting held at Barnsley, Mr. A. H. Green, M.A., of H.M. Geological Survey, read a paper on the Geology of the Barnsley Coal-field. The rocks in this district of Yorkshire consist of Coal Measures, Millstone Grit, and Mountain Limestone. The latter is a mass of pure Limestone, of great but unknown thickness, with very few thin layers of interbedded shale, and two or three beds of lava and volcanic ash. The latter are interbedded with the limestone, and must, therefore, have been deposited during its formation. The limestone is very fossiliferous, and was formed in a clear sea, unstained by mud. In the course of time the sea-bottom was, from time to time, alternately raised and depressed, and beds of sand and mud in large quantities were carried into it, the result being the aggregation of the Yoredale Series and the Millstone Grits. The Coal Measures resemble the latter to some extent, but the sandstones are less coarse and persistent, and workable beds of coal are numerous and important. The fact that each of these required for its formation a land surface shows that during the coal measure period the oscillation of the sea-bottom was more pronounced than during the millstone grit times, and this is, no doubt, the reason for the greater subdivisions of the beds. The physical characteristics of the surface of the district, due to the peculiar characters of the underlying rocks, were described. The more or less tame and monotonous flats, with large rolling hills of Mountain Limestone; the gentle slopes on the one hand, and precipitous edges on the other, of the Millstone Grit; and the softer and more undulating scenery of the Coal Measures; are each characteristic of the rocks of which they are composed.

Mr. John Hutchinson, of Barnsley, gave the result of some observations on Fire Damp and Safety Lamps, and the circumstances under which the fire damp will explode. A number of experiments are described which had been made in conjunction with Mr. Wilson, of the Driffield Lane Colliery, and Mr. Minto, of the Mount Osborne Colliery, to show the comparative merits of the different kinds of Safety Lamps. A rectangular box was constructed 12 feet in length, and 11 inches by 4 inches inside. This was inserted into a flue in connection with the chimney shaft to obtain a current of air. The velocity of this current was regulated by a small sliding door near the inner end, and a second sliding door about the centre was provided of sufficient size to admit a Safety Lamp. A service pipe of coal-gas was connected by means of an india-rubber tube, and allowed to play into the end of the box, the amount of gas and the force of the current of pure air being regulated at pleasure, so as to produce a miniature working of a pit in which an escape of gas may be found. With the current of air passing through the box at the rate of five miles an hour, not an uncommon velocity in a pit, the following comparative results were obtained:—The Davy Lamp exploded in five seconds; the Mousarde in six; the Clanny in 12; the Belgian in 13; and the

Stephenson in 25 secs. These experiments tended to prove that all the Safety Lamps were really unsafe in a current of atmospheric air and gas when mixed to an explosive point ; and secondly, that of the lamps now in use the Stephenson is the most reliable. Somewhat similar experiments with actual coal-gas had been made in the Oaks Pit, the results being practically the same.

Mr. Richard Carter, C.E., made some observations on Ventilation in Relation to Colliery Disasters. The fatality which attended the explosion in the Oaks Colliery in the December previous, when over 300 miners were killed, and a party, at whose head was Parkin Jeffcock, who went down to aid in recovering them, were also lost, led Mr. Carter to again insist on the common-sense method of ventilation, which he had described in papers contributed to the Society in 1857 and 1860 respectively.

In the succeeding year Mr. A. H. Green contributed a second paper on the Coal Measures of the neighbourhood of Rotherham. The Middle Coal Measures, extending between this town and Flockton, were described. The lowest of the thick workable coals was the Silkstone, Sheffield or Black Shale Coal, a bituminous bed of great purity, yielding excellent house coal, and well suited for cokeing. The succeeding beds of coal, with the intervening sandstones and shales, are described *seriatim*. About a hundred yards above the Flockton lies a coal or group of coals, about the identification of which, in different parts of the field, there was some uncertainty. It was known in one place as the Swallow Wood Coal with a dirt parting, altogether about 4 feet 6 inches in thickness. It appears to keep this character as far as Tankersley, where it is worked for local purposes, and is about 3 feet thick. Thence to Barnsley nothing definite is known about the coal, but it is the custom to bore down below the Barnsley Coal, and call the bed that could by any possibility be supposed workable by the name of the Swallow Wood. This caused considerable confusion, and Mr. Green believed that though several beds bear this name, a coal may be fixed upon as the equivalent of the true Swallow Wood in the Sheffield district. It is, however, of inferior quality, and so split up by dirt partings as to be of little worth. Northwards, about Darton and Netherton, there are two beds of coal called the Netherton

Thick and Thin, and still further on these seem to run together and form the valuable seam of the Haigh Moor. They hold about the same position as the Swallow Wood, and may prove to be the same coal. The succeeding measures are traced up to the Shafton Coal, and the red rock of Rotherham was described. This was referred by Prof. Sedgwick to the marls and sandstones beneath the Magnesian Limestone generally as the Rothliegendie. Fairey, Thorp, and other local Geologists looked upon it as a regularly interbedded sandstone of the Coal Measures. Mr. Green was of opinion that it was a member of the Coal Measure Series, but unconformable with the strata composing the coal formation. After the main mass of that formation had been deposited, upheaved, and denuded, the red rock and the beds overlying it were laid down upon the truncated edges of the previously-formed strata, so that these latter rocks rest sometimes on one member, sometimes on another, of the older Carboniferous series. He further considered that the problem of the red rock of Rotherham was by no means solved, and was one to which local observers would do well to turn their attention. A paper was read at the same meeting on the nature of the Graptolitidæ, with notes on the British genera by Dr. H. Alleyne Nicholson, of Keighley, which was not published.

At a meeting held in April, 1869, at Wakefield, the statement of receipts and expenditure for the year ending October, 1868, was presented. The total income was £64 7s. 0d. The principal items of expenditure were for printing, £18 19s. 0d.; Rent of Museum Rooms at the Philosophical Hall, £10 0s. 0d.; and Assistant Secretary, on account, £26 8s. 6d.; which together with smaller items absorb the whole. Messrs. J. G. Marshall and T. W. Embleton were re-appointed Honorary Curators of the joint collections of the Philosophical Society and the West Riding Geological and Polytechnic Society.

A number of natural pits in the valley of the Ure, near Ripon, formed the subject of a paper by the Rev. John Stanley Tute, of Markington. They occur in an area of about a square mile, on the north-east side of the city, and consist of crater-like hollows from 50 to 100 feet across, and sometimes with large and perpendicular shafts. They generally occur within half-a-mile of the river, which at this point flows round an escarpment of red sandstone. Some of the pits are of ancient date; others have been formed within recent years. One fell in in June, 1836, and another in the spring of 1860. The level of the river is about 80 feet below the tops of these pits, and some of the shafts have a depth of between 60 and 80 feet. During wet seasons, and when the river is high, water can be seen at the bottom of them; usually they are dry. Mr. Tute is of opinion that the pits have been formed by the washing away of the red marl and gypsum by subterranean streams connected with the river. This would cause dome-shaped caverns in the magnesian limestone which overlie the gypsum, and when the pit had become sufficiently large so that it did not afford a support for the overlying limestone, it naturally fell in, and the large dome-shaped hollows were the result.

At the same meeting, Mr. Louis C. Miall, Curator of the Bradford Philosophical Society, read a paper on a new carboniferous labyrinthodont, which had been discovered in the roof of the black-bed coal at Toftshaw, near Bradford. Remains of amphibia are by no means rare in the coal shales of the British Islands, and specimens of their vertebræ, skulls, and teeth, have frequently been found. The specimens found in the West Riding coal field have hitherto been very fragmentary. The specimen described was the most complete that had been discovered; nearly 6 feet in length, it possessed twenty-six vertebræ, eighteen ribs, and a well-marked skull showing forty-two teeth, and a large number of scutes in their proper relative position. The specimen had been sent for description to Professor Huxley, and was described in the Quarterly Journal of the Geological Society as a new generic and specific form under the name of *Pholiderpeton scutigerum*. Mr. Miall gave a detailed description of the fossil, and considered the classificatory position of the group of amphibians to which it belongs.

The Seventy-fifth meeting of the members of the Society was held at the Cutlers' Hall, Sheffield, on the 29th April, 1870; Lord Wharncliffe, a Vice-President, occupied the chair. The following gentlemen were appointed local secretaries :—Dr. Sorby at Sheffield;

Dr. Alexander, Halifax ; Mr. T. W. Tew, Pontefract ; Mr. Louis C. Miall, Bradford ; Rev. S. F. Surtees, Doncaster ; Mr. Bentley Shaw, Huddersfield ; Mr. Richard Carter, Barnsley ; Dr. Paley, Ripon ; Mr. J. Guest, Rotherham. Mr. William Sykes Ward was re-elected Honorary Secretary, and Mr. Henry Denny, Assistant Secretary. The balance sheet showed an income to January, 1870, amounting to £69 11s. 0d.; the whole of this amount was disbursed ; the principal items as before being for printing, &c., £25 12s. 6d.; rent of museum, £10 ; and the Assistant Secretary, in part payment, £24 4s. 6d.

At this meeting a paper was read by Mr. D. Mackintosh on the Drift Deposits of the West Riding of Yorkshire, with some remarks on the origin of escarpments, valleys, and outlet gorges. Mr. Mackintosh described between 40 and 50 sections in the drifts which he had examined in the valleys of the Aire, the Wharfe, and the Nidd ; and on the hills extending between them. He found that the lowest beds in the drifts consisted of a greyish-blue and variegated boulder clay ; above this was a yellowish-brown boulder clay gradually merging into sand and stratified gravel. Superimposed on this was an upper boulder clay or loam, and in the lower part of the valley he had found deposits to which the vague term of warp had been applied. Occasionally the yellow clays were absent, and the blue clay merged in the sand and gravel. He considered that all these deposits were made when the land was at a considerably lower level than at present; that the detritus brought down by ice from the adjoining lands was deposited in the waters, and so the beds accumulated. The scratches on Rombalds Moor and other elevated positions he considered were proof that the land must have been to that extent completely submerged, and that the boulders and glacial scratchings were due to floating ice. With respect to the excavation of river gorges Mr. Mackintosh considered that those of the rivers Don and Went were first opened by one or more fractures or faults, and that whilst the land was submerged the ocean currents probably cleared out and enlarged the gorges, and that afterwards the river availed itself of this outlet from the plains of the west. The paper concluded with some remarks on the origin of the Plumpton and Brimham Rocks, and of Gordale Scar and Malham Cove.

Mr. E. Sewell read a paper on some Geological features of Rombolds Moor, and Mr. Walter Rowley, mining engineer, of Leeds, contributed some observations on Coal and Coal-mining and the economical working of our Coal-fields. Mr. Rowley described in detail the two methods of coal-getting in Yorkshire, viz., the pillar and stall and long-wall systems. He strongly advocated getting the coal on the latter system on end, by which means the coal is worked or broken off at right angles to its natural cleavage, and is obtained in much larger pieces than by working it along the face. He was of opinion that the extension of this system in coal-mining was the pioneer paving the way for the working at greater depths than we are accustomed to at present; for, under no system of pillar workings could we get adequate ventilation at such depths as necessity will compel those following after us to venture to; when it is necessary to work at depths of 1,200 yards and upwards we should strive to convey all the air we can collect direct to the working faces unimpaired, avoiding all structures or courses which would so diminish the amount as to render the ventilation totally inadequate. He considered that it would also pave the way for the extensive use of machinery in coal-getting. Already several inventions had been made for the purpose of getting coal both by hydraulic and compressed air machines, which he trusted might afford material for an interesting paper at another time.

In April, 1868, Mr. A. H. Green, who was then engaged making a Geological Survey of the Yorkshire Coal-field, wrote to the Rev. Scott F. Surtees, drawing his attention to the fact that he and his colleague, Mr. Holmes, had picked up a number of flint-flakes and some rude fragments of pottery at Clifton Common, near Conisboro'. This drew Mr. Surtees' attention to the district, and he found a number of pit dwellings which had formed an old British camp, one of the most perfect and symmetrical in England. The pits are in parallel rows, as if for defence as well as for habitation. The site is singularly well chosen to command a ford of the river, which is still called Strafford Sands. "Stratfod," the ford of the great Roman strata or street, running north and south. On the hill on which these pits occur is obtained one of the most extensive views in this part of the country, and it affords an admirable position for placing a camp for the maintenance of the ford and the protection of the district. The earth from each dwelling is thrown up in a horse-shoe form to make a platform for the erection of the stakes or trees to cover their dwellings and uphold the roof of ling or turf, as well as for protection against the wind. Similar dwellings, which the author attributes to the old Brigantes, occur near Danby Beacon, and on the top of Ingleboro', as well as other places. In addition to the 50 pits on this eminence, others are found in the fields adjoining, more or less obliterated by farming. Other implements were found, as well as a quantity of iron slag, which was evidently the result of some process of iron smelting, and very similar to large quantities of the same material which had been obtained from the cliffs between Cromer and Weyburn, where an immense number of pit dwellings had been found.

Mr. F. A. Leyland read a paper in 1870 on certain Roman Roads in Yorkshire in use at the present day. He traced a road from Ribchester, the Coccium of the Romans, to York; the distance is about 70 miles, and was divided into four stages, the first at Colne, the second at Ilkley (Olicana), the third at Wetherby, and the fourth at York. A second iter was traced from York to Chester, the intermediate stations being Leeds; Slack, at Longwood, between Halifax and Huddersfield; the third, Mancunium, or Manchester; and Chester. A third road was traced between Doncaster and Ribchester, with Halifax as an intermediate station. Much valuable information is given of discoveries of Roman remains at the places mentioned and along the lines of the several roads. Mr. Leyland concluded that most itinera improved by Ostorius or Agricola, have been in use ever since, and constitute the turnpike and packhorse roads of the present day. He infers that the numerous roads were rendered necessary by the vast military operations of the Romans at the time that they were formed, and indicate a continually impeding resistance somewhere within or about the district, which rendered these costly and formidable defences necessary, though history is for the most part silent on the important and stirring events which necessarily accompanied, at frequent and sudden intervals, the subjugation of this province.

CHAPTER XV.

PROCEEDINGS, 1871—1877.

After the death of the assistant secretary, Mr. Denny, in 1870, it became necessary to consider the position of the Society and its future prospects, and at a meeting held in July, 1871, at Leeds, when Mr. Thomas Wilson occupied the chair, a resolution was passed that the chairman, Messrs. W. Sykes Ward, T. W. Tew, T. W. Embleton, E. Filliter, Richard Reynolds, and L. C. Miall, with power to add to their number, be requested to prepare a report on the position and prospects of the Society, with suggestions for increasing its numbers and efficiency. Subsequent to the conclusion of the meeting the following letter was addressed to Mr. Embleton by Mr. Thomas Wilson, who continued to exhibit that interest in, and care for, the Society which had characterized him when occupying the position of Honorary Secretary during its earliest years.

Mr. Wilson to Mr. Embleton.

3, HILARY PLACE, LEEDS,
MY DEAR SIR, *28th July, 1871.*

The death of Mr. Denny has caused us to look into the position of the Geological and Polytechnic Society, and we find it somewhat in debt, and with an income not adequate to its present wants.

Our new curator, Mr. Miall, is wishful to work it with spirit, if we can manage to get such a list of subscribers as will pay its way. This ought not to be difficult, as £150 a year will cover all our expenses, that is about 230 members, towards which we have about 100, and could easily increase the number in Leeds and Bradford.

We had a meeting on Wednesday last, and appointed a small committee to examine into the state of the Society, and to advise as to its future. We ventured to put your man upon it, and I hope you will allow it to remain. If you could attend one or two meetings it is all we need ask from you. We will prepare a report, both as to the present state and the future working of the Society, and an hour some day when you are in Leeds will enable you to consider and to give us your advice. I should hope you will allow your name to remain on the Council, though I fear it would be hopeless to expect, with your engagements, that you could give us more than a temporary assistance. I am, my dear Sir, Yours truly,

T. W. Embleton, Esq., THOMAS WILSON.

The committee presented a report at a meeting held in January, 1872, at Keighley, Mr. John Brigg, J.P., in the chair, in which the following items occur :—They had investigated the position of the Society and found the number of members on the books to be 121. The arrears of subscriptions for 1871 amounted to £63 1s., and those for the previous year to £28 14s. The annual income of the Society was estimated at £78 13s., and its necessary expenditure at £73. The committee considered it possible to add largely to the number of members by an active canvass. It was considered a matter of great importance to support and strengthen an institution which had rendered good service to local geology for 34 years; and that there was an extensive field of work open to it in the future, the geological features of the West Riding being still imperfectly understood. The committee had considered the various ways in which the Society might be most useful, and they offered suggestions for its future management :—

"1.—That the proceedings of the Society should be more exclusively confined to geology and technology, the two branches of science which were contemplated as the proper field of the Society at its first institution. The department of local archæology is now occupied by a Yorkshire Society, which is labouring with energy and success to discharge those duties which this Society, inconsistently perhaps with its title, but still usefully, had taken upon itself.

"2.—That a small committee of revision, composed of five persons, of whom three should form a quorum, be appointed to examine all papers read at the Society's meetings, and to select such only as are specially suited for publication. That it be a standing instruction to this committee to recommend only those papers which contain valuable original matter on some of the subjects which are taken into consideration by the Society, or which had a special reference to the geology or industries of the West Riding.

"3.—That photographs of interesting geological phenomena within the Riding be issued periodically to the members, accompanied by descriptive letter-press. The photographs should be on a good scale, and if possible rendered permanent by some of the processes now in use. The committee had made enquiries as to the probable cost of such photographs, and they are of opinion that one or two plates, 14 inch by 9 inch, may be issued annually without incurring too heavy an expense.

"4.—That a summary of geological literature relating to the West Riding, published within the preceding year, be inserted in the annual report of the proceedings. The committee also recommend that a list of titles of papers on West Riding geology, contained in the transactions and journals for past years of the various Geological Societies, as well as of separate publications on the same subject, be issued in an early report."

Mr. Miall offered to undertake for one year, without salary, the duties of assistant secretary, and the committee recommended that this arrangement be sanctioned by the Society. It was further considered highly desirable to retain a collection of local fossils in some central part of the West Riding, and they urged the necessity of increasing and improving the collection of the Society under such regulations as may add to its usefulness as a means of public instruction.

This report was presented to the general meeting and adopted, and the proceedings of the Society for the years 1871-2 were issued to the members, together with a photograph of the contorted limestone at Draughton, and the Society from that time appears to have remained in a state of quiescence until the year 1875, when meetings were held at Halifax and Bradford, the former in April and the latter in October.

At the meeting held at Leeds in July, 1871, Mr. L. C. Miall read a paper recording the result of some experiments to illustrate the contortion of rocks. At a previous meeting he had drawn attention to the remarkable anticlinals in the limestone rocks of Skipton and Draughton, and during the past three years he had made experiments to show how these phenomena could have been produced, and under what conditions rocks once hard and laid horizontally, could be bent to an acute angle without fracture. Sir James Hall, in the early part of the century, had made some experiments to imitate the condition which he supposed to have resulted in the contorted strata on the Berwickshire coast. He placed pieces of cloth of various kinds on a flat surface, over which was placed a board loaded with weights. Pressure was then applied to each end of the layers of cloth, so that they were constrained to assume folds bent up and down, which very much resembled the convoluted beds on the coast. The result of these experiments seemed to prove that strata, originally horizontal, had been carved and folded, and that the disturbing force acted in a horizontal direction. He further considered that this force was accompanied by some volcanic action, but so far as the contortions in the Craven district are concerned there is no evidence of volcanic agency having been an accessory. Mr Miall's experiments were conducted on thin slabs of various rocks, four inches by three, and having a thickness of ·07 of an inch. After several experiments, he constructed a machine, in conjunction with Mr. Thomas Prince, of Bradford, by which pressure could be applied to these slabs conjointly and continuously for a period reaching over several months. Slabs of limestone and sandstone could be bent to a considerable angle without fracture ; but, on the pressure being removed, cracks slowly extended themselves across the part where the deflection was greatest. Thin plates of Mountain Limestone, especially the bituminous kind, proved indefinitely plastic, and it may be doubted whether there is any limit to the bending which a careful and patient observer could produce in them. Flagstone could be bent to a certain extent, but slate was very intractable. The frequent destruction of the plates by spontaneous fracture, when removed from the machine, seemed to indicate that unbroken anticlinals and synclinals are only formed under a considerable weight of subjacent strata, and to test this proposition Mr. Miall embedded the thin slabs of limestone in pitch, and fitted them into a cast-iron box, the two sides of which were removed so that horizontal pressure could be applied to the edges of the plates of rock. This arrangement proved successful, and slabs nine inches long were bent until they rose two-thirds of an inch in the centre.

The result of other experiments is given, and reference made to instances of contortion occurring in the rocks of several parts of the country, as well as others described by Dr. Hitchcock in New England.

At a succeeding meeting, Mr. Miall read papers on the formation of anthracite, and on the structure of ganoid fishes, introductory to an account of the ganoid fishes of the Yorkshire Coal-field. The latter entered into an elaborate discussion of the history and characters of the ganoid fishes, the author explaining at considerable length the result of the labours of Müller, described in a memoir, 'Ueber den Bau und die Grenzen der Ganoiden,' and further considered the position of the dipnous lepidosiren and ceratodus to the ganoids, indicating that the former would be included in the latter sub-division.

Mr. W. H. Dalton, of Her Majesty's Geological Survey, communicated a paper on the Geology of Craven. He described the physical geography and geology of the Aire Valley, dividing the latter into three districts. The first, from its source to Malham Cove, extends over a plateau of Mountain Limestone, with a small area of Silurian rocks; the second, including the contorted limestones and shales, extending southwards to Skipton; and the third area, composed of Millstone Grits and Lower Coal Measures, reaches to the base of the Permian limestones, in the lower part of the valley. The outcrop and lithological character of the several rocks are described, together with some remarks on their fossil contents.

Mr. Charles Bird, B.A., Honorary Secretary to the Bradford Philosophical Society, read a paper on the Red Beds at the base of the Carboniferous Limestone in the North-west of England. He gave a description of red and yellow sandstones and conglomerates which occur between the Silurian and Carboniferous systems. They appeared to have been deposited in shallow, brackish, or fresh waters, caused by the gradual contracting of the Silurian sea. After describing the red beds in several districts in England, Scotland, and the South of Ireland, he proceeded to indicate the localities in which they occur in the north-west of Yorkshire and neighbouring counties. At Kirby Lonsdale they appear as a very coarse, thick-bedded conglomerate, apparently dipping in the same direction as the Carboniferous Limestone, which may also be seen a little lower down in the banks of the river. They are also seen on the banks of a small brook flowing into the Lune, two miles north of Kirby Lonsdale, and in Barbon Beck, near the railway station. In each instance these conglomerates are bounded by faults. Two miles from Sedbergh, in the valley of the Rawthey, good sections may be seen. The red-beds occupy a cliff, 50 feet or 60 feet high, resting unconformably on the Coniston grits, and does not, in this locality, pass into the carboniferous limestone. Near Kendal, there are several patches, as well as at Tebay and Shap, where the series may be seen in ascending order by proceeding up the Birk Beck. In this series the lowest beds are of a red colour, gradually changing upwards to a fine whitish substance marked with dark spots. The whole series is about 270 feet in thickness. At Mell Fell, near Ullswater, the beds attain a thickness of 1,600 feet and 1,700 feet; and Mr. Goodchild, has recorded a series, about 2 feet in thickness, of these rocks east of the Penine fault, near Kirby Stephen and Brough. In all these localities, the red conglomerates rest upon, but are unconformable to the Upper Silurian rocks, and pass upwards into the Carboniferous Limestone. They probably represent a part of the waste of the old Silurian region before the deposition of the Carboniferous Limestone. Mr. Bird considers that they may indicate glacial action, but the absence of scratches on the stones also points to their having been subject to the action of water before being finally deposited, and it does not appear improbable that they may have formed beaches whilst the mountain limestone was being accumulated in the deeper waters adjoining.

Professor A. H. Green gave the result of his investigations on the variations in thickness and character of the Silkstone and Barnsley Coal Seams in the southern part of the Yorkshire Coal-field, and the probable manner in which these and similar changes have been produced. In the southern part of the Yorkshire Coal-field, the Silkstone coal maintains a fairly constant character, it consists of two beds, each averaging 2 feet 6 inches in thickness, separated by a band of dirt. The latter occasionally swells out to a considerable thickness. Near Cawthorne, additional dirt partings set in and break up the coal into several beds, which become thinner still towards the north-west, and in this part no attempt has been made to work it. Still further northwards there is a workable coal known as the Blocking coal, which holds a position in the measures exactly corresponding to that of the Silkstone coal, and which Mr. Green considers to be its equivalent. The Barnsley coal is distinguished by the occurrence in it of a band of hard or steam coal, lying in the middle of the seam, in the neighbourhood of Sheffield. The coal ranges from 4 feet to 4 feet 6 inches in thickness; its thickness increases northwards, and at Rotherham reaches 7 feet or 8 feet; whilst about Barnsley, where it is at its best, the thickness is between 9 feet and 10 feet. At Darton, a parting of dirt set in, and still further northwards at Crigglestone, it becomes split up into so many small seams by dirt partings as to be quite worthless. Beyond this point was unexplored ground, but on approaching Wakefield, the coal called the Warren House, probably corresponds with the Barnsley. It is for the most part a mixture of thin bands of coal and dirt, whilst, north-west, a coal called the Gawthorpe, a seam from 2 feet to 3 ft. in thickness, is probably the equivalent of the Barnsley coal. The author gave detailed sections of the coals in several parts of the district, and explained the method by which the coal becomes divided into thin beds by intercallations of dirt and shale during its formation.

Professor Green also contributed a paper on the Geology of the central portion of the Yorkshire Coal-field, lying between Pontefract and Bolton-on-Dearne. This is one of the least known portions of the Yorkshire Coal-field. Its edges are pierced by workings to a small extent, but the larger part of the tract remains unpierced by a single shaft or bore-hole. The south-western boundary of the district is formed by the outcrop of the seam of coal known as the Shafton, Billingley, Denaby or Nostell Top Coal, which lies some 430 yards above the Barnsley Bed. A line of fault, ranging from Royston Station to Pontefract, bounds it on the north-west; on the up-cast or north-western side of this fault, collieries are plentiful, but on the down-cast there is no information from actual exploration beyond a few unimportant bore-holes. The country for some distance is flat and tame, but two tracts, one extending from Clayton-in-the-Clay towards Brierley, and the other lying around Ackworth and Pontefract, are more elevated, and afford some information. These higher grounds are occupied by a thickly-bedded, softish sandstone, which Mr. Green named the Houghton Common Rock. Below this is a second thick bed of similar sandstone, which he named the Brierley Rock. It may be seen on the north around the village of Hemsworth, and on the south-west side at the village of Brierley. They were calculated to be at a distance of 560 yards and 680 yards respectively above the Barnsley Coal. Near Pontefract there are a couple of similar thickly-bedded, softish, light-brown sandstones. The lower is largely quarried, and forms the bold bluff on which stands the Castle. The upper is less conspicuous. These very much resemble, and, it is conjectured, are the equivalents of the Houghton Common and Brierley rocks. It is probable that the rocks over the whole district undulate gently in broad, shallow folds. In each basin an outlier of the upper sandstone occupies the centre, encircled more or less completely by the lower sandstone. For further details the author refers his hearers to a memoir on the Geology of the Yorkshire Coal-fields, then in preparation, and since published.

At a meeting in 1876, held at Barnsley, Professor Green described a section of boulder-clay near Barnsley. The distribution of the drift on the eastern side of the Penine Chain is very limited. It is, however, not altogether absent, and scattered patches have been detected here and there over the district. One of the most remarkable of these he proceeded to describe. It was exposed while cutting a mineral railway near the Carlton Main Tollgate, on the Barnsley and Wakefield road, about two miles north of Barnsley. It consists of stiff, blue boulder-clay, occupying a hollow in the Woolley Edge rock. The clay contained small pebbles, mostly derived from the neighbouring rocks, but containing a few ice-scratched carboniferous limestone, chert, and trap rocks. Northwards this lower boulder-clay is covered by a deposit of what Professor Green denominated upper boulder-clay. It is more sandy, but has fewer stones. It is more or less bedded, contains interbedded laminated clays or warps. The warp is a bluish-brown, finely-laminated rough clay, with small, well-rounded pebbles of carboniferous sandstone and coal. Having described the beds, Professor Green indicated the succession of events to which they owed their origin.

At a meeting held at Halifax in 1875, Mr. Tiddeman, of H.M. Geological Survey, gave an account of the exploration of the Victoria Cave, near Settle. It is situated in a picturesque locality, in a line of limestone scars behind Settle, at an elevation of about 1,450 feet above the sea level ; the mouth of the cave has a southern aspect, with extensive views over the district of Craven. It was discovered by the dog of Mr. Joseph Jackson entering it through a small orifice in pursuit of a rabbit, on the day of Her Majesty's Coronation in 1837, the year in which this Society was formed. Mr. Jackson's attention having been drawn to the cave, he was led to commence and carry on the exploration of its contents. Prof. Boyd Dawkins states that he discovered a remarkable series of ornaments and implements of bronze, iron, and bone, along with pottery and broken bones of animals. Fragments of Samian ware, and other Roman pottery, coins of Trajan, Constantius, and Constantine, proved that the stratum in which they were found was accumulated after the Roman invasion. There were also bronze fibulæ, iron spear heads, nails, and daggers ; as well as bronze needles, pins, finger rings, armlets, bracelets, buckles, and studs. The broken bones belong to the red-deer, roebuck, pig, horse, Celtic short-horn, sheep or goat, badger, fox and dog. The whole collection was of that sort which is very generally found in the neighbourhood of Roman villas and towns, and was doubtless formed while the cave was a place of habitation.* Objects resulting from his researches are now placed in the British Museum, in the Museum at Leeds, and in his own private collection. In the year 1869 Prof. T. McKenny Hughes saw Mr. Jackson's collection, and considered it of such importance as to render it advisable that a systematic exploration of the cave should be made. He formed a committee, with Sir James Kay-Shuttleworth as chairman, and obtained the permission of Mr. Stackhouse, the owner of the property, to explore the cave. Subscriptions and donations came in liberally. Professor Dawkins undertook the scientific direction of the work, and Mr. John Birkbeck accepted the post of honorary treasurer and secretary ; whilst Mr.

---

* Journ. Anthrop. Inst., Vol. i., p. 61.

Jackson gave his assistance as superintendent. Mr. Jackson's previous work had been entirely inside the cave. It was now decided to remove the screes from the outside, which blocked up the aperture. On the surface was a mass 2 feet thick, of angular fragments, broken from the cliff above by the action of frost. This rested on a dark layer, composed of more or less fragments of burnt bone, burnt stones, which had formed fireplaces, fragments of pottery, and other objects. The dark layer was found to be continuous with the stratum from which Mr. Jackson had obtained his ornaments and implements inside the cave, and there could be no doubt fires had been kindled on the spot for the purpose of cooking food. Similar objects were found to those already accumulated by Mr. Jackson. Some of the bronze ornaments were beautifully enamelled in red, blue, yellow, and green; they were of graceful form, and were considered by Mr. Franks, of the British Museum, to be of Celtic workmanship. Others are of a more distinctly Roman type. The bones found strewn about indicate that the Celtic short-horn formed the staple animal food; a variety of goat was also abundant, and a domestic breed of pigs furnished pork. The remains of roebuck and stag were rare, and there was evidence of the use of horse-flesh. Domestic fowl, wild duck, and grouse complete the list of the animals which can with certainty be affirmed to have been eaten by the cave-dwellers. Professor Dawkins is of opinion that the cave was used in the troublous times during which the Romans evacuated Britain in the fifth century, when the unfortunate provincials were obliged to flee from their homes and exchange the luxuries of civilized life for a hard struggle for common necessaries. Beneath this Roman Celtic layer was a thickness of five or six feet of fragments of rock, bound together by the deposition of carbonate of lime from dripping water. At the base of this was discovered a singular bone harpoon, with double barbs facing in one direction, and a third reversed barb at the base, the last, no doubt, being intended to serve for attachment to a shaft; a hexagonal bone bead, and three flint flakes. Amongst Mr. Jackson's finds inside the cave was a small adze of melaphyr, which was probably from this layer, which has been termed neolithic. The beds beneath the neolithic layer consist of upper cave earth, laminated clay, and lower cave earth. In some positions the upper and lower cave earths coalesce, and the laminated clay is absent. The cave earths consist of large and small angular blocks of limestone, intermingled with a stiff buff clay, occasional beds of stalagmite, and fallen blocks of stalactite. The limestone and stalactite have fallen from the roof. The upper cave earth appears to be derived to some extent from the laminated clay beneath by being trampled on by the animals whose bones are found in it. The laminæ of the laminated clay are exceedingly thin, and flake away easily when pulled asunder. It varies in thickness up to 12 feet, relatively to the conformation of the surface of the lower clay. It has been found to run continuously from the entrance of the cave inwards, a distance of more than 70 feet, as far as the explorations have gone in that direction. Mr. Tiddeman considers that the laminated clay may be the result of glacial conditions, which imply the running of muddy water in alternating periods of flow and rest. This opinion was communicated in a report to the Cave Committee in 1871, and has since been confirmed by finding glaciated boulders in the laminated clay itself, and still later the important discovery of a great accumulation of boulders and glacial till at the cave mouth, resting on the edges of the lower cave-earth. These boulders vary in size, from blocks weighing tons to mere pebbles. They consisted partly of carboniferous limestone, of a darker colour than that in which the cave is situated; and a large proportion of Silurian grit, and occasional boulders of carboniferous gritstones from Ingleborough or Pennyghent, were present. Their presence indicates a period when the glacier of the Ribble valley extended up to this point; and, still higher, the ice-scratches on the rocks at the base of King's Scar, a short distance away, show the direction in which the glacier travelled across from Stainforth towards Long Preston, by way of Attermire; and there are evidences that this ice-sheet covered all the country visible from the cave mouth and many miles beyond. The boulders accumulated from this ice-sheet lie at the base of the screes, which are 19 feet to 20 feet thick. The animal remains found in the lower cave-earth include hyæna, fox, the brown and grizzly bears, Elephas antiquus, Rhinoceros leptorhinus, hippopotamus, Bos primogenius, bison, and red deer.

The bones present the characteristic appearance due to the gnawing and cracking of the hyæna, and the dung of this animal occurs in great abundance. A fibula which was submitted to Professor Busk and other specialists, was stated to be that of a man who lived in the district when the animals were roaming over the hills of Craven. The presence of these animals appears on the whole to indicate a warm climate. The hyæna floor is situated about 20 feet below the base of the laminated clay. On the surface of the laminated clay are several antlers of reindeer, and above the laminated clay the bed of mud and fallen stones. The upper cave-earth contains the following animals :—Fox, grizzly bear, brown bear, badger, horse, pig, reindeer, red-deer, and goat or sheep. Included amongst these remains have been found bones which have been cut or scratched by man, probably with a flint implement. The chief value of the exploration of the Victoria Cave lies in the opportunity which it gives of correlating the ancient fauna contained in it, and which are elsewhere associated with the bones or handiwork of man, with certain great events in geological time. The fibula found in the hyæna bed gave rise to a large amount of discussion, and the opinion of Professor Busk that it was the fibula of a man has been to a large extent discredited. One of the scratched bones was obtained in deposits 25 feet below the original surface, it is the dorsal end of a rib, the articulating surface being broken off. On it there are at least nine transverse scratches, with others less distinct joining them obliquely, and one longitudinally near the head. They are quite unlike the gnawings of either rodents or carnivorous animals. This was discovered in 1875. In 1876, another small bone was found, bearing evident tool marks. It occurred at a depth of 15 feet in the hyæna bed, surrounded by bones and teeth of hyæna, bear, elephant and rhinoceros. The marks upon it are clean cuts made by a sharp instrument. As these bones appear to show evidence of the presence of man at the same period as the animals indicated, it only remains to prove that they were pre-glacial, and the age of man is carried back to a similar period. There can be little doubt that the laminated clay, with ice-scratched stones and the glacial deposits outside the cave, were accumulated at a period subsequent to the formation of the lower cave-earth, in which the remains of these animals occur. Additional evidence in support of this has since been provided by the investigation of the Raygill fissure, where earth, containing remains of similar animals, was covered up and enveloped by glacial clays washed into the fissure at a subsequent period to the animal remains. There is every probability, therefore, that the animals existed in this part of the country before the glacial deposits were made, but whether they are altogether pre-glacial, or whether they have existed intermediate between two periods of glaciation, there is no evidence to prove.

The glacial deposits of the Bradford basin formed the subject of a communication by Mr. Thomas Tate. These deposits are interesting as indicating the southerly extent on the east of the Penine Chain of the North of England ice-sheet. Whilst the Thornton railway was being formed in Ripley Fields, a bed of till, 8 feet thick, was exposed, at a depth of 25 feet. It is a tough, fine-grained, blue clay, which effervesces freely on the application of hydrochloric acid. Numerous sub-angular and well-rounded boulders of limestones, grits, and shales are included in it. The harder rocks are polished and ice-scratched. This till closely resembles similar beds near Skipton. Resting upon an eroded surface of the till is a second blue clay 15 feet thick. It differs from the former in containing a larger percentage of well-rounded small pebbles of the crystalline limestone of Settle. It is of a looser and more open texture, and on exposure to the air acquires a brownish tint. The same clay is seen in the new siding on the Midland Railway at Shipley Fields, where the lower till may be seen resting upon a pre-glacial river gravel. Other exposures have been observed at Bowling Park, at Bowling Ironworks, Bradford Moor, and in Leeds-road it was exposed in an excavation for the new gasworks. Outside the Bradford area it has been seen in Beck-road, at Keighley, and at the head of Shipley Glen, behind Tong Park, and at Esholt Hall; but it is nowhere present east, south, or west of the area drained by the Bradford Beck. The upper clay had been regarded by some geologists as re-arranged till. The author contested this view, and considered that the two beds are essentially one continuous deposit, resting where the land-ice left it. The lower beds, with Skipton blue limestone, were the first to be pushed into the Bradford area by the ice-sheet ; whilst the upper, with Settle limestone, coming from a greater distance, would constitute a later deposit. Another glacial till on the east side of the watershed ranges from Quarry Gap, across Calverley Moor, to Eccleshill and Idle. It is outside the Bradford basin, and differs from that within by the absence of any boulders of limestone, large blocks of sub-angular grit and sandstone alone being present, the contained stones all pointing to an origin at some point north of the Aire, between Shipley and Skipton.

At a general meeting of the members of the Society held at Barnsley on April 27th, 1876, Mr. L. C. Miall tendered his resignation of the office of honorary secretary, and Mr. James W. Davis, on the motion of Professor Green, seconded by Mr. Stott, was elected to fill that office. At the same meeting, Mr. John Brigg was elected treasurer. Mr. Richard Carter presided, and delivered an address on the mineral aspects of the West Riding Coal-field, in which he gave some information as to the great development of the coal-field, the correlation of the several beds of coal worked out to a large extent by members of the Society, and since further developed by the Geological Survey. The extraordinary stimulus during the two or three previous years in the coal and iron trades had vastly extended the area over which the Barnsley and Silkstone coal-seams were being worked, and an additional area of some eight miles in length, by two in breadth, had been added to the proved extent of the coal. If these were regarded with reference to the Barnsley bed alone, it would represent in weight about one hundred million tons of coal. He made especial reference to the Barrow and Hoyland Silkstone Companies, which had just completed very deep pits in the localities of Worsboro' and Hoyland Nether, to the Silkstone seam, the former sinking to a depth of 460 yards from the surface.

At the same meeting, Mr. B. Holgate read a paper, in which he described the character and extent of the several minerals of the Yorkshire Coal-field which are applied to the modern manufacture of iron ; the several fire-clays within this area were described, and the peculiar capability of each to resist the action of fire received due consideration.

Dr. William Watts, of Giggleswick, contributed a valuable paper on the physical properties of ice in connection with the glacial period. He briefly called attention to the fact that water expands in freezing no less than nine per cent. Ice, subject to great pressure, is melted at a considerably lower temperature than freezing point. This remarkable property goes far to explain how a mass of glacial ice can behave like a viscous body. If the bed of the glacier were smooth, and it could move without friction, it would simply slide down by its own weight; but the bed not being smooth, but offering projections of rock, the pressure exerted by these obstacles on the ice would be very great. The ice cannot yield like a viscous body, but it can melt, and this comes to much the same thing. The water which has been formed by this pressure shifts its position, and thus pressure is removed; being again subject to the cold it is re-frozen, but a considerable proportion escapes through crevasses and other cracks in the ice, and forms a stream which issues from the foot of the glacier.

Mr. J. R. Dakyns, of H.M. Geological Survey, described some Silurian erratics which he had found in Wharfedale. Wharfedale consists of two distinct portions, one extending from its source to the southern edge of Grass Wood, in which the river runs in a narrow valley. From Grass Wood to Beamsley, the river is bounded on the east side by Fells, but on the west it is an open drift-covered country, stretching away westward beyond the river Ribble. Below Beamsley, the river again flows in a narrow dale to Otley. In the lower part, only carboniferous series exist, and no other rocks are found in the drift as boulders. Between Beamsley and Chapelhouse, Silurian erratics are plentiful, they have being largely cleared off the land and used as "throughs" in the walls. Mr. Dakyns considered that the explanation of the occurrence of these Silurian erratics is to be found in the occurrence beneath the mountain limestone of Silurian beds probably in the neighbourhood of Kilnsey Crag. At the foot of the crag some strong springs are thrown out, which he considered as evidence of the presence of the Silurian rocks. The whole of the valley bottom is covered by an artificial detritus, and beneath this, though unseen, it is possible that the Silurian rocks exist from which the boulders were obtained now found in the lower part of the valley.

A paper was read by Mr. Walter Rowley, C.E., on Deep Mining, and recent achievements of Engineering in connection with it. He described the great growth in the coal mining industry in this country, and compared the deep mines on the continent with those in England. The several methods of boring were described, and the various systems of lighting and ventilation, together with the use of machinery in coal-getting, were enumerated. The author considered that the increase in temperature in deep mining is not so. great as has generally been supposed, and the deepest mines hitherto sunk appear to bear out this supposition. Such being the case, he sees no reason why mines should not be worked at a great depth provided that this can be done at a sufficiently reasonable cost to pay expenses.

Two papers were read by Mr. James W. Davis, one descriptive of a photograph issued with the volume of proceedings, representing stems and roots of fossil trees discovered in making an extension of the Wadsley Asylum, near Sheffield ; the other on a stratum of shale containing fish-remains, occurring immediately above the Better Bed Coal, known to extend over a surface of four or five miles in length and two in breadth, and having an average thickness of about a quarter of an inch. Thirty-five species of fossil fish are enumerated from this bed, together with the bones of a labyrinthodont, identified by Mr. Miall as those of Loxomma.

At the annual meeting held in October, 1876, Professor Green presiding, the honorary secretary stated in his annual report that the number of members had been increased to 115. A debt owing to Messrs. Edward Baines and Sons for printing, which had accumulated up to the year 1870, and amounted to more than £20, had been paid, the money being subscribed by a few of the members for this purpose. Local secretaries were appointed in Barnsley, Bradford, Halifax, and Huddersfield, and in accordance with the resolution passed at a meeting held at Leeds a summary of geological literature relating to the West Riding had been prepared. This was inserted in the annual report of proceedings. During the year an interesting excursion had been made to the Victoria Cave, near Settle. The members were met at the Giggleswick Museum by Mr. R. H. Tiddeman, who conducted the party to the cave, and explained its early history and the important results that had been obtained from its investigation. The large collection of remains of animals, and other objects found at the cave were deposited in the museum at Giggleswick School, and were exhibited by the master, Mr. Styles. The statement of receipts and expenditure showed a balance in favour of the Society of nearly £11.

The first meeting of the Society in 1877 was held at Halifax. The president, the Marquis of Ripon, occupied the chair, and delivered an address on scientific research.

The Rev. J. Stanley Tute described the glacial drifts near Ripon. They appear to be of three distinct ages, probably separated from each other by long intervals of time. The earliest is a bed of black boulder clay, on the south side of the valley of the Laver. Upon the eroded surface of this lies the brown boulder-clay which is the common drift of the district; over this, again, on each side of the Ure, near Ripon, is a mass of sand, clay, and gravel, derived partly from the boulder clays, and partly from the new red sandstone against which they rest. He drew attention to the curious circumstance that the stream coming down from Haddock's Stones, flowing eastward by Markington and East Stainley into the Ure at Newby, appears to have run at some previous time by Dole Bank, and then southwards to Ripley, where there is a well-marked gorge which is in some places fully as wide and deep as that of the river Nidd at Knaresborough, and considerably larger than that in which the present stream flows. It has been diverted to its present course by a bank of clay and sand, which appears to have been left by a retreating glacier; and as the north and south valley forms a natural boundary between the local drift and glacial drift, Mr. Tute is of opinion that there was here the edge of an ice cap which covered all the hills to the west, and was cut off along this line by the glacial sea. The sea, covered with floating ice, burdened with boulders from the carboniferous rocks, pieces of greenstone, and Shap granite which had been carried over Stainmoor, deposited the clay and boulders to the southwards, whilst the ice cap, bearing only local drift, deposited the beds to the north, and formed at its edge a definite boundary of the boulder clay.

Dr. H. Franklin Parsons described the alluvial strata of the Lower Ouse Valley. The Keuper and Bunter sandstones form the base of this district, and occasionally rise to the surface, as in the

Isle of Axholme, Brayton Barf, and Hambleton Hough, as well as other places. Upon these Triasic rocks rest the post-tertiary beds, the aggregate thickness of which is, in some cases, several hundred feet. At the base is boulder clay exposed on the surface as far south as Escrick, but occurring much lower down in the valley, at a considerable depth beneath the surface. Above the boulder-clay is a coarse gravel, with alternations of sand. A fine section is exposed at the railway station at Heck. Resting on the gravel is a bed of laminated clay of very constant character over a large area. It has a dark grey colour, and splits, when dry, into fine laminæ. At Selby it is 48 feet thick, and at Cawood 57 feet. It contains no fossils, but from its laminated character and its resemblance to modern warp, Dr. Parsons is of opinion that it must have been formed in a tidal estuary similar to that of the Humber. Above this is usually a bed of sand, and then a considerable thickness of peat and forest bed. On Thorne Waste, the peat attains a depth of 20 feet, which northwards is considerably reduced. At Goole, it is only 6 inches in thickness. At the bottom of the peat, and rooted in the sand, are innumerable stumps of trees; the majority are Scotch fir; but oak, willow, birch, hazel, and others are met with. Elytræ of beetles and other insects are common. Horns of deer have been found, but other animal remains have not occurred. The whole thickness of this peat appears to have been formed during the historic period, shown by the fact that the trees which lie beneath it have been felled by the agency of man, which is proved by the marks of tools and of fire on the stumps, and felled timber. The uppermost bed of the series is composed of warp, a name locally given to a peculiar sediment held in suspension in the tidal waters of the Humber and its tributaries. It is probable that this sediment is derived from the rapidly perishing coast of Holderness, and consists of the disintegrated materials of the boulder clay. The land adjoining is at a considerably lower level than the bed of the river, and this fact has been taken advantage of, for many years past, in artificially warping the land. To effect this large drains have been cut from the river; the land intended to be warped is enclosed in a high bank, and a communication is then made with the warping drain, which allows the water to flow over the land at every tide.

This process is continued two or three years, at the end of which time a deposit of rich soil, sometimes three or four feet in thickness, has been accumulated. The physical features of the district have been greatly changed by embanking the rivers, which is said to have been done in the reign of Edward III., and again by Vermuyden's drainage of Hatfield Chase in the 17th century. Prior to that time the country must have been overflowed by every tide, and the whole district been an expanded series of bogs and marshes. In an appendix the author gives an analysis of the ancient and modern warps, and eighteen sections of the alluvial deposits obtained in borings and well sinkings extended over the district.

Mr. J. R. Dakyns described the sections exposed at Falcon Clints, and in the neighbourhood of the Old Pencil Mill below Cronkley, in Upper Teesdale. In each of these the uppermost beds consist of whinsill beneath which are altered limestones and shales. At the base of the latter an altered breccia more or less similar to breccias which had been found in other parts of the country separating the Carboniferous series from the Silurian rocks, and he was led to the inference, which was afterwards demonstrated to be correct, that the Silurian rocks formed the bed of the valley.

Mr. W. Percy Sladen, now honorary secretary of the Linnean Society of London, contributed a paper on the Genus Poteriocrinus and Allied Forms. Twenty-four species described by Müller, Phillips, Austin, McCoy, and De Koninck, were enumerated. These were shown to possess characters which necessitate their re-distribution into the Genus Poteriocrinus, Dactylocrinus, Scaphiocrinus, and Zeacrinus, the second a new genus suggested by the author, who remarks that it is necessary to bear in mind that naturalists have been content hitherto, in the classification and grouping of crinoids, to base their determinations upon differences in the arrangements and relative proportions of those plates alone which enter into the composition of the calyx or body-wall of the crinoid, and have neglected almost entirely any consideration of the general morphology, or physiology even, of the forms to which they have assigned type characters. The continuous increase which has been made of late years in palæontological knowledge has rendered the solution of many problems possible with which formerly we were unable to cope. Perhaps few better examples could be named than the subjects of the present communication. The four groups of crinoids herein described all agree in the number and general arrangement of the plates which form the calyx or body cup. In other words, the numerical elements of the essential portions of their generic formulæ are identical. The special proportions of these plates, however and the general characters of the crinoids differ in each, and when the whole sum of the resemblances and differences of genus with genus is compared, and when the types are examined in their entirety few will dispute the propriety of establishing the groups as above indicated.

Mr. G. H. Parke drew attention to the discovery of a mineral new to Britain, called vermiculite, which had been found in the boulder-clay of Walney Island. The mineral occurs in both red and grey granite, taking the place of mica, with quartz and felspar. Examples were exhibited which varied in size from 1-32nd to 5-32nd of an inch. Being carefully detached from the matrix and placed on a platinum dish exposed to the flame of a spirit lamp, the water held in combination was driven off, and each piece of mineral exfoliated, lengthened, and twisted about like a worm, attaining a length of about ¾ of an inch. The author suggested that the name vermiculite granite should be applied to the rocks which contained this mineral.

An introductory paper on the structure, habits, and distribution, together with the classification of existing Cephalopoda, was communicated by Mr. W. Cash; his intention being to describe in future papers the fossil examples of this group existing in the strata of Yorkshire.

Mr. James W. Davis read a paper on the unconformability of the Permian Limestone to the Red Rocks west of its escarpment in Central Yorkshire, in which, after describing the character of the carboniferous rocks to the westwards and the Permian beds eastwards of its escarpment, he drew the conclusion that the red grits and shales occurring immediately beneath the limestone at Scriven, Knaresbro', in the St. Helen's Quarry at Newsome Bridge, and other places, were rocks of a carboniferous age, the colours of which had been changed by the oxidation of iron due to the permeation of

Carbonate of Lime from the superincumbent strata. The same author contributed a description of the Silurian rocks, with the overlying Mountain Limestone, at Monghton Fell, in Ribblesdale, explanatory of the photograph issued with this year's proceedings.

The annual meeting was held at Huddersfield in October, 1877, Mr. Thomas Brooke, F.S.A., presiding. Revised Rules which had been prepared by Professor Miall, Messrs. Carter, Atkinson, and the Hon. Secretary, were read to the meeting and adopted, and ordered to be printed and circulated amongst the members. On the motion of Mr. Davis, the sphere of the Society's operations was extended from the West Riding so as to embrace the whole of the county, and it was resolved that in future the title of the Society should be the Yorkshire Geological and Polytechnical Society. The Marquis of Ripon was re-elected president. The balance in the hands of the treasurer, after all accounts were paid, was £28 17s. 6d. In accordance with a resolution passed at a previous meeting, a photograph was issued to the members, along with the proceedings, the one for the current year exhibiting the junction of the Silurian Rocks and the Carboniferous Limestone on Monghton Fells in Ribblesdale.

CHAPTER XVI.

BIOGRAPHICAL NOTICES.

The notices of members of the Society which follow have been derived in part from 'Men of the Times,' from the proceedings of the Society, and from other sources, and of necessity are brief and in many respects imperfect.

MARQUIS OF RIPON, K.G., F.R.S.

The Marquis of Ripon was elected President of the Society on December 8th, 1858, about a year after the death of its first president, Earl Fitzwilliam. He was at that time member of parliament for the West Riding of Yorkshire, under the title of Viscount Goderich. He was born in London, October 24th, 1827, and succeeded to his father's title of Earl of Ripon on January 28th, 1859, and to that of his uncle, Earl de Grey, on November 14th, in the same year. He was at this time, as he has been since, devoted to political life. At the general election of 1852 Lord Goderich was returned to the House of Commons as member for Hull, and continued to sit for that borough until 1853, when he vacated his seat to oppose Mr. Starkey at Huddersfield, where he succeeded in winning the seat for the Liberals by a majority of 80. At the general election in 1857 he was returned for the West Riding without opposition. In June, 1859, the year in which he took his seat in the House of Lords, Lord Herbert selected him for the post of Under-Secretary for War, and in February, 1861, he was made Under-Secretary for India. Upon the death of Sir G. C. Lewis, in April, 1863, his lordship, who had shown great efficiency in his subordinate office, became Secretary for War, with a seat in the Cabinet. He remained at the War Office nearly three years, and in February, 1866, when Sir

Charles Wood, afterwards Viscount Halifax, withdrew from the Ministry, he was appointed Secretary of State for India. On Mr. Gladstone's accession to office in December, 1868, he received the appointment of Lord President of the Council, which he retained until August, 1873. He was created a Knight of the Garter in 1869. In 1871 the joint commission which arranged the Treaty of Washington was appointed, and Lord Ripon was selected as chairman. In recognition of the services which he rendered in that capacity he was, soon after his return from the United States, created Marquis of Ripon. The University of Oxford conferred upon him the honorary degree of D.C.L. in 1870, and in April of the same year he was installed as Grand Master of the Freemasons of England in succession to the Earl of Zetland; four years afterwards his Lordship joined the Roman Catholic Church, which necessitated his resignation of that position. During the whole of the period since his election as president of this Society, his Lordship has been engaged in political matters and frequently in office, which has rendered his attendance at the meetings of the Society infrequent. Since the year 1876 except during a period of more than five years when he was absent as Viceroy of India, his Lordship has shown a considerable interest in everything that pertained to the well-being and prosperity of the Society, and has continually taken an active part in its affairs. In April, 1877, his Lordship presided at a meeting held at Ripon and delivered an address on scientific research, in which he stated that in his earlier life he had been devoted to the study of entomology, and had succeeded, whilst making a collection of saw flies, in discovering a specimen which the late Mr. John Curtis pronounced to be a species hitherto unknown. He mentioned this to show that if any study was pursued with accuracy and with care new facts might turn out, which ultimately would be of value to science. The basis of all scientific investigation was the spirit of careful and accurate observation. Those who gave any portion of their time to scientific enquiries must not think that they could be taken up like a novel and read hastily or investigated in a superficial manner. If the study of science were to do any good, or to advance the general knowledge of the world, it must be conducted in a painstaking manner, and whatever they did should be done with the utmost thoroughness they could command. The true spirit of an investigator should be a modest, teachable, reverent spirit, that of a man open to receive all facts from whatever quarter they might come, ready to test them to the utmost, and ready to accept the conclusions to which these facts might lead. Surely it must be encouraging to all, and particularly to young students of science, to know, that providing they devoted themselves to their studies in the manner he had attempted to describe, that new fields of ever-increasing beauty, attraction, and delight would be open to them, though they might never reach the end. On January 14th, 1880, his Lordship presided at a meeting held at Halifax, and referred in his opening address, at some length, to the investigation then proceeding at the Raygill Fissure. He also spoke of the extension of the Society's operations to the North and East Riding. He trusted that this extension would prove successful, and give an impulse to the study of geological science in those parts of Yorkshire, remarking that it must be borne in mind that the visits of the Society to different parts of the county were not merely intended to benefit the members of the Society themselves, but the meetings and excursions being open to others they were intended to propagate an interest in science, and to encourage its study in the districts which they might visit. He then entered at considerable length on the question of general education, and its bearings and relationship to the teaching of science in this country, and deprecated too great an interference by the state in higher education. He believed the latter was not an imaginary danger, and he submitted the consideration to those who were dissatisfied with the English system of teaching. In all experimental branches of knowledge the first essential element of success was freedom; freedom of investigation, freedom of discussion, the honest search of facts, the faithful report of them, and their unprejudiced examination. One of the great objects of this Society was to encourage individual enquiry, to collect facts all over the surface of this great county, and to test the truth and reality of the facts so collected by open and free discussions at the meetings of the Society. He thought the Society should devote special attention to young men when they left the Universities, or the Higher Schools, or Mechanics' Institutes, and help them to carry on in after life the studies which they had begun there. It should be their business to take these young men, from whatever class of life they might have sprung, to test, and to guide, and to encourage them, and to enable them to apply the teachings which they might have received at the school or the college, in the field of actual experiment, and to carry on throughout life, and in the midst of the business engagements of life, not only the cultivation of their own minds but the advance and progress of scientific enquiry in the county. Very shortly after this meeting the Marquis of Ripon left England as the Viceroy of India, which honourable position he held for upwards of five years. Shortly after his return he presided at a meeting held at York on September 9th, 1885. He assured the members that it afforded him great pleasure to meet once more the members of the Society after having been so long separated from them, and from his other friends in the county, by the public duties which he had been discharging in a distant part of Her Majesty's dominions. Those duties had prevented him keeping abreast with geological science, and though he dwelt for a large portion of the year not very far from those Sewalik Hills which were so interesting to geologists, he was not able to study any of the Geology of India; but he could say that the Government of India were well alive to the importance of scientific investigation, and recognised it as part of their duty to it, as far as they could consistently with their financial means. He then reviewed the work of the Society for the past few years, especially referring to the papers of Mr. Lamplugh, which had served to some extent as the basis of a portion of the report of the Geological Survey referring to Holderness prepared by Mr. Clement Reid, and to the work of Mr. Vine, who had been requested by the British Association to prepare a report on Fossil Polyzoa. It was also pleasing to find that two students of the Yorkshire College, Mr. Easterfield and Mr. Whiteley, had contributed original papers to the proceedings of the Society. Referring to the latter, he took the opportunity of urging strongly upon other students of that college and similar institutions to follow the example of those gentlemen, and thus do something to establish, what he would like to see, a recognised connection between the Yorkshire College and other institutions of that kind and this Society. Two years afterwards his Lordship presided at the Jubilee meeting of the Society at Ripon. He reviewed to some extent the work of the Society during its fifty years of existence, and referred to some of the members who had conduced mostly to its success. He thought that the Society in its relation to mining industries and to the general progress and the commercial prosperity of the West Riding had been one of considerable benefit, and he considered that it was a duty of scientific men to see that science should be brought to bear upon the great industries of the country, and that its aid should be afforded largely to the promotion of those industries in every direction. He would indeed go so far as to say that, while scientific investigation should be conducted in a thoroughly scientific spirit, from a pure love for science, and without a mercenary regard to the pecuniary results which may attend it, yet the foremost work for us in a great industrial district like this, during the next fifty years, will be to bring science and industry into the closest possible union, and thus to afford to science the opportunity of making her great conquests available for the advantage of mankind.

LORD HOUGHTON.

The late Lord Houghton was a member of this Society from its earliest years, and for a period of forty years was one of its Vice-Presidents. A large proportion of the following notice has been derived from an article contributed to the *Leeds Mercury* by Mr. J. Wemyss Reid, soon after his Lordship's death in August, 1885. Richard Monckton Milnes was born on the 19th of June, 1809, and was the son of Mr. Robert Pemberton Milnes, of Fryston Hall, who represented Pontefract in the House of Commons from 1806 to 1818. The family of Milnes is one of considerable antiquity in the county of York, its origin being traced to one William Milnes, who was living at Ashford, in Derbyshire, in the time of Queen Elizabeth. Towards the close of the seventeenth century, the Richard Milnes of his day settled at Wakefield, where representatives of the family are still to be found, the Milnes-Gaskells being descendants on the female side of the ancestors of Lord Houghton. It was not until the close of the last century that Richard Slater Milnes became possessed of the Great Houghton and Fryston estates, and took up his residence at Fryston Hall. This Mr. Milnes, who was the grandfather of the deceased peer, represented the city of York in Parliament from 1784 until 1802. His son, Mr. Robert Pemberton Milnes, of whom mention has already been made, married the Hon. Henrietta Maria Monckton, daughter of Robert, fourth Viscount Galway, in 1808, and the eldest child of this union was Richard Monckton Milnes, afterwards Lord Houghton. Mr. Pemberton Milnes was a man of great distinction, who might, if he had been disposed, have taken a very important place in the political world. It was, if we mistake not, in the Ministry of Mr. Canning that Mr. Milnes received the offer of the Chancellorship of the Exchequer. This offer he declined, and during the latter part of his life he lived in comparative retirement at Fryston Hall. His only son, Richard, was educated at Trinity College, Cambridge, where he graduated in 1831. Even at that early time he had won distinction for himself, and had formed many notable friendships. He was already known as a speaker of singular felicity and as a poet of high promise. After leaving Cambridge he travelled extensively in the East, and the fruits of his observations of Eastern life have been preserved for us, not merely in the memorial of "A Tour in Greece," but in poems which are destined to live in English literature, and which have given their author no mean place among the poets of England. In 1837, having returned from abroad, he was elected one of the Members for Pontefract in the House of Commons. He began his political career under the influence of Sir Robert Peel, and he was, of course, at that time a supporter of the Conservative party. But his instincts were far too liberal, and his mind too enlightened, to permit him to remain in the Conservative ranks at the time when the great feud over the repeal of the Corn Laws took place. He clung to Sir Robert Peel, supporting him warmly in the great work; and after his death he gradually advanced further in his Liberalism, transferring his allegiance from Peel to Palmerston, and eventually becoming distinguished as a thorough-going supporter of Liberal principles and Liberal statesmen. He declined an offer from Lord Palmerston, of a seat on his Administration; but he gave it his entire support. Well versed in foreign affairs, and personally acquainted with many of the leading men on the Continent, it was not unnatural that Mr. Milnes should give a great part of his attention to questions of foreign policy. For many years there was no man in the House of Commons whose criticisms upon foreign questions were marked by greater knowledge and intelligence, or were listened to with more respect than were his. But whilst this was the direction in which he showed most activity as a politician, he exhibited a great interest in those social questions affecting the welfare of the great masses of the population which are again at the present moment coming to the front. He had the honour of bringing in the first bill for the establishment of juvenile reformatories so far back as 1846; and throughout his long life he never failed to give his warmest support to all movements directed against the crimes which endanger, and the vices which afflict society. In 1863, his long connection with Pontefract terminated in a manner gratifying both to his constituents, to his friends, and to himself. On the recommendation of Lord Palmerston, the Queen conferred a peerage upon him, and he took his place in the House of Lords as Baron Houghton of Great Houghton.

His elevation to the Peerage did nothing to diminish the interest of Lord Houghton in those social and political questions which had engaged his attention in the House of Commons. He was still distinguished for the attention which he gave to foreign affairs, whilst in the advocacy of all measures of social reform there was no one who took a more consistent or useful part. He might fairly have been described as one of the most prominent and devoted followers of that great philanthropist whom he himself was in the habit of styling the most distinguished of living Englishmen, and who still happily survives, the Earl of Shaftesbury. The warm heart, the vivid imagination, perhaps in part, the poetic temperament of Lord Houghton, led him steadily to espouse and warmly to support nearly all those great efforts for the amelioration of the condition of the people of this country which are associated with the venerable name of Lord Shaftesbury.

It is not, however, as a politician that Lord Houghton will be chiefly remembered. We have incidently made mention of his poetical works. No one who is acquainted with them will doubt that those "Poems of Many Years" are instinct with the fire of genius, and that if he had never been an active politician, a peer, a philanthropist, or a distinguished member of society, he would still have been remembered as the author of some of the most exquisite verses in the English language. One or two of his minor pieces have attained a world-wide popularity. There is, for example, the charming song of which the refrain is, "The beating of my own heart was the only sound I heard." In conversation with a friend not very long ago Lord Houghton described how he had composed that well-known song whilst riding on an Irish car from a railway station in Ireland to the house of a friend whom he was about to visit. When he arrived at the residence of his friend he committed the verses to paper, and after dinner read them to his host and the other guests. The advice given to him was to destroy the trifle as not being worthy of his reputation and his genius. He thought better of it himself, however, and sent it to London, where it was immediately published, and attained a popularity such as few modern songs have ever gained. "Less than twelve months after," said Lord Houghton, when relating the incident, "I had a letter from a friend who was travelling in the United States, and who told me that as he sailed down the Mississippi he heard the slaves upon the banks of the great river singing my song, and keeping time to the refrain with their feet as they worked among the ridges of the cotton fields." Of prose works, his most important was that entitled, "Monographs: Personal and Social," published in 1873, in which he gave the world a charming account of the Miss Berries and some of the other notable personages with whom he became acquainted during the earlier part of his career in London. Shortly before he died he completed a work which for several years past had engaged his time at intervals, and the appearance of which, at the time of his death, was awaited with the greatest interest by his friends. This was his "Reminiscences." How valuable such a book from such a pen must be will be known to all who have had the privilege of Lord Houghton's acquaintance. As we have already said, in the course of this sketch, he had known during his long life an extraordinary number of celebrated persons. Some years ago, in conversation with the present writer, he stated that there was only one man of real genius whom he had the opportunity of knowing with whom he had never been acquainted. This was none other than Goethe, and it was not a little remarkable that the great German's name was not added to the long roll of Lord Houghton's friends, seeing that the latter had actually been in Weimar at the time when Goethe resided there. Innumerable stories, some humorous and some pathetic, are related in society with regard to the variety and indeed universality of Lord Houghton's friendships.

He frequently attended the meetings of this Society, and took considerable interest in the relation of geological science to agricultural pursuits. In 1865 he presided at a meeting at Doncaster, at which he gave an address, the report of which has not been preserved, and on October 23rd, 1878, his Lordship presided at the Annual Meeting, held at Wakefield, when he delivered an address full of genial encouragement to the younger members, in which the following sentences occur. 'There were men in the early part of this century, and who have continued through a very considerable portion of this century, who had a kind of suspicion of science as being something antagonistic to the higher and more important qualities of the mind. People seemed to think that because men knew more they would either think less or feel less. That was a most erroneous opinion, and it has been completely answered by the facts of the world in which we live. Never has there been a time in our history in which so much interest has been taken in Science. At the same time, never has there been a time in which greater interest has been taken in all those developments of the imagination which are generally comprised in the name Art, nor in those deeper developments of mankind which are generally comprised in the word Religion. No doubt there will be certain minds which addict themselves specially to science, and which seem to take very little interest in what are considered still higher aspects of humanity; but it does not at all follow that because a man devotes himself to science he would be any the better for not knowing science at all. The condition of that man would be that he would be deprived of that one development of his nature, and not that he would be inclined to anything else. Therefore do not let anybody be persuaded that it is a disadvantage to young people to show a special interest in the observation of the world about them. The study itself is acquiring far more remarkable interest than it could have done in its earlier commencement. The foundations of it have been taught in some of our best schools, and the direction of it was given to youths in many of our most important centres as a valuable source of information. We must all feel that this is a right and a natural thing, because there is no study which could be suggested to the minds of young people in which they would be better able to connect the material world in which they are immediately living with the processes of their own intelligence.'

Lord Houghton married, in 1851, the Hon. Arabella Hungerford Crewe, sister of the present Lord Crewe. In his wife he found a most admirable and sympathetic helpmeet, and for many years she assisted him with her gracious tact and her unfailing smypathy in the discharge of those social duties in which he took so warm an interest. Lady Houghton was herself a woman of no ordinary intelligence. She possessed considerable talents as an artist, and proofs of her ability as a portrait painter are to be seen upon the walls of Fryston Hall. In those breakfast parties which Lord Houghton was in the habit of giving during the London season; parties at which all that was distinguished in politics, in science, in literature, and in art, might be found represented; Lady Houghton played a conspicuous and most admirable part, whilst under her care the hospitalities of Fryston attained a fame that might almost be described as world-wide. She died in the spring of 1874, after a very brief illness, leaving behind her a son, the Hon. Robert Milnes, and two daughters, now the Hon. Lady Fitzgerald and the Hon. Mrs. Henniker. Her death was a blow from which Lord Houghton never entirely recovered. He sought to find relief in travel, and visited America in company with his son. His journey was full of interest, and he returned to this country more firmly devoted to the American alliance than he had been even during the passionate struggle of the Civil War. And here, it should be said, that at that critical time the cause of the North had no warmer or truer friend than Lord Houghton. During the course of his travels in the United States he had greatly extended his circle of acquaintances. Prior to his journey many Americans of distinction had found their way to Fryston, but since then he has been still more intimately associated with all that is best in American society. During his later years more than one serious blow fell upon him. One of these was the partial destruction of Fryston Hall by fire a few years ago. Upon that occasion the magnificent library, which it had been the work of Lord Houghton's life to accumulate, was happily spared from the flames, but it was saved amid so much confusion that not a few valuable volumes were never recovered, whilst the work of re-arranging them was one which engaged the noble owner's attention and taxed his energies down to a very recent period. It is impossible in the space at our disposal to mention even a small proportion of the men and women of eminence whom Lord Houghton entertained from time to time at Fryston. We must not however, pass by the great name of Carlyle. Between the author of "Sartor Resartus" and Lord Houghton there was a friendship of the very warmest kind, one which lasted from the days of Carlyle's struggles and obscurity down to the moment of his death. It is, indeed, no small tribute to the character of the noble qualities of the man whose death we now mourn that of all the persons mentioned in the "Memorials" of Carlyle recently given to the world, he is the only one of whom the Sage of Chelsea invariably speaks with admiration and affection, the only man apparently who never fell under the lash of his bitter and censorious criticism. Thackeray, too, was another of the intimate friends of Lord Houghton, and the admirers of the author of "Vanity Fair" who remember a certain little sketch, entitled "Going to see a man hanged," will be interested to learn that "X.," the Member of Parliament to whose companionship Thackeray alluded, was Mr. Monckton Milnes. Of the great poet who so recently deprived Lord Houghton of the claim to be the only poet in the House of Lords he was the life-long friend, and it is no secret that the pension that was conferred upon Tennyson while still a young man, by Sir Robert Peel, a pension which bore such noble fruit in the shape of those great poems which the Poet Laureate was subsequently enabled to produce, was obtained for him through the instrumentality of Lord Houghton. Charles Dickens, with whose ancestors the family of

Lady Houghton had an interesting connection, was another of the Peer's intimate literary friends. We believe that it was at Lord Houghton's town house that the Prince of Wales, at his own request, met at dinner, for the first and only time, the immortal author of "The Pickwick Papers." The limits of space dictate caution, or an indefinite enlargement of this imperfect sketch of the great friendships which Lord Houghton formed during his long and illustrious career might be made, and of the work he did both as legislator, poet, and philanthropist. Of late years his health had been steadily failing. About three years ago he went to Egypt to visit his elder daughter, who shortly before had become the wife of Mr., now Sir Gerald, Fitzgerald. On his return, whilst staying at Athens, he was struck down by paralysis, and for a time was in imminent danger. His son and Mrs. Fitzgerald hastened to his bedside. His sister, the Dowager Lady Galway, who during his later years was his most constant companion, also went to Greece. Happily he rallied in a surprising manner from the attack; but though his mental faculties remained to the last unimpaired, and his interest in life was, as has already been told, as keen as it had ever been, his physical infirmities visibly increased, and his death, sudden as it was, was not quite unexpected by those who have seen him during the last twelve months. Few men will be more widely or sincerely mourned, and few men more richly deserve the tribute of a genuine regard. We must not close this sketch without referring to the important part which Lord Houghton took in connection with the Newspaper Press Fund, of which he had been chairman from the time of its establishment. It was characteristic of his benevolence that no class of literary workers were beyond the reach of his sympathy, and that he devoted both time and care during many years to the services of the journalists of Great Britain. His son, the Hon. Robert Offley Ashburton Milnes, who now succeeds to the title, was born in 1858, and is married to Miss Sybil Graham, daughter of Sir Frederick Graham, of Netherby, and granddaughter of the eminent statesman Sir James Graham.

No man of his day had made so many distinguished friendships as he had done; no man has figured more constantly or more conspicuously in contemporary memoirs. Let any one take up the biography of any celebrated personage who has passed away in England within the last forty years, and the chances are ten to one that he will find in it some reference to Lord Houghton. There is another class of memoirs in which also his name constantly occurs. That is in the history of those struggling poets and men of letters, who, in spite of the endowment of genius, have failed to attain success. Of such men Lord Houghton through his whole life had been the generous and unfailing friend ; and if he had no other claim to be remembered, his memory would deserve to be cherished with gratitude by all, because of the apparently boundless kindness which he has shown to genius in distress.

VISCOUNT HALIFAX.

Viscount Halifax was born December 20th, 1800, and graduated as a double first at Oriel College, Oxford, in 1821. He succeeded his father as third baronet on December 31st, 1846, and became Sir Charles Wood. In 1866 he was raised to the peerage as Viscount Halifax. He took his seat in the House of Commons as member for Great Grimsby in 1826, and afterwards sat for Wareham. In December, 1832, he was elected Member of Parliament for Halifax, and retained that position until 1865, when he was elected to represent Ripon. In 1832, he was Secretary of the Treasury, and in 1835, Secretary to the Admiralty. From 1846 to 1852, he was Chancellor of the Exchequer in Lord Russell's first administration. On the formation of the Aberdeen Cabinet in December, 1852, he became President of the Board of Control. He was First Lord of the Admiralty in Lord Palmerston's first administration from 1855 to 1858, and Secretary of State for India and President of the Indian Council from 1859 to 1866. In Mr. Gladstone's administration he became Lord Privy Seal in July, 1870. Viscount Halifax, as well as his father, Sir F. L. Wood, were amongst the founders of the Society, and took considerable interest in its proceedings. His Lordship's constant attendance on public affairs in London, however, prevented, during the later years of his life, his frequent attendance at the meetings of the Society, but reference will be found on previous pages to matters in which he took an interest, pertaining to its welfare.

Sir F. Lindley Wood, the father of the subject of this notice, was one of the original members of the Society, a frequent attender at its meetings, and one who took great interest in its welfare and proceedings. It is satisfactory to know that the present Viscount Halifax is also a member of the Society and one of its Vice-Presidents.

REV. WILLIAM THORP.

Since the record of the works of the Rev. W. Thorp, on page 213 and succeeding ones was printed, the following letter has been received from Mr. J. B. Charlesworth, together with a biographical notice of Mr. Thorp, prepared by his niece, Miss Thorp, for which we are much indebted :—

Mr. Charlesworth to Mr. Davis.

HATFIELD HALL, NEAR WAKEFIELD,
DEAR SIR, *January 6th, 1889.*

After long delay, which may cause my communication to be too late, I am forwarding to you by parcel post a sketch by Miss Thorp of the life of the late Rev. W. Thorp, who was her uncle, and I also enclose a letter from Colonel Drayson, who was one of Mr. Thorp's intimate friends. Miss Thorp has found out that a great number of papers were destroyed which were thought useless, as no business matters were contained. One lecture on the "Food of Nations" has been found, and that is all. I hope this communication may not be too late. Very truly yours,

J. B. CHARLESWORTH.

The memoranda communicated by Miss Thorp afford a considerable amount of information, and are given below.

The Rev. William Thorp was the second surviving son of Samuel Thorp, Esq., of Banks Hall, Cawthorne, by his second wife, Miss Mary Hirst, and grandson of William Thorp, gentleman, of Gawber Hall, in the Parish of Darton, Yorkshire. He was born in 1804, at Banks Hall. His first schooling was with the Rev. Mr. Wagg, Vicar of Darton, who had several boarders, and the usual characters of clerical schoolmasters of that day, viz., one of great severity. His two younger brothers were educated at Giggleswick, but I do not know if my uncle William was educated there.

Mr. William Thorp was sent, after he first left School, into the office of Messrs. Littledale & Co., of Liverpool, with whom he always maintained friendly relations. He was, I have heard, at this time a very handsome man, and of remarkable strength, one feat he accomplished in these days, for which, he always considered, he had to pay in after years, he made a wager with his friend, young Mr. Littledale, that he would swim across the Mersey, against the tide ; he accomplished it, but afterwards suffered somewhat from his back. My father, the late Mr. Richard Thorp, a man of the rarest veracity, told me this several times, remarking it was a greater feat of strength than Lord Byron swimming the Hellespont.

Mr. Thorp's half-sister was married in Liverpool to a cousin of influential position, and nearly related to the well-known writer, Mr. Roscoe, and the families were intimate, but "belles-lettres" were not the attraction to the calibre of Mr. Thorp's mind. The bent of his inclination and where his strength lay, was unfortunately in youth unknown, viz., in science. Afterwards, he considered to take Holy Orders, and went to Jesus College, Cambridge. He had the advantage of taking with him an introduction to the well-known family of Thackeray. Dr. Martin Thackeray being Provost of Kings' at that time, and his brother had married into the Thorp family. I believe Mr. Thorp met here many of the "savants" of the day. He was ordained by the Archbishop of York as Curate to Dr. Sharp, Vicar of Doncaster, and preached his first sermon in Doncaster Parish Church, but about the year 1833 he went as Curate in charge of Womersley, living at the Vicarage. The Rev. Mr. Caton holding the livings of Womersley and Kirk Smeaton.

It was to Womersley he brought his wife, Miss Annie Preston, of Newcastle-on-Tyne, whom he had met when curate at Doncaster. They had eight children, two sons and six daughters :—William, late Captain 78th Highlanders ; Henry Preston ; Emma, married to Mr. William Alexander, Indian Civil Service ; Annie, (deceased), married to Mr. T. W. Jobling, of Point Pleasant, Tynemouth ; Frances Elizabeth, married to Captain Furnivall, Lancashire Militia ; Adela Sophia, married to Mr. Adderley ; Emily, married to Mr. Swain ; Helen Mary, married to the Rev. Charles Perry Reeve, of Dean Priory Vicarage, Devon.

Through the influence of the late Lord Fitzwilliam, he was presented by the Lord Chancellor to the Vicarage of Misson, in Nottinghamshire, in 1848. He was vicar of Misson when he died, suddenly, in 1860. I do not know when first my uncle began to be interested in geology. He had a son's interest in the Gawber Hall Colliery 'the Exors. of Samuel Thorp, Esq.,' and was partner with my father, Richard Thorp, in the North Gawber Colliery. This probably directed his interest in geology. My grandfather was the first to begin the Barnsley Coal Trade, I remember reading, in one of my uncle's lectures. He began on his own property at Gawber. This was the beginning of this great industry. My uncle was also greatly interested in chemistry, astronomy, and very much in medicine, and had a friendship of long-standing with the celebrated Dr. Addison, of London, and the late Mr. Teale, of Leeds. I cannot help thinking if Colonel Drayson, R.A., is still living, he may have many of his papers, for he stayed at Misson often, and for long visits, discussing scientific questions. I know my cousin, the late Captain Thorp, 78th Highlanders, destroyed hundreds of letters from Sedgwick, Murchison, Conybeare, and many scientists of the day, and I hear from my cousins many papers were again destroyed on the death of my aunt at Norwood, a few years ago.

The following is the letter from Colonel Drayson referred to above :—

Colonel Drayson to Miss Thorp.

20, ASHBURTON ROAD, SOUTHSEA,

DEAR MADAM, *17th November, 1888.*

Your letter has at length reached me. I regret that all my correspondence with your late uncle has disappeared, as my travels (since his death) in India and America obliged me to reduce my baggage to a minimum. Mr. Thorp had very advanced views on geology, which, as is usual, were ignored at the time, but have since been generally received. He gave, with me, a lecture at Doncaster on geology, but I have not even a record of it.

During my various visits to him we discussed many of the unsolved problems in geology, and he entirely agreed with the views I afterwards published in a work entitled 'The Last Glacial Epoch.'

If there are any special questions I can answer I shall be happy to do my best in that way. Faithfully yours,

A. W. DRAYSON.

The following extract has been made from the *Barnsley Times* *of December 23rd, 1860* :—We refer to the death of the Rev. William Thorp beyond the notice in our obituary. We feel justified because of his earliest years having their date from our neighbourhood, and because of his resemblance to the family generally in kindness of manner and amiability of disposition. It appears that Mr. Thorp had arranged to be at Doncaster on Saturday last for the purpose of having an interview with Mr. Sutcliffe, the manager of the North Gawber Colliery, near Barnsley, one of the most extensive pits of coal in South Yorkshire, of which he was a partner, the name of the firm being Richard Thorp & Co. Mr. Sutcliffe met him at the Great Northern Railway Station at half-past twelve o'clock. At that time the Rev. William Thorp apparently enjoyed his wonted health. . . . They walked along the line towards the Great Northern Company's Mineral Yard, conversing on colliery topics. As they were walking Mr. Sutcliffe felt Mr. Thorp frequently press his arm; at length Mr. Sutcliffe spoke and received no reply; he then looked and observed a changed appearance in Mr. Thorp. When near the offices they were met by Mr. Middlemiss who spoke and moved, but again there was no reply, only a nod of the head. Mr. Middlemiss and Mr. Sutcliffe felt sure he was the subject of a paralytic stroke, and at once carried him into the private office of Mr. Middlemiss, who immediately sent a message for Dr. Scholefield, and a telegraphic message for Mrs. Thorp and family. Mr. Thorp was removed to the house of Mr. Middlemiss, and the rev. gentleman occupied a bed there until the time of his decease on Sunday night, the 16th of December. On the arrival of Mrs. Thorp, Dr. Thompson of Sheffield, was telegraphed for, who, in consultation with Dr. Scholefield, concluded recovery was hopeless. Mr. Middlemiss sat up with him all night and was most kind. The deceased was the second son of the late Samuel Thorp, Esq., of Banks Hall, near Barnsley; was in the 57th year of his age. He formerly resided at Doncaster as one of the curates of the parish church, and afterwards at Womersley. Through the influence of his kind and intimate friend Lord Fitzwilliam, he was presented by the Lord Chancellor in 1848 to the vicarage of Misson, near Bawtry. The faithful discharge of his ministerial duties was his earnest desire. The poor of Misson have lost a friend. His highest sympathies were exercised at all times towards the alleviation of distress, and in mitigating the physical sufferings of his poorer neighbours, his knowledge of medicine helping him in this. His purse was never closed, and what he did was with so little ostentation, as to be worthy of all praise, and to render the help more gratifying. . . . Every year he caused to be distributed amongst the poor of Misson about 100 tons of coal, and also through Mr. Middlemiss the same amongst the poor of Doncaster. During the twelve years Mr. Thorp was Vicar of Misson he made considerable improvements at the Vicarage. . . With his bereaved family we deeply sympathise, and we are sure this feeling is shared by the people of Misson, and by the gentry of the neighbourhood. Mr. Thorp's remains were removed to Misson Church. The funeral brought together nearly the whole village; sorrow and grief were on every countenance. Rich and poor paid the last tribute of esteem to his memory, and deep sorrow pervaded the large assembly.

THOMAS LISTER.

Mr. Thomas Lister was born in February, 1810, at Old Mill, Barnsley. His parents were members of the Society of Friends, and he was educated at the Friends' School, Ackworth. Mr. Lister was widely known as a poet and naturalist, and many contributions from his pen have appeared in the pages of current periodicals. His best known works were "The Rustic Wreath," a collection of poems published in 1834; "Temperance Rhymes," published in 1837, and "Rhymes of Progress," in 1862. He was a friend of Professor Wilson, Wm. Chambers, Robert Chambers, Ebenezer Elliott, Wm. Miller, Robert Burns, son of the poet, and many other literary and other celebrities. It may be mentioned that in 1832, Lord Morpeth, having taken a great liking to the young aspirant for literary honours, nominated him for the mastership of Barnsley Post-office. The appointment would have been a valuable one to him, but an oath was required, and the young Quaker, rather than offend his conscience, declined to accept the situation. Afterwards the post again became vacant, and the disability having then been removed, Mr. Lister became postmaster, a position he held until 1870, when he retired on a pension. He was presented with a handsome testimonial by the inhabitants on resigning his post. As a student of natural history and meteorology he was very diligent. The deceased gentleman finds favourable mention in many works, including Newsam's " Poets of Yorkshire," Grainge's "Poets and Poetry of Yorkshire," Searle's " Life of Ebenezer Elliott," Dr. Spencer Hall's " Sketches of Remarkable People ;" in an article by a friend and contemporary. Mr. John Hugh Burland, on "Country words of the West Riding ;" and by Mrs. G. Linnæus Banks, in her story, " Wooers and Winners," Mr. Lister for many years filled the office of local secretary to this Society at Barnsley, and to his assiduous attentions much of its successful appreciation in this district was due. He was rarely absent from the meetings of the Society, and contributed one paper to its proceedings which will be found mentioned on another page.

CHAPTER XVII.

THE LAST DECADE.

The history and proceedings of the Society during the past ten years must be fresh in the memories of many of its members, and if this account were intended only for those, it might well be drawn to a close, but as, doubtless, it will reach the hands of others who have not the benefit of this experience, it is proposed, as briefly as may be consistent with the importance of the subjects, to give an indication of the work it has done, and the papers its members have contributed. With the exception of the first ten years of the existence of the Society, the last have been the most important. It has grown in wealth, not only financially, but also in the size and quality of its proceedings. Previous to 1870, the latter were largely composed of papers on antiquarian and archæological subjects, but after the institution of the Yorkshire Archæological and Topographical Society, of which the late Mr. Fairless Barber, F.S.A., was the honorary secretary, these subjects were eliminated, and the authors transferred the result of their investigations to the new Society. The death of Mr. Denny about the same time resulted in a period of comparative quietude for this Society, and it was not until the action of Professor Miall, along with Mr. Thomas Wilson and others, infused new life into the Society, that it resumed its former state of activity. Since that time it has flourished, and its proceedings have been more purely geological than at any previous period. It will be gathered from succeeding pages that several excursions have been made and a considerable amount of field work done. In two instances, special investigations, involving considerable outlay, have been prosecuted. The papers contributed to its proceedings have not only treated on isolated subjects, but in some instances have acquired an increased value by their connected sequence extending over several years. The photographic illustration of important geological sections occurring in the county have been regularly issued with the proceedings since the year 1871. The photographs have been highly appreciated, not only by the members of the Society, but by others, and notably by some of the most important educational institutions in the country. It is satisfactory to find this method of illustration gaining in favour with other Societies having kindred objects to our own ; and the hope may be expressed, that the recollection of many remarkable and instructive geological phenomena may be preserved by this means, which would otherwise be speedily lost.

In the secretary's report, presented at the annual meeting in October, 1878, when Lord Houghton occupied the chair, an addition of 48 members, or 30 per cent. of the entire number constituting the Society, was reported, and was regarded as a justification of the extension of the Society to the whole of the county at the previous annual meeting. During 1878, meetings were held at Selby, Scarbro', and Wakefield, and ten papers were contributed, four of which were by members outside the West Riding. At the Scarbro' meeting Mr, J. W. Woodall presided, and after the meeting placed his yacht at the disposal of the members, and several of them availed themselves of the opportunity, and proceeded with him on a short dredging expedition. The financial statement was satisfactory, and showed a considerable balance to the credit of the Society. Five additional local secretaries were appointed, at Sowerby Bridge, Thirsk, Bridlington, Huddersfield, and Wakefield.

During the year 1879 the number of members was increased to 207, and the balance to the credit of the Society at the end of the year was over twenty-eight pounds. Three meetings were held, in each instance combined with some practical work in the mine or field. In April the members met at Barnsley at noon, and drove to the Barrow Colliery, the property of the Hematite Steel Co., Limited. Under the guidance of Messrs. Kells, the engineers to the Company, a descent was made into the mine, which is especially interesting from its being the first in which the Silkstone Coal has been won below the Barnsley Bed. The depth of the coal is four hundred and sixty-nine yards below the surface. At the meeting which was afterwards held at the Queen Hotel, the chair was occupied by Mr. W. S. Stanhope, M.P., one of the vice-presidents, who delivered an address. In July, the Society had a two days' excursion amongst the Yorkshire Wolds. Alighting at North Grimston Station the members were met and entertained at luncheon by Sir Charles W. Strickland, who, together with the Rev. E. Maule Cole and Mr. Mortimer, acted as guides throughout the day. The Oolitic quarries at Grimston were visited, and the party proceeded thence to Wharram Percy, and after a visit to the Burdale Tunnel, a circuit was made to Deepdale, one of the most characteristic in the district. From thence to Burdale Station in Thixendale, where the party took the train to Driffield. At Driffield a visit was paid to the museum of Mr. J. R. Mortimer, and his rich collection of remains from the tumuli in the district and other pre-historic objects, together with a large collection of fossils from the chalk, afforded considerable interest to the members. The party dined at the Bell Hotel, and afterwards held a meeting, over which Sir Chas. Strickland presided. On the following day, the members again took train to Wetwang, where arrangements had been made to convey the party to Huggate, a distance of four and a half miles. There the Huggate Dykes and Millington Dale were visited, and the scenery of these and other extensive dales, marvellous in their development and striking in their effect, were investigated. The party was entertained at luncheon by the Rev. G. P. Keogh. After an examination of the red chalk at Millington Springs, they proceeded to Warter, where extensive views of the plain of York were obtained, and a well exposed section of red chalk and lias was visited in Warter brickyard. The members afterwards walked to Pocklington, and thence sought their several destinations.

The annual meeting was held at Skipton. The members met at Cononley at one p.m., and walked to Raygill Quarries, visiting the Cononley Lead Mines *en route*, under the guidance of Mr. J. Ray Eddy, who explained the method of mining, and also of obtaining the lead from the ore. At Raygill the members inspected a fissure in the limestone quarry of Mr. Spencer, from which bones of elephas, rhinoceros, bison, bear, hyæna, and other animals had been obtained. ·Prof. Miall gave an explanation of the discovering of the cave, and briefly described its contents so far as they were known. After partaking of luncheon, provided by Mr. John Brigg, the party walked to Skipton, and a meeting was held at the Devonshire Arms, at which Mr. Walter Morrison, J.P., presided. At this meeting it was decided to make the following addition to Rule VI., viz.: That members may compound for their annual subscriptions and become life members on payment of six guineas.

At a succeeding meeting of the Council it was considered desirable that steps should be taken to secure a thorough investigation of the Raygill fissure and its contents, and Professors Green and Miall, and Messrs. Brigg and Davis were appointed a committee, and empowered to collect subscriptions, to make necessary arrangements, and to carry out the exploration. It was further decided that any specimens which should be found during the exploration should be deposited in the Museum at the Philosophical Hall at Leeds. Early in the following year, 1880, a circular was issued to the members, with the result that sixty pounds was speedily subscribed, and on June 7th, Mr. Spencer placed at the disposal of the committee, workmen skilled in the class of work required, and instructed his manager, Mr. Todd, to give every assistance that he was able. The work was carried on energetically during the remaining part of the year, and a report was presented at the next annual meeting. The fissure, which occurs in an anticlinal of limestone, was formerly open to the surface, and from thence extended in a southerly direction, and with only a slight inclination from the vertical line. It had been repeatedly cut across during quarrying operations, each exposure being at a lower level and exhibiting some new feature of the clays and sands, with which it was filled. When the Society began operations the fissure opened into the face of the quarry towards the north, the limestone dipping at a sharp angle into the hill southwards. The diameter of the fissure was about nine feet, and it was situated sixty feet below the surface of the ground, and about the same distance above the floor of the quarry. The contents of the fissure consisted mainly of three strata. The uppermost one was composed of fine, unctuous, laminated clay, of a blueish colour, which turned brown on exposure to the atmosphere. The middle stratum consisted of sand, and contained boulders of stone, mostly of sub-angular form, and appeared to be principally composed of limestone and grit rock, derived from the adjoining country; no bones were found in this bed. The third, or lowest stratum, was a brown, sandy clay, containing numerous well-rounded, waterworn pebbles of limestone, and of similar derivation to those in the middle stratum. Intermixed with these, especially near the base of the section, were numerous bones and teeth. The sands and clays surrounding or forming the matrix of the bones were cemented, and formed a hard mass. The bones for the most part, when newly exposed, were soft and friable, and it rarely happened that a bone could be secured which retained its original form. They remained embedded in the matrix, and broke with it in any direction. After penetrating a distance of fifteen feet, the fissure terminated by a vertical wall of limestone, whose surface was well rounded and waterworn, and from this point the fissure descended almost vertically for a distance of twenty-seven feet. This vertical portion of the fissure was filled up in a great portion of its depth by the bone-earth, but towards the bottom there was a large mass of yellow clay, with angular blocks of limestone. The animal remains obtained from the bone-earth included tusks and teeth of elephas antiquus, well preserved teeth and tusks of the hippopotamus, teeth of rhinoceros leptorhinus, and a portion of the horn of a roebuck. Teeth of hyæna were numerous, and appeared mostly to be those of adult animals. At the lower extremity of the vertical portion of the fissure already mentioned, it branches in two directions, one proceeding eastwards, nearly horizontally. This was penetrated to a distance of twenty-five feet, where further progress was stopped by a mass of fallen limestone. The second branch extends in a southerly direction, and falls somewhat rapidly. The roof and sides of the fissure afford abundant signs of errosion, the surfaces smoothened and the corners rounded off by running water. This branch of the fissure was excavated to some extent, and a number of bones and teeth were found, affording examples, in additon to those already named, of the bear, the lion, a smaller animal, probably a fox, and the bones of a bird. Operations had now to be stopped, partly on account of bad weather and partly to give the proprietors of the quarry an opportunity to remove a large mass of limestone which extended from the fissure to the surface of the quarry. For a considerable time the operations of the committee were practically suspended, during which the obstructing mass of limestone was removed. In the summer of 1866 work was re-commenced, and it was found that the branch of the fissure which had been investigated to a short extent extended to a distance of one hundred and fourteen feet, with a gradual declination in a southeasterly direction. At a distance of sixty feet it expands and forms a lofty cave. Thence, forwards, the diameter again diminishes. At the further extremity which has been explored it appears to receive a tributary extending almost vertically in a north-westerly direction. The general direction of the fissure is towards a neighbouring valley forming the channel of a watercourse at present running at no great distance, and it appears probable that the fissure formerly opened into this valley, although no direct evidence at present exists of the exit. Borings in the fissure showed the bottom to be filled with clay, varying from six inches to several feet in thickness, with slight alternating layers of sand and gravel, and occasionally fragments of grit and limestone at the bottom. A few remains of mammals were found near the entrance, similar to those already recorded. The work of investigation was found to be increasingly laborious, and the expense proportionately heavy; and as there was little probability that the knowledge of the fauna buried in the clays would be extended to any great extent, it was thought advisable to suspend operations until a more favourable opportunity. The importance of the investigation of this fissure was recognised by the British Association, who, during the period that operations were carried on, made grants of money to assist the committee.

Four general meetings were held in 1880, the first in January, at Halifax, when the Marquis of Ripon presided. It was immediately before his Lordship's departure to preside over a great nation as the Viceroy of India, and the opportunity was taken to congratulate him on his appointment, and to assure his Lordship of the continued good wishes of the Society. In April, the Society met at York, and under the guidance of the Rev. Canon Raine and Dr. Tempest Anderson, visited some of the principal antiquarian objects in the city and the museum. In the latter the Reed collection, recently presented to the Philosophical Society, attracted large attention, and was exhibited and explained by Dr. Purvis, the curator. A meeting was held in the lecture theatre during the afternoon, and the members afterwards dined at the Station Hotel. A third meeting was held at Middlesborough, in the North Riding, Mr. Bell, the President of the Literary and Philosophical Society, presiding. On the following day, members, accompanied by several members of the Tees Valley Field Club, and Mr. Barrow, of H.M. Geological Survey, proceeded by train to Lofthouse, where the inferior oolites were examined, and numerous fossils obtained. The magnificent section exposed in the cliffs of lower lias between Rockcliffe and Saltburn were examined, and their features described by Mr. Barrow. The annual meeting was held at Leeds, Dr. T. Clifford Allbutt, President of the Literary and Philosophical Society, in the chair. The number of members had increased during 1880 to 234, being a gain of twenty-seven during the year, and the balance to the credit of the Society was thirty-six pounds. Several members had availed themselves of the opportunity to compound for their annual subscriptions, and eighty-eight pounds, four shillings, stood to the credit of this fund.

In 1881, the number of members declined to two hundred and seven. The funds of the Society had, however, increased to forty-two pounds in the general account, and one hundred and twenty-one pounds stood to the credit of the Society as composition fees. Two meetings were held during the year, one af them at Hull, at which Sir A. K. Rollitt presided. This was followed by an excursion to the coast at Withernsea, where Prof. James Geikie explained the drift deposited in the neighbourhood, with a general exposition of the geological phenomena they indicate. The second meeting was held at Bradford, Arthur Briggs, Esq., presiding, and eleven papers were presented or read.

During 1883 three meetings were held, one at Dewsbury; the second took the form of an excursion, and the third was held at Pontefract. The excursion was made in conjunction with the

Geologists' Association of London. The combined societies met at Harrogate on July 17th, and the geological features of the district were examined, under the guidance of Mr. Hudleston. On the following day the members visited Knaresbro' and Plumpton, and on the 19th the party, under the guidance of the Honorary Secretary of this Society, left Harrogate and drove to Skipton, spending some pleasant hours at Bolton Abbey and its beautiful environment. At Skipton the somewhat numerous party was located at the several hotels in the town, having their headquarters at the Devonshire Arms. On Thursday, Malham and Gordale were visited, and the more energetic portion of the party walked across the moors to the Victoria Cave, and thence to Settle and Giggleswick. The museum in connection with the Grammar School at the latter place was inspected, and the remains which were obtained during the exploration of the Victoria Cave, which are deposited in this museum, were examined. On Friday, the 21st, the members of the joint societies proceeded to Clapham and visited the Ingleboro' Cave, Trougill and Gaping Gill Hole. They thence proceeded to Norber, where the immense assemblage of ice-borne Silurian blocks, resting on limestone, is located, and continuing their walk round the spur of Monghton Fell, inspected the quarries of slate, with superimposed limestone, which form its summit. From Horton in Ribblesdale the party returned by train to Skipton. On account of the bad weather which had set in, a projected excursion to Lothersdale and Raygill was abandoned. A detailed and interesting description of this excursion was prepared by Mr. Hudleston and the Honorary Secretary, and is printed in the proceedings of the Society.

The visit of the Society to Pontefract was rendered very agreeable by the kind entertainment of one of the vice-presidents, Mr. T. W. Tew, who presided on the occasion. Before the meeting the members visited a portion of the new Hull and Barnsley line of railway at Upton. A fine section was exposed by a cutting in the Permian limestone, showing this rock resting uncomformably on the coal measures.

It was during this year that the hand of the assassin deprived the Society of one of its most esteemed vice-presidents. Lord

Frederick Cavendish was always anxious to support any cause which had for its object advanced education or the promotion of original scientific research, and worthily adhered to the example set by so many of his ancestors. He was intimately connected with scientific societies in Yorkshire, and had been for several years a vice-president of this one. A resolution was passed at the meeting at Dewsbury expressing the greatest regret and sorrow at his untimely end, and was forwarded to Lady Frederick Cavendish, and Lord Edward Cavendish, on behalf of the Duke of Devonshire.

The number of members, which had been two hundred and three in 1882, was increased in 1883 to two hundred and twelve. The amount standing to the credit of the capital account was increased to one hundred and sixty-five pounds, and there was a balance of forty-four pounds on the general account. In July, 1883, a number of members of the Society met at Hull, and proceeded *via* Patrington to Kilnsea and Spurn Point. The ancient kitchen middens at Kilnsea were examined, and a number of bones and some bronze ornaments were obtained from them. On the third day, the party, proceeding by way of Hull, went to Hornsea, and after inspecting Hornsea Mere, a large lake below the level of the sea, drove to Skipsea, where Mr. Thomas Boynton, of Ulrome Grange, met the party. A section of an ancient lake exposed in the cliff was first inspected, and thence by way of Skipsea Howe the party walked along the sides of the Barmston Drain to the lake dwelling which Mr. Boynton had discovered and excavated. After inspecting the collection of remains found in the lake-dwelling and in the locality generally, at Mr. Boynton's residence, and partaking of his hospitality, the members proceeded to Bridlington.

Meetings were held at Leeds, Ripon, and Halifax. At the latter, Mr. Louis J. Crossley, President of the Literary and Philosophical Society, presided, and Mr. John Brigg, of Keighley, who had been treasurer during the past eight years, resigned this office, and Mr. William Cash, of Halifax, was elected to the post.

In April of the following year the Society met at Harrogate, where Mr. Richard Carter presided, and a number of papers of peculiar interest, all treating, with one exception, of some subject connected with the geological or chemical constitution of the mineral waters of Harrogate, were read. The interest of this meeting, combined with the hospitality of its chairman, will long be remembered. The annual meeting was held at the Philosophical Hall, Leeds, the chair being occupied by Professor Bodington, Principal of the Yorkshire College. The number of members during the year had been increased to two hundred and twenty, twenty-six of whom had compounded for their annual subscription.

In 1885 three meetings were held, the first at Malton, in the East Riding. Before the meeting the members proceeded to Setrington and North Grimston, where Mr. C. Fox Strangways, of H.M. Geological Survey, pointed out and explained the geological features of the district. Quarries in coralline oolite were visited and fossils obtained. The meeting was held at the Talbot Hotel, and the Rev. E. Maule Cole, in the absence of Sir Charles Strickland, occupied the chair. The second meeting was held at York in September, and the President, the Marquis of Ripon, who had returned from India, occupied the chair. He received a very hearty reception, and congratulations on his successful occupancy of the position of Viceroy during the last five years; the members afterwards adjourned to the Station Hotel. The third meeting was at Leeds in October. The honorary secretary, in his annual report, had to state the unfortunate loss the Society had sustained by the deaths of Viscount Halifax and Lord Houghton. The number of members was two hundred and ten, which, in the following year was increased to two hundred and fifteen. The finances of the Society were in a flourishing condition, eighty-two pounds standing to the credit of the general account, and two hundred and seventeen pounds to that of the composition fees. These sums were still further increased, and early in 1887 it was decided to invest three hundred and fifty pounds in a mortgage with the Halifax Corporation, an additional twenty pounds still standing to the credit of the Society.

In 1886, the members met at Barnsley; they had an excursion to Leyburn in Wensleydale; and the annual meeting was held at Wakefield. At the latter, Mr. T. W. Embleton, one of the founders of the Society, presided, and delivered an address on the history of coal mining, which will be found printed in the Society's proceedings.

At the first general meeting at Halifax, in 1887, a recommendation of the council was adopted, that a sum of ten pounds might with advantage be devoted to the purpose of investigating a pre-glacial deposit at the foot of an ancient escarpment of the chalk near Bridlington, from which portions of the skeleton of an elephant had been obtained, and to Messrs. Lamplugh and Boynton, and the honorary secretary, was entrusted the duty of superintending the excavation. At this meeting Mr. James Booth, F.G.S., presided, and afterwards entertained the members at his residence, Spring Hall. During the summer an excursion meeting was held at Bridlington Quay, and the glacial beds exposed by the washing away of the Beaconsfield seawall were examined; the excavation of the buried cliff at Sewerby was visited, and the party then proceeded to Speeton to examine the Speeton clay and the red and white chalk of the cliffs at Bempton, Flamborough. Thence the excursion was extended to Filey and Gristhorpe, where the oolitic series are exposed. Mr. Lamplugh acted as guide in the first part of the excursion, and Mr. C. Fox Strangways accompanied the members to Filey and Gristhorpe.

The year 1887 was the fiftieth anniversary of the formation of the Society, and a Jubilee meeting, in celebration of this, was held in the Town Hall, Ripon, on October 22nd, 1887. The President, the Marquis of Ripon, presided, and Prof. J. W. Judd, the president of the Geological Society of London, together with Principal Bodington and Professors Green and Miall, of the Yorkshire College, were present. Professor Judd gave an address on the relation between great central societies and local ones, and Principal Bodington on the new seats of learning. The meeting was a large one, and the opportunity was taken to present the honorary secretary with a valuable miscroscope in recognition of his services to the Society, extending over a period of more than twelve years. The members afterwards dined together at the Unicorn Hotel.

A paper was read in 1878 by Dr. H. C. Sorby, at that time president of the Geological Society of London, on a new method of studying the optical characters of minerals. These characters afforded a valuable means for identifying the various species, but their practical application had been restricted by the difficulty of obtaining crystals sufficiently large and transparent to be cut into appropriate sections, so that the properties of some of the commonest minerals are very imperfectly known. The methods described by Dr. Sorby appeared to overcome these difficulties. If a pure, transparent crystal be merely magnified, little or nothing can be learnt, but if instead of viewing the crystal itself, it be looked through with a suitable magnifying power, at some appropriate object, more facts of interest and importance can be learnt than by any other single method whatever. The object Dr. Sorby examined through the crystals was the image of a small circular hole or of rectangular lines ruled on a piece of glass, formed at the focal point of a well-corrected achromatic condenser, fixed below the stage, and so arranged that the image is placed either just below or just above the lower surface of the crystal. The divergent rays passing through it to the object glass are bent, so that the focal length is, as it were, increased by an amount depending on the thickness of the crystal and its refractive power. The method of testing these values was treated at considerable length and reduced to mathematical formulæ. The data thus obtained are so remarkably characteristic that they alone would amply suffice to identify a large proportion of natural minerals. In many cases all the necessary observations can be made with small crystals in their natural state, which alone is a very great gain for practical mineralogy. The chief value of the method is, however, that portions of minerals, of microscopic size, may be identified in sections of rocks as thin or even thinner than 1-400ths of an inch, with an amount of certainty that leaves little to be desired.

The Geological History of the Strata of East Yorkshire formed the subject of an admirable paper by the Rev. J. F. Blake. Yorkshire may be broadly divided into two parts by the great Triassic plain running north and south, midway between the Penine Chain and the sea-coast. To the eastwards of this plain the formations consist mainly of lias, oolites, and chalk. The liassic beds in all probability were derived from the denudation of the coal measures, and their varying characteristics of fine clay or more sandy deposits depended on the source from which the materials were derived. When the coal measures became exhausted the millstone grits were attacked ; their denudation was less rapid, but the results may be seen in the beds which form the middle lias; and the increasingly calcareous rocks with which these beds terminated are attributed to the denudation of the Yoredale and Scar limestones. Most of these are now ironstones, and whence the iron was derived is not known, but there can be little doubt that the iron has taken the place of the calcareous matter which originally formed the beds. The large oysters occurring so abundantly in these beds indicate a shallowness of the water, and the consequent close proximity of the land. During the formation of the upper lias shales, the sea and land were again much depressed, and the coal measures were again broken up and redeposited to form the upper lias. The aggregation of the several beds constituting the oolitic rocks are considered in detail ; the cornbrash, the Kelloway rock, and the thick beds of Oxford clay are all traced to their origin in older rocks. The accumulation of great coral reefs which formed the coralline oolites were gradually depressed, so that the great thickness of Kimmeridge clay could be deposited above them. At the close of this period East Yorkshire ceased to be local, and became, during the deposition of the cretaceous rocks, part of a wide area ; and whilst in the south the gault and green sands were being accumulated, the more northern sea appears to have been deeper, and only a thin seam of red chalk represents the period. Above this the great thickness of the chalk was formed, and so ended the accumulation of the solid rocks which form the moors and wolds of East Yorkshire. The furthur action of atmospheric agencies on the surface is referred to, as well as the action of the glaciers which covered that part of the country during the glacial epoch.

The Rev. E. Maule Cole, M.A., contributed a paper on the Red Chalk. He traced the occurrence of the red chalk at the base of the white chalk through a considerable area, the best sections probably occurring near Wharram and Burdale, a district visited by the Society a short time afterwards. The white chalk of Yorkshire somewhat resembles a basin in form, the rim of which has been raised to the highest points by subterranean forces, and is now the thinnest portion, whilst in the centre of the basin the chalk has a thickness probably reaching

800 feet. The colour of the red chalk is very variable. At Speeton it is rich in colour and in fossils, whilst at Burdale it is a duller colour and in some places grey. Mr. Cole refers to the discovery at the bottom of the Atlantic of the red clay during the voyage of the "Challenger," and expresses the opinion that the two had probably a similar origin.

The occurrence of certain fish-remains in the Coal Measures, and the evidence they afford of fresh water origin, formed the subject of a paper by Mr. James W. Davis. The objects of this paper were to describe a bed of cannel coal existing over a limited area of the West Riding of Yorkshire, and to enumerate the remains of fossil fishes which occur in it, and further, to consider the relation of these fishes to each other, and the evidence they afford as to the circumstances attending their deposition. The cannel coal extends over an area of sixteen to twenty square miles, and appears to be the result of the decay of vegetable matter in inland lagoons or depressions. The coal is thickest in the centre of these depressions, and thins off towards the margin. The extent and character of the coal is traced throughout the district which comprises Adwalton, Gildersome, Morley, Tingley, and Ardsley. At Tingley, a large number of fish-remains had been obtained from the cannel coal and the shale immediately contiguous to it. Twelve species had been identified. Besides these were the bones of a labyrinthodont, some unios, and entomostraca. The relationship of the fish-remains with others existing at the present time is traced, and the inference drawn that they lived and the coal was deposited in fresh water.

At a meeting at Selby, held in March, Mr. J. T. Atkinson presided, and gave an interesting resumé of the history and objects of the Society, together with a brief notice of the geology of the district around Selby. Mr. J. R. Dakyns, of H.M. Geological Survey, contributed a paper on the southward flow of Shap granite boulders. These boulders are plentiful in the neighbourhood of Kendal, and to have reached that district must have passed over the Silurian rocks which form the high ground between the two areas. Shap granite occurs at a height of 1,659 feet above the sea level on Sleadale Pike. The author arrives at the conclusion that an ordinary glacier would be incapable of surmounting so great an obstacle as would be presented by these hills. The theory of floating ice is also considered untenable, and he is driven to the conclusion that a great ice sheet extended over the district, pushed southwards under an enormous pressure from behind.

Messrs. W. Cash and T. Hick contributed a notice of the flora of the lower coal measures of the Parish of Halifax. It was only during the ten previous years that a considerable impetus had been given to the study of fossil plants which flourished in the carboniferous age by the discovery of their remains, preserved with great fidelity in calcareous nodules, (locally termed coal-balls), found above the hard bed coal at Halifax, in Yorkshire, and at Oldham, in Lancashire. The organization of these fossils is preserved even to the most minute microscopical detail. The researches of Professor Williamson and others have thrown considerable light on the structure and affinities of the plants which flourished during the coal period. The observations of the authors were confined to the plants from the Halifax district, and the stratigraphical position and chemical composition of the coal-balls were explained. The fossils are roughly placed in four groups, namely, stems, organs of fructification, undetermined forms, and fungi. Of the first, eight are referred to, together with five species of Rachiopteris, a genus of ferns. The organs of fructification comprise the macrospores and microspores of lepidostrobi, cardiocarpon, the sporangia of ferns, and detached spore-like bodies which have not been determined. Amongst the undetermined organisms, the stomata, existing on fragments of epidermis, are perhaps the most remarkable, and of fungus one example of a mycelium has been found by Mr. Binns.

A paper on the triassic boulder, pebble, and clay beds at Sutton Coldfield, was contributed by Mr. J. E. Clarke; and the Rev. J. Stanley Tute described a species of Orthoceras which he had found in a bed of black shale immediately underlying the Cayton Gill beds near Ripon.

Amongst the contributors to the proceedings who have followed a well-defined line of research must be mentioned Mr. George W. Lamplugh, whose work on the Glacial Geology of the East Coast, and especially the neighbourhood of Bridlington, has been prosecuted in a well-organised and persistent manner for several years past; of eleven papers printed during the last eight years no fewer than eight have been on this subject. The papers deal chiefly with the coast between Filey and Bridlington Quay, and each paper is so far independent of the others that it contains a description of the glacial section at some particular locality, but in any one paper it will generally be found that one part of the glacial system receives greater attention, and is described in fuller detail than the other parts, and in this way the whole series of papers, if taken together, forms a continuous account of the glacial system as developed in the neighbourhood of Bridlington Quay and Flambro'.

The first of the papers was published in the Proceedings for 1879, on the divisions of the Glacial beds in Filey Bay. In it the author pointed out that the divisions made in the drifts south of Flambro' could also be traced in those lying to the north of the headland, and that the supposition of Messrs. Wood & Rome (Q. J. G. S., Vol. XXIV., p. 14) that the whole of the boulder clays north of Flambro' could be referred to one only of the divisions which they had instituted in the drifts of Holderness, was not borne out by the facts, but that on the other hand the glacial sequence was possibly more fully developed in Filey Bay than in the more southerly parts of the county. The value of differences in colour and texture in tracing divisions in boulder clay was also referred to.

In the Proceedings for the following year is a short paper on a fault in the chalk of Flambro' Head, with some notes on the Drift of the locality. After a short description of the fault, which lets down the chalk on the north side of Selwick's Bay, he drew attention to the drift deposits under the Lighthouse, where the lower boulder clay is chiefly derived from the Neocomian and Kimeridge clays, and in places consists of pure Neocomian clay, simply removed and in the condition of a boulder. Mr. Lamplugh also mentioned that in his opinion the patches of secondary clay that occur in the cliff near Filey, supposed to be of Middle Kimeridge age, are not in place, but are, similarly, boulders in drift.

In 1881 the Proceedings contain the first paper of a series

on the Glacial Sections near Bridlington. Of this series a second instalment was printed in 1882, and a third in 1883.

The principal object of these papers was to place on record sections which artificial works, such as the erection of sea-walls, etc., were closing to the geologist. For this purpose Mr. Lamplugh made drawings of the threatened sections to a natural scale of 1 inch to 60 feet, with enlargements to 1 inch to 10 feet of those parts that contained features which might prove of importance. The drawings have been lithographed by the Society, and as the original sections are now nearly all obliterated, they should hereafter prove of value. Indeed they have already been found useful to the Geological Survey, and three of the drawings have been reproduced in the Survey Memoirs on Holderness. (C. Reid, 1885, pp. 12, 30 and 76).

The first paper described the cliff section lying to the north of Bridlington Quay between Sands Cut and Carr Lane (opposite the Alexandra Hotel), where the cliff is now hidden by a strong sea-wall. Another drawing carries the section northwards as far as Sands Lane, this part of the cliff being still visible, though it has been somewhat altered by the encroachments of the sea. The deductive part of this paper deals chiefly with the extraordinary way in which the upper surface of the uppermost boulder clay is contorted and drawn out into the overlying gravels, and it is attempted to explain this by supposing that the gravels have been frozen solid in shallow water, and have then been moved in masses over and into the clays.* It is also shown that these gravels are of fresh water origin, and have been deposited in the streamways and lakelets that covered this area at the close of the glacial period.

In the second of the series, published in 1882, nine hundred yards of the cliff lying to the south of the town is described, and the sections are drawn on the same scales as before. The Purple Clay is more fully described and attention drawn to the presence in it of a 'stratified band,' along which lenticular patches of sand and gravel frequently make their appearance. It is also suggested that the constant recurrence of chalky gravels, interstratified among the

---

* C. Reid, however, thinks these contortions may be of the nature of 'pipes,' and due to weathering. (Holderness, p. 76-77).

glacial clays, is evidence that an exposed chalk surface existed in the neighbourhood during the deposition of the boulder clays.

In the third paper Mr. Lamplugh records the facts observed during the deep drainage of the town, and illustrates the geology of the town-site by giving actual sections as noted along extended lines of streets in various directions. These drawings, owing to their great length as compared with their depth, he was obliged to print on a scale reduced horizontally to one-third of that of the previous sections, but the vertical scale remained unaltered.

Mr. Lamplugh gave a summary of his previous work, and made a geological map of the town and its surroundings, to a scale of six inches to one mile. This map was reproduced in colours by the Society. In these concluding notes views are stated as to the origin of the beds, dealing more especially with the gravel and other deposits newer than the boulder clay. Reasons are given for believing that the 'Bridlington Gravels,' (certain rough gravels on the north side of the town), the 'Sewerby Gravels,' (finer gravel, well seen in the cliff opposite Sewerby), and the 'Hilderthorpe Sands,' (the sand and warp series lying south of the harbour), were contemporaneous deposits, the results of a strong current issuing from the main Wold Valley that here debouched either into a lake or estuary, more probably the former; and the term Bridlington Series, is proposed to include the whole of these deposits.

The view is put forward that the great flow of water down the valley during the deposition of this series, as compared with the insignificant stream now running there, might be due not only to a greater rainfall, but also to the surface layers of the chalk, being saturated and frozen, and thus forming an impervious subsoil that shed the rainfall rapidly into the valley.*

An idea is given of the state of the neighbourhood during the deposition of the 'Bridlington Series' as a region of bleak frozen chalk wolds, silent and deserted, and deeply covered by snow in

---

* This theory has been considerably strengthened by observations made by the Rev. E. Maule Cole during the winter of 1887, when the conditions required actually obtained on the Wolds, and resulted in floods. (See Proc. Yorksh. Geol. and Polyt. Soc., vol. IX., pt. iii., p. 343).

winter, and in summer streaked and drenched with melting snow and muddy chalk detritus; and of dales, sometimes ice-bound, sometimes held by rills and streams and floods of icy water, sweeping out into the low ground with swift floe-laden currents. It is also stated in this paper that there is reason to believe the ice-flow during the glacial period did not wholly cover the Wolds.

For the fine chalky low level gravels found on either side of the stream known as the Gypsey Race, the term 'Gypsey Gravel' is proposed. These are supposed to have been formed as valley gravels of the Gypsey, at a period later than the deposition of the Bridlington Series.

In the Proceedings issued in 1882, will be found a description of Thornwick Bay, Flambro', in explanation of the photograph issued by the Society. It includes some account of the drift deposits of that part of the coast, and also shows how much the shape of the coast is affected by the presence of a pre-glacial valley on the headland running close to and nearly parallel with the coast line on the north side; this valley by its influence on the erosive action of the sea, being the chief cause of the extremely jagged outline of the shoreline northwestward from the lighthouse.

In 1885 Mr. Lamplugh contributed a paper 'On Icegroved Rock-surfaces near Victoria, Vancouver Island, with notes on the glacial phenomena of the neighbouring region, and on the Muir Glacier of Alaska,' in which he described observations made during a visit in 1884 to the Pacific Coast of North America.

In the proceedings for 1887 are three papers by Mr. Lamplugh, one on the larger Boulders of Flambro' Head, is the first instalment of a study of the glacially-transported blocks to be found lying on the shore and elsewhere on the headland. This study, which was undertaken at the instigation of the Yorkshire Boulder Committee, aims, by cataloguing all the boulders within a given area that have any dimension exceeding twelve inches, to determine whether any of these may be localized, or whether the various rocks are evenly diffused over the whole area. One somewhat unexpected result has already been brought out, for it appears that, at any rate on the south side of the headland, somewhere between 60 and 80 per cent.

of the blocks have been derived from the carboniferous system, and that secondary blocks of the requisite size are rare.

A Report on the Buried Cliff at Sewerby, near Bridlington, is the outcome of an investigation, carried on by means of a grant of £10 made by the Society, into the fossiliferous deposits banked against an ancient sea cliff of chalk on the south side of Flambro' Head. These deposits consist of an old sea beach at the foot of the cliff, overlaid by the remains of land surface, which is, in turn, covered and overlapped by a thick dune of blown sand reaching to the top of the old cliff. The whole series is overlaid and overlapped by the lowest boulder clay. A large number of bones and other remains were obtained in process of excavation, among other mammals are the Elephant (*Elephas antiquus*), Rhinoceros and hippopotamus. The paper is illustrated by a lithograph and a woodcut.

Another paper in the Proceedings for 1887 is on a Mammaliferous Gravel at Elloughton, in the Humber Valley. It is a description of a high level gravel with mammalian remains, (chiefly of the Mammoth), recently exposed in a pit near Brough-on-the-Humber. A tusk about 10 feet long was found there, but was badly preserved and could not be removed. The gravel is evidently of glacial age, and it is suggested that it may have been accumulated when the mouth of the Humber was blocked with ice. A description of the Photograph for the year, a section in the cross-bedded 'Hilderthorpe Sands,' is also contributed by Mr. Lamplugh.

The Rev. E. Maule Cole during the past ten years has contributed six papers to the Society, five of which have had reference to the Wold district of the East Riding. The origin and formation of the dales, together with the physical geography of this district, have received from him much careful attention. The Wolds consist of a series of level plateaus divided by deep valleys in which there is at present no running water. These dales, Mr. Cole is of opinion, have received their present conformation to a large extent from the action of glaciers which ploughed their way from the hills towards the sea, and left their detritus scattered over the plains of Holderness. The sinuous windings, the deep indentations, the beautifully rugged, steep and curved outlines, the level gently-sloping bottoms, added to the fact that the *debris* of the upper dales has been removed and deposited at a lower level of several hundred feet, all point to this agency as the grand feature of their formation. He ventures an opinion that the origin of the dales is due to a series of inequalities or synclinals of the surface shown by the fact that the beds of chalk repeatedly dip in different directions, though the general dip of the mass is towards the south-east. This paper was followed, in 1885, by one read by Mr. J. R. Mortimer, who endeavoured to demonstrate that the valleys were due in the first instance and in a great measure to cracks or fissures caused by the elevation of the beds of chalk into dry land, and that since the commencement of that elevation those gaping cracks have been widened and acted upon by sub-marine, sub-ærial, and all the denuding and abraiding forces of nature, some of which are still at work. Mr. Mortimer cites a number of instances in which faults have been proved to exist at the bottom of the dale, for example, that of Thixendale, Backdale, Fairydale, and near Wharram Station. The contortions in the chalk at Flamborough Head were described by Mr. James W. Davis, in a paper explanatory of photographs issued to the Society in the same year. The contortions which are exhibited in the cliffs at Staple Nook, a small bay in the Bempton Cliffs, extend about 300 yards, and are more than 400 feet in height. The strata are bent and doubled into a series of anticlinals and synclinals, and in one place are broken and faulted. The action causing these contortions probably took place long after the deposition of the chalk when it had become hard and consolidated, the pressure in all probability having been applied laterally. In 1882, the Rev. Mr. Cole contributed a paper on the White Chalk, in which he contests the opinion that the chalk was deposited in an area forming a deep sea. Europe, before the deposition of the chalk, which extends over a large part of its surface, had certainly attained a continental form, and it is probable that a slight depression of the surface allowed the waters of the Atlantic to pour over its central portion. The constant flow eastward of a stream, similar to the Gulf Stream, would supply an enormous quantity of foraminifera, which, by their decay, aided by the disintegration of coral reefs, caused the accumulation of calcareous sediment known as chalk. The fossils which are found in chalk are indicative of animal life existing in shallow water. The chalk in Yorkshire is characterised by different forms of flint, which, in the several beds, maintain a characteristic appearance. The uppermost beds are devoid of flint, but on analysis the chalk is found to yield twice as much silicia distributed throughout its mass as the chalk which contains flint nodules. During 1885 the same author contributed papers describing some sections formed during the construction of the Hull and Barnsley Railway at Cave and Drewton, and the physical geography of the East Riding of the county. He also described a series of parallel roads in Glengloy, of similar structure to those of the far-famed Glenroy. In 1887 Mr. Cole contributed a paper on the dry valleys in the chalk; during the month of January, a succession of frosts had frozen the bare ground so hard that no rain could penetrate, but was quickly converted into ice. Snow also fell, and was repeatedly melted and re-frozen. The snow and ice gradually descended and accumulated in the bottom of the valleys. On a sudden a rapid thaw ensued, and in a few hours the dale bottoms were converted into roaring torrents, in some cases three feet deep. The ground was still frozen hard underneath, so that the water could not penetrate. Large quantities of loose chalk and rubbish were carried considerable distances and re-deposited further down the valleys. The author referred to a paper by Mr. Clement Reid, read at the Geological Society of London, on the origin of dry chalk valleys, in which he showed that with a frozen sub-soil the drainage system of the chalk might be entirely modified and the underground circulation stopped. Mr. Cole recorded the above instance as affording some confirmation to this view.

In 1881 Mr. J. R. Mortimer described a series of sections in the drift obtained whilst forming the new drainage works at Driffield. They were cut in the purple clay and Hessle clay, frequently intricately dove-tailed and squeezed together so as to obliterate every well-marked line of separation, intermixed with patches of chalk gravel, and sand. These Mr. Mortimer attempted to correlate with more extensive deposits throughout Holderness. In 1886 Mr. Mortimer also described a series of lance-pointed terraces or platforms occurring on the steep hillsides of some of the Yorkshire Wold valleys. They are quite distinct from any other form of earthworks or hillside ledges, and are usually found on slopes facing southwards. The author considers that these platforms were constructed for the purpose of erecting habitations, and cites instances described by Mr. Foote, of the Indian Geological Survey, in which similar pre-historic artificial terraces have been discovered in India. In both instances, though so widely separated, the terraces are accompanied by the discovery of flint implements.

Mr. J. R. Dakyns contributed in 1879-80 two papers on the Glacial Beds in the neighbourhood of Bridlington. In the latter he describes a large number of sections of the glacial beds around Flamborough Head. In the following year the same author read a paper on Flots. Flot is a term used by miners to describe pockets of ore lying between the beds at certain definite horizons in the strata; They are of two kinds. The first is found where two veins cross, and only bears lead where a spar-vein intersects it. The second kind is found in connection with courses of dun limestone; the latter is a dolomitized limestone of a brown colour, and wherever this peculiar feature is observed it is usually accompanied by lead, the metal being found up and down between the dun and the white limestone.

In addition to the paper already referred to, read in 1878, the Fossil Flora of the lower coal measures in the neighbourhood of Halifax has received valuable attention from Messrs. Wm. Cash and Thos. Hick, and they have published joint papers between the years 1879 and 1884. In 1879 they described a series of examples of fossilised fungoid growths which, though not sufficiently perfect for complete identification, still presented many interesting characters deserving detailed description. The fungus was found in a rootlet of some plant, and the tissues of the rootlet bear obvious marks of the ravages which the fungus has made upon it. Its cell walls are crude and less sharply defined in the infected part, so that the two can be readily distinguished even under the lower powers of the microscope. The vegetative part of the fungus consists of a large number of very delicate hyphæ, the majority finer than the threads of Penicillium glaucum, and can scarcely be more than 1-7000 inch in diameter. So perfectly are the structural details preserved that it is possible to distinguish the protoplasmic contents from the enclosing cellulose wall. The authors describe as fully as possible the general characters of the fungus, and are inclined to refer it to the sub-order Peronospora. Another slide, exhibiting a number of disconnected fragments of vegetable tissue, contained, intermixed with these, an immense number of small round bodies which are considered to be the spores of some fungus. There was no trace of mycelium or any other filamentous structure. The authors are of opinion that these may be related to the Myxomycetes. The latter usually occur on old and decaying stumps and sticks of trees, and when in fructification consist mainly of an extremely thin-walled sporangium filled with small pores. These, when released by the rupture of the sporangium, are scattered in immense quantities, and often form a thick layer of dust on the substratum on which the fungus has grown. The authors contributed a note on certain minute globular organisms which Mr. Carruthers described as Traquairia, and considered that they presented affinities with the radiolarian group of animals. Prof. Williamson, in 1878, described the same bodies as of vegetable origin, and the authors were now able to confirm this view, and were able to state that the enclosure of Traquairia within the sporangium wall was sufficient evidence in favour of the view that they were of vegetable and not animal origin.

In 1881 Messrs. Cash and Hick described a representative of a new genus of fossil plants which have many points of resemblance to the structure of the stem of Myriophyllum, and which they designated Myriophylloides Williamsoni. This was followed by a fresh contribution in 1884, in which the structure of Calamites was given; and a further reference to Myriophylloides. In 1887 Mr. William Cash contributed the first of a series of papers on the fructifications of the fossil plants of the Yorkshire coal measures, and described and illustrated the interesting cone-like fruit spikes of Calamostachys. A description of the section in which the hard-bed coal occurs is given, as well as the chemical structure of the coal-balls containing the plants which occur in this coal. Calamostachys is nearly related to calamites and to the existing equisetum, and a comparison between the structure of the latter and the fossil is given. Two species of Calamostachys are known, C. Binneyana, of Schimper, and C. Casheana, named by Professor Williamson after the author, and described in his 11th memoir on the organization of the fossil plants of the coal measures, from a specimen discovered in the Halifax beds by the late Captain Aitken. Illustrations are given of the features distinguishing the two species. The paper is supplemented by a bibliographical list of works and authors who had previously dealt with the subject. In addition to the palæo-botanical papers already referred to, Mr. James Spencer read a paper on Astromyelon and its affinities. The genus was described by Professor Williamson in 1878. Since that time Mr. Spencer had discovered a number of other specimens which he described, and expressed his opinion that the genus occupied an intermediate position between the lepidodendroid plants and the gymnosperm dadoxylons.

To Mr. George Robert Vine the Society is indebted for a series of ten papers treating of the microscopic organisms in the strata between the Wenlock Shales and the Greensand, but mainly describing those of the Carboniferous Rocks of Yorkshire. Mr. Vine is a recognized authority on the Polyzoa of these strata, and his papers are necessary for reference in any country where the Polyzoa are studied.

In 1881 he contributed to the proceedings notes on the Carboniferous Polyzoa of North Yorkshire. In it the author deals with, and partly describes, the Polyzoan fauna found in the shales of North Yorkshire, at Richmond and Hurst. Some years previously to the date of the paper, Mr. Vine received from Mr. John Harker, of Richmond, a packet of unwashed clay, from some locality in the neighbourhood of Hurst. The sample, after careful washing, was found to be rich in fragments of Polyzoa, Entomostraca and Foraminifera. Twenty-two species of Polyzoa are either described or referred to, many of which differ from the forms so abundant in the Lower Limestone Shales of Scotland, but in all probability the whole may be referred to as belonging to the Upper Limestone Series of Scotland, more particularly those found in Gair and Belstonburn (Yoredale ?).

A second paper on the Carboniferous Entomostraca and Foraminifera of North Yorkshire was read in 1883; the specimens were found in the Hurst and Richmond shales, from which are described, and the range given of, eleven species of Carboniferous Entomostraca. The author also catalogues nineteen species of Carboniferous Foraminifera, all of which had been described and figured in the admirable Monograph of Carboniferous and Permian Foraminifera by Mr. H. B. Brady. Mr. Brady does not catalogue Saccammina Carteri as a Yorkshire form ; yet Mr. Vine discovered in the shales of Downholm, both Nodosinella concinna, Brady, and S. Carteri, Brady, in the Hurst debris.

Further notes on new species and other Yorkshire Carboniferous Polyzoa. In this paper the author deals with and revises the early work of Phillips, as described in the Geology of Yorkshire. Calamopora tumida, Phill. is redescribed, and illustrated and placed in the Monticuliporidæ group of Nicholson. There are, however, certain characters pointed out in this and other species, regarded by the author as new, which have since been fully investigated by Messrs. Young, and Nicholson and Foord. The latter authors restore the Ceramopora megastoma, M'Coy, of the present paper to the Fistulipora group as F. incrustans, Phillips.* In the Family Rhabdomesontidæ Vine, species closely allied to American forms, are described or referred to. Certain forms found in the shales were new, and some of these were placed in the Genus Rhombopora, Meek, by the author, while others were described and illustrated and placed in the (M.S.) Genus Streblotrypa, Ulrich, which has been since then fully established by Mr. Ulrich in American Palæontological Works.† This is an important paper, and its contents and references were overlooked by Nicholson and Foord, and also by Mr. John Young in their later descriptions.‡

The Carboniferous Polyzoa of West Yorkshire and Derbyshire, read in 1884. Mr. Vine wrote this paper to attempt the identification of Phillips' species from material placed in his hands by the late Mr. John Aitken. This paper deals with species of Polyzoa which up to the time of writing were either rare or little known from any Derbyshire locality. Mr. Aitken obtained his examples from a thin layer

---

* Ann. Mag. Nat. Hist., Dec., 1885 (S. 5, vol. xvi.)
† III. Geol. Survey, vol. vii.
‡ Ann. Mag. Nat. Hist., April, 1888.

or bind in the Castleton Limestone. Twelve species are described, and the author gave the history of Glauconome bipinnata? Phill, and described an example identical with, or closely related to that peculiar species.

In 1885 Mr. Vine read some notes on the Yoredale Polyzoa of North Lancashire, and described a fine series of Polyzoa from the Yoredale horizon of North Lancashire. In 1884 Mr. J. W. Kirkby, F.G.S., was working these shales for Entomostraca, and the fragments of Polyzoa were handed over to Mr. Vine. Thirty-five species and varieties are described, new species illustrated, and the range, in tabular form, of Carboniferous Polyzoa in Yoredale rocks given.

Mr. Vine also contributed Notes on the Polyzoa and Foraminifera of the Cambridge Greensand. In this paper the author described, and partially illustrated, twenty-three species of Polyzoa and Foraminifera, most of which were new to British rocks of this horizon. Since the paper was written the author finds that a species described as new (Entalophora striatopora, Vine), is closely related to, if not identical with Entalophora lineata, Beissel. The species is described by Beissel (Ueber d. Bry. d. Aachen Kreid, p. 80, taf. 9, figs. 116-119), and a variety of Beissel's species is described and illustrated by Prof. Reuss in Das Ethalg. in Sach. Geinitz, (Die Foram. Bry. and Ostracod. des Pläners, p. 133, taf. II, 25, figs. 5-6). A new interest is lent to this discovery on account of the peculiar range, British and Foreign, of this singular form, as one of the citations of Reuss, following that of Beissels, 1865, is 1872, Stoliczka, Palæont. indica. IV, 2. The Ciliopoda, p. 31, taf. 3, figs. 9-10.

Another species, re-described in this paper by the author, (Quart. Journ. Geol. Soc., 1884), properly belongs to this series, and the specimens were handed over for description by the late lamented Mr. G. Busk, and the form though named Lichenopora (?) paucipora, Vine, is unlike any other known Upper Greensand Lichenoporidæ.

During 1886-7 Mr. Vine read three papers on the Palæontology of the Wenlock Shales; on the Polyzoa of the Wenlock Shales; and on the Distribution of Entomostraca in the Wenlock Shales. The papers on the Wenlock Shales of Shropshire are the outcome of much laborious investigation on the part of the author, other papers on the same horizon being published in the Quart. Journ. of the Geological Society, and in the Annals and Magazine of Natural History. Previously to Mr. Vine's labours, very little was known respecting the fauna of the Wenlock Shales of Shropshire. The shales, about 22 tons, were originally washed by Mr. Maw, for the purpose of assisting the late Dr. Davidson in his illustration of the Upper Silurian Brachiopoda, the residue being handed over (about 2½ cwts. of washed material), to Mr. Vine. After several years labour the author was able to describe and catalogue a fine series of Polyzoa and Annelida tubicola, many of which were new, and with the assistance of Prof. T. Rupert Jones, about 100 species of Entomostraca have been catalogued and illustrated in the Annals and Magazine of Natural History by Prof. Jones and Dr. Holl. These papers represent the work accomplished, but much still remains to be done; other groups of fossil organisms are only partially catalogued in the first of these papers.

In 1887 the same author contributed Notes on Classifications of Polyzoa, new and old. To working students especially this is a most important contribution to scientific literature, as in it the author records all the varied attempts at classifying the Cyclostomata, from the time of Busk's Crag Polyzoa Monograph to the present. The author, however, limits himself in this paper, practically to the Cyclostomata of the various Mesozoic horizons. The number of new species and varieties described in these papers are given below, under the dates when published :—

1883. Ptylopora Phillipsia, Vine.
    (Thamniscus dubius? King).
        Var. carbonaria, Vine.
    Ichthyorachis sp., Vine.
    Glauconome bipinnata? Phill. (Vine).
    Heterotrypa delicatula, Vine.
    Diplotrypa petrapolitanaforma, (new var. ?)
    (Rhombopora lepidodendroidea, Meek.
        ,,   persimilis, Ulrich
    Streblotrypa nicklisi, (Ulrich M.S.)
        ,,   genus and species (new to Yorkshire).

1885. Pinnatopora, Vine.
,, ornata, Vine.
,, ? simplex, Vine.
,, sp. (grandis, ? M'Coy).
Polypora verrucosa, ? M'Coy. (Provisional, Vine).
Thamniscus gracilis, Vine.
Rhombopora vinculariformis, Vine.
Streblotrypa minuta, Vine.
Entalophora striatopora, Vine.
(=? E. lineata, Beiss).
,, gigantopóra, Vine.
Diastopora cretacea, Vine.
,, ,, var. lineata, Vine.
,, fecunda, Vine.
Lichenopora ? paucipora, Vine.
Membranipora Dumerelli, Aud.
,, var. cantabrigensis, Vine.
Microporella sp., (? antiquata), Vine.

Mr. James W. Davis has contributed eighteen papers on a variety of subjects during the period covered by this chapter. Six have reference to fossil fish remains, and one to fossil trees. The erratic boulders in the Calder Valley, and at Norber are described. Reports of the excavation of Raygill fissure, three or four stratigraphical papers; two referring to pre-historic man in Yorkshire, and a biographical notice of John Phillips.

At the meeting held at Barnsley in 1879 Mr. Davis read a paper on the source of the erratic boulders in the valley of the River Calder, entering at greater detail into the question which formed the subject of a communication at a previous meeting. At the same meeting Dr. H. Franklin Parsons, then of Goole, explained some researches he had made on the Trias of the southern part of the Vale of York. Two years previously he had read a paper on the alluvial strata of this district which envelops the Trias with the exception of a few isolated patches. The Triassic-rocks are divided into two parts, the Keuper consisting of variegated marls, and the Bunter or new Red Sandstone. The Keuper rises to the surface in the Isle of Axholme and at Crowle, in Lincolnshire, and it is reached by borings at several places in the neighbourhood of Goole. At Holme-on-Spalding Moor it rises into a detached hill 150 feet in height. At a boring at Reedness the Keuper extends to a depth of 342 feet, where it rests on the Bunter. The total thickness of the former is estimated at 700 feet, and of the latter at 1,270 feet. The Bunter rises into hills at Brayton Barf and Hambledon Haugh respectively 175 feet and 150 feet in height. The junction of the Bunter Sandstone with the underlying Permian Limestone is nowhere exposed. An appendix to the paper gives a number of sections in wells and borings which illustrate the relation of the two series of rocks.

Mr. Stephen Seal gave an account of the fossil plants found at the Darfield Quarries near Barnsley.

The source of the water which issues at the foot of Malham Cove had been for many years a subject of dispute, and during 1879 Mr. Thomas Tate, with some other members of the Society, prosecuted a series of experiments to determine the question. The co-operation of Mr. Walter Morrison, M.P., vice-president, was readily obtained, and the results of the experiments formed the subject of a communication to this Society during the same year. They proved conclusively that the streams issuing at the Cove, as well as at Aire Head about a mile and a half lower down the stream, were both supplied from Malham Tarn by way of the Tarn water sinks. They also rendered it probable that behind Malham Cove there exists a water cave of greater or less extent as suggested by Prof. Boyd Dawkins. The theory that Malham Cove is supplied by the stream which disappears at the Streets Smelting Mill was completely refuted. Whilst these investigations were proceeding, Mr. Morrison called attention to an interesting phenomenon at Cowden Hill, north-east of Malham. This hill is ordinarily without a spring, but about once in every five years a body of water rushes out at its foot and down Fingal-street with such violence as to tear away the macadam off the road. This discharge continues for seven or eight hours, after which the scene resumes its wonted stillness, and grass reclothes the denuded slopes. The phenomenon may be explained by the existence of a deep funnel-shaped reservoir, near the base of which exists a syphon whose bend is nearly on a level with its roof.

Professor Arnold Lupton, of the Yorkshire College, contributed notes on the Midland Coal-field. In the proceedings for 1880, the Rev. J. Magens Mello gave an account of investigations which he with others had made in Cresswell Caves in Derbyshire, and Mr. W. H. Wood gave the result of experiments which enabled him to distinguish obsidian from black blast furnace slag, the former containing nearly double the percentage of silicia as compared with the slag. Professor L. C. Miall read a paper on the structure of the skull and some other bones of Ctenodus. Mr. Davis read a paper on the distribution of fossil fishes in the Yorkshire Coalfields, and enumerated all the genera which had been found associated with the several beds of coal. The total number of species of fossil fishes hitherto discovered was fifty-one. The same author also described a group of erratic boulders at Norber, near Clapham. Norber is the southern extremity of a long promontory of mountain limestone extending from the base of that portion of Ingleboro' called Simon's Fell. On its western flank are escarpments overlooking Clapdale, and on the opposite one precipitous ridges extend for nearly two miles in a northerly direction, towards the head of the dale overlooking the Crummack Valley. The escarpments of the limestone extend across the upper part of the dale, and on the eastern side constitute Moughton Fell. The whole of the surface of this limestone plateau is thickly strewn with masses of Silurian grit, some of immense size and weighing many tons. Blocks, sixteen to twenty feet in diameter, are not uncommon, and many of them are raised on a pedestal of limestone, in some instances nearly two feet in height, the surrounding limestone having been denuded to this extent since the Silurian blocks gained the present locality. Towards the head of the valley the limestone becomes much thinner, and Silurian rocks are exposed, and it is from this source that the perched blocks have been derived. They have been carried by a great glacier which descended on the western flank of Ingleboro' towards the vale of the Ribble. Numerous scratches on the rocks show the direction of this glacier, and its power and thickness are indicated by the force with which it tore up the Silurian grits and carried them over the limestone deposit, in some instances two or three hundred feet higher than their original position.

At a meeting held at Hull in April, 1881, Mr. A. G. Cameron, of H.M. Geological Survey, drew attention to subsidences over the Permian boundary between Hartlepool and Ripon. The phenomena are similar to those described by the Rev. J. Stanley Tute, in a previous communication to this Society. A number of instances are cited of pits which occur northwards from Ripon. The initiative to a number of the pits may have been given by the river at a time when confined between high and overhanging crags, as it must once have been about Ripon. It beat ceaselessly against the walls of the narrow gorge which would become caverned and rugged by the force of the torrent. On the boundary walls of this ravine the subsidences took place more frequently than elsewhere, and this may be due to the strata being in greater dilapidation from the above causes, areas less compact than this determining the locality of the pits. A more probable explanation is that where the underground water, flowing over the limestone surface, reaches the margin of the sandstone it receives a check whereby it accumulates, forming a chain of dams or pools along the line of junction of these rocks, as denudation proceeds hollows will form above and below until ultimately the phenomena of the pits appear. In the neighbourhood of Hartlepool the Permian and Triassic rocks dip or roll towards each other indicating a trough extending longitudinally in the direction of their boundary. There are thick beds of salt only a 'very short way from Hartlepool, and it is possible that when the coast line extended further into the present bay the drainage off the land may have found access to beds of salt below, and dissolving them caused a cavity into which the overlying strata has sunk, giving rise to the large pool called the Slake. Other instances in neighbouring formations are given and compared with those of the Permian. Bearing on a similar subject, Mr. T. Fairley contributed a paper on the blowing wells near Northallerton. Three of these wells occur at Salberg, Langton, and Ornhams. In each of them currents of air flow from the shafts of the wells during a falling period of the barometer, and inward currents flow into the shafts of the wells while the barometer is rising. When the rise or fall of the barometer is considerable, the currents are very powerful, producing a strong draught or wind in the openings leading to the shaft. Mr. Fairley, by means of a vane-anemometer fixed to the top of the closed well, was able to ascertain the amount of air which passed in and out of the wells in a given time; and in one instance at Salberg, between July 3rd and July 6th, he found that with a rise of the barometer of ·4 inches an undercurrent of 11·76 millions of cubic feet In the following year Mr. Fairley obtained a large dry gasometer, constructed to pass 3,000 cubic feet per hour, and coupled this to his pipe at the top of the well, and frequent readings were taken. The results corroborated his former experiment, and demonstrated that the currents vary in nature with the changes of the barometer, just as the volume of the air in any closed reservoir varies strictly with the atmospheric pressure when the influence of temperature has been eliminated. Hence the observations were considered to prove the existence of large cavities or fissures in the underlying strata adjacent to the wells. In the case of the well at Salberg, this cavity has a capacity approximating to ten million of cubic feet, which would occupy a chamber two hundred and seventeen feet in length, width, and height.

Mr. Joseph Lucas contributed an interesting account of the vestiges of ancient forests, which formerly covered the moors in the neighbourhood of Nidderdale; and a paper on some sections in the lower palæozoic rocks of the Craven district was read by Mr. J. E. Marr, in which an unconformity was shown to exist at the base of the Mayhill beds, occurring between the Mayhill and Bala beds, occurring at Crummack Beck Head in Craven.

Previous to the year 1859, Mr. Jackson, of Settle, Mr. Farrar, and Mr. Denny, (formerly secretary of this Society), had conducted explorations in the Dowkabottom Cave, near Kilnsey, the results of which were described in the proceedings of this Society for that year. In 1865 a further contribution to the subject was made by Mr. Farrar and Mr. Denny, and from that time to the year 1881 no further investigations were made. During the summer of 1881 Mr. E. B. Poulton and a number of gentlemen from Oxford spent a portion of their vacation in a further exploration of the cave, the results of which are published in the proceedings for that year. The cave is described as consisting of a series of chambers connected by narrow passages, the entrance descending vertically from the surface down into the cave, from which the chambers extend in an easterly and westerly direction. The total length of the easterly division is 463 feet 6 inches, and consists of three chambers and two passages. Westward the cave extends about 200 feet, and consists of two chambers and two passages. At the western extremity of the cave he found that the limestone roof terminated, and its place was occupied by stones and earth. The latter were removed, and it was found that the cave opens out on the slope of the hill, terminating with a vertical cliff face 20 feet in height. After clearing out the opening it was found that the side walls of the cave continue onwards as a ravine for about 50 feet, being entirely filled with the loose mixture of earth and stones, and only discernable on the ground above by its covering of unbroken turf; this, Mr. Poulton regards as the true opening of the cave. About fifty yards distant from the ravine is a pot-hole, and it is probable that there was formerly a connection between this and the cave by a passage now denuded away. The cave would thus drain into the pot-hole, and the stream on the eastern side of the vertical opening is in this direction, although it sinks in the second chamber. Inside the cave a considerable amount of work was done. It was found that the investigations of the previous explorers had extended superficially to the most productive portions of the caves, and that little remained to be done. The second chamber on the east side was found to have been as little worked as any, and it was to this that the party principally devoted their attention. Near the surface was found a blackish earth containing pottery, bones, and in some cases metal implements. This corresponds with the historic layers in the Victoria Cave. Near the centre of the cave they found a circular pit which had been dug by the men who lived at the time when this layer was being formed. It was about a yard in diameter and four feet deep; in it were found bones and ornaments, frequently encrusted with stalagmite; three small bronze pins occurred close together, half a broken spindle whorl of Samian pottery, and a small piece of flint were found; many rugged and cut bones, probably used as handles, knives, or rough pins. They also found the bowl end of a spoon-shaped fibula, pierced by a central hole, and ornamented with circles, with dots in their centres. In this cave several implements or ornaments of bronze were obtained, brooches, rings, a needle, and others, some iron implements were discovered, and numerous fragments of pottery, mostly bearing a Roman character. Indications of the use of fire were frequent. Fragments of charred wood and pot boilers for heating water were not uncommon. After investigating the black superficial deposit, a shaft was sunk to ascertain the depth of the floor and its contents. They first passed through alternating layers of hard and soft stalagmite, which carried them down to a depth of four feet. Then large blocks of limestone encrusted with hard stalagmite were met with, and below this horizon all chemical deposits ceased, and those of mechanical origin alone succeeded. For a depth of ten feet there was an extremely tough, stiff, brown clay, and huge blocks of limestone were abundant, rough and angular, and uncovered by stalagmite. At the depth of twelve feet the left wall of the cave was found sloping downwards. This was followed for two feet more, and had then taken a vertical direction. Beneath this thick bed of mechanical deposits it is possible that the older cave-earth exists. The further investigation, however, was stopped by the constant and great influx of water. No remains of any kind were found beneath the surface layer of black earth, except in the hard stalagmite immediately below it, in which the remains of a dog or wolf are common, and in excellent preservation. Whilst there is no evidence so far for the existence of older remains, there is no reason to doubt their presence. They were found in abundance in one chamber of the Victoria Cave under very similar circumstances to those existing in the Dowkabottom Cave, and it is probable that further investigations may render their presence known in the latter as well. Mr. Poulton was greatly aided in his labour by the kindly assistance rendered by Mr. Eddy, of Carlton, near Skipton.

The excavations necessary for the erection of the new railway station at York afforded an opportunity for the investigation of the glacial beds in that district, of which Mr. J. Edmund Clarke readily availed himself, and subsequently formed the basis of an elaborate and interesting paper which he contributed to the Society at a meeting held at Hull in 1881. The glacial beds are divided into two divisions, the lowermost much resembling the purple boulder clays of Holderness. This appearance indicates a deposition from floating ice rather than from the moraine profonde of an ice-sheet; otherwise it would be difficult to account for beds of gravel, boulders, and current-bedded sands so closely associated with the tough stone clays. Judging from the material, the ice-sheet or flows must have come from the north-west. The upper division appears to indicate a period much less severe than the lower, and consisted principally of sand, gravels, and boulders, with occasional beds of clay. Post-glacial beds probably derived from the glacial of the district have been formed to a considerable depth. Brickclays are worked for thirty feet in thickness, and the river deposits seem to go up much deeper. The Ouse now runs at a height of sixty or seventy feet above its pre-glacial bed; the slight protrusions from the general dead level are of glacial origin, whilst the river flood and tidal deposits have largely obliterated these undulations by filling them up perhaps as much as fifty feet above the level to which the river first cut down its bed in the opening of the post-glacial epoch.

In 1882 the Council decided that biographical notices of eminent Yorkshire Geologists should be printed in the proceedings, if possible annually. In accordance with this resolution, the Editor of the Proceedings contributed the first notice, his subject being John Phillips. In the following year a very instructive and interesting biography of Prof. Adam Sedgwick was contributed from the pen of Prof. T. M'Kenny Hughes, of Cambridge. In 1884 Dr. W. C. Williamson, Professor of Botany at the Owen's College, Manchester, contributed a biographical notice of his father, John Williamson, late of Scarborough. The article is full of interest, not only illustrating the salient features in the life of Mr. Williamson, but also of that group of scientists for which Scarbro' was for many years famous, including the Rev. Geo. Young, Wm. Bean, and John Bird, together with reminiscences of Wm. Smith, Prof. Phillips and others.

At a meeting held at Dewsbury in May, 1882, Mr. Jas. W. Davis contributed some notes on the occurrence of fossil fish-remains in the Carboniferous Limestone of Yorkshire. The fish-remains in this district are neither numerous nor are they found in a great number of localities, considering the large area occupied by the Mountain Limestone extending from Clitheroe and Slaidburn, Thornton, Skipton, to Greenhow Hill in the south, to the limits of the county westwards and northwards, and that in all these localities the rock is exposed for commercial and agricultural purposes in quarries of enormous extent. There can remain but one conclusion that whilst these rocks are replete with fossil mollusca, corals, and encrinites, there appears to have been a most remarkable absence of fishes in the seas of that period. The non-discovery may, perhaps, be attributed to a want of interest in this branch of palæontology, but with collectors in every district, searching for fossils of other kinds, it seems scarcely credible that the fishes would have escaped attention if they had been present. Occasionally localities are found in which fish-remains are abundant; one such occurs in the red beds of limestone in Wensleydale, from which a large number of fossil teeth have been collected by Mr. Wm. Horne, of Leyburn. Occasional specimens have also been found at Settle, Kettlewell, and Richmond, and in all thirty species are recorded. The author compares the Yorkshire fish-remains with those from the Mountain Limestone of Armagh, Bristol, and other localities, and arrives at the conclusion that the fishes occurring most frequently in the thick-bedded lower limestone of other parts of the British Islands are absent or only represented by dwarf specimens. The great spines of Ctenacanthus and Oracanthus are not present. The great teeth of Orodus, most of the genera of the Cochliodonts, the large palates of Psammodus, and the teeth of the Petalodonts, have in each case become dwarfed and comparatively insignificant. They present the appearance of groups which have previously reached the climax of their existence, and were gradually succumbing to a more or less unfavourable environment. With the advent of the coal measures they almost entirely disappeared.

Mr. J. Ray Eddy took the opportunity of the Society visiting the Raygill Quarries to conduct the members through the lead mining district of Cononley, and contributed a paper on the lead veins in the neighbourhood of Skipton, the most southern lead-producing district in the county. He gave a history of the discovery of various workings of the lead mines, and described the strata in which the veins occur. The total quantity of ore which has been produced from the Cononley veins is about fifteen thousand tons. The only other places near, where any ore has been produced from the Kinderscout grit is Cowling, about one and a half miles west of Cononley, where a trial was made, and three and a half tons of ore raised. In the limestone of the district there are, north and south, veins running across the Carleton Park Head, and also of the Skipton Haw Bank Quarries. From the former place about fifteen tons have been obtained, and from the latter about thirteen tons. These veins are very uncertain, but carry ore of good quality in self lumps in the clay lode. The paper was illustrated by a plan and longitudinal section of the upper veins.

For several years prior to 1879 occasional chips and implements of flint had been found on the moors covering the Penine Hills. These incited Messrs. Robert Law and James Horsfall to a more thorough investigation of the surface of the moors from which the peat had been denuded. Wherever patches of the surface thus exposed were found one or more fragments of flint were nearly always discovered. The most striking example was met with on March Hill, a conical eminence overlooking the Vale of Marsden; from a few small patches of bare ground on its southern surface more than two thousand flints were obtained. They included flint cores and one leaf-shaped arrow tip. The flints occurred in a dark-grey sand beneath the peat and a peaty clay. The sand is about six inches thick, and flints appear to occur indiscriminately throughout the whole thickness. Beneath this the sand assumes a red ochreous tint, about twelve inches in thickness, resting on Yoredale shale. Middle Hill, near Whitworth, also proved very remunerative. The peat had been burnt off some years previously, and atmospheric agents had lowered the loamy sub-soil at least an inch, proved by little earth pillars, capped with stones, and occasionally flints, here and there on the surface. Three hundred and fifty pieces of flint were gathered at this spot. Broken flints and arrow-heads were found at Knowl Hill, and on Midgley Moor, two miles north of Mytholmroyd, and also in numerous other localities. A total of 3,824 flints were found, and of these 83 had been worked into one or other kind of implement, including arrow and spear-heads, scrapers, and a few very small and neatly pointed flints, which Dr. John Evans considered unique, and may have been used as carving tools.

In 1883 the Rev. J. Stanley Tute, of Markington, read a paper on the sequence of the Permian Rocks near Ripon, and described some indications of a raised beach at Redcar. Mr. W. Y. Veitch also described some evidences of a submerged forest and peat beds in the neighbourhood of Hartlepool and Redcar, and a raised beach at Saltburn. The latter consists of a band of alluvial sand containing shells of marine species, such as purpura, litorina, and others. The beach is thirty-five feet above high-water mark. The existence of this raised beach at Saltburn only on this part of the coast indicates the extremely slow denuding action carried on by the sea. At Robin Hood's Bay, where the sea's action is accurately marked, its inroad is about twenty feet a year, three coastguard flagstaffs having been washed away in twenty years, which were placed respectively 140 feet from the shore.

Mr. Thos. H. Easterfield described a glacial deposit near Doncaster, at the Balby Brickworks. It consists of a tough, dark-blue clay, packed with boulders up to half a ton in weight, the latter mainly of local origin, though a few Carboniferous limestones are found. The extent of the deposit is stated to be about a quarter of a mile in greatest diameter. In a letter which was received in the following year Mr. Easterfield stated that the deposit extended as far as Warmsworth, so that it is over a mile in extent. Papers on the Geology of Palestine by Mr. W. H. Hudleston, and notes on a visit to the Channel Tunnel by Prof. Arnold Lupton, were also contributed to the proceedings of this year.

At a meeting held at Ripon in May, the Rev. W. C. Lukis, Rector of Wath, occupied the chair. In an address which he gave he stated his opinion that the Polytechnic side of the Society might very well include the results of archæological investigation. In previous years papers on British, Roman, and other remains had been freely inserted in its proceedings, and he considered that the tools and weapons of the primitive inhabitants of Yorkshire, and the materials from which they had been formed; the clothing which covered the people, whether manufactured out of woollen stuff or of leather, the art of the primeval potter, the implements employed in agricultural and mining purposes, the design, material, and fabrication of personal ornaments, and other kindred matters were legitimate branches of scientific study which no Polytechnic Society could fairly exclude, for in tracing out the development of industry no hard and fast line could be drawn beyond which research would be unnecessary and uninstructive. The explorations of antiquarians have been instrumental not only in bringing to light numerous articles of various kinds which for honest purity of materials, elegance of form and design, and excellence of workmanship cannot be excelled at the present day, but which on being reproduced by our manufacturers had found a ready sale because the public eye has been captivated and public taste educated.

A meeting was held at Harrogate in April, 1884, at which Mr. Richard Carter, one of the oldest members of the Society, occupied the chair, and gave an address. The population of Harrogate had doubled since 1861, and then stood at about 11,000, and on the 1st of February of that year had received its charter of incorporation as a borough. Mr. Carter gave an historical *resumé* of the rise and increased importance of the town, due to its mineral waters, and was of opinion that the anticlinal on which the town rested formed the output for an inexhaustible storehouse of mineral waters existing in the strata extending westwards. A paper was read by Mr. C. Fox-Strangways, of H.M. Geological Survey, on the mineral waters of Harrogate considered under geological aspects.. The beds at Harrogate are a portion of the Yoredale series, lying below the millstone grit, and above the scar limestone, and the anticlinal upon which Harrogate stands is a continuation of that at Skipton and Bolton Abbey. The axis of disturbance is well shown in the town of Low Harrogate by the quarries which have been opened for roadstone on either side of the bogs, where the impure limestone of the Yoredale series may be seen dipping respectively N.W. and S.E., at high angles on either side of this little valley. After describing the constituents of the several wells he summarises by stating the Harro-

gate waters consist of four distinct classes, each of which has a
certain marked peculiarity in its chemical constitution. The strong
sulphur is very rich in chlorides and sulphides, with a large bulk of
free gases. The mild sulphur has nearly the same constituents, but
in a less concentrated condition, and is also slightly richer in carbonates. The saline chalybeate is very rich in chlorides and carbonates,
but contains no sulphides, and the pure chalybeate contains a much
smaller proportion of saline ingredients than either of the preceding,
in fact, it more nearly resembles the ordinary kinds of drinking water,
with a rather larger per centage of carbonate of magnesia and iron.
Mr. Fox-Strangways was of opinion that each of these waters owed
its peculiarity to the separate strata through which it passed, and
that each one was distinctly separate from the others. The strong
sulphur water issues from some of the lower strata which occur at
Harrogate, within a short distance of the roadstone ; the mild sulphur
waters for the most part are found coming from some of the highest
strata that occur in the neighbourhood, the saline chalybeate waters,
of which there are only two springs, both issue from the same beds,
whilst the pure chalybeate waters rise irrespectively from both high
and low measures, although some of the principal springs issue from
the highest strata of the millstone grit. The chemical impregnation
of the water is caused during its passage through these strata, and it
is from these sources that the bases of all the salts are derived. Dr.
George Oliver contributed an elaborate paper on the chemico-geological
aspect of the springs. He described wells occurring not only at
Harrogate and other places in its immediate neighbourhood, but also
westward at Bolton Wood, Skipton and district, Wigglesworth and
Aldfield, and coincided with the opinion previously expressed that
the source of the Harrogate waters extended westwards. He was of
opinion that the salts which were found in the waters were due to
some extent to the ancient sea-water from which the rocks were
deposited. He discusses at some length the chemical constitution of
the waters, and the source from which they individually have derived
their particular ingredients. The existence of a relatively large
quantity of a soluble salt of barium in waters free of sulphates is
remarkable, and the author considers it probable that thus was derived

Witherite, which has been found in association with metallic sulphites in the lower carboniferous rocks. The mineral wealth of Harrogate was the subject of a paper at the same meeting by Mr. R. Hayton Davis, who had recently made a complete examination of all the public sulphur springs. He found that the springs in the cellars beneath the Royal Pump Room yielded 240,000 gallons per annum, and taking the whole of the wells in the district he found that the solid constituents would amount to no less than a hundred tons in a year, if separated. If a well be sunk in a part of Harrogate to a depth of eighteen or twenty feet under favourable conditions, the alluvial deposit will first be penetrated, then perhaps sand, afterwards yellow clay, then a blue or almost black clay is reached, after which black shiver or shale cross the upper part finely laminated, and which, as the excavations proceed, becomes harder and of a more rock-like character, almost like slate. The characteristics of the water met with in these proceedings would be found as variable as the strata. There is first, surface water containing carbonate of iron in solution, to a more or less degree. From the blue clay a weak saline water, charged with iron either as carbonate or in some other combination would be obtained, and as the excavation continued the water would become more saline and less chalybeate. Eventually, strong saline water containing only traces of iron would be found, and lower still a saline sulphur water would be the result. He considered the Spas as a mine only partially explored, and might be regarded as only an indication of the mineral wealth of Harrogate. Mr. R. Lloyd Whiteley, a student in the Yorkshire College, described analyses of the Kissengen Saline Chalybeate water made in 1883, and compared them with others done in 1845, 1854, 1867, and 1879, in which he found considerable differences. These were attributed to the amount of water in the well, and to the relative rate at which the various springs were flowing when the analyses was made.

Mr. W. E. Garforth contributed an important paper on the firedamp detector with recent improvements in the miners' safety lamp. After describing the lamps invented by Stephenson, Davy, Clanny, and others, and stating their points of weakness and the difficulty of overcoming them, he proceeded to describe a detector for fire-damp which he had invented. It consists of an indiarubber ball so small that all the air within it is expelled by the compression of one hand, to which is attached a tube. The tube can be placed in a break in the roof or any other position from which it is supposed that there is an escape of combustible gas, and by squeezing the bag so as to expel the contained air and drawing in that suspected of inflammability, sufficient is obtained to test it. This is done by forcing the gas through the tube near the flame of a lamp, and if gas be present it is at once revealed by the elongation of the flame in the ordinary way, at the same time burning with a blue flame at the top of the test tube. By means of this simple apparatus the lamp may be kept at a distance from the suspected atmosphere, whilst a small quantity is obtained and brought to it. It also prevents the lamp becoming extinguished by foul air, and the necessity to go perhaps a mile to re-light it.

Mr. Davis described a new species of Heterolepidotus, a fossil fish from the lias, of which a figure is given.

The Rev. J. Stanley Tute described Spirangium carbonarium, a fossil plant not hitherto found in this country, from the Carboniferous Sandstone near Harrogate.

Three species of fossils not hitherto described, viz., Chonetes Clevelandicus, Pleuromya navicula, and Isis liasica, all from the lias beds, formed the subject of a communication from Mr. W. Y. Veitch.

Mr. H. B. Stocks described the analyses of the composition of coal-balls and baum-pots found in the Lower Coal Measures at Halifax, and afterwards of a hydraulic limestone obtained from Sewerby, near Flamborough. It occurs in nodules, grey and very hard sometimes, containing fossils which are burnt so as to form cement. The nodules consist essentially of a mixture of carbonate of lime and clay, with some phosphoric acid probably due to fossil molluscan remains which the nodules contained.

At a meeting held at Barnsley in 1866, Mr. Joseph Mitchell presided, and gave a brief abstract of the final report on the Royal Commission on Accidents in Mines. The principal points in the report referred to the lighting of mines and to the use of explosives. With respect to the former, Mr. Mitchell considered that a lamp of the Mueseler type, fitted with a bonnet, was most suitable, and he agreed with the commission that a quick explosive was the most desirable, and with the explosive recommended viz., gelatine dynamite which is fired surrounded by water, the effect being instantaneous and giving off no flame.

At a meeting held at Barnsley in 1866, Dr. H. C. Sorby read a paper on some remarkable properties of the characteristic constituents of steel. The microscopical examination of suitably prepared specimens of iron and steel shows that there are two well marked constituents. One of these is comparatively soft, and is iron which is free from carbon ; the other is intensely hard, and probably contains combined carbon, since it occurs in white cast iron, blistered steel, and other varieties known to contain carbon in that state. Besides these there is another which gives beautiful colours like mother-of-pearl. With very high magnifying powers this pearly constituent is shown to have a structure closely like that of pearl, being made up of alternating thin plates. Dr. Sorby came to the conclusion that these plates are alternating layers of soft iron, free from carbon, and of the intensely hard compound with carbon. The only satisfactory explanation for this remarkable structure appears to be that at a high temperature the stable compound of iron and carbon exists, which is not stable at a lower temperature, but breaks up into extremely thin laminated alternations of the two.

Mr. H. B. Stocks described a concretion found in sandstones, and consisting of a grey or brown friable sand which is called Acrespire. A chemical examination of this concretion showed it to contain about 30 per cent. of carbonate of lime.

Mr. Wm. Horne, of Leyburn, gave an account of the discovery of a tumulus and some ancient burials, about three-quarters of a mile to the west of Leyburn, on a plateau beneath the Shawl. He incidentally discovered a portion of a human skeleton on the edge of a small landslip, and further investigation proved that the place had been used as one of interment by some pre-historic people. With the human remains he found several bones of the reindeer, quantities of charcoal, and several burnt stones and pot boilers. The plateau seemed to have been used as a camping ground for a long period, as well as to inter the dead. About a mile further along the cliff he had also discovered and described a small cave. Whilst removing the earth from the cave fragments of Roman Samian pottery and the bones of rabbit, hare, fox, sheep, red deer, wild ox, a human lower jaw, and other bones were found. Outside the cave there was evidence of burnt stones and charcoal, together with slightly burnt pottery, and the whole presented the appearance of having served for human habitation. All the objects found, as well as those from the ancient burial ground, are deposited in a room set apart for a museum by the Honourable W. Orde Powlett at Bolton Castle.

During the same year a meeting was held at Wakefield, at which Mr. T. W. Embleton presided, and contributed a lengthy account of ancient coal mining. He traced the historical evidence of the use of coal by the ancient British tribes, and of the Romans who succeeded them, in the occupation of this part of the country. Near Stanley, in Derbyshire, some years ago, some colliers were driving in the Kilburn coal, and broke into some old excavations, in which they found picks made of solid oak. The implements were entirely destitute of metal, and cut out of one piece of timber. In other instances stone hammer heads, and wedges of flint, bound to hazel sticks, had been discovered, as well as wheels of solid wood. The evidences that the Romans were acquainted with the use of coal are more numerous, and excavations have repeatedly been found which contained more or less indisputable traces of their having been made by this people. In the 13th and 14th centuries, grants of right to obtain coal are not infrequent in the districts around Newcastle. When coal was first taken by sea to London, an impression arose that the smoke arising therefrom contaminated the atmosphere, and was injurious to the public health; and it was said that the nice dames in London would not come into any house where sea coals were burnt, or willingly eat of the meat that was roasted with it. For a long time there appeared to be great objection to the use of coal, and King Edward the First and his Parliament issued a proclamation forbidding the use of this fuel, which was repeated at several subsequent periods. The prohibition, however, did not last very long, and in the reign of Queen Elizabeth the coal trade flourished greatly, and was regarded as an important source, not only of local but national revenue, by succeeding monarchs, and it speedily became used all over the country.

An interesting and instructive paper, on the microscopical structure of rocks, was contributed by the Rev. J. Magens Mello.

Mr. Richard Reynolds recorded some abnormal barometrical disturbances, which had been noted by himself and Mr. Bransome, at Leeds, in 1883-4. On the 27th of August of the former year, the violent volcanic outburst in the Straits of Sunda, by which, in the course of a few hours the greater part of the Island of Krakatoa was literally blown to pieces occurred. The atmospheric perturbations caused by this eruption were so violent as to be felt over the whole surface of the globe where observations were taken, and the self-registering aneroid at Leeds registered remarkable oscillations, occurring during the next two or three days. In the following year a remarkable earthquake occurred in the Eastern Counties, doing considerable damage, especially in the County of Essex. As earthquake disturbances spread outwards from their origin the vibrations become longer in wave-length and period, and decrease in amplitude, so that the short and rapid movements which cause damage at the focus become slow, wave-like pulsations of the ground at greater distances. Mr. Reynolds' recording barometer traced a diagram which indicated the slow, wave-like motion extending between the hours of 9-30 and 1-30 on the same day the earthquake happened, April 22nd, the distances from the focus being 171 miles, showing that the disturbances originating in Essex were sufficiently intense to cause the ground 170 miles away to be tilted slowly to and fro, for a period of four hours after the event.

The Rev. J. Stanley Tute contributed a paper on the Cayton Gill beds, north-west of Ripley, with especial reference to a highly fossiliferous bed worked for roadstone. Mr. Tute enumerates the fossils obtained from this bed, and the localities from which they have been obtained.

The relative age of the remains of man which have been found in Yorkshire was the subject of an interesting and comprehensive summary of the facts which had hitherto been discovered referring to pre-historic man in this county, by Mr. James W. Davis. The same author contributed a paper descriptive of fossil trees found in the lower coal measures at Clayton, near Halifax, one of which had been photographed, and was issued to the members of the Society for that year; the specimen has since been removed to Owen's College, Manchester, where it has been set up in the museum as it was obtained from the quarry, under the direction of Professor W. C. Williamson.

Mr. S. A. Adamson described sections which had been revealed by the excavation of a gas-holder tank at Old Mill, near Barnsley, consisting of alternations of silt, gravel, and stony clay, resting on the shale of the Middle Coal-Measures. The gravels, besides local rocks, contained some boulders of basalt and a felspathic stone, and in the uppermost parts had been discovered vegetable accumulations which included pieces of oak, hazel nuts and leaves, as well as a freshwater bivalve shell, and the remains of a beetle. In the same gravel a remarkable implement composed of mica-schist, smooth, and having at the sides peculiar groovings which had evidently been produced by man, was found. It has every appearance of having been used to sharpen some implement.

Mr. John Holmes, of Roundhay, read a learned and elaborate paper on the pre-historic remains of Rumbalds Moor. The earthworks on Baildon Common, the cairns known as the big and little Skirtfull of Stones, and the Lanshaw Delves were described, and records of their investigations were given. The greater part of the paper, however, was taken up with a description of the cup and ring marks which cover several large stones and rock surfaces on the Ilkley and Addingham moors, and the origin and use of these peculiar rock markings were discussed with some detail, and compared with similar carvings in several other parts of the world.

In the proceedings of the following year notes on the discovery of bronze implements in the West Riding were contributed by the same author, and Mr. Thomas Boynton also gave a list of bronze implements discovered in the East Riding, nearly all of which are in his private collection.

The Rev. J. Stanley Tute recorded the occurrence of a Lingula in the black shale occurring below the Follyfort grit which had been found during the excavation in making a reservoir on Lumley Moor for the supply of Ripon with water. The occurrence of a large boulder, 2 feet 6 inches in diameter, of coarse grit stone of nearly spherical form, was recorded from the black bed coal at Wortley, near Leeds, by Mr. Charles Brownridge. Three other smaller boulders of quartzite were also found in the same stratum near the same locality. The author advanced the theory that these boulders had been carried to their position by masses of floating vegetation in a manner similar to that recorded by travellers on such rivers as the Amazon, where in the swamps and shallows such masses are seen floating, carrying foreign matters along with them.

Mr. Jas. E. Bedford described the discovery of a number of flint implements which he had found in the Isle of Man.

Mr. Thomas Tate gave the first of a proposed series of papers on Yorkshire Petrology, in which he described the Lamprophyres occurring in the erupted rocks in the neighbourhood of Ingleton. Three dykes of intrusive rock, more or less closely associated, occur in the Borrowdale and Conistone limestone groups, which form the bed of the Chapel-le-dale Beck. These are described both in bulk, and after microscopical examination of thin slices. The paper is illustrated with coloured figures of the sections, as well as by enlarged details of the constituent parts of the rocks.

The formation of the line of railway from Skipton to Ilkley afforded Mr. S. A. Adamson an opportunity to study the contorted limestone and shales of the district and the superincumbent glacial beds, a description of which he contributed to the Proceedings of the Society.

Mr. James W. Davis recorded the identification of a fossil species of Chlamydoselachus, and contributed a paper on the ancient flint-users of Yorkshire.

CHAPTER XVIII.

LIST OF OFFICERS AND MEMBERS, WITH THE DATE OF THEIR ELECTION.
COMPILED BY J. PERCY A. DAVIS.

In accordance with suggestions that it is desirable, and would be interesting, to have a list of all the officers and members printed, the following has been prepared. The earliest records of the Society are imperfectly preserved, and it is probable that many of the names which have the earliest *recorded* dates attached, are those of members who were elected in 1837 or 1838, but as no list was preserved, it is thought best to give the dates which are known.

PRESIDENTS :

Elected.
1837. Earl Fitzwilliam.
1858. Marquis of Ripon.

VICE-PRESIDENTS :

1840. Duke of Norfolk.
1840. Earl of Effingham.
1840. Earl of Scarborough.
1840. Earl of Dartmouth.
1841. Lord Wharncliffe.
1840. Lord Stourton.
1840. Viscount Milton.
1840. Viscount Howard.
1840. Hon. W. S. Lascelles.
1840. Hon. J. Stuart Wortley.
1840. Rev. Theophilus Barnes.
1840. T. W. Beaumont.
1840. J. Spencer Stanhope.
1840. R. O. Gascoigne.

Elected.
1840. G. Lane Fox.
1840. Godfrey Wentworth.
1840. W. Bennett Martin.
1840. Charles John Brandling.
1840. J. Garth Marshall.
1840. M. Ellison.
1840. Rev. Samuel Sharp.
1841. Sir F. Lindley Wood, Bart.
1841. Sir W. B. Cooke, Bart.
1841. Rev. W. Scoresby, D.D., F.R.S.
1841. E. B. Beaumont.
1841. T. D. Bland, Jun.
1841. J. W. Childers.
1842. Hon. G. W. Fitzwilliam.
1842. P. D. Cooke.
1842. William West, F.R.S.
1846. Rt. Hon. Charles Wood (afterwards Sir C. Wood and Viscount Halifax.
1846. R. Monckton Milnes (Lord Houghton).
1854. E. Beckett Denison.
1854. Viscount Galway.
1854. William Beckett.
1854. Rev. William Thorp.
1854. Thomas Wilson.
1854. John Waterhouse, F.R.S.
1854. Edward Akroyd, F.S.A.
1859. Duke of Leeds.
1859. Earl Fitzwilliam.
1859. Lord Londesborough.
1870. Edmund Denison.
1877. W. Beckett Denison.
1877. W. T. W. S. Stanhope.
1879. Lord Frederick C. Cavendish.
1879. Sir Charles W. Strickland, Bart.
1879. Thomas Shaw.
1879. Walter Morrison.

VICE-PRESIDENTS.

Elected.
1880. T. Clifford Allbutt, M.D., F.R.S.
1882. H. C. Sorby, LL.D., F.R.S.
1882. Thos. W. Tew.
1885. Lord Houghton.
1885. Viscount Halifax.
1887. James Booth.
1887. F. H. Bowman, D.Sc.
1887. Richard Carter, C.E.
1887. Professor A. H. Green, F.R.S.

TRUSTEES:
1840. Earl Fitzwilliam.
1840. Earl of Effingham.
1840. Lord Wharncliffe.
1840. Viscount Milton.
1840. Viscount Howard.
1840. Hon. W. S. Lascelles.
1840. Hon. J. S. Wortley.
1840. T. W. Beaumont.
1840. J. S. Stanhope.
1840. W. B. Martin.
1840. Charles J. Brandling.
1840. Godfrey Wentworth.

SECRETARY AND TREASURER:
1837. Thomas Wilson.
1842. Joseph Travis Clay.
1844. Rev. William Thorp.
1854. William Sykes Ward.

HONORARY SECRETARY:
1871. Louis C. Miall.
1876. James W. Davis.

HONORARY TREASURER:
1876. John Brigg.
1883. William Cash.

ASSISTANT SECRETARY:
1846. Henry Denny, A.L.S.
1875. J. Crowther, (resigned 1881).

COUNCIL:

Elected.
1840. J. Charlesworth, Jun.
1840. Joseph Charlesworth, Jun.
1840. Henry Briggs.
1840. T. W. Embleton.
1840. Charles Morton.
1840. Henry Hartop.
1840. Rev. William Thorp.
1840. J. Brackenridge.
1840. J. Milnes Stansfeld.
1840. Henry Holt.
1840. Joshua Smithson.
1840. W. T. Hall.
1841. W. Billington.
1841. J. Brackenridge.
1841. J. C. D. Charlesworth.
1841. George Wilson.
1842. Thomas Wilson.
1842. W. R. H. Johnstone.
1842. Henry Clarkson.
1842. W. H. Dikes.
1842. Charles Clapham.
1843. George Welch.
1843. J. Westmoreland.
1843. Charles Locke.
1846. J. Travis Clay.
1846. William Alexander, M.D.
1846. J. W. Leather.
1846. Ambrose Butler.
1846. Dr. Chadwick.
1846. Edward Waud.
1846. John D. Heaton, M.D.
1848. W. Sykes Ward.
1854. H. Clifton Sorby, F.R.S.
1854. Michael Stocks.
1854. John Jebson.

Elected.

1854. Thomas Pitt.
1854. Benjamin Biram.
1854. Dr. William Paley.
1854. Richard Carter, C.E.
1859. Bentley Shaw.
1859. T. Pridgin Teale.
1859. John Hope Shaw.
1859. Dr. Scholefield.
1859. E. W. Shaw.
1859. H. Brown.
1860. William Chadwick.
1860. Samuel Baines.
1862. Rev. Dr. Burnet.
1870. Thomas W. Tew.
1870. Rev. W. C. Lukis.
1870. Rev. S. F. Surtees.
1870. Rev. H. C. Middleton.
1870. Richard Reynolds.
1870. Archibald Briggs.
1875. George Bailey.
1875. E. Filliter.
1875. W. Sykes Ward.
1875. Professor Louis C. Miall.
1875. Professor A. H. Green, F.R.S.
1875. John Brigg.
1875. James W. Davis.
1877. H. P. Holt.
1878. Fairless Barber.
1880. Walter Rowley.
1880. W. Percy Sladen.
1881. J. Ray Eddy.
1882. W. Cheetham.
1883. George H. Parke.
1884. J. E. Bedford.
1885. C. Fox Strangways.
1886. Thomas H. Gray.

LIST OF OFFICERS.

CURATORS:

Elected.
- 1840. Thomas W. Embleton.
- 1840. Henry Holt.
- 1844. J. Garth Marshall.

(Messrs. Embleton and Marshall Remained in office until 1871).

RESIDENT CURATOR:
- 1842. Martin Simpson.

LOCAL TREASURERS AND SECRETARIES:

Elected	Name	Location
1846.	W. Alexander, M.D.	Halifax.
1846.	Thomas Pitt	Huddersfield.
1846.	Phineas Beaumont	Sheffield.
1846.	George C. Walker	Doncaster.
1854.	Henry Briggs	Wakefield.
1854.	H. C. Sorby	Sheffield.
1854.	R. D. Baxter	Doncaster.
1859.	Dr. Scholefield	Doncaster.
1859.	Bentley Shaw	Huddersfield.
1859.	Richard Carter	Barnsley.
1862.	Rev. Dr. Burnet	Bradford.
1863.	Dr. Paley	Ripon.
1870.	Thomas W. Tew	Pontefract.
1870.	Louis C. Miall	Bradford.
1870.	Rev. S. F. Surtees	Doncaster.
1870.	John Guest	Rotherham.
1876.	Thomas Lister	Barnsley.
1876.	Thomas Tate	Bradford.
1876.	William Cash	Halifax.
1876.	Peace Sykes	Huddersfield.
1878.	John Marshall	Sowerby Bridge.
1878.	Ed. Gregson	Thirsk.
1878.	George W. Lamplugh	Bridlington.
1878.	George Bailey	Wakefield.
1878.	Thomas W. Helliwell	Brighouse.
1879.	Rev. E. Maule Cole	Driffield.
1879.	H. F. Parsons, M.D.	Goole.
1879.	J. E. Bedford	Leeds.

Elected.

1879.	R. Gascoigne	- Mexborough.
1879.	Rev. J. Stanley Tute	- Ripon.
1879.	J. T. Atkinson	- Selby.
1880.	W. Y. Veitch	- Middlesborough.
1880.	Rev. Thomas Adams	- York.
1881.	G. J. Wilson, M.A.	- Hull.
1881.	William Horne	- Wensleydale
1883.	P. F. Lee	- Dewsbury.
1883.	George Patchett, Junr.	- Halifax.
1884.	George Paul	- Leeds.
1885.	Robert Peach	- Harrogate.
1886.	Thomas Ormerod	- Brighouse.
1886.	S. A. Adamson	- Leeds.
1886.	H. M. Platnauer	- York.

HONORARY MEMBERS.

1842. Professor John Phillips, York.
1842. Rev. W. Buckland, Oxford.
1842. Rev. Professor Sedgwick, Norwich.
1842. Professor Johnstone, Durham.
1842. Charles Babbage, London.
1842. Sir Roderick I. Murchison, London.
1842. J. B. Greenhough, London.
1842. Rev. Dr. Lardner, LL.D.
1842. John Lindley, LL.D.
1842. Professor Henslow, Cambridge.
1842. Thomas Sopwith, Newcastle-on-Tyne.
1842. Nicholas Wood, "
1842. John Buddle, "
1842. William Hutton, "
1842. H. M. Witham, Barnard Castle.
1842. John Taylor.
1842. Rev. Frederick Watkins, Lewes.
1842. Charles Vignoles, C.E.
1842. E. W. Binney, Manchester.
1879. Edward Akroyd, F.S.A., Halifax.
1887. Professor John W. Judd, F.R.S., London.

LIST OF OFFICERS. 443

Elected.
1887. Dr. Henry Woodward, F.R.S., London.
1887. Professor N. Bodington, Leeds.
1887. Professor T. Mc Kenny Hughes, F.R.S., Cambridge.
1887. Professor W. C. Williamson, F.R.S., Manchester.

MEMBERS.

The first list of members was prepared in 1839; many of the members whose names follow this date joined the Society at its initiation in 1837.

Elected.
1839. Armstrong, Rev. C. E., Hemsworth, Pontefract.
1839. Arthington, Robert, Leeds.
1839. Aldred, John, Rotherham.
1840. Alexander, Dr. Wm., Lord Street, Halifax.
1840. Atkinson, John, Chesterfield.
1840. Aldam, Wm., Jun., M.P., Frickley Hall, Doncaster.
1840. Alexander, James, Doncaster.
1841. Alexander, E. N., F.S.A., Halifax.
1841. Akroyd, Edward, F.S.A., Bankfield, Halifax.
1841. Akroyd, Henry, Woodside, Halifax.
1841. Abbot, Joseph, Normanton, Wakefield.
1842. Alderson, Rev. C., M.A., Kirkheaton, Huddersfield.
1843. Aldam, William, Warmsworth.
1854. Appleyard, Joshua, Clare Hall, Halifax.
1864. Atkinson, Rev. J. C., Danby, York.
1875. Atkinson, J. T., Selby.
1878. Adamson, S. A., 52, Well Close Terrace, Leeds.
1879. Adams, Thomas, Clifton Grove House, York.
1880. Allison, Thomas, Belmont, Guisborough.
1881. Allbutt, T. Clifford, M.D., F.R.S., Leeds.
1881. Anderton, C. P., Cleckheaton.
1882. Arnold, C. Comber, Clare Hall, Halifax.
1883. Abbott, R. T. G., Quarry Cottage, Norton, Malton.

1839. Beckett, J., Stainforth.
1839. Beaumont, T. W., Bretton Park, Wakefield.

LIST OF MEMBERS.

Elected.
1839. Bischoff, G. W.
1839. Beaumont, E. B., Finningley Park, Bawtry.
1839. Bateson, Mr.
1839. Brandling, C. J., Middleton Lodge, Leeds.
1839. Brandling, Mrs. C., Middleton Lodge, Leeds.
1839. Brandling, Rev. R.,
1839. Blayds, John, Oulton Hall, Leeds.
1839. Banks, George, St. Catherine's, Doncaster.
1839. Bland, T. D., Jun., Kippax Park, Pontefract.
1839. Biram, B., Wentworth, Rotherham.
1839. Briggs, Henry, Overton House, Wakefield.
1839. Brakenridge, John, Bretton Lodge, Wakefield.
1839. Birks, John, Hemingfield, Barnsley.
1839. Booth, Thomas, Park Iron Works, Sheffield.
1839. Blackburn, Rev. J., Attercliffe Rectory, Sheffield.
1839. Baxter, Robert, Doncaster.
1839. Brooke, T. S., Dewsbury.
1839. Barnes, Rev. T., Castleford Rectory, Pontefract.
1839. Billinton, W., C.E., Westgate, Wakefield.
1839. Bull, W., Westgate, Wakefield.
1839. Boultbee, Henry, Norfolk Street, Sheffield.
1839. Butler, T., Kirkstall Forge, Leeds.
1839. Butler, A., Kirkstall Forge, Leeds.
1839. Beecroft, George, Kirkstall Forge, Leeds.
1839. Bean, Joseph, Gas Works, Bradford.
1839. Bourne, T. R., Chesterfield.
1840. Bradshaw, B., Upper Thong, Huddersfield.
1840. Baxter, Ed., Doncaster.
1840. Brooke, Thomas, Doncaster.
1840. Baker, C., Yorkshire Institute for Deaf and Dumb, Doncaster.
1840. Bower, J. S., M.D., Broxholm.
1841. Briggs, W., Halifax.
1842. Brooke, John, Armitage Bridge, Huddersfield.
1842. Battye, Thomas, Huddersfield.
1842. Barker, Samuel, Mexborough, Doncaster.
1842. Beaumont, Phineas, Sheffield Canal Office, Sheffield.

LIST OF MEMBERS.

Elected.
1842. Butler, J. O., Kirkstall Forge, Leeds.
1848. Brown, John, Wingerworth Hall, Derbyshire.
1849. Brodrick, Geo., Hamphall Stubbs.
1852. Baxter, R. D., Doncaster.
1853. Beckett, Wm., M.P., Kirkstall Grange.
1856. Beecroft, G. S., Abbey House, Kirkstall.
1856. Brown, John, Barnsley.
1857. Baines, Sir Edward, Leeds.
1857. Brook, Edward. jun., Fieldhouse Clay Works, Huddersfield.
1858. Brereton, Dr. J. Le-Gay, Horton Lane, Bradford.
1858. Brown, H., Bradford.
1858. Baines, Samuel, Holroyd House, Lightcliffe.
1859. Brown, James, Rossington.
1859. Bentley, R. J., Finningley Park.
1860. Booth, Edwin, Barnsley.
1862. Burnett, Rev. Dr., Vicar of Bradford.
1862. Brinstead, C. H., C.E., Wakefield.
1865. Bartholomew, Charles, Broxholme.
1866. Barber, Fairless, F.S.A., Brighouse.
1867. Burgess, Mr., Brighouse.
1867. Briggs, A., Wakefield.
1869. Banks, Mr., Wakefield.
1869. Barton, J. H., Stapleton Park, Pontefract.
1870. Bradley, Geo., Aketon Hall, Pontefract.
1875. Bedford, James, Woodhouse Ridge, Leeds.
1875. Booth, James, F.G.S., Spring Hall, Halifax.
1875. Brigg, John, J.P., Broomfield, Keighley.
1875. Bird, C., F.G.S., Grammar School, Bradford.
1875. Balme, E. B. W., J.P., Cote Hall, Mirfield.
1875. Baily, Walter, 176, Haverstock Hill, London.
1875. Bustard, John, Barnsley.
1876. Binns, L., Grove House, Oakenshaw, Bradford.
1876. Boothroyd, W., Brighouse.
1876. Bowman, F. H., D.Sc.F.R.S., Ed., &c., Halifax.
1878. Bailey, George, Wakefield.
1878. Barber, W. C., F.R.A.S., &c., The Orphanage, Halifax.

Elected.
1878. Battinson, George, Savile Mount, Halifax.
1878. Beaumont, Henry, Elland.
1878. Bedwell, F. A., Fort Hall, Bridlington Quay.
1878. Berry, William, King Cross Street, Halifax.
1878. Binnie, A. R., C.E., &c., Town Hall, Bradford.
1878. Blakey, James K., 23, Fountain Street, Leeds.
1878. Brookes, Rev. W. J., Elmfield Terrace, Halifax.
1879. Barbour, J. M., Broad Street, Halifax.
1879. Bartholomew, C. W., Blakesley Hall, near Towcaster.
1879. Blake, Rev. Prof. J. F., 11, Gauden Road, Clapham, London.
1879. Broadhead, John, St. John's Colliery, Normanton.
1879. Bury, Captain, Barnsley.
1880. Bayley, Rev. T., Weaverthorpe.
1880. Belk, J. T., Middlesborough.
1880. Bingley, Godfrey, Ash Lea, Cardigan Road, Headingley.
1881. Briggs, Arthur, J.P., Cragg Royd, Rawdon, Leeds.
1882. Brierley, H. G., Clare Street, Huddersfield.
1882. Buckley, George, Jun., Waterhouse Street, Halifax.
1883. Butler, J. Dyson, Estate Buildings, Huddersfield.
1885. Bould, Charles H., Huddersfield.
1887. Binns, J. A., 11, Oak Lane, Manningham.
1887. Brownridge, C., C.E., Horsforth, Leeds.

1839. Croft, W.,
1839. Carr, Dr., Knostrop.
1839. Cooper, William, Mount Vernon, Barnsley.
1839. Cooper, Samuel, Park House, Barnsley.
1839. Charlesworth, J. D., Chapelthorp Hall, Wakefield.
1839. Charlesworth, J. C. D., Chapelthorp Hall, Wakefield.
1839. Charlesworth, Joseph, Lofthouse, Wakefield.
1839. Charlesworth, Joseph, jun,, Lofthouse, Wakefield.
1839. Chambers, G. W., Clough House, Rotherham.
1839. Clayton, J. G., Byerley, Bradford.
1839. Clarke, R. C., Noblethorp, Barnsley.
1839. Casson, Thomas, Hatfield Hall, Wakefield.
1839. Clay, J. T., Rastrick, Huddersfield.
1839. Clapham, C., Northgate, Wakefield.

LIST OF MEMBERS.

Elected.
1839. Carr, William, Wath, Rotherham.
1839. Crowther, C., M.D., Wakefield.
1839. Chantrell, R. D., Leeds.
1839. Chambers, T., Thorncliffe Ironworks, Sheffield.
1839. Chambers, M., Thorncliffe Ironworks, Sheffield.
1839. Chambers, J., Thorncliffe Ironworks, Sheffield.
1839. Chambers, G., High Green House, Sheffield.
1839. Cash, Newman, Scarcroft Lodge, Leeds.
1839. Chadwick, C., M.D., Park Row, Leeds.
1839. Cross, J., Commercial Street, Leeds.
1839. Copperthwaite, W. C., Leeds.
1839. Cooper, W., Railway Terrace, Sheffield.
1840. Chandler, Rev. G., Treeton Rectory, Rotherham.
1840. Cooke, Sir W. B., Bart., Wheatley, Doncaster.
1840. Cooke, P. D., Owston, Doncaster.
1840. Cooke, Geo., Carr House, Doncaster.
1840. Childers, J. W., M.P., Cantley, Doncaster.
1841 Clarkson, Henry, Wakefield.
1841. Charnock, Charles, Holmfield House, Pontefract.
1841. Clay, John, Huddersfield.
1845. Cassels, Rev. A., Morley.
1848. Carter, Richard, (Halifax), Spring Bank, Harrogate.
1849. Childe, Rowland, Wakefield.
1850. Child, J. W., Halifax.
1853. Champneys, Rev. Phipps, Skellon, Doncaster.
1856. Chadwick, W., Arksey, Doncaster.
1857. Carter, Nicholas, Huddersfield.
1857. Crosland, T. P., J.P., Gledholt, Huddersfield.
1857. Cocking, William, Architect, New Street, Huddersfield.
1864. Crowther, Benjamin, Wakefield.
1870. Childers, Mrs. Walbanke, Cantley Hall, Doncaster.
1875. Cash, William, 38, Elmfield Terrace, Halifax.
1875. Charlesworth, J. B., Hatfield Hall, Wakefield.
1875. Carr, J. O., Barnsley.
1876. Carrington, Thomas, High Hazels, Sheffield.
1876. Clark, J. E., Friends School, York.

LIST OF MEMBERS.

Elected.
1878. Cameron, A. G., Stokesley, Northallerton.
1878. Carr, William, Heathfield, Halifax.
1878. Clegg, John, Church Street, Halifax.
1878. Cole, Rev. E. Maule, Wetwang Vicarage, York.
1878. Colefax, J., Mannville Terrace, Bradford.
1878. Crebbin, A., Mannville, Horton Road, Bradford.
1878. Cudworth, W. J., Upperthorpe, Darlington.
1879. Cavendish, Lord F. C., Carlton House Terrace, London.
1879. Clay, J. T., Rastrick, Brighouse.
1879. Crossley, Newman, Barnsley.
1879. Cheetham, W., Horsforth, near Leeds.
1880. Child, H., The Beeches, Whitkirk.
1880. Cole, George B., Wakefield Road, Wakefield.
1880. Cross, Benjamin, Dewsbury.
1881. Crowther, F., Northowram.
1883. Carter, James, Burton House, Bedale.
1884. Crossley, Newman, Barnsley.

1839. Dartmouth, Earl of, Sandwell Park, Birmingham.
1841. Denison, E. B., M.P., Doncaster.
1839. Dennings, Joshua.
1839. Dibb, W., Churwell, Leeds.
1839. Dunn, R., Heath, Wakefield.
1839. Davis, Gabriel, Boar Lane, Leeds.
1839. Dixon, B., Kirkgate, Wakefield.
1839. Dunn, T., Richmond Hill, Sheffield.
1841. Dawson, C., jun., Halifax.
1841. Dawson, J., Halifax.
1841. Dikes, Wm. Hey, F.G.S., Wakefield.
1841. Dewhirst, William, Huddersfield.
1848. Donisthorp, G. E., Leeds.
1854. Dartmouth, Earl of, Patshull House, Wolverhampton.
1857. Dowse, William, Doncaster.
1870. Denys, Sir G. W., Bart., Draycott Hall, Richmond.
1870. Durham, Maken, Thorne, Doncaster.
1875. Davis, James William, F.G.S., F.S.A., &c., Chevinedge, Halifax.

LIST OF MEMBERS.

Elected.
1875. Day, Rev. H. J., Barnsley.
1875. Denison, W. B., Meanwood Park.
1878. Davey, Henry, Hyde Lodge, Leeds.
1878. Denham, Charles, Halifax.
1878. Dunning, Jno., Middlesborough.
1879. Dakyns, J. R., of H.M. Geological Survey, Driffield.
1879. Dent, G., Selby.
1879. Dewhurst, J. B., Skipton.
1879. Drury, Ed., Halifax.
1880. Dixon, Wayman, Grove Hill, Middlesborough.
1880. Dolan, T. M., Halifax.
1880. Dunhill, C. H., Gray's Court, York.
1881. Dyson, W. Colbeck, Wilton Park, Batley.
1883. Dalton, Thomas, Albion Street, Leeds.
1883. Davidson, J., F.C.S., Holywell Green, near Halifax.
1883. Dodsworth, Sir Charles, Bart., Thornton Watlass, Bedale.
1884. Davis, R. H., Harrogate.
1884. Dobson, M. G., Stannary Hall, Halifax.
1887. Duncan, Surr W., Horsforth Hall, Leeds.

1839. Effingham, Earl of, The Grange, Rotherham.
1839. Embleton, T. William, Methley, Leeds.
1839. Ellison, Michael, The Farm, Sheffield.
1839. Eddison, Edwin, Headingley, Leeds.
1840. Eddison, William, Huddersfield.
1840. Elmsall, J. G., Woodlands, Doncaster.
1862. Ellison, George, Birkenhead.
1862. Edwards, Sir Henry, M.P., Pye Nest, Halifax.
1879. Eddy, J. R., Carlton Grange, Skipton.
1879. Emmott, W., The Square, Halifax.

1839. Furbank, Rev. Thomas, Bramley.
1839. Fitzwilliam, Earl, Wentworth House, Rotherham.
1839. Fitzwilliam, Hon. G. W., M.P., Wentworth House, Rotherham.
1839. Fox, George Lane, Bramham Park, Wetherby.
1839. Fullerton, John, Thriberg Park, Rotherham.
1839. Foljambe, Thomas, Holmfield, Wakefield.

Elected.
1839. Fernandes, J. L., Belle Vue, Wakefield.
1839. Fairbank, W. F., East Parade, Sheffield.
1839. Faulds, Andrew, Darley Hall, Barnsley.
1839. French, J. K., Blenheim Terrace, Leeds.
1839. Fowler, Charles, Park Row, Leeds.
1840. Fennel, Rev. S., D.D., Wakefield.
1840. Faber, C. Wilson, North Deighton, Wetherby.
1841. Farrar, Timothy, Jun., Wragby, Wakefield.
1841. Freeman, John, Huddersfield.
1841. Firth, Thomas, Jun., Huddersfield.
1842. Firth, Thomas, Toothill, Huddersfield.
1853. Fairbairn, Sir Peter, Bart., Woodsley House, Leeds.
1857. Firth, Joseph, J.P., Carr Hill, Huddersfield.
1857. Filliter, Edward, C.E., Borough Surveyor, Leeds.
1860. Farrar, James, M.P., Ingleborough House, near Settle.
1869. Flooks, John, Elliot's Terrace, West Tarring, Worthing.
1875. Fraser, J., Grove House, Headingley.
1875. Fraser, H. J., Grove House, Headingley.
1875. Ford, J. R., Adel Grange, near Leeds.
1875. Farrer, James, Old Foundry, Barnsley.
1878. Fox, M., Jun., Mirfield.
1879. Fish, Rev. I., Huttons Ambo Vicarage, York.
1883. Fleming, Francis, Halifax.
1885. Field, Joseph, Huddersfield.
1887. Fennel, Charles W., Westgate, Wakefield.

1839. Gaskell, D., Lupset Hall, Wakefield.
1839. Gascoigne, R. O., Parlington, Aberford.
1839. Greaves, Geo., Elmsall Lodge, Pontefract.
1839. Greaves, H. M., Hesley, Bawtry.
1839. Graham, William, Milton Ironworks, Barnsley.
1839. Gibson, Rev. J., Wilkinson Street, Sheffield.
1839. Gully, John, Ackworth Park, Pontefract.
1839. Greaves, A., Purston, Pontefract.
1839. Greaves, Jno., Ossett, Wakefield.
1839. Gowthwaite, Richard, Lumby, Ferrybridge.

Elected.
1839. Gott, William, Hanover Square, Leeds.
1840. Green, Sir Ed., Bart., Phœnix Works, Wakefield.
1842. Garnett, James, Bradford.
1845. Galway, Lord, Serlby, near Bawtry.
1864. Gott, William Ewart, Wyther Grange, Leeds.
1868. Guest, Jno., Rotherham.
1869. Greaves, J. D., Wakefield.
1875. Greaves, J. O., Wakefield.
1875. Green, Professor A. H., F.R.S., &c., 11, Hyde Park Terrace, Leeds.
1875. Gascoigne, Col. T., Parlington Park.
1875. Goody, James, Darfield.
1876. Garnett, William, Fairlawn, Ripon.
1878. Gregson, William, Baldersby Park, Thirsk.
1879. Gascoigne, R., Denaby Collieries, Mexbro'.
1880. Gough, Thomas, B.Sc., Elmfield College, York.
1881. Gleadhow, F., 12, Ash Grove, Victoria Road, Leeds.
1881. Gray, Thomas H., Brookleigh, Calverley, Leeds.
1882. Gregson, W., Baldersby, Thirsk.
1883. Gaukroger, W., Fernside, Halifax.
1885. Gough, W. C., Wykeham, York.

1839. Howard, Viscount, M.P., Barbot Hall, Rotherham.
1839. Hare, S.
1839. Hawke, Lord, Womersley Park, Pontefract.
1839. Hebden, T.
1841. Heywood, James, F.G.S., Acrefield, Manchester.
1839. Hollow, R. W.
1839. Hartop, Henry, Barnborough Hall, Rotherham.
1839. Hook, Rev. Dr., The Vicarage, Leeds.
1839. Hartop, John, Barnborough Hall, Rotherham.
1839. Hamilton, Rev. R. W.
1839. Hopwood, William, Barnsley.
1839. Holt, Henry, Bond Street, Wakefield.
1839. Hall, W. F., C.E., Sandal Cliff, Wakefield.
1839. Hurst, William, Doncaster.

Elected.
1839. Harpin, John, Birk House, Holmfirth.
1839. Hird, L. W., Low Moor, Bradford.
1839. Hatfield, John, Wakefield.
1839. Hague, Thomas, Stanley Hall, Wakefield.
1839. Hounsfield, George, Sheffield.
1839. Holland, G. C., M.D., Sheffield.
1839. Hindle, William, J., Barnsley.
1839. Hey, William, Jun., Albion Place, Leeds.
1839. Hunter, Adam, M.D., Leeds.
1839. Hubbard, J. R., Park Place, Leeds.
1840. Harris, Henry, Bradford.
1840. Harris, Alfred, Bradford.
1840. Hagen, Henry.
1839. Horsfall, John G., Bolton Royd, Bradford.
1839. Hanson, William, Derby.
1841. Haigh, William, Shay, Halifax.
1841. Hammerton, James, Hellifield Peel, Skipton.
1841. Hardy, Thomas, Kirkgate, Huddersfield.
1841. Hanson, George, Market Place, Huddersfield.
1842. Hailstone, Samuel, F.G.S., Bradford.
1842. Hailstone, Edward, F.S.A., Bradford.
1842. Hall, M., Wortley, near Leeds.
1843. Hatfield, William, Newton Kyme, Tadcaster.
1845. Hind, Rev. T., Featherstone, Pontefract.
1845. Hirst, S., Kellington, Pontefract.
1845. Hepworth, William, Pontefract.
1846. Howard, Hon. and Rev. W., Whiston.
1848. Horton, R. G., Leeds.
1849. Hewitson, W. W., Leeds.
1849. Hastings, William, Huddersfield.
1850. Hodgson, Thomas, Huddersfield.
1855. Haigh, Jno., Honley, near Huddersfield.
1857. Hirst, Joseph, Wilshaw, Meltham, Huddersfield.
1864. Husband, Charles, Ripon.
1865. Harewood, Right Hon. the Earl of.
1867. Hutchinson, Jno., Barnsley.

LIST OF MEMBERS.

Elected.
1869. Holdsworth, Dr., Wakefield.
1870. Hepworth, J. M., Ackworth Hall, Pontefract.
1870. Heslop, M., Doncaster.
1845. Houghton, Lord (formerly R. M. Milnes), Fryston Hall.
1875. Holmes, Jno., Methley.
1875. Holt, H. P., Cavendish Road.
1875. Harrison, H. D., Moortown.
1875. Holgate, Benjamin, 3, Atkinson Street, Hunslet.
1875. Herring, Ed., Birkwood House, Normanton.
1875. Hopkinson, Jno., Old Hall, Normanton.
1875. Hardcastle, Jno., jun., South Milford.
1843. Halifax, Viscount (formerly Charles Wood), Hickleton Hall, Doncaster.
1876. Helliwell, T. W., Brighouse.
1876. Hirst, Jno., Tadcaster, Dobcross, Saddleworth.
1876. Hobkirk, C. P., Huddersfield.
1878. Hallilay, J., Burley Road, Leeds.
1878. Heaton, J. A., Brighouse.
1878. Howgate, William, Leeds.
1880. Hawking, S., Feversham Street, Bradford.
1880. Hedley, J., M.D., Middlesborough.
1880. Hewson, Charles, Albion Street, Leeds.
1881. Horne, William, Leyburn.
1882. Haigh, John, Eightlands, Dewsbury.
1882. Hepworth, S. C., West Park Street, Dewsbury.
1883. Hanstock, John, Denby Grange, near Wakefield.
1883. Heslington, T. C., North Road, Ripon.
1883. Hewitson, H. B., 11, Hanover Place, Leeds.
1883. Huddleston, W. H., F.R.S., Culverden Lodge, Oaklands Park, Weybridge.
1884. Holroyd, A., Savile Park, Halifax.
1884. Hunt, H. J., Surgeon, Harrogate.
1885. Harding, E., Bridlington Quay.
1885. Harrison, G., East View, Huddersfield.
1887. Harry, E. W., C.E., Borough Engineer, Harrogate.

1839. Ingham, Joshua, Blake Hall, Dewsbury.

Elected.
1839. Ikin, Jno. A., Seacroft, Leeds.
1839. Ikin, Joshua Ingham, Leeds.
1841. Inglis, James, M.D., Halifax.
1860. Ingram, Hugo Charles Meynell, Temple Newsam.

1838. Johnston, Jas. F. W., M.A., F.R.S.L., and E.
1839. Johnstone, W. R. H., St. John's, Wakefield.
1839. Jackson, William, Bank Street, Sheffield.
1839. Jeffcock, William, High Hazles, Sheffield.
1839. Jeffcock, Jno., Cowley, Sheffield.
1839. Jeffcock, Thomas D., Brush House, Sheffield.
1839. Jackson, Henry, St. James' Row, Sheffield.
1840. Jackson, Charles, Doncaster.
1841. Jubb, Abraham, Halifax.
1841. Jones, F. R., Birk House, Huddersfield.
1851. Jeffcock, W. H., Sheffield.
1851. Jebson, John, Huddersfield.
1864. Jackson, Samuel, Leeds.
1885. Jury, Samuel, Huddersfield.

1839. Kell Thomas, Bramham.
1848. Kitson, James, Leeds.
1857. Kaye, Anthony Knowles, Mold Green, Huddersfield.
1858. Knowles, George, Leeds Road, Bradford.
1875. Kell, Arthur A., Barnsley.
1875. Kell, George, Barnsley.
1880. Kirby, Joel, Mexbro'.
1880. Kirk, Robert Samuel, Buckingham Villa, Leeds.
1887. Kirby, Rev. W. W., M.A., Rectory, Barnsley.

1839. Lascelles, Hon. William G., Harewood, Leeds.
1839. Lapage, John.
1839. Lucas, William, The Mills, Sheffield.
1839. Land, W.
1839. Leah, Henry, Leeds.
1839. Lee, T., New Lodge, Wakefield.
1839. Leather, James T., C.E., Sheffield Water Works,

Elected.
1839. Locke, Charles, Shapethorp, Wakefield.
1839. Leather, J. W., Springfield House, Wellington Road, Leeds.
1839. Longeridge, James.
1841. Lumb, Richard K., Savile Green, Halifax.
1841. Leatham, William, Heath, Huddersfield.
1842. Lythall, W., Bradford.
1855. Leather, J. T., Leventhorpe Hall, Leeds.
1855. Londesborough, Right Hon. Lord, Grimston Park.
1856. Leeds, Duke of, Hornby Castle, Bedale.
1860. Lowther, Sir J. H., Swillington House, Leeds.
1861. Lister, Dr., Shibden Hall, Halifax.
1864. Lukis, Rev. W. C., M.A., Wath Rectory.
1864. Lloyd, Rev. G., Thurstonland.
1869. Lowther, Sir Charles, Bart., Swillington House.
1869. Lord, Edmund, East Hardwick, Pontefract.
1875. Lupton, F. M., Wellington Street, Leeds.
1875. Lister, T., Victoria Crescent, Barnsley.
1875. Lancaster, Ed., Barnsley.
1875. Lawrence, John, Barnsley.
1878. Lamplugh, G. W., Bridlington Quay.
1878. Laxton, F., Brighouse.
1878. Lupton, Prof. Arnold, Eldon Terrace, Leeds.
1880. Lee, P. F., West Park Villas, Dewsbury.
1880. Lister, Charles, Halifax.
1881. Lee, J. Banks, Ripon.
1883. Lund, Percy, Ilkley.
1884. Leach, John, Linden Road, Halifax.
1885. Learoyd, S., F.G.S., Sherwood House, Huddersfield.

1840. Milton, Viscount, Wentworth House, Rotherham.
1840. Marshall, J. G., Headingley House, Leeds.
1840. Martin, William B., Worsborough Hall, Barnsley.
1840. Musgrave, Archdeacon, Vicarage, Halifax.
1840. Morley, Sir Isaac, Doncaster.
1840. Morton, Charles, Normanton.
1840. Marchant, F., M.D., Hemsworth, Pontefract.

Elected.
1840. Micklethwaite, Daniel, South Parade, Wakefield.
1840. Martin, S. D., Leeds.
1840. Maclea, C. G., Leeds.
1840. March, J. O., Leeds.
1840. Mann, Joshua, Bradford.
1840. Marsden, William, Chapeltown Iron Works, Sheffield
1840. Moffatt, William, Doncaster.
1840. Morton, Henry, Wakefield.
1840. Machell, Joseph, Kirkstall.
1840. Maxfield, John, Wath, Rotherham.
1840. Morey, J. E., Doncaster.
1840. Masser, George, Leeds.
1840. Maudall, T. R., Doncaster.
1840. Monk, Rev. W., Owston, Doncaster.
1841. Morris, Rev. J. G., St. Austin's, Wakefield.
1841. Macaulay, Henry, Huddersfield.
1841. Mellin, R. S., Wakefield.
1841. Makin, Samuel, Huddersfield.
1841. Moore, William, Huddersfield.
1842. Milner, William Pashley, Attercliffe, Sheffield.
1841. Moxon, John, King Street, Huddersfield.
1841. Morley, Isaac, Doncaster.
1842. Madden, Rev. W., M.A., Woodhouse, Huddersfield.
1842. Mason, Thomas, Copt Hewick, near Ripon.
1842. Mallison, James, Brighouse.
1842. Macintosh, D., Blair-gowrie, Perthshire.
1842. Milligan, Robert, Bradford.
1845. Moxon, Mr., Pontefract.
1846. Mason, Rev. William.
1849. Marshall, Arthur, Headingley.
1853. McLandsborough, John, C.E., Otley.
1855. Maude, E., Chapeltown, Leeds.
1855. Morton, H. C., Leeds.
1857. Morley, George, Leeds.
1858. Mowbray, Fred. Wm., Shipley.
1858. Milnes, E.

LIST OF MEMBERS.

Elected.
1868. Middleton, Rev. C. H., Badsworth.
1875. Myers, W. B., 13, Park Square, Leeds.
1875. Mammatt, J. E., Barnsley.
1875. Miall, Professor L. C., Belle Vue Road, Leeds.
1875. Mitchell, John, Swaith Hall, Barnsley.
1875. Mitchell, Josh., Jun., Worsbro' Dale, Barnsley.
1875. Marshall, Stephen A., Weetwood.
1875. Mallinson, John, Blacker Colliery, Barnsley.
1875. Marsden, Thomas, Paper Mills, Barnsley.
1876. Moiser, H. R., 2, South View, Heworth, York.
1876. Morril, Robert W., Bradford.
1878. Marshall, John, Sowerby Bridge.
1878. Mason, C. L., Leeds and County Bank, Leeds.
1878. Menzies, James, Halifax.
1878. Milne, S. M., Calverley House, Calverley, near Leeds.
1878. Mortimer, J. R., Driffield.
1878. Müller, Harry, Rawdon, near Leeds.
1879. Morrison, Walter, M.P., Malham Tarn, near Leeds.
1882. Marriott, C. H., Manor Lawn, Dewsbury.
1883. Mitchell, T. C., Topcliff, Thirsk.
1884. Middleton, Charles, Lord Street, Halifax.

1840. Norfolk, Duke of, St. James' Square, London.
1840. Norton. Hon. G. C., Kettlethorp Hall, Wakefield.
1840. Newman, William, Darley Hall, Barnsley.
1840. Newman, Edward, Barnsley.
1840. Nicholls, Richard, Wakefield.
1840. Newbould, William, Intake Colliery, Sheffield.
1840. Newton, Thomas, Thorncliffe Iron Works, Sheffield.
1840. Neill, John, Wakefield.
1840. Nesbitt, David, Chapeltown Iron Works, Sheffield.
1841. Nowell, John, Farnley Wood, Huddersfield.
1841. Nelson, Thomas, Huddersfield.
1868. Nicholson, Prof. H. A., D.Sc., Keighley.
1875. Nelson, Henry, St. John's Cottage, St. John's Road, Leeds.
1875. North, S. W., Castlegate, York.

Elected.
1878. Newhouse, William Henry, Bird Cage, Skircoat, Halifax.
1879. Norton, Walter, J.P., Denby Dale, near Huddersfield.

1840. Outhwaite, John, M.D., Bradford.
1840. Overend, Wilson, Sheffield.
1842. Oldham, Rev. R., Huddersfield.
1858. O'Callaghan, P., Bradford.
1875. Oxley, Henry, Weetwood.
1876. Ormerod, Hanson, Brighouse.
1880. Ogden, John Preston, 13, Carr Road, Leeds.
1881. Ormerod, Thomas, Brighouse.

1839. Palfreyman, Luke, Sheffield.
1839. Parker, Hugh, Jun., Woodthorp, Sheffield.
1839. Proctor, Richard, Hemsworth, Pontefract.
1839. Price, Mr.
1839. Porter, Joseph, Barnsley.
1839. Pearson, Thomas, Commercial Buildings, Sheffield.
1839. Poppleton, Richard, Westgate Moor, Wakefield.
1839. Priestley, Joseph, St. John's, Wakefield.
1839. Pitchforth, Charles, Boothroyd, Halifax.
1839. Pitt, Thomas, Huddersfield.
1839. Perring, Robert, Commercial Street, Leeds.
1839. Pease, T. B., South Parade, Leeds.
1841. Peel, William, Frickley Hall, Doncaster.
1850. Paley, Dr., Halifax.
1850. Pearsall, T. J., Agent to the Yorkshire Union of Mechanics' Institutes, Leeds.
1864. Pattison, Captain, St. Agnesgate, Ripon.
1869. Parker, Right Hon. J., Darrington Hall, Pontefract.
1875. Peacock, W., Thornhill Collieries, Dewsbury.
1875. Parke, G. H., Infield Lodge, Furness Abbey.
1875. Parsons, H. F., M.D., Goole.
1876. Pratt, Thomas, Ripon.
1876. Pocklington, Henry, Cedar Grove, Armley.
1882. Preston, A. Eley, C.E., The Exchange, Bradford.
1883. Patchett, George, Jun., Halifax.

Elected.
1883. Peach Robert, Harrogate.
1884. Paul, George, F.G.S., Moortown, Leeds.
1885. Platnauer, H. M., The Museum, York.
1885. Pollock, Rev. Dr., Neville Hall, Middleham, Bedale.
1887. Pole, Charles, Halifax.
1887. Pole, M., H.M. Inspector of Schools, Sowerby Bridge.

1839. Robinson, A. G.
1839. Read, John, Derwent Hall, Sheffield.
1839. Ridsdale, George, Old Hall, Wakefield.
1839. Rhodes, James, Tintwhistle.
1839. Rand, John, Bradford.
1839. Ray, James, Sheffield.
1841. Ralph, John R., Halifax.
1841. Russell, Rev. F., Halifax.
1841. Rawson, Thomas W., Bradford.
1842. Rangely, Henry, Sheffield.
1843. Rogerson, John, Doncaster.
1848. Ramsbotham, F. H., Fixby Hall, Huddersfield.
1848. Radcliffe, J., Huddersfield.
1848. Ramsden, William, Wakefield.
1852. Ripley, Sir H. W., Bart., Holme House, Lightcliffe.
1856. Ripon, Marquis of, Studley Royal, Ripon.
1857. Radcliffe, James, Westgate, Huddersfield.
1859. Ross, Rear Admiral Sir James Clark, F.R.S.
1859. Ramsden, Sir J. W., Bart., M.P., Byram Hall, Pontefract.
1860. Richardson, John, Barnsley.
1864. Rhodes, John, Leeds.
1864. Reynolds, Richards, Leeds.
1869. Rowley, Mr. Walter, Leeds.
1875. Ryder, Charles, Regent Villas, Headingley.
1875. Roebuck, W. Denison, 9, Sunny Bank Terrace, Leeds.
1881. Rigge, S. T., Balmoral Place, Halifax.
1881. Rollitt, Sir A. K.. LL.D., D.C.L., Cogan House, Hull.
1882. Reuss, F. W., Dewsbury.

Elected.
1839. Sanderson, J. P.
1839. Stourton, Lord, Allerton Park, Wetherby.
1839. Smith, Sam.
1839. Stanhope, J. S., Cannon Hall, Barnsley.
1839. Smith, Dr. Pyemont.
1839. Smith, J. G., Heath Hall, Wakefield.
1839. Simes, Mr.
1839. Sharp, Rev. S., Vicarage, Wakefield.
1839. Stead, William.
1839. Sharp, Rev. J., Horbury, Wakefield.
1839. Scoresby, Rev. W., D.D., Bradford.
1839. Simpson, Rev. T. W., Thurnscoe Hall, Doncaster.
1840. Scott, Joseph, Badsworth Hall, Pontefract.
1840. Stephenson, George, C.E., Tapton House, Chesterfield.
1840. Smithson, Joshua, Northgate, Wakefield.
1840. Stansfeld, J. M., Flockton Manor House, Wakefield.
1840. Sorby, John, Spital Hill, Sheffield.
1840. Sorby, J. F., Spital Hill, Sheffield.
1840. Sorby, R., Rotherwood, Rotherham.
1840. Sorby, W., Rotherwood, Rotherham.
1840. Sidebottom, J., Hollingworth, Manchester.
1840. Smith, T., Gildersome, Leeds.
1840. Smith, W., Brotherton, Ferrybridge.
1840. Smith, C. J., Springfield Place, Leeds.
1840. Swanwick, F., C.E., Whittington, Chesterfield.
1840. Shaw, George, Park Square, Leeds.
1840. Sanderson, Charles, Sheffield.
1840. Stephenson, Joseph, Arundel Street, Sheffield.
1840. Sharp, William, Bradford.
1840. Sharp, Samuel, 7, Benson's Buildings, Leeds.
1840. Smith, Joseph, Land Agent, Bradford.
1840. Scholey, John, Wakefield.
1840. Schofield, M. D., Doncaster.
1840. Shepherd, T., Victoria House, Huddersfield.
1840. Storrs, Robert, Doncaster.
1840. Sheardown, Ed., Doncaster.

LIST OF MEMBERS.

Elected.
1841. Stocks, Joseph, Upper Shibden Hall, Halifax.
1841. Shaw, Foster, Huddersfield.
1841. Shaw, Bentley, Woodfield House, Lockwood.
1841. Simpson, George, Huddersfield.
1842. Solly, Richard, Sandon Place, Sheffield.
1842. Statter, Mr., Wakefield.
1845. Stainforth, Rev. R., Pontefract.
1845. Simpson, Dr., Pontefract.
1849. Simpson, William, Thurnscoe.
1851. Sorby, H. C., LLD., F.R.S., &c., Sheffield.
1854. Salt, Sir Titus, Bart., Saltaire.
1856. Sanderson, E. F., Sheffield.
1857. Shaw, E. W., Leeds.
1857. Sheard, Joseph, Brooklyed, Mirfield.
1857. Stockwell, Charles, Grange Moor, Huddersfield.
1857. Swallow, David, Gas Works, Bradford.
1857. Sylvester, Rev. W. T. M., Castleford Rectory.
1858. Stansfield, T. W., Bradford.
1859. Sewell, E , Fulneck.
1864. Staveley, Miles, Slenningford, near Ripon.
1869. Surtees, Rev. S. F., Rector of Sprotburgh.
1839. Seal, Stephen, Goldthorpe Hall, Darfield.
1870. Southern, Robert, Silkstone, Barnsley.
1870. Stott, William, Greetland.
1875. Stanhope, W. T. W. S., Cannon Hall, Barnsley.
1875. Sladdin, W. H., The Mount, Brighouse.
1875. Shaw, Thomas, M.P., Allangate, Halifax.
1875. Sladen, W. Percy, Ewell, Surrey.
1875. Sadler, M. T., Barnsley.
1876. Smeeton, G. F., Savile Road, Halifax.
1876. Smith, F., Huddersfield Road, Halifax.
1878. Sadd, W. E., Highfield Terrace, Halifax.
1878. Scarborough, George, Whinney Field, Halifax.
1878. Smithies, J. W., Elland.
1878. Stott, Alfred, Brighouse.
1878. Strangways, C. Fox., 5, Belgrave Crescent, Scarborough.

Elected.

1878. Stubbins, Jno., Chester Cottage, Old Lane, Halifax.
1878. Sykes, Peace, Estate Buildings, Huddersfield.
1879. Singleton, Thomas, Great Givendale, Pocklington.
1879. Slingsby, W. C., Carleton, near Skipton.
1879. Strickland, Sir Charles W., Hildenley, Malton.
1880. Steel, R. Elliott, B.A., 28, Blenheim Road, Bradford.
1880. Stevenson, Jno., Ormesby Packend, Middlesborough.
1881. Stansfeld, A., Weetwood Grove, near Leeds.
1882. Scarborough Philosophical Society, (J. H. Phillips.)
1882. Shaw, Jno.. Darrington Hall, Pontefract.
1882. Smith, Wm., Osborne House, Morley, near Leeds.
1883. Scargill, Alfred, East Parade, Sheffield.
1883. Scratcherd, T. C., Halifax.
1885. Slater, E., Ashville, Stanningley, Leeds.
1885. Stockdale, T., Spring Lea, Leeds.
1887. Slater, M. B., Malton.
1887. Sugden, R., Ye Farre Close, Brighouse.
1887. Sykes, Sir Tatton, Bart, Sledmere, York.

1839. Titley, F.
1839. Teale, Rev. W. H.,
1839. Thorp, Rev. Wm., Womersley Vicarage, Pontefract.
1839. Thorp, R., Burton, Barnsley.
1839. Torre, Rev. H., Thornhill Rectory, Wakefield.
1840. Turner, Rev. W., jun., Halifax.
1840. Trappes, Rev. M., St. Patricks, Huddersfield,
1840. Thornely, Jno., Dodworth Green, Barnsley.
1840. Thornely, Jno., jun., Chiswick, Glossop.
1840. Twibell, Jno., Barnsley.
1840. Tottie, T. W., Beech Grove, Leeds.
1840. Tottie, J. W., Beech Grove, Leeds,
1840. Teale, Henry, Stourton Lodge, Leeds.
1840. Teale, Henry, jun., Stourton Lodge, Leeds.
1840. Taylor, Thomas, St. John's, Wakefield.
1840. Teale, T. P., M. D., Albion Street, Leeds.
1840. Tee, Charles, Pindar Oak, Barnsley,

Elected.
1840. Tinker, E., Bent House, Meltham, Huddersfield.
1840. Thomas, Henry, Norfolk Street, Sheffield.
1840. Teal, E. J., Leeds.
1840. Titley, A., Wortley Lodge, Leeds.
1840. Twiton, G., Sheffield.
1840. Thorp, Wm., Thorne.
1842. Tattersfield, Jno., Huddersfield.
1848. Taylor, James, Huddersfield.
1857. Tolson, E. S., Dalton, Hudddersfield.
1859. Tinker, Uriah, Holmfirth.
1859. Tinker, Thomas Shaw, Holmfirth.
1866. Thompson, Leonard, Sheriff Hutton Park.
1867. Tetley, F. W., Leeds.
1869. Tew, T. W., Carlton Villa, Pontefract.
1875. Tate, Thomas, 5, Bagby Road, Leeds.
1875. Tennant, J. R., Kildwick Hall.
1875. Tiddeman, R. H., 15, West Place, Lancaster.
1875. Turner, R. B., South Parade, Leeds.
1875. Tute, Rev. J. S., B.A., Markington, near Ripley.
1878. Thompson, Joseph, Norton Towers, Halifax.
1880. Tetley, C. H., Spring Road, Headingley.
1880. Townend, W.. Lightcliffe.
1887. Taylor, Jas., Borough Surveyor, Barnsley.

1839. Upton, Rev. James, Wentworth, Rotherham.

1839. Vickers, William, Firs Hill, Sheffield.
1839. Vickers, Hervey, Far Gate, Sheffield.
1839. Vickers, Edward, Western Bank, Sheffield.
1841. Varley Thomas, Edgerton House, Sheffield.
1878. Villiers, J., Barnsley.
1880. Veitch, W. Y., 37, Grange Road, Middlesborough.
1883. Vine, G. R.. 112, Hilltop, Attercliffe, Sheffield.

1839. Warris, Rev. R., Chesterfield.
1839. Wood, Neville, Campshull Hall.

LIST OF MEMBERS.

Elected.
1839. Wharncliffe, Lord, Wortley Hall, Sheffield.
1839. Wortley, Hon. J. S., M.P., Wortley Hall, Sheffield.
1839. Wood, Sir F. L., Bart, Hickleton Hall, Doncaster.
1839. Wentworth, Hon. G., Woolley Park, Wakefield.
1839. Wentworth, Hon. F. T. W. Vernon, Wentworth Castle, Barnsley.
1839. Wright, Dr., Wakefield.
1839. Williamson, Dr.
1839. Wilcock, W.
1839. Woodhead, William, Bradford Moor.
1840. Wrightson, W. B., M.P., Cusworth, Doncaster.
1840. Walker, Henry, Clifton, Rotherham.
1840. Watkins, Rev. H., Silkstone Vicarage, Barnsley.
1840. Wright, Rev. Godfrey, Bilham House, Doncaster.
1840. Wicksteed, Rev. Charles, Leeds.
1840. Wilson T., Crimbles House, Leeds.
1840. Waud, Edward, Chester Court, Selby.
1840. Wilson, John, Flockton Colliery, Wakefield.
1840. Wilson, George, Cross Square, Wakefield.
1840. Westmoreland, M., Jun., Astley Colliery, Leeds.
1840. Wordsworth, William, Black Gates, Wakefield.
1840. Walker, John, Wakefield.
1840. Williams, M., Pule Hill Hall, Sheffield.
1840. Wilson, T. W., Oak House, Barnsley.
1840. Westmoreland, Joseph, Wakefield.
1840. Walker, J. K., M.D., Huddersfield.
1840. Walker, S., Clifton Colliery, Halifax.
1840. Walker. E., Calder Ironworks, Dewsbury.
1840. Willans, John, Roundhay, Leeds.
1840. Ward, W. Sykes, Hunslet Lane, Leeds.
1840. West, William, F.R.S., Highfield House, Leeds.
1840. Wright, J. F., Sheffield.
1840. Wheatley, William, Hopton, Dewsbury.
1840. Wheatley, C., Jun., Hopton, Dewsbury.
1840. Walker, T., Wilsick, Doncaster.
1840. Wigglesworth, W. W.,
1840. Walker, G. C., Doncaster.

LIST OF MEMBERS.

Elected.
1840. Wimberley, W. C., Doncaster.
1841. Wallen, Wm., F.S.A., West Parade, Huddersfield.
1841. Wordsworth, William, jun., Leeds.
1841. Welsh, Robert, Huddersfield.
1842. Wheatley, E. B.. Hopton.
1842. Walker, Charles, Bradford.
1843. Wilson, Jno., Sheffield.
1843. Wilson, J. C., Sheffield.
1851. Wilson, Thomas, jun., Sheffield.
1857. Waterhouse, Edward, Lindley, Huddersfield.
1858. Woodhead, John, Eccleshill, Bradford.
1869. Wall, G. P., Sheffield.
1875. Ward, Christopher, Halifax.
1875. Ward, J. W., Halifax.
1875. Waterhouse, Jno., F.R.S., Well Head, Halifax.
1875. Warrington, Jno., Worsbro', near Barnsley.
1875. Warburton, J., Pease's Buildings, South Parade, Leeds.
1878. Ward, Jno., Longton, Staffordshire.
1878. Whiteley, J., Uxbridge Street, Edgehill, Liverpool.
1878. Woodall, J. W., jun,, Old Bank, Scarborough.
1878. Woodhead, Jos., Woodthorpe, Huddersfield.
1879. Walker, Charles, Barnsley.
1880. Ward, J. F., Park Road, Middlesborough.
1880. Wilcock, W. A., Idle.
1880. Wood, W. H., Albion Place, Leeds.
1880. Wood, W. H., Halifax.
1881. Ward, Geo., F.C.S.. Leeds.
1881. Whiteley, Fredk., Clare Hall Road, Halifax.
1881. Wilson, E. J., M.A., 6, Whitefriars Gate, Hull.
1884. Walmisley, A. T., C. E., 5, Westminster Chambers, Victoria Street, London, S.W.

1840. Yarburgh, George Cooke, Camps Mount, Doncaster.
1846. Yates, James, F.R.S., Norton Hall, Derbyshire.
1857. York, Archbishop of, York.
1868. Yates, Jno., Rotherham.

INDEX.

Abdy, 236.
Aberford, 95.
Aberystwith, 251.
Acanthodes, 73, 198.
Ackworth Rock, 96.
Adamson, S. A., 434, 435.
Adel 323, 324.
Adwalton, 198.
Agassiz, Prof. Lousia, 4, 11, 72, 73, 130, 142, 143, 144, 149, 198, 286, 287, 288, 289.
Agricultural Geology, Wold District, 223, 224, 228.
Agricultural Geology, South Cave, 223, 224.
Aire and Calder Canal, 195.
Airy, G. B., 211, 212.
Aitkin, J., 412.
Aldborough, 95, 322, 333.
Aldfield, 335.
Alexander, Dr. R., 252, 253.
Alexander, Dr. Wm., 168, 169, 184, 199, 262, 264, 338, 345.
Alexander, Dr. Wm., Biographical Notice of, 251.
Alexander, Dr. Wm., Paper by, 253.
——— Ed., 252.
——— Gervase, 252.
——— Mrs., 214.
——— R. G., 252.
Allandale, 176.
Allbutt, Dr. T. C., 394.
Allen T., 128.
Almondbury, 333.
Alpine Limestones, 127.
Alston Moor, 80, 279.
Althorp, Lord, 42.
Altofts Colliery, 112.
Anning, Miss Mary, 148.
Ancient Coal Mining, Paper on, 432.
Anderson, Dr. F., 394.
Andrew, James, 2.
Ansell, Mr., 334.
Ansted, Mr., 141.
Austwick, 326.
Anthropological Society, 251.
Antiquarian Society, 306, 314.

Appletreewick Moor, 258.
Appold, Mr., 276.
Ardsley, 22, 23, 75, 174, 230.
Argyll, Duke of, 288.
Arkendale, 124.
Arncliffe, 305.
Arran, Isle of, 138.
Ashton, 96, 236.
Aspect of Springs, Chemico-Geological 428.
Astromyelon, and its Affinities, 412.
Athenæum, 119.
Atkinson, J. C., 300, 301, 302, 338, 368.
Atkinson, J. T., 401.
Attercliff, 241.
Auld Gang Lead Mines, 124.
Avebury, 321.
Aveline, W. T., 117.
Axminster, 145.

Bacillaria, 197.
Baddle, Mr., 17.
Baildon Moor, 322.
Bailiffe Bridge, 108.
Baines, Samuel, 330, 338.
Baker, W., 264, 280.
Baldwin, J. R., 214, 215.
Ball, Sir R., 295, 298, 311.
Balta Sound, 202.
Banks, Sir J., 203, 204, 205.
Barber, Fairless, 322, 323, 388.
Barham Rectory, 245.
Barmston, 65.
Barnes, Rev. Theo., 74, 161, 171, 173.
Barnes, Thomas, 253.
Barnsley, 95, 96, 97, 105, 106, 110, 214, 231, 233, 256, 270, 274, 298, 340, 342, 355, 389, 397, 430, 431.
Barometrical Disturbances, 433.
Barrett, Mr., 141.
Barrow, Mr., 394.
Barrows and Tumuli, 298, 299, 300, 301, 302, 303, 304, 305, 306, 307, 308, 309, 310, 311, 312, 313, 314, 315, 316, 317, 318.
Bartholomew, W. H., 266, 278.
Baxter, R. D , 262, 264.

INDEX.

Bawtry, 95.
Batty, Mr., 156, 157, 160.
Bath, 120, 121, 126.
Bean, W., 180, 423.
Beaumont, E. B., 176, 218, 220.
Beaumont, T. W., 5, 26, 150, 152.
Beche, Sir H. de la, 92, 100, 101, 103, 131, 215, 243, 270.
Beckett, William, 259.
Beckwith, Mr., 14.
Bedford, J. E., 435.
Beeston, 75, 76, 77, 91, 112.
Beetham Fell, 196.
Bell, Mr., 394.
Belmore, 130.
Bempton, 317, 398, 408.
Ben Jochlin, 130.
Bessingby, 208.
Beverley, 323.
Billingley, 110.
Billington, Mr., 172.
Biloculina, 265.
Bingley, Dr. C. W., 329.
Binney, Ed. W., 29, 71, 91, 93, 94, 96, 192, 193, 266, 272, 338.
Binns, J. Arthur, 200.
Biram, B., 2, 5, 83, 271.
Birchoff, G. W., 171.
Bird, C., 352, 353.
Bird, J., 423.
Birkbeck, J., 356.
Birmingham, 122, 128.
Black, Dr., 104.
Blackmore Museum, 248.
Blackwell, 132.
Blake, Rev. J. F., 399.
Blaydes, Mr., 337.
Blean-y-ddol, 119.
Blenkinsop, Mr., Biographical Notice of, 253.
Blubberhouses, 337.
Board of Ordnance, 25, 100, 101.
Bodington, Dr. G., 270.
Bodington, Prof. N., 397, 398.
Bolland, 126.
Boltby, 303.
Bolton Bridge, 130, 337.
Bolton Castle, 432.
Bolton-on-Dearne, 110.
Booth, J., 398.
Booth, Mr., 2, 160.
Boston Spa, 299.
Bosworth Field, 252.
Boué Mr., 103.
Boulsworth, 286.
Bourne, 269.
Bowling, 271.
Bowman, F. H., 248.

Bowman, Mr., 29, 71, 93, 94, 104, 184.
Boynton, T., 396, 398, 434.
Brackenridge, J., 266, 273, 274, 275.
Bradford, 72, 78, 104, 179, 186, 200, 209, 210, 231, 266, 267, 280, 318, 394.
Bradford Basin, Glacial Deposits of, 360, 361.
Bradford Literary and Philosophical Society, 77, 177, 344.
Bradford Rock, 33.
Bradgate Rock, 23, 76, 89, 90, 91, 96, 109.
Brage, Sir R., 252.
Brakenridge, Mr., 2.
Brandling, C. J., 5, 11, 26, 150, 151, 152, 172, 253, 255.
Brandling, Ralph, 253.
Bramham Moor, 91.
Bransome, Mr., 433.
Brayley, E. W., 262, 280.
Brayton Barf, 417.
Brereton, Dr., 323.
Bretton, 109, 110, 117, 180.
Brewster, Sir D., 123, 127, 128, 239.
Briar, Mr., 161.
Bridgewater Treatises, 149.
Bridlington, 197, 256, 265, 296, 298, 299, 302, 316, 317, 323, 389, 396, 398.
Bridlington, Glacial Sections near, 404, 405, 410.
Brierley, 110, 117, 180.
Brigg, J., 349, 361, 391, 396.
Briggs, A. C., 60, 394.
Briggs, Henry, 2, 5, 14, 20, 21, 22, 24, 28, 29, 32, 33, 65, 71, 80, 91, 107, 109, 111, 117, 150, 155, 159, 160, 164, 166, 167, 180, 184, 192, 194, 199, 230, 231, 262, 263, 264, 268, 273, 338
Briggs, Henry, Biographical Notice of, 60, 61.
Brighouse, 108.
Bright, Miss, 44.
Brignell, 124.
British Association, 20, 25, 31, 36, 46, 72, 80, 100, 115, 116, 122, 126, 127, 128, 130, 131, 132, 140, 144, 146, 176, 180, 182, 185, 197, 208, 246, 266, 287, 289, 393.
British Museum, 146, 306, 309, 315, 334, 356.
Bristol, 124, 126.
Bristow, Mr., 118.
Broderip, W., 128, 145.
Brompton Cemetery, 244.
Brook, Ed., 338.
Brooke, T., 274, 368.
Brown, Captain, 93, 199.
Brown, Major H., 267.
Brownridge, C., 435.

INDEX.

Byng, Sir John, 47.
Byrom, B., 190.
Bach, Baron von, 205.
Buckland, Dr. W., 69, 73, 102, 103, 126, 128, 131, 151, 153, 159, 160, 171, 172, 174, 190, 226, 232, 283, 284, 285, 286, 287, 306, 309.
Buckland, Wm., Biographical Notice of, 145, 146, 147, 148, 149.
Buckton, 302.
Buddle, Mr., 234.
Bull, Mr., 97, 111, 115, 117, 179.
Bunsen, Chevalier, 279.
Burdale, 400, 401.
Burdiehouse, 72, 73.
Burnley, 124.
Burnsall, 130.
Busk, Prof., 359.
Bute, Isle of, 204.
Buxton, 105.

Calamoporæ, 196.
Calamostachys, 411, 412.
Calcareous Grit, 126, 257.
Calder River, 23, 39, 90, 113, 174, 189, 195, 289, 292.
Calder Valley, Erratic Boulders in, 416.
Callernish, 321.
Cambrian System, 140, 141.
Cambridge Greensand, 141.
Cambridge Philosophical Society, 137.
Cambridge University, 132, 140, 141, 145.
Cameron, A. G., 419.
Cape, Mr., 299.
Carboniferous Limestone, 195, 352, 353.
Carboniferous Limestone, Fish Remains in, 423, 424.
Carcharopsis, 198.
Carlisle, 147.
Carlisle, Earl of, 101.
Carlton, 110.
Carnaby, 323.
Carnac, 324.
Carroll, J. B., 299.
Carruthers, Dr. W., 411.
Carter, R., 263, 265, 271, 272, 273, 274, 275, 332, 338, 342, 345, 361, 368, 396, 427.
Cash, Wm., 367, 396, 402, 410, 411, 412.
Casson, Mr., 2.
Cavendish, Lady F., 396.
Cavendish, Lord E., 396.
Cavendish, Lord F., 396.
Cawood, 324.
Cayton Gill Beds, 402, 433.
Cephalopoda, 367.
Chadwick, Mr., 166.

Chalk, Contortions in, 408
Chalk Fossils, Image Collection of, 141,
Chalk, White, 408.
Chalk, Valleys in, 405, 409.
Chambers, John, 2, 160.
Chambers, Matthew, 2, 160.
Channel Tunnel, 426.
Chantrell, R. D., 156, 160, 173, 264, 282.
Charlesworth, J. B., 63, 64, 110, 214.
Charlesworth, Jno., 2, 5, 110.
Charlesworth, Jos., 2, 4, 5, 110.
Charlesworth, Jos., Biographical Notice of, 63, 64.
Charlesworth, Joseph, jun., 2, 110.
Charlesworth, Joseph, jun., Biographical Notice of, 63, 64.
Charnwood, 183.
Charpentier, Prof., 286.
Cheetham, William, 238.
Chemical Society of London, 238, 241.
Cheshire, 147, 294.
Chester, 122.
Chevet Rock, 20, 96, 113.
Cheviot Hills, 124.
Childers, J. W., 218.
Chlamydoselachus, 435.
Chonetes Clevelandicus, 430.
Clanney, Dr., 27, 429.
Clark, S., 2, 185.
Clarke, J. E., 402, 422.
Clarke, Mr., 2.
Clay, J. T., 163, 164, 165, 166, 167, 174, 179, 180, 181, 184, 213, 226, 227, 231, 288, 289, 290, 291, 292.
Clayton, Fossil Trees at, 434.
Cleet, 16, 17, 18.
Cleveland, 263, 275, 300, 302.
Cleave Dyke, 304.
Clifton, 180.
Coal Measures, 139.
Coal Mines, Ventilation of, 233.
Coal Mining, 75.
Cobden, Mr., 240.
Cocconema, 197.
Cochliodonts, 424.
Cœlacanthus, 198.
Cole, Rev. E. Maule, 390, 397, 399, 407, 408, 409.
Collie Weston, 126.
Collingham, 282.
Collision, Captain, 302.
Coniston, 181.
Cononley, 275, 390, 424, 425.
Contortion of Rocks, 350, 351.
Conybeare, Wm., 128.
Cook, Captain, 200, 205.
Cooper, P., 339.

Cooper, S., 2.
Cooper, W,. 2.
Copenhagen, 203.
Coralline Oolite, 126, 257.
Cornwall, 24, 33, 74, 131, 137, 215, 243, 279.
Cowden Hill, Spring near, 417.
Cowthorpe, 293.
Cracoe, 130.
Crania Britannica, 304.
Craster, Mr., 303.
Craven, 292, 319.
Craven District, Sections in Lower Palæozoic Rocks of, 420.
Craven Fault. 124, 130, 352.
Craven, Geology of, 352.
Crawford, Mr., 148.
Creswell Caves, Investigations at, 418.
Crigglestone, 117, 180.
Crimsworth Dean, 169.
Crole, Mr., 277.
Cromwell Bed, 109, 174.
Cropton, 200.
Crossley, L. J., 396.
Crowther, Dr., 230.
Ctenacanthus, 198, 424.
Ctenodus, 73, 198.
Ctenodus, Bones of. 418.
Ctenoptychius, 73, 198.
Cudworth, 110, 113.
Culvers, 250.
Cumberland, 138, 286, 290.
Cumming, Rev. J. G., 292, 295.
Curtis, Mr., 245.
Cuvier, M., 137.
Cyathophylla, 196.
Cytheridea Sorbyana, 265.
Cytheridea concinna, 265.

Daguerre, 243.
Dakyns, J. R., 118, 362, 366, 401, 410.
Dalton, W. H., 118, 128, 129, 239, 352.
Dampier, 205.
Danby, 300.
Danes Dyke, 317.
Darfield, 110, 113.
Darfield Quarries, Fossil Plants at, 417.
Darton, 110, 342.
Darwin, C., 132, 133, 134, 142, 247.
Daubeny, Prof., 123, 127, 128, 129, 179, 226, 239.
Davidson, Dr., 415.
Davis, Barnard, 304.
Davis, J. W., 58, 60, 61, 63, 64, 251, 361, 363, 367, 368, 391, 395, 397, 398, 401, 408, 416, 418, 423, 430, 433, 434, 435.
Davis, R. Hayton, 429.
Davy, Sir Humphrey, 13, 20, 24, 27, 218, 272, 429.

Dawson, Christ., 2, 22, 78.
Dawson, Matthew, 137.
Dawkins, Prof. Boyd, 317, 356, 417.
Dean, Forest of, 124, 176, 226.
De Blainville, M., 137.
Denby Dale, 109.
Denny, H., 77, 91, 184, 197, 198, 213, 241, 256, 260, 264, 293, 295, 297, 298, 303, 304, 305, 307, 308, 310, 311, 312, 323, 324, 326, 332, 337, 339, 345, 348, 388, 420.
Denny, Henry, Biographical Notice of, 244.
Denny, Prof. A., 244.
Dent, 136, 145, 336.
Dentalium communis, 265.
Derbyshire, 105. 106, 188, 228, 231.
Devon, 131, 137, 143, 144, 215, 243, 309.
Devonport, 243.
Dewsbury, 21, 280, 282, 394, 423.
Diplodus, 73, 198.
Diplopteris, 198.
Doncaster, 179, 214, 229, 256, 259, 293, 316.
Doncaster, Glacial Deposit at, 426.
Don, Geology of the, 11, 33, 36, 83, 105, 106.
Dowkabottom, 305, 306, 307, 308, 310.
Dowkabottom Cave, Explorations at, 420, 421, 422.
Drabble, Mr., 198.
Draper, Dr., 232.
Draughton, 337.
Drayson, Capt., 327, 328.
Dresser, C. L., 281.
Driffield, 326.
Driffield, Sections in Drift at, 409.
Drift Deposits of the West Riding of Yorkshire, 345.
Drighlington, 21.
Dublin, 130, 140, 185.
Dublin University, 132.
Duckinfield, 96, 105.
Dundas, Lord, 41, 48.
Dunford Bridge, 98.
Dunmore, 250.
Durden, E. H., 262.
Durham, 124, 138, 236, 270, 288, 320.
Durham Coal-field, 36, 231, 233.
Durham, Natural History Society of, 3, 4, 8, 15, 19.

Early Ethnology of Britain, 296.
Earthquake in Essex, 433.
Easingwold, 230.
Eastern Alps, Geology of, 138.
Easterfield, Thomas H., 426.
Ebberstone Lodge, 236, 319.

Eddy, J. Ray, 390, 422, 424.
Eddy, Stephen, 269, 280.
Edinburgh, 202, 203, 204, 207, 209, 252, 258.
Edinburgh Encyclopædia, 203.
Edinburgh, Philosophical Society of, 127, 185, 208.
Effingham, Earl of, 5, 152.
Egerton, Sir Philip, 127, 130.
Elland, 108, 170.
Elland Flag Rock, 178.
Elloughton, 407.
Elsecar, 159, 160, 271.
Embleton, T. W., 2, 3, 4, 5, 7, 8, 9, 10, 11, 12, 14, 15, 16, 17, 18, 19, 20, 23, 24, 27, 29, 33, 34, 35, 37, 38, 39, 60, 65, 66, 67, 75, 77, 78, 80, 81, 89, 90, 91, 92, 93, 97, 98, 104, 106, 107, 111, 112, 113, 114, 115, 150, 155, 156, 157, 158, 159, 160, 161, 162, 163, 164, 165, 166, 167, 168, 171, 172, 174, 176, 179, 180, 181, 191, 220, 221, 223, 226, 255, 260, 262, 264, 339, 343, 348, 349, 397, 432.
Emerson's Mechanics, 25.
Encyclopædia Brittanicæ, 285.
Enniskillen, Earl of, 130, 288.
Entomostraca, 158, 412, 413, 414.
Esk, Vale of, 236, 237, 263, 331.
Eskwith, 303.
Eston Hall, 236, 237, 275.
Eunotia, 197.
Evans, Dr. John, 131, 135, 312, 314, 316, 426.
Exeter, 160, 209.

Fairbairn, Mr., 185.
Fairey, Mr., 343.
Fairley, T., 419.
Falcon Clints, Sections at, 366.
Faraday, Dr., 270.
Farrer, Mr., 161, 306, 307, 310, 420.
Faulkner, Dr., 314.
Fenton, Mr., 21, 254.
Ferrybridge, 130, 292.
Ffooks, J., 316, 317, 324, 325.
Field, Mr., 2, 4, 5, 150.
Filey, 257, 267, 398.
Filey Bay, Glacial Beds in, 403.
Filliter, E., 348.
Fisher, W., 263.
Fish Remains in the Coal Measures, 401.
Fitton, Mr., 103.
Fitzwilliam, Charles W., 48, 150.
Fitzwilliam, Earl, 3, 5, 11, 21, 26, 31, 39, 41, 42, 43, 44, 45, 46, 47, 49, 82, 90, 127, 128, 150, 152, 153, 159, 160, 161, 174, 184, 213, 223, 226, 227, 231, 233, 236, 241, 256, 264, 266, 267, 268, 271.
Fitzwilliam, Hon. George W., 48, 150.
Flamborough, 296, 324.
Flamborough Head, Boulders of, 406.
Flamborough Head, Fault in the Chalk, 403.
Fletcher, Mr., 29.
Flitcroft, Mr., 47.
Flockton, 20, 21, 90, 96, 109, 158, 192, 236.
Flora of the Lower Coal Measures, 402.
Flots, 410.
Fossilised Fungus, 410, 411.
Foljambe, George Savile, 45.
Foraminifera, 196, 412, 413.
Foramenifera in Cambridge Greensand, 414.
Forbes, J., 123, 128, 239.
Fossil Icthyology of the Yorkshire Coal-field, 71.
Fourness, Mr., 25.
Fowler, Rev. J. T., 326.
Fox, G. L., 5, 152, 259, 279, 303.
Fox-Strangways, C., 118.
Franks, Mr., 357.
French Revolution, 43.
Fyffe, Mr., 311.

Gaillonella, 197.
Gainsboro', 95.
Garforth, W. E., 429.
Garlick, M., 170.
Gascoigne, R. O., 5, 8.
Gatty, Rev. A., 41.
Gawber Hall, 214.
Gea Fell, 120.
Geikie, Prof. J., 127, 394.
Geographical Society, 251.
Geological Society of London, 72, 125, 126, 127, 131, 132, 137, 138, 139, 143, 146, 182, 222, 223, 227, 241, 251, 285, 295, 338.
Geology, Treatise on, 135.
Geology, Guide to, 135.
George, Ed. S., 72, 124.
Gibson, J., 130, 169.
Gilbertson, Mr., 130.
Gildersome, 21.
Gill, Francis, 124.
Girtanner, Dr., 79.
Glasgow, 185, 246, 287.
Glen Gloy, Parallel Roads in, 409.
Glennan, Mr., 311.
Goderich, Viscount, 49, 267, 268.
Gooch, Mr., 113.
Goodchild, Mr., 353.

Goole, 229.
Graham, W., 2, 186.
'Grassdale, 336.
Grassington, 281.
Great Houghton, 110, 117, 180.
Green, A. H., 118, 270, 338, 340, 342, 343, 346, 353, 354, 355, 356, 361, 363, 391. 393.
Green, John, 311.
Greenland, 201, 202, 203, 204, 205, 206, 207.
Greenough, G. B., 20, 25, 26, 103, 125, 127, 147, 153, 154, 155, 285, 286.
Greenwell, Rev. W., 303, 318, 321, 322.
Greetland, 170, 333.
Gretta Bridge, 282.
Grey, Lord, 43.
Griffith, Mr., 130.
Gristhorpe, 257, 398.
Grove Colliery, 191.
Guest, J., 345.
Guisborough, 300.
Gulf Stream, 292.
Guttulina, 265.
Guy's Hospital, 153.
Gyracanthus, 73, 198.

Hackness, 282.
Hague's Patent Pumping Apparatus, 27.
Haigh, D. H., 264, 282, 326.
Haigh Moor, 18, 21, 22, 24, 32, 71, 76, 77, 91, 172, 174, 343.
Hailstone, Prof., 137.
Halifax, 21, 28, 72, 95, 108, 122, 124, 129, 157, 168, 169, 179, 192, 198, 229, 230, 231, 248, 249, 251, 256, 261, 271, 275, 289, 316, 333.
Halifax Agricultural Society, 252.
Halifax Literary and Philosophical Society, 192, 198, 249, 252, 334, 338.
Halifax, Lord, 101, 397.
Halifax Mechanics' Institute, 249, 252.
Halifax, Viscount, 381, 382.
Hall, Sir J., 351.
Hall, T. W., 37, 105, 111, 117, 166, 180, 184.
Hambledon Haugh, 417.
Hambleton Hills, 303, 304.
Hamilton, Rev. R. W., 166.
Hampsthwaite, 335.
Hammerton, J., 189, 190, 226.
Hanwick, 311.
Harcourt, Rev. W. V., 46, 96, 123, 126, 127, 128, 160, 224.
Harewood, 124.
Harewood, Earl of, 150.
Harrogate, 124, 129, 337, 396, 427.
Harrogate, Mineral Waters of, 427.
Harrogate, Wealth of, 429.
Harte, Dr., 294.

Hartop, H., 2, 5, 7, 11, 27, 28, 29, 33, 36, 65, 66, 73, 75, 78, 79, 80, 83, 88, 90, 92, 98, 106, 107, 111, 160, 161, 164, 167, 173, 174, 184, 185, 186, 223.
Hartop, Henry, Biographical Notice of, 240.
Hartshead, 108, 109, 117, 180, 282.
Hatfield Chase, 268.
Hawke, Right Hon. Lord, 91, 213.
Hawkins, Mr., 251.
Hawkshaw, Mr., 104.
Hawnby, 303.
Headley, William, 255.
Heaton, J. B., 194.
Hebden Bridge, 169.
Hebburn Colliery, 11.
Helmsley, 230, 283.
Helodus, 73, 198.
Henry, D., 126.
Henslow, Prof., 137.
Henwood, Mr., 280.
Heptonstall, 170.
Heterolepidotus, 430.
Heywood, James, 83, 105, 199.
Hick, Thomas, 402, 410, 411.
Higher Wood, 169.
High Pressure Boilers, 33.
Hindle, Mr., 160.
Hipperholme, 338.
Hird, L., 2, 160.
History of Craven, 305.
Hitchcock, Prof., 178, 352.
Hoare, Sir R. C., 312.
Hodgson, Mr., 306, 338.
Holderness, 95, 96, 224, 286, 288.
Holderness, Geological Survey of, 404.
Holgate, B., 361.
Holmes, J., 434.
Holmes, T. S., 2, 118, 173, 346.
Holoptychius, 73, 198.
Holt, Henry, 2, 5, 14, 27, 28, 32, 49, 79, 80, 92, 107, 111, 112, 113, 117, 153, 155, 159, 166, 172, 179, 180, 236, 241.
Holt, Henry, Biographical Notice of, 52, 53.
Holt, H. P., 49.
Holme Fell, 336.
Holroyd, J., 171.
Hook, Rev. Dr., 66, 68, 69, 75.
Hoolebottom Clough, 169.
Hopkins, Mr., 174.
Hopwood, Mr., 2.
Horbury Rock, 91.
Horley Green, 190.
Hornblower, Mr., 74.
Horne, Wm., 424, 431.
Horner, Leonard, 122.
Hornsea, 396.

Horsfall, A., 303, 338.
Houghton, Lord, 316, 389, 397.
Houghton, Lord, Biographical Notice of, 373, 381.
House of Commons, 35, 41.
Howard, Lord, 35, 37.
Howgill Fells, 130, 336.
Huddersfield, 178, 187, 229, 231, 266, 275, 288, 339, 389.
Huddersfield, Annual Meeting at, 1, 117.
Huddleston, Prof., 395, 426.
Hudson, Mr., 205, 206.
Hughes, Prof. T. M., 335, 356, 423.
Hull, 122, 219, 222, 223, 230, 394, 396, 419, 422.
Hull and Barnsley Railway, 395, 409.
Hull Literary and Philosophical Society, 223.
Hull, Prof. Ed., 117.
Humbolt, Mr., 79, 232.
Humfrey, M., 337.
Hunt, Prof., 259, 262, 275, 279, 280, 331.
Hunt, Robert, Biographical Notice of, 243.
Hunt, Robert, Papers by, 244.
Hunton, 298.
Hutchinson, J., 341.
Hutton, Dr., 98, 99.
Hutton, W., 4, 8, 128.
Huxley, Prof., 344.
Hybodus, 73, 198.
Hydraulic Limestone, Analysis of, 430.

Ichthyosaurus, 180.
Idle, 72.
Ingham, Mr., 2, 109, 180.
Ingleborough, 335.
Inglis, Dr. J., 191, 192, 230, 231.
Institute of Civil Engineers, 238.
Irrawaddy, 148.
Isis liassica, 430.
Isle of Wight, Geology of, 137.

Jackson, Mr., 305, 306, 307, 356, 357, 358, 359, 420.
Jameson, Mr., 103, 203, 204.
Jardine, Sir William, 246.
Jarrow, 270.
Jebson, J., 267, 274, 275, 232.
Jeffcock, P., 2, 342.
Jefferies, Dr. Gwyn, 265.
Jones, Prof. T. Rupert, 265, 415.
Jordan, T. B., 175, 242.
Judd, Prof. J. W., 393.
Jukes, Prof, 102, 141.
Johnston, Prof. J. F. W., 3, 4, 7, 8, 9, 11, 14, 15, 16, 17, 18, 19, 20, 24, 32, 36, 38, 75, 103, 123, 128, 221.

Kaye, Sir J. L. L., 5, 152, 192.
Kell, Messrs., 389.
Keller, Dr. F., 313.
Kelloway Rock, 400.
Kenrick, Rev. J., 264, 308, 310, 315.
Kent's Hole, 369.
Keogh, Rev. G. P., 390.
Kepwick Moor, 303.
Kettleness, 331.
Kettlewell, 424.
Ketton, 126.
Kidd, Dr., 145.
Kidderminster, 229.
Killingworth Colliery, 255.
Kilnsea, 396.
Kilnsea Range, 305, 306.
Kimmeridge Clay, 102, 400.
King's Scar, 305.
Kirby Lonsdale, 124, 336.
Kirby, Rev. W., 245.
Kirkdale Cave, 148, 149, 283, 284, 285, 291, 293, 318.
Kissengen Saline Chalybeate, Analysis of, 429.
Knaresbro', 337, 395.
Knowles, Mr., 338.
Krakatoa, 433.
Kulkeagh, 130.

Lagena striata, 265.
Lamplugh, G. W., 265, 398, 402, 407.
Lancashire, 147, 228, 288, 294.
Lancashire Coal-field, 28, 34, 89, 94, 96, 97, 98, 101, 104, 105, 106, 107, 117, 174, 193, 308.
Lancaster, 33.
Lankester, Dr. E., 246.
Lartet, M., 314.
Lascelles, Hon. H., 41, 42.
Lascelles, Hon. W. S., 20, 26, 67.
Law, Robert, 425.
Lawrence, Mr., 174.
Lead Mines, History of, 424, 425.
Leah, H., 2, 78, 160.
Leather, J. W., 167.
Leeds, 8, 19, 21, 25, 49, 77, 95, 98, 104, 106, 108, 111, 112, 122, 124, 152, 156, 164, 170, 173, 179, 186, 222, 228, 229, 230, 231, 238, 241, 253, 254, 259, 263, 264, 266, 282, 292, 297, 303, 308, 310, 324, 338, 340, 350, 396.
Leeds Literary and Philosophical Society, 4, 11, 49, 65, 77, 164, 166, 167, 177, 181, 183, 198, 228, 238, 239, 240, 241, 245, 259, 293, 297, 308, 322, 324, 337, 394, 397.
Leeds Mechanics' Institute, 238.
Leeds School of Medicine, 239, 247.

Leeds Museum, 72, 73, 158, 304, 310, 311, 322, 324, 356, 391.
Lee, William, 177, 178.
Legard, Mr., 220.
Leigh, Dr., 294.
Lepidosteus, 72.
Leyburn, 124, 397.
Leyland, F. A., 333, 334, 338, 347.
Lias, The, 139, 148, 163.
Liebig, Prof., 179, 218, 226.
Life on the Earth, 132.
Lightcliffe, 316.
Lime and its uses in Agriculture, 195.
Lincolnshire, 268.
Lingula, Occurrence of, 434.
Linnean Society, 247.
Lister, John, Biographical Notice of, 250.
Lister, Thomas, 266.
Lister, Thomas, Biographical Notice of, 386, 387.
Liverpool, 122, 208.
Liverpool, Earl of, 45.
Livingstone, Dr., 247.
Lloyd, Dr., 128, 265, 299, 317.
Lofthouse, 18, 23, 71, 75, 76.
Londesborough, Lord, 264, 265, 299.
London and Birmingham Railway, 194.
London Clay, 218.
London College of Physicians, 250, 252.
Looney, Mr., 130.
Lords, House of, 43.
Lothersdale, 337.
Lower Coal Measures, 169.
Lower Coal Measures at Halifax, Analysis of Coal Balls in, 430.
Lower Coal Measures at Halifax, Fossil Trees in, 434.
Lubbock, Sir John, 313, 314.
Lucas, J., 420.
Lukis, Rev. W. C., 80, 177, 302, 312, 426.
Lund Hill, 271, 274.
Lupton, Prof. A., 418, 426.
Lyell, Sir C., 270, 290, 314, 339.
Lyme Regis, 148.
Lyxidicula, 197.
Lower Ouse Valley, 364, 365, 366.
Low Moor, 4, 91, 108, 112, 186, 197, 198, 236, 263, 271.

Macculloch, Mr., 103, 105.
Mackintosh, D., 345.
Maclean, Mr., 165.
Magnesian Limestone, 108, 110, 118, 125, 138, 139, 147, 195, 196, 218, 325, 343.
Major, Mr., 189.
PP

Malaria, 199.
Malham Cove, Source of the stream at the foot of, 417.
Maltby, 95.
Malton, 44, 230, 397.
Manchester, 29, 104, 122, 126, 162, 173, 185, 192, 198, 334.
Manchester Geological Society, 70, 71, 92, 93, 94, 98, 104, 105, 337, 338.
Manchester Railway, 95, 97, 98, 193.
Mantell, G. A., 148, 295.
Mapleton, Rev. R. J., 322.
Marden, 119.
Marr, J. E., 420.
Marsh, Mr., 75.
Marshall, J. G., 4, 74, 165, 166, 167, 171, 172, 181, 182, 262, 264, 339, 340, 343.
Marshall, J. Garth, Biographical Notice of, 58, 59, 60.
Marshall, Stephen A., 58, 65.
Martin, W. B., 5, 79, 98, 111, 152.
Masham, 124.
Maunsell, Archdeacon, 293.
Mauritius, 296.
M'Coy, Prof., 141.
McDougall, Sir T., 204.
M'Enery, Rev. Mr., 308, 309, 310.
Mello, Rev. J. Magens, 433.
Megaceros Hibernicus, 293, 310.
Megalicthys, 4, 66, 72, 73, 197, 198.
Megalosaurus, 148.
Metalliferous Mines in the United Kingdom, 244.
Meteorology, 203, 204, 249.
Methley, 75.
Mexborough, Earl of, 5.
Miall, Prof. L. C., 336, 344, 345, 348, 350, 351, 352, 361, 363, 368, 388, 390, 391, 398, 418.
Microscopic Animals in the Rocks of Yorkshire, Paper on, 195.
Middlesboro', 236, 263, 394.
Middleton, 4, 7, 8, 11, 16, 18, 20, 21, 22, 23, 24, 33, 71, 75, 76, 77, 90, 91, 109, 112, 158, 172, 192, 198, 253, 254, 255.
Midland Coal-field, Notes on, 418.
Milleporidæ, 196.
Millstone Grit, 28, 102, 139, 169, 174, 269, 335, 340, 341.
Millwood, 169.
Milton Ironworks, 241.
Milton, Lady, 42.
Milton, Lord, 41, 42, 44, 150.
Milner, W. R., 332.
Mineral Springs in the Parish of Halifax, Paper on, 168.
Mining, Agriculture, and Arts, Paper on, 36.

Minto, Mr. 341.
Mirfield Moor Coal, 90, 109, 117.
Mitchell, J., 430.
Moffatt, Mr., 160.
Monk Hill, 324.
Monmouthshire, 270.
Monographia Anoplurarum Britanniæ, 246, 247.
Monographia Pselaphidarum et Scydmænidarum Britanniæ, 245.
Moortown, 71, 72, 76.
Morley, Mr., 2.
Morny, Chevalier W. P. Barbel de, 338.
Morpeth, Lord, 129, 228.
Morrison, W., 391, 416.
Mortimer, J. R., 390, 408, 409.
Morton, C., 2, 12, 14, 20, 22, 23, 24, 25, 27, 29, 34, 35, 37, 38, 65, 66, 70, 74, 75, 79, 80, 83, 89, 91, 92, 93, 94, 96, 98, 104, 105, 106, 107, 111, 112, 153, 155, 161, 164, 166, 167, 171, 172, 184, 230.
Morton, Charles, Biographical Notice of, 61, 62, 63.
Morton, H. J., 61, 62, 63, 115.
Mottram, 97, 105.
Moughton Fell, 395.
Mountain Limestone, 130, 147, 168, 196, 228, 335, 336, 340.
Muir Glacier of Alaska, 406.
Munster, Count, 141.
Murchison, Sir R., 123, 125, 126, 127, 129, 130, 138, 140, 147, 232, 239, 287.
Murray, Mr., 254, 303.
Myriophylloides, 411.
Myxomycetes, 411.

Nasmyth, James, 263, 270, 278.
Navicula, 197.
Netherton, 117, 180, 342.
Newcastle, 4, 8, 9, 11, 20, 25, 122, 124, 153, 156, 230, 233, 234.
Newlay, Mr., 188.
Newman, Mr., 294.
Newmarket, 21, 22, 23, 27, 124.
New Red Sandstone, 139, 147, 177, 215, 335.
Newton, 22, 191, 198.
Newton, T. W., 242.
Nicholson, Dr. H. A., 343.
Nidderdale, 130.
Nidderdale, Ancient Forests of, 420.
Nonionina, 265.
Norber, Erratic Boulders at, 418.
Norfolk, 291.
Norfolk and Norwich Museum, 248.
Norland Moor, 169.

Normanton, 113, 177.
Northallerton, Blowing Wells at, 419.
Northamptonshire, 42, 237, 263, 268, 331.
North Grimston, 397.
North Midland Railway, 36, 172.
Northmore, Mr., 309.
Northowram, 108.
Northumberland, 231, 255, 258, 320.
Northumberland, Natural History Society of, 3, 4.
Norwich, 297.
Nottinghamshire, 291.
Notton Park, 110, 113, 117.
Nunneley, Mr., 4.
Nutton, 180.

Observations on the process of Petrifaction, 195.
O'Callaghan, P., 305, 312, 3 5, 338.
Old Red Sandstone, 144, 147, 336.
Oliver, Dr. George, 428.
Oolite Fossils, Leckenby Collection of, 141.
Oolitic Rocks, 99, 283.
Oracanthus, 424.
Origin of Species, 132, 133, 134.
Ormskirk, 97.
Ornithicnites, 178.
Ornithosauria, 141.
Orodus, 424.
Orthacanthus, 198.
Orthoceras, 402.
Osbaldiston, Mr., 236.
Oulton, 292.
Overton, 109, 192, 198, 293.
Owen, Prof., 294, 297, 311.
Owlerton, 178.
Oxford, 146, 147, 232.
Oxford and the Valley of the Thames, Geology of, 135.
Oxford, Bishop of, 283.
Oxford Clay, 102, 218, 257, 400.
Oxford, Lord, 102.
Oxfordshire, 99.
Oxford University, 131, 132, 145, 146.
Oxon, 314.

Palæozoic Rocks, 137, 138, 141, 143.
Palestine, Geology of, 426.
Paley, Dr., 345.
Paramoudra, 148.
Parke G. H., 367.
Parker, Mr., 338.
Parkgate Coal, 90, 96, 109, 236.
Parry, Admiral, 202.
Parsons, Dr. H. F., 364, 365, 366, 416.
Patrington, 396.
Pattinson, Mr., 280, 331.

INDEX. 475

Pearce, F. H., 267, 274.
Pearsall, T. J., 259.
Pecten papyraceus, 28, 72, 97.
Peel, Sir Robert, 147.
Pendle Hill, 126.
Pengelly, W., 309.
Penine Chain, 89, 91, 93, 94, 95, 96, 97, 98, 104, 333.
Penine Hills, Flints in, 425.
Penistone, 105, 124.
Penyghent, 130, 335, 336.
Penzance, 243.
Permian Boundary between Hartlepool and Ripon, Subsidences over, 419.
Permian Limestone, 228, 367.
Permian Rocks near Ripon, Sequence of, 426.
Perthes, M. Boucher de, 314.
Petalodonts, 424.
Petalodus, 198.
Peterborough, 331.
Petroleum, 19, 20.
Phillips, Prof. John, 3, 6, 7, 8, 10, 46, 65, 92, 101, 103, 117, 119, 151, 168, 182, 195, 196, 197, 215, 219, 228, 232, 233, 236, 252, 259, 267, 280, 285, 288, 423.
Phillips, Prof. J., Biographical Notice of, 119-135.
Philosophical Magazine, 243.
Philosophy, Annals of, 138, 224.
Pholiderpeton scutigerum, 344.
Pickering, 239, 236, 319.
Pierceall, Mr, 281.
Pilkington, Lady, 20,
Pitt, T., 166, 184, 262.
Platysomus, 73, 198.
Playfair, Dr. Lyon, 179, 226, 270, 277.
Pleuracanthus, 73, 198.
Pleuromya navicula, 430.
Plumpton, 395.
Pocklington, 95, 236, 390.
Polar Ice, Description of, 205.
Polymorphina lactea, 265.
Polyzoa, Cambridge Greensand, 414.
Polyzoa, Carboniferous, of North Yorkshire, 412, 413.
Polyzoa, Carboniferous, West Yorkshire and Derbyshire, 413.
Polyzoa, List of New Species and Varieties of, 415, 416.
Polyzoa, Notes on the Classification of, 415.
Polyzoa, Yoredale, of North Lancashire, 414.
Ponsonby, Lady Charlotte, 41.
Pontefract, 229, 235, 394, 395.
Pontefract Rock, 138.

Pontypool, 124.
Porter, Mr., 2.
Portlock, Captain, 130.
Portman, Lord, 45.
Poteriocrinus, 366.
Poulton, E. B., 420, 421, 422.
Powlett, W. Orde, 432.
Pre-Historic Man, 317, 318, 319, 320, 321, 322, 323, 324, 325, 326.
Pre-Historic Man in Yorkshire, 433.
Prestwich, Dr., 314.
Priestley, Dr., 79.
Prince, Thomas, 351.
Pritchard, Dr., 267.
Prospectus of York. Geological and Polytechnic Society, 12, 13, 14.
Pryme, De la, 268.
Psammodus, 424.
Pterodactylus macromyx, 148.
Purvis, Dr., 394.
Pusey, Dr., 69.

Quinqueloculina seminulum, 265.

Rachiopteris, 402.
Raine, Canon, 394.
Rainhill, 336.
Ramsay, Prof., 336.
Rastrick, 282.
Rawson, C., 129, 251.
Raygill, 337, 390, 391, 424.
Reade, Rev. J. B., 249.
Reche, 312.
Redcar and Hartlepool, Submerged Forests at, 426.
Redcar, Raised Beach at, 426.
Red Chalk, 400.
Red Marl, 139.
Reeth, 124.
Reid, J. Wemyss, 373.
Reliquiæ Diluvianæ, 148, 285.
Rennie, 223.
Reynolds, Richard, 238, 334, 348, 433.
Rhodes, Green, 23.
Rice, Spring, 100.
Richardson, Rev. Benjamin, 121, 294.
Richardson, Sir J., 247, 338.
Richmond, 424.
Ripon, 124, 300, 335, 343, 364, 396, 398, 426.
Ripon, Marquis of, 364, 368, 393, 397, 398.
Ripon, Marquis of, Biographical Notice of, 369, 373.
Risca, 270.
Rishworth, 170.
Roberts, Martin J., 173, 191, 270.
Robin Hood, 22.

INDEX.

Robin Hood's Bay, 124.
Robulina calcar, 265.
Rockingham, Marquis of, 44.
Rocking Stones, 312.
Rocks, Microscopical Structure of, 433.
Rollit, Sir A. K., 394.
Roman Remains, 346, 347.
Rombolds Moor, 346, 434.
Ross, Sir J., 247.
Rotalia, 196.
Rotherham, 112, 236, 343.
Rothwell Haigh, 21, 22, 23, 32, 75, 158, 198, 292.
Rowley, W., 346, 362, 363.
Royal Astronomical Society, 250.
Royal College of Surgeons, 250.
Royal Commission on Accidents in Mines, Report on, 430.
Royal Cornwall Polytechnic Society, 243.
Royal Dublin Society, 294.
Royal Institution, 251.
Royal Irish Academy, 311.
Royal Microscopical Society, 250.
Royal Physical Society or Wernerian Society, 204, 205, 211.
Royal Society, 79, 132, 137, 143, 146, 238, 244, 250, 314.
Royal Society of Edinburgh, 72, 206.
Roy, Rammohun, 208.
Royston, 110, 117, 180.
Rules of the Society formed, 4, 5, 84, 85, 86, 87, 88.
Russell, Lord John, 47.
Russell, R., 118.

Sabine, General, 132.
Safety Fuse and Iron Ropes, 33.
Salby, P. S., 246,
Saltburn, Raised Beach at, 426.
Salter, J. W., 141, 251, 337.
Salter's Brook, 97, 105.
Sandstone, Concretion found in, 431.
Savile, Sir John, 334,
Sayle, Mr., 2.
Scattergood, Thomas, 214.
Scarborough, 122, 125, 256, 257, 389.
Scarborough, Earl of, 5.
School of Mines, 242, 243.
Scott, Sir W., 207.
Scoresby, Dr., 77, 78, 104, 186, 187, 188, 197.
Scoresby, W., jun., Biographical Notice of, 200.
Scoresby, W., Papers by, 211.
Scrope, Mr., 103.
Seal, Stephen, 417.
Sedgwick, Prof. A., 82, 102, 103. 128, 130, 136. 153. 217, 335, 343, 423.
Sedgwick, Adam, Biographical Notice of, 136.
Seeley, Prof., 141.
Selby, 8, 229, 389.
Setrington, 397.
Settle, 124, 130, 305, 336, 424.
Sewell, E, 346.
Sewerby, 296, 317, 398.
Sewerby, Report on the Buried Cliff at, 407.
Seyffarth, Dr. G., 337.
Shafton, 110, 113, 117, 180, 343.
Shap Fell, 286.
Shap Granite Boulders, 401.
Sharp, Rev. S., 5, 20, 26, 77, 91, 153, 155, 160, 177.
Sharpe, Prof., 259.
Shaw, B., 345.
Shaw, George, 165, 171.
Shaw, J. H., 259, 264, 281.
Sheffield, 122, 159, 177, 188, 229, 230, 231, 241, 263, 290, 305, 329.
Sheffield, Geology of, 36, 90, 95.
Sheffield, Meeting at. 79, 290, 344.
Sheffield Quarterly Meeting, 85.
Shetland, 202.
Shuttleworth, Sir J. K., 356.
Sigillaria, 193.
Silkstone, 90, 96.
Silurian Collection, Fletcher's, 141.
Silurian System, 140, 141.
Simes, N. P., 171.
Simpson, Martin, 161, 162, 163, 164, 180, 191.
Simpson, W. L., 256, 276, 277.
Skelton, 300.
Skiddaw, 182, 183.
Skipsey, 323.
Skipton, 124, 130, 189. 280, 390, 391, 395, 424, 428.
Slack, 333, 334.
Sladen, W. P., 366.
Slaidburn, 130, 337.
Smith, Archibald, 214.
Smith, Dr. C., 243, 306.
Smith, Dr. W., 6, 7, 23, 37. 76, 91, 98, 99, 102, 119, 120, 121, 123, 124, 125, 128, 129, 131, 138, 145, 252, 423.
Smith, H. E., 322.
Smith, Sir J. E., 245.
Smithson, Mr., 2.
Smyth, Warrington, S., 117. 270.
Sollitt, Mr., 331.
Solly, Richard, 188, 259, 279.
Somerset, West, 131, 215.
Sopwith, T., 65, 80, 83, 160, 171, 172, 174, 175, 190, 226, 290.

INDEX. 477

Sorby, H. C., 256, 257, 258, 259, 262, 263, 264, 265, 269. 290, 291, 329, 338, 340, 344, 398, 399, 431.
Southowram, 251, 338.
South Pacific Ocean, 296.
Southwoods, 303.
Sowerby Bridge, 389.
Sowerby, Prof., 239.
Soyland, 170.
Speeton, 398, 401.
Spence, Mr, 246.
Spencer, J., 224, 390, 391, 412.
Spencer, Lord, 228.
Spirangium carbonarium, 430.
Spitzbergen, 206.
Spurn Point, 396.
Stackhouse, Mr., 356.
Stainland, 170.
Stainmoor, 286.
Staithes, 200.
Stamford, 331.
Stanhope, J. S., 5, 152, 390
Stanley, 75, 76, 174, 191, 192, 198.
Stanley, Lord, 252.
Stansfield, Mr., 2, 109, 192.
Stapleton Estate, 236.
Steel, Characteristic Constituents of, 431.
Stennis, 321.
Stephenson, G., 255, 429.
Stigmaria, 193.
Stocks, H. B., 430. 431.
Stockwell, 250.
Stokes, Mr., 128.
Stonehenge, 321.
Stott, Wm., 361.
Stourton, Lord, 5, 67, 152.
Strafford, Lord, 44, 45, 48.
Strangways, C. F., 397, 398, 427, 428.
Strata of England and Wales, Map of, 121.
Strickland, H. E., 131.
Strickland, Sir Charles, 390, 397.
Stuart, Dr., 204.
Styles, Mr., 364.
Sutton, 275, 323.
Surtees, Rev. S. F., 323, 345, 346.
Swaledale, 124, 275.
Swallow Wood Coal, 236, 342, 343.
Swansea, 194, 250.
Swanwick, Mr., 111, 112.
Swarth Fell, 181.
Swinefleet, 95, 96, 236.
Sydenera, 197.

Tankersley Park, 236.
Tate, Thomas, 360, 361, 417, 435.
Teale, Dr., T. P., 4, 49, 65, 66, 67, 68, 71, 72, 73, 77, 97, 83, 152, 165, 166, 167, 171, 172, 214, 297.

Teale, Dr. T. P., Biographical Notice of, 54.
Teale, T. P., jun., 49.
Tees, 288.
Teesdale, 130.
Temple Newsome, 315.
Tennant, Mr., 251.
Tew, T. W., 324, 345, 348, 395.
Texilaria, 196.
Tickhill, 95.
Tiddeman, R. H., 356, 358, 363.
Tidswell, 105.
Tindall, E., 265, 296, 297, 299, 302, 323.
Tingley, 401.
Titanium in Blast Furnaces, Paper on, 173.
Thames, 121.
Thirsk, 256, 389.
Thompson, Mr., 220,
Thoresby, Mr., 324.
Thorne, 229.
Thornecliffe, 236.
Thornhill, 90, 109, 117, 180.
Thornwick Bay, 406.
Thornton, 336.
Thorp, 22, 29.
Thorp Rev. Wm., 2, 11, 14, 26, 28, 32, 35, 36, 37, 39, 65, 66, 76, 78, 79, 80, 83, 89, 90, 91, 92, 96, 104, 105, 106, 107, 111, 112, 117, 150, 160, 168, 172, 173, 174, 179, 181, 184, 221, 222, 223, 225, 226, 227, 228, 229, 230, 231, 232, 233, 235, 236, 237, 260, 261, 262, 263, 291, 292, 293, 343.
Thorp, Rev. W., Biographical Notice of, 213, 382, 386.
Thorpe Arch, 299.
Todd, C., 165, 173, 186, 391.
Todmorden, 124, 169, 275.
Torquay, 210, 212, 309.
Tottenham, 277.
Townend, Rev. J., 145.
Traice, H. J., 262, 271.
Traquaria, 411.
Treadgold, Mr., 234.
Trevelyan, Mr., 309.
Trevithick, Mr., 254.
Triassic Beds at Sutton Coal Field, 402,
Trimmer, Mr., 290, 292.
Trollope, Rev. Ed., 268, 315.
Truncatulina tuberculata, 265.
Tumulus and Burials, Discovery of, 431.
Turner, Rev. William, 251.
Tute, Rev. J. S., 335, 343, 344, 364, 402, 419, 426, 430, 433, 434.
Twedale, Mr., 110.
Twibell, 2.

Twigg, Mr., 323.

University College, 122.
Ulswater, 181.
Upton, Mr., 27, 173, 270.
Upton, 395.
Uredale, 130.

Vancouver, Island, 406.
Veitch, W. Y., 426, 430.
Victoria Cave, 305, 307, 356, 357, 358, 359, 363, 395, 421.
Victoria Pit, 22.
Vindiciæ Geologiæ, 146.
Vine, G. R., 412, 413, 414, 415.
Verity, Mr., 303.
Vesuvius, Description of, 135.
Vivian, Mr., 303.

Wakefield, 21, 22, 150, 157, 160, 164, 166, 215, 226, 227, 230, 256, 269, 343, 389, 397.
Wakefield, Committee Meeting at, 2, 14, 65, 91, 150.
Wakefield, Meeting at, 2, 5, 6, 11, 20, 26, 29, 39, 81, 115, 153, 161, 178, 180, 185, 389, 432.
Wakefield, Museum at, 46, 151, 153, 158, 159, 160, 161, 162, 163, 166, 179.
Wakefield, Preliminary Meeting at, 2.
Walker, 253.
Walker, John, 2, 20, 67, 108, 109, 226.
Walkley, 178.
Wallen, W., 160, 174.
Walney Island, 367.
Wandsworth, 238.
Wardle, James, 297.
Ward, J. C., 118.
Ward, W. Sykes, 75, 166, 171, 193, 194, 242, 256, 259, 261, 262, 264, 270, 271, 274, 281, 338, 345, 348.
Ward, W. Sykes, Biographical Notice of, 241.
Warter, 264.
Warwickshire Coal-field, 36.
Water Crag, 130.
Waterhouse, John, 251, 261, 333, 338.
Waterhouse, John, Biographical Notice of, 248.
Watson John, 331.
Watts, Dr. William, 361.
Waud, Ed., 171.
Wealden, 148.
Wellington, Duke of, 43.
Wenlock Shales, Distribution of Entomostraca in, 414.
Wenlock Shales, Palæontology of, 414.
Wenlock Shales, Polyzoa of, 414.

Wensleydale, 275.
Wentworth, 41, 46, 47.
Wentworth, Godfrey, 26.
Wentworth, Lady Anne Watson, 44.
Wentworth Park, 44.
Wentworth, W., 42.
Wentworth Woodhouse, 46, 47, 48.
Werner, Prof., 98.
Westerdale, 300.
Westmoreland, 286.
West, Theodore, 258.
West, Tuffen, 240.
West, W., 4, 11, 75, 78, 83, 165, 166, 170, 171, 172, 177, 184, 191, 197, 199, 239, 240, 256, 270.
West, W., Biographical Notice of, 238.
Westwood, Prof., 247.
Wharncliffe, Lord, 5, 26, 65, 152, 344.
Wharfedale, 124, 130, 275, 362.
Wharram 400, 408.
Wharton, Mr. 8.
Whetby, Mrs., 333.
Whitby, 125, 164, 201, 208, 331.
Whitby, Philosophical Society of, 163.
Whiteley, R. Lloyd, 429.
Whitwood, 75, 76, 113.
Wrenthorpe, 75, 76.
Wilberforce, Mr., 41.
Wildboar Fell, 130, 336.
Willand, 126.
Willey-How, 265, 299.
Williamson, Dr. W. C., 411, 423, 434.
Williamson, John, Biographical Notice of, 423.
Willoughby-on-Wold, 319.
Wilson, G., 2, 184.
Wilson, Henry, 49.
Wilson, John, 2.
Wilson, Thomas, 1, 2, 3, 5, 6, 7, 8, 9, 14, 15, 26, 29, 37, 49, 60, 65, 66, 67, 77, 78, 80, 81, 83, 90, 96, 104, 106, 107, 112, 114, 115, 150, 152, 156, 157, 158, 159, 160, 161, 163, 164, 165, 166, 167, 171, 172, 174, 176, 178, 179, 183, 189, 220, 221, 222, 226, 260, 261, 266, 268, 269, 338, 341, 348, 349, 388.
Wilson, Thomas, Biographical Notice of, 49, 50, 51, 52.
Wiltshire, 319.
Winter, 110.
Witham, Harry, 128.
Wold-Newton, 265, 299.
Wold Valleys during Glacial Period, 405.
Wolds, Origin of, 407, 408.
Woolley Edge Rock, 23, 96, 110.
Woolrow, 108.
Wood, W. H., 254, 418.
Wood, Sir F. L., 152, 217.

INDEX.

Woodall, J. W., 389.
Woodhead, E., 338.
Woodmoor, 110.
Woodwardian Museum, 140,
Wortley, 108, 117, 180, 293, 294, 297.
Wortley, Hon. J. S., 26.
Wrangham, Archdeacon, 207.
Wright, Dr. T., 39, 153, 264, 265, 296, 298, 302.
Wycliffe, 282.

Xanthidia, 196.

Yates, Mr., 127,
Yarrell, W., 246.
Yedmandale, 257.
Yoredale Shales, 169, 341, 400.
York, 46, 119, 122, 123, 152, 153, 156, 172, 176, 221, 222, 231, 239, 334, 393, 397.
York, Archbishop of, 46.
York, Glacial Beds at, 422.
York Museum, 46, 123, 125, 126, 172.
York, Vale of, Trias in, 416.

Yorkshire Agricultural Society, 46, 159, 171, 173, 179, 215, 216, 219, 221, 222, 223, 227.
Yorkshire Archæological and Topographical Society, 388.
Yorkshire Coal Field, 11, 18, 28, 34, 89, 94, 97, 98, 101, 104, 105, 106, 107, 117, 118, 131, 151, 152, 154, 168, 197, 199, 228, 229, 231, 233, 235, 247, 256, 330, 340, 346, 352, 353, 354, 355, 361.
Yorkshire, Flint-users of, 435.
Yorkshire, Geology of, 123, 126, 131, 137, 138, 140, 147, 148, 174.
Yorkshire Petrology, 435.
Yorkshire Philosophical Society, 122, 123, 124, 125, 126, 176, 248.
Yorkshire, West Riding of, 152, 153, 154, 155, 166.
Yorkshire Wolds, 390.
Young, Rev. George, 423.

Zmütt Glacier, 120.
Zoological Society, 251.

www.ingramcontent.com/pod-product-compliance
Lightning Source LLC
Chambersburg PA
CBHW051234300426
44114CB00011B/732